ETHICS FOR MODERN LIFE

SIXTH EDITION

ETHICS FOR MODERN LIFE

SIXTH EDITION

RAZIEL ABELSON
New York University

MARIE-LOUISE FRIQUENON
William Patterson College

BEDFORD/ST. MARTIN'S
Boston ◆ New York

For Bedford/St. Martin's

Developmental Editor: Jane Smith
Production Editor: Maria Teresa Burwell
Production Supervisor: Christie Gross
Marketing Manager: Brian Wheel
Art Director: Lucy Krikorian
Text Design: Lee Goldstein
Copy Editor: Alice Vigliani
Cover Design: Lucy Krikorian
Cover Photo: David Heald © The Solomon Guggenheim Foundation, New York
Composition: the dotted i
Printing and Binding: Haddon Craftsmen

President: Joan E. Feinberg
Editorial Director: Denise B. Wydra
Director of Marketing: Karen R. Melton
Director of Editing, Design, and Production: Marcia Cohen
Managing Editor: Erica T. Appel

Library of Congress Control Number: 2002107338

Manufactured in the United States of America.

8 7 6 5 4 3
f e d c b a

For information, write: Bedford/St. Martin's, 75 Arlington Street, Boston, MA 02116
(617-399-4000)

ISBN: 0-312-15761-4

For Aimee and Carmel

PREFACE

Ethics for Modern Life sprang from our struggle as teachers of ethics to meet the rival demands of theory and practice by illustrating the connection between ethical theory and ethical practice, between philosophical principles and concrete decisions and policies. We hope that this book will demonstrate how philosophical analysis can be relevant to the solution of problems we face in our personal and social lives.

The format of the sixth edition is similar to that of the fifth. Part I presents the main theories offered by philosophers to explain and guide our ethical judgments (Chapter 1) and those that attempt to define the grounds of moral responsibility (Chapter 2). Parts II and III provide discussions of social issues to which the principles proposed in Part I can be applied. To make the book more flexible, we have replaced the lengthy part introductions with streamlined and focused chapter introductions.

NEW TO THIS EDITION

In this sixth edition of *Ethics for Modern Life,* we have increased the number of readings from 39 to 50 (34 are new to this edition) and added three timely new topics. In addition, each of the three main parts now begins with a literary selection dramatizing the problem to which the subsequent philosophical essays offer solutions. In Part I an excerpt from *Philoctetes* by Sophocles dramatizes the philosophical conflict between individual human rights and the needs of the community. Part II begins with the prize-winning science fiction story "The Cold Equations" by Tom Godwin that illustrates the dilemmas involved in taking human life. The heatedly disputed social issues covered in Part III are introduced by two chapters from Aldous Huxley's *Brave New World* that provide an early warning about the dangers of excessive social engineering.

A large part of this revision involved the selection of the readings themselves. Our goal: to increase the number of contemporary selections and to take a fresh look at some of the classical offerings with an eye to finding even clearer expressions of a particular philosophical stance. For example, we replaced Bishop Mortimer's statement of religious absolutism with Robert M. Adams's subtle and persuasively argued formulation of the divine command theory. An excerpt from Simon Blackburn's *Think* (Free Will) now represents soft determinism, and Peter van Inwagen's powerfully argued brief for indeterminism replaces the William James essay. The arguments on abortion have been augmented with one from a recent book by Paul Wilkes, a devout Catholic who questions and proposes to moderate the Church's official position on the subject. The chapter on affirmative action now includes recent essays by Gertrude Ezorsky (in favor) and Charles Murray (against). Indeed, every chapter—with the exception of that on Privacy—contains new readings.

Chapters 11, 12, and 13 introduce debates over issues drawn from today's headlines: genetic engineering (Robert Sinsheimer, Stephen P. Stich, Hilary Putnam, John Harris); multiculturalism and political correctness (Lawrence Foster, Jan Narveson); and war and terrorism (B. T. Wilkins, Alfred Louch).

NEW MEDIA RESOURCE

We are very excited about the new media resource that has been designed for our anthology, a TopLinks Web site <www.bedfordstmartins.com/ethicsforlife>. TopLinks—a topical links database—guides you to the best links available on the most common research topics.

TopLinks will enable students to further explore the issues in *Ethics for Modern Life* and find out what other people have to say about those topics. Each link includes a critical annotation to help students choose the best Web sources for their search.

ACKNOWLEDGMENTS

We would like to thank those who carefully reviewed the fifth edition and offered suggestions for this sixth edition: David ButleRichie, The College of New Jersey; Michael Connelley, Longview Community College; Evelyn Pluhar, Pennsylvania State University—Fayette; T. A. Torgerson, University of Minnesota—Duluth; and Karen Wendling, University of Guelph.

At Bedford/St. Martin's, we would like to give special thanks to Jane Smith, who guided our efforts and saw the manuscript to completion; Maria Burwell, who coordinated the project from manuscript stage through typesetting; and Gregory J. Johnson, who created the content for the TopLinks Web site.

CONTENTS

ETHICS FOR MODERN LIFE

SIXTH EDITION

General Introduction

WHY STUDY ETHICAL PHILOSOPHY?

A small child keeps asking "Why?" and drives us wild with exasperation. We cannot silence the child by giving an answer that cannot be questioned in turn, because our knowledge lacks an absolute foundation.

In ethics, this problem is especially prickly. Faced with the bewildering variety of customs around the world, how are we to decide on the correct rules of moral conduct? As Al-Ghazali, an Arab philosopher, observed many centuries ago, a Christian child grows up Christian, a Zoroastrian child grows up Zoroastrian, and a Muslim child grows up Muslim. Are our moral codes just a matter of our upbringing? Why not—how could it be otherwise? But then, what if our upbringing is bad? Think of the Artful Dodger in Dickens's *Oliver Twist,* brought up to be a thief. Surely there must be some more basic criterion of right and wrong.

The rise of moral philosophy in Western civilization was owing to a conflict between cultures. Ancient Greece was divided into isolated sections on account of its islands and mountain ranges. Initially most of these sections were governed by local kings, and customs (which were considered to represent the will of the gods) were passed down from parents to children. However, the special geography of the Greeks' homeland gave rise to challenges and changes. The islands formed commercial stepping stones to Africa and Asia Minor as well as to the various sections of the Greek mainland. Sailors learned to navigate from island to island and eventually to other continents, where they absorbed new customs and ways of life, and merchants accumulated new ideas as well as great wealth. Because money is power, this resulted in both oligarchies and democracies that rejected the traditions of the old monarchies. In Athens, especially, in order to succeed in influencing the democratic assembly, it was necessary for the newly rich merchants, who lacked the training of the landed aristocrats and royal families, to become skilled in persuasive rhetoric.

Bolstered by their newly developed knowledge of the diversity of cultures and moral codes, itinerant teachers such as Protagoras and Thrasymachus, as

1

described by Plato in his *Dialogues,* prospered by educating the newly rich and teaching them how to plead their cases, under the slogan "Man is the measure of all things" (meaning that we, not the gods or the kings, decide what is right and wrong, good and bad). These teachers pointed out, for example, that whereas the Greeks believed one must always bury the dead (witness Antigone's sacrificing of her own life in order to bury her brother), members of another culture encountered in the travels of seafaring merchants believed one must always eat one's dead relatives. So, right and wrong depended on who was judging. In fact, it was natural for these teachers (called Sophists, meaning wise men) to advertise that they could "make the worse appear the better" and to train the financial elite to persuade the assembly to rule in their favor, regardless of the true merit of their case.

Into this maelstrom of argumentation and moral skepticism came Socrates, arguing that ethical truth was to be found neither in the decrees of gods and kings nor in the passionate assertions of individual claimants, but through reasoning, by showing what claims could not be true because they were self-contradictory. Although he made no final judgments himself, Socrates exposed the claims of the Sophist teachers to be mere pretenses of ethical wisdom for which thoughtful people must continue to search.

Plato, a disciple of Socrates, recorded these debates in a series of dialogues. In one of these dialogues, the *Euthyphro,* Socrates encounters a self-righteous young man on his way to denounce his own father for (accidentally) killing a slave. When Socrates questions the propriety of this decision, the young man (Euthyphro) claims it is the will of the gods, whereupon Socrates asks if an act is right because the gods will it, or if the gods will it because it is right. Euthyphro is hard-pressed to answer satisfactorily. This exchange marks the beginning of ethical philosophy, the attempt to find an objective foundation for ethical reasoning. The subsequent history of philosophy has consisted of the Herculean labors of philosophers to provide the foundation Socrates was searching for, and to apply it to resolving the moral dilemmas of both personal and social life.

Social problems provoke more philosophical reflection and debate than personal dilemmas because of their far-reaching consequences. When many people are affected by a practice, many points of view will be voiced, and the resulting disputes call for rational deliberation. When we look beyond the horizon of our personal affairs and take an active interest in political and social issues, we find ourselves having to choose, for example, between social upheaval and infringement of minority rights, between national loyalty and moral conscience, between abundance at home and alleviation of misery abroad. In this broader perspective our automatic responses to familiar situations now seem crude and inappropriate. Few of us have been trained to make large-scale decisions in a routine way. The rules of conduct we have been following in our daily lives without conscious deliberation must now be modified or even replaced, and such revisions require philosophical reflection.

Ethical philosophy results from the effort to resolve conflicts rationally, when our automatic responses guided by implicit rules of action collide with contrary responses and rules. When opposition from others or from our own consciences makes us aware of reasons against our actions or policies, it becomes necessary for us to defend them by engaging in philosophical discussion. The purpose of doing so is not to improve our moral character but to refine our conceptual equipment for supporting or rejecting disputed courses of action, so that the course we choose will be rationally justifiable.

But weighing reasons for and against particular actions and policies is only the practical side of ethical philosophy. People skilled in distinguishing the better from the worse and in giving cogent reasons for their judgments are, in this sense, ethical philosophers even if they have never taught a course in ethics or written articles on the subject. But reflection on practice leads eventually to theory; and on the theoretical level, special training is needed for philosophical clarity. When plausible reasons are cited for both sides of a practical issue, one begins to wonder not just which course of action is best, but which of the competing reasons are the more compelling, and why. Reasoning about actions and policies then requires an ascent to theoretical reasoning about standards of judgment and general principles—whereupon one finds oneself on the lofty terrain of ethical theory.

ETHICAL THEORY AND SCIENTIFIC THEORY

The term "ethical theory" should not mislead anyone into thinking that there can be a science of ethics that is in any way analogous to the science of physics or chemistry. Theories in the natural sciences are generalizations from observed patterns of events combined with explanatory hypotheses that make possible the prediction of new events. The experimental natural scientist discovers new facts, and the theoretical scientist constructs a theory that explains them and also predicts new discoveries. In contrast, an ethical theory is formulated to explain commonsense facts already known; and it consists of principles and standards whose function is not to predict anything but to guide our choices and actions. This difference is often summed up by saying that natural science is *descriptive* whereas ethics is *normative*—meaning that science tells us what was, is, or will be the case, whether we like it or not, whereas ethics tells us what we ought to do. Science gives us information about the world, whereas ethics gives us rules and standards for changing the world. A scientific theory provides a hypothesis for predicting what will happen, whereas an ethical theory provides rules for making things happen.

Of course, there are standards in science as well as in ethics—the meter bar was, and now the hydrogen atom spectrum is, the standard of length; a certain extremely small amount of foreign substances is the standard of chemical purity of a solution. But these are standards of measurement and classification, not standards of choice and action. Scientific standards are adopted by all because of (1) their uniformity under varying environmental conditions, and (2) the ease with which they can be applied. The meter bar is, for most purposes, unchanging—it does not shrink or expand or bend—and everyone who uses it can agree on the result, independently of their particular desires, needs, or aspirations. In contrast, ripeness and sweetness are standards for evaluating apples as better or worse because we prefer ripe and sweet apples; likewise, integrity and intelligence are standards for evaluating political leaders because those are the qualities needed for social stability and growth.

Finally, ethical standards differ from scientific standards and ethical principles differ from scientific laws in their logical relations to the particular judgments they support. Once a scientific standard has been agreed on, any object that meets it must be judged to have passed the test. For example, if a boat measures ten feet in length, then all people must acknowledge that it is ten feet long, whether they like it or not. But an ethical standard, such as politeness, is variable in application, depending on our needs and preferences (e.g., belching is considered polite in some cultures and impolite in others). Moreover, when a particular ethical standard is met by something we strongly disapprove of, we may decide to modify the standard rather than approve of the object or action that satisfies it. For example, a teacher grading term papers will normally look for features such as accuracy of information, clarity of expression, and unity of structure as the standards for judging a paper to be good. But suppose a paper that satisfies these standards is nevertheless a dull and mechanical repetition of the classroom lectures. The teacher may then decide that another standard should prevail in deciding on the appropriate grade. The paper lacks originality, and this fact should outweigh the others. In this manner, ethical standards are subject to modification when they support individual judgments that conflict with our preferences and sensitivities.

These differences between science and ethics may account for the difference in the kind of knowledge we have in these areas. Whereas theories, laws, and standards of measurement are well known by all qualified scientists in a given field, ethical principles and standards remain for the most part obscurely at work in our actions and judgments, and it takes philosophical reflection to bring them to conscious attention. We often know what we approve or disapprove of without knowing why—that is, without being able to state just what features justify our approval or condemnation. In ordinary circumstances this lack of awareness of our reasons for our judgments does not cause any difficulty. But when we are uncertain of our decisions, when we vacillate between alternative choices or courses of action, we find it necessary to engage in philosophical reflection in order to make clear to ourselves the reasons on both sides of the issue and to assess their relative weights. Whereas scientific knowledge advances through new discoveries, ethical wisdom advances through clarification of what we already obscurely believe.

THE ROLE OF ETHICAL PHILOSOPHY TODAY

In our world of rapid change and continuous conflict, many long-established principles of action and standards of evaluation have proven inadequate or outdated. "Defend free elections" seems irrelevant to a starving and illiterate peasantry in a feudal society in Asia or Africa. "Grade everyone alike" strikes the teacher, who is sensitive to the enormous differences in the upbringing of pupils with different socioeconomic backgrounds, as masking the perpetuation of social injustice behind a facade of impartiality. "All violations of the law must be punished" sounds unrealistic to the police officer faced with a possible riot if he arrests a teenager for opening a fire hydrant on a hot summer night. Situations like these indicate a need to re-evaluate our standards and principles by means of philosophical analysis.

THE NATURE OF MORALITY

Theoretical efforts to articulate the proper standards of right conduct and the conditions for ascribing moral responsibility are presented in Chapters 1 and 2. We begin this Part with a selection from the timeless drama *Philoctetes,* by the ancient Greek tragedian Sophocles, in which the issues of what standard of right takes precedence and whether individual moral responsibility does or does not take precedence over military orders, are confronted and explored—perhaps for the first time.

The Greek warrior Neoptolemus, son of Achilles, is ordered by his general, Odysseus, to steal a magic bow from Philoctetes, who has been marooned on an island because his "rotting foot" was weakening the Greek army's siege of Troy. Philoctetes' golden bow, which enables him to obtain food, is his only means of survival. In facing the order to steal this bow, Neoptolemus is forced to choose between deceiving Philoctetes, which violates his moral conscience, and failing to do what his commanding officer and his nation require.

Both theoretical issues of Part I are illustrated in this drama: the conflict between the standards of social benefit and universal moral law, and that between individual moral responsibility and military necessity.

from PHILOCTETES

Sophocles

[Scene: Lemnos, a volcanic island not far from the coast of Asia Minor. A part of the shore where there is a steep cliff riddled with caves.]

[Enter NEOPTOLEMOS, *a young officer from the Greek army,* ODYSSEUS, *and some* SAILORS, *part of the crew of* NEOPTOLEMOS' *ship.]*

ODYSSEUS   The island of Lemnos . . . Sea . . . sand . . . rock! No one comes here, no one lives here—and this is where I put him ashore, Neoptolemos, on this island. Yes, this is where I left Philoctetes all those years ago . . . I had my orders, I carried them out. His foot was a mass of rotting flesh, eaten right down to the bone. The sounds that came from him—we couldn't hold sacrifices, couldn't pray to heaven . . . it would have been blasphemy with him shrieking, screaming . . . But why need we talk of that? We must be quick. The one thing we cannot do is talk. If he knows I'm here, our journey's wasted. I have a plan to catch him—I hope—it's quick and it's clever. Your function here is to carry out that plan . . . Go and see if you can find a cave with two entrances. Look for a place where you could lie in the sun all day in cold weather, or sleep in a cool breeze if the weather was hot . . . And further down to the left you should see a spring of drinking water . . . [NEOPTOLEMOS *has begun to climb.*] Still there? . . . Go in as close as you can . . . [NEOPTOLEMOS *dislodges a stone.*] . . . but keep it *quiet!* . . . If it looks as if he's still living there, wave . . . After that I want you back here, and I'll tell you the rest of my plan. Then our mission can proceed.

NEOPTOLEMOS   Easily done, Odysseus. I think I can see the cave you mean.

ODYSSEUS   Up there, or further down? I can't tell from here . . .

NEOPTOLEMOS   Just above me here . . . No tracks, though, no sign of life . . .

ODYSSEUS   Careful! He could be lying there asleep.

[NEOPTOLEMOS *peers into the opening.*]

NEOPTOLEMOS   No, I can see inside . . . Empty, no one at home.

ODYSSEUS   Does it seem lived in? . . . Any food?

NEOPTOLEMOS   A few leaves . . . they've been pressed down flat. Someone slept there last night.

ODYSSEUS   But otherwise empty. Nothing lying around?

NEOPTOLEMOS   A cup hollowed out of wood, very rough. Not well made, whoever did it . . . Some pieces of kindling wood . . .

ODYSSEUS   Yes, all his wealth is in that cave.

NEOPTOLEMOS   *[letting out a cry of disgust]* These rags left out here to dry— they're stiff with matter . . . pus!

ODYSSEUS   This is the place. Good. We've found our man. He's living here, may even be close to us now . . . He's a sick man, you see, one limb useless, he can't get far. He probably went looking for food, or perhaps he knows of some leaves that relieve the pain . . . Send one of them to keep watch.

[NEOPTOLEMOS *signals to one of his* SAILORS]

I mustn't let him find me here. He'd rather lay hands on me than all the Greek army put together!

NEOPTOLEMOS   One of my men is going now. He'll guard the path . . . Next?

ODYSSEUS   And now, my boy, you have a mission to fulfill. You are the son of Achilles and I want to see you fulfill it like your father. I don't mean just physical courage. I mean, if what I tell you now comes as a surprise, appears somewhat . . . unusual . . . I want complete obedience. Remember, you are here to assist me.

NEOPTOLEMOS   Your orders, sir?

ODYSSEUS   I want Philoctetes. And you must get him for me. And for that you will tell any lie that may be necessary . . . You will be asked who you are and where you come from. You will say: "Son of Achilles, from Skyros." So far—no deception. But . . . you are sailing home, having withdrawn from the Greek army—the Greeks, remember, you hate, you loathe! They came to you with an appeal for help, they humbly asked you to leave your home and sail to Troy where, they assured you, you were the one man who could take the city for them. You went to Troy. There, you naturally and correctly asked for the return of your father's armor. You were most unreasonably refused, and the armor was handed over to . . . Odysseus. Say anything you like about me, the worst insults you can think of—you won't hurt me . . . But if you fail me, then I will be hurt, and so will all of us in the Greek army. You see, without Philoctetes and his bow, you can't take Troy. Now, Philoctetes hates me, but you he will trust. I'll tell you why. You took no oath like the rest of us who sailed on the original expedition; no one forced you to come; . . . none of which applies to me. If he finds me here and that bow is in his hands, I die, and since we are here together—so will you. . . . No, this requires management, skill. For the sake of that bow, young man, that invincible weapon, you are about to become a thief! [*seeing* NEOPTOLEMOS *about to protest*] I know, I know, Neoptolemos, it isn't your nature. To you, lying is wrong, intrigue is wrong. Yes, but victory is sweet—seize it! Dare! Time will put us in the right—you'll see. Today, just for today, forget shame, and place yourself in my hands. Then, for the rest of your life you can be as virtuous as you like.

NEOPTOLEMOS   Odysseus, some things—at the very mention of them I feel disgust—and when I have to do them, I rebel. Deceit is not my way. I'm not made like that, nor was my father, so they tell me. If we must use force to take this man off Lemnos, look I'm ready. But deceive him— no . . . He has one good leg; he can't be strong enough to fight us all. I was sent here under your command and I shall be accused of mutiny. I don't enjoy the thought. But if I have to do wrong in order to succeed, sir, I would rather remain honest—and fail.

ODYSSEUS   How like your father, your upright, honorable father . . . When I was your age, I was the same. I had no use for words, I believed in action. But now I realize that in this life it is not what you do that counts. Words are what matter; words have power. I know, believe me.

NEOPTOLEMOS   You are ordering me to tell a lie. Is that the case or not?

ODYSSEUS   I am asking you to bring me Philoctetes by a strategy.

NEOPTOLEMOS   Why strategy? Why not persuade him?

ODYSSEUS   He will never be persuaded. And you can't take him by force.

NEOPTOLEMOS   Why not? Is he so strong, so terrible, so brave?

ODYSSEUS   The arrows. They are deadly and they never miss.

NEOPTOLEMOS   Even to go near him is a risk, then?

ODYSSEUS   Yes, unless you use strategy, as I said.

NEOPTOLEMOS   But don't you think lying is wrong?

ODYSSEUS   Not necessarily . . . Suppose the lie saves my life.

NEOPTOLEMOS   But how does one say the words and not blush?

ODYSSEUS   Think of what you gain and don't be shy. This is no time to be shy.

NEOPTOLEMOS   What do I gain if he goes to Troy . . . ?

ODYSSEUS   His bow will take the city. Nothing else can.

NEOPTOLEMOS   But everyone said I was going to conquer Troy. Wasn't that true?

ODYSSEUS   It was. And that bow can do nothing without you. But you can do nothing without the bow.

[NEOPTOLEMOS *reflects.*]

NEOPTOLEMOS   I see . . . The bow is essential, then. That is the prize.

ODYSSEUS *[quickly]*   Do what I ask and you win two prizes.

NEOPTOLEMOS   How do you mean? If I could be sure, I think I would agree.

ODYSSEUS   Two prizes, Neoptolemos, one for courage and one for brains.

[Pauses]

NEOPTOLEMOS   Right, I'll do it! I'm not ashamed. That's gone—

ODYSSEUS   You remember what I said.

NEOPTOLEMOS   Yes, yes, I've told you—I agree to everything.

ODYSSEUS   You wait and meet Philoctetes here. I'll leave you. I don't want him to catch sight of me. I'll dismiss your sentry back to his ship, but if I think you're taking too long I'll send the same man back to you disguised as a merchant so that his uniform isn't recognized. He'll probably say some puzzling things, my boy, but you improvise as best you can and take your cue from him. I'm going back to the ship. You are in charge now . . . May Hermes, patron of all conspirators, assist us now, and the Goddess Athene of victories, who watches over my interests always.

[*Exit* ODYSSEUS]

QUESTIONS FOR DISCUSSION: PHILOCTETES

1. Is Neoptolemus's reluctance to deceive Philoctetes owing to his sympathy for Philoctetes' suffering, or owing to his conviction that it is dishonorable to deceive a comrade? Discuss which motive should be morally more compelling. Would either motive justify a soldier's disobeying a military command? Explain your response.

2. After you have read the selections in Chapter 1 from Immanuel Kant and John Stuart Mill, discuss which moral theory—rational absolutism or utilitarianism—morally supports the point of view of Odysseus, and which one supports the reluctance of Neoptolemus to obey Odysseus.

1

STANDARDS OF RIGHT AND WRONG

How do we know when our actions are morally right or wrong? No doubt we learned such things from our parents and teachers. But how did *they* know? Did they *really* know? Are they infallible? We can hardly answer these questions unless we know the answer to the first question, so let's return to it. How do we know when an action is right or wrong? Is there a standard we can match against the action, or a principle that the action satisfies or violates, and if so, what justifies that standard or that principle? A satisfactory answer requires a general theory.

Many ethical theories have been formulated by philosophers, and in this chapter we will examine the most persuasive of them. Such theories fall into two groups that might be called absolutist and relativist. Theories in the former group offer standards that are thought to be independent of any other conditions such as social customs, group or individual needs, personal preferences, or stage of historical development. Theories in the latter group derive their ethical standards from precisely such variable factors. An absolutist argues for the invariant character of ethical standards on the grounds that they are the commands of a divine authority, or that they are deducible from the concept of a rational agent, or that they are intuitively self-evident. A relativist holds that what is right conduct varies with social agreements, or with established customs, or with political, psychological, economic, or biological needs. The history of ethical philosophy has been a continuing dialogue between progressively more refined forms of absolutism and relativism.

Although the basic issue between these two main viewpoints is still (and may always be) unsettled, each view we will consider contributes important insights into the meaning of our ethical judgments. As the dialogue continues, we progress in untangling the complex logic of such judgments.

Space does not permit a complete survey here of the many philosophical theories of morality that history offers. We shall limit our study to eight major schools of thought: religious absolutism, rational absolutism, social benefit, convention, contractualism, virtue ethics, self-assertion, and feminist ethics.

The many other views that philosophers have offered can be seen as variations on these eight major themes.

(1) DIVINE COMMAND

In our first selection, Robert M. Adams defends what is probably the oldest and most deeply entrenched conception of morality: the religious view that right action consists in obedience to divine commands. Assuming that natural human tendencies reflect the will of their creator and that conscience is, so to speak, the voice of God in the human soul, almost all the world's religions acknowledge the absolute authority of their divine lawgiver over what humans should or should not do. Most philosophers, beginning with Plato in his Socratic dialogue *Euthyphro,* have criticized this view on the grounds that, for those who believe that God sometimes commands murderous actions (e.g., ordering Abraham to slay his son, Isaac), it flagrantly violates our intuitive sense of moral right and wrong.

The identification of moral conduct with obedience to a higher authority has been linked by some psychologists, most notably Jean Piaget and Lawrence Kohlberg, with the earliest stage of moral awareness in childhood. A child first learns to distinguish "right" from "wrong" on the basis of what his parents command him to do and not to do. Later on, it is held, the child adopts the unstated rules of his social milieu; still later, assuming healthy development in a democratic society, the child learns to employ his or her own reasoning ability to refine the rules and make independent judgments of how to act. Not so for adherents of religious absolutism. In their view, human reason must not presume to correct divine authority, but only to be guided by it.

The possibility of conflict between divine authority and human reason has tended to undermine religious faith ever since the eighteenth-century Enlightenment and the rise of democratic social institutions in the industrialized nations of the world. The idea of a divine lawgiver with absolute authority over us, so absolute that we must obey even if we are commanded to do what we deeply believe is morally abominable (e.g., killing innocent people), goes against the modern grain and undermines religious faith.

Robert M. Adams, a professor of philosophy and an ordained minister, proposes a compromise between secular reason and religious faith that avoids this head-on conflict by conceding that moral right does not mean the same thing as obedience to divine command; the former need not be defined by the latter. Nevertheless, he maintains, one may have faith (and he does) that God would, in fact, never command that His creatures perform immoral actions. To believe that He might do so is either to follow a false religion or to lack a clear understanding of moral right and wrong.

By holding it to be a factual claim, rather than a matter of definition, that whatever God commands is morally right, Adams successfully avoids embarrassing possibilities, such as Abraham being commanded to sacrifice his son—which, if morally right *meant* commanded by God, would entail that killing one's innocent child can be morally right. No doubt Adams would maintain that the biblical story of Abraham and Isaac should be interpreted more sympathetically (e.g., perhaps Abraham was mistaken in thinking that God had ordered him to slay his son) or, as Kierkegaard seems to have understood it in his book *Fear and Trembling,* Abraham was being tested by God and had a strong enough faith to be confident that God would not let it happen. By basing this factual claim on religious faith, Adams avoids the need to support it with evidence that would be extremely hard to come by.

(2) RATIONALITY

The religious view of divine command is absolutist in the sense that it regards such commands as allowing of no excuses or exceptions, thus as universally binding. An equally absolutist position, but one that appeals to reason rather than divine authority, was developed by Immanuel Kant, the most influential thinker of the eighteenth-century Enlightenment. His rational absolutism is often referred to by later philosophers as deontological ethics, meaning an ethics of absolutely strict rules.

According to Kant, good will or moral character is the willingness to obey rules ("maxims") that each person legislates for all to obey. Such rules are "categorical imperatives," requiring action independent of what the agent, or anyone else, happens to want, rather than "hypothetical imperatives" that guide action toward desired goals. Most people, Kant suggests, confuse hypothetical imperatives (which, being conditional on desire for the ends to which they prescribe the means, lack universal binding force) with moral rules that hold unconditionally.

Kant may have unearthed for the first time the distinguishing feature of genuinely moral rules as contrasted with mere custom or prudence, namely, their binding force that makes us feel guilty when we violate them. But many have argued that his rules are too strict in allowing for no exceptions. When Kant was asked if one may lie to a would-be murderer when asked where his victim is hiding, Kant said no. His answer was consistent with his theory; but, his critics say, so much the worse for his theory.

(3) SOCIAL BENEFIT (UTILITARIANISM)

The Kantian account of moral right as conformity to universal and unconditional rules prompts this question: Which rules satisfy that condition without exception? The difficulty of answering this question to everyone's satisfaction leads relativists to conclude that the question itself is a mistake and that the criterion of moral right must be something other than universalizability. Utilitarians offer the more relativistic criterion of social benefit, that yields different results under different conditions. They classify moral right as that species of good which affects other people, rather than oneself alone; and they propose that an action be considered morally right if it increases pleasure or decreases suffering for most, if not all, of those affected by it. John Stuart Mill, a nineteenth-century British philosopher, summed up this view in the "greatest happiness principle": "Aim at the greatest good for the greatest number."

Mill acknowledges that it is good for people to develop the habits of good conduct we call virtues, such as honesty, helpfulness, fairness, and temperance, because such "habits" contribute to social benefit, but they should prevail only when an action is uncontroversial enough to be appropriately automatic. However, when a situation is complex enough to require deliberation, a utilitarian estimate of social benefits as against harms should take the place of virtuous habits and sometimes override them.

The most vulnerable aspect of utilitarianism lies in its approach to problems of justice. There are situations in which satisfying the demands of justice would require actions that produce more harm than benefit—for example, ancient Athens prosecuted its generals for violating their duty to rescue drowning sailors, as a predictable result of which Athens lost the Peloponnesian War. In such cases, utilitarian considerations would seem to override those of justice. But should they?

(4) CONVENTION

For the utilitarian, what is morally right varies with, and thus is relative to, what can be expected to produce more benefit than harm, which in turn varies with many other conditions. In this sense it is a form of ethical relativism, in contrast with the religious absolutism of Adams and the rational absolutism of Kant. But when philosophers talk of ethical relativism, they usually mean a position more extremely relativistic than utilitarianism—one that makes morality vary in a less rational way, depending not on the objective facts of the matter but on the traditions, customs, and, in general, conventions accepted by the social group in which the policy or action is carried out. This more extreme form of relativism, which Gilbert Harman calls "conventionalism," is especially popular among anthropologists who are particularly sensitive to the differences among cultures.

In this view, as Harman points out, it is morally wrong in this society to practice cannibalism, but not in certain primitive societies in which cannibalism is the accepted practice. One may wonder what Harman would say about certain modern-day extremist subcultures, such as the Irish Republican Army, or the Muslim fundamentalist groups like al Quaeda, which is believed to have perpetrated the World Trade Center and Pentagon atrocities on September 11, 2001. Did they simply have a different moral code according to their conventional agreements or customs; or are they, like the rest of us, committed to basic moral principles common to all members of modern civilization— more fundamental conventions that override those of any particular ideology, so that their violent actions merit world condemnation as morally evil?

(5) CONTRACTUALISM

Still another and more moderate kind of ethical relativism, approaching, but not quite reaching, the absolutism of Kantian deontology, is the "contractualist" view of Thomas Scanlon, which applies to individual ethics the ideal contractarian theory of social and political justice for which John Rawls is famous. Rawls had proposed, in his *Theory of Justice,* that social justice can be defined in terms of general principles that all people would agree to behind a "veil of ignorance" about their own situations in life. Scanlon proposes that the same is true of the principles of individual moral conduct that provide the reasons for morally justifying or condemning particular actions. Such morally supporting reasons are those to which anyone would appeal in justifying his or her own actions. According to Scanlon, "This leads me to describe the subject matter of judgments of right and wrong by saying that they are judgments that would be permitted by principles that could not reasonably be rejected, by people who were moved to find principles for the general regulation of behavior that others, similarly motivated, could not reasonably reject."

What might these principles be, that "others . . . could not reasonably reject"? This question is similar to that asked, above, about Kant's criterion of universalizability: What rules of conduct would people want to be obeyed universally, that is, without exception? Scanlon does not insist, like Kant, that moral principles must hold without exception, but only that they "could not be reasonably be rejected by people who were moved to find principles . . . that others, similarly motivated, could not reasonably reject." But what about people who might not be moved to find such principles—for example, Harman's cannibals, or Osama bin Laden and his terrorist followers? Clearly, they are not "similarly motivated" if we regard ourselves as typical moral judges. Do moral judgments then not apply to such recalcitrant examples?

(6) VIRTUE ETHICS

Many philosophers today, in agreement with Philippa Foot, consider all the theorists so far discussed to be too preoccupied with formulating rules of action, rather than clarifying the traits of character (virtues) that dispose people to act well and that serve as goals of moral education. Issues regarding how we should behave are less important, they claim, than issues regarding what we should be like, because a person of good character can be trusted to do the right thing whether guided by a rule or not, whereas a person of bad character will often act badly no matter what general ethical principles he or she professes. Therefore, the main task of ethical theory should be to identify and clarify the various moral virtues that make up good character and to resolve possible conflicts between them (such as justice vs. charity).

This point of view is not in competition with the others with respect to offering an alternative standard of morally right action as against divine command, universalizability, social benefit, convention, or ideal agreement (contractualism). Philippa Foot's own implicit standard seems to be the Aristotelian one of personal well-being, or *eudaimonia;* but other virtue theorists favor somewhat different standards. For example, Bernard Williams inclines toward some kind of generalizability, and A. C. MacIntyre seems closer to social traditions. What these theorists have in common is a focus on what we ought to be, rather than what we ought to do.

For models of moral theory, Foot refers to Aristotle and St. Thomas Aquinas to define the central moral virtues such as courage, temperance, prudence, and justice; explain how they contribute to individual and social well-being; and resolve apparent conflicts among them. Unlike Aristotle, Foot distinguishes genuinely moral virtues from what are often called "social virtues," such as charm and diplomacy, as well as from desirable skills, such as athletic or musical virtuosity. She prefers to focus on virtues rather than on rules because she believes that moral conduct is best encouraged by showing that it is to the long-run advantage of the agent as well as to the beneficiaries of the action to behave morally. Foot holds that the classical emphasis on rules—whether religious, Kantian, utilitarian, culturally relative, or ideally agreed upon—fails to perform the critical task of showing that morality and self-interest really coincide. The theorists in question might reply either that they do not always coincide, so that morality sometimes requires self-sacrifice, or that even if and when they do, it should not be for the sake of one's self-interest that one does the morally right thing.

(7) SELF-ASSERTION

Friedrich Nietzsche was perhaps the most eloquent spokesperson for the nineteenth-century romantic revolt against the sovereignty of reason professed by the eighteenth-century Enlightenment. Nietzsche fused elements of idealism, Darwinian evolutionary naturalism, and egoistic psychology into an ideal of life that stressed the "will to power" of the strong and creative individual. Nietzsche has been one of the few philosophers to denounce conventional morality as inimical to the values of sincere self-expression and emotional health. He denounces Judaism and Christianity as the sources of a "slave morality" that replaced the more natural "master-morality" of pre-Socratic Greece and the barbarian tribes that overran the Roman Empire. Master-morality, he claims, is the way of life of the naturally superior and creative individual, whose unrepressed instincts and passions create ever new standards of taste and conduct. Nietzsche holds that qualities such as courage, emotional and intellectual strength, and bold self-assertion are the true virtues that were appreciated in the ancient world but were subverted and replaced by the Christian virtues of humility, self-sacrifice, and meekness, which were appropriate only for slaves. His view might be considered a form of virtue ethics, but a rather inverted form.

(8) FEMINIST ETHICS

The distinguished contemporary philosopher Annette Baier disdains offering a rival set of moral principles as what she considers the too narrow limitation of moral theory to "a systematic account of a large area of moral philosophy with a keystone (i.e., a principle) supporting all the rest." She proposes instead a focus on the concept of trust, in contrast to the concept of obligation preferred by most male philosophers and also that of love preferred by some feminist philosophers. Baier thinks trust combines the partial merits of the other two approaches, so that a moral theory should inform us whom to trust and why, for the enforcement of moral obligations, as well as whom to trust to care for and assist us and thus to do the work of love. She does not try to formulate a general theory of trust but merely to establish the need for it.

Baier claims that an ethic of obligation, such as those of Adams or Kant, emphasizes coercive restraints on liberty—what one must not do, under coercive threat of blame or punishment—and thus does weakly what the criminal law does better, because a would-be miscreant would be more effectively deterred by the threat of criminal sanctions than by that of moral disapproval. This is a controversial claim, worth exploring in depth by both psychologists and philosophers. On the other hand, Baier argues, a pure ethic of love, such as that of early Christianity, supports a more cooperative and pleasant way of life but fails to provide us with guidelines as to whom to trust and to what degree. Moreover, it fails to explain the specific kind of trust involved in authorizing some persons to coerce others into behaving decently. Baier seems to be claiming that obligations can only be enforced by social authorities such as police, prosecutors, and judges, rather than by means of public and private criticism and exhortation. Is it true that the rules of obligatory conduct can be entrusted to the police and the courts to uphold, rather than to the conscience of the individual? As for love, does it really need an ethic? Can anyone tell us whom to love and why? These are questions well worth exploring, as Baier insists we should do.

DIVINE COMMAND

Robert Merrihew Adams

I

It is widely held that all those theories are indefensible which attempt to explain in terms of the will or commands of God what it is for an act to be ethically right or wrong. In this paper I shall state such a theory, which I believe to be defensible; and I shall try to defend it against what seem to me to be the most important and interesting objections to it. I call my theory a *modified* divine command theory because in it I renounce certain claims that are commonly made in divine command analyses of ethical terms. (I should add that it is *my* theory only in that I shall state it, and that I believe it is defensible — not that I am sure it is correct.) I present it as a theory of ethical *wrongness* partly for convenience. It could also be presented as a theory of the nature of ethical obligatoriness or of ethical permittedness. Indeed, I will have occasion to make some remarks about the concept of ethical permittedness. . . . I am not prepared to claim that the theory can be extended to all ethical terms; and it is therefore important that it not be presented as a theory about ethical terms in general.

It will be helpful to begin with the statement of a simple, *un*modified divine command theory of ethical wrongness. This is the theory that ethical wrongness *consists in* being contrary to God's commands, or that the word "wrong" in ethical contexts *means* "contrary to God's commands." It implies that the following two statement forms are logically equivalent.

> (1) It is wrong (for A) to do X.
> (2) It is contrary to God's commands (for A) to do X.

Of course that is not all that the theory implies. It also implies that (2) is conceptually prior to (1), so that the meaning of (1) is to be explained in terms of (2), and not the other way round. It might prove fairly difficult to state or explain in what that conceptual priority consists, but I shall not go into that here. I do not wish ultimately to defend the theory in its unmodified form, and I think I have stated it fully enough for my present purposes.

I have stated it as a theory about the meaning of the word "wrong" in ethical contexts. The most obvious objection to the theory is that the word

Robert M. Adams. "Divine Command." Excerpted from "A Modified Divine Command Theory of Ethical Wrongness" by Robert M. Adams, in *Religion and Morality* edited by G. Outka and J. Reeder. Copyright © 1987 Doubleday/Anchor (Garden City). Reprinted by permission of Doubleday, a division of Random House, Inc. [Original footnotes have been omitted.]

"wrong" is used in ethical contexts by many people who cannot mean by it what the theory says they must mean, since they do not believe that there exists a God. This objection seems to me sufficient to refute the theory if it is presented as an analysis of what *everybody* means by "wrong" in ethical contexts. The theory cannot reasonably be offered except as a theory about what the word "wrong" means as used by *some but not all* people in ethical contexts. Let us say that the theory offers an analysis of the meaning of "wrong" in Judeo-Christian religious ethical discourse. This restriction of scope will apply to my modified divine command theory too. . . .

In Section II, I will discuss what seems to me the most important objection to the unmodified divine command theory, and suggest how the theory can be modified to meet it. Section III will be devoted to a brief but fairly comprehensive account of the use of "wrong" in Judeo-Christian ethical discourse, from the point of view of the modified divine command theory. . . .

II

The following seems to me to be the gravest objection to the divine command theory of ethical wrongness, in the form in which I have stated it. Suppose God should command me to make it my chief end in life to inflict suffering on other human beings, for no other reason than that He commanded it. (For convenience I shall abbreviate this hypothesis to "Suppose God should command cruelty for its own sake.") Will it seriously be claimed that in that case it would be wrong for me not to practice cruelty for its own sake? I see three possible answers to this question.

(1) It might be claimed that it is logically impossible for God to command cruelty for its own sake. In that case, of course, we need not worry about whether it would be wrong to disobey if He did command it. It is senseless to agonize about what one should do in a logically impossible situation. This solution to the problem seems unlikely to be available to the divine command theorist, however. For why would he hold that it is logically impossible for God to command cruelty for its own sake? Some theologians (for instance, Thomas Aquinas) have believed (a) that what is right and wrong is independent of God's will, *and* (b) that God always does right by the necessity of His nature. Such theologians, if they believe that it would be wrong for God to command cruelty for its own sake, have reason to believe that it is logically impossible for Him to do so. But the divine command theorist, who does not agree that what is right and wrong is independent of God's will, does not seem to have such a reason to deny that it is logically possible for God to command cruelty for its own sake.

(2) Let us assume that it is logically possible for God to command cruelty for its own sake. In that case the divine command theory seems to imply that it would be wrong not to practice cruelty for its own sake. There have been at least a few adherents of divine command ethics who have been prepared to accept this consequence. William Ockham held that those acts which we call "theft," "adultery," and "hatred of God" would be meritorious if God

had commanded them. He would surely have said the same about what I have been calling the practice of "cruelty for its own sake."

This position is one which I suspect most of us are likely to find somewhat shocking, even repulsive. We should therefore be particularly careful not to misunderstand it. We need not imagine that Ockham disciplined himself to be ready to practice cruelty for its own sake if God should command it. It was doubtless an article of faith for him that God is unalterably opposed to any such practice. The mere logical possibility that theft, adultery, and cruelty might have been commanded by God (and therefore meritorious) doubtless did not represent in Ockham's view any real possibility.

(3) Nonetheless, the view that if God commanded cruelty for its own sake it would be wrong not to practice it seems unacceptable to me; and I think many, perhaps most, other Jewish and Christian believers would find it unacceptable too. I must make clear the sense in which I find it unsatisfactory. It is not that I find an internal inconsistency in it. And I would not deny that it may reflect, accurately enough, the way in which some believers use the word "wrong." I might as well frankly avow that I am looking for a divine command theory which at least might possibly be a correct account of how *I* use the word "wrong." I do not use the word "wrong" in such a way that I would say that it would be wrong not to practice cruelty if God commanded it, and I am sure that many other believers agree with me on this point.

But now have I not rejected the divine command theory? I have assumed that it would be logically possible for God to command cruelty for its own sake. And I have rejected the view that if God commanded cruelty for its own sake, it would be wrong not to obey. It seems to follow that I am committed to the view that in certain logically possible circumstances it would not be wrong to disobey God. This position seems to be inconsistent with the theory that "wrong" means "contrary to God's commands."

I want to argue, however, that it is still open to me to accept a modified form of the divine command theory of ethical wrongness. According to the modified divine command theory, when I say, "It is wrong to do X," (at least part of) what I *mean* is that it is contrary to God's commands to do X. "It is wrong to do X" *implies* "It is contrary to God's commands to do X." But "It is contrary to God's commands to do X" implies "It is wrong to do X" only if certain conditions are assumed—namely, only if it is assumed that God has the character which I believe Him to have, of loving His human creatures. If God were really to command us to make cruelty our goal, then He would not have that character of loving us, and I would not say it would be wrong to disobey Him.

But do I say that it would be wrong to obey Him in such a case? This is the point at which I am in danger of abandoning the divine command theory completely. I do abandon it completely if I say both of the following things.

(A) It would be wrong to obey God if He commanded cruelty for its own sake.

(B) In (A), "wrong" is used in what is for me its normal ethical sense.

If I assert both (A) and (B), it is clear that I cannot consistently maintain that "wrong" in its normal ethical sense for me means or implies "contrary to God's commands."

But from the fact that I deny that it would be wrong to disobey God if He commanded cruelty for its own sake, it does not follow that I must accept (A) and (B). Of course someone might claim that obedience and disobedience would both be ethically permitted in such a case; but that is not the view that I am suggesting. If I adopt the modified divine command theory as an analysis of my present concept of ethical wrongness (and if I adopt a similar analysis of my concept of ethical permittedness), I will not hold either that it would be wrong to disobey, or that it would be ethically permitted to disobey, or that it would be wrong to obey, or that it would be ethically permitted to obey, if God commanded cruelty for its own sake. For I will say that my concept of ethical wrongness (and my concept of ethical permittedness) would "break down" if I really believed that God commanded cruelty for its own sake. Or to put the matter somewhat more prosaically, I will say that my concepts of ethical wrongness and permittedness could not serve the functions they now serve, because using those concepts I could not call any action ethically wrong or ethically permitted, if I believed that God's will was so unloving. This position can be explained or developed in either of two ways, each of which has its advantages.

I could say that by "X is ethically wrong" I mean "X is contrary to the commands of a *loving* God" (i.e., "There is a *loving* God and X is contrary to His commands") and by "X is ethically permitted" I mean "X is in accord with the commands of a *loving* God" (i.e., "There is a *loving* God and X is not contrary to His commands"). On this analysis we can reason as follows. If there is only one God and He commands cruelty for its own sake, then presumably there is not a *loving* God. If there is not a loving God then neither "X is ethically wrong" nor "X is ethically permitted" is true of any X. Using my present concepts of ethical wrongness and permittedness, therefore, I could not (consistently) call any action ethically wrong or permitted if I believed that God commanded cruelty for its own sake. This way of developing the modified divine command theory is the simpler and neater of the two, and that might reasonably lead one to choose it for the construction of a theological ethical theory. On the other hand, I think it is also simpler and neater than ordinary religious ethical discourse, in which (for example) it may be felt that the statement that a certain act is wrong is *about* the will or commands of God in a way in which it is not about His love.

In this essay I shall prefer a second, rather similar, but somewhat untidier, understanding of the modified divine command theory, because I think it may lead us into some insights about the complexities of actual religious ethical discourse. According to this second version of the theory, the statement that something is ethically wrong (or permitted) says something about the will or commands of God, but not about His love. Every such statement, however, *presupposes* that certain conditions for the applicability of the believer's concepts of ethical right and wrong are satisfied. Among these conditions is that God does not command cruelty for its own sake—or, more generally, that God loves His human creatures. It need not be assumed that God's love is the only such condition.

The modified divine command theorist can say that the possibility of God commanding cruelty for its own sake is not provided for in the Judeo-Christian religious ethical system as he understands it. The possibility is not provided for, in the sense that the concepts of right and wrong have not been developed in such a way that actions could be correctly said to be right or wrong if God were believed to command cruelty for its own sake. The modified divine command theorist agrees that it is logically possible that God should command cruelty for its own sake; but he holds that it is unthinkable that God should do so. To have *faith* in God is not just to believe that He exists, but also to trust in His love for mankind. The believer's concepts of ethical wrongness and permittedness are developed within the framework of his (or the religious community's) religious life, and therefore within the framework of the assumption that God loves us. The concept of the will or commands of God has a certain function in the believer's life, and the use of the words "right" (in the sense of "ethically permitted") and "wrong" is tied to that function of that concept. But one of the reasons why the concept of the will of God can function as it does is that the love which God is believed to have toward men arouses in the believer certain attitudes of love toward God and devotion to His will. If the believer thinks about the unthinkable but logically possible situation in which God commands cruelty for its own sake, he finds that in relation to that kind of command of God he cannot take up the same attitude, and that the concept of the will or commands of God could not then have the same function in his life. For this reason he will not say that it would be wrong to disobey God, or right to obey Him, in that situation. At the same time he will not say that it would be wrong to obey God in that situation, because he is accustomed to use the word "wrong" to say that something is contrary to the will of God, and it does not seem to him to be the right word to use to express his own personal revulsion toward an act against which there would be no divine authority. Similarly, he will not say that it would be "right," in the sense of "ethically permitted," to disobey God's command of cruelty; for that does not seem to him to be the right way to express his own personal attitude toward an act which would not be in accord with a divine authority. In this way the believer's concepts of ethical rightness and wrongness would break down in the situation in which he believed that God commanded cruelty for its own sake—that is, they would not function as they now do, because he would not be prepared to use them to say that any action was right or wrong.

III

It is clear that according to this modified divine command theory, the meaning of the word "wrong" in Judeo-Christian ethical discourse must be understood in terms of a complex of relations which believers' use of the word has, not only to their beliefs about God's commands, but also to their attitudes toward certain types of action. I think it will help us to understand the theory better if we can give a brief but fairly comprehensive description of the most important features of the Judeo-Christian ethical use of "wrong," from the point of view of the modified divine command theory. That is what I shall try to do in this section.

(1) "Wrong" and "contrary to God's commands" at least contextually imply each other in Judeo-Christian ethical discourse. "It is wrong to do X" will be assented to by the sincere Jewish or Christian believer if and only if he assents to "It is contrary to God's commands to do X." This is a fact sufficiently well known that the known believer who says the one commits himself publicly to the other.

Indeed "wrong" and such expressions as "against the will of God" seem to be used interchangeably in religious ethical discourse. If a believer asks his pastor, "Do you think it's always against the will of God to use contraceptives?" and the pastor replies, "I don't see anything wrong with the use of contraceptives in many cases," the pastor has answered the same question the inquirer asked.

(2) In ethical contexts, the statement that a certain action is wrong normally expresses certain volitional and emotional attitudes toward that action. In particular it normally expresses an intention, or at least an inclination, not to perform the action, and/or dispositions to feel guilty if one has performed it, to discourage others from performing it, and to react with anger, sorrow, or diminished respect toward others if they have performed it. I think this is true of Judeo-Christian ethical discourse as well as of other ethical discourse.

The interchangeability of "wrong" and "against the will of God" applies in full force here. It seems to make no difference to the expressive function of an ethical statement in a Judeo-Christian context which of these expressions is used. So far as I can see, the feelings and dispositions normally expressed by "It is wrong to commit suicide" in a Judeo-Christian context are exactly the same as those normally expressed by "It is against God's will to commit suicide," or by "Suicide is a violation of the commandments of God."

I am speaking of attitudes *normally* expressed by statements that it is wrong to do a certain thing, or that it would be against God's will or commands to do that thing. I am not claiming that such attitudes are *always* expressed by statements of those sorts. Neither am I now suggesting any analysis of the *meaning* of the statements in terms of the attitudes they normally express. The relation between the meaning of the statements and the attitudes expressed is a matter about which I shall have somewhat more to say, later in this section . . . At this point I am simply observing that in fact statements of the forms "It is wrong to do X," "It is against God's will to do X," "X is a violation of the commandments of God," normally do express certain attitudes, and that in Judeo-Christian ethical discourse they all typically express the same attitudes.

Of course these attitudes can be specified only within certain very wide limits of normality. The experience of guilt, for instance, or the feelings that one has about conduct of others of which one disapproves, vary greatly from one individual to another, and in the same individual from one occasion to another.

(3) In a Judeo-Christian context, moreover, the attitudes expressed by a statement that something is wrong are normally quite strongly affected and colored by specifically religious feelings and interests. They are apt to be motivated in various degrees by, and mixed in various proportions with, love, devotion, and loyalty toward God, and/or fear of God. Ethical wrongdoing is seen and experienced as *sin,* as rupture of personal or communal relationship with God. The normal feelings and experience of guilt for Judeo-Christian believers surely cannot be separated from beliefs, and ritual and devotional practices, having to do with God's judgment and forgiveness.

In all sin there is offense against a person (God), even when there is no offense against any other human person—for instance, if I have a vice which harms me but does not importantly harm any other human being. Therefore in the Judeo-Christian tradition reactions which are appropriate when one has offended another person are felt to be appropriate reactions to any ethical fault, regardless of whether another human being has been offended. I think this affects rather importantly the emotional connections of the word "wrong" in Judeo-Christian discourse.

(4) When a Judeo-Christian believer is trying to decide, in an ethical way, whether it would be wrong for him to do a certain thing, he typically thinks of himself as trying to determine whether it would be against God's will for him to do it. His deliberations may turn on the interpretation of certain religiously authoritative texts. They may be partly carried out in the form of prayer. It is quite possible, however, that his deliberations will take forms more familiar to the nonbeliever. Possibly his theology will encourage him to give some weight to his own intuitions and feelings about the matter, and those of other people. Such encouragement might be provided, for instance, by a doctrine of the leading of the Holy Spirit. Probably the believer will accept certain very general ethical principles as expressing commandments of God, and most of these may be principles which many nonbelievers would also accept (for instance, that it is always, or with very few exceptions, wrong to kill another human being). The believer's deliberation might consist entirely of reasoning from such general principles. But he would still regard it as an attempt to discover God's will on the matter.

(5) Typically, the Judeo-Christian believer is a nonnaturalist objectivist about ethical wrongness. When he says that something is (ethically) wrong, he means to be stating what he believes to be a fact of a certain sort—what I shall call a "nonnatural objective fact." Such a fact is objective in the sense that whether it obtains or not does not depend on whether any human being thinks it does. It is harder to give a satisfactory explanation of what I mean by "nonnatural" here. Let us say that a nonnatural fact is one which does not consist simply in any fact or complex of facts which can be stated entirely in the languages of physics, chemistry, biology, and human psychology. That way of putting it obviously raises questions which it leaves unanswered, but I hope it may be clear enough for present purposes.

That ethical facts are objective and nonnatural has been believed by many people, including some famous philosophers—for instance, Plato and G. E. Moore. The term "nonnaturalism" is sometimes used rather narrowly, to refer to a position held by Moore, and positions closely resembling it. Clearly, I am using "nonnaturalist" in a broader sense here.

Given that the facts of wrongness asserted in Judeo-Christian ethics are nonnatural in the sense explained above, and that they accordingly do not consist entirely in facts of physics, chemistry, biology, and human psychology, the question arises, in what they do consist. According to the divine command theory (even the modified divine command theory), in so far as they are nonnatural and objective, they consist in facts about the will or commands of God. I think this is really the central point in a divine command theory of ethical wrongness. This is the point at which the divine command theory is distinguished from alternative theological theories of ethical wrongness, such as the theory that facts of ethical rightness and wrongness are objective, nonnatural facts about ideas or essences subsisting eternally in God's understanding, not subject to His will but guiding it.

The divine command account of the nonnatural fact-stating function of Judeo-Christian ethical discourse has at least one advantage over its competitors. It is clear, I think, that in stating that X is wrong a believer normally commits himself to the view that X is contrary to the will or commands of God. And the fact (if it is a fact) that X is contrary to the will or commands of God is surely a nonnatural objective fact. But it is not nearly so clear that in saying that X is wrong, the believer normally commits himself to belief in any *other* nonnatural objective fact. (The preceding sentence presupposes the rejection of the Moorean view that the fact that X is wrong is an objective nonnatural fact which cannot and should not be analyzed in terms of other facts, natural or nonnatural.)

(6) The modified divine command theorist cannot consistently claim that "wrong" and "contrary to God's commands" have exactly the same meaning for him. For he admits that there is a logically possible situation which he would describe by saying, "God commands cruelty for its own sake," but not by saying, "It would be wrong not to practice cruelty for its own sake." If there were not at least some little difference between the meanings with which he actually, normally uses the expressions "wrong" and "contrary to God's commands," there would be no reason for them to differ in their applicability or inapplicability to the far-out unthinkable case. We may now be in a position to improve somewhat our understanding of what the modified divine command theorist can suppose that difference in meaning to be, and of why he supposes that the believer is unwilling to say that disobedience to a divine command of cruelty for its own sake would be wrong.

We have seen that the expressions "It is wrong" and "It is contrary to God's commands" or "It is against the will of God" have virtually the same uses in religious ethical discourse, and the same functions in the religious ethical life. No doubt they differ slightly in the situations in which they are most likely to be used and the emotional overtones they are most apt to carry. But in all situations experienced or expected by the believer as a believer they at least contextually imply each other, and normally express the same or extremely similar emotional and volitional attitudes.

There is also a difference in meaning, however, a difference which is normally of no practical importance. All three of the following are aspects of the normal use of "it is wrong" in the life and conversation of believers. (a) It is used to state what are believed to be facts about the will or commands of God. (b) It is used in formulating decisions and arguments about what to do (i.e., not just in deciding what one *ought* to do, but in deciding *what to do*). (c) It expresses certain emotional and volitional attitudes toward the action under discussion. "It is wrong" is commonly used to do all three of those things at once.

The same is true of "It is contrary to God's commands" and "It is against the will of God." They are commonly used by believers to do the same three things, and to do them at once. But because of their grammatical form and their formal relationships with other straightforwardly descriptive expressions about God, they are taken to be, first and last, descriptive expressions about God and His relation to whatever actions are under discussion. They can therefore be used to state what are supposed to be facts about God, even when one's emotional and decision-making attitude toward those supposed facts is quite contrary to the attitudes normally expressed by the words "against the will of God."

In the case of "It is wrong," however, it is not clear that one of its functions, or one of the aspects of its normal use, is to be preferred in case of conflict with the others. I am not willing to say, "It would be wrong not to do X," when both my own attitude and the attitude of most other people toward the doing of X under the indicated circumstances is one of unqualified revulsion. On the other hand, neither am I willing to say, "It would be wrong to do X," when I would merely be expressing my own personal revulsion (and perhaps that of other people as well) but nothing that I could regard as clothed in the majesty of a divine authority. The believer's concept of ethical wrongness therefore breaks down if one tries to apply it to the unthinkable case in which God commands cruelty for its own sake.

None of this seems to me inconsistent with the claim that part of what the believer normally means in saying "X is wrong" is that X is contrary to God's will or commands.

RATIONALITY

Immanuel Kant

PART ONE

Nothing in the whole world, or even outside of the world, can possibly be regarded as good without limitation except a *good will.* No doubt it is a good and desirable thing to have intelligence, sagacity, judgment, and other intellectual gifts, by whatever name they may be called; it is also good and desirable in many respects to possess by nature such qualities as courage, resolution, and perseverance; but all these gifts of nature may be in the highest degree pernicious and hurtful, if the will which directs them, or what is called the *character,* is not itself good. The same thing applies to *gifts of fortune.* Power, wealth, honor, even good health, and that general well-being and contentment with one's lot which we call *happiness,* give rise to pride and not infrequently to insolence, if a man's will is not good; nor can a reflective and impartial spectator ever look with satisfaction upon the unbroken prosperity of a man who is destitute of the ornament of a pure and good will. A good will would therefore seem to be the indispensable condition without which no one is even worthy to be happy.

A man's will is good, not because the consequences which flow from it are good, nor because it is capable of attaining the end which it seeks, but it is good in itself, or because it wills the good. By a good will is not meant mere well-wishing; it consists in a resolute employment of all the means within one's reach, and its intrinsic value is in no way increased by success or lessened by failure.

This idea of the absolute value of mere will seems so extraordinary that, although it is endorsed even by the popular judgment, we must subject it to careful scrutiny.

If nature had meant to provide simply for the maintenance, the well-being, in a word the happiness, of beings which have reason and will, it must be confessed that, in making use of their reason, it has hit upon a very poor way of attaining its end. As a matter of fact the very worst way a man of refinement and culture can take to secure enjoyment and happiness is to make use of his reason for that purpose. Hence there is apt to arise in his mind a certain degree of *misology,* or hatred of reason. Finding that the arts which minister to luxury, and even the sciences, instead of bringing him happiness, only lay a heavier yoke on his neck, he at length comes to envy, rather than to despise, men of less refinement, who follow more closely the promptings of their natural impulses, and pay little heed to what reason tells them to do or to leave undone. It must at least be admitted, that one may deny reason to have much or indeed any value in the production of happiness and contentment, without taking a morose or ungrateful view of the goodness with which the world is governed. Such a judgment really means that life has another and a much nobler end than happiness, and that the true vocation of reason is to secure that end.

The true object of reason then, in so far as it is practical, or capable of influencing the will, must be to produce a will which is *good in itself,* and not merely good *as a means* to something else. This will is not the only or the whole good, but it is the highest good, and the condition of all other good, even of the desire for happiness itself. It is therefore not inconsistent with the wisdom of nature that the cultivation of reason which is essential to the furtherance of its first and unconditioned object, the production of a good will, in this life at least, in many ways limits, or even makes impossible, the attainment of happiness, which is its second and conditioned object.

To bring to clear consciousness the conception of a will which is good in itself, a conception already familiar to the popular mind, let us examine the conception of *duty,* which involves the idea of a good will as manifested under certain subjective limitations and hindrances.

I pass over actions which are admittedly violations of duty, for these, however useful they may be in the attainment of this or that end, manifestly do not proceed *from* duty. I set aside also those actions which are not actually inconsistent with duty, but which yet are done under the impulse of some natural inclination, although *not a direct inclination* to do these particular actions; for in these it is easy to determine whether the action that is consistent with duty, is done *from duty* or with some selfish object in view. It is more difficult to make a clear distinction of motives when there is a *direct* inclination to do a certain action, which is itself in conformity with duty. The preservation of one's own life, for instance, is a duty; but, as everyone has a natural inclination to preserve his life, the anxious care which most men usually devote to this object, has no intrinsic value, nor the maximum from which they act any moral import. They preserve their life *in accordance with* duty, but not *because of* duty. But, suppose adversity and hopeless sorrow to have taken away all desire for life; suppose that the wretched man would welcome death as a release, and yet takes means to prolong his life simply from a sense of duty; then his maxim has a genuine moral import.

But, secondly, an action that is done from duty gets its moral value, *not from the object* which it is intended to secure, but from the maxim by which it is determined. Accordingly, the action has the same moral value whether the object is attained or not, if only the *principle* by which the will is determined to act is independent of every object of sensuous desire. What was said above makes it clear, that it is not the object aimed at, or, in other words, the consequences which flow from an action when these are made the end and motive of the will, that can give to the action an unconditioned and moral value. In what, then, can the moral value of an action consist, if it does not lie in the will itself, as directed to the attainment of a certain object? It can lie only in the principle of the will, no matter whether the object sought can be attained by the action or not. For the will stands as it were at the parting of the ways, between its *a priori* principle, which is formal, and its *a posteriori* material motive. As so standing it must be determined by something, and, as no action which is done from duty can be determined by a material principle, it can be determined only by the formal principle of all volition.

From the two propositions just set forth a third directly follows, which may be thus stated: *Duty is the obligation to act from reverence for law.* Now, I may have a natural *inclination* for the object that I expect to follow from my action, but I can never have *reverence* for that which is not a spontaneous activity of my will, but merely an effect of it; neither can I have reverence for any natural inclination, whether it is my own or another's. If it is my own, I can at most only approve of it; if it is manifested by another, I may regard it as conducive to my own interest, and hence I may in certain cases even be said to have a love for it. But the only thing which I can reverence or which can lay me under an obligation to act, is the law which is connected with my will, not as a consequence, but as a principle; a principle which is not dependent upon natural inclination, but overmasters it, or at least allows it to have no influence whatever in determining my course of action. Now if an action which is done out of regard for duty sets entirely aside the influence of natural inclination and along with it every object of the will, nothing else is left by which the will can be determined but objectively the *law* itself, and subjectively *pure reverence* for the law as a principle of action. Thus there arises the maxim, to obey the moral law even at the sacrifice of all my natural inclinations.

The supreme good which we call moral can therefore be nothing but the *idea of the law* in itself, in so far as it is this idea which determines the will, and not any consequences that are expected to follow. Only a *rational* being can have such an idea, and hence a man who acts from the idea of the law is already morally good, no matter whether the consequences which he expects from his action follow or not.

Now what must be the nature of a law, the idea of which is to determine the will, even apart from the effects expected to follow, and which is therefore itself entitled to be called good absolutely and without qualification? As the will must not be moved to act from any desire for the results expected to follow from obedience to a certain law, the only principle of the will which remains is that of the conformity of actions to universal law. In all cases I must act in such a way *that I can at the same time will that my maxim should become a universal law.* This is what is meant by conformity to law pure and simple; and this is the principle which serves, and must serve, to determine the will, if the idea of duty is not to be regarded as empty and chimerical. As a matter of fact the judgments which we are wont to pass upon conduct perfectly agree with this principle, and in making them we always have it before our eyes.

May I, for instance, under the pressure of circumstances, make a promise which I have no intention of keeping? The question is not, whether it is prudent to make a false promise, but whether it is morally right. To enable me to answer this question shortly and conclusively, the best way is for me to ask myself whether it would satisfy me that the maximum to extricate myself from embarrassment by giving a false promise should have the force of a universal law, applying to others as well as to myself. And I see at once, that, while I can certainly will the lie, I cannot will that lying should be a universal law. If lying were universal, there would, properly speaking, be no promises whatever. I might say that I intended to do a certain thing at some future time, but nobody would believe me, or if he did at the moment trust to my promise, he would afterwards pay me back in my own coin. My maxim thus proves itself to be self-destructive, so soon as it is taken as a universal law.

Duty, then, consists in the obligation to act from *pure* reverence for the moral law. To this motive all others must give way, for it is the condition of a will which is good *in itself,* and which has a value with which nothing else is comparable.

There is, however, in man a strong feeling of antagonism to the commands of duty, although his reason tells him that those commands are worthy of the highest reverence. For man not only possesses reason, but he has certain natural wants and inclinations, the complete satisfaction of which he calls happiness. These natural inclinations clamorously demand to have their seemingly reasonable claims respected; but reason issues its commands inflexibly, refusing to promise anything to the natural desires, and treating their claims with a sort of neglect and contempt. From this there arises a *natural dialectic,* that is, a disposition to explain away the strict laws of duty, to cast doubt upon their validity, or at least, upon their purity and stringency, and in this way to make them yield to the demands of the natural inclinations.

Thus men are forced to go beyond the narrow circle of ideas within which their reason ordinarily moves, and to take a step into the field of *moral philosophy,* not indeed from any perception of speculative difficulties, but simply on practical grounds. The practical reason of men cannot be long exercised any more than the theoretical, without falling insensibly into a dialectic, which compels it to call in the aid of philosophy; and in the one case as in the other, rest can be found only in a thorough criticism of human reason.

PART TWO

So far, we have drawn our conception of duty from the manner in which men employ it in the ordinary exercise of their practical reason. The conception of duty, however, we must not suppose to be therefore derived from experience. On the contrary, we hear frequent complaints, the justice of which we cannot but admit, that no one can point to a single instance in which an action has undoubtedly been done purely from a regard for duty; that there are certainly many actions which are not *opposed* to duty, but none which are indisputably done *from* duty and therefore have a moral value. Nothing indeed can secure us against the complete loss of our ideas of duty, and maintain in the soul a well-grounded respect for the moral law, but the clear conviction, that reason issues its commands on its own authority, without caring in the least whether the actions of men have, as a matter of fact, been done purely from ideas of duty. For reason commands inflexibly that certain actions should be done, which perhaps never have been done; actions, the very possibility of which may seem doubtful to one who bases everything upon experience. Perfect disinterestedness in friendship, for instance, is demanded of every man, although there may never have been a sincere friend; for pure friendship is bound up with the idea of duty as duty, and belongs to the very idea of a reason which determines the will on *a priori* grounds, prior to all experience.

It is, moreover, beyond dispute, that unless we are to deny to morality all truth and all reference to a possible object, the moral law has so wide an application that it is binding, not merely upon man, but upon all *rational beings*, and not merely under certain contingent conditions, and with certain limitations, but absolutely and necessarily. And it is plain, that no experience could ever lead us to suppose that laws of this apodictic character are even possible.

There is, therefore, no genuine supreme principle of morality, which is not independent of all experience, and based entirely upon pure reason. If, then, we are to have a philosophy of morality at all, as distinguished from a popular moral philosophy, we may take it for granted without further investigation, that moral conceptions, together with the principles which flow from them, are given *a priori* and must be presented in their generality (*in abstracto*).

Such a metaphysic of morality, which must be entirely free from all admixture of empirical psychology, theology, physics and hyperphysics, and above all from all occult or, as we may call them, hypophysical qualities, is not only indispensable as a foundation for a sound theory of duties, but it is also of the highest importance in the practical realization of moral precepts. For the pure idea of duty, unmixed with any foreign ingredient of sensuous desire, in a word, the idea of the moral law, influences the heart of man much more powerfully through his reason, which in this way only becomes conscious that it can of itself be practical, than do all the motives which have their source in experience. Conscious of its own dignity, the moral law treats all sensuous desires with contempt, and is able to master them one by one.

From what has been said it is evident, that all moral conceptions have their seat and origin in reason entirely *a priori,* and are apprehended by the ordinary reason of men as well as by reason in its purely speculative activity. We have also seen that it is of the greatest importance, not only in the construction by speculative reason of a theory of morality, but also with a view to the practical conduct of life, to derive the conceptions and laws of morality from pure reason, to present them pure and unmixed, and to mark out the sphere of this whole practical or pure knowledge of reason. Nor is it permissible, in seeking to determine the whole faculty of pure practical reason, to make its principles dependent upon the peculiar nature of human reason, as we were allowed to do, and sometimes were even forced to do, in speculative philosophy; for moral laws must apply to every rational being, and must therefore be derived from the very conception of a rational being as such.

To show the need of advancing not only from the common moral judgments of men to the philosophical, but from a popular philosophy, which merely gropes its way by the help of examples, to a metaphysic of morality, we must begin at the point where the practical faculty of reason supplies general rules of action, and exhibit clearly the steps by which it attains to the conception of duty.

Everything in nature acts in conformity with law. Only a rational being has the faculty of acting in conformity with the *idea* of law, or from principles; only a rational being, in other words, has a will. And as without reason actions cannot proceed from laws, will is simply practical reason. If the will is infallibly determined by reason, the actions of a rational being are subjectively as well as objectively necessary; that is, will must be regarded as a faculty of choosing *that only* which reason, independently of natural inclination, declares to be practically necessary or good. On the other hand, if the will is not invariably determined by reason alone, but is subject to certain subjective conditions or motives, which are not always in harmony with the objective conditions; if the will, as actually is the case with *man,* is not in perfect conformity with reason; actions which are recognized to be objectively necessary, are subjectively contingent. The determination of such a will according to objective laws is therefore called *obligation.* That is to say, if the will of a rational being is not absolutely good, we conceive of it as capable of being determined by objective laws of reason, but not as by its very nature necessarily obeying them.

The idea that a certain principle is objective, and binding upon the will, is a command of reason, and the statement of the command in a formula is an *imperative.*

All imperatives are expressed by the word *ought,* to indicate that the will upon which they are binding is not by its subjective constitution necessarily determined in conformity with the objective law of reason. An imperative says, that the doing, or leaving undone of a certain thing would be good, but it addresses a will which does not always do a thing simply because it is good. Now, that is practically *good* which determines the will by ideas of reason, in other words, that which determines it, not by subjective influences, but by principles which are objective, or apply to all rational beings as such. *Good* and *pleasure* are quite distinct. Pleasure results from the influence of purely subjective causes upon the will of the subject, and these vary with the susceptibility of this or that individual, while a principle of reason is valid for all.

A perfectly good will would, like the will of man, stand under objective laws, laws of the good, but it could not be said to be under an *obligation* to act in conformity with those laws. Such a will by its subjective constitution could be determined only by the idea of the good. In reference to the Divine will, or any other holy will, imperatives have no meaning; for here the will is by its very nature necessarily in harmony with the law, and therefore *ought* has no application to it. Imperatives are formulae, which express merely the relation of objective laws of volition in general to the imperfect will of this or that rational being, as for instance, the will of man.

Now, all imperatives command either *hypothetically* or *categorically.* A hypothetical imperative states that a certain thing must be done, if something else which is willed, or at least might be willed, is to be attained. The categorical imperative declares that an act is in itself or objectively necessary, without any reference to another end.

Every practical law represents a possible action as good, and therefore as obligatory for a subject that is capable of being determined to act by reason. Hence all imperatives are formulae for the determination of an action which is obligatory according to the principle of a will that is in some sense good. If the action is good only because it is a means to *something else,* the imperative is *hypothetical;* if the action is conceived to be good *in itself,* the imperative, as the necessary principle of a will that in itself conforms to reason, is *categorical.*

An imperative, then, states what possible action of mine would be good. It supplies the practical rule for a will which does not at once do an act simply because it is good, either because the subject does not know it to be good, or because, knowing it to be good, he is influenced by maxims which are opposed to the objective principles of a practical reason.

The hypothetical imperative says only that an action is good relatively to a certain *possible* end or to a certain *actual* end. In the former case it is *problematic,* in the latter case *assertoric.* The categorical imperative, which affirms that an action is in itself or objectively necessary without regard to an end, that is, without regard to any other end than itself, is an *apodictic* practical principle.

Whatever is within the power of a rational being may be conceived to be capable of being willed by some rational being, and hence the principles which determine what actions are necessary in the attainment of certain possible ends, are infinite in number.

Yet there is one thing which we may assume that all finite rational beings actually make their end, and there is therefore one object which may safely be regarded, not simply as something that they *may* seek, but as something that by a necessity of their nature they actually *do* seek. This object is *happiness.* The hypothetical imperative, which affirms the practical necessity of an action as the means of attaining happiness, is *assertoric.* We must not think of happiness as simply a possible and problematic end, but as an end that we may with confidence presuppose *a priori* to be sought by everyone, belonging as it does to the very nature of man. Now skill in the choice of means to his own greatest well-being may be called *prudence,* taking the word in its more restricted sense. An imperative, therefore, which relates merely to the choice of means to one's own happiness, that is, a maxim of prudence, must be hypothetical; it commands an action, not absolutely, but only as a means to another end.

Lastly, there is an imperative which directly commands an action, without presupposing as its condition that some other end is to be attained by means of that action. This imperative is *categorical*. It has to do, not with the matter of an action and the result expected to follow from it, but simply with the form and principle from which the action itself proceeds. The action is essentially good if the motive of the agent is good, let the consequences be what they may. This imperative may be called the imperative of *morality*.

How are all these imperatives possible? The question is not, How is an action which an imperative commands actually realized? but, How can we think of the will as placed under obligation by each of those imperatives? Very little need be said to show an imperative of skill is possible. He who wills the end, wills also the means in his power which are indispensable to the attainment of the end. Looking simply at the act of will, we must say that this proposition is analytic. If a certain object is to follow as an effect from my volition, my causality must be conceived as active in the production of the effect, or as employing the means by which the effect will take place. The imperative, therefore, simply states that in the conception of the willing of this end there is directly implied the conception of actions necessary to this end. No doubt certain synthetic propositions are required to determine the particular means by which a given end may be attained, but these have nothing to do with the principle or act of the will, but merely state how the object may actually be realized.

Were it as easy to give a definite conception of happiness as of a particular end, the imperatives of prudence would be of exactly the same nature as the imperatives of skill, and would therefore be analytic. For, we should be able to say, that he who wills the end wills also the only means in his power for the attainment of the end. But, unfortunately, the conception of happiness is so indefinite, that, although every man desires to obtain it, he is unable to give a definite and self-consistent statement of what he actually desires and wills. The truth is, that, strictly speaking, the imperatives of prudence are not commands at all. They do not say that actions are objective or *necessary*, and hence they must be regarded as counsels (*consilia*), not as commands (*praecepta*) of reason. Still, the imperative of prudence would be an analytic proposition, if the means to happiness could only be known with certainty. For the only difference in the two cases is that in the imperative of skill the end is merely possible, in the imperative of prudence it is actually given; and as in both all that is commanded is the means to an end which is assumed to be willed, the imperative which commands that he who wills the end should also will the means, is in both cases analytic. There is therefore no real difficulty in seeing how an imperative of prudence is possible.

The only question which is difficult of solution, is, how the imperative of morality is possible. Here the imperative is not hypothetical, and hence we cannot derive its objective necessity from any presupposition. Nor must it for a moment be forgotten, that an imperative of this sort cannot be established by instances taken from experience. We must therefore find out by careful investigation, whether imperatives which seem to be categorical may not be simply hypothetical imperatives in disguise.

One thing is plain at the very outset, namely, that only a categorical imperative can have the dignity of a practical *law,* and that the other imperatives, while they may no doubt be called *principles* of the will, cannot be called laws. An action which is necessary merely as a means to an arbitrary end, may be regarded as itself contingent, and if the end is abandoned, the maxim which prescribes the action has no longer any force. An unconditioned command, on the other hand, does not permit the will to choose the opposite, and therefore it carries with it the necessity which is essential to a law.

It is, however, very hard to see how there can be a categorical imperative or law of morality at all. Such a law is an *a priori* synthetic proposition, and we cannot expect that there will be less difficulty in showing how a proposition of that sort is possible in the sphere of morality than we have found it to be in the sphere of knowledge.

In attempting to solve this problem, we shall first of all inquire, whether the mere conception of a categorical imperative may not perhaps supply us with a formula, which contains the only proposition that can possibly be a categorical imperative. The more difficult question, how such an absolute command is possible at all, will require a special investigation, which must be postponed to the last section.

If I take the mere conception of a hypothetical imperative, I cannot tell what it may contain until the condition under which it applies is presented to me. But I can tell at once from the very conception of a categorical imperative what it must contain. Viewed apart from the law, the imperative simply affirms that the maxim, or subjective principle of action, must conform to the objective principle or law. Now the law contains no condition to which it is restricted, and hence nothing remains but the statement, that the maxim ought to conform to the universality of the law as such. It is only this conformity to law that the imperative can be said to represent as necessary.

There is therefore but one categorical imperative, which may be thus stated: *Act in conformity with that maxim, and that maxim only, which you can at the same time will to be a universal law.*

Now, if from this single imperative, as from their principle, all imperatives of duty can be derived, we shall at least be able to indicate what we mean by the categorical imperative and what the conception of it implies, although we shall not be able to say whether the conception of duty may not itself be empty.

The universality of the law which governs the succession of events, is what we mean by *nature,* in the most general sense, that is, the existence of things, in so far as their existence is determined in conformity with universal laws. The universal imperative of duty might therefore be put in this way: *Act as if the maxim from which you act were to become through your will a universal law of nature.*

If we attend to what goes on in ourselves in every transgression of a duty, we find, that we do not will that our maxim should become a universal law. We find it in fact impossible to do so, and we really will that the opposite of our maxim should remain a universal law, at the same time that we assume the liberty of making an exception in favor of natural inclination in our own case, or perhaps only for this particular occasion. Hence, if we looked at all cases from the same point of view, that is, from the point of view of reason, we should see that there was here a contradiction in our will. The contradiction is, that a certain principle is admitted to be necessary objectively or as a universal law, and yet is held not to be universal subjectively, but to admit of exceptions. What we do is, to consider our action at one time from the point of view of a will that is in perfect conformity with reason, and at another time from the point of view of a will that is under the influence of natural inclination. There is, therefore, here no real contradiction, but merely an antagonism of inclination to the command of reason. The universality of the principle is changed into a mere generality, in order that the practical principle of reason may meet the maxim half way. Not only is this limitation condemned by our impartial judgment, but it proves that we actually recognize the validity of the categorical imperative, and merely allow ourselves to make a few exceptions in our own favor which we try to consider as of no importance, or as a necessary concession to circumstances.

This much at least we have learned, that if the idea of duty is to have any meaning and to lay down the laws of our actions, it must be expressed in categorical and not in hypothetical imperatives. We have also obtained a clear and distinct conception (a very important thing), of what is implied in a categorical imperative which contains the principle of duty for all cases, granting such an imperative to be possible at all. But we have not yet been able to prove *a priori,* that there actually is such an imperative; that there is a practical law which commands absolutely on its own authority, and is independent of all sensuous impulses; and that duty consists in obedience to this law.

In seeking to reach this point, it is of the greatest importance to observe, that the reality of this principle cannot possibly be derived from the *peculiar constitution of human nature.* For by duty is meant the practically unconditioned necessity of an act, and hence we can show that duty is a law for the will of all human beings, only by showing that it is applicable to all rational beings, or rather to all rational beings to whom an imperative applies to all.

The question, then, is this: Is it a necessary law *for all rational beings* that they must always estimate the value of their actions by asking whether they can will that their maxims should serve as universal laws? If there is such a law, it must be possible to prove entirely *a priori,* that it is bound up with the very idea of the will of a rational being. To show that there is such a connection we must, however reluctantly, take a step into the realm of metaphysic; not, however, into the realm of speculative philosophy, but into the metaphysic of morality. For we have here to deal with objective practical laws, and therefore with the relation of the will to itself, in so far as it is determined purely by reason. All relation of the will to what is empirical is excluded as a matter of course, for if reason determines the relation *entirely by itself,* it must necessarily do so *a priori.*

Will is conceived of as a faculty of determining itself to action *in accordance with the idea of certain laws.* Such a faculty can belong only to a rational being. Now that which serves as an objective principle for the self-determination of the will is an *end,* and if this end is given purely by reason, it must hold for all rational beings. On the other hand, that which is merely the condition of the possibility of an action the effect of which is the end, is called the *means.* The subjective ground of desire is natural inclination, the objective ground of volition is a motive; hence there is a distinction between subjective ends, which depend upon natural inclination, and objective ends, which are connected with motives that hold for every rational being. Practical principles that abstract from all subjective ends are *formal;* those that presuppose subjective ends, and therefore natural inclinations, are *material.* The ends which a rational being arbitrarily sets before himself as material ends to be produced by his actions, are all merely relative; for that which gives to them their value is simply their relation to the peculiar susceptibility of the subject. They can therefore yield no universal and necessary principles, or practical laws, applicable to all rational beings, and binding upon every will. Upon such relative ends, therefore, only hypothetical imperatives can be based.

Suppose, however, that there is something the existence of which has in itself an absolute value, something which, *as an end in itself,* can be a ground of definite laws; then, there would lie in that, and only in that, the ground of a possible categorical imperative or practical law.

Now, I say, that man, and indeed every rational being as such, *exists* as an end in himself, *not merely as a means* to be made use of by this or that will, and therefore man in all his actions, whether these are directed towards himself or towards other rational beings, must always be regarded as an end. No object of natural desire has more than a conditional value; for if the natural desires, and the wants to which they give rise, did not exist, the object to which they are directed would have no value at all. So far are the natural desires and wants from having an absolute value, so far are they from being sought simply for themselves, that every rational being must wish to be entirely free from their influence. The value of every object which human action is the means of obtaining, is, therefore, always conditioned. And even beings whose existence depends upon nature, not upon our will, if they are without reason, have only the relative value of means, and are therefore called *things.* Rational beings, on the other hand, are called *persons,* because their very nature shows them to be ends in themselves, that is, something which cannot be made use of simply as a means. A person being thus an object of respect, a certain limit is placed upon arbitrary will. Persons are not purely subjective ends, whose existence has a value *for us* as the effect of our actions, but they are *objective ends,* or beings whose existence is an end in itself, for which no other end can be substituted. If all value were conditioned, and therefore contingent, it would be impossible to show that there is any supreme practical principle whatever.

If, then, there is a supreme practical principle, a principle which in relation to the human will is a categorical imperative, it must be an *objective* principle of the will, and must be able to serve as a universal practical law. For, such a principle must be derived from the idea of that which is necessarily an end for every one because it is an *end in itself.* Its foundation is this, that *rational nature exists as an end in itself.* Man necessarily conceives of his own existence in this way, and so far this is a *subjective* principle of human action. But in this way also every other rational being conceives of his own existence, and for the very same reason; hence the principle is also *objective*, and from it, as the highest practical ground, all laws of the will must be capable of being derived. The practical imperative will therefore be this: *Act so as to use humanity, whether in your own person or in the person of another, always as an end, never as merely a means.*

The principle, that humanity and every rational nature is an end in itself, is not borrowed from experience. For, in the first place, because of its universality it applies to all rational beings, and no experience can apply so widely. In the second place, it does not regard humanity subjectively, as an end of man, that is, as an object which the subject of himself actually makes his end, but as an objective end, which ought to be regarded as a law that constitutes the supreme limiting condition of all subjective ends, and which must therefore have its source in pure reason. The objective ground of all practical laws consists in the *rule* and the form of universality, which makes them capable of serving as laws, but their *subjective* ground consists in the *end* to which they are directed. Now, by the second principle, every rational being, as an end in himself, is the subject of all ends. From this follows the third practical principle of the will, which is the supreme condition of its harmony with universal practical reason, namely, the idea of *the will of every rational being as a will which lays down universal laws of action.* . . .

At the point we have now reached, it does not seem surprising that all previous attempts to find out the principle of morality should have ended in failure. It was seen that man is bound under law by duty, but it did not strike anyone, that the *universal* system of laws to which he is subject are laws which he *imposes upon himself,* and that he is only under obligation to act in conformity with his own will, a will which by the purpose of nature prescribes universal laws. Now so long as man is thought to be merely subject to law, no matter what the law may be, he must be regarded as stimulated or constrained to obey the law from interest of some kind; for as the law does not proceed from *his* own will, there must be *something external* to his will which compels him to act in conformity with it. This perfectly necessary conclusion frustrated every attempt to find a supreme principle of duty. Duty was never established, but merely the necessity of acting from some form of interest, private or public. The imperative was therefore necessarily always conditioned, and could not possibly have the force of a moral command. The supreme principle of morality I shall therefore call the principle of the *autonomy* of the will, to distinguish it from all other principles which I call principles of *heteronomy*.

The conception that every rational being in all the maxims of his will must regard himself as prescribing universal laws, by reference to which himself and all his actions are to be judged, leads to a cognate and very fruitful conception, that of a *kingdom of ends.*

By *kingdom,* I mean the systematic combination of different rational beings through the medium of common laws. Now, laws determine certain ends as universal, and hence, if abstraction is made from the individual differences of rational beings, and from all that is peculiar to their private ends, we get the idea of a complete totality of ends combined in a system; in other words, we are able to conceive of a kingdom of ends, which conforms to the principles formulated above.

All rational beings stand under the law, that each should treat himself and others, *never simply as means,* but always as *at the same time ends in themselves.* Thus there arises a systematic combination of rational beings through the medium of common objective laws. This may well be called a kingdom of ends, because the object of those laws is just to relate all rational beings to one another as ends and means. Of course this kingdom of ends is merely an ideal.

Morality, then, consists in the relation of all action to the system of laws which alone makes possible a kingdom of ends. These laws must belong to the nature of every rational being, and must proceed from his own will. The principle of the will, therefore, is, that no action should be done from any other maxim than one which is consistent with a universal law. This may be expressed in the formula: *Act so that the will may regard itself as in its maxims laying down universal laws.* Now, if the maxims of rational beings are not by their very nature in harmony with this objective principle, the principle of a universal system of laws, the necessity of acting in conformity with that principle is called practical obligation or *duty.* No doubt duty does not apply to the sovereign will in the kingdom of ends, but it applies to every member of it, and to all in equal measure. *Autonomy* is thus the foundation of the moral value of man and of every other rational being.

The three ways in which the principle of morality has been formulated are at bottom simply different statements of the same law, and each implies the other two.

An absolutely good will, then, the principle of which must be a categorical imperative, will be undetermined as regards all objects, and will contain merely the *form of volition* in general, a form which rests upon the *autonomy* of the will. The one law which the will of every rational being imposes upon itself, and imposes without reference to any natural impulse or any interest, is, that the maxims of every good will must be capable of being made a universal law.

SOCIAL BENEFIT

John Stuart Mill

WHAT UTILITARIANISM IS

The creed which accepts as the foundation of morals, Utility, or the Greatest Happiness Principle, holds that actions are right in proportion as they tend to promote happiness, wrong as they tend to produce the reverse of happiness. By happiness is intended pleasure, and the absence of pain; by unhappiness, pain, and the privation of pleasure. To give a clear view of the moral standard set up by the theory, much more requires to be said; in particular, what things it includes in the ideas of pain and pleasure; and to what extent this is felt an open question. But these supplementary explanations do not affect the theory of life on which this theory of morality is grounded—namely, that pleasure, and freedom from pain, are the only things desirable as ends; and that all desirable things (which are as numerous in the utilitarian as in any other scheme) are desirable either for the pleasure inherent in themselves, or as means to the promotion of pleasure and the prevention of pain.

Now, such a theory of life excites in many minds, and among them in some of the most estimable in feeling and purpose, inveterate dislike. To suppose that life has (as they express it) no higher end than pleasure—no better and nobler object of desire and pursuit—they designate as utterly mean and grovelling; as a doctrine worthy only of swine, to whom the followers of Epicurus were, at a very early period, contemptuously likened; and modern holders of the doctrine are occasionally made the subject of equally polite comparisons by its German, French, and English assailants.

When thus attacked, the Epicureans have always answered, that it is not they, but their accusers, who represent human nature in a degrading light; since the accusation supposes human beings to be capable of no pleasures except those of which swine are capable. If this supposition were true, the charge could not be gainsaid, but would then be no longer an imputation: for if the sources of pleasure were precisely the same to human beings and to swine, the rule of life which is good enough for the one would be good enough for the other. The comparison of the Epicurean life to that of beasts is felt as degrading, precisely because a beast's pleasures do not satisfy a human being's conceptions of happiness. Human beings have faculties more elevated than the animal appetites, and when once made conscious of them, do not regard anything as happiness which does not include their gratification. I do not, indeed, consider the Epicureans to have been by any means faultless in drawing out their scheme of consequences from the utilitarian principle. To do this in any sufficient manner, many Stoic, as well as Christian elements require to be included. But there is no known Epicurean theory of life which does not assign to the pleasures of the intellect, of the feelings and imagination, and of the moral sentiments, a much higher value as pleasures than to those of mere sensation. It must be admitted, however, that utilitarian writers in general have placed the superiority of mental over bodily pleasures chiefly in the greater permanency, safety, uncostliness, &c., of the former—that is, in their circumstantial advantages rather than in their intrinsic nature. And on all these points utilitarians have fully proved their case; but they might have taken the other, and, as it may be called, higher ground, with entire consistency. It is quite compatible with the principle of utility to recognise the fact, that some *kinds* of pleasure are more desirable and more valuable than others. It would be absurd that while, in estimating all other things, quality is considered as well as quantity, the estimation of pleasures should be supposed to depend on quantity alone.

If I am asked, what I mean by difference of quality in pleasures, or what makes one pleasure more valuable than another, merely as a pleasure, except its being greater in amount, there is but one possible answer. Of two pleasures, if there be one to which all or almost all who have experience of both give a decided preference, irrespective of any feeling of moral obligation to prefer it, that is the more desirable pleasure. If one of the two is, by those who are competently acquainted with both, placed so far above the other that they prefer it, even though knowing it to be attended with a greater amount of discontent, and would not resign it for any quantity of the other pleasure which their nature is capable of, we are justified in ascribing to the preferred enjoyment a superiority in quality, so far outweighing quantity as to render it, in comparison, of small account.

Now it is an unquestionable fact that those who are equally acquainted with, and equally capable of appreciating and enjoying, both, do give a most marked preference to the manner of existence which employs their higher faculties. Few human creatures would consent to be changed into any of the lower animals, for a promise of the fullest allowance of a beast's pleasures; no intelligent human being would consent to be a fool, no instructed person would be an ignoramus, no person of feeling and conscience would be self-ish and base, even though they should be persuaded that the fool, the dunce, or the rascal is better satisfied with his lot than they are with theirs. They would not resign what they possess more than he, for the most complete satisfaction of all the desires which they have in common with him. If they ever fancy they would, it is only in cases of unhappiness so extreme, that to escape from it they would exchange their lot for almost any other, however undesirable in their own eyes. A being of higher faculties requires more to make him happy, is capable probably of more acute suffering, and is certainly accessible to it at more points, than one of an inferior type; but in spite of these liabilities, he can never really wish to sink into what he feels to be a lower grade of existence. We may give what explanation we please of this unwillingness; we may attribute it to pride, a name which is given indiscriminately to some of the most and to some of the least estimable feelings of which mankind are capable; we may refer it to the love of liberty and personal independence, an appeal to which was with the Stoics one of the most effective means for the inculcation of it; to the love of power, or to the love of excitement, both of which do really enter into and contribute to it: but its most appropriate appellation is a sense of dignity, which all human beings possess in one form or another, and in some, though by no means in exact, proportion to their higher faculties, and which is so essential a part of the happiness of those in whom it is strong, that nothing which conflicts with it could be, otherwise than momentarily, an object of desire to them. Whoever supposes that this preference takes place at a sacrifice of happiness—that the superior being, in anything like equal circumstances, is not happier than the inferior—confounds the two very different ideas, of happiness, and content. It is indisputable that the being whose capacities of enjoyment are low, has the greatest chance of having them fully satisfied; and a highly-endowed being will always feel that any happiness which he can look for, as the world is constituted, is imperfect. But he can learn to bear its imperfections, if they are at all bearable; and they will not make him envy the being who is indeed unconscious of the imperfections, but only because he feels not at all the good which those imperfections qualify. It is better to be a human being dissatisfied than a pig satisfied; better to be Socrates dissatisfied than a fool satisfied. And if the fool, or the pig, is of a different opinion, it is because they only know their own side of the question. The other party to the comparison knows both sides.

It may be objected, that many who are capable of the higher pleasures, occasionally, under the influence of temptation, postpone them to the lower. But this is quite compatible with a full appreciation of the intrinsic superiority of the higher. Men often, from infirmity of character, make their election for the nearer good, though they know it to be the less valuable; and this no less when the choice is between two bodily pleasures, than when it is between bodily and mental. They pursue sensual indulgences to the injury of health, though perfectly aware that health is the greater good. It may be further objected, that many who begin with youthful enthusiasm for everything noble, as they advance in years sink into indolence and selfishness. But I do not believe that those who undergo this very common change, voluntarily choose the lower description of pleasures in preference to the higher. I believe that before they devote themselves exclusively to the one, they have already become incapable of the other. Capacity for the nobler feelings is in most natures a very tender plant, easily killed, not only by hostile influences, but by mere want of sustenance; and in the majority of young persons it speedily dies away if the occupations to which their position in life has devoted them, and the society into which it has thrown them, are not favourable to keeping that higher capacity in exercise. Men lose their high aspirations as they lose their intellectual tastes, because they have not time or opportunity for indulging them; and they addict themselves to inferior pleasures, not because they deliberately prefer them, but because they are either the only ones to which they have access, or the only ones which they are any longer capable of enjoying. It may be questioned whether any one who has remained equally susceptible to both classes of pleasures, ever knowingly and calmly preferred the lower; though many, in all ages, have broken down in an ineffectual attempt to combine both.

From this verdict of the only competent judges, I apprehend there can be no appeal. On a question which is the best worth having of two pleasures, or which of two modes of existence is the most grateful to the feelings, apart from its moral attributes and from its consequences, the judgment of those who are qualified by knowledge of both, or, if they differ, that of the majority among them, must be admitted as final. And there needs be the less hesitation to accept this judgment respecting the quality of pleasures, since there is no other tribunal to be referred to even on the question of quantity. What means are there of determining which is the acutest of two pains, or the intensest of two pleasurable sensations, except the general suffrage of those who are familiar with both? Neither pains nor pleasures are homogeneous, and pain is always heterogeneous with pleasure. What is there to decide whether a particular pleasure is worth purchasing at the cost of a particular pain, except the feelings and judgment of the experienced? When, therefore, those feelings and judgment declare the pleasures derived from the higher faculties to be preferable *in kind*, apart from the question of intensity, to those of which the animal nature, disjoined from the higher faculties, is susceptible, they are entitled on this subject to the same regard.

I have dwelt on this point, as being a necessary part of a perfectly just conception of Utility or Happiness, considered as the directive rule of human conduct. But it is by no means an indispensable condition to the acceptance of the utilitarian standard; for that standard is not the agent's own greatest happiness, but the greatest amount of happiness altogether; and if it may possibly be doubted whether a noble character is always the happier for its nobleness, there can be no doubt that it makes other people happier, and that the world in general is immensely a gainer by it. Utilitarianism, therefore, could only attain its end by the general cultivation of nobleness of character, even if each individual were only benefited by the nobleness of others, and his own, so far as happiness is concerned, were a sheer deduction from the benefit. But the bare enunciation of such an absurdity as this last, renders refutation superfluous.

According to the Greatest Happiness Principle, as above explained, the ultimate end, with reference to and for the sake of which all other things are desirable (whether we are considering our own good or that of other people), is an existence exempt as far as possible from pain, and as rich as possible in enjoyments, both in point of quantity and quality; the test of quality, and the rule for measuring it against quantity, being the preference felt by those who, in their opportunities of experience, to which must be added their habits of self-consciousness and self-observation, are best furnished with the means of comparison. This, being, according to the utilitarian opinion, the end of human action, is necessarily also the standard of morality; which may accordingly be defined as the rules and precepts for human conduct, by the observance of which an existence such as has been described might be, to the greatest extent possible, secured to all mankind; and not to them only, but, so far as the nature of things admits, to the whole sentient creation.

Against this doctrine, however, rises another class of objectors, who say that happiness, in any form, cannot be the rational purpose of human life and action; because, in the first place, it is unattainable: and they contemptuously ask, What right hast thou to be happy? a question which Mr. Carlyle clenches by the addition, What right, a short time ago, hadst thou even *to be*? Next, they say, that men can do *without* happiness; that all noble human beings have felt this, and could not have become noble but by learning the lesson of *Entsagen,* or renunciation; which lesson, thoroughly learnt and submitted to, they affirm to be the beginning and necessary condition of all virtue.

The first of these objections would go to the root of the matter were it well founded; for if no happiness is to be had at all by human beings, the attainment of it cannot be the end of morality, or of any rational conduct. Though, even in that case, something might still be said for the utilitarian theory; since utility includes not solely the pursuit of happiness, but the prevention or mitigation of unhappiness; and if the former aim be chimerical, there will be all the greater scope and more imperative need for the latter, so long at least as mankind think fit to live, and do not take refuge in the simultaneous act of suicide recommended under certain conditions by Novalis. When, however, it is thus positively asserted to be impossible that human life should be happy, the assertion, if not something like a verbal quibble, is at least an exaggeration. If by happiness be meant a continuity of highly pleasurable excitement, it is evident enough that this is impossible. A state of exalted pleasure lasts only moments, or in some cases, and with some intermissions, hours or days, and is the occasional brilliant flash of enjoyment, not its permanent and steady flame. Of this the philosophers who have taught that happiness is the end of life were as fully aware as those who taunt them. The happiness which they meant was not a life of rapture; but moments of such, in an existence made up of few and transitory pains, many and various pleasures, with a decided predominance of the active over the passive, and having as the foundation of the whole, not to expect more from life than it is capable of bestowing. A life thus composed, to those who have been fortunate enough to obtain it, has always appeared worthy of the name of happiness. And such an existence is even now the lot of many, during some considerable portion of their lives. The present wretched education, and wretched social arrangements, are the only real hindrance to its being attainable by almost all.

The objectors perhaps may doubt whether human beings, if taught to consider happiness as the end of life, would be satisfied with such a moderate share of it. But great numbers of mankind have been satisfied with much less. The main constituents of a satisfied life appear to be two, either of which by itself is often found sufficient for the purpose: tranquillity, and excitement. With much tranquillity, many find that they can be content with very little pleasure: with much excitement, many can reconcile themselves to a considerable quantity of pain. There is assuredly no inherent impossibility in enabling even the mass of mankind to unite both; since the two are so far from being incompatible that they are in natural alliance, the prolongation of either being a preparation for, and exciting a wish for, the other. It is only those in whom indolence amounts to a vice, that do not desire excitement after an interval of repose; it is only those in whom the need of excitement is a disease, that feel the tranquillity which follows excitement dull and insipid, instead of pleasurable in direct proportion to the excitement which preceded it. When people who are tolerably fortunate in their outward lot do not find in life sufficient enjoyment to make it valuable to them, the cause generally is, caring for nobody but themselves. To those who have neither public nor private affections, the excitements of life are much curtailed, and in any case dwindle in value as the time approaches when all selfish interests must be terminated by death: while those who leave after them objects of personal affection, and especially those who have also cultivated a fellow-feeling with the collective interests of mankind, retain as lively an interest in life on the eve of death as in the vigour of youth and health. Next to selfishness, the principal cause which makes life unsatisfactory, is want of mental cultivation. A cultivated mind—I do not mean that of a philosopher, but any mind to which the foundations of knowledge have been opened, and which has been taught, in any tolerable degree, to exercise its faculties—finds sources of inexhaustible interest in all that surrounds it; in the objects of nature, the achievements of art, the imaginations of poetry, the incidents of history, the ways of mankind past and present, and their prospects in the future. It is possible, indeed, to become indifferent to all this, and that too without having exhausted a thousandth part of it; but only when one has had from the beginning no moral or human interest in these things and has sought in them only the gratification of curiosity.

Now there is absolutely no reason in the nature of things why an amount of mental culture sufficient to give an intelligent interest in these objects of contemplation, should not be the inheritance of everyone born in a civilised country. As little is there an inherent necessity that any human being should be a selfish egotist, devoid of every feeling or care but those which centre in his own miserable individuality. Something far superior to this is sufficiently common even now, to give ample earnest of what the human species may be made. Genuine private affections, and a sincere interest in the public good, are possible, though in unequal degrees, to every rightly brought up human being. In a world in which there is so much to interest, so much to enjoy, and so much also to correct and improve, everyone who has this moderate amount of moral and intellectual requisites is capable of an existence which may be called enviable, and unless such a person, through bad laws, or subjection to the will of others, is denied the liberty to use the sources of happiness within his reach, he will not fail to find this enviable existence, if he escape the positive evils of life, the great sources of physical and mental suffering—such as indigence, disease, and the unkindness, worthlessness, or premature loss of objects of affection. The main stress of the problem lies, therefore, in the contest with these calamities, from which it is a rare good fortune entirely to escape; which, as things now are cannot be obviated, and often cannot be in any material degree mitigated. Yet no one whose opinion deserves a moment's consideration can doubt that most of the great positive evils of the world are in themselves removable, and will, if human affairs continue to improve, be in the end reduced within narrow limits. Poverty, in any sense implying suffering, may be completely extinguished by the wisdom of society, combined with the good sense and providence of individuals. Even that most intractable of enemies, disease, may be indefinitely reduced in dimensions by good physical and moral education, and proper control of noxious influences; while the progress of science holds out a promise for the future of still more direct conquests over this detestable foe. And every advance in that direction relieves us from some, not only of the chances which cut short our own lives, but, what concerns us still more, which deprive us of those in whom our happiness is wrapt up. As for vicissitudes of fortune, and other disappointments connected with worldly circumstances, these are principally the effect either of gross imprudence, of ill-regulated desires, or of bad or imperfect social institutions. All the grand sources, in short, of human suffering are in a great degree, many of them almost entirely, conquerable by human care and effort; and though their removal is grievously slow—though a long succession of generations will perish in the breach before the conquest is completed, and this world becomes all that, if will and knowledge were not wanting, it might easily be made—yet every mind sufficiently intelligent and generous to bear a part, however small and inconspicuous, in the endeavour, will draw a noble enjoyment from the contest itself, which he would not for any bribe in the form of selfish indulgence consent to be without.

And this leads to the true estimation of what is said by the objectors concerning the possibility and the obligation, of learning to do without happiness. Unquestionably it is possible to do without happiness. It is done involuntarily by nineteen-twentieths of mankind, even in those parts of our present world which are least deep in barbarism; and it often has to be done voluntarily by the hero or the martyr, for the sake of something which he prizes more than his individual happiness. But this something, what is it, unless the happiness of others, or some of the requisites of happiness? It is noble to be capable of resigning entirely one's own portion of happiness or chances of it, but after all, this self-sacrifice must be for some end. It is not its own end; and if we are told that its end is not happiness but virtue, which is better than happiness, I ask, would the sacrifice be made if the hero or martyr did not believe that it would earn for others immunity from similar sacrifices? Would it be made if he thought that his renunciation of happiness for himself would produce no fruit for any of his fellow creatures, but to make their lot like his, and place them also in the condition of persons who have renounced happiness? All honour to those who can abnegate for themselves the personal enjoyment of life, when by such renunciation they contribute worthily to increase the amount of happiness in the world; but he who does it, or professes to do it, for any other purpose is no more deserving of admiration than the ascetic mounted on his pillar. He may be an inspiriting proof of what men *can* do, but assuredly not an example of what they *should*.

Though it is only in a very imperfect state of the world's arrangements that anyone can best serve the happiness of others by the absolute sacrifice of his own, yet so long as the world is in that imperfect state, I fully acknowledge that the readiness to make such a sacrifice is the highest virtue which can be found in man. I will add that in this condition of the world, paradoxical as the assertion may be, the conscious ability to do without happiness gives the best prospect of realizing such happiness as is attainable. For nothing except that consciousness can raise a person above the chances of life, by making him feel that, let fate and fortune do their worst, they have no power to subdue him, which, once felt, frees him from excess of anxiety concerning the evils of life and enables him, like many a Stoic in the worst times of the Roman Empire, to cultivate in tranquillity the sources of satisfaction accessible to him without concerning himself about the uncertainty of their duration any more than about their inevitable end.

Meanwhile, let us utilitarians never cease to claim the morality of self devotion as a possession which belongs by as good a right to them as either to the Stoic or to the Transcendentalist. The utilitarian morality does recognize in human beings the power of sacrificing their own greatest good for the good of others. It only refuses to admit that the sacrifice is itself a good. A sacrifice which does not increase, or tend to increase, the sum total of happiness, it considers as wasted. The only self-renunciation which it applauds is devotion to the happiness, or to some of the means of happiness, of others — either of mankind collectively or of individuals within the limits imposed by the collective interests of mankind.

I must again repeat what the assailants of utilitarianism seldom have the justice to acknowledge, that the happiness which forms the utilitarian standard of what is right in conduct is not the agent's own happiness but that of all concerned. As between his own happiness and that of others, utilitarianism requires him to be as strictly impartial as a disinterested and benevolent spectator. In the golden rule of Jesus of Nazareth, we read the complete spirit of the ethics of utility. To do as you would be done by and to love your neighbour as yourself constitute the ideal perfection of utilitarian morality. As the means of first making the nearest approach to this ideal, utility would enjoin, first, that laws and social arrangements should place the happiness or (as speaking practically it may be called) the interest of every individual as nearly as possible in harmony with the interest of the whole and, secondly, that education and opinion, which have so vast a power over human character, should so use that power as to establish in the mind of every individual an indissoluble association between his own happiness and the good of the whole—especially between his own happiness and the practice of such modes of conduct, negative and positive, as regard for the universal happiness prescribes—so that not only he may be unable to conceive the possibility of happiness to himself consistently with conduct opposed to the general good, but also that a direct impulse to promote the general good may be in every individual one of the habitual motives of action, and the sentiments connected herewith may fill a large and prominent place in every human being's sentient existence. If the impugners of the utilitarian morality represented it to their own minds in this its true character, I know not what recommendation possessed by any other morality they could possibly affirm to be wanting to it, what more beautiful or more exalted developments of human nature any other ethical system can be supposed to foster, or what springs of action, not accessible to the utilitarian, such systems rely on for giving effect to their mandates.

The objectors to utilitarianism cannot always be charged with representing it in a discreditable light. On the contrary, those among them who entertain anything like a just idea of its disinterested character sometimes find fault with its standard as being too high for humanity. They say it is exacting too much to require that people shall always act from the inducement of promoting the general interests of society. But this is to mistake the very meaning of a standard of morals and confound the rule of action with the motive of it. It is the business of ethics to tell us what are our duties or by what tests we may know them, but no system of ethics requires that the sole motive of all we do shall be a feeling of duty; on the contrary, ninety-nine hundredths of all our actions are done from other motives, and rightly so done, if the rule of duty does not condemn them. It is the more unjust to utilitarianism that this particular misapprehension should be made a ground of objection to it, inasmuch as utilitarian moralists have gone beyond almost all others in affirming that the motive has nothing to do with the morality of the action, though much with the worth of the agent. He who saves a fellow creature from drowning does what is morally right, whether his motive be duty or the hope of being paid for his trouble; he who betrays the friend that trusts him is guilty of a crime, even if his object be to serve another friend to whom he is under greater obligations. But to speak only of actions done from the motive of duty and in direct obedience to principle, it is a misapprehension of the utilitarian mode of thought to conceive it as implying that people should fix their minds upon so wide a generality as the world, or society at large. The great majority of good actions are intended not for the benefit of the world but for that of individuals, of which the good of the world is made up; and the thoughts of the most virtuous man need not on these occasions travel beyond the particular persons concerned, except so far as is necessary to assure himself that in benefiting them he is not violating the rights, that is, the legitimate and authorized expectations, of anyone else. The multiplication of happiness is, according to the utilitarian ethics, the object of virtue. The occasion on which any person (except one in a thousand) has it in his power to do this on an extended scale—in other words, to be a public benefactor—are but exceptional, and on these occasions alone is he called on to consider public utility; in every other case, private utility, the interest or happiness of some few persons, is all he has to attend to. Those alone the influence of whose actions extends to society in general need concern themselves habitually about so large an object. In the case of abstinences indeed—of things which people forbear to do from moral considerations, though the consequences in the particular case might be beneficial—it would be unworthy of an intelligent agent not to be consciously aware that the action is of a class which, if practised generally, would be generally injurious and that this is the ground of the obligation to abstain from it. The amount of regard for the public interest implied in this recognition is no greater than is demanded by every system of morals, for they all enjoin to abstain from whatever is manifestly pernicious to society.

The same considerations dispose of another reproach against the doctrine of utility, founded on a still grosser misconception of the purpose of a standard of morality and of the very meaning of the words right and wrong. It is often affirmed that utilitarianism renders men cold and unsympathizing; that it chills their moral feelings towards individuals; that it makes them regard only the dry and hard consideration of the consequences of actions, not taking into their moral estimate the qualities from which those actions emanate. If the assertion means that they do not allow their judgment respecting the rightness or wrongness of an action to be influenced by their opinion of the qualities of the person who does it, this is a complaint not against utilitarianism but against having any standard of morality at all; for certainly no known ethical standard decides an action to be good or bad because it is done by a good or bad man, still less because done by an amiable, a brave, or a benevolent man, or the contrary. These considerations are relevant not to the estimation of actions but of persons; and there is nothing in the utilitarian theory inconsistent with the fact that there are other things which interest us in persons besides the rightness and wrongness of their actions. The Stoics, indeed, with the paradoxical misuse of language which was part of their system and by which they strove to raise themselves above all concern about anything but virtue, were fond of saying that he who has that has everything, that he, and only he, is rich, is beautiful, is a king. But no claim of this description is made for the virtuous man by the utilitarian doctrine. Utilitarians are quite aware that there are other desirable possessions and qualities besides virtue and are perfectly willing to allow to all of them their full worth. They are also aware that a right action does not necessarily indicate a virtuous character and that actions which are blamable often proceed from qualities entitled to praise. When this is apparent in any particular case, it modifies their estimation, not certainly of the act but of the agent. I grant that they are, notwithstanding, of the opinion that in the long run the best proof of a good character is good actions and resolutely refuse to consider any mental disposition as good of which the predominant tendency is to produce bad conduct. This makes them unpopular with many people; but it is an unpopularity which they must share with everyone who regards the distinction between right and wrong in a serious light, and the reproach is not one which a conscientious utilitarian need be anxious to repel.

If no more be meant by the objection than that many utilitarians look on the morality of actions, as measured by the utilitarian standard, with too exclusive a regard and do not lay sufficient stress upon the other beauties of character which go towards making a human being lovable or admirable, this may be admitted. Utilitarians who have cultivated their moral feelings but not their sympathies nor their artistic perceptions do fall into this mistake; and so do all other moralists under the same conditions. What can be said in excuse for other moralists is equally available for them—namely, that, if there is to be any error, it is better that it should be on that side. As a matter of fact, we may affirm among utilitarians, as among adherents of other systems, there is every imaginable degree of rigidity and of laxity in the application of their standard: some are even puritanically rigorous, while others are as indulgent as can possibly be desired by sinner or by sentimentalist. But on the whole, a doctrine which brings prominently forward the interest that mankind have in the repression and prevention of conduct which violates the moral law, is likely to be inferior to no other in turning the sanctions of opinion against such violations. It is true, the question, What does violate the moral law? is one on which those who recognize different standards of morality are likely now and then to differ. But difference of opinion on moral questions was not first introduced into the world by utilitarianism, while that doctrine does supply, if not always an easy, at all events a tangible and intelligible mode of deciding such differences.

CONVENTION

Gilbert Harman

1. MORAL CONVENTIONS

Hume says that some, but not all, aspects of morality rest on "convention." There is a convention in Hume's sense when each of a number of people adheres to certain principles so that each of the others will also adhere to these principles. I adhere to the principles in my dealings with the others because I benefit from their adherence to these principles in their dealings with me and because I think that they will stop adhering to these principles in their dealings with me unless I continue to adhere to the principles in my dealings with them. For example, two farmers have a convention of helping each other till their fields. Farmer A helps farmer B till his fields so that when it comes time to till farmer A's fields, farmer B will help farmer A. Each farmer benefits from this practice, which depends upon their expectation that the other will continue it.

Hume mentions other conventions of this sort, for example those that give rise to the institutions of money. Certain pieces of paper can be traded for goods only because they will be accepted in turn by others in exchange for their goods. The conventions of language provide another example, one which indicates that conventions may be extremely subtle and even impossible for an ordinary person to describe in any precise and explicit way.

Conventions are reached through a process of implicit bargaining and mutual adjustment. Two people rowing a boat will adjust their actions with respect to each other so that they pull at the same time. It does not matter what their rate is, as long as both row at the same rate. If one tries to row more quickly and the other tries to row more slowly, some sort of compromise will have to be reached.

Among the most important conventions, according to Hume, are those having to do with property. It is useful to each person that there should be a system of security regarding possessions. This system is entirely conventional; and until it develops, there is no such thing as property. Another important convention is the one that makes possible explicit contracts and promises. The convention is that, by using a certain form of words (or other sign), a person binds himself to do what he says he will do. The obligation to keep your promises therefore itself derives from a prior convention, according to Hume.

Hume says that the original motive to observe conventions is "natural" rather than moral, by which he means that it is a self-interested motive. Initially, each person continues to adhere to the conventional principles in his dealings with others so that they will continue to do so in their dealings with him. Eventually habits develop. Action in accordance with those principles becomes relatively automatic; it would be hard to change. Obligations based on those principles come to seem natural and obvious. According to Hume, these "natural" obligations will strike us as moral as soon as we reflect sympathetically on the usefulness of the relevant conventions to human society. For, as you will recall, Hume accepts a kind of ideal observer theory. In his view, moral judgments express feelings based on sympathy.

Hume himself does not think that everything about morality is conventional, although he thinks that much is. He holds that sympathy can lead us to approve or disapprove of some things apart from prior conventions—for example, we will approve of kindness to others even in a state of nature—and, in Hume's view, this is moral approval. But he would probably agree that moral *obligations* and *duties* depend on convention; in any event, I will assume in what follows that this is part of Hume's theory.

A more extreme theory than Hume's would treat every aspect of morality as conventional. For example, when Hume believes that a weak sympathy for others is built into people, it might be supposed instead that sympathy itself derives from a convention whereby people tacitly agree to respect each other at least to the extent of trying to feel sympathy for others. But we do not need to decide between Hume's theory and this more extreme version.

Hume's tacit convention theory of morality is a more specific version of the social custom theory. It has a number of advantages. For one thing, it provides a more specific account of the way in which morality involves social utility: certain rules are conventionally adopted because each person benefits from everyone else acting in accordance with those rules. We therefore expect rules to be adopted if they promote social utility in the sense that they are beneficial to all.

To take another example . . . we do not normally assume that you are obligated to help someone when you know that he would not help you if the situation were reversed; we feel that to help such a person would be to do something that is above and beyond the call of duty, a generous act rather than something you are obligated to do. But this is just what we would expect given Hume's theory. There are reasons of self-interest for people to adopt a convention of *mutual* aid, but no obvious reasons of this sort to extend this convention to aid those who do not participate in the convention. So, given Hume's theory, we would not expect an obligation or duty to help the person who would not help you. On the other hand, sympathy would lead an observer to approve of your helping this person; so, given Hume's theory, it would be a good thing if you were to help him even though you are not obligated to do so.

We noted . . . our reluctance to blame cannibals for eating human flesh, despite our abhorrence of their doing so and our view that it would be wrong for any of us to do so while visiting a society that practiced cannibalism. Given Hume's theory we might explain our own aversion to the eating of human flesh in the following way. We have a tacit convention in our society that we will respect each other as people. We will, in Kant's phrase, "treat people as ends," as if they were sacred and possessed a special kind of dignity. Furthermore, there are various conventional forms in which we have come to express our respect and we have therefore come to see it as demeaning to human dignity if persons are not treated according to these conventions. For example, if someone dies, we think it appropriate to hold a funeral and bury the body or perhaps cremate it. Given our current conventions, we will not eat the body. To do that would strike us as an insult to the memory of the person who has died. It would indicate a lack of respect for persons as persons. Our respect for people and our conventional habits of expressing that respect lead us automatically to reject the idea that we could eat human flesh; indeed, we have come to find the very idea disgusting.

Our reactions to the cannibals are complicated, however, because two moralities are relevant, theirs and ours. In judging the situation, we can simply appeal to our own morality: "Eating people is wrong!" But in judging the cannibals themselves, we must take their morality into account. We cannot simply blame them for what they do, because their moral understanding is not the same as ours. They see nothing wrong with eating people; and there is no obvious reason why they should. This makes it difficult for us to judge that it is wrong *of them* to eat human flesh. We do not feel comfortable in judging the cannibals themselves to be wrong. It does not seem right to say that each of them ought morally not to eat human flesh or that each of them has a moral duty or obligation not to do so. At best we might say that it ought not to be the case that they eat human flesh; but . . . that is not the same sort of judgment at all. From our own point of view we can judge their acts and their situation, even their society and morality; but we cannot, it seems, judge *them*.

. . . We are inclined to suppose that a person ought morally not to have done a particular thing only if we can also assume that he had a reason not to do it. We could not suppose that the cannibals ought morally not to eat human flesh unless we also supposed that they have a reason not to eat human flesh. The trouble is that we are presently assuming that they have no such reason, because their morality is not the same as ours. Given this assumption, we can make certain moral or evaluative judgments about the cannibals; for example, we can call them "ignorant savages." But we cannot correctly say of them that they are morally wrong to eat human flesh or that they ought morally not to do it.

2. JUDGING OUTSIDERS

Now, it is very difficult to get a clear grasp on such examples just because it is not always clear when someone has a reason to do something and when he does not. To take a very different sort of example, Hitler, who had millions of people killed, was an extraordinarily evil man. In some sense we can say that he ought not to have killed those people and that what he did was wrong. Yet the following remarks are weak and even in some way odd: "It was wrong of Hitler to have ordered the extermination of the Jews." "Hitler ought morally not to have ordered the extermination of the Jews."

One might suppose that it is the enormity of Hitler's crime against humanity that makes such remarks seem too weak. He killed so many people; it would have been wrong of him to have killed only one. To say simply that it was wrong of him to have ordered the extermination of the Jews suggests that it was *only* wrong—that it is wrong only in the way in which murder is wrong. And, given what Hitler did, that is as if one were to say that it was *naughty* of Hitler to have ordered the extermination of the Jews.

This explanation, however, is not completely satisfactory. First of all, there are things we can say about Hitler without the same sort of oddity. Although it would be odd to say that it was wrong of Hitler to have acted as he did, it is not equally odd to say that what Hitler did was wrong. Similarly, there is no oddness in the remark, "What Hitler did ought never to have happened." That is not odd in the way that it is odd to say, "Hitler ought morally not to have ordered the extermination of the Jews." But, if the enormity of his crime makes the one remark odd, why doesn't it make the other remark as odd?

Another reason for doubting that the enormity of the crime, by itself, is the reason for the oddness in certain of these judgments is that we can make these very judgments about someone who has committed an equally enormous crime, at least if enormity is measured in numbers of people killed. For example, Stalin was also a mass murderer who ordered the purges of the thirties knowing that millions of people would be killed. Yet it is possible to think that Stalin was really only trying to do the right thing, that he hated the prospect of the purges, that he was however also alarmed at the consequences of not ordering the purges because he was afraid that the revolution was in danger of collapse. He found himself faced with a terrible choice and he opted for what he took to be the lesser of two evils. I am not suggesting that this is the truth about Stalin; it probably is not. I mean only that this is a possible view of Stalin. Of course, even someone taking such a sympathetic view of Stalin can suppose that Stalin was terribly mistaken. To take this view of Stalin is certainly not to condone Stalin's actions. It can never be right to order the deaths of millions of people like that, no matter what you hope to gain. Indeed, taking this view of Stalin, it is natural to say that it was wrong of Stalin to have ordered the purges; Stalin was morally wrong to have done so. The interesting question, then, is why is it not odd to say this about Stalin in the way that it is odd to say the same thing about Hitler. It cannot be the vast numbers of people killed that makes a difference, since vast numbers were killed by both men. And certainly the judgment that it was wrong of Stalin to have ordered the purges is not the judgment that it was *naughty* of him to have done so. Why then does it seem that if you say that it was wrong of Hitler to have done what he did you are saying something as odd and ridiculous as if you had said that it was naughty of Hitler to have done that?

Part of the answer has to do with our conception of the attitudes that we think Hitler and Stalin took toward their crimes, with the moral principles we think of them accepting, with our views of what they considered to be reasons for action. Hitler's attitude was in this respect much more extreme than Stalin's. Hitler is farther from us than Stalin is (or as Stalin is imagined to be in the view of him that I have sketched). Hitler is beyond the pale in a way that Stalin was not. Hitler was not just immoral, he was amoral, he was evil. Stalin was terrible and also, perhaps, evil; but he was not wholly beyond the reaches of morality as I have imagined him. We cannot but think of Hitler as beyond the reaches of morality or at least that part of morality that we invoke in judging him to be an evil man.

In saying that it was wrong of Hitler to have ordered the extermination of the Jews we would be saying that Hitler had a reason (every reason in the world) not to do what he did. But what is horrible about someone who did what he did is that he could not have had such a reason. If he was willing to exterminate a whole people, there was no reason for him not to do so: that is just what is so terrible about him. That is why it sounds too weak to say that it was wrong of him to do what he did. It suggests that he had a reason not to act as he did and we feel that any man who could have done what Hitler did must be the sort of man who would not have had a reason not to do it. Such a man is evil rather than wrong.

This is why it is odd to say that it was wrong of Hitler to have acted as he did but it is not odd to say that Hitler's act was wrong. The judgment that Hitler's act was wrong and the judgment that it never ought to have happened do not imply that Hitler had a reason not to do what he did. The fact that we feel that Hitler was not the sort of person who could have had such a reason does not undermine judgments of his *acts* in the way that it undermines certain judgments about *him*.

All this is explicable in Hume's tacit convention theory. Hitler, like the cannibals, is outside our morality, although in a different direction. We can judge his acts with reference to our morality, but not Hitler himself, since that would imply that he was someone who acknowledged the moral standards we use to judge him. To say, "It was wrong of Hitler" or "Hitler ought morally not to have done it" would imply that Hitler accepted the relevant moral conventions. But his actions show that he does not accept those conventions. He is therefore beyond the pale and an enemy of humanity.

There are other examples that confirm the same point. Consider judgments that we might make about Martians who felt no concern for us. Suppose that these Martians would not be deterred from a given course of action simply by the reflection that that course of action would harm some human being. These Martians would not treat such a consideration as any sort of reason. For them, the consideration would simply not tell against that course of action at all. In that case, we cannot say that it would be morally wrong of the Martians to harm us.

This is to disagree with Kant, who would say that, since a Martian is a rational being, it has a reason not to harm any of us, because we too are rational beings. "The Martian would not agree to our harming it; so how can it agree to its harming us?" Kant believes that reflection of this sort can provide the Martian with motivation not to harm us. If Kant were right, there would be no need for moral conventions. We could make do with pure practical reason alone.

Now a defender of Hume's tacit convention theory will assume, plausibly, that Kant is mistaken about the powers of pure practical reason. When we first come across the Martians, they may well have no reason to be concerned about us at all, and, in that case, there are no moral constraints on them in their dealings with us. If they harm us, that is not a matter of morality or immorality, although it may well be a matter of war between the planets. If it turns out that there is no way for us to harm the Martians, so that they do not need to be concerned about us even for reasons of self-interest, then a morality that encompasses us and them may never develop.

On the other hand, if a conflict develops that is in neither their interest nor ours, we and they may try to arrive at conventions that would reduce or eliminate this sort of conflict. For example, we and they might adopt a convention of respect for each other as rational beings that would involve, among other things, trying to avoid actions that would harm other rational beings. In that case, there would be a morality encompassing us and them.

This is how a morality would arise from a state of nature, according to a tacit convention theory. Before any conventions were established, there would be no such thing as right and wrong; it would not make sense to judge what people morally ought or ought not to do. But once a group of people developed conventional patterns of action in order to avoid conflicts with each other, their actions could be judged with reference to those conventions. People who remained outside the relevant group and still in a state of nature could, however, not be so judged.

3. CONVENTIONAL ASPECTS OF MORALITY

One reason for thinking that morality has arisen like this, as the result of convention, is that certain elements in our actual moral views seem to reflect what would be the result of implicit bargaining and mutual adjustments between people of different powers and resources. For example, consider a point I have alluded to several times. In our morality, harming someone is thought to be much worse than not helping someone. That is why we suppose that a doctor cannot cut up one patient in order to save five other patients by distributing the one patient's organs according to need. Now, this general principle about harming and not helping may seem irrational and unmotivated, but it makes sense if we suppose that our moral views derive from a tacit convention that arose among people of different wealth, status, and power. For, whereas everyone would benefit equally from a conventional practice of trying not to harm each other, some people would benefit considerably more than others from a convention to help those who needed help. The rich and powerful do not need much help and are often in the best position to give it; so, if a strong principle of mutual aid were adopted, they would gain little and lose a great deal, because they would end up doing most of the helping and would receive little in return. On the other hand, the poor and weak might refuse to agree to a principle of noninterference or noninjury unless they also reached some agreement on mutual aid. We would therefore expect a compromise, as in our example of the two rowers who arrive at a rate intermediate between the rates that each prefers to row at. In the present case, the expected compromise would involve a strong principle of noninjury and a much weaker principle of mutual aid—which is just what we now have. If our moral principles were not in this way a result of bargaining and adjustment, it would be hard to see why we would suppose that there is this moral difference between harming and not helping; and it would be hard to understand how our moral principles could be the result of bargaining and adjustment in this way unless they were derived from some sort of convention in Hume's sense. So, this aspect of our moral views is evidence in favor of Hume's tacit convention theory.

Now, it is important that Hume's theory is an *actual* convention theory. Duties and obligations are seen as deriving from actual, not hypothetical, conventions. Hume's theory is therefore to be distinguished from hypothetical agreement theories that say that the correct moral rules are those that people *would* agree to under certain conditions of equality. Hume's explanation of moral motivation requires his actual convention theory and does not work on any sort of hypothetical agreement theory. Hume says that we act morally first out of self-interest and then out of a habit of following certain conventional rules. We cannot in the same way explain why someone would be motivated to adhere to principles he *would have* agreed to adhere to in a position of equality.

CONTRACTUALISM

Thomas Scanlon

1. INTRODUCTION

The idea that an act is right if and only if it can be justified to others is one that even a noncontractualist might accept. Utilitarians, for example, who hold that an act is right only if it would produce a greater balance of happiness than any alternative available to the agent at the time, presumably also believe that an act is justifiable to others just in case it satisfies this utilitarian formula, so they too will hold that an act is right if and only if it is justifiable to others on terms they could not reasonably reject. For utilitarians, however, what makes an action right is having the best consequences; justifiability is merely a consequence of this.

What is distinctive about my version of contractualism is that it takes the idea of justifiability to be basic in two ways: this idea provides both the normative basis of the morality of right and wrong and the most general characterization of its content. According to contractualism, when we address our minds to a question of right and wrong, what we are trying to decide is, first and foremost, whether certain principles are ones that no one, if suitably motivated, could reasonably reject. In order to make the content of my view clearer I need to say more about the ideas of justifiability and reasonable rejection on which it rests. This is the aim of the present chapter.

Many theories have been offered that are like mine in suggesting that we can understand the content of morality (or of justice) by considering what principles people would (perhaps under special conditions) have reason to agree to, or what principles could be willed (from a certain point of view) to hold universally. These include, to mention only a few well-known examples, Kant's view and the theories offered more recently by David Gauthier, Jürgen Habermas, R. M. Hare, and John Rawls. Most of these theories appeal to some idea of rationality or of what it would be rational to choose (perhaps under special conditions). In Gauthier's case, rationality is identified, initially, with doing or choosing what conduces to the fulfillment of one's aims, and his aim is to show how we could have good reason to comply with principles that it would be rational, in this sense, for all to agree to. Hare identifies the rational action with the action that would maximize the satisfaction of one's present preferences as they would be if purged of logical error and modified by exposure to the facts. Since he takes moral principles to be universal imperatives (applying not only to things as they are but also to the possible worlds in which one occupies the position of any of the other people performing or affected by actions of the kind in question), a rational decision about which principles to accept must take into account not only one's present preferences but also the preferences one would have in any of these other positions. Rationally defensible moral principles will thus be those that lead to maximum satisfaction of the rational preferences of all affected parties.

Kant famously held that an action is morally permissible if it would be allowed by a principle that one could rationally will to hold "as a universal law." Rawls maintains, as one part of his theory, that the principles of justice (standards for determining the legitimacy of basic social institutions) are those that it would be rational for parties to accept if they were to choose with the aim of doing as well as they can for those they represent but under conditions in which they lacked any information about their social position, their natural advantages, and their distinctive values and commitments (that is to say, if they were to choose behind a "veil of ignorance" that obscures these facts).

Each of the theories I have mentioned proposes that we can reach conclusions about the content of morality by asking certain questions about what it would be rational to do or choose or will. In each case these questions are understood in a way that requires us, in one way or another, to take the interests of others into account in answering it. In the case of Gauthier's theory, we must take account of what others have reason to do because we are trying to gain the benefits of cooperative arrangements and it would not be rational for others to accept a plan of action if doing so would not advance their interests. In Hare's theory, and in the part of Rawls's that I have mentioned, the rational choice in question is defined in a way that makes the fates of others relevant in a different way. In Hare's theory this is accomplished by adding information and motivation: information about other people's preferences, which then shapes our own preferences about how we would want to be treated if we were in their position. In Rawls's theory it is done by subtracting information (imposing a veil of ignorance) and by focusing on motivation of one particular kind—the desire of mutually disinterested parties to do as well as they can for themselves and those whom they represent. Contracting parties are moved to protect the interests of the least advantaged and of cultural and religious minorities because, for all they know, they may belong to these groups themselves.

According to the version of contractualism that I am advancing here our thinking about right and wrong is structured by a different kind of motivation, namely the aim of finding principles that others, insofar as they too have this aim, could not reasonably reject. This gives us a direct reason to be concerned with other people's points of view: not because we might, for all we know, actually *be* them, or because we might occupy their position in some other possible world, but in order to find principles that they, as well as we, have reason to accept. . . . There is on this view a strong continuity between the reasons that lead us to act in the way that the conclusions of moral thought require and the reasons that shape the process through which we arrive at those conclusions. My version of contractualism is distinguished from these otherwise similar theories, then, by its particular motivational claim and by its appeal to the notion of reasonableness rather than rationality.

2. REASONABLENESS

This second feature, in particular, may seem questionable. Why speak of "principles which no one could reasonably reject" rather than "principles which no one could rationally reject"? The "reasonableness" formulation seems more obscure. Why use it, then, especially in view of the fact that I add the rider "given the aim of finding principles which others, insofar as they share this aim, could not reasonably reject"? Why not rely upon the idea of what would be *rational* for a person who has this aim?

. . . "Rationality" can be understood in a number of different ways. But in recent years "the (most) rational thing to do" has most commonly been taken to mean "what most conduces to the fulfillment of the agent's aims." The primacy of this usage is indicated by the contemporary theories I have just discussed, which despite their differences almost all make use of the idea of rationality in more or less this same sense. As I have indicated, I believe that this conception of rationality is mistaken, but it is so familiar that it is what any unqualified use of the term is likely to call to mind.

"Reasonable" also has an established meaning, which is much closer to what I take to be basic to moral thinking. A claim about what it is reasonable for a person to do presupposes a certain body of information and a certain range of reasons which are taken to be relevant, and goes on to make a claim about what these reasons, properly understood, in fact support. In the contractualist analysis of right and wrong, what is presupposed first and foremost is the aim of finding principles that others who share this aim could not reasonably reject. This aim then brings other reasons in its train. Given this aim, for example, it would be unreasonable to give the interests of others no weight in deciding which principles to accept. For why should they accept principles arrived at in this way? This then leads to further, more complicated questions about how, more exactly, we can be asked to "take others' interests into account" in various situations.

The distinction between what it would be reasonable to do in this sense and what it would be rational to do is not a technical one, but a familiar distinction in ordinary language. Suppose, for example, that we are negotiating about water rights in our county, and that there is one landowner who already controls most of the water in the vicinity. This person has no need for our cooperation. He can do as he pleases, and what he chooses to do will largely determine the outcome of the negotiations. Suppose also that while he is not ungenerous (he would probably provide water from his own wells for anyone who desperately needed it) he is extremely irritable and does not like to have the legitimacy of his position questioned. In such a situation, it would not be unreasonable for one of us to maintain that each person is entitled to at least a minimum supply of water, and to reject any principle of allocation which does not guarantee this. But it might not be rational to make this claim or to reject such principles, since this is very likely to enrage the large landholder and lead to an outcome that is worse for almost everyone. Moreover, it is natural to say that it would be unreasonable of the large landholder to reject our request for principles guaranteeing minimum water rights. What it would be rational for him to do (in the most common understanding of that term) is a different question, and depends on what his aims are.

There is, then, a familiar distinction between reasonableness and rationality. It might be objected that in calling attention to this distinction I have concentrated exclusively on what would be rational *simpliciter,* and have not considered what would be rational given the particular aim I have specified. Why not, it might be asked, take rightness to be determined by the principles no one could *rationally* reject given the aim of finding principles which others, who share this aim, could also not rationally reject? This seems to offer a way of capturing the idea that I have in mind while avoiding the obscure notion of reasonableness in favor of the clearer and better-understood idea of rationality.

My first reason for not formulating the contractualist account of right and wrong in this way is that so formulated it is most likely to be understood as a question of strategy, of how best to bring about the desired end of agreement on principles. So interpreted, it is unlikely to have a determinate answer, in light of the fact, noted above, that what it is rational to do will depend on what others can be expected to do in response. If there is one principle which would make everyone better off than he or she would be under any other, then it may be obvious that it is rational for everyone to choose this principle, and the question "What principle could no one rationally reject given the aim of finding principles that others, who share this aim, could not rationally reject?" may therefore have a determinate answer. But in more common situations we must choose among principles each of which would benefit some at the expense of others. In such cases, there may be no determinate answer, in the abstract, to the question whether a given principle is or is not one that no one with the aim in question could rationally reject.

The answer to this question in a given situation may become determinate once the details of that situation—the psychologies of the individuals involved and the options open to them—are fully specified. In the water rights case mentioned above, for example, even if all of us (the large landowner included) share the aim of finding principles which no one else could rationally reject, it remains true that none of us has reason to reject the terms which he prefers. Adding the aim of rational agreement makes little difference in this case, since the landowner is in a position to make it rational for his neighbors to accept whatever principle he chooses. In this example the answer, though determinate, carries little moral weight. If we rule out the features of this example which make it morally objectionable—by requiring, for example, that there be full information and a no-agreement point which leaves everyone in a position that is at least minimally acceptable—then determinateness may be lost again, since the outcome may depend on the individual psychologies of the parties, and their relations and loyalties. One familiar strategy is to impose further constraints on the agreement in question, with the aim of preserving both determinateness and moral relevance. This strategy may well succeed in particular cases. My present aim is not to argue against theories employing this strategy but rather to distinguish it from the strategy that I am pursuing.

According to my version of contractualism, deciding whether an action is right or wrong requires a substantive judgment on our part about whether certain objections to possible moral principles would be reasonable. In the argument over water rights, for example, our judgment that it would not be unreasonable for the neighbors to demand better terms than the large landowner is offering reflects a substantive judgment about the merits of their claims. It is not a judgment about what would be most likely to advance their interests or to produce agreement in their actual circumstances or in any more idealized situation, but rather a judgment about the suitability of certain principles to serve as the basis of mutual recognition and accommodation.

If my analysis is correct then the idea of what would be reasonable in this sense is one that underlies and guides our ordinary thinking about right and wrong. It is thus an idea with moral content. This moral content makes it inviting as a component in moral theory, but also invites the charge of circularity. By basing itself on reasonableness, it may be charged, a theory builds in moral elements at the start. This makes it easy to produce a theory which *sounds* plausible, but such a theory will tell us very little, since everything we are to get out of it at the end we must put in at the beginning as part of the moral content of reasonableness. A strategy which relies on the idea of rationality (together, perhaps, with structural features of an ideal situation in which the rational choices are to be made) therefore seems to promise a more successful theory, or at least an account of right and wrong which is less threatened with circularity. Before responding to this objection, I will describe my version of contractualism in somewhat greater detail. By making clearer the ways in which judgments about reasonable rejection "have moral content" I hope to clarify both the force of the charge of circularity and my way of responding to it.

Before turning to this task, however, I want to say more about how the idea of reasonableness figures in the process of deciding whether or not an action is wrong. According to contractualism, in order to decide whether it would be wrong to do X in circumstances C, we should consider possible principles governing how one may act in such situations, and ask whether any principle that permitted one to do X in those circumstances could, for that reason, reasonably be rejected. In order to decide whether this is so, we need first to form an idea of the burdens that would be imposed on some people in such a situation if others were permitted to do X. Call these the objections to permission. We then need, in order to decide whether these objections provide grounds for reasonably rejecting the proposed principle, to consider the ways in which others would be burdened by a principle forbidding one to do X in these circumstances. Suppose that, compared to the objections to permission, the objections to prohibition are not significant, and that it is therefore reasonable to reject any principle that would permit one to do X in the circumstances in question. This means that this action is wrong, according to the contractualist formula. Alternatively, if there were some principle for regulating behavior in such situations that would permit one to do X and that it would not be reasonable to reject, then doing X would not be wrong: it could be justified to others on grounds that they could not reasonably refuse to accept.

Returning to the former case for the moment, if it would be reasonable to reject any principle that permitted one to do X in circumstances C, then it would seem that there must be some principle that it would not be reasonable to reject that would disallow doing X in these circumstances. One would expect this to be true because of the comparative nature of the question of reasonable rejection. If the objections to permission are strong enough, *compared to the objections to prohibition,* to make it reasonable to reject any principle permitting doing X in C, then one would not expect the objections to prohibition to be strong enough, *compared to the objections to permission,* to make it reasonable to reject any principle that forbids doing X in C.

But it may seem that there could be cases in which this might be true. Consider, for example, the case of two people swimming from a sinking ship, one of whom finds a life jacket floating in the water. May the other person take the jacket by force? It might seem that, even though any principle that permitted this could reasonably be rejected, any principle forbidding it could also be rejected, since taking the jacket is the only way for the other person to avoid drowning. Put in a general form, the idea might be that there is a threshold of reasonable rejection: a level of cost such that it is reasonable to reject any principle that would lead to one's suffering a cost that great, and reasonable to do this no matter what objections others might have to alternative principles. It does not seem to me that there is such a threshold. It does not seem, for example, that the fact that a principle would forbid one to do something that was necessary in order to save one's life always makes it reasonable to reject that principle. The reasonableness of rejecting such a principle will depend not only on the costs that alternative principles would impose on others but also on how those costs would be imposed. This reflects the general fact, which I will discuss later in this chapter, that the strength of a person's objection to a principle is not determined solely by the difference that the acceptance of that principle would make to that person's welfare. In the shipwreck case, for example, the costs of the two principles to the parties may be the same (one will drown if not permitted to seize the life jacket, and the other will drown if it is taken from him). But it may still make a difference to the force of their objections that one of them now has the jacket (perhaps he has looked hard to find it) and is therefore not now at risk.

Even if the general idea of a threshold of reasonable rejection is incorrect, however, there could still be cases in which opposing parties have strong objections that are evenly balanced. Suppose, for example, that the two swimmers, one of whom is much stronger than the other, arrive at the life jacket at the same moment. May each use force to try to seize it? It might seem that if a principle permitting this could reasonably be rejected then so too could a principle forbidding it, since the considerations on the two sides are the same. This conclusion depends on an overly simple view of the alternatives. A principle permitting each to struggle for the jacket at least has the merit of recognizing the symmetry of their claims and the need for some decisive solution. It would be reasonable to reject this principle if, but only if, there were some alternative that did this better (such as a principle requiring them to take turns or, unrealistic as it may seem, to draw lots). Similarly, a principle forbidding the use of force could not reasonably be rejected if there were some other (nonrejectable) method for resolving the matter.

It thus does not follow, from the fact that the situations of the people who would suffer from an action's being permitted and those who would suffer from its being forbidden are virtually the same, that if any principle that permits the action can reasonably be rejected then so too can any principle that forbids it. The very fact that these objections are symmetrical may point the way toward a class of principles that are not rejectable.

3. PRINCIPLES

I have said that an act is wrong if it would be disallowed by any *principle* that no one could reasonably reject. The aim of this section is to explain what is meant here by a principle and to say something about the role that such principles play in our thinking about right and wrong. Taking familiar controversies about act and rule utilitarianism as a background, it would be natural to ask why justification of our actions to others should proceed by way of principles at all. Why not consider individual acts instead? Put in this way, the question is misconceived. To justify an action to others is to offer reasons supporting it and to claim that they are sufficient to defeat any objections that others may have. To do this, however, is also to defend a principle, namely one claiming that such reasons are sufficient grounds for so acting under the prevailing conditions. There is a question (corresponding to the debate between act and rule utilitarianism) as to whether the justification for an action should appeal only to consequences of that act (as compared with the consequences of alternative actions available to the agent) or whether other considerations are also relevant. I will address this question in the following section. But it is a question about the form that the relevant principles should take, not about whether justification should involve principles at all.

The emphasis that contractualism places on justification, hence on reasons and principles, captures a central feature of everyday judgments of right and wrong. Typically, our intuitive judgments about the wrongness of actions are not simply judgments *that* an act is wrong but that it is wrong for some reason, or in virtue of some general characteristic. Judgments of right and wrong are in this respect quite different from many other types of evaluative judgment such as judgments that something is beautiful, or ugly, or funny. In the latter cases the evaluative judgment comes first—we "see" that the thing is beautiful or funny—and the explanation comes later, if in fact we can supply it at all. But we rarely, if ever, "see" that an action is wrong without having some idea *why* it is wrong. There may be cases in which some action "just seems wrong," even though one cannot say what the objection to it is. But these reactions have the status of "hunches" or suspicions which need to be made good: there is pressure to come up with an explanation or else withdraw the judgment if we cannot explain what our objection is.

People in different cultures regard different things as funny and have different views about what constitutes a beautiful face. They thus have "different standards" of humor and (at least some kinds of) beauty, and it is plausible to say that when a member of one of these groups makes a judgment about what is funny or good-looking, the claim that this judgment makes has to be understood as relative to the standards of that group (so that opposing assessments of the same joke, made in Omsk and Los Angeles, could both be true). But even if there are, in this sense, standards of humor and beauty, these standards do not play the same role in individual judgments that moral standards generally do. A person who regards a joke as funny, or a person or scene as beautiful, may be quite unable to articulate the standards, if any, to which his or her judgment is relative. But I cannot claim that an action is morally wrong without having some idea what objection there is to it.

Contractualism offers a natural explanation of this feature of our judgments about right and wrong. In another respect, however, the claim that moral judgments involve conscious reference to principles may seem implausible. Suppose I believe that while McCormick had a legal right to build his house where he did, it was wrong of him to put it so close to the property line, thereby ruining his neighbor's view. In this example I have a definite idea what the moral objection to McCormick's action is: insufficient consideration for his neighbor's interests. But it is unlikely that I could formulate a principle to back this up, if by a principle we mean a rule specifying what weight one is supposed to give to others' interests when they conflict with one's own interests of a similar sort. So the claim I have been making may seem very implausible insofar as it is taken to suggest that we make decisions of this kind by invoking or "applying" a principle or rule.

This observation is quite correct. But the idea that it constitutes an objection to what I have been claiming rests on an overly narrow idea of what a principle is. If a principle is taken to be a rule that can be "applied" to settle quite a wide range of questions with little or no room left for the exercise of judgment, then there are very few moral principles at all, and it would certainly be false to claim that every judgment about right and wrong must be backed by one. If the claim that moral judgments must be backed by principles is to have any plausibility, the notion of a principle will have to be understood much more broadly. Principles, as I will understand them, are general conclusions about the status of various kinds of reasons for action. So understood, principles may rule out some actions by ruling out the reasons on which they would be based, but they also leave wide room for interpretation and judgment.

Consider, for example, moral principles concerning the taking of human life. It might seem that this is a simple rule, forbidding a certain class of actions: Thou shalt not kill. But what about self-defense, suicide, and certain acts of killing by police officers and by soldiers in wartime? And is euthanasia always strictly forbidden? The parts of this principle that are the clearest are better put in terms of reasons: the fact that a course of action can be foreseen to lead to someone's death is normally a conclusive reason against it; the fact that someone's death would be to my personal advantage is no justification for aiming at it; but one may use deadly force when this seems the only defense against a person who threatens one's life; and so on.

Much the same can be said of the principle of fidelity to promises. We are not morally required to keep a promise no matter what. The clearest part of the principle is this: the fact that keeping a promise would be inconvenient or disadvantageous is not normally a sufficient reason for breaking it, but "normally" here covers many qualifications. There are, for example, questions of proportionality (the kind of disadvantage that may not be appealed to in order to justify backing out depends on what is at stake in the promise) and questions about the conditions under which the promise was given (such as whether there was duress and whether crucial information was withheld).

So even the most familiar moral principles are not rules which can be easily applied without appeals to judgment. Their succinct verbal formulations turn out on closer examination to be mere labels for much more complex ideas. Moral principles are in this respect much like some legal ones. The constitutional formula "Congress shall make no law abridging freedom of speech, or of the press" may sound like a simple prohibition. But the underlying idea is much more complicated. There is of course considerable controversy about what, more precisely, this amendment covers. What is striking, however, and more relevant for present purposes, is the breadth and complexity of the area of agreement. Presented with a range of examples of governmental regulation of expression, people who understand freedom of expression will agree on a wide range of judgments about which of these involve violations of the First Amendment and which do not. These cases are sufficiently varied that it would be difficult to explain our convergent judgments as applications of any statable rule. How, then, do we arrive at these judgments? We do so, I believe, by appeal to a shared sense of what the point of freedom of expression is and how it is supposed to work: why restrictions on governmental power to regulate expression are necessary, what threats they are supposed to rule out, and what it is that they are trying to promote.

Similarly, it is a familiar moral principle that promises freely made must be kept, although we must add "at least in the absence of special justification." How do we decide what forms of justification are sufficient? It is sometimes suggested that this is a matter of "balancing" the competing considerations. But this metaphor is misleading insofar as it suggests that what is involved is only a process of weighing or comparing the seriousness of conflicting interests. The costs at stake for promiser and promisee are of course among the relevant factors in deciding whether a given promise must be kept, but these must be considered within a more complex structure which the metaphor of balancing conceals. Anyone who understands the point of promising—what it is supposed to ensure and what it is to protect us against—will see that certain reasons for going back on a promise could not be allowed without rendering promises pointless, while other exceptions must be allowed if the practice is not to be unbearably costly.

For example, the point of promising would be defeated if a minor inconvenience, or even a major cost that was clearly foreseeable at the time the promise was made, counted as adequate ground for failing to perform as promised. On the other hand it would not render promises pointless to recognize, as grounds for default, a cost which is both quite unexpected and much more serious than what is at stake for the promisee. Perhaps this exception is even required in order not to make promising too risky. Factors such as whether a cost to a promisee was foreseeable, foreseen, or unexpected are made relevant by the interests to which a principle of fidelity to agreements must be responsive. . . .

All of this structure and more is part of what each of us knows if we understand the principle that promises ought to be kept. In making particular judgments of right and wrong we are drawing on this complex understanding, rather than applying a statable rule, and this understanding enables us to arrive at conclusions about new and difficult cases, which no rule would cover.

When we judge a person to have acted in a way that was morally wrong, we take her or him to have acted on a reason that is morally disallowed, or to have given a reason more weight than is morally permitted, or to have failed to see the relevance or weight of some countervailing reason which, morally, must take precedence. Each of these judgments involves a principle in the broad sense in which I am using that term. There may be no rule we can invoke as telling us that a certain reason is not morally sufficient (that my reason for breaking my promise is not sufficiently weighty, or that McCormick did not have good reason for disregarding his neighbor's interest in preserving his view). But we make such judgments by drawing on our understanding of why there should be a moral constraint on actions of the kind in question (why principles that left us free to do as we liked in such situations are "reasonably rejectable") and of the structure that that constraint takes (in what way we can be asked to take the relevant interests into account). When, in the light of our best understanding of this moral rationale, we make a judgment about the sufficiency of the reasons for an action in a particular case, this judgment is guided by, and expresses, our understanding of a moral principle.

How many valid moral principles are there, then? An indefinite number, I would say. This, again, may seem implausible. How are we supposed to know what principles there are? By the same kind of thinking that we use to understand the content of familiar principles like fidelity to promises and freedom of speech. That is: we can see the need for limits on certain patterns of action (patterns of justification) by seeing the ways in which we are at risk if people are left free to decide to act in these ways; and by understanding the rationale for these moral constraints we can see why it is that certain reasons for action, and certain ways of giving some reasons priority over others, are morally inadmissible. Some familiar principles are generally learned through explicit moral teaching, but we can see, on reflection, that they have a basis of the kind I have just described. Other principles we may never have thought of until we are presented with a situation (real or hypothetical) to which they would apply; but when this happens we can see immediately that they are valid.

For example: we are all taught that it is wrong to break one's promises (although, as I have said, our understanding of this principle goes far beyond the content of any explicit teaching). But . . . there are many other ways in which one can behave wrongly in regard to other people's expectations about what one will do: one can fail to take care about the expectations one leads others to form, fail to warn them that their expectations are mistaken, or (without promising anything) intentionally lead others to form false expectations when their doing so is to one's advantage. Not every action falling under the last two descriptions is wrong, but many are. There are no familiar and widely taught principles—analogous to "Keep your promises"—that cover these cases. Yet once the question arises we are able to see the wrongness of these actions in much the same way that we see the wrongness of breaking a promise or of making a promise that one does not intend to keep. That is to say, we are able to see that principles licensing such actions would be ones that people could reasonably reject.

Virtues and Vices

Philippa Foot

I

For many years the subject of the virtues and vices was strangely neglected by moralists working within the school of analytic philosophy. The tacitly accepted opinion was that a study of the topic would form no part of the fundamental work of ethics; and since this opinion was apparently shared by philosophers such as Hume, Kant, Mill, G. E. Moore, W. D. Ross, and H. A. Prichard, from whom contemporary moral philosophy has mostly been derived, perhaps the neglect was not so surprising after all. However that may be, things have recently been changing. During the past ten or fifteen years several philosophers have turned their attention to the subject; notably H. W. von Wright and Peter Geach. Von Wright devoted a not at all perfunctory chapter to the virtues in his book *The Varieties of Goodness*[1] published in 1963, and Peter Geach's book called *The Virtues*[2] appeared in 1977. Meanwhile a number of interesting articles on the topic have come out in the journals.

In spite of this recent work, it is best when considering the virtues and vices to go back to Aristotle and Aquinas. I myself have found Plato less helpful, because the individual virtues and vices are not so clearly or consistently distinguished in his work. It is certain, in any case, that the most systematic account is found in Aristotle, and in the blending of Aristotelian and Christian philosophy found in St. Thomas. By and large Aquinas followed Aristotle — sometimes even heroically — where Aristotle gave an opinion, and where St. Thomas is on his own, as in developing the doctrine of the theological virtues of faith, hope and charity, and in his theocentric doctrine of happiness, he still uses an Aristotelian framework where he can: as for instance in speaking of happiness as man's last end. However, there are different emphases and new elements in Aquinas's ethics: often he works things out in far more detail than Aristotle did, and it is possible to learn a great deal from Aquinas that one could not have got from Aristotle. It is my opinion that the *Summa Theologica* is one of the best sources we have for moral philosophy, and moreover that St. Thomas's ethical writings are as useful to the atheist as to the Catholic or other Christian believer.

There is, however, one minor obstacle to be overcome when one goes back to Aristotle and Aquinas for help in constructing a theory of virtues, namely a lack of coincidence between their terminology and our own. For when we talk about the virtues we are not taking as our subject everything to which Aristotle gave the name *aretē* or Aquinas *virtus,* and consequently not everything called a virtue in translations of these authors. "The virtues" to us are the moral virtues whereas *aretē* and *virtus* refer also to arts, and even to excellences of the speculative intellect whose domain is theory rather than practice. And to make things more confusing we find some dispositions called moral virtues in translations from the Greek and Latin, although the class of virtues that Aristotle calls *aretai ēthikai* and Aquinas *virtutes morales* does not exactly correspond with our class of moral virtues. For us there are four cardinal moral virtues: courage, temperance, wisdom and justice. But Aristotle and Aquinas call only three of these virtues moral virtues; practical wisdom (Aristotle's *phronēsis* and Aquinas's *prudentia*) they class with the intellectual virtues, though they point out the close connexions between practical wisdom and what they call moral virtues; and sometimes they even use *aretē* and *virtus* very much as we use "virtue."

I will come back to Aristotle and Aquinas, and shall indeed refer to them frequently in this paper. But I want to start by making some remarks, admittedly fragmentary, about the concept of a moral virtue as we understand the idea.

First of all it seems clear that virtues are, in some general way, beneficial. Human beings do not get on well without them. Nobody can get on well if he lacks courage, and does not have some measure of temperance and wisdom, while communities where justice and charity are lacking are apt to be wretched places to live, as Russia was under the Stalinist terror, or Sicily under the Mafia. But now we must ask to whom the benefit goes, whether to the man who has the virtue or rather to those who have to do with him? In the case of some of the virtues the answer seems clear. Courage, temperance and wisdom benefit both the man who has these dispositions and other people as well; and moral failings such as pride, vanity, worldliness, and avarice harm both their possessor and others, though chiefly perhaps the former. But what about the virtues of charity and justice? These are directly concerned with the welfare of others, and with what is owed to them; and since each may require sacrifice of interest on the part of the virtuous man both may seem to be deleterious to their possessor and beneficial to others. Whether in fact it is so has, of course, been a matter of controversy since Plato's time or earlier. It is a reasonable opinion that on the whole a man is better off for being charitable and just, but this is not to say that circumstances may not arise in which he will have to sacrifice everything for charity or justice.

Nor is this the only problem about the relation between virtue and human good. For one very difficult question concerns the relation between justice and the common good. Justice, in the wide sense in which it is understood in discussions of the cardinal virtues, and in this paper, has to do with that to which someone has a right—that which he is owed in respect of non-interference and positive service—and rights may stand in the way of the pursuit of the common good. Or so at least it seems to those who reject utilitarian doctrines. This dispute cannot be settled here, but I shall treat justice as a virtue independent of charity, and standing as a possible limit on the scope of that virtue.

Let us say then, leaving unsolved problems behind us, that virtues are in general beneficial characteristics, and indeed ones that a human being needs to have, for his own sake and that of his fellows. This will not, however, take us far towards a definition of a virtue, since there are many other qualities of a man that may be similarly beneficial, as for instance bodily characteristics such as health and physical strength, and mental powers such as those of memory and concentration. What is it, we must ask, that differentiates virtues from such things?

As a first approximation to an answer we might say that while health and strength are excellences of the body, and memory and concentration of the mind, it is the will that is good in a man of virtue. But this suggestion is worth only as much as the explanation that follows it. What might we mean by saying that virtue belongs to the will?

In the first place we observe that it is primarily by his intentions that a man's moral dispositions are judged. If he does something unintentionally this is usually irrelevant to our estimate of his virtue. But of course this thesis must be qualified, because failures in performance rather than intention may show a lack of virtue. This will be so when, for instance, one man brings harm to another without realising he is doing it, but where his ignorance is itself culpable. Sometimes in such cases there will be a previous act or omission to which we can point as the source of the ignorance. Charity requires that we take care to find out how to render assistance where we are likely to be called on to do so, and thus, for example, it is contrary to charity to fail to find out about elementary first aid. But in an interesting class of cases in which it seems again to be performance rather than intention that counts in judging a man's virtue there is no possibility of shifting the judgement to previous intentions. For sometimes one man succeeds where another fails not because there is some specific difference in their previous conduct but rather because his heart lies in a different place; and the disposition of the heart is part of virtue.

Thus it seems right to attribute a kind of moral failing to some deeply discouraging and debilitating people who say, without lying, that they mean to be helpful; and on the other side to see virtue *par excellence* in one who is prompt and resourceful in doing good. In his novel *A Single Pebble* John Hersey describes such a man, speaking of a rescue in a swift flowing river:

> It was the head tracker's marvellous swift response that captured my admiration at first, his split second solicitousness when he heard a cry of pain, his finding in mid-air, as it were, the only way to save the injured boy. But there was more to it than that. His action, which could not have been mulled over in his mind, showed a deep, instinctive love of life, a compassion, an optimism, which made me feel very good . . .

What this suggests is that a man's virtue may be judged by his innermost desires as well as by his intentions; and this fits with our idea that a virtue such as generosity lies as much in someone's attitudes as in his actions. Pleasure in the good fortune of others is, one thinks, the sign of a generous spirit; and small reactions of pleasure and displeasure often the surest signs of a man's moral disposition.

None of this shows that it is wrong to think of virtues as belonging to the will; what it does show is that "will" must here be understood in its widest sense, to cover what is wished for as well as what is sought.

A different set of considerations will, however, force us to give up any simple statement about the relation between virtue and will, and these considerations have to do with the virtue of wisdom. Practical wisdom, we said, was counted by Aristotle among the intellectual virtues, and while our *wisdom* is not quite the same as *phronēsis* or *prudentia* it too might seem to belong to the intellect rather than the will. Is not wisdom a matter of knowledge, and how can knowledge be a matter of intention or desire? The answer is that it isn't, so that there is good reason for thinking of wisdom as an intellectual virtue. But on the other hand wisdom has special connexions with the will, meeting it at more than one point.

In order to get this rather complex picture in focus we must pause for a little and ask what it is that we ourselves understand by wisdom: what the wise man knows and what he does. Wisdom, as I see it, has two parts. In the first place the wise man knows the means to certain good ends; and secondly he knows how much particular ends are worth. Wisdom in its first part is relatively easy to understand. It seems that there are some ends belonging to human life in general rather than to particular skills such as medicine or boatbuilding, ends having to do with such matters as friendship, marriage, the bringing up of children, or the choice of ways of life; and it seems that knowledge of how to act well in these matters belongs to some people but not to others. We call those who have this knowledge wise, while those who do not have it are seen as lacking wisdom. So, as both Aristotle and Aquinas insisted, wisdom is to be contrasted with cleverness because cleverness is the ability to take the right steps to any end, whereas wisdom is related only to good ends, and to human life in general rather than to the ends of particular arts.

Moreover, we should add, there belongs to wisdom only that part of knowledge which is within the reach of any ordinary adult human being: knowledge that can be acquired only by someone who is clever or who has access to special training is not counted as part of wisdom, and would not be so counted even if it could serve the ends that wisdom serves. It is therefore quite wrong to suggest that wisdom cannot be a moral virtue because virtue must be within the reach of anyone who really wants it and some people are too stupid to be anything but ignorant even about the most fundamental matters of human life. Some people are wise without being at all clever or well informed: they make good decisions and they know, as we say, "what's what."

In short wisdom, in what we called its first part, is connected with the will in the following ways. To begin with it presupposes good ends: the man who is wise does not merely know *how* to do good things such as looking after his children well, or strengthening someone in trouble, but must also want to do them. And then wisdom, in so far as it consists of knowledge which anyone can gain in the course of an ordinary life, is available to anyone who really wants it. As Aquinas put it, it belongs "to a power under the direction of the will."[3]

The second part of wisdom, which has to do with values, is much harder to describe, because here we meet ideas which are curiously elusive, such as the thought that some pursuits are more worthwhile than others, and some matters trivial and some important in human life. Since it makes good sense to say that most men waste a lot of their lives in ardent pursuit of what is trivial and unimportant it is not possible to explain the important and the trivial in terms of the amount of attention given to different subjects by the average man. But I have never seen, or been able to think out, a true account of this matter, and I believe that a complete account of wisdom, and of certain other virtues and vices must wait until this gap can be filled. What we can see is that one of the things a wise man knows and a foolish man does not is that such things as social position, and wealth, and the good opinion of the world, are too dearly bought at the cost of health or friendship or family ties. So we may say that a man who lacks wisdom "has false values," and that vices such as vanity and worldliness and avarice are contrary to wisdom in a special way. There is always an element of false judgement about these vices, since the man who is vain for instance sees admiration as more important than it is, while the worldly man is apt to see the good life as one of wealth and power. Adapting Aristotle's distinction between the weak-willed man (the *akratēs*) who follows pleasure though he knows, in some sense, that he should not, and the licentious man (the *akolastos*) who sees the life of pleasure as the good life,[4] we may say that moral failings such as these are never purely "*akratic*." It is true that a man may criticise himself for his worldliness or vanity or love of money, but then it is his values that are the subject of his criticism.

Wisdom in this second part is, therefore, partly to be described in terms of apprehension, and even judgement, but since it has to do with a man's attachments it also characterises his will.

The idea that virtues belong to the will, and that this helps to distinguish them from such things as bodily strength or intellectual ability has, then, survived the consideration of the virtue of wisdom, albeit in a fairly complex and slightly attenuated form. And we shall find this idea useful again if we turn to another important distinction that must be made, namely that between virtues and other practical excellences such as arts and skills.

Aristotle has sometimes been accused, for instance by von Wright, of failing to see how different values are from arts or skills;[5] but in fact one finds, among the many things that Aristotle and Aquinas say about this difference, the observation that seems to go to the heart of the matter. In the matter of arts and skills, they say, voluntary error is preferable to involuntary error, while in the matter of virtues (what we call virtues) it is the reverse.[6] The last part of the thesis is actually rather hard to interpret, because it is not clear what is meant by the idea of involuntary viciousness. But we can leave this aside and still have all we need in order to distinguish arts or skills from virtues. If we think, for instance, of someone who deliberately makes a spelling mistake (perhaps when writing on the blackboard in order to explain this particular point) we see that this does not in any way count against his skill as a speller: "I did it deliberately" rebuts an accusation of this kind. And what we can say without running into any difficulties is that there is no comparable rebuttal in the case of an accusation relating to lack of virtue. If a man acts unjustly or uncharitably, or in a cowardly or intemperate manner, "I did it deliberately" cannot on any interpretation lead to exculpation. So, we may say, a virtue is not, like a skill or art, a mere capacity: it must actually engage the will.

II

I shall now turn to another thesis about the virtues, which I might express by saying that they are *corrective*, each one standing at a point at which there is some temptation to be resisted or deficiency of motivation to be made good. As Aristotle put it, virtues are about what is difficult for men, and I want to see in what sense this is true, and then to consider a problem in Kant's moral philosophy in the light of what has been said.

Let us first think about courage and temperance. Aristotle and Aquinas contrasted these virtues with justice in the following respect. Justice was concerned with operations and courage and temperance with passions.[7] What he meant by this seems to have been, primarily, that the man of courage does not fear immoderately nor the man of temperance have immoderate desires for pleasure, and that there was no corresponding moderation of a passion implied in the idea of justice. This particular account of courage and temperance might be disputed on the ground that a man's courage is measured by his action and not by anything as uncontrollable as fear; and similarly that the temperate man who must on occasion refuse pleasures need not *desire* them any less than the intemperate man. Be that as it may (and something will be said about it later) it is obviously true that courage and temperance have to do with particular springs of action as justice does not. Almost any desire can lead a man to act unjustly, not even excluding the desire to help a friend or to save a life, whereas a cowardly act must be motivated by fear or a desire for safety, and an act of intemperance by a desire for pleasure, perhaps even for a particular range of pleasures such as those of eating or drinking or sex. And now, going back to the idea of virtues as correctives one may say that it is only because fear and the desire for pleasure often operate as temptations that courage and temperance exist as virtues at all. As things are we often want to run away not only where that is the right thing to do but also where we should stand firm; and we want pleasure not only where we should seek pleasure but also where we should not. If human nature had been different there would have been no need of a corrective disposition in either place, as fear and pleasure would have been good guides to conduct throughout life. So Aquinas says, about the passions

> They may incite us to something against reason, and so we need a curb, which we name *temperance*. Or they may make us shirk a course of action dictated by reason, through fear of dangers or hardships. Then a person needs to be steadfast and not run away from what is right; and for this *courage* is named.[8]

As with courage and temperance so with many other virtues: there is, for instance, a virtue of industriousness only because idleness is a temptation; and of humility only because men tend to think too well of themselves. Hope is a virtue because despair too is a temptation; it might have been that no one cried that all was lost except where he could really see it to be so, and in this case there would have been no virtue of hope.

With virtues such as justice and charity it is a little different, because they correspond not to any particular desire or tendency that has to be kept in check but rather to a deficiency of motivation; and it is this that they must make good. If people were as much attached to the good of others as they are to their own good there would no more be a general virtue of benevolence than there is a general virtue of self-love. And if people cared about the rights of others as they care about their own rights no virtue of justice would be needed to look after the matter, and rules about such things as contracts and promises would only need to be made public, like the rules of a game that everyone was eager to play.

On this view of the virtues and vices everything is seen to depend on what human nature is like, and the traditional catalogue of the two kinds of dispositions is not hard to understand. Nevertheless it may be defective, and anyone who accepts the thesis that I am putting forward will feel free to ask himself where the temptations and deficiencies that need correcting are really to be found. It is possible, for example, that the theory of human nature lying behind the traditional list of the virtues and vices puts too much emphasis on hedonistic and sensual impulses, and does not sufficiently take account of less straightforward inclinations such as the desire to be put upon and dissatisfied, or the unwillingness to accept good things as they come along.

It should now be clear why I said that virtues should be seen as correctives; and part of what is meant by saying that virtue is about things that are difficult for men should also have appeared. The further application of this idea is, however, controversial, and the following difficulty presents itself: that we both are and are not inclined to think that the harder a man finds it to act virtuously the more virtue he shows if he does act well. For on the one hand great virtue is needed where it is particularly hard to act virtuously; yet on the other it could be argued that difficulty in acting virtuously shows that the agent is imperfect in virtue: according to Aristotle, to take pleasure in virtuous action is the mark of true virtue, with the self-mastery of the one who finds virtue difficult only a second best. How then is this conflict to be decided? Who shows most courage, the one who wants to run away but does not, or the one who does not even want to run away? Who shows most charity, the one who finds it easy to make the good of others his object, or the one who finds it hard?

What is certain is that the thought that virtues are corrective does not constrain us to relate virtue to difficulty in each individual man. Since men in general find it hard to face great dangers or evils, and even small ones, we may count as courageous those few who without blindness or indifference are nevertheless fearless even in terrible circumstances. And when someone has a natural charity or generosity it is, at least part of the virtue that he has; if natural virtue cannot be the whole of virtue this is because a kindly or fearless disposition could be disastrous without justice and wisdom, and these virtues have to be learned, not because natural virtue is too easily acquired. I have argued that the virtues can be seen as correctives in relation to human nature in general but not that each virtue must present a difficulty to each and every man.

Nevertheless many people feel strongly inclined to say that it is for moral effort that moral praise is to be bestowed, and that in proportion as a man finds it easy to be virtuous so much the less is he to be morally admired for his good actions. The dilemma can be resolved only when we stop talking about difficulties standing in the way of virtuous action as if they were of only one kind. The fact is that some kinds of difficulties do indeed provide an occasion for much virtue, but that others rather show that virtue is incomplete.

To illustrate this point I shall first consider an example of honest action. We may suppose for instance that a man has an opportunity to steal, in circumstances where stealing is not morally permissible, but that he refrains. And now let us ask our old question. For one man it is hard to refrain from stealing and for another man it is not: which shows the greater virtue in acting as he should? Is it not difficult to see in this case that it makes all the difference whether the difficulty comes from circumstances, as that a man is poor, or that his theft is unlikely to be detected, or whether it comes from something that belongs to his own character. The fact that a man is *tempted* to steal is something about him that shows a certain lack of honesty: of the thoroughly honest man we say that it "never entered his head," meaning that it was never a real possibility for him. But the fact that he is poor is something that makes the occasion more *tempting,* and the difficulties of this kind make honest action all the more virtuous.

A similar distinction can be made between different obstacles standing in the way of charitable action. Some circumstances, as that great sacrifice is needed, or that the one to be helped is a rival, give an occasion on which a man's charity is severely tested. Yet in given circumstances of this kind it is the man who acts easily rather than the one who finds it hard who shows the most charity. Charity is a virtue of attachment, and that sympathy for others which makes it easier to help them is part of the virtue itself.

These are fairly simple cases, but I am not supposing that it is always easy to say where the relevant distinction is to be drawn. What, for instance, should we say about the emotion of fear as an obstacle to action? Is a man more courageous if he fears much and nevertheless acts, or if he is relatively fearless? Several things must be said about this. In the first place it seems that the emotion of fear is not a necessary condition for the display of courage; in the face of a great evil such as death or injury a man may show courage even if he does not tremble. On the other hand even irrational fears may give an occasion for courage: if someone suffers from claustrophobia or a dread of heights he may require courage to do that which would not be a courageous action for others. But not all fears belong from this point of view to the circumstances rather than to a man's character. For while we do not think of claustrophobia or a dread of heights as features of character, a general timorousness may be. Thus, although pathological fears are not the result of a man's choices and values some fears may be. The fears that count against a man's courage are those that we think he could overcome, and among them, in a special class, those that reflect the fact that he values safety too much.

In spite of problems such as these, which have certainly not all been solved, both the distinction between different kinds of obstacles to virtuous action, and the general idea that virtues are correctives, will be useful in resolving a difficulty in Kant's moral philosophy closely related to the issues discussed in the preceding paragraphs. In a passage in the first section of the *Groundwork of the Metaphysics of Morals* Kant notoriously tied himself into a knot in trying to give an account of those actions which have as he put it "positive moral worth." Arguing that only actions done out of a sense of duty have this worth he contrasts a philanthropist who "takes pleasure in spreading happiness around him" with one who acts out of respect for duty, saying that the actions of the latter but not the former have moral worth. Much scorn has been poured on Kant for this curious doctrine, and indeed it does seem that something has gone wrong, but perhaps we are not in a position to scoff unless we can give our own account of the idea on which Kant is working. After all it does seem that he is right in saying that some actions are in accordance with duty, and even required by duty, without being the subjects of moral praise, like those of the honest trader who deals honestly in a situation in which it is in his interest to do so.

It was this kind of example that drove Kant to his strange conclusion. He added another example, however, in discussing acts of self-preservation; these he said, while they normally have no positive moral worth, may have it when a man preserves his life not from inclination but without inclination and from a sense of duty. Is he not right in saying that acts of self-preservation normally have no moral significance but that they may have it, and how do we ourselves explain this fact?

To anyone who approaches this topic from a consideration of the virtues the solution readily suggests itself. Some actions are in accordance with virtue without requiring virtue for their performance, whereas others are both in accordance with virtue and such as to show possession of a virtue. So Kant's trader was dealing honestly in a situation in which the virtue of honesty is not required for honest dealing, and it is for this reason that his action did not have "positive moral worth." Similarly, the care that one ordinarily takes for one's life, as for instance on some ordinary morning in eating one's breakfast and keeping out of the way of a car on the road, is something for which no virtue is required. As we said earlier there is no general virtue of self-love as there is a virtue of benevolence or charity, because men are generally attached sufficiently to their own good. Nevertheless in special circumstances virtues such as temperance, courage, fortitude, and hope may be needed if someone is to preserve his life. Are these circumstances in which the preservation of one's own life is a duty? Sometimes it is so, for sometimes it is what is owed to others that should keep a man from destroying himself, and then he may act out of a sense of duty. But not all cases in which acts of self-preservation show virtue are like this. For a man may display each of the virtues just listed even where he does not do any harm to others if he kills himself or fails to preserve his life. And it is this that explains why there may be a moral aspect to suicide which does not depend on possible injury to other people. It is not that suicide is "always wrong," whatever that would mean, but that suicide is *sometimes* contrary to virtues such as courage and hope.

Let us now return to Kant's philanthropists, with the thought that it is action that is in accordance with virtue and also displays a virtue that has moral worth. We see at once that Kant's difficulties are avoided, and the happy philanthropist reinstated in the position which belongs to him. For charity is, as we said, a virtue of attachment as well as action, and the sympathy that makes it easier to act with charity is part of the virtue. The man who acts charitably out of a sense of duty is not to be undervalued, but it is the other who most shows virtue and therefore to the other that most moral worth is attributed. Only a detail of Kant's presentation of the case of the dutiful philanthropist tells on the other side. For what he actually said was that this man felt no sympathy and took no pleasure in the good of others because "his mind was clouded by some sorrow of his own," and this is the kind of circumstances that increases the virtue that is needed if a man is to act well.

III

It was suggested above that an action with "positive moral worth," or as we might say a positively good action, was to be seen as one which was in accordance with virtue, by which I mean contrary to no virtue, and moreover one for which a virtue was required. Nothing has so far been said about another case, excluded by the formula, in which it might seem that an act displaying one virtue was nevertheless contrary to another. In giving this last description I am thinking not of two virtues with competing claims, as if what were required by justice could nevertheless be demanded by charity, or something of that kind, but rather of the possibility that a virtue such as courage or temperance or industry which overcomes a special temptation, might be displayed in an act of folly or villainy. Is this something that we must allow for, or is it only good or innocent actions which can be acts of these virtues? Aquinas, in his definition of virtue, said that virtues can produce only good actions, and that they are dispositions "of which no one can make bad use,"[9] except when they are treated as objects, as in being the subject of hatred or pride. The common opinion nowadays is, however, quite different. With the notable exception of Peter Geach hardly anyone sees any difficulty in the thought that virtues may sometimes be displayed in bad actions. Von Wright, for instance, speaks of the courage of the villain as if this were a quite un-problematic idea, and most people take it for granted that the virtues of courage and temperance may aid a bad man in his evil work. It is also sup-posed that charity may lead a man to act badly, as when someone does what he has no right to do, but does it for the sake of a friend.

There are, however, reasons for thinking that the matter is not as simple as this. If a man who is willing to do an act of injustice to help a friend, or for the common good, is supposed to act out of charity, and he so acts where a just man will not, it should be said that the unjust man has more charity than the just man. But do we not think that someone not ready to act un-justly may yet be perfect in charity, the virtue having done its whole work in prompting a man to do the acts that are permissible? And is there not more difficulty than might appear in the idea of an act of injustice which is never-theless an act of courage? Suppose for instance that a sordid murder were in question, say a murder done for gain or to get an inconvenient person out of the way, but that this murder had to be done in alarming circumstances or in the face of real danger; should we be happy to say that such an action was an act of courage or a courageous act? Did the murderer, who certainly acted boldly, or with intrepidity, if he did the murder, also act courageously? Some people insist that they are ready to say this, but I have noticed that they like to move over to a murder for the sake of conscience, or to some other act done in the course of a villainous enterprise but whose immediate end is in-nocent or positively good. On their hypothesis, which is that bad acts can easily be seen as courageous acts or acts of courage, my original example should be just as good.

What are we to say about this difficult matter? There is no doubt that the murderer who murdered for gain was *not a coward:* he did not have a sec-ond moral defect which another villain might have had. There is no difficulty about this because it is clear that one defect may neutralise another. As Aquinas remarked, it is better for a blind horse if it is slow.[10] It does not fol-low, however, that an act of villainy can be courageous; we are inclined to say that it "took courage," and yet it seems wrong to think of courage as equally connected with good actions and bad.

One way out of this difficulty might be to say that the man who is ready to pursue bad ends does indeed have courage, and shows courage in his ac-tion, but that in him courage is not a virtue. Later I shall consider some cases in which this might be the right thing to say, but in this instance it does not seem to be. For unless the murderer consistently pursues bad ends his cour-age will often result in good; it may enable him to do many innocent or pos-itively good things for himself or for his family and friends. On the strength of an individual bad action we can hardly say that in him courage is not a virtue. Nevertheless there is something to be said even about the individual action to distinguish it from one that would readily be called an act of courage or a courageous act. Perhaps the following analogy may help us to see what it is. We might think of words such as "courage" as naming characteristics of human beings in respect of a certain power, as words such as "poison" and "solvent" and "corrosive" so name the properties of physical things. The power to which virtue-words are so related is the power of producing good action, and good desires. But just as poisons, solvents and corrosives do not always operate characteristically, so it could be with virtues. If P (say arsenic) is a poison it does not follow that P acts as a poison wherever it is found. It is quite natural to say on occasion "P does not act as a poison here" though P is a poison and it is P that is acting here. Similarly courage is not operating as a virtue when the murderer turns his courage, which is a virtue, to bad ends. Not surprisingly the resistance that some of us registered was not to the expression "the courage of the murderer" or to the assertion that what he did "took courage" but rather to the description of that action as an act of courage or a courageous act. It is not that the action *could* not be so described, but that the fact that courage does not here have its characteristic operation is a reason for finding the description strange.

In this example we were considering an action in which courage was not operating as a virtue, without suggesting that in that agent it generally failed to do so. But the latter is also a possibility. If someone is both wicked and foolhardy this may be the case with courage, and it is even easier to find examples of a general connexion with evil rather than good in the case of some other virtues. Suppose, for instance, that we think of someone who is over-industrious, or too ready to refuse pleasure, and this is characteristic of him rather than something we find on one particular occasion. In this case the virtue of industry, or the virtue of temperance, has a systematic connexion with defective action rather than good action; and it might be said in either case that the virtue did not operate as a virtue in this man. Just as we might say in a certain setting "P is not a poison here" though P is a poison and P is here, so we might say that industriousness, or temperance, is not a virtue in some. Similarly in a man habitually given to wishful thinking, who clings to false hopes, hope does not operate as a virtue and we may say that it is not a virtue in him.

The thought developed in the last paragraph, to the effect that not every man who has a virtue has something that is a virtue in him, may help to explain a certain discomfort that one may feel when discussing the virtues. It is not easy to put one's finger on what is wrong, but it has something to do with a disparity between the moral ideals that may seem to be implied in our talk about the virtues, and the moral judgements that we actually make. Someone reading the foregoing pages might, for instance, think that the author of this paper always admired most those people who had all the virtues, being wise and temperate as well as courageous, charitable, and just. And indeed it is sometimes so. There are some people who do possess all these virtues and who are loved and admired by all the world, as Pope John XXIII was loved and admired. Yet the fact is that many of us look up to some people whose chaotic lives contain rather little of wisdom or temperance, rather than to some others who possess these virtues. And while it may be that this is just romantic nonsense I suspect that it is not. For while wisdom always operates as a virtue, its close relation prudence does not, and it is prudence rather than wisdom that inspires many a careful life. Prudence is not a virtue in everyone, any more than industriousness is, for some it is rather an over-anxious concern for safety and propriety, and a determination to keep away from people or situations which are apt to bring trouble with them; and by such defensiveness much good is lost. It is the same with temperance. Intemperance can be an appalling thing, as it was with Henry VIII of whom Wolsey remarked that

> rather than he will either miss or want any part of his will or appetite, he will put the loss of one half of his realm in danger.

Nevertheless in some people temperance is not a virtue, but is rather connected with timidity or with a grudging attitude to the acceptance of good things. Of course what is best is to live boldly yet without imprudence or intemperance, but the fact is that rather few can manage that.

Author's postscript added July 2002:

When I wrote this essay, some twenty years ago, no one was talking about "virtue ethics," and it was not necessary for me to deny that I was committed to a view of ethics in which *all* moral judgements were seen as based on a consideration of virtues and vices. Nowadays, however, I must explicitly refuse the title of "virtue ethicist" understood in such a way. As my discussion of promise-keeping, stealing, and such things in my recent book *Natural Goodness*, should make clear, I do not believe that considerations about the motives, dispositions, emotions, and such of an agent who performs an action *alone* determine the moral status of that action. Virtues and vices are not all!

NOTES

1. H.W. von Wright, *The Varieties of Goodness* (London, 1963).
2. Peter Geach, *The Virtues* (Cambridge, 1977).
3. Aquinas, *Summa Theologica,* 1a2ae Q.56 a.3.
4. Aristotle, *Nicomachean Ethics,* especially bk. VII.
5. von Wright op. cit. Chapter VIII.
6. Aristotle op. cit. 1140 b 22–25. Aquinas op. cit. 1a2ae Q.57 a.4.
7. Aristotle op. cit. 1106 b 15 and 1129 a.4 have this implication; but Aquinas is more explicit in op. cit. 1a2ae Q.60 a.2.
8. Aquinas op. cit. 1a2ae Q.61 a.3.
9. Aquinas op. cit. 1a2ae Q.56 a.5.
10. Aquinas op. cit. 1a2ae Q.58 a.4.

SELF-ASSERTION

Friedrich Nietzsche

FROM *"THE BIRTH OF TRAGEDY"*

It is an eternal phenomenon: the insatiate will can always, by means of an illusion spread over things, detain its creatures in life and compel them to live on. One is chained by the Socratic love of knowledge and the delusion of being able thereby to heal the eternal wound of existence; another is ensnared by art's seductive veil of beauty fluttering before his eyes; still another by the metaphysical comfort that beneath the flux of phenomena eternal life flows on indestructibly: to say nothing of the more ordinary and almost more powerful illusions which the will has always at hand. These three planes of illusion are on the whole designed only for the more nobly formed natures, who in general feel profoundly the weight and burden of existence, and must be deluded by exquisite stimulants into forgetfulness of their sorrow. All that we call culture is made up of these stimulants; and, according to the proportion of the ingredients, we have either a dominantly *Socratic* or *artistic* or *tragic* culture: or, if historical exemplifications are wanted, there is either an Alexandrian or a Hellenic or a Buddhistic culture.

Our whole modern world is entangled in the net of Alexandrian culture. It proposes as its ideal the theoretical man equipped with the greatest forces of knowledge, and laboring in the service of science, whose archetype and progenitor is Socrates. All our educational methods have originally this ideal in view: every other form of existence must struggle on wearisome beside it, as something tolerated, but not intended. In an almost alarming manner, the cultured man was for a long time found only in the form of the scholar: even our poetical arts have been forced to evolve from learned imitations, and in the main effect, that of rhyme, we still recognize the origin of our poetic form from artistic experiments with a nonindigenous, thoroughly learned language. How unintelligible must *Faust,* the modern cultured man, who is in himself intelligible, have appeared to a true Greek—Faust, storming unsatisfied through all the faculties, devoted to magic and the devil from a desire for knowledge; Faust, whom we have but to place beside Socrates for the purpose of comparison, in order to see that modern man is beginning to divine

Friedrich Nietzsche. "Self-Assertion." Excerpted from *Birth of Tragedy and the Case of Wagner* by Friedrich Nietzsche, translated by Walter Kaufmann. Copyright © 1967 by Walter Kaufmann. Used by permission of Random House, Inc. Excerpts from *Beyond Good and Evil* and *The Genealogy of Morals* by Friedrich Nietzsche. Copyright © Allen & Unwin, England. Reprinted by permission.

the limits of this Socratic love of perception and yearns for a coast in the wide waste of the ocean of knowledge. When Goethe on one occasion said to Eckermann with reference to Napoleon: "Yes, my good friend, there is also a productiveness of deeds," he reminded us in a charmingly naive manner that the non-theorist is something incredible and astounding to modern man; so that we again have need of the wisdom of Goethe to discover that such a surprising form of existence is not only comprehensible, but even pardonable.

Now, we must not hide from ourselves what is concealed at the heart of this Socratic culture: Optimism, with its delusion of limitless power! Well, we must not be alarmed if the fruits of this optimism ripen—if society, leavened to the very lowest strata by this kind of culture, gradually begins to tremble with wanton agitations and desires, if the belief in the earthly happiness of all, if the belief in the threatening demand for such an Alexandrian earthly happiness, into the conjuring up of a Euripidian *deus ex machina*. Let us mark this well: the Alexandrian culture, to be able to exist permanently, requires a slave class, but, with its optimistic view of life, it denies the necessity of such a class, and consequently, when the effect of its beautiful seductive and tranquilizing utterance about the "dignity of man" and the "dignity of labor" is over, it gradually drifts toward a dreadful destruction. There is nothing more terrible than a barbaric slave class, who have learned to regard their existence as an injustice, and now prepare to avenge, not only themselves, but all future generations. In the face of such threatening storms, who dares to appeal with any confidence to our pale and exhausted religions, whose very foundations have degenerated into "learned" religions?— so that myth, the necessary prerequisite of every religion, is already paralyzed everywhere, and even in this domain the optimistic spirit—which we have just designated as the destroying germ of society—has attained the mastery.

While the evil slumbering in the heart of theoretical culture gradually begins to disquiet modern man, while he anxiously ransacks the stores of his experience for means to avert the danger, though he has no great faith in these means; while he, therefore, begins to divine the consequences of his position: great, universally gifted natures have contrived, with an incredible amount of thought, to make use of the paraphernalia of science itself, in order to point out the limits and the relativity of knowledge generally, and thus definitely to deny the claim of science to universal validity and universal aims: with which demonstration the illusory notion was for the first time recognized as such, which pretends, with the aid of causality, to be able to fathom the innermost essence of things. The extraordinary courage and wisdom of *Kant* and *Schopenhauer* have succeeded in gaining the most difficult victory, the victory over the optimism hidden in the essence of logic, which optimism in turn is the basis of our culture. While this optimism, resting on apparently unobjectionable *aerternae veritates,* had believed in the intelligibility and solvability of all the riddles of the universe, and had treated space, time, and causality as totally unconditioned laws of the most universal validity, Kant, on the other hand, showed that in reality these served only to elevate the mere phenomenon, the work of Maya, to the position of the sole and highest reality, putting it in place of the innermost and true essence of things, and thus making impossible any knowledge of this essence or, in Schopenhauer's words, lulling the dreamer still more soundly asleep. With this knowledge a culture is inaugurated which I venture to call a tragic culture; the most important characteristic of which is that wisdom takes the place of science as the highest end, wisdom, which uninfluenced by the seductive distractions of the sciences, turns with unmoved eye to a comprehensive view of the world, and seeks to conceive therein, with sympathetic feelings of love, the eternal suffering as its own. Let us imagine a rising generation with this bold vision, this heroic desire for the magnificent, let us imagine the valiant step of these dragonslayers, the proud daring with which they turn their backs on all the effeminate doctrines of optimism that they may "live resolutely," wholly, and fully: Would it not be necessary for the tragic man of this culture, with his self-discipline of seriousness and terror, to desire a new art, the art of metaphysical comfort—namely, tragedy—to claim it as Helen, and exclaim with Faust:

> Und sollt ich nicht, sehnsuechtigster Gewald,
> Ins Leben ziehn die einzigste Gestalt?
> [And must I not satisfy my longing,
> By bringing this incomparable beauty to life?]

But now that the Socratic culture can only hold the scepter of its infallibility with trembling hands; now that it has been shaken from two directions— once by the fear of its own conclusions which it at length begins to surmise, and again, because it no longer has its former naive confidence in the eternal validity of its foundations—it is a sad spectacle to see how the dance of its thought rushes longingly on ever-new forms, to embrace them, and then, shuddering, lets them go suddenly as Mephistopheles does the seductive Lamaiae. It is certainly the sign of the "breach" which all are wont to speak of as the fundamental tragedy of modern culture that the theoretical man, alarmed and dissatisfied at his own conclusions, no longer dares entrust himself to the terrible ice-stream of existence: he runs timidly up and down the bank. So thoroughly has he been spoiled by his optimistic views, that he no longer wants to have anything whole, with all of nature's cruelty attaching to it. Besides, he feels that a culture based on the principles of science must be destroyed when it begins to grow *illogical*, that is, to retreat before its own conclusions. Our art reveals this universal trouble: in vain does one depend imitatively on all great productive periods and natures; in vain does one accumulate the entire "World-Literature" around modern man for his comfort; in vain does one place one's self in the midst of the art-styles and artists of all ages, so that one may give names to them as Adam did to the beasts: one still continues eternally hungry, the "critic" without joy and energy, the Alexandrian man, who is at bottom a librarian and corrector of proofs, and who, pitiable wretch, goes blind from the dusty books and printers' errors.

FROM *"BEYOND GOOD AND EVIL"*

In a tour through the many finer and coarser moralities which have hitherto prevailed or still prevail on the earth, I found certain traits recurring regularly together, and connected with one another, until finally two primary types revealed themselves to me, and a radical distinction was brought to light. There is *master-morality* and *slave-morality.* I would at once add, however, that in all higher and mixed civilizations, there are also attempts at the reconciliation of the two moralities; but one finds still oftener the confusion and mutual misunderstanding of them, indeed, sometimes their close juxtaposition— even in the same man, within one soul. The distinctions of moral values have either originated in a ruling caste, pleasantly conscious of being different from the ruled—or among the ruled class, the slaves and dependents of all sorts. In the first case, when it is the rulers who determine the conception "good," it is the exalted, proud disposition which is regarded as the distinguishing feature, and that which determines the order of rank. The noble type of man separates from himself the beings in whom the opposite of this exalted, proud disposition displays itself: he despises them. Let it at once be noted that in this first kind of morality the antithesis "good" and "bad" means practically the same as "noble" and "despicable"; the antithesis "good" and *"evil"* is of a different origin. The cowardly, the timid, the insignificant, and those thinking merely of narrow utility are despised; moreover, also, the distrustful, with their constrained glances, the self-abasing, the doglike kind of men who let themselves be abused, the mendicant flatterers, and above all the liars:—it is a fundamental belief of all aristocrats that the common people are untruthful. "We truthful ones"—the nobility in ancient Greece called themselves. It is obvious that everywhere the designations of moral value were at first applied to *men,* and were only derivatively and at a later period applied to *actions;* it is a gross mistake, therefore, when historians of morals start questions like, "Why have sympathetic actions been praised?"

The noble type of man regards *himself* as a determiner of values: he does not require to be approved of; he passes the judgment: "What is injurious in itself"; he knows that it is he himself only who confers honor on things; he is a *creator of values.* He honors whatever he recognizes in himself: such morality is self-glorification. In the foreground there is the feeling of plenitude, of power which seeks to overflow, the happiness of high tension, the consciousness of a wealth which would fain give and bestow: the noble man also helps the unfortunate, but not—or scarcely—out of pity, but rather from an impulse generated by the super-abundance of power. The noble man honors in himself the powerful one, him also who has power over himself, who knows how to speak and how to keep silence, who takes pleasure in subjecting himself to severity and hardness and has reverence for all that is severe and hard. "Wotan placed a hard heart in my breast," says an old Scandinavian Saga: it is thus rightly expressed from the soul of a proud Viking. Such a type of man is even proud of *not* being made for sympathy; the hero of the Saga therefore adds warningly: "He who has not a hard heart when young, will never have one." The noble and brave who think thus are the furthest removed from the morality which sees precisely in sympathy, or in acting for the good of others, or in *désinteressement,* the characteristic of the moral; faith in oneself, pride in oneself, a radical enmity and irony towards "selflessness," belong as definitely to noble morality, as do a careless scorn and precaution in presence of sympathy and the "warm heart"—it is the powerful who *know* how to honor, it is their art, their domain for invention. The profound reverence for age and for tradition—all law rests on this double reverence, the belief and prejudice in favor of ancestors and unfavorable to newcomers, is typical in the morality of the powerful; and if, reversely, men of "modern ideas" believe almost instinctively in "progress" and the "future," and are more and more lacking in respect for old age, the ignoble origin of these "ideas" has complacently betrayed itself thereby. A morality of the ruling class, however, is more especially foreign and irritating to present-day taste in the sternness of its principle that one has duties only to one's equals; that one may act towards beings of a lower rank, towards all that is foreign, just as seems good to one, or "as the heart desires," and in any case "beyond good and evil": it is here that sympathy and similar sentiments can have a place. The ability and obligation to exercise prolonged gratitude and prolonged revenge—both only within the circle of equals, artfulness in retaliation, *raffinement* of the idea in friendship, a certain necessity to have enemies (as outlets for the emotions of envy, quarrelsomeness, arrogance— in fact in order to be a good *friend*): all these are typical characteristics of the noble morality, which, as has been pointed out, is not the morality of "modern ideas," and is therefore at present difficult to realize, and also to unearth and disclose.

It is otherwise with the second type of morality, *slave-morality.* Supposing that the abused, the oppressed, the suffering, the unemancipated, the weary, and those uncertain of themselves, should moralize, what will be the common element in their moral estimates? Probably a pessimistic suspicion with regard to the entire situation of man will find expression, perhaps a condemnation of man, together with this situation. The slave has an unfavorable eye for the virtues of the powerful; he has a skepticism and distrust, a *refinement* of distrust of everything "good" that is there honored—he would fain persuade himself that the very happiness there is not genuine. On the other hand, *those* qualities which serve to alleviate the existence of sufferers are brought into prominence and flooded with light; it is here that sympathy, the kind, helping hand, the warm heart, patience, diligence, humility, and friendliness attain to honor; for here these are the most useful qualities, and almost the only means of supporting the burden of existence. Slave-morality is essentially the morality of utility. Here is the seat of the origin of the famous antithesis "good" and "evil": power and dangerousness are assumed to reside in the evil, a certain dreadfulness, subtlety, and strength, which do not admit of being despised. According to slave-morality, therefore, the "evil" man arouses fear; according to master-morality it is precisely the "good" man who arouses fear and seeks to arouse it, while the bad man is regarded as the despicable being. The contrast attains its maximum when, in accordance with the logical consequences of slave-morality, a shade of depreciation—it may be slight and well-intentioned—at last attaches itself to the "good" man of his morality; because, according to the servile mode of thought, the good man must in any case be the *safe* man: he is good-natured, easily deceived, perhaps a little stupid, *un bonhomme.* Everywhere that slave-morality gains the ascendency, language shows a tendency to approximate the significations of the words "good" and "stupid." A last fundamental difference: the desire for *freedom,* the instinct for happiness, and the refinements of the feeling of liberty belong as necessarily to slave-morals and morality, as artifice and enthusiasm in reverence and devotion are the regular symptoms of an aristocratic mode of thinking and estimating. Hence we can understand without further detail why love *as a passion*—it is our European specialty—must absolutely be of noble origin; as is well known, its invention is due to the Provençal poet-cavaliers, those brilliant ingenious men of the *"gaisaber,"* to whom Europe owes so much, and almost owes itself.

FROM *"THE GENEALOGY OF MORALS"*

The revolt of the slaves in morals begins in the very principle of *resentment* becoming creative and giving birth to values—a resentment experienced by creatures who, deprived as they are of the proper outlet of action, are forced to find their compensation in an imaginary revenge. While every aristocratic morality springs from a triumphant affirmation of its own demands, the slave morality says "no" from the very outset to what is "outside itself," and "not itself": and this "no" is its creative deed. This volte-face of the valuing standpoint—this *inevitable* gravitation to the objective instead of back to the subjective—is typical of "resentment": the slave-morality requires as the condition of its existence an external and objective world; to employ physiology terminology, it requires objective stimuli to be capable of action at all—its action is fundamentally a reaction. The contrary is the case when we come to the aristocrat's system of values: it acts and grows spontaneously, it merely seeks its antithesis in order to pronounce a more grateful and exultant "yes" to its own self; its negative conception, "low," "vulgar," "bad," is merely a pale lateborn foil in comparison with its positive and fundamental conception (saturated as it is with life and passion), of "we aristocrats, we good ones, we beautiful ones, we happy ones."

When the aristocratic morality goes astray and commits sacrilege on reality, this is limited to that particular sphere, with which it is *not* sufficiently acquainted—a sphere, in fact, from the real knowledge of which it disdainfully defends itself. It misjudges, in some cases, the sphere which it despises, the sphere of the common vulgar man and the low people: on the other hand, due weight should be given to the consideration that in any case the mood of contempt, of disdain, of superciliousness, even on the supposition that it *falsely* portrays the object of its contempt, will always be far removed from that degree of falsity which will always characterize the attacks—in effigy, of course—of the vindictive hatred and revengefulness of the weak in onslaughts on their enemies. In point of fact, there is in contempt too strong an admixture of nonchalance, of casualness, of boredom, of impatience, even of personal exultation, for it to be capable of distorting its victim into a real caricature or a real monstrosity. Attention again should be paid to the almost benevolent *nuances* which, for instance, the Greek nobility imparts into all the words by which it distinguishes the common people from itself; note how continuously a kind of pity, care, and consideration imparts its honeyed *flavor,* until at last almost all the words which are applied to the vulgar man survive finally, as expressions for "unhappy," "worthy of pity"—and how, conversely, "bad," "low," "unhappy" have never ceased to ring in the Greek ear with a tone in which "unhappy" is the predominant note: this is a heritage of the old noble aristocratic morality, which remains true to itself even in contempt. The "well-born" simply *felt* themselves the "happy"; they did not have to manufacture their happiness artificially through looking at their enemies, or in cases to talk and lie themselves into happiness (as is the custom with all resentful men); and similarly, complete men as they were, exuberant with strength, and consequently *necessarily* energetic, they were too wise to dissociate happiness from action—activity becomes in their minds necessarily counted as happiness—all in sharp contrast to the "happiness" of the weak and the oppressed, with their festering venom and malignity, among whom happiness appears essentially as a narcotic, a deadening, a quietude, a peace, a "Sabbath," an enervation of the mind and relaxation of the limbs, in short, a purely *passive* phenomenon. While the aristocratic man lived in confidence and openness with himself, the resentful man, on the other hand, is neither sincere nor naive, nor honest and candid with himself. His soul *squints;* his mind loves hidden crannies, tortuous paths and backdoors, everything secret appeals to him as *his* word, *his* safety, *his* balm; he is past master in silence, in not forgetting, in waiting, in provisional self-depreciation and self-abasement. A race of such *resentful* men will of necessity eventually prove more *prudent* than any aristocratic race, it will honor prudence on quite a distinct scale, as, in fact, a paramount condition of existence, while prudence among aristocratic men is apt to be tinged with a delicate flavor of luxury and refinement: so among them it plays nothing like so integral a part as that complete certainty of function of the governing *unconscious* instincts, or as indeed a certain lack of prudence, such as a vehement and valiant charge, whether against danger or the enemy, or as those ecstatic bursts of rage, love, reverence, gratitude, by which at all times noble souls have recognized each other. When the resentment of the aristocratic man manifests itself, it fulfills and exhausts itself in an immediate reaction, and consequently instills no *venom:* on the other hand, it never manifests itself at all in countless instances, when in the case of the feeble and weak it would be inevitable. An inability to take seriously for any length of time their enemies, their disasters, their *misdeeds*—that is the sign of the full strong natures who possess a superfluity of molding plastic force, that heals completely and produces forgetfulness: a good example of this in the modern world is Mirabeau, who had no memory for any insults and meannesses which were practised on him, and who was only incapable of forgiving because he forgot. Such a man indeed shakes off with a shrug many a worm which would have buried itself in another; it is only in characters like these that we see the possibility (supposing, of course, that there is such a possibility in the world) of the real "*love* of one's enemies." What respect for his enemies is found, forsooth, in an aristocratic man—and such a reverence is already a bridge to love! He insists on having his enemy to himself as his distinction. He tolerates no other enemy but a man in whose character there is nothing to despise and much to honor! On the other hand, imagine the "enemy" as the resentful man conceives him—and it is here exactly that we see his work, his creativeness; he has conceived "the evil enemy," the "evil one," and indeed that is the root idea from which he now evolves as a contrasting and corresponding figure, a "good one," himself—his very self!

The method of this man is quite contrary to that of the aristocratic man, who conceives the root idea "good" spontaneously and straight away, that is to say, out of himself, and from that material then creates for himself a concept of "bad"! This "bad" of aristocratic origin and that "evil" out of the cauldron of unsatisfied hatred—the former an imitation, an "extra," an additional nuance; the latter, on the other hand, the original, the beginning, the essential act in the conception of a slave-morality—these two words "bad" and "evil," how great a difference do they mark, in spite of the fact that they have an identical contrary in the idea "good." But the idea "good" is *not* the same: much rather let the question be asked, "Who is really evil according to the meaning of the morality of resentment?" In all sternness let it be answered thus: *just* the good man of the other morality, just the aristocrat, the powerful one, the one who rules, but who is distorted by the venomous eye of resentfulness, into a new color, a new signification, a new appearance. This particular point we would be the last to deny: the man who learned to know those "good" ones only as enemies, learned at the same time not to know them only as *"evil enemies,"* and the same men who *inter pares* were kept so rigorously in bounds through convention, respect, custom, and gratitude, though much more through mutual vigilance and jealousy *inter pares,* these men who in their relations with each other find so many new ways of manifesting consideration, self-control, delicacy, loyalty, pride and friendship, these men are in reference to what is outside their circle (where the foreign element, a *foreign* country, begins) not much better than beasts of prey, which have been let loose. They enjoy their freedom from all social control, they feel that in the wilderness they can give vent with impunity to that tension which is produced by enclosure and imprisonment in the peace of society, they *revert* to the innocence of the beast-of-prey conscience, like jubilant monsters, who perhaps come from a ghostly bout of murder, arson, rape, and torture, with bravado and a moral equanimity, as though merely some wild student's prank had been played, perfectly convinced that the poets have now an ample theme to sing and celebrate. It is impossible not to recognize at the core of all these aristocratic races a beast of prey; the magnificent *blond brute,* avidly rampant for spoil and victory; this hidden core needed an outlet from time to time, the beast must get loose again, must return into the wilderness—the Roman, Arabic, German, and Japanese nobility, the Homeric heroes, the Scandinavian Vikings, are all alike in this need. It is the aristocratic races who have left the idea "Barbarian" on all the tracks in which they have marched; nay, a consciousness of this very barbarianism, and even a pride in it, manifests itself even in their highest civilization (for example, when Pericles says to his Athenians in that celebrated funeral oration, "Our audacity has forced a way over every land and sea, rearing everywhere imperishable memorials of itself for *good* and for *evil*").

. . . Granted the truth of the theory now believed to be true, that the very *essence of all civilizations is* to *train* out of man the beast of prey, a tame and civilized animal, it follows indubitably that we must regard as the real tools of civilization all those instincts of reaction and resentment, by the help of which the aristocratic races, together with their ideas, were finally degraded and overpowered; though that has not yet come to be synonymous with saying that the bearers of those tools also *represented* the civilization. It is rather the contrary that is not only probable—nay, it is *palpable* today; these bearers of vindictive instincts that have to be bottled up, these descendants of all European and non-European slavery, especially of the pre-Aryan population—these people, I say, represent the *decline* of humanity! These "tools of civilization" are a disgrace to humanity, and constitute in reality more of an argument against civilization, more of a reason why civilization should be suspected. One may be perfectly justified in being always afraid of the blond beast that lies at the core of all aristocratic races, and in being on one's guard: but who would not a hundred times prefer to be afraid, when one at the same time admires, than to be immune from fear, at the cost of being perpetually obsessed with the loathsome spectacle of the distorted, the dwarfed, the stunted, the envenomed? And is that not our fate? What produces today our repulsion towards "man"? For we *suffer* from "man," there is no doubt about it. It is not fear; it is rather that we have nothing more to fear from men; it is that the worm "man" is in the foreground and pullulates; it is that the "tame-man," the wretched mediocre and unedifying creature, has learned to consider himself a goal and a pinnacle, an inner meaning, an historic principle, a "higher man"; yes, it is that he has a certain right so to consider himself, in so far as he feels that in contrast to that excess of deformity, disease, exhaustion, and effeteness whose order is beginning to pollute present-day Europe, he at any rate has achieved a relative success, he at any rate still says "yes" to life. . . .

But let us come back to it; the problem of *another* origin of the good—of the good, as the resentful man has thought it out—demands its solution. It is not surprising that the lambs should bear a grudge against the great birds of prey for taking the little lambs. And when the lambs say among themselves, "Those birds of prey are evil, and he who is far removed from being a bird of prey, who is rather its opposite, a lamb—is he not good?" then there is nothing to cavil at in the setting up of this ideal, though it may also be that the birds of prey will regard it a little sneeringly, and perchance say to themselves, "We bear no grudge against them, these good lambs, we even like them: nothing is tastier than a tender lamb." To require of strength that it should *not* express itself as strength, that it should not be a wish to over-power, a wish to overthrow, a wish to become master, a thirst for enemies and antagonisms and triumphs, is just as absurd as to require of weakness that it should express itself as strength. A quantum of force is just such a quantum of movement, will, action; rather it is nothing else than just those very phe-nomena of moving, willing, acting, and can only appear otherwise in the mis-leading errors of language (and the fundamental fallacies of reason which have become petrified therein), which understands, and understands wrongly, all working as conditioned by a worker, by a "subject." And just exactly as the people separate the lightning from its flash, and interpret the latter as a thing done, as the working of a subject which is called lightning, so also does the popular morality separate strength from the expression of strength, as though behind the strong man there existed some indifferent neutral *substratum,* which enjoyed a *caprice and option* as to whether or not it should express strength. But there is no such *substratum,* there is no "being" behind doing, working, becoming; "the doer" is a mere appanage to the action. The action is everything. In point of fact, the people duplicate the doing, when they make the lightning lighten, that is a "doing-doing"; they make the same phe-nomenon first a cause, and then, secondly, the effect of that cause. The sci-entists fail to improve matters when they say, "Forces move, forces cause," and so on. Our whole science is still, in spite of all its coldness, of all its free-dom from passion, a dupe of the tricks of language, and has never succeeded in getting rid of that superstitious changeling "the subject" (the atom, to give another instance, is such a changeling just as the Kantian "Thing-in-itself").

What wonder if the suppressed and stealthily simmering passions of re-venge and hatred exploit for their own advantage their belief, and indeed hold no belief with a more steadfast enthusiasm than this—"that the strong has the *option* of being weak, and the bird of prey of being a lamb." Thereby do they win for themselves the right of attributing to the birds of prey the *responsibility* for being birds of prey: when the oppressed, downtrodden, and overpowered say to themselves with the vindictive guile of weakness, "Let us be otherwise than the evil, namely, good! and good is everyone who does not oppress, who hurts no one, who does not attack, who does not pay back, who hands over revenge to God, who holds himself, as we do, in hid-ing; who goes out of the way of evil, and demands, in short, little from life; like ourselves the patient, the meek, the just"—yet all this, in its cold and un-prejudiced interpretation, means nothing more than "once for all, the weak are weak; it is good to do *nothing for which we are not strong enough*"; but this dismal state of affairs, this prudence of the lowest order, which even insects possess (which in a great danger are fain to sham death so as to avoid doing "too much") has, thanks to the counterfeiting and self-deception of weak-ness, come to masquerade in the pomp of an ascetic, mute, and expectant virtue, just as though the *very* weakness of the weak—that is, forsooth, its *being,* its working, its whole unique inevitable inseparable reality—were a strong result, something wished, chosen, a deed, an act of *merit.* This kind of man finds the belief in a neutral, free-choosing "subject" *necessary* from an instinct of self-preservation, of self-assertion, in which every lie is fain to sanctify itself. The subject (or to use popular language, the *soul*) has perhaps proved itself the best dogma in the world simply because it rendered possible to the horde of mortal, weak, and oppressed individuals of every kind, that most sublime specimen of self-deception, the interpretation of weakness as freedom, of being this, or being that, *as merit.*

FEMINIST ETHICS

Annette Baier

When I finished reading Carol Gilligan's *In a Different Voice,* I asked myself the obvious question for a philosopher reader: what differences should one expect in the moral philosophy done by women, supposing Gilligan's sample of women to be representative and supposing her analysis of their moral attitudes and moral development to be correct? Should one expect women to want to produce moral theories, and if so, what sort of moral theories? How will any moral theories they produce differ from those produced by men?

Obviously one does not have to make this an entirely a priori and hypothetical question. One can look and see what sort of contributions women have made to moral philosophy. Such a look confirms, I think, Gilligan's findings. What one finds *is* a bit different in tone and approach from the standard sort of moral philosophy as done by men following in the footsteps of the great moral philosophers (all men). Generalizations are extremely rash, but when I think of Phillipa Foot's work on the moral virtues, Elizabeth Anscombe's work on intention and on modern moral philosophy, Iris Murdoch's philosophical writings, Ruth Barcan Marcus's work on moral dilemmas, the work of the radical feminist moral philosophers who are not content with orthodox Marxist lines of thought, Jenny Teichman's book on illegitimacy, Susan Wolf's articles, Claudia Card's essay on mercy, Sabina Lovibond's writings, Gabriele Taylor's work on pride, love, and on integrity, Cora Diamond's and Mary Midgeley's work on our attitude toward animals, Sissela Bok's work on lying and on secrecy, Virginia Held's work, the work of Alison Jaggar, Marilyn Frye, and many others, I seem to hear a different voice from the standard moral philosophers' voice. I hear the voice Gilligan heard, made reflective and philosophical. What women want in moral philosophy is what they are providing. And what they are providing seems to me to confirm Gilligan's theses about women. One has to be careful here, of course, for not all important contributions to moral philosophy by women fall easily into the Gilligan stereotype or its philosophical extension. Nor has it been only women who have been proclaiming discontent with the standard approach in moral philosophy and trying new approaches. Michael Stocker, Alasdair MacIntyre, and Ian Hacking when he assesses the game-theoretic approach to morality, all should be given the status of honorary women, if we accept the hypothesis that there are some moral insights for whatever reason women seem to attain more easily or more reliably than men do. Still, exceptions confirm the rule, so I shall proceed undaunted by these important exceptions to my generalizations.

If Hacking is right, preoccupation with prisoner's and prisoners' dilemmas is a big boys' game, and a pretty silly one too. It is, I think, significant that women have not rushed into the field of game-theoretic moral philosophy, and that those who have dared enter that male locker room have said distinctive things there. Edna Ullmann Margalit's book *The Emergence of Norms* put prisoner's dilemma in its limited moral place. Supposing that at least part of the explanation for the relatively few women in this field is disinclination rather than disability, one might ask if this disinclination also extends to the construction of moral theories. For although we find out what sort of moral philosophy women want by looking to see what they have provided, if we do that for moral theory, the answer we get seems to be "none." None of the contributions to moral philosophy by women really counts as a moral theory, nor is seen as such by its author.

Is it that reflective women, when they become philosophers, want to do without moral theory, want no part in the construction of such theories? To conclude this at this early stage, when we have only a few generations of women moral philosophers to judge from, would be rash indeed. The term "theory" can be used in wider and narrower ways, and in its widest sense a moral theory is simply an internally consistent fairly comprehensive account of what morality is and when and why it merits our acceptance and support. In that wide sense, a moral theory is something it would take a skeptic, or one who believes that our intellectual vision is necessarily blurred or distorted when we let it try to take in too much, to be an antitheorist. Even if there were some truth in the latter claim, one might compatibly with it still hope to build up a coherent total account by a mosaic method, assembling a lot of smaller-scale works until one had built up a complete account—say, taking the virtues or purported virtues one by one until one had a more or less complete account. But would that sort of comprehensiveness in one's moral philosophy entitle one to call the finished work a moral theory? If it would, then many women moral philosophers today can be seen as engaged in moral theory construction. In the weakest sense of "theory," as a coherent near-comprehensive account, there are plenty of incomplete theories to be found in the works of women moral philosophers. And in *that* sense of theory, most of what are recognized as the current moral theories are also incomplete, because they do not yet purport to be really comprehensive. Wrongs to animals and wrongful destruction of our physical environment are put to one side by John Rawls, and in most "liberal" theories there are only hand waves concerning our proper attitude toward our children, toward the ill, toward our relatives, friends, and lovers.

Is comprehensiveness too much to ask of a moral theory? The paradigm examples of moral theories—those that are called by their authors "moral theories"—are distinguished not by the comprehensiveness of their internally coherent account but by the *sort* of coherence which is aimed at over a fairly broad area. Their method is not the mosaic method but the broad brushstroke method. Moral theories, as we know them, are, to change the art form, vaults rather than walls—they are not built by assembling painstakingly made brick after brick. In *this* sense of theory—a fairly tightly systematic account of a large area of morality, with a keystone supporting all the rest—women moral philosophers have not yet, to my knowledge, produced moral theories or claimed that they have.

Leaving to one side the question of what purpose (other than good clean intellectual fun) is served by such moral theories, and supposing for the sake of argument that women can, if they wish, systematize as well as the next man and, if need be, systematize in a mathematical fashion as well as the next mathematically minded moral philosopher, then what key concept or guiding motif might hold together the structure of a moral theory hypothetically produced by a reflective woman, Gilligan-style, who has taken up moral theorizing as a calling? What would be a suitable central question, principle, or concept to structure a moral theory which might accommodate those moral insights which women tend to have more readily than men, and to answer those moral questions which, it seems, worry women more than men? I hypothesized that the women's theory, expressive mainly of women's insights and concerns, would be an ethics of love, and this hypothesis seems to be Gilligan's too, since she has gone on from *In a Different Voice* to write about the limitations of Freud's understanding of love as women know it. But presumably women theorists will be like enough to men to want their moral theory to be acceptable to all, so acceptable both to reflective women and reflective men. Like any good theory, it will need not to ignore the partial truth of previous theories. It must therefore accommodate both the insights men have more easily than women and those women have more easily than men. It should swallow up its predecessor theories. Women moral theorists, if any, will have this very great advantage over the men whose theories theirs supplant, that they can stand on the shoulders of male moral theorists, as no man has yet been able to stand on the shoulders of any female moral theorist. There can be advantages as well as handicaps in being latecomers. So women theorists will need to connect their ethics of love with what has been the men theorists' preoccupation, namely, obligation.

The great and influential moral theorists have in the modern era taken *obligation* as the key and the problematic concept, and have asked what justifies treating a person as morally bound or obliged to do a particular thing. Since to be bound is to be unfree, by making obligation central one at the same time makes central the question of the justification of coercion, of forcing or trying to force someone to act in a particular way. The concept of obligation as justified limitation of freedom does just what one wants a good theoretical concept to do—to divide up the field (as one looks at different ways one's freedom may be limited, freedom in different spheres, different sorts and versions and levels of justification) and at the same time to hold the subfields together. There must in a theory be some generalization and some speciation or diversification, and a good rich key concept guides one both in recognizing the diversity and in recognizing the unity in it. The concept of obligation has served this function very well for the area of morality it covers, and so we have some fine theories about that area. But as Aristotelians and Christians, as well as women, know, there is a lot of morality *not* covered by that concept, a lot of very great importance even for the area where there are obligations.

This is fairly easy to see if we look at what lies behind the perceived obligation to keep promises. Unless there is some good moral reason why someone should assume the responsibility of rearing a child to be *capable* of taking promises seriously, once she understands what a promise is, the obligation to obey promises will not effectively tie her, and any force applied to punish her when she breaks promises or makes fraudulent ones will be of questionable justice. Is there an *obligation* on someone to make the child into a morally competent promisor? If so, on whom? Who has failed in his or her obligations when, say, war orphans who grew up without parental love or any other love arrive at legal adulthood very willing to be untrue to their word? Who failed in what obligation in all those less extreme cases of attempted but unsuccessful moral education? The parents who didn't produce promise-keeping offspring? Those who failed to educate the parents in how to educate their children (whoever it might be who could plausibly be thought to have the responsibility for training parents to fulfill their obligations)? The liberal version of our basic moral obligations tends to be fairly silent on who has what obligations to new members of the moral community, and it would throw most theories of the justification of obligations into some confusion if the obligation to rear one's children lovingly were added to the list of obligations. Such evidence as we have about the conditions in which children do successfully "learn" the morality of the community of which they are members suggests that we cannot substitute "conscientiously" for "lovingly" in this hypothetical extra needed obligation. But an obligation to love, in the strong sense needed, would be an embarrassment to the theorist, given most accepted versions of "ought implies can."

It is hard to make fair generalizations here, so I shall content myself with indicating how this charge I am making against the current men's moral theories, that their version of the justified list of obligations does not ensure the proper care of the young and so does nothing to ensure the stability of the morality in question over several generations, can be made against what I regard as the best of the men's recent theories, Rawls's theory of justice. One of the great strengths of Rawls's theory is the careful attention given to the question of how just institutions produce the conditions for their continued support, across generations, and in particular of how the sense of justice will arise in children, once there are minimally just institutions structuring the social world into which they are born. Rawls, more than most moral theorists, has attended to the question of the stability of his just society, given what we know about child development. But Rawls's sensitive account of the conditions for the development of that sense of justice needed for the maintenance of his version of a just society takes it for granted that there will be loving parents rearing the children in whom the sense of justice is to develop.

"The parents, we may suppose, love the child, and in time the child comes to love and trust the parents." Why may we suppose this? Not because compliance with Rawls's version of our obligations and duties will ensure it. Rawls's theory, like so many other theories of obligation, in the end must take out a loan not only on the natural duty of parents to care for children (which he will have no trouble including) but on the natural *virtue* of parental love (or even a loan on the maternal instinct?). The virtue of being a *loving* parent must supplement the natural duties and obligations of justice, if the just society is to last beyond the first generation. And as Nancy Chodorow's work indicates, the loving parents must also accept a certain division of child-care responsibility if their version of the obligations and virtues of men and women is, along with their version of the division of labor accompanying that allocation of virtues, to be passed on.

Reliance on a recognized obligation to turn oneself into a good parent or else to avoid becoming a parent would be a problematic solution. Good parents tend to be the children of good parents, so this obligation would collapse into the obligation to avoid parenthood unless one expected to be a good parent. That, given available methods of contraception, may itself convert into the obligation, should one expect not to be a good parent, to sexual abstinence, or sterilization, or resolute resort to abortion when contraception fails. The conditional obligation to abort, and in effect also the conditional obligation to sterilization, falls on the women. There may be conditions in which the rational moral choice is between obligatory sexual abstinence and obligatory sterilization, but obligatory abortion, such as women in China now face, seems to me a moral monster. I do not believe that liberal moral theorists will be able to persuade reflective women that a morality that in any conditions makes abortion obligatory, as distinct from permitted or advisable or, on occasion, best, is in their own as well as their male fellows' long-term self-interest. It would be tragic if such moral questions in the end came to the question of whose best interests to sacrifice, men's or women's. I do not believe that they *do* come to this, but should they, then justice would require that, given the long history of the subordination of women's to men's interests, men's interests be sacrificed. Justice, of course, never decides these issues unless power reinforces justice, so I am not predicting any victory for women, should it ever come to a fight over obligatory abortion or over who is to face obligatory sterilization.

No liberal moral theorist, as far as I know, is advocating obligatory abortion or obligatory sterilization when necessary to prevent the conception of children whose parents do not expect to love them. My point rather is that they escape this conclusion only by avoiding the issue of what is to ensure that new members of the moral community do get the loving care they need to become morally competent persons. Liberal moral theories assume that women either will provide loving maternal care, or will persuade their mates to provide loving paternal care, or when pregnant will decide for abortion, encouraged by their freedom-loving men. These theories, in other words, exploit the culturally encouraged maternal instinct and/or the culturally encouraged docility of women. The liberal system would receive a nasty spanner in its works should women use their freedom of choice as regards abortion to choose *not* to abort, and then leave their newborn children on their fathers' door-steps. That would test liberal morality's ability to provide for its own survival.

At this point it may be objected that every moral theory must make some assumptions about the natural psychology of those on whom obligations are imposed. Why shouldn't the liberal theory count on a continuing sufficient supply of good loving mothers, as it counts on continuing self-interest and, perhaps, on a continuing supply of pugnacious men who are able and willing to become good soldiers, without turning any of these into moral *obligations?* Why waste moral resources recognizing as obligatory or as virtuous what one can count on getting without moral pressure? If, in the moral economy, one can get enough good mothers and good warriors "for free," why not gladly exploit what nature and cultural history offer? I cannot answer this question fully here, but my argument does depend upon the assumption that a decent morality will *not* depend for its stability on forces to which it gives no moral recognition. Its account books should be open to scrutiny, and there should be no unpaid debts, no loans with no prospect of repayment. I also assume that once we are clear about these matters and about the interdependencies involved, our principles of justice will not allow us to recognize either a special obligation on every woman to initiate the killing of the fetus she has conceived, should she and her mate be, or think they will be, deficient in parental love, or a special obligation on every young man to kill those his elders have labeled enemies of his country. Both such "obligations" are prima facie suspect, and difficult to make consistent with any of the principles supposedly generating obligations in modern moral theories. I also assume that, on reflection, we will not want to recognize as *virtues* the character traits of women and men which lead them to supply such life and death services "for free." Neither maternal servitude, nor the resoluteness needed to kill off one's children to prevent their growing up unloved, nor the easy willingness to go out and kill when ordered to do so by authorities seems to me to be a character trait a decent morality will encourage by labeling a virtue. But the liberals' morality must somehow encourage such traits if its stability depends on enough people showing them. There is, then, understandable motive for liberals' avoidance of the question of whether such qualities are or are not morally approved of, and of whether or not there is any obligation to act as one with such character traits would act.

It is symptomatic of the bad faith of liberal morality as understood by many of those who defend it that issues such as whether to fight or not to fight, to have or not to have an abortion, or to be or not to be an unpaid maternal drudge are left to individual conscience. Since there is no coherent guidance liberal morality can give on these issues, which clearly are *not* matters of moral indifference, liberal morality tells each of us, "the choice is yours," hoping that enough will choose to be self-sacrificial life providers and self-sacrificial death dealers to suit the purposes of the rest.

Rawls's theory does explicitly face the question of the moral justification of refusal to bear arms, and how a just society justly provides for its own defense. The hardships imposed on conscripted soldiers are, he says, a necessary evil, and the most that just institutions can do is to "make sure that the risks of suffering from those misfortunes are more or less evenly shared by all members of society over the course of their life, and that there is no avoidable class bias in selecting those who are called for duty." What of sex/gender bias? Or is that assumed to be unavoidable? Rawls's principles seem to me to imply that women should be conscripted, if anyone is (and I think that is right), but since he avoids the questions of justice between men and women one does not know whether he intended this implication. His suggestion that one argument in favor of a conscripted army is that it is less likely to be an instrument of unjustified foreign adventures will become even stronger, I believe, if half the conscripts are women. Like most male moral theorists, Rawls does not discuss the morality of having children, refusing to have them, refusing to care for them, nor does he discuss how just institutions might equalize the responsibilities involved in ensuring that there be new members of society and that they become morally competent members of it, so one does not know whether he accepts a gender-based division of social service here, leaving it to the men to do the dangerous defensive destruction of life and cities, while the support of life, and any costs going or contrived to go with that, are left to the women. I hope that is not what he meant.

I do not wish, by having myself spoken of these two traditionally gender-based allocations of responsibility (producing and caring for new human life and the destruction of the lives of those officially labeled enemies) together, to leave the impression that I see any parallel between them except that they have both been treated as gender based and that both present embarrassments for liberal moral theory. Not all allocations of responsibility are allocations of burdens, and parenthood, unlike unchosen military life, need not be seen as essentially burden bearing. Good mothers and good soldiers make contributions of [very different sorts and sort of importance] to the ongoing life of a moral community, and they should not be seen, as they sometimes are, as fair mutual substitutes, as forms of social service. Good mothers will always be needed by a moral community, in the best conditions as well as the worst; the need for good military men, though foreseeably permanent, is a sign of some failure of our morality, a failure of our effectively acted upon moral laws to be valid theorems for the conservation of men in multitudes. Nor do the burdens of soldiering have any real analogue in the case of motherhood, which today *need* not impose real costs on the mother. If there are significant costs—loss of career opportunity, improperly recompensed drudgery in the home, or health risks—this is due to bad but largely remediable social arrangements, as the failure of parents to experience any especially parental satisfactions may be also due to bad but remediable socially produced attitudes toward parental responsibility. We do not, I think, want our military men to enjoy killing the enemy and destroying their cities, and any changes we made in social customs and institutions to make such pleasures more likely would be deplorable ones. Military life in wartime should always be seen as a sacrifice, while motherhood should never need to be seen as self-sacrificial service. If it is an honor and a privilege to bear arms for one's country, as we understandably tell our military conscripts and volunteers, part of the honor is being trusted with activities that are a necessary evil, being trusted not to enjoy their evil aspects, and being trusted to see the evil as well as the necessity. Only if we contrive to make the bringing into the world of new persons as nasty a business as killing already present persons will there be any just reason to exclude young women from conscripted armies or to exclude men from equal parental responsibility.

Granted that the men's theories of obligation need supplementation, to have much chance of integrity and coherence, and that the women's hypothetical theories will want to cover obligation as well as love, then what concept brings them together? My tentative answer is—the concept of appropriate trust, oddly neglected in moral theory. This concept also nicely mediates between reason and feeling, those tired old candidates for moral authority, since to trust is neither quite to believe something about the trusted nor necessarily to feel any emotion toward them—but to have a belief-informed and action-influencing attitude. To make it plausible that the neglected concept of appropriate trust is a good one for the enlightened moral theorist to make central, I need to show, or begin to show, how it could include obligation, indeed shed light on obligations and their justification, as well as include love, the other moral concerns of Gilligan's women, and many of the topics women moral philosophers have chosen to address, mosaic fashion. I would also need to show that it could connect all of these in a way which holds out promise both of synthesis and of comprehensive moral coverage. A moral theory which looked at the conditions for proper trust of all the various sorts we show, and at what sorts of reasons justify inviting such trust, giving it, and meeting it, would, I believe, not have to avoid turning its gaze on the conditions for the survival of the practices it endorses, so it could avoid that unpleasant choice many current liberal theories seem to have—between incoherence and bad faith. I do not pretend that we will easily agree once we raise the questions I think we should raise, but at least we may have a language adequate to the expression of both men's and women's moral viewpoints.

My trust in the concept of trust is based in part on my own attempts to restate and consider what is right and what wrong with men's theories, especially Hume's, which I consider the best of the lot. I have found myself reconstructing his account of the artifices of justice as an account of the progressive enlargement of a climate of trust, and have found that a helpful way to see it. It has some textual basis, but it is nevertheless a reconstruction, and one I have found, immodestly, an improvement. So it is because I have tried the concept and explored its dimensions a bit—the variety of goods we may trust others not to take from us, the sort of security or insurance we have when we do, the sorts of defenses or potential defenses we lay down when we trust, the various conditions for reasonable trust of various types—that I am hopeful about its power as a theoretical, and not just an exegetical, tool. I also found myself needing to use it when I made a brief rash attempt at that women's topic, caring (invited in by a male philosopher, I should say). I am reasonably sure that trust does generalize some central moral features of the recognition of binding obligations and moral virtues and of loving, as well as of other important relations between persons such as teacher-pupil, confider-confidante, worker to co-worker in the same cause, and professional to client. Indeed it is fairly obvious that love, the main moral phenomenon women want attended to, involves trust, so I anticipate little quarrel when I claim that, if we had a moral theory spelling out the conditions for appropriate trust and distrust, that would include a morality of love in all its variants—parental love, love of children for their parents, love of family members, love of friends, of lovers in the strict sense, of co-workers, of one's country and its figure-heads, of exemplary heroines and heroes, of goddesses and gods.

Love and loyalty demand maximal trust of one sort, and maximal trust-worthiness, and in investigating the conditions for maximal trust and maxi-mal risk we must think about the ethics of love. More controversial may be my claim that the ethics of obligation will also be covered. I see it as covered because to recognize a set of obligations is to trust some group of persons to instill them, to demand that they be met, possibly to levy sanctions if they are not, and this is to trust persons with very significant coercive power over others. Less coercive but still significant power is possessed by those shap-ing our conception of the virtues and expecting us to display them, approving when we do, disapproving and perhaps shunning us when we do not. Such coercive and manipulative power over others requires justification, and is justified only if we have reason to trust those who have it to use it properly and to use the discretion which is always given when trust is given in a way which serves the purpose of the whole system of moral control, and not merely self-serving or morally improper purposes. Since the question of the justifi-cation of coercion becomes, at least in part, the question of the wisdom of trusting the coercers to do their job properly, the morality of obligation, in as far as it reduces to the morality of coercion, is covered by the morality of proper trust. Other forms of trust may also be involved, but trusting enforc-ers with the use of force is the most problematic form of trust involved.

The coercers and manipulators are, to some extent, all of us, so to ask what our obligations are and what virtues we should exhibit is to ask what it is reasonable to trust us to demand, expect, and contrive to get from one another. It becomes, in part, a question of what powers we can in reason trust ourselves to exercise properly. But self-trust is a dubious or limit case of trust, so I prefer to postpone the examination of the concept of proper self-trust at least until proper trust of others is more clearly understood. Nor do we distort matters too much if we concentrate on those cases where moral sanctions and moral pressure and moral manipulation is not self-applied but applied to others, particularly by older persons to younger persons. Most moral pressuring that has any effect goes on in childhood and early youth. Moral sanctions may continue to be applied, formally and informally, to adults, but unless the criminal courts apply them it is easy enough for adults to ignore them, to brush them aside. It is not difficult to become a sensible knave, and to harden one's heart so that one is insensible to the moral con-demnation of one's victims and those who sympathize with them. Only if the pressures applied in the morally formative stage have given one a heart that rebels against the thought of such ruthless independence of what others think will one see any reason *not* to ignore moral condemnation, not to treat it as mere powerless words and breath. Condemning sensible knaves is as much a waste of breath as arguing with them—all we can sensibly do is to try to protect children against their criminal influence, and ourselves against their knavery. Adding to the criminal law will not be the way to do the latter, since such moves will merely challenge sensible knaves to find new knavish exceptions and loopholes, not protect us from sensible knavery. Sensible knaves are precisely those who exploit us without breaking the law. So the whole question of when moral pressure of various sorts, formative, reformative, and punitive, ought to be brought to bear by whom is subsumed under the question of whom to trust when and with what, and for what good reasons.

In concentrating on obligations, rather than virtues, modern moral theorists have chosen to look at the cases where more trust is placed in enforcers of obligations than is placed in ordinary moral agents, the bearers of obligations. In taking, as contractarians do, contractual obligations as the model of obligations, they concentrate on a case where the very minimal trust is put in the obligated person, and considerable punitive power entrusted to the one to whom the obligation is owed (I assume here that Hume is right in saying that when we promise or contract, we formally subject ourselves to the penalty, in case of failure, of never being trusted as a promisor again). This is an interesting case of the allocation of trust of various sorts, but it surely distorts our moral vision to suppose that *all* obligations, let alone all morally pressured expectations we impose on others, conform to that abnormally coercive model. It takes very special conditions for it to be safe to trust persons to inflict penalties on other persons, conditions in which either we can trust the penalizers to have the virtues necessary to penalize wisely and fairly, or else we can rely on effective threats to keep virtuous penalizers from abusing their power—that is to say, rely on others to coerce the first coercers into proper behavior. But that reliance too will either be trust or will have to rely on threats from coercers of the coercers of coercers, and so on. Morality on this model becomes a nasty, if intellectually intriguing, game of mutual mutually corrective threats. The central question of who should deprive whom of what freedom soon becomes the question of whose anger should be dreaded by whom (the theory of obligation), supplemented perhaps by an afterthought on whose favor should be courted by whom (the theory of the virtues).

Undoubtedly some important part of morality does depend in part on a system of threats and bribes, at least for its survival in difficult conditions when normal goodwill and normally virtuous dispositions may be insufficient to motivate the conduct required for the preservation and justice of the moral network of relationships. But equally undoubtedly life will be nasty, emotionally poor, and worse than brutish (even if longer), if that is all morality is, or even if that coercive structure of morality is regarded as the backbone, rather than as an available crutch, should the main support fail. For the main support has to come from those we entrust with the job of rearing and training persons so that they can be trusted in various ways, some trusted with extraordinary coercive powers, some with public decision-making powers, all trusted as parties to promise, most trusted by some who love them and by one or more willing to become co-parents with them, most trusted by dependent children, dependent elderly relatives, sick friends, and so on. A very complex network of a great variety of sorts of trust structures our moral relationships with our fellows, and if there is a *main* support to this network it is the trust we place in those who respond to the trust of new members of the moral community, namely, children, and prepare them for new forms of trust.

A theory which took as its central question "Who should trust whom with what, and why?" would not have to forego the intellectual fun and games previous theorists have had with the various paradoxes of morality—curbing freedom to increase freedom, curbing self-interest the better to satisfy self-interest, not aiming at happiness in order to become happier. For it is easy enough to get a paradox of trust to accompany or, if I am right, to generalize the paradoxes of freedom, self-interest, and hedonism. To trust is to make oneself or to let oneself be more vulnerable than one might have been to harm from others—to give them an opportunity to harm one, in the confidence that they will not take it, because they have no good reason to. Why would one take such a risk? For risk it always is, given the partial opaqueness to us of the reasoning and motivation of those we trust and with whom we cooperate. Our confidence may be, and quite often is, misplaced. That is what we risk when we trust. If the best reason to take such a risk is the expected gain in security which comes from a climate of trust, then in trusting we are always giving up security to get greater security, exposing our throats so that others become accustomed to not biting. A moral theory which made proper trust its central concern could have its own categorical imperative, could replace obedience to self-made laws and freely chosen restraint on freedom with security-increasing sacrifice of security, distrust in the promoters of a climate of distrust, and so on.

Such reflexive use of one's central concept, negative or affirmative, is an intellectually satisfying activity which is bound to have appeal to those system lovers who want to construct moral theories, and it may help them design their theory in an intellectually pleasing manner. But we should beware of becoming hypnotized by our slogans or of sacrificing truth to intellectual elegance. Any theory of proper trust should not *prejudge* the question of when distrust is proper. We might find more objects of proper distrust than just the contributors to a climate of reasonable distrust, just as freedom should be restricted not just to increase human freedom but to protect human life from poisoners and other killers. I suspect, however, that all the objects of reasonable distrust are more reasonably seen as falling into the category of ones who contribute to a decrease in the scope of proper trust than can all who are reasonably coerced be seen as themselves guilty of wrongful coercion. Still, even if all proper trust turns out to be for such persons and on such matters as will increase the scope or stability of a climate of reasonable trust, and all proper distrust for such persons and on such matters as increase the scope of reasonable distrust, overreliance on such nice reflexive formulae can distract us from asking all the questions about trust which need to be asked if an adequate moral theory is to be constructed around that concept.

These questions should include when to *respond* to trust with *un*trustworthiness, when and when not to invite trust, as well as when to give and refuse trust. We should not assume that promiscuous trustworthiness is any more a virtue than is undiscriminating distrust. It is appropriate trustworthiness, appropriate trustingness, appropriate encouragement to trust which will be virtues, as will be judicious untrustworthiness, selective refusal to trust, discriminating discouragement of trust.

Women are particularly well placed to appreciate these last virtues, since they have sometimes needed them to get into a position even to consider becoming moral theorizers. The long exploitation and domination of women by men depended on men's trust in women and women's trustworthiness to play their allotted role and so to perpetuate their own and their daughters' servitude. However keen women now are to end the lovelessness of modern moral philosophy, they are unlikely to lose sight of the cautious virtue of appropriate distrust or of the tough virtue of the principled betrayal of the exploiters' trust.

Gilligan's girls and women saw morality as a matter of preserving valued ties to others, of preserving the conditions for that care and mutual care without which human life becomes bleak, lonely, and after a while, as the mature men in her study found, not self-affirming, however successful in achieving the egoistic goals which had been set. The boys and men saw morality as a matter of finding workable traffic rules for self-assertors, so that they not needlessly frustrate one another and so that they could, should they so choose, cooperate in more positive ways to mutual advantage. Both for the women's sometimes unchosen and valued ties with others and for the men's mutual respect as sovereigns and subjects of the same minimal moral traffic rules (and for their more voluntary and more selective associations of profiteers), trust is important. Both men and women are concerned with cooperation, and the dimensions of trust-distrust structure the different cooperative relations each emphasize. The various considerations which arise when we try to defend an answer to any question about the appropriateness of a particular form of cooperation with its distinctive form of trust or distrust, that is, when we look into the terms of all sorts of cooperation, at the terms of trust in different cases of trust, at what are fair terms and what are trust-enhancing and trust-preserving terms, are suitably many and richly interconnected. A moral theory (or family of theories) that made trust its central problem could do better justice to men's and women's moral intuitions than do the going men's theories. Even if we don't easily agree on the answer to the question of who should trust whom with what, who should accept and who should meet various sorts of trust, and why, these questions might enable us better to reason morally together than we can when the central moral questions are reduced to those of whose favor one must court and whose anger one must dread. But such programmatic claims as I am making will be tested only when women standing on the shoulders of men, or men on the shoulders of women, or some theorizing Tiresias actually works out such a theory. I am no Tiresias, and have not foresuffered all the labor pains of such a theory. I aim here only to fertilize.

QUESTIONS FOR DISCUSSION
STANDARDS OF RIGHT AND WRONG

1. What danger do you see in using the theory of divine command as the criterion of morally right action? What revision does Robert Adams propose to avoid the danger?

2. Discuss the biblical stories of Abraham being told to sacrifice Isaac, and of Job complaining about God's injustice. How are they (or are they not) counterexamples to the traditional divine command theory of morality? Does Adams's revision make better moral sense of these stories? If so, how? If not, why?

3. Aristotle held that the person who gets pleasure from doing what is right is superior to the person who does the right thing, but does it reluctantly. Compare Kant's claim that only action contrary to one's natural inclination deserves moral credit. Which philosopher do you agree with? Explain why.

4. Discuss Kant's contention that doing the right thing because one is naturally so inclined has less moral worth than doing it out of a sense of duty. Do you agree? Why or why not?

5. Explain the difference, for Kant, between "hypothetical" and "categorical" imperatives. Which kind are moral laws, and why?

6. What does Mill mean by the "quality" of pleasure, and how does he think it can be reliably measured? Is his emphasis on quality consistent with his greatest happiness principle of morally right action? Take a position and defend it.

7. On what grounds do some critics claim that utilitarianism is too difficult an ethics to live up to, and why do others claim it is too permissive? How does Mill reply to each of these criticisms?

8. Do you agree with Harman that it seems odd to say that it was wrong of Hitler to exterminate millions, but it does not seem odd to say this of Stalin? What difference does Harman point out?

9. Is Harman right to claim that cannibalism is not morally wrong in certain primitive societies but is morally wrong in advanced societies? Explain his reason for this claim, and defend your reaction to it.

10. Define "contractualism" as Scanlon uses the term. Explain his distinction between "rational" and "reasonable."

11. What is the relation, for Scanlon, between a moral principle and reasons for action? If a principle neither permits a certain reason for an action nor prohibits it, can it have any moral significance? Explain.

12. According to Philippa Foot, the acquisition of moral virtues such as courage and justice is beneficial to the individual agent as well as to society, although there are some situations in which their interests come into

conflict—but she considers such situations to be rare. Do you agree? Does Kant agree? Defend your response.

13. Nietzsche makes a distinction between "master morality" and "slave morality." He also praises the "transcendence of morality" by superior people. Explain his distinction between the two moralities, and identify the morality he proposes to transcend.

14. Discuss Annette Baier's contention that the emphasis of past philosophers on moral obligation rather than on trust and love was owing to the fact that most philosophers were men. Can one morally command oneself to love or to trust, rather than to do certain things or refrain from them? Or has ethics nothing to do with commanding oneself? Defend your position on this issue.

SELECTED READINGS

Divine Command

ADAMS, R. M. "A Modified Divine Command Theory of Ethical Wrongness." In *Religion and Morality,* edited by G. Outka and J. Reeder. Garden City, NY: Anchor Books, 1987.

AQUINAS, ST. THOMAS. *Selections on Politics and Ethics.* Trans. P. Sigmund. New York: W. W. Norton, 1998.

DONAGAN, A. *Reflections on Morality and Religion.* New York: Oxford University Press, 1998.

———. *The Theory of Morality.* Chicago: University of Chicago Press, 1978.

GIL, ROBIN, ed. *The Cambridge Companion to Christian Ethics.* New York: Cambridge University Press, 2001.

GUSTAFSON, J. *Ethics from a Theocratic Perspective.* Chicago: University of Chicago Press, 1981.

PHILLIPS, D. Z. *Religion and Morality.* New York: St. Martin's Press, 1995.

RAMSEY, P. *Basic Christian Ethics.* New York: Scribners, 1950.

Rationality

GEWIRTH, A. *Reason and Morality.* Chicago: University of Chicago Press, 1978.

GUYER, P., ed. *The Cambridge Companion to Kant.* New York: Cambridge University Press, 1992.

KANT, I. *Grounding for the Metaphysics of Morals.* Trans. J. Ellington. Indianapolis: Hackett, 1981.

KORNER, S. *Kant.* Baltimore: Penguin, 1955.

PRICHARD, H. *Moral Obligation.* Oxford: Clarendon Press, 1949.

SINGER, M. *Generalization in Ethics.* New York: Knopf, 1961.

WOOD, ALAN. *Kant's Ethical Thought.* New York: Cambridge University Press, 1999.

Social Benefit (Utilitarianism)

ASHFORD, ELIZABETH. "Utilitarianism, Integrity and Partiality." *Journal of Philosophy,* August 1997.

BENTHAM, J. *Introduction to the Principles of Morals and Legislation.* New York: Hafner, 1948.

DEWEY, JOHN. *Human Nature and Conduct.* New York: Modern Library, 1957.

HAMPSHIRE, S. *Two Theories of Morality.* New York: Oxford University Press, 1977.

KAGAN, S. *The Limits of Morality.* New York: Oxford University Press, 1989.

LYONS, D. *Forms and Limits of Utilitarianism.* Oxford: Clarendon, 1965.

PARFIT, DEREK. *Reasons and Persons.* New York: Oxford University Press, 1984.

SCHEFFLER, S. A. *The Rejection of Consequentialism.* New York: Oxford University Press, 1989.

SIDGWICK, H. *The Methods of Ethics.* London: Macmillan, 1922.

SMART, J., and B. WILLIAMS. *Utilitarianism For and Against.* New York: Cambridge University Press, 1973.

Convention (Cultural Relativism)

BENEDICT, RUTH. *Patterns of Culture.* Boston: Houghton Mifflin, 1961.

HARMAN, G. *Explaining Value.* Oxford: Clarendon Press, 2000.

———. *The Nature of Morality.* New York: Oxford University Press, 1978.

MACKIE, J. *Ethics: Inventing Right and Wrong.* Baltimore: Penguin, 1977.

SUMNER, G. *Folkways.* Boston: Ginn, 1934.

WESTERMACK, E. *Ethical Relativity.* New York: Greenwood, 1970.

Contractualism (Ideal Social Contract Theory)

RAWLS, J. *A Theory of Justice.* Cambridge, MA: Harvard University Press, 1971. Rev. ed., 1999.

ROUSSEAU, J. J. *On "The Social Contract with Geneva Manuscript and Political Economy."* Ed. R. D. Masters, trans. J. R. Masters. New York: St. Martin's Press, 1978.

SCANLON, T. *What We Owe to Each Other.* Cambridge, MA: Harvard University Press, 1998.

Virtue Ethics

FOOT, P. *Virtues and Vices.* Berkeley: University of California Press, 1978.

GEACH, P. *The Virtues.* New York: Cambridge University Press, 1977.

MACINTYRE, A. *After Virtue.* Ann Arbor: University of Notre Dame, 1984.

NUSSBAUM, M. "Virtue Ethics: A Misleading Category?" *Ethics,* 1999.

SLOTE, M. *From Morality to Virtue.* New York: Oxford University Press, 1992.

WALLACE, J. D. *Virtues and Vices.* Ithaca, NY: Cornell University Press, 1978.

Self-Assertion

CARUS, P. *Nietzsche.* New York: Haskell House, 1972.

DANTO, A. *Nietzsche as a Philosopher.* New York: Macmillan, 1965.

KAUFMAN, W. *Nietzsche as a Moral Philosopher.* New York: Random House, 1968.

NIELSEN, K. "Nietzsche as a Moral Philosopher." *Man and World,* 1973.

RICHARDSON, J. *Nietzche's System.* New York: Oxford University Press, 1996.

Feminist Ethics

BAIER, A. *Moral Prejudices.* Cambridge, MA: Harvard University Press, 1995.

BELL., L. *Rethinking Ethics.* Lanham, MD: Rowland and Littlefield, 1993.

CARD, C. *Feminist Ethics.* Lawrence: University of Kansas Press, 1981.

GILLIGAN, CAROL. *In a Different Voice.* Cambridge, MA: Harvard University Press, 1982.

JAGGAR, A. *Feminist Politics and Human Nature.* Totowa, NJ: Rowman and Allanheld, 1983.

2

WHEN ARE WE RESPONSIBLE?

Assuming that we now understand how to judge actions and people to be moral or immoral, what can we do with our acquired wisdom? Suppose that whatever people do is necessitated by causes beyond their control. Would deliberation about right and wrong be pointless if we were powerless to change our conduct in response to moral judgment, so that it makes no difference what we believe to be right or wrong? In short, without free will, isn't ethical evaluation useless?

Using ethical standards to judge the conduct and character of others would seem to require that our judgments can affect those we judge. We say, for example, that Smith behaved badly or that Jones has a vicious character, in the hope of reforming Smith and Jones by blaming and perhaps punishing them. But to do so is to hold them responsible for their conduct. The usefulness of moral theory thus depends on knowledge of the conditions under which people can be held responsible for what they do. To say that a person has done the right thing is to praise that person. To say that someone is vicious is to punish that person verbally and sometimes to suggest more tangible modes of punishment. But the question arises: When, if ever, are we justified in meting out praise and blame, reward and punishment?

Knowledge of the conditions for assigning moral responsibility is needed in deciding whether, and how severely, to punish wrongdoers. Everyday rules of procedure that are products of centuries of human experience often serve well enough, but at times they become rather slippery. For example, were the Germans all responsible for the atrocities of the Third Reich? Or were some more responsible than others, and if so, to what degree? Is a person who is clinically insane responsible for a brutal murder? To what extent does neurosis excuse bad conduct? Is a juvenile delinquent from a broken home in a slum less responsible for theft or drug dealing than a pampered teenager who rebels against wealthy and overindulgent parents? In such matters the line between free and compulsive, excusable and inexcusable seems to melt away, and we turn to philosophy for clearer definitions of "free will," "voluntary," and "responsible."

Classical thought addressed the problem of moral responsibility by considering whether or not the will is free, assuming that only freely willed action is responsible action. Plato ascribed all good powers to the intellect and all bad ones to the desires, concluding that wrong action is always owing to lack of knowledge, so that "no one does evil voluntarily." Aristotle rejected that account, noting that blame and punishment are justified only if we can distinguish voluntary from involuntary infractions of law or moral principle; he suggested that a freely willed or voluntary action is one whose cause is internal to the agent, which can be taken to mean that the agent was not coerced or suffering from ignorance or compulsion.

The Greek Stoics held the fatalistic view that no one can help acting as he or she does, and yet they made self-control the cornerstone of their system of ethics, unaware of the paradox until it was pointed out by Cicero. Epicurus and his followers rejected Stoic fatalism and accounted for free will as owing to the unpredictable swerves of the atoms that they thought make up the soul.

Christian theologians, agreeing with Plato that the soul is intangible and indestructible, thought of the will as a part of the soul substance that causes the body to act. They argued over whether this personalized will was free to direct the body independently of other causes, including the intellect, until St. Augustine formulated a compromise doctrine that became authoritative in Christianity but was sufficiently vague to be interpreted in diverse ways by later theologians. Augustine transformed the Stoic notion of a blind, naturalistic fatalism into a doctrine of divine predestination, according to which God has so arranged the world that He knows in advance how everyone will freely choose to act.

The rise of modern science in the seventeenth century inspired a new and more secular form of causal determinism, proclaimed by Thomas Hobbes and Benedict Spinoza and accepted by most scientists and science-oriented philosophers ever since. In this view, every event could, in principle (if we had sufficient knowledge of initial conditions and the laws of nature), be explained as a necessary outcome of antecedent causes. Some of these scientists and philosophers concluded that free will is an illusion and that blame and punishment are not morally deserved but only justified by their deterrent value. In any given situation, if we knew all the causal factors, we would know that the agent had no real alternative and thus was not really morally responsible for what he or she did. This view, which holds that free will is illusory because it is incompatible with causal determinism, was labeled "hard determinism" by the American philosopher William James. He distinguished it from what he called "soft determinism," which holds that determinism is compatible with free will when the latter concept is properly understood. James accepted neither form of determinism because he believed that free will is a fact of human life whereas determinism is an abstract hypothesis inconsistent with our experience of causally inexplicable choices. Galen Strawson is one of the few contemporary philosophers who defends the hard determinist view, although it is also held by most scientists.

Strawson's argument is simple and powerfully persuasive. He suggests that no one would deny that we do not choose or decide to be "the way we are," that is, having a certain character and personality that develops as we grow. Nor can it be denied that we act as we do because of "the way we are." Because we are not responsible for the way we are, which is the cause of what we do, it follows that we are not responsible for what we do; thus, free will is an illusion.

But is it true that what we are is the determining cause of what we do, in the sense that we cannot choose to act "out of character"? Peter van Inwagen denies this assumption in favor of an indeterminist view somewhat like that of William James. However, unlike James, he rejects the conclusion that our free actions are random or, as James put it, matters of chance.

Van Inwagen develops his form of indeterminism by means of a technical analysis in terms of possible worlds, in an attempt to show that the agent's reasons for action, even if they are the causes of her action, need not determine (i.e., necessitate) her action. Determinists argue that if such causes do not determine the action, then the action has occurred randomly and cannot really be ascribed to the will of the agent, any more than the way the dice fall can be ascribed to the will of the person who throws them. Van Inwagen rebuts this criticism by arguing that a random event is not an action and that there is no reason to believe that a free action is random just because it is not causally necessitated.

Libertarians like Roderick Chisholm agree with hard determinists like Galen Strawson that determinism is incompatible with free will and therefore with moral responsibility; but, contending that the latter are facts of life that cannot be denied, they conclude that where human action is concerned, determinism is false. We know that we are free, they reason, although we can only conjecture that our actions are causally determined. Because these two beliefs are in conflict, it is the conjecture that must go, not the known fact. However, in proposing a special kind of causation that Chisholm calls "immanent," whereby the agent in some inscrutable manner causes his own action, the libertarian seems merely to push the difficulty back one step—to a point where one must ask whether the agent's causing his own action is in turn determined by some antecedent cause, at which point the libertarian has to fall back on either some form of determinism or some form of indeterminism.

Soft determinists like Simon Blackburn differ from hard determinists like Strawson, indeterminists like James and van Inwagen, and libertarians like Chisholm in denying that free will, when properly understood, is incompatible with causal determinism. Agreeing with Aristotle, who distinguished voluntary from involuntary actions in terms of whether their causes are internal (desires) or external (constraints), soft determinists propose that freely willed action be defined in terms of the kind of causes that produce it, rather than as having no cause at all. Their problem is to explain how the internal causes of free action genuinely determine their effects and yet, unlike ordinary physical causes, permit freely willed decision.

Blackburn's refinement of the soft determinist view that causal determinism and freely willed action are compatible is very persuasive. He offers what he calls a "revised revised compatibilist definition" of freely willed action.

According to Blackburn, an action is freely willed if it is determined by causes that would not have determined the action had the agent taken note (as she could have and should have) of the reasons for choosing differently. This account conforms to and explains our commonsense criteria of responsibility while avoiding obscure notions of "immanent" or "agent" causation exercised by a "self" distinct from one's formed character (libertarianism), as well as that of an undetermined action (indeterminism). It makes no advance commitments as to just which of our actions are free and responsible, leaving these matters to psychologists to decide after thorough empirical investigation.

But Blackburn's persuasive formulation of soft determinism is not invulnerable to criticism. After all, it broadens the concept of cause to what may be an unwarranted extent, to include reasons for acting that are not, like physical causes, compelling—in which case it would be not wrong, but perhaps not really different from an equally sophisticated form of indeterminism such as that of van Inwagen.

Susan Wolf offers a controversially broad interpretation of the term "determine" in holding that actions are determined by motives, and motives by heredity and environment. She calls this kind of determination "psychological determination." The concept enables Wolf to offer a compromise between the compatibilism of soft determinism and the incompatibilism of hard determinism. She proposes an "asymmetrical" account of freely willed action, whereby it is compatible with psychological determinism when the action is determined by good reasons, but not when it is determined by bad reasons. It follows that "an agent can be morally praiseworthy even though he is determined . . . but . . . an agent cannot be morally blameworthy if he is determined."

Wolf arrives at the paradoxical conclusion that responsibility is asymmetrical with respect to free will as against causal determinism. We are free to perform good actions despite being caused to do so, and so we deserve moral praise; but we are not free when we are caused to do bad things, and therefore moral blame is inappropriate. Wolf does not address the question of when, if ever, a person is causally determined by good or bad reasons or motives, and when only influenced by them but capable of refraining from acting on them. This crucial question remains in need of a final answer.

Hard determinism

Galen Strawson

I. WHAT DO WE WANT?

The question may still be asked—are we or are we not free agents? Are we ever truly responsible for our actions in what I call the ordinary strong sense of "truly responsible"? Are we ever truly responsible for our actions in such a way as to be—among other things—capable of being truly or ultimately deserving of praise and blame for them? Or is the right conclusion simply that we are not really truly responsible agents at all, although we cannot help believing we are?

Roughly, this is my conclusion, and I will summarize the essential reasons for it in the next section. First, though, consider an objection that comes in the form of a couple of questions: Why this concentration on the notion of true responsibility? Certainly we want to be free, but do we really want to be *truly responsible* for our actions? We are very often entirely free in the "basic," Humean, wholly compatibilist sense: that is, we are very often entirely free in the sense of being able to do what we want or choose or decide to do. Isn't this enough? Isn't this all that really matters, in the way of freedom? What more could anyone possibly reasonably want?

The principal answer to this objection is simple: from the theoretical point of view, the centrally important question about freedom is not what we want (or might on reflection want), but rather what we believe. And it is indubitable that we do ordinarily behave as if we believed that we (and others) have free will in the ordinary, strong sense—true responsibility. This belief plays a central role in our lives. That is why it is of fundamental importance for philosophy to examine this belief, its nature, origins, and consequences, and to try to determine its truth or falsity.

Suppose, though, that it is conceded that the belief is false: true responsibility is impossible. It may then again be asked: Why should anyone want it anyway? The question deserves consideration. For it can sometimes seem very plausible to say that "basic" freedom to do what one wants or chooses to do is all that one could ever reasonably want in the way of freedom, as one pursues one's various concerns from day to day. Surely, to be able to do (or attempt) what one wants or chooses to do (or attempt) is to have complete freedom of action? So why should anyone want true responsibility? What does it really add? These are powerful questions for the compatibilist to ask. Once again it is reasonable to make the question-pre-empting response that it is not so much what we want but what we believe that matters most. But it is worth facing the questions directly.

One can first of all concede that some (perhaps highly pragmatic and single-minded) individual human agents may have no reason at all to want any sort of freedom other than the "basic" freedom described above. It depends entirely on what other things they want. In particular, it seems clear that someone who pursues goals, ideals, projects, opportunities, and satisfactions that have little to do with the entertaining of affective relations with other people may have no reason at all to want any sort of freedom other than "basic" compatibilist freedom. This is undoubtedly an important point.

Things look different when one considers agents who give weight to the entertaining of certain sorts of moral and affective relations with other people. But these relations are not all of equal importance: the fact that we ordinarily behave as if we firmly believed people to be proper objects of blame, resentment, grudges, contempt, scorn, moral indignation, and so on, does not seem particularly important. For although we ordinarily behave as if we firmly believed that people can be proper objects of certain at least of these (predominantly negative) reactions, it is not obvious that this is something we particularly want to be the case.

Clearly, our more positive attitudes to other people are the best cases to consider. For when we consider these attitudes, the idea that people can be true originators of their actions in such a way as to be truly responsible for them emerges as integral to some of our strongest beliefs about what is valuable (and therefore worth wanting) in human life and interaction. It seems that we very much want people to be proper objects of gratitude, for example. And they cannot be proper objects of gratitude unless they can be truly responsible for what they do. Our ordinary conception of love also seems to require ascription of true responsibility to the one who is loved. True, one can love a person sexually, one can love their looks, their wit, their forgetfulness, their childishness; and none of these things presupposes any ascription of true responsibility to them. Infatuation, too, can happily treat the person who is its object as an entirely determined phenomenon, just as it can happily accept the idea that the infatuation is itself an entirely determined phenomenon. Nevertheless there is a leading notion of what it is to love someone in the fullest sense—to love someone as a person, so one might say, rather than as some collocation of desirable features—which makes ascription of true responsibility to the one who is loved an ineliminable part of love.

But why? What is it to consider and love a person "as a person"? A familiar and off-putting sort of vagueness appears to be creeping in. Perhaps one could make the point this way. To take x seriously as a person, in the way that one must if one loves x not in a merely infatuated way, but in a way that involves the kind of emotional reciprocity that is commonly seen as that which is most valuable in love, is—at least—to conceive of x as a being that is independent and self-determining in such a way that one *could* properly feel gratitude to him or her for some action or gesture. Love implies a view of the one who is loved as a self-determining agent to whom gratitude can be an appropriate response. But the possible appropriateness of gratitude implies true responsibility. Hence love implies ascription of true responsibility. So to want love to be possible is to want people to be truly responsible.

Again this may not be thought very satisfactory. Perhaps the best thing to do, in order to see the point, is to imagine someone one loves, or to imagine loving someone, and then, in thought, to strip away any idea of that person as a truly responsible agent—to think of him or her as just a determined phenomenon with a given character, an entirely determinately given range of responses. Most people who do this will find that something extremely valuable, real or imagined, seems to drain away from the relation—except perhaps lovers like Pygmalion, or those who are merely infatuated (or very self-centred or hard-headed—but then it may be said that they don't really know what love is). No doubt there is something vertiginously agreeable about the ineluctability of pure infatuation. But we find it hard to renounce the possibility of gratitude.

Some may find that generalizing this thought-experiment leaves them feeling that they are all alone—alone in the world. If it does, this is because they have in pursuing the thought-experiment been unable to stop thinking of themselves as truly responsible; and so they have found that the thought-experiment leaves them surrounded by entirely determined entities with whom any interaction is ultimately only a mockery of "true" communication—being essentially like interaction with a programmed character in a computer game (there being only a difference of degree, not of kind). People who have this reaction will again have a reason for wanting true responsibility to exist (in other people).

No doubt the thing that seems to drain away in the thought-experiment is, in some ineliminable sense or other, an illusion—since true (ultimate) responsibility is demonstrably impossible. But that does not alter the fact that the thought-experiment may help to show that we *want* true responsibility, and want it because we want love (or want love to be possible, at least). Love is only the most dramatic case of what we want to be possible in human relations, moreover—and perhaps it is not even the best case. The possibility of gratitude seems even more important: we very much want it to be true that we can stand in relations to other people in which reactions like the reaction of feeling gratitude are appropriate, in that sense of "appropriate" which requires that people can be truly responsible for what they do in the ordinary, strong sense. This is profoundly important to us; many people's lives would lose much of their point without it. And those people whose lives would not lose much of their point are perhaps the worse for that.

It could be said that the collective and inescapable illusion of true (ultimate) responsibility is as good as the real thing, and that therefore we don't have reason to want the real and impossible thing itself. But this is a point without much significance. If it is true, then it is true simply in the sense in which any inescapable illusion that something one desires is the case is as good as its actually being the case. The illusion fulfils the desire only because we desire the real thing. And if the illusion were impossible or unreliable, then we would want the real thing.

It is arguable, then, that we do have reason to want true responsibility. Most simply, perhaps, we want it to be true that people really can be truly *morally* responsible for what they do. But certain people—who may be highly egocentric, or devoted to researches that have little to do with other people, or just naturally solitary—may have very little reason to want true responsibility. And for this reason they may have difficulty in seeing (or feeling) the philosophical problem—even, perhaps, when facing some momentous choice between duty and desire. Some of us are far more naturally compatibilist in our attitude to free will than others.

Finally, it is arguable that long familiarity with the philosophical problem of free will may produce something of the same effect. It may work indirectly, like a practice of meditation, and slowly erode the basis of belief in true responsibility. And those to whom this happens may not feel that they have lost very much, when they reflect. For in losing the belief in true responsibility they may also lose the sorts of attitudes that made it seem important in the first place. No doubt they will also lose the sense that the philosophical problem of free will is a deep problem. And perhaps this will be a sign that their understanding of reality has become more profound. But perhaps they should imagine facing a choice between their own torture and the torture of others.

II. WHAT SHOULD WE BELIEVE?

I now return to the main topic, and a summary of the reasons given for the conclusion that we are not really free and truly responsible agents at all, even if we cannot help believing we are.

(1) There is a clear and fundamental sense in which no being can be truly self-determining in respect of its character and motivation in such a way as to be truly responsible for how it is in respect of character and motivation.

There can be no serious dispute about this. There can be serious dispute only about whether it follows from this that we cannot be truly responsible for our actions (i.e., about (3) below).

(2) When we act, at a given time, the way we act is, in some quite straightforward sense, a function of the way we then are, in respect of character and motivation. We act as we act *because of* how we then are, in respect of character and motivation.

However one understands the "because" in this statement, there can be no serious dispute about its truth.

(3) It follows that there is a fundamental sense in which we cannot possibly be truly responsible for our actions. For we cannot be truly responsible for the way we are, and we act as we act because of the way we are.

There are all sorts of ways of objecting to this line of thought. But none of them, I suggest, can touch the fundamental sense in which it is correct.

Given that this is so, it seems that there is really only one way left in which to try to show that we are truly responsible for our actions: somehow or other, we have to show that fully self-conscious rational deliberation, of the sort creatures like ourselves are capable of, has some very special features indeed—features which can somehow or other make it true that when we act we can, on account of our general ability to engage in deliberation of this sort, correctly be said to be truly responsible for our actions even though we cannot be truly responsible for the way we are.

Is this at all plausible? Well, the nature of our experience of agency strongly suggests to us that fully self-conscious rational deliberation, of the sort of which we are capable, does indeed have the property of making us truly responsible for our actions in the strongest possible sense, despite the fact that we cannot be truly responsible for the way we are. Somehow or other, we feel, our capacity for such deliberation suffices to *constitute* us as truly responsible agents in the strongest possible sense.

But one must not be swept away by the apparently self-validating *experience* of freedom or true responsibility. Here again one must review the arguments against it. The principal point is this: however much one deliberates, and whatever one does finally do when one actually acts, one does what one does for reasons R that one just finds one has (or finds occurring to one or seeming right or relevant to one) in the situation in which one then is. And whatever the precise nature of the processes by which one has come to have those reasons, R, for which one then acts in the way one does—heredity or environment, calculation or accident, rage or love, inference or impulse, "existential choice" or successful fulfilment of some long-term plan of character development— there is a simple and fundamental sense in which one is demonstrably not truly or ultimately responsible for the fact that one has them (see (1) above). And yet these reasons R are the reasons why one acts as one does; they are finally responsible for one's acting as one does (see (2) above). And so it follows, from the fact that one is not finally responsible for the fact that one has them, that one is not finally responsible for acting as one does (see (3) above).

It may well be objected that this sense in which it is demonstrable that we cannot be truly or ultimately responsible for our *reasons* for action (such true responsibility being logically impossible) is not decisive, when it is our true responsibility for our *actions,* as ordinarily understood, that is in question. To make such an objection is once again to challenge the derivation of (3) from (1) and (2). But it is in fact *precisely* this sort of logically impossible true responsibility that is required by our ordinary notion of true responsibility for action; and this is particularly easy to see when one considers the fact that we believe people can be truly responsible for their actions in such a way as to be truly deserving of moral praise and blame for them.

It is not only the supposedly romantic or metaphysically woozy incompatibilists or libertarians who are inclined to agree that this extremely strong notion of true responsibility is the one that matters, so far as our ordinary, strong notion of (desert-entailing) freedom is concerned. Nearly all supposedly tough-minded or clear-headed compatibilists agree. That, after all, is why they propose to abandon our ordinary strong notion of freedom altogether: they want to define the predicate "free" in such a way that it can be fully satisfied, and they see that it cannot be fully satisfied, as ordinarily understood.

I conclude that appeal to the special nature of fully self-conscious rational deliberation cannot—demonstrably cannot—overcome the initial objection to the idea that we are truly responsible for our actions (in such a way that we can be truly deserving of praise and blame for them). It goes on seeming that this is not so—for such is the nature of our experience of agency. But it is so—as most compatibilists would agree.

There is, it appears, one last alternative. It seems that one can, without being swept away by the apparently self-validating experience of freedom, argue that the fact that this experience is as it is is a fact of crucial importance. It seems that one can argue that the way some things are may be partly a function of how they seem; and that if x has a belief B to the effect that it, x, is a truly responsible agent, then, if it is also a self-conscious, motivationally "integrated" rational agent, the presence of B can change the situation B is meant to be a belief about in such a way that B is made true partly by the fact of its own presence—so that it is true that x is a truly responsible agent, given that x believes it is true, although it is not true if x does not believe it is true. One can, it seems, argue that this is so *even though true responsibility (or freedom) is not in any sense a conventional property,* but a straightforwardly non-conventional property like being bald or asleep.

To argue in this way is, it seems, to seek to revise our ordinary criteria of truth and falsity in some quite fundamental fashion—in the way envisaged by Sidgwick at the end of *The Methods of Ethics,* perhaps. At present I have no idea how such an argument can succeed; but, in conclusion, it is worth briefly considering one more attempt at such an argument.

Consider the suggestion that truth, for us, is "our" truth; that "our" truth is "human" truth; that "human" truth is just a matter of human "forms of life"; and that, on these terms, the facts of science (for example) are, in the end, exactly on a par with the "experiential fact"—so one might call it—that we are free agents truly responsible for our actions: thus there is, on the one hand, the "doing science" form of life, in which certain things appear to be undeniably the case; and there is, on the other hand, the "experiencing ourselves and others as free and truly responsible agents" form of life, in which certain things appear to be undeniably the case; and these forms of life are, as forms of life, and, therefore, as sources of truth ("truth," "our" truth, "human" truth), exactly on a par.

On the whole, such arguments fail to convince. But even if they do work in some cases, they lead at best to stand-off in the present case. For it is precisely within and on the terms of one of our most central forms of life—our theorizing, philosophizing, ratiocinative form of life—that the argument that true responsibility is impossible has such force. And so the truth enshrined in (or generated by) one form of life is directly at odds with the truth enshrined in (or generated by) another form of life; and it looks as if the only clear solution to this difficulty is to abandon belief in the *unity of (theoretical) truth,* and to grant that one truth may be inconsistent with another.

Now the philosophical conclusion that we are indeed truly responsible agents is a very desirable one. But abandonment of the belief in the unity of theoretical truth is a very high price to pay for it. It involves, to say the least, an earth-quaking revision of our ordinary criteria of truth and falsity. And it is a price that has to be paid in a currency that we value above all others, as theorists: the currency of consistency and completeness. It is a price we cannot pay except at great cost to (A) our belief in the basic consistency and coherence of our actual, admittedly incomplete overall view of the world, and (B) our commitment to belief in the existence of some one, single, *complete,* overall conception of the world that is internally consistent and coherent and is in principle attainable by human beings.

To give up in this way the idea that there is, in some fundamental sense, one truth—and to do so specifically in order to derive the conclusion that we are indeed truly responsible agents partly from the fact that we do and cannot but so experience ourselves—is, I think, to pay a higher price (in the currency of consistency and possible completeness of world-view) than the price one pays when one grants that true responsibility is impossible, and then patently continues to believe in it without question in one's daily thought and action (continuing to think and act as if one believed in it without question). For to choose to pay the first price is simply to give up belief in the unity of truth. It is, to put it dramatically, to say that there is a sense in which truth itself is perhaps necessarily inconsistent. Whereas to choose to pay the second price is not to give up belief in the unity of truth. It is, rather, to say that *we* are perhaps necessarily inconsistent; it is simply to admit that we are not only finite and imperfect, considered as theorizing and speculative beings who are seeking to achieve a consistent and complete world-view, but are also severely hobbled in a certain quite specific respect, because our actual, overall, admittedly incomplete world-view is already demonstrably and perhaps irreparably inconsistent in a certain respect.

This is too simple (there are no doubt some genuine arguments in favour of abandoning the unity of truth). Still, one thing that can be invoked to support the view that the second price is less high than the first is the claim that a being like the Genuine Incompatibilist Determinist could possibly exist, or equally the claim that exceptional human beings may—as Buddhists, say— possibly be able to achieve a true view of the way things are that involves no sort of belief in true responsibility at all. For if such a claim is correct, then although we as we ordinarily are must admit our imperfection, as theorists, and abandon (A) above, we need not abandon (B).

Hume may be cited as someone who cheerfully chooses to pay something like the second price, and manages to make light of it in a convincing fashion. His position may be summarized roughly as follows: "(i) as a 'first-order' philosopher I reach certain unattractive but seemingly inescapable conclusions; (ii) in common life I find that I can (and cannot but) simply ignore these conclusions; (iii) as a 'second-order' philosopher, I can produce reasons for being unperturbed by the fact that both (i) and (ii) are true." This response is not as strong here as it is in the sorts of cases Hume is usually concerned with, however. For Hume's characteristic sceptical conclusion is not that something we firmly believe to be true cannot be true; it is, rather, that we cannot know it to be true, and cannot provide any rational foundation for our firm belief that it is true. The present conclusion is different; it is that something we firmly believe is actually demonstrably false. So the Humean option is not obviously available.

Which price should one pay? I cannot decide this dispute in a general way; many considerations bear on it, and they extend far beyond the particular problem of freedom. There is, in any case, a price to pay, if one takes the problem of freedom seriously. This is what many compatibilists have wrongly tried to deny. Pay one price, or pay the other. And if you pay the second, do not underestimate it.

Indeterminism

Peter van Inwagen

If determinism is true, then one's acts are determined by states of affairs that obtained before one was born. Whatever dialectical advantage an appeal to this fact may win the incompatibilist, however, it has no more logical or philosophical significance than has an appeal to the fact that if determinism is true, then one's acts are determined simply by *past* events. As Agathon observed, not even the gods can change the past, and this is no *more* true of the events of a thousand years ago than it is of the events of one second ago. Therefore, if a man's acts were determined by events that occurred earlier than those acts—by *however* short an interval—then one could show that his acts were unfree. . . . Therefore, if the incompatibilist is right, a free act must be an undetermined act, or, at least, the immediate result of undetermined deliberations.

But now let us see what an undetermined act would really be like. Let us consider the case of a hardened thief who, as our story begins, is in the act of lifting the lid of the poor-box in a little country church. He sneers and curses when he sees what a pathetically small sum it contains. Still, business is business: he reaches for the money. Suddenly there flashes before his mind's eye a picture of the face of his dying mother and he remembers the promise he made to her by her deathbed always to be honest and upright. This is not the first occasion on which he has had such a vision while performing some mean act of theft, but he has always disregarded it. This time, however, he does *not* disregard it. Instead, he thinks the matter over carefully and decides not to take the money. Acting on this decision, he leaves the church empty-handed.

We may suppose that this decision was undetermined. That is, we may assume that there are possible worlds in which things were absolutely identical in every respect with the way they were in the actual world up to the moment at which our repentant thief made his decision—worlds in which, moreover, the laws of nature are just what they are in the actual world—and in which he takes the money.

According to the incompatibilist, this indetermination is necessary for the thief's act of repentance to have been a free act. But if we look carefully at the idea of an undetermined act, we shall see that such an act could not be a free act. . . .

(i) If the incompatibilist's account of free action is correct, then a free act is an act that is undetermined by prior states of affairs. But an act that is undetermined is a mere *random* or *chance* occurrence, and a random or chance occurrence is hardly the kind of thing that could be called a free act.

Reply: The doubtful premiss in this argument is the assertion that if our acts are undetermined they are mere "random" or "chance" events. What does this mean? The words "random" and "chance" most naturally apply to *patterns* or *sequences* of events. (If the argument is that if our acts were undetermined they would issue from us in a meaningless and incoherent jumble, as if we were perpetually deciding what to do by consulting a table of random numbers, there seems to be no reason whatever to believe this. There are computers that sometimes change state in ways that are not determined by their earlier states and their input, but their output is not random in the way in which a table of random numbers is random.) It is not clear what "random" and "chance" mean when they are applied to single events. These words *might* simply mean "undetermined"; but in that case we should have no argument but only an assertion that undetermined events are not the sort of thing that can be called free acts. A more interesting possibility is that, in this strand of the *Mind* Argument, "chance" and "random" are being used, properly or not, to mean "uncaused." But, as we shall discover when we discuss the second strand, an undetermined act need *not* be an uncaused act. Therefore, if "random" and "chance" mean "uncaused" the first strand is invalid. I know of no other things that "random" or "chance" might mean, and I therefore conclude that the first strand fails to disprove incompatibilism. Let us turn to the second strand.

(ii) If an act, or what *looks* superficially like an act, is not determined to occur by prior states of affairs, then it is not really an act at all. (It should be clear that something can look like an act and yet not be an act. If a clever brain-physiologist stimulated the motor centres of your brain in the right way, then he might make it look as if you had raised your hand when you had not.) This is because, whatever else an act may be, it is a production of its agent. But if an "act" is undetermined, it is not a production of its putative agent and hence not really his act at all. Let us consider our thief who refrained—or so we should say if we went by outward appearances—from robbing the poor-box. His refraining, or the event that we should initially be inclined to call his refraining, was *ex hypothesi* undetermined. Let us examine this event carefully. We shall assume that some version or other of the mind-body identity theory is true, but this assumption will be only an aid to our intuition, and not a premiss of our argument: it is easier to visualize changes in a material substance than changes in a spiritual substance, but the point of our argument would remain if it were restated on the assumption that, for example, Cartesian Dualism provided the correct description of our nature. On the assumption of psychophysical identity, the thief's act of refraining was identical with a certain event in his brain. Now suppose that some event in your brain is identical with one of your acts. And suppose that this event was undetermined by earlier events in your brain. Let us call this undetermined event E. There would seem to be no reason to suppose that E or any other undetermined event is *essentially* undetermined. Suppose, for example, that a cup sitting untouched on a table suddenly breaks at *t* and that this event—the cup's breaking at *t*—is undetermined by earlier states of affairs. It would seem that it *might* have been determined by earlier states of affairs: a hammer might have struck the cup at just the proper moment that its breaking at *t* should have been causally determined by this blow. (Some philosophers might want to raise the question whether the event that would have occurred in such a case was numerically the same as the event that in fact happened, but we need not consider this question. It will do for our purposes to note that if an undetermined event happens, it is logically possible for a *descriptively* identical determined event to have happened at the same moment.) Let us suppose that this had happened in the case of E: suppose that an event just like E and having the same consequences had happened—it may have been E itself or some other event— and that it was determined. Let us suppose that it was determined by the action of some supernatural power: a freakish demon caused it. The sequence of events is this: the freakish demon performs some supernatural act such that it is causally impossible for this act to be performed and E—or an event just like E—not to occur; E is identical with the event we also call "the thief's deliberations," under which description we include the outcome of these deliberations; this outcome then determines that the thief shall refrain from robbing the poor-box and shall depart.

Or we may describe the case as follows. In the "actual" case the thief's deliberations take a certain course that results in his refraining from stealing. These deliberations are identical with a certain rather protracted event in the thief's brain. If his act is free, and if incompatibilism is true, then this protracted brain-event is undetermined. We then imagine something that *might have* happened: a freakish demon might have done something that rendered it causally impossible for this in fact undetermined event not to occur.

Suppose the demon *had* done this. Then the thief would not really have *acted* at all, because he would not have been the *producer* of the event in his brain that initiated the bodily motions characteristic of a man leaving a poor-box empty-handed. The case is really no different from the case of the man whose brain has been "wired" by a brain-physiologist and whose arm rises whenever the physiologist presses a certain button. That man does not *raise* his arm when the physiologist presses the button; rather, his arm *rises* as a consequence of what the physiologist does.

The thief, therefore, if his (supposed) act is caused by the freakish demon, does *not* act. Now let us restore the "actual" situation: we remove from our imagined case the demon and his works, leaving an uncaused event and its consequences. Does this somehow change the "demon" story to a story in which the thief *does* act? How could that be? If a certain change in one's body is determined to occur by events that were produced at the pleasure of some rational being other than oneself, this shows that neither this change nor its consequences could be, or be a part or component of, one's act. But it shows this only by bringing into prominence the fact that the determinants of the change are not to be found within *oneself.* Now if an event is *undetermined,* then it is just as true that the determinants of that event are not to be found within oneself as it would be if these determinants were to be found in the capricious acts of a demon, for if the determinants of one's act are not to be found, then, *a fortiori,* they are not to be found within *one.* If we are asking whether a certain event is a production of *mine,* then we must admit that there is no *philosophical* difference between this event's being undetermined and its being determined by an external force, for each of these cases is quite simply a case of *interference* with my plans, desires, deliberations, and hopes. In the one case we have a causally explicable sort of interference. In both cases we have *some* sort of interference.

If this is not sufficiently obvious, perhaps we can make it so by elaborating the story of the freakish demon. Let us suppose he exercises his influence over the thief in this way: there is an invisible wire that passes through the thief's skull and into his brain (no hole is required, for the wire is made of the subtle matter that the Stoics postulated); at the other end of the wire is a sort of piano that is also made of subtle matter and upon the keyboard of which the demon plays; by what he plays, he can "direct," via the subtle wire, the motions of the atoms in the thief's brain and can thereby direct the thief's inner life, including his deliberations. And that is just what he has done in the case we have imagined: by striking the keys in a certain order, he has guided the thief's brain through just that sequence of states that correspond to the deliberations of a man who refrains from stealing. It is clear, in this case, that neither the thief's bodily motions nor the pseudo-deliberations that preceded them were things *he* produced: he was merely the demon's instrument and *acted* only in the etiolated sense in which a fiddle acts in the hands of a violinist or a scalpel acts in the hands of a surgeon.

Let us now gradually, very gradually, modify this case. Let us first suppose that the demon's actions at the keyboard are undetermined by the demon's own inner states and by anything else. This change in the case does not weaken the argument for our earlier conclusion (that the thief did not act). Now let us remove the demon and suppose that the "sort of piano" we imagined the demon to be playing is a sort of *player* piano: let us imagine that the keyboard is worked by a mechanism internal to the piano; and let us suppose that this internal mechanism is an indeterministic one. This further change in the case does not weaken our argument for the conclusion that the thief does not act. Now let us remove the piano and suppose that impulses simply *appear* in the subtle wire (which now protrudes from the thief's skull, its far end unattached to anything) undetermined by prior states of affairs. Again, this change does not weaken our argument for the conclusion that the thief did not act. Now let us imagine the wire becoming shorter and shorter till only the part inside the thief's skull remains. This change, too, does not weaken our argument: if impulses undetermined by past states of affairs appear in the wire and if these impulses determine the putative acts of the thief—determine what movements are made by his limbs and what thoughts pass through his mind—then these putative acts are not real acts, are not among the things he *does* or produces. Now let us suppose that the subtle wire is replaced by one of too, too solid flesh, by a "wire," or wire-shaped thing, made of brain cells. This change does not weaken our argument. What difference does it make *what* the wire that delivers undetermined impulses to the thief's brain is *made of?* The important thing is that the impulses of which it is the carrier should be undetermined by past states of affairs. Let us now make one final change: let us suppose that the wire-shaped thing made of brain cells is a *natural part* of the thief's brain.

Does this make a difference? It's hard to see why it should. Take any part of an agent's brain and replace it with an artificially produced perfect duplicate; then, assuming the replaced part of the brain was not something essential to the agent's *identity,* this would certainly not affect the agent's free will. If this is true, such a replacement performed "in reverse" should be equally irrelevant to the agent's free will. Our thief has a wire-shaped thing made of brain cells within his brain, in which there arise impulses, undetermined by past states of affairs, which determine his every action. If we now suppose that this thing is a *natural part* of the thief, we are making a supposition not about its momentary operations, but only about its origins. But only the present, momentary operations of the parts of one's brain should be relevant to the question whether one is *now* acting freely. Facts about the *origin* of a part of one's brain can be relevant to questions of free will only in so far as they are relevant to questions about the momentary operations of the part. Thus, to replace a part of one's brain with a perfect duplicate of different origins can have no effect on one's free will—always assuming that the replacement leaves one's identity intact.

We have now got to the point of imagining our thief's "acts" being the result of undetermined impulses originating in a certain section of his brain. This section of his brain plays the same part in our final story that a freakish demon played in our original story. We moved from one point to the other by gradually modifying the freakish demon and his apparatus until we had turned them into a natural part of the thief's brain. Now in our original story, it was clear that the thief did not *act.* We have seen that none of our series of modifications introduced any "opportunity" for him to act. We must therefore conclude that in our *final* story the thief did not act. But our final story is just exactly the tale the incompatibilist tells when he is asked what goes on inside someone who acts freely. Therefore, the incompatibilist's story is incoherent.

All this window-dressing, of course, is not strictly necessary. Anyone whose "analytical imagination," as Hobart calls it, is in good working order can see right at the outset that a person whose "acts" are the consequences of undetermined events—whether these undetermined events occur within a natural part of him or not—is not really an agent at all. Such a person is not acting, but is merely being pushed about or interfered with. People whose analytical powers are modest, however, may find our technique of telling a sequence of stories, each of which is very slightly closer than its predecessor to the incompatibilist's story of the inner nature of a free act, a useful substitute for adequate analytical powers.

We have seen, therefore, that an act, and *a fortiori* a free act, cannot be an undetermined act, for an undetermined act is a contradiction in terms.

Reply: My analytical powers are apparently inadequate. The "longer story" helps me to see why someone would say that an apparent act that is undetermined is not really an act at all. This story is, of course, a "slippery-slope" argument. Such arguments are, to my mind, a useful but dangerous tool for philosophers. They are dangerous because, when they are moving briskly along, they acquire a kind of dialectical momentum that can carry the unwary audience smoothly over gaps in the argument.

I think there is a gap in the argument. That is, I think there is a point at which the allegedly philosophically unimportant alteration that the proponent of the *Mind* Argument makes in his story *does* make a philosophical difference. At a certain point in the story, the reader will remember, the freakish demon and his keyboard of subtle matter have been reduced to a wire-shaped thing of brain-stuff. The next step is to suppose that this thing is a *natural part* of the thief. This next step is, in my view, the one that makes the difference. I do not, of course, say that an undetermined change in a natural part of a human being will *necessarily* have an action of that human being's among its consequences; I do say that it's not clear that it *couldn't*. If I am right in supposing this, then the *Mind* Argument—or the strand of it that we are currently investigating—errs in supposing that the step from "wire-shaped thing" to "*natural* wire-shaped thing" is an obviously harmless step. And therefore, if I am right, this strand of the *Mind* Argument does not succeed in showing that an undetermined act is a contradiction in terms.

I shall now attempt to show that it is not clear that an apparent act of a human being that was the consequence of an undetermined change in a natural part of a human being *could not* be a real act. I shall attempt to show this by constructing two "models" of human action according to which this *is* possible. Since neither of these models is known to be impossible or incoherent, it will follow that there may well be a gap in the apparently continuous progression of modifications of the "freakish demon" case that the *Mind* Argument presents us with. And if that is true, then the *Mind* Argument fails to establish its conclusion.

I shall not contend that either of the models is right. I do not know—except as we all know—what human action is. I shall not contend that either of these models entails that an undetermined *free* act is possible. . . . I shall show only that if either of these models is correct, then an undetermined *act* is possible.

The first model I shall mention only briefly, since so many philosophers are convinced of its incoherence—on what grounds, I am not clear—that it would be a tactical mistake for me to discuss it at length. The model I am alluding to is that of *immanent* or *agent* causation.

The medieval philosophers, like all theists, believed that God was the cause of all things other than himself. Unlike many theists, they—or most of them—believed that God was *changeless*. This raised a difficult philosophical problem, since the causes we observe in nature produce their effects only at the expense of some change in themselves. So far as I know, the Schoolmen never solved this problem, though they postulated a solution and gave this solution a label. They postulated a type of causation that does *not* involve a change in the cause and called it *immanent* causation. (Garden-variety causation they called *transeunt* causation.)

In our own time, this medieval idea has been revived by Roderick Chisholm and applied not to God but to the human agent. More or less the same idea has been employed by Richard Taylor, who prefers the term "agent causation." (Chisholm has lately come to prefer this second term himself.) According to Chisholm and Taylor, the *agent himself* is sometimes (when he acts freely) the cause of his own acts, or, perhaps, the cause of the bodily or mental changes that manifest them. This does not mean that a change in the agent causes these acts or changes; rather the agent *causes* without himself changing in any way. (Save accidentally. The human agent, unlike the God of the Philosophers, is not only mutable but is *constantly* undergoing change. But, according to the Chisholm-Taylor theory, none of these changes he undergoes is the cause of his free acts.)

Now let us ignore the contention that an immanently caused act would be a *free* act, which is not our present concern, and consider only the thesis that we are the immanent causes of at least some of our acts. If this thesis is true—and it is not my purpose here to argue that it is coherent, much less that it is true—then it is easy to see that an act can be an undetermined act. Let us return to the case of our thief. To say that it was not determined that he should refrain from stealing is to say this: there is a possible world that (a) is *exactly* like the actual world in every detail up to the moment at which the thief refrained from stealing, and (b) is governed by the same laws of nature as the actual world, and (c) is such that, in it, the thief robbed the poor-box.

It is plain that immanent causation allows for the possibility of such a world: its divergence from the actual world is possible because the immanent causation of an event does not imply that that event is determined by earlier states of affairs—if anything, the immanent causation of an event implies that that event is *not* determined by earlier states of affairs. Moreover, there is no basis for the caution implied by the use of phrases like "what looks superficially like an act" or by writing "act" inside scare-quotes. If the thief moves in a way typical of a man who very nearly robs a poor-box but draws back from doing so at the last moment, and if the same thoughts pass through his mind that would typically pass through the mind of a man who considers but refrains from robbing a poor-box, and if these thoughts and movements are caused *by the agent himself,* then it surely follows that if we say "He refrained from robbing the poor-box," we are describing his *action* and describing it in words that are literally correct.

Therefore, *if* immanent causation is a coherent concept, the second strand of the *Mind* Argument fails to show that the notion of an undetermined act is a contradiction in terms. The proponent of the *Mind* Argument is likely to concede this and to argue, or assert, that immanent causation is *not* a coherent concept. I will not dispute this. I have mentioned immanent causation because it is an idea that has won the allegiance of highly respected philosophers and which is therefore worthy of the attention of anyone who is troubled by the *Mind* Argument. I commend their writings to you. Let us proceed to the second "model" of human action I have promised.

Donald Davidson has proposed an account of human action that is an elaboration—an elaboration constructed with great sophistication and philosophical sensitivity—of the following very simple idea: an act is *caused* by the very factors its agent would adduce if asked to give his reason for performing it, to wit, by the agent's desire that a certain state of affairs should be realized and his belief that an act of that type was the best—or, at least, an unsurpassed—means to realizing that state of affairs. Suppose, for example, that a certain man has raised his hand; and suppose that, when he is asked why he raised his hand, he says that he did this because he wanted to vote for the measure before the meeting and believed that the way to vote for this measure was to raise his hand. If what he says about the reasons for his act is correct, then, according to Davidson, the cause of his act is his desire to vote coupled with his belief that he could realize his desire by raising his hand. . . .

Many, perhaps most, philosophers believe that causes *determine* their effects. They believe, that is, that given the cause—we are talking once more about "normal" causation, a relation that takes *events* or *states of affairs* or some such, and not *persons,* as its terms—the effect *must* follow. (This "must," of course, is the "must" of physical, not logical, necessity.) They believe that if A is the cause of B, then, if A had happened and had *not* been followed by B, this could only have been because the laws of nature were different. Some of the philosophers I am alluding to think that laws of nature are merely exceptionless regularities; others think that only some exceptionless regularities are laws and differ as to what makes a regularity a law. These disputes are important, but they need not concern us at present. I shall count a philosopher a proponent of the standard or Humean view if he thinks that the effect is determined by the cause together with the laws of nature, however he may understand "the laws of nature."

Considering its vast army of adherents, the really striking thing about the standard theory is that there seems to be no reason to think it is true. . . .

Suppose someone throws a stone at a window and that the stone strikes the glass and the glass shatters in just the way we should expect glass to shatter when struck by a cast stone. Suppose further that God reveals to us that the glass did not *have* to shatter under these conditions, that there are possible worlds having exactly the same laws of nature as the actual world and having histories identical with that of the actual world in every detail up to the instant at which the stone came into contact with the glass, but in which the stone rebounded from the intact glass. It follows from what we imagine God to have told us that determinism is false. But does it also follow that the stone did not break the glass, or that the glass did not break *because* it was struck by the stone? It is not easy to see why we should say this follows; perhaps the only reason we could have for saying this is that we accept a corollary of the standard theory of causation: that instances of causation simply *are* instances of universal, exceptionless laws, that the concept of the instantiation of the exceptionless law and the concept of causation are one and the same concept. But this proposition is very doubtful.

Let us suppose that we are watching a slow-motion film taken by a camera trained on the point at which our stone came into contact with our pane of glass. We observe the following: the stone moves through the air toward the point of impact; the stone touches the glass; the glass bends ever so slightly; cracks appear in the glass, radiating outward from the point of impact; shorter cracks appear, joining these radial cracks, thus producing detached shards of glass; the stone moves through the space formerly occupied by the unbroken pane, pushing, or apparently pushing, shards of glass out of its way; the stone continues along its path, trailing a rough cone of spinning shards. Watching this slow-motion film several times should make it very hard to believe that the stone did not break the glass. We could perhaps construct some wild hypothesis, logically consistent with our visual evidence, according to which the stone did not cause the glass to break (for example, the stone didn't touch the glass; a demon caused the pane to shatter a thousandth of a second before the stone would have touched it, carefully counterfeiting the appearance of what would have happened if things had been left to themselves). And if God revealed to us that something like this had happened, then we should have to admit that, despite appearances, the stone hadn't really caused the glass to break. But what about the revelation we earlier imagined God's having delivered? Could this revelation really lead us to say that, despite appearances, the stone didn't cause the glass to break? That this is a *logical consequence* of this revelation? Wouldn't it be more reasonable to say this: that, while the stone did cause the window to break, it was not *determined* that it should; that it *in fact* caused the window to break, though, even if all conditions had been precisely the same, it might not have?

This case convinces me that whatever the *facts* of the matter may be, it is at any rate not part of the *concept* of causation that a cause—or even a cause plus the totality of its accompanying conditions—determines its effect. (A similar case: whatever the facts of the matter may be, it is not part of the *concept* of a human being that a human being should have a liver. If a madman says he is a man who has no liver, we can't simply tell him that it's part of the concept of a human being that a human being has a liver. But just as all human beings *do* have livers, it may be that all causes *do* determine their effects.)

Suppose that some causes don't determine but merely, as we might say, *produce* their effects. Suppose that our simple-minded version of Davidson's theory of the causes of human action is correct. Suppose that among the causes that merely produce their effects are (some of) the "Davidsonian" causes of action. This is our "second model." Let us look once more at our thief. If the model of the causes of action we are considering is correct, then his refraining from robbing the poor-box (R) was caused but not necessitated by his desire to keep the promise he made to his dying mother coupled with his belief that the best way to do this would be to refrain from robbing the poor-box (DB). Let us suppose that the second model is correct: R was caused by DB and DB did not *have* to cause R; it just *did*. We may suppose that God has thousands of times caused the world to revert to precisely its state at the moment just before the thief decided not to steal, and has each time allowed things to proceed without interference for a few minutes, and that DB caused R on about half these occasions. On the other occasions, we may suppose, DB did *not* cause R: instead the thief's desire for money, coupled with his belief that the best way for him to get money was to rob the poor-box, caused him to rob the poor-box. (If we are right in supposing that causes may *produce* their effects without *determining* them, then our supposition about the distribution of outcomes that results from God's thousands of "resettings" of the world is a perfectly possible one.)

Does it follow that the thief *didn't* refrain from robbing the poor-box? I don't see why it should be supposed to follow. The thief's act—or what looks very much like his act—was *caused* by his desires and beliefs, after all. What more do we want? (Remember, I am not saying that the thief acted freely in refraining from taking the money but only that he *acted*.)

I do not know what to say about this case to make it more persuasive. It seems to me to be at least possible that some sort of Davidsonian theory of the causes of action is correct. It seems to me to be at least possible that some causes do not determine their effects. If these two things could be severally true, then I do not see anything to prevent their being jointly true. If they could be jointly true, then the case we have presented seems to show that it is possible for an agent's *act* to be undetermined by antecedent states of affairs. We can now see why the compatibilist's move from "wire-shaped thing made of brain cells" to "natural part" was not so innocent as he alleged. A change in a natural part of one may well be identical with one's coming to have a certain desire or with one's acquiring a certain belief. But a change in something that is *not* a part of one—even if it is inside one's head and made of brain cells—could not possibly be identical with either of these things.

LIBERTARIANISM

Roderick M. Chisholm

> *A staff moves a stone, and is moved by a hand, which is moved by a man.*
>
> —ARISTOTLE, *PHYSICS,* 256A

I

The metaphysical problem of human freedom might be summarized in the following way: "Human beings are responsible agents; but this fact appears to conflict with a deterministic view of human action (the view that every event that is involved in an act is caused by some other event); and it *also* appears to conflict with an indeterministic view of human action (the view that the act, or some event that is essential to the act, is not caused at all)." To solve the problem, I believe, we must make somewhat far-reaching assumptions about the self of the agent—about the man who performs the act.

Perhaps it is needless to remark that, in all likelihood, it is impossible to say anything significant about this ancient problem that has not been said before.

Let us consider some deed, or misdeed, that may be attributed to a responsible agent: one man, say, shot another. If the man *was* responsible for what he did, then, I would urge, what was to happen at the time of the shooting was something that was entirely up to the man himself. There was a moment at which it was true, both that he could have fired the shot and also that he could have refrained from firing it. And if this is so, then, even though he did fire it, he could have done something else instead. (He didn't find himself firing the shot "against his will," as we say.) I think we can say, more generally, then, that if a man is responsible for a certain event or a certain state of affairs (in our example, the shooting of another man), then that event or state of affairs was brought about by some act of his, and the act was something that was in his power either to perform or not to perform.

But now, if the act which he *did* perform was an act that was also in his power *not* to perform, then *it* could not have been caused or determined by any event that was not itself within his power either to bring about or not to bring about. For example, if what we say he did was really something that was brought about by a second man, one who forced his hand upon the trigger,

---

Roderick M. Chisholm. "Libertarianism." Excerpted from *Freedom and Determinism* edited by K. Lehrer. Reprinted by permission.

It is a violation of the law to reproduce this selection by any means whatsoever without the written consent of the copyright holder.

say, or who, by means of hypnosis, compelled him to perform the act, then, since the act was caused by the *second* man, it was nothing that was within the power of the *first* man to prevent. And precisely the same thing is true, I think, if instead of referring to a second man who compelled the first one, we speak instead of the *desires* and *beliefs* which the first man happens to have had. For if what we say he did was really something that was brought about by his own beliefs and desires, if these beliefs and desires in the particular situation in which he happened to have found himself caused him to do just what it was they say he did do, then, since *they* caused it, *he* was unable to do anything other than just what he did do. It makes no difference whether the cause of the deed was internal or external: if the cause was some state or event for which the man himself was not responsible, then he was not responsible for what we have been mistakenly calling his act. If a flood caused the poorly structured dam to break, then, given the flood and the constitution of the dam, the break, we may say, *had* to occur and nothing could have happened in its place. And if the flood of desire caused the weak-willed man to give in, then he too, had to do just what it was that he did do and he was no more responsible than was the dam for the results that followed. (It is true, of course, that if the man is responsible for the beliefs and desires that he happens to have, then he may also be responsible for the things they lead him to do. But the question now becomes: *is* he responsible for the beliefs and desires he happens to have? If he is, then there was a time when they were within his power either to acquire or not to acquire, and we are left, therefore, with our general point.)

One may object: But surely if there were such a thing as a man who is really *good,* then he would be responsible for things that he would do; yet, he would be unable to do anything other than just what he does do, since, being good, he will always choose to do what is best. The answer, I think, is suggested by a comment that Thomas Reid makes upon an ancient author. The author had said of Cato, "He was good because he could not be otherwise," and Reid observes: "This saying, if understood literally and strictly, is not the praise of Cato, but of his constitution which was no more the work of Cato than his existence." If Cato was himself responsible for the good things that he did, then Cato, as Reid suggests, was such that, although he had the power to do what was not good, he exercised his power only for that which was good.

All of this, if it is true, may give a certain amount of comfort to those who are tender-minded. But we should remind them that it also conflicts with a familiar view about the nature of God—with the view that St. Thomas Aquinas expresses by saying that "every movement both of the will and of nature proceeds from God as the Prime Mover." If the act of the sinner *did* proceed from God as the Prime Mover, then God was in the position of the second agent we just discussed—the man who forced the trigger finger, or the hypnotist—and the sinner, so-called, was *not* responsible for what he did. (This may be a bold assertion, in view of the history of western theology, but I must say that I have never encountered a single good reason for denying it.)

There is one standard objection to all of this and we should consider it briefly.

The objection takes the form of a stratagem—one designed to show that determinism (and divine providence) is consistent with human responsibility. The stratagem is one that was used by Jonathan Edwards and by many philosophers in the present century, most notably, G. E. Moore.

One proceeds as follows: The expression

(a) He could have done otherwise,

it is argued, means no more nor less than

(b) If he had chosen to do otherwise, then he would have done otherwise.

(In place of "chosen," one might say "tried," "set out," "decided," "undertaken," or "willed.") The truth of statement (b), it is then pointed out, is consistent with determinism (and with divine providence); for even if all of the man's actions were causally determined, the man could still be such that, *if* he had chosen otherwise, then he would have done otherwise. What the murderer saw, let us suppose, along with his beliefs and desires, *caused* him to fire the shot; yet he was such that *if,* just then, he had chosen or decided *not* to fire the shot, then he would not have fired it. All of this is certainly possible. Similarly, we could say, of the dam, that the flood caused it to break and also that the dam was such that, *if* there had been no flood or similar pressure, then the dam would have remained intact. And therefore, the argument proceeds, if (b) is consistent with determinism, and if (a) and (b) say the same thing, then (a) is also consistent with determinism; hence we can say that the agent *could* have done otherwise, even though he was caused to do what he did do; and therefore determinism and moral responsibility are compatible.

Is the argument sound? The conclusion follows from the premises, but the catch, I think, lies in the first premise—the one saying that statement (a) tells us no more nor less than what statement (b) tells us. For (b), it would seem, could be true while (a) is false. That is to say, our man might be such that, if he had chosen to do otherwise, then he would have done otherwise, and yet *also* such that he could not have done otherwise. Suppose, after all, that our murderer could not have *chosen,* or could not have *decided,* to do otherwise. Then the fact that he happens also to be a man such that, if he had chosen not to shoot he would not have shot, would make no difference. For if he could *not* have chosen *not* to shoot, then he could not have done anything other than just what it was that he did do. In a word: from our statement (b) above ("If he had chosen to do otherwise, then he would have done otherwise"), we cannot make an inference to (a) above ("He could have done otherwise"), unless we can *also* assert:

(c) He could have chosen to do otherwise.

And therefore, if we must reject this third statement (c), then, even though we may be justified in asserting (b), we are not justified in asserting (a). If the man could not have chosen to do otherwise, then he would not have done otherwise — *even if* he was such that, if he *had* chosen to do otherwise, then he would have done otherwise.

This stratagem in question, then, seems to me not to work, and I would say, therefore, that the ascription of responsibility conflicts with a deterministic view of action.

Perhaps there is less need to argue that the ascription of responsibility also conflicts with an indeterministic view of action — with the view that the act, or some event that is essential to the act, is not caused at all. If the act — the firing of the shot — was not caused at all, if it was fortuitous or capricious, happening so to speak "out of the blue," then, presumably, no one — and nothing — was responsible for the act. Our conception of action, therefore, should be neither deterministic nor indeterministic. Is there any other possibility?

We must not say that every event involved in the act is caused by some other event, and we must not say that the act is something that is not caused at all. The possibility that remains, therefore, is this: We should say that at least one of the events that are involved in the act is caused, not by any other events, but by something else instead. And this something else can only be the agent — the man. If there is an event that is caused, not by other events, but by the man, then there are some events involved in the act that are not caused by other events. But if the event in question is caused by the man, then it *is* caused and we are not committed to saying that there is something involved in the act that is not caused at all.

But this, of course, is a large consequence, implying something of considerable importance about the nature of the agent or the man.

If we consider only inanimate natural objects, we may say that causation, if it occurs, is a relation between *events* or *states of affairs.* The dam's breaking was an event that was caused by a set of other events — the dam being weak, the flood being strong, and so on. But if a man is responsible for a particular deed, then, if what I have said is true, there is some event, or set of events, that is caused, *not* by other events or states of affairs, but by the man himself, by the agent, whatever he may be.

I shall borrow a pair of medieval terms, using them, perhaps, in a way that is slightly different from that for which they were originally intended. I shall say that when one event or state of affairs (or set of events or states of affairs) causes some other event or state of affairs, then we have an instance of *transeunt* causation. And I shall say that when an *agent,* as distinguished from an event, causes an event or state of affairs, then we have an instance of *immanent* causation.

The nature of what is intended by the expression "immanent causation" may be illustrated by this sentence from Aristotle's *Physics:* "Thus, a staff moves a stone, and is moved by a hand, which is moved by a man" (VII, 5, 256a. 6–8). If the man was responsible, then we have in this illustration a number of instances of causation—most of them transeunt, but at least one of them immanent. What the staff did to the stone was an instance of transeunt causation, and thus we may describe it as a relation between events: "the motion of the staff caused the motion of the stone." And similarly for what the hand did to the staff: "the motion of the hand caused the motion of the staff." And, as we know from physiology, there are still other events which caused the motion of the hand. Hence we need not introduce the agent at this particular point, as Aristotle does—we *need* not, though we *may*. We *may* say that the hand was moved by the man, but we may *also* say that the motion of the hand was caused by the motion of certain muscles; and we may say the motion of the muscles was caused by certain events that took place within the brain. But some event, and presumably one of those that took place within the brain, was caused by the agent and not by any other events.

There are, of course, objections to this way of putting the matter; I shall consider the two that seem to me to be the most important.

One may object, firstly: "If the *man* does anything, then, as Aristotle's remark suggests, what he does is to move the *hand*. But he certainly does not *do* anything to his brain—he may not even know that he *has* a brain. And if he doesn't do anything to the brain, and if, as physiology seems to tell us, the motion of the hand was caused by something that happened within the brain, then there is no point in appealing to 'immanent causation' as being something incompatible with 'transeunt causation'—for the whole thing, after all, is a matter of causal relations among events or states of affairs. The motion of the hand was caused by the brain and not by the man."

The answer to this objection, I think, is this: It is true that the agent does not *do* anything with his brain, or to his brain, in the sense in which he *does* something with his hand and does something to the staff. But from this it does not follow that the agent was not the immanent cause of something that happened within his brain.

We should note a useful distinction that has been proposed by Professor A. I. Melden—namely, the distinction between "making something A happen" and "doing A." If I reach for the staff and pick it up, then one of the things that I *do* is just that—reach for the staff and pick it up. And if it is something that I do, then there is a very clear sense in which it may be said to be something that I know that I do. If you ask me, "Are you doing something, or trying to do something, with the staff?," I will have no difficulty in finding an answer. But in doing something with the staff, I also make various things happen which are not in the same sense things that I do: I will make various air-particles move; I will free a number of blades of grass from the pressure that had been upon them; and I may cause a shadow to move from one place to another. If these are merely things that I make happen, as distinguished from things that I do, then I may know nothing whatever about them; I may not have the slightest idea that, in moving the staff, I am bringing about any such thing as the motion of air-particles, shadows, and blades of grass.

We may say, in answer to the first objection, therefore, that it is true that our agent does nothing to his brain or with his brain; but from this it does not follow that the agent is not the immanent cause of some event within his brain, for the brain event may be something which, like the motion of the air-particles, he made happen in picking up the staff. The only difference between the two cases is this: in each case, he made something happen when he picked up the staff; but in the one case—the motion of the air-particles or of the shadows—it was the motion of the staff that caused the event to happen; and in the other case—the event that took place in the brain—it was this event that caused the motion of the staff.

The point is, in a word, that whenever a man does something A, then (by "immanent causation") he makes a certain cerebral event happen, and this cerebral event (by "transeunt causation") makes A happen.

The second objection is more difficult, and it concerns the very concept of "immanent causation," or causation by an agent, as this concept is to be interpreted here. The concept is subject to a difficulty which has long been associated with that of the prime mover unmoved. We have said that there must be some event A, presumably some cerebral event, which is caused not by any other event, but by the agent. Since A was not caused by any other event, then the agent himself cannot be said to have undergone any change or produced any other event (such as "an act of will" or the like) which brought A about. For if the cerebral event is caused by some change *within* the agent, then it *is* caused by an event and we have lost the solution to our problem. But now: if, when the agent made A happen, there was no event involved other than A itself, no event which could be described as *making* A happen, what did the agent's causation consist of? What, for example, is the difference between A's just happening, and the agent's *causing* A to happen? We cannot attribute the difference to any event that took place within the agent. And so far as the event A itself is concerned, there would seem to be no discernible difference—no discernible difference between A just happening and the agent causing A to happen. Thus Aristotle said that the activity of the prime mover is nothing in addition to the motion that it produces, and Suarez said that "the action is in reality nothing but the effect as it flows from the agent." Must we conclude, then, that there is no more to the man's action in causing event A than there is to the event A's happening by itself? Here we would seem to have a distinction without a difference—in which case we have failed to find a *via media* between a deterministic and an indeterministic view of action.

The only answer, I think, can be this: that the difference between the man's causing A, on the one hand, and the event A just happening, on the other, lies in the fact that, in the first case but not the second, the event A *was* caused and was caused by the man. There was a brain event A; the agent did, in fact, cause the brain event; but there was nothing that he did to cause it.

This answer may not entirely satisfy and it will be likely to provoke the following question: "But what are you really *adding* to the assertion that A happened when you utter the words 'The agent *caused* A to happen'?" As soon as we have put the question this way, we see, I think, that whatever difficulty we may have encountered is one that may be traced to the concept of causation generally—whether "immanent" or "transeunt." The problem, in other words, is not a problem that is peculiar to our conception of human action. It is a problem that must be faced by anyone who makes use of the concept of causation at all and therefore, I would say, it is a problem for everyone but the complete indeterminist.

For the problem, as we put it, referring just to "immanent causation," or causation by an agent, was this: "What is the difference between saying, of an event A, that A just happened and saying that someone caused A to happen?" The analogous problem, which holds for "transeunt causation," or causation by an event, is this: "What is the difference between saying, of two events A and B, that B happened and then A happened, and saying that B's happening was the *cause* of A's happening?" And the only answer that one can give is this—that in the one case the agent was the cause of A's happening, and in the other case event B was the cause of A's happening. The nature of transeunt causation is no more clear than is that of immanent causation. In short, as long as we talk about causation at all (and we cannot avoid it) the difficulty is one that we will have on our hands. It is not a difficulty that is peculiar, therefore, to our treatment of the problem of freedom.

But we may plausibly say—and there is a respectable philosophical tradition to which we may appeal—that the notion of immanent causation, or causation by an agent, is in fact more clear than that of transeunt causation, or causation by an event, and that it is only by understanding our own causal efficacy, as agents, that we can grasp the concept of *cause* at all. Hume may be said to have shown that we do not derive the concept of *cause* from what we perceive of external things. How, then, do we derive it? The most plausible suggestion, it seems to me, is that of Reid, once again: namely, that "the conception of an efficient cause may very probably be derived from the experience we have had . . . of our own power to produce certain effects." If we did not understand the concept of immanent causation, we would not understand that of transeunt causation.

It may have been noted that I have avoided the term "free will" in all of this. For even if there is such a faculty as "the will," which somehow sets our acts a-going, the question of freedom, as John Locke said, is not "the question whether the will be free"; it is the question "whether a man be free." For if there is a "will," as a moving faculty, the question is whether the man is free to will to do those things that he does will to do—and also whether he is free *not* to will any of those things that he does will to do, and, again, whether he is free to will any of those things that he does not will to do. Jonathan Edwards tried to restrict himself to the question—"Is the man free to do what it is that he wills?"—but the answer to this question will not tell us whether the man is responsible for what it is that he *does* will to do. Using still another pair of medieval terms, we may say that the metaphysical problem of freedom does not concern the *actus imperatus:* it does not concern the question whether we are free to accomplish whatever it is that we will or set out to do; it concerns the *actus elicitus,* the question whether we are free to will or to set out to do those things that we will or set out to do. It is one thing to ask whether the things that a man wills are things that are within his power: this is the problem of the *actus imperatus.* It is quite a different thing to ask whether his willing itself is something that is within his power: this is the problem of the *actus elicitus.* And this latter—the problem of the *actus elicitus*—is the problem, not of the freedom of the will, but of the freedom of the man.

If we are responsible, and if what I have been trying to say is true, then we have a prerogative which some would attribute only to God: each of us, when we act, is a prime mover unmoved. In doing what we do, we cause certain events to happen, and nothing—or no one—causes us to cause those events to happen.

If we are thus prime movers unmoved and if our actions, or those for which we are responsible, are not causally determined, then they are not causally determined by our *desires.* And this means that the relation between what we want or what we desire, on the one hand, and what it is that we do, on the other, is not as simple as most philosophers would have it.

We may distinguish between what we might call the "Hobbist approach" and what we might call the "Kantian approach" to this question. The Hobbist approach is the one that is generally accepted at the present time, but the Kantian approach, I believe, is the one that is true. According to Hobbism, if we *know,* of some man, what his beliefs and desires happen to be and how strong they are, if we know what he feels certain of, what he desires more than anything else, and if we know the state of his body and what stimuli he is being subjected to, then we may *deduce,* logically, just what it is that he will do—or, more accurately, just what it is that he will try, set out, or undertake to do. Thus Professor Melden has said that "the connection between wanting and doing is logical."

But according to the Kantian approach to our problem, and this is the one that I would take, there is no such logical connection between wanting and doing, nor need there even be a causal connection. No set of statements about a man's desires, beliefs, and stimulus situation at any time implies any statement, telling us what the man will try, set out, or undertake to do at that time. As Reid put it, "Though we may reason from men's motives to their actions and, in many cases, with great probability," we can never do so "with absolute certainty."

This means that, in one very strict sense of the terms, there can be no complete science of man. If we think of science as a matter of finding out what laws happen to hold, and if the statement of a law tells us what kinds of events are caused by what other kinds of events, then there will be human actions that we cannot explain by subsuming them under any laws. We cannot say, "It is causally necessary that, given such and such desires and beliefs, and being subject to such and such stimuli, the agent will do so and so." For at times the agent, if he chooses, may rise above his desires and do something else instead.

But all of this is consistent with saying that, perhaps more often than not, our desires do exist under conditions such that those conditions necessitate us to act. And we may also say, with Leibniz, that at other times our desires may "incline without necessitating."

Leibniz's phrase presents us with still another philosophical problem. What does it mean to say that a desire, or a motive, might "incline without necessitating"? There is a temptation, certainly, to say that "to incline" means to cause and that "not to necessitate" means not to cause, but obviously we cannot have it both ways.

Nor will Leibniz's own solution do. In his letter to Coste, he puts the problem as follows: "When a choice is proposed, for example to go out or not to go out, it is a question whether, with all the circumstances, internal and external, motives, perceptions dispositions, impressions, passions, inclinations taken together, I am still in a contingent state, or whether I am necessitated to make the choice, for example, to go out; that is to say, whether this proposition, true and determined in fact, *In all these circumstances taken together I shall choose to go out,* is contingent or necessary." Leibniz's answer might be put as follows: in one sense of the terms "necessary" and "contingent," the proposition "In all these circumstances taken together I shall choose to go out," may be said to be contingent and not necessary, and in another sense of these terms, it may be said to be necessary, and not contingent. But the sense in which the proposition may be said to be contingent, according to Leibniz, is only this: there is no logical contradiction involved in denying the proposition. And the sense in which it may be said to be necessary is this: since "nothing ever occurs without cause of determining reason," the proposition is causally necessary. "Whenever all the circumstances taken together are such that, the balance of deliberation is heavier on one side than on the other, it is certain and infallible that that is the side that is going to win out." But if what we have been saying is true, the proposition "In all these circumstances taken together I shall choose to go out" may be causally as well as logically contingent. Hence we must find another interpretation for Leibniz's statement that our motives and desires may incline us, or influence us, to choose without thereby necessitating us to choose.

Let us consider a public official who has some moral scruples but who also, as one says, "could be had." Because of the scruples that he does have, he would never take any positive steps to receive a bribe—he would not actively solicit one. But morality has its limits and he is also such that, if we were to confront him with a *fait accompli* or to let him see what is about to happen ($10,000 in cash is being deposited behind the garage), then he would succumb and be unable to resist. The general situation is a familiar one and this is one reason that people pray to be delivered from temptation. (And it also justifies Kant's remark: "How many there are who may have led a long blameless life, who are only *fortunate* in having escaped so many temptations.") Our relation to the misdeed that we contemplate may not be a matter simply of our being able to bring it about or not to bring it about. As St. Anselm noted, there are at least four possibilities. We may illustrate them, by reference to our public official and the event which is his receiving the bribe, in the following way: (i) he may be able to bring the event about himself *(facere esse)*, in which case he would actively cause himself to receive the bribe; (ii) he may be able to refrain from bringing it about himself *(non facere esse)*, in which case he would not himself do anything to insure that he receive the bribe; (iii) he may be able to do something to prevent the event from occurring *(facere non esse)*, in which case he would make sure that the $10,000 was *not* left behind the garage; or (iv) he may be unable to do anything to prevent the event from occurring *(non facere non esse)*, in which case, though he may not solicit the bribe, he would allow himself to keep it. We have envisaged our official as a man who can resist the temptation to (i) but cannot resist the temptation to (iv): he can refrain from bringing the event about himself, but he cannot bring himself to do anything to prevent it.

Let us think of "inclination without necessitation," then, in such terms as these. First we may contrast the two propositions:

(1) He can resist the temptation to do something in order to make A happen;

(2) He can resist the temptation to allow A to happen (i.e., to do nothing to prevent A from happening).

We may suppose that the man has some desire to have A happen and thus has a motive for making A happen. His motive for making A happen, I suggest, is one that *necessitates,* provided that, because of the motive, (1) is false: he cannot resist the temptation to do something in order to make A happen. His motive for making A happen is one that *inclines,* provided that, because of the motive, (2) is false: like our public official, he cannot bring himself to do anything to prevent A from happening. And therefore we can say that his motive for making A happen is one that *inclines* but does not *necessitate,* provided that, because of the motive, (1) is true and (2) is false; he can resist the temptation to make it happen but he cannot resist the temptation to allow it to happen.

Let us now consider the concept of an act, or a deed, in more detail.

II

The concept of an act, or a deed, is both imputative and descriptive. When we say of a man that he *did* something, we may be declaring, by way of imputation, that the man is to be held responsible for making a certain thing happen; that is to say, we may be pronouncing a verdict, notifying our hearers that forthwith we are holding this man responsible. But we are also making a descriptive statement; we are saying that the man was a causal factor in making something happen, or in keeping something from happening. Let us now try to lay bare this descriptive element in the concept of an act, stripping from it all implications of moral and legal responsibility. The point of doing this is to throw light upon the interrelations among several important and perplexing concepts and to contribute toward the solution of certain additional philosophical puzzles.

H. L. A. Hart has suggested that the descriptive facts we presuppose in applying our action concepts might consist simply of facts about the state of the agent's body and what it causes or fails to cause ("His arm went up and knocked over the lamp" as distinguished from "He knocked over the lamp with his arm"). But this suggestion, it seems to me, is clearly mistaken. If we ask ourselves, for example, "What facts, in the absence of defeating considerations, would warrant our saying that one man has killed another?" we will find, I think, that these facts cannot be described merely by reference to what is caused by some state of the agent's body; similarly for some, at least, of those facts that would defeat the ascription of killing.

What more is there, then, to the concept of an act? First, there is the fact that the agent himself, as we have seen, is a causal factor. We must say that at least one of the events that is involved in any act is caused, not by any other event, but by the agent, by the man. Causation is a relation that holds, not only between states or events, but also between agents, as causes, and states or events, as effects. And, secondly, there is the fact that the concept of an act is essentially teleological. Action involves *endeavor* or *purpose,* one thing occurring *in order that* some other thing may occur. And this concept of endeavor, or purpose, must be distinguished from that of *want* or *desire.* A man may endeavor, or undertake, to bring about what he does not desire and what he does not even believe to be a means to anything that he desires; and he may refrain from undertaking to bring about what he does desire.

Some philosophers, however, have attempted to define purpose, or endeavor, in terms of belief, causation, and desire. It has been suggested, for example, that a man might be said to bring about something X *for the purpose of* bringing about something Y, provided that the following three conditions hold: (i) he desires Y; (ii) he believes that, if he brings about X, then he will bring about Y; and (iii) this belief and desire jointly cause him to bring about X. But this type of definition is too broad and does not in fact capture the concept of purpose. Suppose, for example: (i) a certain man desires to inherit a fortune; (ii) he believes that, if he kills his uncle, then he will inherit a fortune; and (iii) this belief and this desire agitate him so severely that he drives excessively fast, with the result that he accidentally runs over and kills a pedestrian who, unknown to the nephew, was none other than the uncle. The proposed definition of purpose would require us to say, incorrectly, that the nephew killed the uncle in order to inherit the fortune.

Let us attempt to set forth the descriptive element in the concept of action by an undefined locution, one indicating both that the agent is a cause and that the action is purposive or teleological. I propose the following:

> There is a state of affairs A and a state of affairs B, such that, at time *t,* he makes B happen in the endeavor to make A happen.

As an alternative for the English expression, "He makes B happen," we might use "He realizes B," "He brings it about that B," or, if "state of affairs" is replaced by "proposition," then "He makes it true that B." The letters may be replaced, in obvious ways, by propositional clauses. The relation of "making happen" is transitive and asymmetrical: if A makes B happen, then B does not make A happen. The states of affairs to which our locution refers may be "unchanges" as well as changes; they may also be complex (e.g., "He makes B happen with an end to making it happen that A and that A makes C happen"). And the subject term of "makes happen" may designate either a state of affairs or a person.

"Make happen" is to be taken in such a way that we may say, of a man who raises his arm, not only that he makes it happen that his arm goes up, but also that he makes it happen, just before, that certain other physiological events occur inside his body, and that he makes it happen, just subsequently, that air particles move in various ways.

The teleological component of our locution (viz., "in the endeavor to make A happen") should be taken as intentional. This means, for example, that a man may make something happen in the endeavor to make A happen without thereby actually making A happen. It also means that, from "He made something happen in the endeavor to make A happen and he did thereby make A happen" and "A is the same concrete event as B," we may not infer "He made something happen in the endeavor to make B happen." And it also means that, if a man makes something B happen in the endeavor to make something A happen, then he can *know,* directly or immediately, that he is making something happen in the endeavor to make A happen, but, as the example from the previous paragraph will indicate, he may not know at all that he is making B happen.

Since we are attempting to describe *action* in terms of *making happen*—or, more accurately, in terms of making things happen *in the endeavor* to make things happen—the "A's" and "B's" of our formulae will not normally be replaceable by expressions which themselves refer to actions. If I am right, the man who raises his arm under ordinary circumstances will make something happen in the endeavor to make it happen, *not* that he raises his arm, but that his arm goes up. (But the paralytic, in the course of his exercises, may make things happen now in the endeavor to make it happen that later he raises his arm.) To act, therefore, is to endeavor to make happen. But from this it does not follow that when a man acts he therefore endeavors to act. What the liar endeavors to do, for example, is not to *lie,* but to make it happen that his hearers are deceived.

SOFT DETERMINISM

Simon Blackburn

The argument for hard determinism does not talk of the *kinds* of causal influences in play as an agent performs a given action. Now sometimes the causal routes are totally independent of what we think. The causal route that leads from my being irreversibly under water to my drowning is one of them. The same outcome is inevitable for Einstein and for a donkey. But sometimes the causal routes only go via high-level neural processes. This is no more than to say that we often move as we do because our brains are functioning properly.

So let us try a primitive model. Think of the brain in "software" terms, as having various "modules." One (a "scanner") takes in information about a situation. Another (a "tree producer") delivers options for behaviour in the light of what the scanner says. A third (an "evaluator") ranks the options in the light of concerns that it has programmed into it. It may work by attaching emotional indicators such as fear or joy to the different paths. Finally a fourth (a "producer") fixes on the option ranked best by the preceding processes, and outputs neural signals that move muscles and limbs. Here is a schematic diagram:

Remember that all this is supposed to be just a "software" description of parts of the brain. Now suppose a decision is the upshot of these modules functioning. Suppose it is one of your decisions, and these parts function to produce it in the way that they normally do. If we call these modules, "decision" modules, and if these modules are engaged in producing the output, then we can say that *you* chose the output. It was not forced on you, in the way that drowning is forced on the trapped swimmer.

Suppose the decision was to do something really bad. You come into my room, and chuck my peaceable old dog out of the window. I am outraged, and minded to blame you. Suppose you try to defend yourself by invoking the incompatibilist argument.

> Look, this action was the result of the way my scanner/producer system had been "set." Perhaps events in my childhood, quite outside my control, "set it" so that making the environment dog-free has for me the highest priority.

My tree producer told me it was an option, after my scanner had told me that there was a dog present and a window nearby. My evaluator immediately selected that option, and my producer smoothly initiated the action of chucking the dog out of the window. Why blame me?

Surely I am not likely to be very impressed. I might reply something like this:

I am not all that interested in how you came to be "set" like you are. What bothers me is that this *is* your set. I don't care how it came to be your set, or what deterministic forces brought you to have these systems set that way. All I am concerned about is that now, at the end of the day, you are a nasty piece of work, and I am going to thump you. Maybe it was indeed bad luck your getting to be like you are. And now it is doubly bad luck, because you are going to get thumped for it.

At least I have the consolation that, following your own argument, you cannot blame me for thumping you! It's just the way I am set: I react badly to people who do this to my peaceable old dog.

Thumping you may have a point—in fact, several points. It might readjust your evaluator. Next time round, this module may rank throwing the dog out of the window below putting up with its presence. In a more complex picture, we could imagine this happening by means of a number of other mechanisms: perhaps it attaches a risk-of-being-thumped flag to the dog-throwing option. Or perhaps my anger shocks you into a more general re-evaluation of strategies of behaviour. And even if thumping you does not succeed in changing you, it sends a signal to other would-be dog-chuckers. It also relieves my feelings.

This is different from blaming someone for drowning, while not blaming him or her for being trapped in the water. The causal route there lies through basic animal physiology that cannot be altered by education or the attitudes of others. Praise and blame cannot "reset" it. The causal route does not lie through modules that are *elastic,* or flexible, capable of being reset by anger or blame. But dog-throwers can be deterred and changed and warned away.

Schoolteachers sometimes say things like this: "I don't mind a stupid pupil, but I do dislike a lazy one." In the grip of the hard determinist argument, you might think that this is just prejudice: some people are born stupid and pitied for it; why should those born lazy not be similarly pitied for that? It is just tough luck, either way. But the schoolteacher's attitude will have a point if laziness responds to incentives in a way that stupidity does not. If respect for the teacher's opinion can make you work harder, whereas it cannot make you smarter, then there is one justification for the asymmetry. The teacher is in the business of resetting your evaluating module. It is an empirical fact, a fact to be learned from human experience, how far modules do get reset by interactions with others, including the unpleasant ones in which the others display their anger or contempt for us.

We have here the beginning—but only the beginning—of the programme of *compatibilism,* or the attempt to show that, properly understood, there is no inconsistency between acknowledging determinism and our practices of holding people responsible for their actions. Compatibilism is sometimes called "soft" determinism, in opposition to "hard" determinism. This is not a very good label for two reasons. First, it is not really a different kind of determinism. It accepts determinism in just the same sense as anybody else. There is no ghostly power stepping in to interfere with the natural causal order of events. Second, in moral or political terms, the "soft" determinist may actually be pretty hard, in the sense of harsh. If you come to her with the heartrending excuse that your biology or your environment made you the way you are, she turns deaf, and vents her anger on you just the same. Not for her the facile equation between crime and illness: people can pull their socks up, and if it seems appropriate, she will use punishment or any other appropriate reaction to make you do so too.

Of course, a compatibilist can accept some kinds of excuse. If you were constrained in some situation so that no matter how well-functioning your "modules," no good upshot was possible, then you are not to blame for events. This is the case of the drowning swimmer: no matter how good their character, there is nothing they can do about it. Equally, if an action is quite "out of character," for instance, because you have had to take some medications whose result is to disorientate you or depress you, then perhaps you can be forgiven, when you are yourself again.

We might think at this point: well, the reaction to the villainous dog-thrower was natural enough. Perhaps it is even justifiable in terms of its *consequences*. Perhaps blame and associated reactions have a function, and we just need things with that function. But all the same, isn't there a hint of injustice? Because we have done nothing to show that the dog-chucker *could have done otherwise*. For on any occasion, the modules will be set one way or another, so the outcome is determined. Compatibilists, so far, seem to blame someone for events, when the person could not have done otherwise. To this they may reply by distinguishing different senses of "could have done otherwise." If the causal route to the agent's action lay through the decision modules, then she "could have done otherwise" in some sense, and may be regarded as being free. To get at the right sense of "could have done otherwise," we might offer what I shall call the *first compatibilist definition:*

> A subject acted freely if she could have done otherwise in the right sense. The subject could have done otherwise in this sense provided she *would* have done otherwise *if* she had chosen differently.

And, says the compatibilist, that is all that is needed to justify our reactions of holding people responsible, and perhaps reacting to them with blame and anger.

The ghostly response to determinism posited a kind of intervention from *outside* the realm of nature: a "contra-causal" freedom, in which the ghost is distinct from the causal order of nature, yet mysteriously able to alter that order. We could call that conception, *interventionist* control. It is sometimes known in the literature as a *libertarian* conception of freedom, although this is confusing, since it has nothing to do with political or economic libertarianism, which is the ideology of free markets and minimal government. I shall stick with calling it interventionist control. Compatibilism on the other hand substitutes a view of you as entirely situated *inside* the causal order of nature. Your freedom lies in the way action flows out of your cognitive processes. So how does the compatibilist respond to the original argument about control? He might suggest that the argument is no better than this:

> The past controls the present and future.
> A thermostat cannot control the past.
> A thermostat cannot control the way in which the past controls the present and future.
> *So,* a thermostat cannot control the future.

There has to be something wrong with this, because a thermostat *can* control the future, in respect of temperature. That is what thermostats do. A thermostat controls the temperature by being *part of the way* in which the past controls the present and future. And according to compatibilism, that is how we control things. We are involved in the causal order. We are part of the way in which the past controls the future. And therein lies our responsibility. We can call this conception of control, *inside* control, control from inside nature. When we exercise inside control, the compatibilist holds, we are responsible for various events. And if we exercise that control badly, we may justly be held responsible for the upshot, and held to blame if blame is an appropriate reaction.

But is this compatibilist freedom what we really wanted? We do not attribute any freedom to the thermostat. And compatibilism can seem more like a dismissal of the problem of freedom, rather than a solution of it. This is how it seemed to the great Immanuel Kant (1724–1804), who dismissed it as giving us only the "freedom of clockwork" and called it nothing better than a "wretched subterfuge."

PUPPETS AND MARTIANS

Here is another way of sharing Kant's worries. The modules and complexities of information processing complicated the causal picture. But do they alter it fundamentally? Imagine counsel for the fig tree, pointing out that it was winter rather than summer. This is a complete defence of the tree. Well, if I acted badly, then does not that show that it was winter too? The modules had been badly set, presumably by events belonging to causal chains that stretch back before my birth. It may be that if you are angry with me that will alter my decision-making system *for the future,* but it does not show that I could have acted differently *in the past.*

As we come to learn about causal regularities lying behind actions and other mental states, we are apt to switch into less moralistic modes. We might blame someone for being depressed all the time, until we learn a chemical story explaining it. We might be angry with someone for being unable to stir himself, until we learn that he has mononucleosis. But according to the determinist, there are *always* things like this to learn. Quite apart from increasing neurophysiological evidence, we may think of cases where we learn of "brain-washing" or "conditioning." Parents may be inclined to blame their teenage daughter for spending time, energy, and income on valueless cosmetics, but a better reaction would be to understand the social and commercial pressures that paralyse her better judgement and bring this state of affairs about.

Things get worse for compatibilism if we indulge in a little science fiction. Imagine the invasion of the mini-Martians. These are incredibly small, organized, and mischievous beings: small enough to invade our brains and walk around in them. If they do so, they can set our modules pretty well at will. We become puppets in their hands. (If this kind of example sounds too far-fetched, reflect that there actually exists a parasite that lives by coloniz-ing the brains of ants. Under its influence, the ant climbs blades of grass. This makes it more likely to be ingested by passing sheep, which the parasite then infects [the particular individual in the ant's brain itself perishes, but others hitch-hike]. For all one knows, the ant feels free as air as it climbs its blade of grass.) Of course, the mini-Martians might set us to do what we would have done anyhow. But they might throw the chemical switches so that we do quite terrible things. Then let us suppose that, fortunately, science invents a scan to detect whether the Martians have invaded us. Won't we be sympathetic to anyone who suffered this misfortune? Wouldn't we immediately recognize that he was not responsible for his wrongdoings?

But, says the incompatibilist, why does it make a difference if it was mini-Martians, or causal agencies of a more natural kind?

This kind of reply takes issue with the compatibilist version of "could not have done otherwise." It is all very well, it points out, to say that some-one would have done otherwise if he or she had chosen differently. But sup-pose they were set so that they *could not* have chosen differently. Suppose at the time of acting, their choosing modules were locked into place by mini-Martians, or chemicals, or whatever. What then? The compatibilist we have so far shrugs the question off—he is not interested in how the subjects got to be as they are, only whether the outcome is good or bad. The objector finds it important, and at least some of our reactions, when we find more about causal routes, show that we agree with the objector.

OBSESSIONS AND TWINKIES

I think the best line for compatibilism, faced with this counterattack, is to query the word "set," when there is talk of the modules being set to produce some outcome. This in effect repeats a similar move to the one he made to distinguish decision-making from drowning. There, he introduced a degree of flexibility into the causal process, by highlighting modules that are capable of being tuned or set differently. When the objector claims that in that case the subject is a mere victim if the modules are "set" wrong, the reply ought to be to introduce another level of flexibility. True, we can say, in the case of the brainwashed teenager, or the mini-Martians, the modules may really be set. We are imagining the modules badly *fixed* by chemical or other processes. But these cases are special, precisely because once they are in them subjects become inflexible: immune to argument, or to additions or changes in the decision-making scenario. But normally agents are not *so* set in their ways. Their freedom consists in the fact that they are responsive to new information, and new differences in the situation. They are not driven or bound to chuck dogs out of windows or to stand all day at the cosmetics counter.

We might pursue the idea with something like this, that I shall call the *revised compatibilist definition:*

> The subject acted freely if she could have done otherwise in the right sense. This means that she would have done otherwise if she had chosen differently *and,* under the impact of other thoughts or considerations, she *would* have chosen differently.

Of course, on an occasion, it may have been bad *luck* that the right thoughts did not arise. Well, says the compatibilist once more, that is indeed bad luck. But perhaps my anger and the fact that I am going to thump you will prevent it recurring.

Some philosophers (Baruch Spinoza [1632–77] is the most famous example) like to associate freedom with increased knowledge and understanding. We are free, they say, in so far as we understand things. This is in many ways an attractive idea: it ties freedom of the will to things like political freedoms: freedom of information and freedom of speech. We are only free in so far as we have opportunities open to us, and lack of information denies us opportunities. We could add this thought to the revised compatibilist definition, by specifying that the "other thoughts or considerations," first, are accurate representations of the agent's situation and options, and second, are *available* to the agent. That is, it is not much use saying that under the impact of other thoughts or considerations she would have chosen differently, if those other thoughts and considerations were simply not in the landscape. Thus, suppose I set about to poison you and cunningly put arsenic in your coffee. You drink it. It is not much use saying that you were free not to do so. For although it is true that you would have avoided the coffee if you had chosen differently, and true that the thought or consideration that perhaps the coffee was laced with arsenic would have made you choose differently, nevertheless, since there was no reason for that thought to enter your mind, you were a victim rather than a free agent. We might incorporate that into a revised revised compatibilist definition:

> The subject acted freely if she could have done otherwise in the right sense. This means that she would have done otherwise if she had chosen differently *and,* under the impact of other *true and available* thoughts or considerations, she *would* have chosen differently. True and available thoughts and considerations are those that represent her situation accurately, and are ones that she could reasonably be expected to have taken into account.

What of the person to whom the thoughts or considerations just didn't occur? Is she a victim rather than a responsible agent? This introduces a new twist to things.

So far we have talked as if "free choice," either of some mysterious interventionist kind or of some substitute "inside" or compatibilist kind, is necessary for responsibility. But is this right? I said above that it might be just bad luck that some crucial consideration does not occur to someone at a moment of decision. But sometimes we do not treat it as "mere" bad luck. We say that the thought *should* have arisen. The agent is liable to censure if it didn't. Someone setting fire to buildings for fun cannot seriously plead that "it never occurred to him" that someone might get hurt—not unless he is a child or mentally deficient. Even if it is true that it never occurred to him, so there was no free choice to put people at risk, he is still responsible. Recklessness and negligence are faults, and we can be held responsible for them, just as much as we are for more controlled decisions. Some philosophers have found it hard to accept that. Aristotle rather desperately held that negligent people have actually chosen to make themselves negligent, perhaps in early childhood, and that this is the only reason they can be held responsible.

There is actually a whole range of interesting thoughts that open up here. Some kinds of bad luck are really incidental: things that do not affect our relationship to the agent. But others in some way cast a reflection on the agent. Imagine a golfer. Suppose on day one he hits a fine ball, but, amazingly, a passing seagull gets in its way and spoils the shot. Then on day two he hits an equally fine ball, but a little breeze blows it off course and again spoils the shot. We might say each of these is bad luck. The first is pure bad luck. But the second is not quite so simple. It is bad luck, yes, but the kind of bad luck that a really good golfer is expected to foresee and play around. It should be within the player's purview. Whereas the seagull represents a pure act of God. Enough bad luck of the second kind, and we start to think less well of the golfer, and it is the same with agency. Hence the reply made by a pianist whose admirer gushed about how lucky he was to have so much talent: "Yes, and the more I practice the luckier I get."

The conceptual engineering we are doing at this point is supposed to tease out or make explicit real elements in our thinking. We want to highlight and try to encapsulate things like this: we do make a distinction between changing the past (cannot do) and acting differently than we do (sometimes can do); we do have discriminating practices of blame; we do make a distinction between being ill and being bad; we do allow some excuses and disallow others. The philosophical analysis is supposed to give us intellectual control of all this. It is supposed to exhibit it all, not just as an irrational jumble of disconnected habits, but as the application of a reasonable and defensible set of concepts and principles. It is because it is hard to do this that the philosophy is hard. The compatibilist account is a piece of engineering, either plotting our extant concepts, or designing improved ones. It has to answer to the ways we often think, or think when we are best in control of the problems that face us. Myself, I believe that the revised revised compatibilist definition does that pretty well. But others take Kant's objection more seriously. They think that our "interpersonal reactions," which include the ways we hold each other and ourselves responsible for things, do depend upon some lingering affection for interventionist freedom. So if that is metaphysically bankrupt, our attitudes ought to change. The philosophical problem would be that interventionist control is untenable, and inside control inadequate.

Sometimes an analysis will settle hard cases. But sometimes it leaves grey areas, and this may not be a bad thing. Return to the teenage girl spending an incredible amount of time and money on cosmetics. Can she do otherwise? If we run the revised revised definition, we may find that the issue hinges now on what other thoughts and considerations are "available" to her. In one sense, we might want to say, it is possible that she should start realizing that her popularity or attractiveness is not greatly improved by cosmetics (it would increase more if she got a decent mind, perhaps by reading a book like this). This may be a true and potentially available thought. But in another sense, perhaps it is not. Perhaps people subjected to the influences she is subjected to just cannot get themselves to believe this. The culture is awfully good at blinding teenagers to this truth. So it would not be reasonable to expect her to believe it. Myself, I would incline to this diagnosis, seeing her as a victim rather than an agent. But the point is that even if the revised revised analysis does not *settle* this issue, it certainly *pinpoints* it. And this is itself a step towards getting the issue of responsibility and freedom under control. But it must in fairness be added that there is still a road to travel. An incompatibilist, for instance, might insist that thoughts are only available if they are themselves the objects of free (interventionist) selection, and this would put us back to square one.

Contemporary culture is not very good on responsibility. Consider the notorious "Twinkie defence." One day in 1978, an ex-employee of the city of San Francisco, Dan White, entered the City Hall with a gun, evading metal detectors by going through a basement window. He went upstairs, and shot and killed Mayor George Moscone and a supervisor, Harvey Milk. In court a defence psychiatrist, Martin Blinder, testified that White had been depressed, which led to his eating too much, and in particular the high-sugar junk food known as Twinkies. According to Blinder, this further deepened his depression, since White was an ex-athlete and knew that Twinkies were not good for him. Blinder claimed that the emotional state White would have got into would have meant it was impossible to have acted with premeditation or real intent, both of which were necessary conditions for first-degree murder. The jury were impressed by the argument, and acquitted White of murder, finding him guilty instead of the lesser crime of "voluntary manslaughter."

California later revised its law to close the space for this kind of defence, and on the face of it the state was right to do so. White *obviously* acted with intention and premeditation, since that is why he procured a gun and went in through the basement. And we can see that the revised revised analysis is not at all hospitable to the Twinkie defence. A defendant would have to work awfully hard to show that enough sugar literally takes our behaviour out of the range of our decision-making modules and our thoughts. It does not seem to be true that with enough Twinkies inside us we become literally incapable of certain thoughts, so that we could not reasonably be expected to realize that murdering people is a bad idea, for example. Even a lot of sugar does not tend to do that. (But then, contemporary juries are not very good on causation either. In Michigan recently a man won a lawsuit for substantial damages because, he claimed, a rear-end collision in his car had made him a homosexual.)

Before leaving compatibilism, it is worth noticing a difficulty in front of all the definitions. Compatibilism tries to generate the right notion of control out of the reflection that under different circumstances the agent *would* have done otherwise. There are nasty cases that suggest that these notions do not fit together quite so tightly. These are called "causal overdetermination" cases. In such a case something does control some outcome, although the outcome would have been the same anyway because of a "fail-safe" mechanism. Thus, a thermostat might control the temperature even if, because of a fail-safe mechanism, the temperature *would* have been the same even *if* the thermostat had malfunctioned. If the thermostat had malfunctioned, something else would have clicked in to keep the temperature at its proper level. Similarly an agent might do something bad, be in control, be acting with intent and responsibility, even if *were* he to choose to do otherwise unknown mechanisms would click in to ensure that he does the bad thing anyhow. Imagine the mini-Martians sitting there not actually interfering with things, but ready to do so whenever the outcome looks set to be one that they don't want. These cases are surprisingly tricky to handle. But the compatibilist can reflect that they make it no harder to define the right sense of control for human beings than they do for thermostats. Since the problem must have a solution in the case of mechanical control, it must have one for people as well.

HARD AND SOFT DETERMINISM
Susan Wolf

In order for a person to be morally responsible, two conditions must be satisfied. First, he must be a free agent—an agent, that is, whose actions are under his own control. For if the actions he performs are not up to him to decide, he deserves no credit or discredit for doing what he does. Second, he must be a moral agent—an agent, that is, to whom moral claims apply. For if the actions he performs can be neither right nor wrong, then there is nothing to credit or discredit him with. I shall call the first condition, *the condition of freedom,* and the second, *the condition of value.* Those who fear that the first condition can never be met worry about the problem of free will. Those who fear that the second condition can never be met worry about the problem of moral skepticism. Many people believe that the condition of value is dependent on the condition of freedom—that moral prescriptions make sense only if the concept of free will is coherent. In what follows, I shall argue that the converse is true—that the condition of freedom depends on the condition of value. Our doubts about the existence of true moral values, however, will have to be left aside.

I shall say that an agent's action is *psychologically determined* if his action is determined by his interests—that is, his values or desires—and his interests are determined by his heredity or environment. If all our actions are so determined, then the thesis of psychological determinism is true. This description is admittedly crude and simplistic. A more plausible description of psychological determination will include among possible determining factors a wider range of psychological states. There are, for example, some beliefs and emotions which cannot be analyzed as values or desires and which clearly play a role in the psychological explanations of why we act as we do. For my purposes, however, it will be easier to leave the description of psychological determinism uncluttered. The context should be sufficient to make the intended application understood.

Many people believe that if psychological determinism is true, the condition of freedom can never be satisfied. For if an agent's interests are determined by heredity and environment, they claim, it is not up to the agent to have the interests he has. And if his actions are determined by his interests as well, then he cannot but perform the actions he performs. In order for an agent to satisfy the condition of freedom, then, his actions must not be psy-

Susan Wolf. "Hard and Soft Determinism." From the *Journal of Philosophy* LXXVII 3 (March 1980). Reprinted by permission of the author and publisher.

chologically determined. Either his actions must not be determined by his interests, or his interests must not be determined by anything external to himself. They therefore conclude that the condition of freedom requires the absence of psychological determinism. And they think this is what we mean to express when we state the condition of freedom in terms of the requirement that the agent "could have done otherwise."

Let us imagine, however, what an agent who satisfied this condition would have to be like. Consider first what it would mean for the agent's actions not to be determined by his interests—for the agent, in other words, to have the ability to act despite his interests. This would mean, I think, that the agent has the ability to act against everything he cares about. It would mean, for example, that if the agent's son were inside a burning building, the agent could just stand there and watch the house go up in flames. Or that the agent, though he thinks his neighbor a fine and agreeable fellow, could just go up one day, ring the doorbell, and punch him in the nose. One might think such pieces of behavior should not be classified as actions at all—that they are rather more like spasms that the agent cannot control. If they are actions, at least, they are very bizarre, and an agent who performed them would have to be insane. Indeed, one might think he would have to be insane if he had even the ability to perform them. For the rationality of an agent who could perform such irrational actions as these must be hung by a dangerously thin thread.

So let us assume that his actions are determined by his interests, but that his interests are not determined by anything external to himself. Then of any of the interests he happens to have, it must be the case that he does not have to have them. Though perhaps he loves his wife, it must be possible for him not to love her. Though perhaps he cares about people in general, it must be possible for him not to care. This agent, moreover, could not have reasons for his interests—at least no reasons of the sort we normally have. He cannot love his wife, for example, because of the way his wife is—for the way his wife is is not up to him to decide. Such an agent, presumably, could not be much committed to anything; his interests must be something like a matter of whim. Such an agent must be able not to care about the lives of others, and, I suppose, he must be able not to care about his own life as well. An agent who didn't care about these things, one might think, would have to be crazy. And again, one might think he would have to be crazy if he had even the ability not to care.

In any case, it seems, if we require an agent to be psychologically undetermined, we cannot expect him to be a moral agent. For if we require that his actions not be determined by his interests, then *a fortiori* they cannot be determined by his moral interests. And if we require that his interests not be determined by anything else, then *a fortiori* they cannot be determined by his moral reasons.

When we imagine an agent who performs right actions, it seems, we imagine an agent who is rightly determined: whose actions, that is, are determined by the right sorts of interests, and whose interests are determined by the right sorts of reasons. But an agent who is not psychologically determined cannot perform actions that are right in this way. And if his actions can never be appropriately right, then in not performing right actions, he can never be wrong. The problem seems to be that the undetermined agent is so free as to be free *from moral reasons.* So the satisfaction of the condition of freedom seems to rule out the satisfaction of the condition of value.

This suggests that the condition of freedom was previously stated too strongly. When we require that a responsible agent "could have done otherwise" we cannot mean that it was determined that he did what he did. It has been proposed that "he could have done otherwise" should be analyzed as a conditional instead. For example, we might say that "he could have done otherwise" means that he would have done otherwise, if he had tried. Thus the bank robber is responsible for robbing the bank, since he would have restrained himself if he had tried. But the man he locked up is not responsible for letting him escape, since he couldn't have stopped him even if he had tried.

Incompatibilists, however, will quickly point out that such an analysis is insufficient. For an agent who would have done otherwise if he had tried cannot be blamed for his action if he could not have tried. The compatibilist might try to answer this objection with a new conditional analysis of "he could have tried." He might say, for example, that "he could have tried to do otherwise" be interpreted to mean he would have tried to do otherwise, if he had chosen. But the incompatibilist now has a new objection to make: namely, what if the agent could not have chosen?

It should be obvious that this debate might be carried on indefinitely with a proliferation of conditionals and a proliferation of objections. But if an agent is determined, no conditions one suggests will be conditions that an agent could have satisfied.

Thus, any conditional analysis of "he could have done otherwise" seems too weak to satisfy the condition of freedom. Yet if "he could have done otherwise" is not a conditional, it seems too strong to allow the satisfaction of the condition of value. We seem to think of ourselves one way when we are thinking about freedom, and to think of ourselves another way when we are thinking about morality. When we are thinking about the condition of freedom, our intuitions suggest that the incompatibilists are right. For they claim that an agent can be free only insofar as his actions are not psychologically determined. But when we are thinking about the condition of value, our intuitions suggest that the compatibilists are right. For they claim that an agent can be moral only insofar as his actions are psychologically determined. If our intuitions require that both of these claims are right, then the concept of moral responsibility must be incoherent. For then a free agent can never be moral, and a moral agent can never be free.

In fact, however, I believe that philosophers have generally got our intuitions wrong. There is an asymmetry in our intuitions about freedom which has generally been overlooked. As a result, it has seemed that the answer to the problem of free will can lie in only one of two alternatives: Either the fact that an agent's action was determined is always compatible with his being responsible for it, or the fact that the agent's action was determined will always rule his responsibility out. I shall suggest that the solution lies elsewhere—that both compatibilists and incompatibilists are wrong. What we need in order to be responsible beings, I shall argue, is a suitable combination of determination and indetermination.

When we try to call up our intuitions about freedom, a few stock cases come readily to mind. We think of the heroin addict and the kleptomaniac, of the victim of hypnosis, and the victim of a deprived childhood. These cases, I think, provide forceful support for our incompatibilist intuitions. For of the kleptomaniac it may well be true that he would have done otherwise if he had tried. The kleptomaniac is not responsible because he could not have tried. Of the victim of hypnosis it may well be true that he would have done otherwise if he had chosen. The victim of hypnosis is not responsible because he could not have chosen.

The victim of the deprived childhood who, say, embezzles some money, provides the most poignant example of all. For this agent is not coerced nor overcome by an irresistible impulse. He is in complete possession of normal adult faculties of reason and observation. He seems, indeed, to have as much control over his behavior as we have of ours. He acts on the basis of his choice, and he chooses on the basis of his reasons. If there is any explanation of why this agent is not responsible, it would seem that it must consist simply in the fact that his reasons are determined.

These examples are all peculiar, however, in that they are examples of people doing bad things. If the agents in these cases were responsible for their actions, this would justify the claim that they deserve to be blamed. We seldom look, on the other hand, at examples of agents whose actions are morally good. We rarely ask whether an agent is truly responsible if his being responsible would make him worthy of praise.

There are a few reasons why this might be so which go some way in accounting for the philosophers' neglect. First, acts of moral blame are more connected with punishment than acts of moral praise are connected with reward. So acts of moral blame are likely to be more public, and examples will be readier to hand. Second, and more important, I think, we have stronger reasons for wanting acts of blame to be justified. If we blame someone or punish him, we are likely to be causing him some pain. But if we praise someone or reward him, we will only add to his pleasures. To blame someone undeservedly is, in any case, to do him an injustice. Whereas to praise someone undeservedly is apt to be just a harmless mistake. For this reason, I think, our intuitions about praise are weaker and less developed than our intuitions about blame. Still, we do have some intuitions about cases of praise, and it would be a mistake to ignore them entirely.

When we ask whether an agent's action is deserving of praise, it seems we do not require that he could have done otherwise. If an agent does the right thing for just the right reasons, it seems absurd to ask whether he could have done the wrong. "I cannot tell a lie," "He couldn't hurt a fly" are not exemptions from praiseworthiness but testimonies to it. If a friend presents you with a gift and says "I couldn't resist," this suggests the strength of his friendship and not the weakness of his will. If one feels one "has no choice" but to speak out against injustice, one ought not to be upset about the depth of one's commitment. And it seems I should be grateful for the fact that if I were in trouble, my family "could not help" but come to my aid.

Of course, these phrases must be given an appropriate interpretation if they are to indicate that the agent is deserving of praise. "He couldn't hurt a fly" must allude to someone's gentleness—it would be perverse to say this of someone who was in an iron lung. It is not admirable in George Washington that he cannot tell a lie, if it is because he has a tendency to stutter that inhibits his attempts. "He could not have done otherwise" as it is used in the context of praise, then, must be taken to imply something like "because he was too good." An action is praiseworthy only if it is done for the right reasons. So it must be only in light of and because of these reasons that the praiseworthy agent "could not help" but do the right thing.

But when an agent does the right thing for the right reason, the fact that, having the right reasons, he *must* do the right should surely not lessen the credit he deserves. For presumably the reason he cannot do otherwise is that his virtue is so sure or his moral commitment so strong.

One might fear that if the agent really couldn't have acted differently, his virtue must be *too* sure or his commitment *too* strong. One might think, for example, that if someone literally couldn't *resist* buying a gift for a friend, his generosity would not be a virtue—it would be an obsession. For one can imagine situations in which it would be better if the agent did resist—if, for example, the money that was spent on the gift was desperately needed for some other purpose. Presumably, in the original case, though, the money was not desperately needed—we praise the agent for buying a gift for his friend rather than, say, a gift for himself. But from the fact that the man could not resist in this situation it doesn't follow that he couldn't resist in another. For part of the explanation of why he couldn't resist in this situation is that in this situation he has no reason to try to resist. This man, we assume, has a generous nature—a disposition, that is, to perform generous acts. But, then, if he is in a situation that presents a golden opportunity, and has no conflicting motive, how could he act otherwise?

One might still be concerned that if his motives are determined, the man cannot be truly deserving of praise. If he cannot help but have a generous character, then the fact that he is generous is not up to him. If a man's motives are determined, one might think, then *he* cannot control them, so it cannot be to his credit if his motives turn out to be good. But whether a man is in control of his motives cannot be decided so simply. We must know not only whether his motives are determined, but how they are determined as well.

We can imagine, for example, a man with a generous mother who became generous as a means of securing her love. He would not have been generous had his mother been different. Had she not admired generosity, he would not have developed this trait. We can imagine further that once this man's character had been developed, he would never subject it to question or change. His character would remain unthinkingly rigid, carried over from a childhood over which he had no control. As he developed a tendency to be generous, let us say, he developed other tendencies—a tendency to brush his teeth twice a day, a tendency to avoid the company of Jews. The explanation for why he developed any one of these traits is more or less the same as the explanation for why he has developed any other. And the explanation for why he has retained some of these tendencies is more or less the same as the explanation for why he has retained any other. These tendencies are all, for him, merely habits which he has never thought about breaking. Indeed, they are habits which, by hypothesis, it was determined he would never think about breaking. Such a man, perhaps, would not deserve credit for his generosity, for his generosity might be thought to be senseless and blind. But we can imagine a different picture in which no such claim is true, in which a generous character might be determined and yet under the agent's control.

We might start again with a man with a generous mother who starts to develop his generosity out of a desire for her love. But his reasons for developing a generous nature need not be his reasons for retaining it when he grows more mature. He may notice, for example, that his generous acts provide an independent pleasure, connected to the pleasure he gives the person on whom his generosity is bestowed. He may find that being generous promotes a positive fellow feeling and makes it easier for him to make friends than it would otherwise be. Moreover, he appreciates being the object of the generous acts of others, and he is hurt when others go to ungenerous extremes. All in all, his generosity seems to cohere with his other values. It fits in well with his ideals of how one ought to live.

Such a picture, I think, might be determined as the former one. But it is compatible with the exercise of good sense and an open frame of mind. It is determined, because the agent does not create his new reasons for generosity any more than he created his old ones. He does not *decide* to feel an independent pleasure in performing acts of generosity, or decide that such acts will make it easier for him to make friends. He discovers that these are consequences of a generous nature—and if he is observant and perceptive, he cannot help but discover this. He does not choose to be the object of the generous acts of others, or to be the victim of less generous acts of less virtuous persons. Nor does he choose to be grateful to the one and hurt by the other. He cannot help but have these experiences—they are beyond his control. So it seems that what reasons he *has* for being generous depends on what reasons there *are*.

If the man's character is determined in this way, however, it seems absurd to say that it is not under his control. His character is determined on the basis of his reasons, and his reasons are determined by what reasons there are. What is not under his control, then, is that generosity be a virtue, and it is only because he realizes this that he remains a generous man. But one cannot say for *this* reason that his generosity is not praiseworthy. This is the best reason for being generous that a person could have.

So it seems that an agent can be morally praiseworthy even though he is determined to perform the action he performs. But we have already seen that an agent cannot be morally blameworthy if he is determined to perform the action he performs. Determination, then, is compatible with an agent's responsibility for a good action, but incompatible with an agent's responsibility for a bad action. The metaphysical conditions required for an agent's responsibility will vary according to the value of the action he performs.

The condition of freedom, as it is expressed by the requirement that an agent could have done otherwise, thus appears to demand a conditional analysis after all. But the condition must be one that separates the good actions from the bad—the condition, that is, must be essentially value-laden. An analysis of the condition of freedom that might do the trick is:

He could have done otherwise if there had been good and sufficient reason.

where the "could have done otherwise" in the analysans is not a conditional at all. For presumably an action is morally praiseworthy only if there are no good and sufficient reasons to do something else. And an action is morally blameworthy only if there are good and sufficient reasons to do something else. Thus, when an agent performs a good action, the condition of freedom is a counterfactual: though it is required that the agent would have been able to do otherwise *had there been* good and sufficient reason to do so, the situation in which the good-acting agent actually found himself is a situation in which there was no such reason. Thus, it is compatible with the satisfaction of the condition of freedom that the agent in this case could not actually have done other than what he actually did. When an agent performs a bad action, however, the condition of freedom is not a counterfactual. The bad-acting agent does what he does in the face of good and sufficient reasons to do otherwise. Thus the condition of freedom requires that the agent in this case could have done otherwise in just the situation in which he was actually placed. An agent, then, can be determined to perform a good action and still be morally praiseworthy. But if an agent is to be blameworthy, he must unconditionally have been able to do something else.

It may be easier to see how this analysis works, and how it differs from conditional analyses that were suggested before, if we turn back to the case in which these previous analyses failed—namely, the case of the victim of a deprived childhood.

We imagined a case, in particular, of a man who embezzled some money, fully aware of what he was doing. He was neither coerced nor overcome by an irresistible impulse, and he was in complete possession of normal adult faculties of reason and observation. Yet it seems he ought not to be blamed for committing his crime, for, from his point of view, one cannot reasonably expect him to see anything wrong with his action. We may suppose that in childhood he was given no love—he was beaten by his father, neglected by his mother. And that the people to whom he was exposed when he was growing up gave him examples only of evil and selfishness. From his point of view, it is natural to conclude that respecting other people's property would be foolish. For presumably no one had ever respected his. And it is natural for him to feel that he should treat other people as adversaries.

In light of this, it seems that this man shouldn't be blamed for an action we know to be wrong. For if we had had his childhood, we wouldn't have known it either. Yet this agent seems to have as much control over his life as we are apt to have over ours: he would have done otherwise, if he had tried. He would have tried to do otherwise, if he had chosen. And he would have chosen to do otherwise, if he had had reason. It is because he couldn't have had reason that this agent should not be blamed.

Though this agent's childhood was different from ours, it would seem to be neither more nor less binding. The good fortune of our childhood is no more to our credit than the misfortune of his is to his blame. So if he is not free because of the childhood he had, then it would appear that we are not free either. Thus it seems no conditional analysis of freedom will do—for there is nothing internal to the agent which distinguishes him from us.

My analysis, however, proposes a condition that is not internal to the agent. And it allows us to state the relevant difference: namely that, whereas our childhoods fell within a range of normal decency, his was severely deprived. The consequence this has is that he, unlike us, could not have had reasons even though there were reasons around. The problem is not that his reason was functioning improperly, but that his data were unfortuitously selective. Since the world for him was not suitably cooperating, his reason cannot attain its appropriate goal.

The goal, to put it bluntly, is the True and the Good. The freedom we want is the freedom to find it. But such a freedom requires not only that we, as agents, have the right sorts of abilities—the abilities, that is, to direct and govern our actions by our most fundamental selves. It requires as well that the world cooperate in such a way that our most fundamental selves have the opportunity to develop into the selves they ought to be.

If the freedom necessary for moral responsibility is the freedom to be determined by the True and the Good, then obviously we cannot know whether we have such a freedom unless we know, on the one hand, that there *is* a True and a Good and, on the other, that there *are* capacities for finding them. As a consequence of this, the condition of freedom cannot be stated in purely metaphysical terms. For we cannot know which capacities and circumstances are necessary for freedom unless we know which capacities and circumstances will enable us to form the *right* values and perform the *right* actions. Strictly speaking, I take it, the capacity to reason is not enough—we need a kind of sensibility and perception as well. But these are capacities, I assume, that most of us have. So when the world cooperates, we are morally responsible.

I have already said that the condition of freedom cannot be stated in purely metaphysical terms. More specifically, the condition of freedom cannot be stated in terms that are value-free. Thus, the problem of free will has been misrepresented insofar as it has been thought to be a purely metaphysical problem. And, perhaps, this is why the problem of free will has seemed for so long to be hopeless.

That the problem should have seemed to be a purely metaphysical problem is not, however, unnatural or surprising. For being determined by the

True and the Good is very different from being determined by one's garden variety of causes, and I think it is not unnatural to feel as if one rules out the other. For to be determined by the Good is not to be determined by the Past. And to do something because it is the right thing to do is not to do it because one has been taught to do it. One might think, then, that one can be determined only by one thing or the other. For if one is going to do whatever it is right to do, then it seems one will do it whether or not one has been taught. And if one is going to do whatever one has been taught to do, then it seems one will do it whether or not it is right.

In fact, however, such reasoning rests on a category mistake. These two explanations do not necessarily compete, for they are explanations of different kinds. Consider, for example, the following situation: you ask me to name the capital of Nevada, and I reply "Carson City." We can explain why I give the answer I do give in either of the following ways: First, we can point out that when I was in the fifth grade I had to memorize the capitals of the fifty states. I was taught to believe that Carson City was the capital of Nevada, and was subsequently positively reinforced for doing so. Second, we can point out that Carson City *is* the capital of Nevada, and that this was, after all, what you wanted to know. So on the one hand, I gave my answer because I was taught. And on the other, I gave my answer because it was right.

Presumably, these explanations are not unrelated. For if Carson City were not the capital of Nevada, I would not have been taught that it was. And if I hadn't been taught that Carson City was the capital of Nevada, I wouldn't have known that it was. Indeed, one might think that if the answer I gave weren't right, I *couldn't* have given it because I was taught. For no school board would have hired a teacher who got such facts wrong. And if I hadn't been taught that Carson City was the capital of Nevada, perhaps I couldn't have given this answer because it was right. For that Carson City is the capital of Nevada is not something that can be known a priori.

Similarly, we can explain why a person acts justly in either of the following ways: First, we can point out that he was taught to act justly, and was subsequently positively reinforced for doing so. Second, we can point out that it is right to act justly, and go on to say why he knows this is so. Again, these explanations are likely to be related. For if it weren't right to act justly, the person may well have been taught that it was. And if the person hadn't been taught that he ought to act justly, the person may not have discovered this on his own. Of course, the explanations of both kinds in this case will be more complex than the explanations in the previous case. But what is relevant here is that these explanations are compatible: that one can be determined by the Good and determined by the Past.

In order for an agent to be morally free, then, he must be capable of being determined by the Good. Determination by the Good is, as it were, the goal we need the freedom to pursue. We need the freedom *to* have our actions determined by the Good, and the freedom to be or to become the sorts of persons whose actions will continue to be so determined. In light of this, it should be clear that no standard incompatibilist views about the conditions of moral responsibility can be right, for, according to these views, an agent is free only if he is the sort of agent whose actions are not causally determined at all. Thus, an agent's freedom would be incompatible with the realization of the goal for which freedom is required. The agent would be, in the words, though not in the spirit, of Sartre, "condemned to be free"—he could not both be free and realize a moral ideal.

Thus, views that offer conditional analyses of the ability to do otherwise, views that, like mine, take freedom to consist in the ability *to be determined* in a particular way, are generally compatibilist views. For insofar as an agent *is* determined in the right way, the agent can be said to be acting freely. Like the compatibilists, then, I am claiming that whether an agent is morally responsible depends not on whether but on how that agent is determined. My view differs from theirs only in what I take the satisfactory kind of determination to be.

However, since on my view the satisfactory kind of determination is determination by reasons that an agent ought to have, it will follow that an agent can be both determined and responsible only insofar as he performs actions that he ought to perform. If an agent performs a morally bad action, on the other hand, then his actions can't be determined in the appropriate way. So if an agent is ever to be responsible for a bad action, it must be the case that his action is not psychologically determined at all. According to my view, then, in order for both moral praise and moral blame to be justified, the thesis of psychological determinism must be false.

Is it plausible that this thesis is false? I think so. For though it appears that some of our actions are psychologically determined, it appears that others are not. It appears that some of our actions are not determined by our interests, and some of our interests are not determined at all. That is, it seems that some of our actions are such that no set of psychological facts are sufficient to explain them. There are occasions on which a person takes one action, but there seems to be no reason why he didn't take another.

For example, we sometimes make arbitrary choices—to wear the green shirt rather than the blue, to have coffee rather than tea. We make such choices on the basis of no reason—and it seems that we might, in these cases, have made a different choice instead.

Some less trivial and more considered choices may also be arbitrary. For one may have reasons on both sides which are equally strong. Thus, one may have good reasons to go to graduate school and good reasons not to; good reasons to get married, and good reasons to stay single. Though we might want, in these cases, to choose on the basis of reasons, our reasons simply do not settle the matter for us. Other psychological events may be similarly undetermined, such as the chance occurrence of thoughts and ideas. One is just struck by an idea, but for no particular reason—one might as easily have had another idea or no idea at all. Or one simply forgets an appointment one has made, even though one was not particularly distracted by other things at the time.

On retrospect, some of the appearances of indetermination may turn out to be deceptive. We decide that unconscious motives dictated a choice that seemed at the time to be arbitrary. Or a number of ideas that seemed to occur to us at random reveal a pattern too unusual to be the coincidence we thought. But if some of the appearances of indetermination are deceptive, I see no reason to believe that all of them should be.

Let us turn, then, to instances of immoral behavior, and see what the right kind of indetermination would be. For indetermination, in this context, is indetermination among some number of fairly particular alternatives—and if one's alternatives are not of the appropriate kind, indetermination will not be sufficient to justify moral blame. It is not enough, for example, to know that a criminal who happened to rob a bank might as easily have chosen to hold up a liquor store instead. What we need to know, in particular, is that when an agent performs a wrong action, he could have performed the right action for the right reasons instead. That is, first, the agent could have had the interests that the agent ought to have had, and second, the agent could have acted on the interests on which he ought to have acted.

Corresponding to these two possibilities, we can imagine two sorts of moral failure: the first corresponds to a form of negligence, the second to a form of weakness. Moral negligence consists in a failure to recognize the existence of moral reasons that one ought to have recognized. For example, a person hears that his friend is in the hospital, but fails to attend to this when planning his evening. He doesn't stop to think about how lonely and bored his friend is likely to be—he simply reaches for the *TV Guide* or for his novel instead. If the person could have recognized his friend's sorry predicament, he is guilty of moral negligence. Moral weakness, on the other hand, consists in the failure to act on the reasons that one knows one ought, for moral reasons, to be acting on. For example, a person might go so far as to conclude that he really ought to pay his sick friend a visit, but the thought of the drive across town is enough to convince him to stay at home with his book after all. If the person could have made the visit, he is guilty of moral weakness.

There is, admittedly, some difficulty in establishing that an agent who performs a morally bad action satisfies the condition of freedom. It is hard to know whether an agent who did one thing could have done another instead. But presumably we decide such questions now on the basis of statistical evidence—and if, in fact, these actions are not determined, this is the best method there can be. We decide, in other words, that an agent could have done otherwise if others in his situation have done otherwise, and these others are like him in apparently relevant ways. Or we decide that an agent could have done otherwise if he himself has done otherwise in situations that are like this one in all apparently relevant ways.

It should be emphasized that the indetermination with which we are here concerned is indetermination only at the level of psychological explanation. Such indetermination is compatible with determination at other levels of explanation. In particular, a sub-psychological, or physiological, explanation of our behavior may yet be deterministic. Some feel that if this is the case, the nature of psychological explanations of our behavior cannot be relevant to the problem of free will. Though I am inclined to disagree with this view, I have neither the space nor the competence to argue this here.

Restricting the type of explanation in question appropriately, however, it is a consequence of the condition of freedom I have suggested that the explanation for why a responsible agent performs a morally bad action must be, at some level, incomplete. There must be nothing that made the agent perform the action he did, nothing that prevented him from performing a morally better one. It should be noted that there may be praiseworthy actions for which the explanations are similarly incomplete. For the idea that an agent who could have performed a morally bad action actually performs a morally good one is no less plausible than the idea that an agent who could have performed a morally good action actually performs a morally bad one. Presumably, an agent who does the right thing for the right reasons deserves praise for his action whether it was determined or not. But whereas indetermination is compatible with the claim that an agent is deserving of praise, it is essential to the justification of the claim that an agent is deserving of blame.

Seen from a certain perspective, this dealing out of praise and blame may seem unfair. In particular, we might think that if it is truly undetermined whether a given agent in a given situation will perform a good action or a bad one, then it must be a matter of chance that the agent ends up doing what he does. If the action is truly undetermined, then it is not determined by the agent himself. One might think that in this case the agent has no more control over the moral quality of his action than does anything else.

However, the fact that it is not determined whether the agent will perform a good action or a bad one does not imply that which action he performs can properly be regarded as a matter of chance. Of course, in some situations an agent might choose to make it a matter of chance. For example, an agent struggling with the decision between fulfilling a moral obligation and doing something immoral that he very much wants to do might ultimately decide to let the toss of a coin settle the matter for him. But, in normal cases, the way in which the agent makes a decision involves no statistical process or randomizing event. It appears that the claim that there is no complete explanation of why the agent who could have performed a better action performed a worse one or of why the agent who could have performed a worse action performed a better one rules out even the explanation that it was a matter of chance.

In order to have control over the moral quality of his actions, an agent must have certain requisite abilities—in particular, the abilities necessary to see and understand the reasons and interests he ought to see and understand and the abilities necessary to direct his actions in accordance with his reasons and interests. And if, furthermore, there is nothing that interferes with the agent's use of these abilities—that is, no determining cause that prevents him from using them and no statistical process that, as it were, takes out of his hands the control over whether or not he uses them—then it seems that these are all the abilities that the agent needs to have. But it is compatible with the agent's having these abilities and with there being no interferences to their use that it is not determined whether the agent will perform a good action or a bad one. The responsible agent who performs a bad action fails to exercise these abilities sufficiently, though there is no complete explanation of why he fails. The responsible agent who performs a good action does exercise these abilities—it may or may not be the case that it is determined that he exercise them.

The freedom required for moral responsibility, then, is the freedom to be good. Only this kind of freedom will be neither too much nor too little. For then the agent is not so free as to be free from moral reasons, nor so unfree as to make these reasons ineffective.

QUESTIONS FOR DISCUSSION
WHEN ARE WE RESPONSIBLE?

1. What does Galen Strawson mean by "the way we are"? How does "the way we are" seem to make free will an illusion?

2. Why does Strawson think that if we believe in free will and moral responsibility, we have to deny the "unity of truth"? Why is this, for him, too high a price to pay?

3. What, according to Chisholm, is the difference between "transeunt" causation and "immanent" causation, and how does it bear on the issue of free will versus determinism?

4. Compare Chisholm's unpacking of the meaning of "could have done otherwise" with that of Simon Blackburn. What do you think the phrase really means?

5. What does van Inwagen mean by saying that "an undetermined act need not be an uncaused act"?

6. Why, for van Inwagen, is an undetermined act not a random or chance event? What do "random" and "chance" mean, according to him?

7. What is Simon Blackburn's "revised-revised" definition of compatibilism? How does it differ crucially from his earlier "revised" definition?

8. Discuss whether there is a real conflict between van Inwagen's indeterminism and Blackburn's soft determinism (compatibilism), or only a difference in terminology.

9. What does Wolf mean by "psychological determination"? Does a motive or a reason determine an action in so strong a way that the agent cannot refrain from performing it? Should phrases like "I could not help stealing the money" or "Logic compels me to vote guilty" be taken at face value, or are they exaggerations like "I'm dying to meet her"? Defend your response to these questions.

10. According to Wolf, when would it be fair to blame someone for wrongdoing and when would it be unfair? Is she right? Explain.

SELECTED READINGS

ABELSON, R. *Lawless Mind.* Philadelphia: Temple University Press, 1988.

ARISTOTLE. *Nichomachean Ethics.* Trans. J. Thomson. Baltimore: Penguin, 1955.

AUGUSTINE, ST. *The Problem of Free Choice.* Trans. M. Pontifex. Westminster: Newman Press, 1955.

BLACKBURN, S. *Think.* New York: Oxford University Press, 1999.

CAMPBELL, C. A. *In Defense of Free Will.* New York: Humanities, 1967.

CHISHOLM, R. *Human Freedom and the Self.* Lawrence: University of Kansas Press, 1964.

DENNETT, D. K. *Elbow Room.* Cambridge, MA: MIT Press, 1984.

FRANKFURT, H. "Freedom of the Will and the Concept of a Person." *Journal of Philosophy* 68 (1971).

FRENCH, P. *The Spectrum of Responsibility.* New York: St. Martin's, 1991.

HOOK, S., ed. *Determinism and Freedom in the Age of Modern Science.* New York: New York University Press, 1958.

JAMES, W. *The Will to Believe.* New York: Longmans Green, 1896.

MELDEN, A. I. *Free Action.* New York: Humanities, 1961.

NOWELL-SMITH, P. H. *Ethics.* New York: Penguin, 1954.

STRAWSON, GALEN. *Freedom and Belief.* New York: Oxford University Press, 1986.

VAN INWAGEN, P. *Essay on Free Will.* New York: Oxford University Press, 1983.

WOLF, SUSAN. *Freedom within Reason.* New York: Oxford University Press, 1990.

THE MORALITY OF TAKING LIFE

Three problems involving the taking of human life are explored in the following three chapters: physician-assisted suicide and mercy killing in Chapter 3, abortion in Chapter 4, and capital punishment in Chapter 5. We begin with Tom Godwin's prize-winning science fiction story that highlights the moral dilemma between the natural inhibition against the taking of human life and the need to do so for a compelling reason—in this case, to save other lives. In Godwin's story the pilot of a space ship, racing to bring life-saving medicine to a far-off planet, will have enough fuel for the trip only if he jettisons an unexpected passenger.

In the philosophical discussions that follow, the presumably compelling reasons for taking life are, in Chapter 3, the desire to terminate unbearable suffering; in Chapter 4, a woman's right to rid her body of an unwanted fetus; and, in Chapter 5, society's right to exact the ultimate penalty for the most vicious crime.

THE COLD EQUATIONS

Tom Godwin

He was not alone.

There was nothing to indicate the fact but the white hand of the tiny gauge on the board before him. The control room was empty but for himself, there was no sound other than the murmur of the drives—but the white hand had moved. It had been on zero when the little ship was launched from the *Stardust;* now, an hour later, it had crept up. There was something in the

---

Tom Godwin. "The Cold Equations." Reprinted by permission.

It is a violation of the law to reproduce this selection by any means whatsoever without the written consent of the copyright holder.

supplies closet across the room, it was saying, some kind of body that radiated heat.

It could be but one kind of a body—a living, human body.

He leaned back in the pilot's chair and drew a deep, slow breath, considering what he would have to do. He was an EDS pilot, inured to the sight of death, long since accustomed to it and to viewing the dying of another man with an objective lack of emotion, and he had no choice in what he must do. There could be no alternative—but it required a few moments of conditioning for even an EDS pilot to prepare himself to walk across the room and coldly, deliberately, take the life of a man he had yet to meet.

He would, of course, do it. It was the law, stated very bluntly and definitely in grim Paragraph L, Section 8, of Interstellar Regulations: *Any stowaway discovered in an EDS shall be jettisoned immediately following discovery.*

It was the law, and there could be no appeal.

It was a law not of men's choosing but made imperative by the circumstances of the space frontier. Galactic expansion had followed the development of the hyperspace drive and as men scattered wide across the frontier there had come the problem of contact with the isolated first-colonies and exploration parties. The huge hyperspace cruisers were the product of the combined genius and effort of Earth and were long and expensive in the building. They were not available in such numbers that small colonies could possess them. The cruisers carried the colonists to their new worlds and made periodic visits, running on tight schedules, but they could not stop and turn aside to visit colonies scheduled to be visited at another time; such a delay would destroy their schedule and produce a confusion and uncertainty that would wreck the complex interdependence between old Earth and the new worlds of the frontier.

Some method of delivering supplies or assistance when an emergency occurred on a world not scheduled for a visit had been needed and the Emergency Dispatch Ships had been the answer. Small and collapsible, they occupied little room in the hold of the cruiser; made of light metal and plastics, they were driven by a small rocket drive that consumed relatively little fuel. Each cruiser carried four EDS's and when a call for aid was received the nearest cruiser would drop into normal space long enough to launch an EDS with the needed supplies or personnel, then vanish again as it continued on its course.

The cruisers, powered by nuclear converters, did not use the liquid rocket fuel but nuclear converters were far too large and complex to permit their installation in the EDS's. The cruisers were forced by necessity to carry a limited amount of the bulky rocket fuel and the fuel was rationed with care; the cruiser's computers determining the exact amount of fuel each EDS would require for its mission. The computers considered the course coordinates, the mass of the EDS, the mass of pilot and cargo; they were very precise and accurate and omitted nothing from their calculations. They could not, however, foresee, and allow for, the added mass of a stowaway.

The *Stardust* had received the request from one of the exploration parties stationed on Woden; the six men of the party already being stricken with fever carried by the green *kala* midges and their own supply of serum destroyed by the tornado that had torn through their camp. The *Stardust* had gone through the usual procedure; dropping into normal space to launch the EDS with the fever serum, then vanishing again in hyperspace. Now, an hour later, the gauge was saying there was something more than the small carton of serum in the supplies closet.

He let his eyes rest on the narrow white door of the closet. There, just inside, another man lived and breathed and was beginning to feel assured that discovery of his presence would now be too late for the pilot to alter the situation. It *was* too late—for the man behind the door it was far later than he thought and in a way he would find terrible to believe.

There could be no alternative. Additional fuel would be used during the hours of deceleration to compensate for the added mass of the stowaway; infinitesimal increments of fuel that would not be missed until the ship had almost reached its destination. Then, at some distance above the ground that might be as near as a thousand feet or as far as tens of thousands of feet, depending upon the mass of ship and cargo and the preceding period of deceleration, the unmissed increments of fuel would make their absence known; the EDS would expend its last drops of fuel with a sputter and go into whistling free fall. Ship and pilot and stowaway would merge together upon impact as a wreckage of metal and plastic, flesh and blood, driven deep into the soil. The stowaway had signed his own death warrant when he concealed himself on the ship; he could not be permitted to take seven others with him.

He looked again at the tell-tale white hand, then rose to his feet. What he must do would be unpleasant for both of them; the sooner it was over, the better. He stepped across the control room, to stand by the white door.

"Come out!" His command was harsh and abrupt above the murmur of the drive.

It seemed he could hear the whisper of a furtive movement inside the closet, then nothing. He visualized the stowaway cowering into one corner, suddenly worried by the possible consequences of his act and his self-assurance evaporating.

"I said *out!*"

He heard the stowaway move to obey and he waited with his eyes alert on the door and his hand near the blaster at his side.

The door opened and the stowaway stepped through it, smiling. "All right—I give up. Now what?"

It was a girl.

He stared without speaking, his hand dropping away from the blaster and acceptance of what he saw coming like a heavy and unexpected physical blow. The stowaway was not a man—she was a girl in her teens, standing before him in little white gypsy sandals with the top of her brown, curly head hardly higher than his shoulder, with a faint, sweet scent of perfume coming from her and her smiling face tilted up so that her eyes could look unknowing and unafraid into his as she waited for his answer.

Now what? Had it been asked in the deep, defiant voice of a man he would have answered it with action, quick and efficient. He would have taken the stowaway's identification disc and ordered him into the air lock. Had the stowaway refused to obey, he would have used the blaster. It would not have taken long; within a minute the body would have been ejected into space—had the stowaway been a man.

He returned to the pilot's chair and motioned her to seat herself on the boxlike bulk of the drive-control units that were set against the wall beside him. She obeyed, his silence making the smile fade into the meek and guilty expression of a pup that has been caught in mischief and knows it must be punished.

"You still haven't told me," she said. "I'm guilty, so what happens to me now? Do I pay a fine, or what?"

"What are you doing here?" he asked. "Why did you stow away on this EDS?"

"I wanted to see my brother. He's with the government survey crew on Woden and I haven't seen him for ten years, not since he left Earth to go into government survey work."

"What was your destination on the *Stardust*?"

"Mimir. I have a position waiting for me there. My brother has been sending money home all the time to us—my father and my mother and I—and he paid for a special course in linguistics I was taking. I graduated sooner than expected and I was offered this job on Mimir. I knew it would be almost a year before Gerry's job was done on Woden so he could come on to Mimir and that's why I hid in the closet, there. There was plenty of room for me and I was willing to pay the fine. There were only the two of us kids—Gerry and I—and I haven't seen him for so long, and I didn't want to wait another year when I could see him now, even though I knew I would be breaking some kind of a regulation when I did it."

I knew I would be breaking some kind of a regulation——In a way, she could not be blamed for her ignorance of the law; she was of Earth and had not realized that the laws of the space frontier must, of necessity, be as hard and relentless as the environment that gave them birth. Yet, to protect such as her from the results of their own ignorance of the frontier, there had been a sign over the door that led to the section of the *Stardust* that housed the EDS's; a sign that was plain for all to see and heed:

UNAUTHORIZED PERSONNEL
KEEP OUT!

"Does your brother know that you took a passage on the *Stardust* for Mimir?"

"Oh, yes. I sent him a spacegram telling him about my graduation and about going to Mimir on the *Stardust* a month before I left Earth. I already knew Mimir was where he would be stationed in a little over a year. He gets a promotion then, and he'll be based on Mimir and not have to stay out a year at a time on field trips, like he does now."

There were two different survey groups on Woden, and he asked, "What is his name?"

"Cross—Gerry Cross. He's in Group Two—that was the way his address read. Do you know him?"

Group One had requested the serum; Group Two was eight thousand miles away, across the Western Sea.

"No, I've never met him," he said, then turned to the control board and cut the deceleration to a fraction of a gravity; knowing as he did so that it could not avert the ultimate end, yet doing the only thing he could do to prolong that ultimate end. The sensation was like that of a ship suddenly dropping and the girl's involuntary movement of surprise half lifted her from her seat.

"We're going faster now, aren't we?" she asked. "Why are we doing that?"

He told her the truth. "To save fuel for a little while."

"You mean we don't have very much?"

He delayed the answer he must give her so soon to ask: "How did you manage to stow away?"

"I just sort of walked in when no one was looking my way," she said. "I was practising my Gelanese on the native girl who does the cleaning in the Ship's Supply Office when someone came in with an order for supplies for the survey crew on Woden. I slipped into the closet there after the ship was ready to go and just before you came in. It was an impulse of the moment to stow away, so I could get to see Gerry—and from the way you keep looking at me so grim, I'm not sure it was a very wise impulse.

"But I'll be a model criminal—or do I mean prisoner?" She smiled at him again. "I intended to pay for my keep on top of paying the fine. I can cook and I can patch clothes for everyone and I know how to do all kinds of useful things, even a little bit about nursing."

There was one more question to ask:

"Did you know what the supplies were that the survey crew ordered?"

"Why, no. Equipment they needed in their work, I supposed."

Why couldn't she have been a man with some ulterior motive? A fugitive from justice, hoping to lose himself on a raw new world; an opportunist, seeking transportation to the new colonies where he might find golden fleece for the taking; a crackpot, with a mission——

Perhaps once in his lifetime an EDS pilot would find such a stowaway on his ship; warped men, mean and selfish men, brutal and dangerous men— but never, before, a smiling, blue-eyed girl who was willing to pay her fine and work for her keep that she might see her brother.

He turned to the board and turned the switch that would signal the *Stardust*. The call would be futile but he could not, until he had exhausted that one vain hope, seize her and thrust her into the air lock as he would an animal—or a man. The delay, in the meantime, would not be dangerous with the EDS decelerating at fractional gravity.

A voice spoke from the communicator. "*Stardust.* Identify yourself and proceed."

"Barton, EDS 34G11. Emergency. Give me Commander Delhart."

There was a faint confusion of noises as the request went through the proper channels. The girl was watching him, no longer smiling.

"Are you going to order them to come back after me?" she asked.

The communicator clicked and there was the sound of a distant voice saying, "Commander, the EDS requests——"

"Are they coming back after me?" she asked again. "Won't I get to see my brother, after all?"

"Barton?" The blunt, gruff voice of Commander Delhart came from the communicator. "What's this about an emergency?"

"A stowaway," he answered.

"A stowaway?" There was a slight surprise to the question. "That's rather unusual—but why the 'emergency' call? You discovered him in time so there should be no appreciable danger and I presume you've informed Ship's Records so his nearest relatives can be notified."

"That's why I had to call you, first. The stowaway is still aboard and the circumstances are so different——"

"Different?" the commander interrupted, impatience in his voice. "How can they be different? You know you have a limited supply of fuel; you also know the law, as well as I do: 'Any stowaway discovered in an EDS shall be jettisoned immediately following discovery.'"

There was the sound of a sharply indrawn breath from the girl. "*What does he mean?*"

"The stowaway is a girl."

"*What?*"

"She wanted to see her brother. She's only a kid and she didn't know what she was really doing."

"I see." All the curtness was gone from the commander's voice. "So you called me in the hope I could do something?" Without waiting for an answer he went on. "I'm sorry—I can do nothing. This cruiser must maintain its schedule; the life of not one person but the lives of many depend on it. I know how you feel but I'm powerless to help you. You'll have to go through with it. I'll have you connected with Ship's Records."

The communicator faded to a faint rustle of sound and he turned to the girl. She was leaning forward on the bench, almost rigid, her eyes fixed wide and frightened.

"What did he mean, to go through with it? To jettison me . . . to go through with it—what did he mean? Not the way it sounded . . . he couldn't have. What did he mean . . . what did he really mean?"

Her time was too short for the comfort of a lie to be more than a cruelly fleeting delusion.

"He meant it the way it sounded."

"*No!*" She recoiled from him as though he had struck her, one hand half up-raised as though to fend him off and stark unwillingness to believe in her eyes.

"It will have to be."

"No! You're joking—you're insane! You can't mean it!"

"I'm sorry." He spoke slowly to her, gently. "I should have told you be-fore—I should have, but I had to do what I could first; I had to call the *Star-dust.* You heard what the commander said."

"But you can't—if you make me leave the ship, I'll *die.*"

"I know."

She searched his face and the unwillingness to believe left her eyes, giv-ing way slowly to a look of dazed terror.

"You—know?" She spoke the words far apart, numb and wonderingly.

"I know. It has to be like that."

"You mean it—you really mean it." She sagged back against the wall, small and limp like a little rag doll and all the protesting and disbelief gone. "You're going to do it—you're going to make me die?"

"I'm sorry," he said again. "You'll never know how sorry I am. It has to be that way and no human in the universe can change it."

"You're going to make me die and I didn't do anything to die for—I didn't *do* anything——"

He sighed, deep and weary. "I know you didn't, child. I know you didn't——"

"EDS." The communicator rapped brisk and metallic. "This is Ship's Records. Give us all information on subject's identification disc."

He got out of his chair to stand over her. She clutched the edge of the seat, her upturned face white under the brown hair and the lipstick standing out like a blood-red cupid's bow.

"*Now?*"

"I want your identification disc," he said.

She released the edge of the seat and fumbled at the chain that sus-pended the plastic disc from her neck with fingers that were trembling and awkward. He reached down and unfastened the clasp for her, then returned with the disc to his chair.

"Here's your data, Records: Identification Number T837——"

"One moment," Records interrupted. "This is to be filed on the grey card, of course?"

"Yes."

"And the time of the execution?"

"I'll tell you later."

"Later? This is highly irregular; the time of the subject's death is required before——"

He kept the thickness out of his voice with an effort. "Then we'll do it in a highly irregular manner—you'll hear the disc read first. The subject is a girl and she's listening to everything that's said. Are you capable of under-standing that?"

There was a brief, almost shocked, silence, then Records said meekly: "Sorry. Go ahead."

He began to read the disc, reading it slowly to delay the inevitable for as long as possible, trying to help her by giving her what little time he could to recover from her first terror and let it resolve into the calm of acceptance and resignation.

"Number T8374 dash Y54. Name: Marilyn Lee Cross. Sex: Female. Born: July 7, 2160. *She was only eighteen.* Height: 5 3. Weight: 110. *Such a slight weight, yet enough to add fatally to the mass of the shell-thin bubble that was an EDS.* Hair: Brown. Eyes: Blue. Complexion: Light. Blood Type: O. *Irrelevant data.* Destination: Port City Mimir. *Invalid data——*"

He finished and said, "I'll call you later," then turned once again to the girl. She was huddled back against the wall, watching him with a look of numb and wondering fascination.

"They're waiting for you to kill me, aren't they? They want me dead, don't they? You and everybody on the cruiser wants me dead, don't you?" Then the numbness broke and her voice was that of a frightened and bewildered child. "Everybody wants me dead and I didn't *do* anything. I didn't hurt anyone—I only wanted to see my brother."

"It's not the way you think—it isn't that way, at all," he said. "Nobody wants it this way; nobody would ever let it be this way if it was humanly possible to change it."

"Then why is it? I don't understand. Why is it?"

"This ship is carrying *kala* fever serum to Group One on Woden. Their own supply was destroyed by a tornado. Group Two—the crew your brother is in—is eight thousand miles away across the Western Sea and their helicopters can't cross it to help Group One. The fever is invariably fatal unless the serum can be had in time, and the six men in Group One will die unless this ship reaches them on schedule. These little ships are always given barely enough fuel to reach their destination and if you stay aboard your added weight will cause it to use up all its fuel before it reaches the ground. It will crash, then, and you and I will die and so will the six men waiting for the fever serum."

It was a full minute before she spoke, and as she considered his words the expression of numbness left her eyes.

"Is that it?" she asked at last. "Just that the ship doesn't have enough fuel?"

"Yes."

"I can go alone or I can take seven others with me—is that the way it is?"

"That's the way it is."

"And nobody wants me to have to die?"

"Nobody."

"Then maybe—— Are you sure nothing can be done about it? Wouldn't people help me if they could?"

"Everyone would like to help you but there is nothing anyone can do. I did the only thing I could do when I called the *Stardust.*"

"And it won't come back—but there might be other cruisers, mightn't there? Isn't there any hope at all that there might be someone, somewhere, who could do something to help me?"

She was leaning forward a little in her eagerness as she waited for his answer.

"No."

The word was like the drop of a cold stone and she again leaned back against the wall, the hope and eagerness leaving her face. "You're sure—you *know* you're sure?"

"I'm sure. There are no other cruisers within forty light-years; there is nothing and no one to change things."

She dropped her gaze to her lap and began twisting a pleat of her skirt between her fingers, saying no more as her mind began to adapt itself to the grim knowledge.

It was better so; with the going of all hope would go the fear; with the going of all hope would come resignation. She needed time and she could have so little of it. How much?

The EDS's were not equipped with hull-cooling units; their speed had to be reduced to a moderate level before entering the atmosphere. They were decelerating at •10 gravity; approaching their destination at a far higher speed than the computers had calculated on. The *Stardust* had been quite near Woden when she launched the EDS; their present velocity was putting them nearer by the second. There would be a critical point, soon to be reached, when he would have to resume deceleration. When he did so the girl's weight would be multiplied by the gravities of deceleration, would become, suddenly, a factor of paramount importance; the factor the computers had been ignorant of when they determined the amount of fuel the EDS should have. She would have to go when deceleration began; it could be no other way. When would that be—how long could he let her stay?

"How long can I stay?"

He winced involuntarily from the words that were so like an echo of his own thoughts. How long? He didn't know; he would have to ask the ship's computers. Each EDS was given a meagre supply of fuel to compensate for unfavourable conditions within the atmosphere and relatively little fuel was being consumed for the time being. The memory banks of the computers would still contain all the data pertaining to the course set for the EDS; such data would not be erased until the EDS reached its destination. He had only to give the computers the new data; the girl's weight and the exact time at which he had reduced the deceleration to •10.

"Barton." Commander Delhart's voice came abruptly from the communicator, as he opened his mouth to call the *Stardust*. "A check with Records shows me you haven't completed your report. Did you reduce the deceleration?"

So the commander knew what he was trying to do.

"I'm decelerating at point ten," he answered. "I cut the deceleration at seventeen fifty and the weight is a hundred and ten. I would like to stay at point ten as long as the computers say I can. Will you give them the question?"

It was contrary to regulations for an EDS pilot to make any changes in the course or degree of deceleration the computers had set for him but the commander made no mention of the violation, neither did he ask the reason for it. It was not necessary for him to ask; he had not become commander of an interstellar cruiser without both intelligence and an understanding of human nature. He said only: "I'll have that given the computers."

The communicator fell silent and he and the girl waited, neither of them speaking. They would not have to wait long; the computers would give the answer within moments of the asking. The new factors would be fed into the steel maw of the first bank and the electrical impulses would go through the complex circuits. Here and there a relay might click, a tiny cog turn over, but it would be essentially the electrical impulses that found the answer; formless, mindless, invisible, determining with utter precision how long the pale girl beside him might live. Then five little segments of metal in the second bank would trip in rapid succession against an inked ribbon and a second steel maw would spit out the slip of paper that bore the answer.

The chronometer on the instrument board read 18.10 when the commander spoke again.

"You will resume deceleration at nineteen ten."

She looked toward the chronometer, then quickly away from it. "Is that when . . . when I go?" she asked. He nodded and she dropped her eyes to her lap again.

"I'll have the course corrections given you," the commander said. "Ordinarily I would never permit anything like this but I understand your position. There is nothing I can do, other than what I've just done, and you will not deviate from these new instructions. You will complete your report at nineteen ten. Now—here are the course corrections."

The voice of some unknown technician read them to him and he wrote them down on a pad clipped to the edge of the control board. There would, he saw, be periods of deceleration when he neared the atmosphere when the deceleration would be five gravities—and at five gravities, one hundred and ten pounds would become five hundred and fifty pounds.

The technician finished and he terminated the contact with a brief acknowledgment. Then, hesitating a moment, he reached out and shut off the communicator. It was 18.13 and he would have nothing to report until 19.10. In the meantime, it somehow seemed indecent to permit others to hear what she might say in her last hour.

He began to check the instrument readings, going over them with unnecessary slowness. She would have to accept the circumstances and there was nothing he could do to help her into acceptance; words of sympathy would only delay it.

It was 18.20 when she stirred from her motionlessness and spoke.

"So that's the way it has to be with me?"

He swung around to face her. "You understand now, don't you? No one would ever let it be like this if it could be changed."

"I understand," she said. Some of the colour had returned to her face and the lipstick no longer stood out so vividly red. "There isn't enough fuel for me to stay; when I hid on this ship I got into something I didn't know anything about and now I have to pay for it."

She had violated a man-made law that said KEEP OUT but the penalty was not of men's making or desire and it was a penalty men could not revoke. A physical law had decreed: *h amount of fuel will power an EDS with a mass of m safely to its destination;* and a second physical law decreed: *h amount of fuel will not power an EDS with a mass of m plus x safely to its destination.*

EDS's obeyed only physical laws and no amount of human sympathy for her could alter the second law.

"But I'm afraid. I don't want to die—not now. I want to live and nobody is doing anything to help me; everybody is letting me go ahead and acting just like nothing was going to happen to me. I'm going to die and nobody *cares.*"

"We all do," he said. "I do and the commander does and the clerk in Ship's Records; we all care and each of us did what little he could to help you. It wasn't enough—it was almost nothing—but it was all we could do."

"Not enough fuel—I can understand that," she said, as though she had not heard his own words. "But to have to die for it. *Me,* alone——"

How hard it must be for her to accept the fact. She had never known danger of death; had never known the environments where the lives of men could be as fragile and as fleeting as sea foam tossed against a rocky shore. She belonged on gentle Earth, in that secure and peaceful society where she could be young and gay and laughing with others of her kind; where life was precious and well-guarded and there was always the assurance that tomorrow would come. She belonged to that world of soft winds and warm suns, music and moonlight and gracious manners and not on the hard, bleak frontier.

"How did it happen to me, so terribly quickly? An hour ago I was on the *Stardust,* going to Mimir. Now the *Stardust* is going on without me and I'm going to die and I'll never see Gerry and Mama and Daddy again—I'll never see anything again."

He hesitated, wondering how he could explain it to her so that she would really understand and not feel she had, somehow, been the victim of a reasonlessly cruel injustice. She did not know what the frontier was like; she thought in terms of safe-and-secure Earth. Pretty girls were not jettisoned on Earth; there was a law against it. On Earth her plight would have filled the newscasts and a fast black Patrol ship would have been racing to her rescue. Everyone, everywhere, would have known of Marilyn Lee Cross and no effort would have been spared to save her life. But this was not Earth and there were no Patrol ships; only the *Stardust,* leaving them behind at many times the speed of light. There was no one to help her, there would be no Marilyn Lee Cross smiling from the newscasts tomorrow. Marilyn Lee Cross would be but a poignant memory for an EDS pilot and a name on a grey card in Ship's Records.

"It's different here; it's not like back on Earth," he said. "It isn't that no one cares; it's that no one can do anything to help. The frontier is big and here along its rim the colonies and exploration parties are scattered so thin and far between. On Woden, for example, there are only sixteen men—sixteen men on an entire world. The exploration parties, the survey crews, the little first-colonies—they're all fighting alien environments, trying to make a way for those who will follow after. The environments fight back and those who go first usually make mistakes only once. There is no margin of safety along the rim of the frontier; there can't be until the way is made for the others who will come later, until the new worlds are tamed and settled. Until then men will have to pay the penalty for making mistakes with no one to help them because there is no one *to* help them."

"I was going to Mimir," she said. "I didn't know about the frontier; I was only going to Mimir and *it's* safe."

"Mimir is safe but you left the cruiser that was taking you there."

She was silent for a little while. "It was all so wonderful at first; there was plenty of room for me on this ship and I would be seeing Gerry so soon . . . I didn't know about the fuel, didn't know what would happen to me——"

Her words trailed away and he turned his attention to the viewscreen, not wanting to stare at her as she fought her way through the black horror of fear toward the calm grey of acceptance.

Woden was a ball, enshrouded in the blue haze of atmosphere, swimming in space against the background of star-sprinkled dead blackness. The great mass of Manning's Continent sprawled like a gigantic hourglass in the Eastern Sea with the western half of the Eastern Continent still visible. There was a thin line of shadow along the right-hand edge of the globe and the Eastern Continent was disappearing into it as the planet turned on its axis. An hour before the entire continent had been in view, now a thousand miles of it had gone into the thin edge of shadow and around to the night that lay on the other side of the world. The dark blue spot that was Lotus Lake was approaching the shadow. It was somewhere near the southern edge of the lake that Group Two had their camp. It would be night there, soon, and quick behind the coming of night the rotation of Woden on its axis would put Group Two beyond the reach of the ship's radio.

He would have to tell her before it was too late for her to talk to her brother. In a way, it would be better for both of them should they not do so but it was not for him to decide. To each of them the last words would be something to hold and cherish, something that would cut like the blade of a knife yet would be infinitely precious to remember, she for her own brief moments to live and he for the rest of his life.

He held down the button that would flash the grid lines on the view-screen and used the known diameter of the planet to estimate the distance the southern tip of Lake Lotus had yet to go until it passed beyond radio range. It was approximately five hundred miles. Five hundred miles; thirty minutes—and the chronometer read 18.30. Allowing for error in estimating, it could not be later than 19.05 that the turning of Woden would cut off her brother's voice.

The first border of the Western Continent was already in sight along the left side of the world. Four thousand miles across it lay the shore of the Western Sea and the Camp of Group One. It had been in the Western Sea that the tornado had originated, to strike with such fury at the camp and destroy half their prefabricated buildings, including the one that housed the medical supplies. Two days before the tornado had not existed; it had been no more than great gentle masses of air out over the calm Western Sea. Group One had gone about their routine survey work, unaware of the meeting of the air masses out at sea, unaware of the force the union was spawning. It had struck their camp without warning; a thundering, roaring destruction that sought to annihilate all that lay before it. It had passed on, leaving the wreckage in its wake. It had destroyed the labour of months and had doomed six men to die and then, as though its task was accomplished, it once more began to resolve into gentle masses of air. But for all its deadliness, it had destroyed with neither malice nor intent. It had been a blind and mindless force, obeying the laws of nature, and it would have followed the same course with the same fury had man never existed.

Existence required Order and there was order; the laws of nature, irrevocable and immutable. Men could learn to use them but men could not change them. The circumference of a circle was always pi times the diameter and no science of Man would ever make it otherwise. The combination of chemical A with chemical B under condition C invariably produced reaction D. The law of gravitation was a rigid equation and it made no distinction between the fall of a leaf and the ponderous circling of a binary star system. The nuclear conversion process powered the cruisers that carried men to the stars; the same process in the form of a nova would destroy a world with equal efficiency. The laws *were,* and the universe moved in obedience to them. Along the frontier were arrayed all the forces of nature and sometimes they destroyed those who were fighting their way outward from Earth. The men of the frontier had long ago learned the bitter futility of cursing the forces that would destroy them for the forces were blind and deaf; the futility of looking to the heavens for mercy, for the stars of the galaxy swung in their long, long sweep of two hundred million years, as inexorably controlled as they by the laws that knew neither hatred nor compassion.

The man of the frontier knew—but how was a girl from Earth to fully understand? *H amount of fuel will not power an EDS with a mass of m plus x safely to its destination.* To himself and her brother and parents she was a sweet-faced girl in her teens; to the laws of nature she was *x,* the unwanted factor in a cold equation.

She stirred again on the seat. "Could I write a letter? I want to write to Mama and Daddy and I'd like to talk to Gerry. Could you let me talk to him over your radio there?"

"I'll try to get him," he said.

He switched on the normal-space transmitter and pressed the signal button. Someone answered the button almost immediately.

"Hello. How's it going with you fellows now—is the EDS on its way?"

"This isn't Group One; this is the EDS," he said. "Is Gerry Cross there?"

"Gerry? He and two others went out in the helicopter this morning and aren't back yet. It's almost sundown, though, and he ought to be back right away—in less than an hour at the most."

"Can you connect me through the radio in his 'copter?"

"Huh-uh. It's been out of commission for two months—some printed circuits went haywire and we can't get any more until the next cruiser stops by. Is it something important—bad news for him, or something?"

"Yes—it's very important. When he comes in get him to the transmitter as soon as you possibly can."

"I'll do that; I'll have one of the boys waiting at the field with a truck. Is there anything else I can do?"

"No, I guess that's all. Get him there as soon as you can and sign me."

He turned the volume to an inaudible minimum, an act that would not affect the functioning of the signal buzzer, and unclipped the pad of paper from the control board. He tore off the sheet containing his flight instructions and handed the pad to her, together with pencil.

"I'd better write to Gerry, too," she said as she took them. "He might not get back to camp in time."

She began to write, her fingers still clumsy and uncertain in the way they handled the pencil and the top of it trembling a little as she poised it between words. He turned back to the viewscreen, to stare at it without seeing it.

She was a lonely little child, trying to say her last good-bye, and she would lay out her heart to them. She would tell them how much she loved them and she would tell them to not feel badly about it, that it was only something that must eventually happen to everyone and she was not afraid. The last would be a lie and it would be there to read between the sprawling, uneven lines; a valiant little lie that would make the hurt all the greater for them.

Her brother was of the frontier and he would understand. He would not hate the EDS pilot for doing nothing to prevent her going; he would know there had been nothing the pilot could do. He would understand, though the understanding would not soften the shock and pain when he learned his sister was gone. But the others, her father and mother—they would not understand. They were of Earth and they would think in the manner of those who had never lived where the safety margin of life was a thin, thin line— and sometimes not at all. What would they think of the faceless, unknown pilot who had sent her to her death?

They would hate him with cold and terrible intensity but it really didn't matter. He would never see them, never know them. He would have only the memories to remind him; only the nights to fear, when a blue-eyed girl in gypsy sandals would come in his dreams to die again——

He scowled at the viewscreen and tried to force his thoughts into less emotional channels. There was nothing he could do to help her. She had unknowingly subjected herself to the penalty of a law that recognized neither innocence nor youth nor beauty, that was incapable of sympathy or leniency. Regret was illogical—and yet, could knowing it to be illogical ever keep it away?

She stopped occasionally, as though trying to find the right words to tell them what she wanted them to know, then the pencil would resume its whispering to the paper. It was 18.37 when she folded the letter in a square and wrote a name on it. She began writing another, twice looking up at the chronometer as though she feared the black hand might reach its rendezvous before she had finished. It was 18.45 when she folded it as she had done the first letter and wrote a name and address on it.

She held the letters out to him. "Will you take care of these and see that they're enveloped and mailed?"

"Of course." He took them from her hand and placed them in a pocket of his grey uniform shirt.

"These can't be sent off until the next cruiser stops by and the *Stardust* will have long since told them about me, won't it?" she asked. He nodded and she went on. "That makes the letters not important in one way but in another way they're very important—to me, and to them."

"I know, I understand, and I'll take care of them."

She glanced at the chronometer, then back at him. "It seems to move faster all the time, doesn't it?"

He said nothing, unable to think of anything to say, and she asked, "Do you think Gerry will come back to camp in time?"

"I think so. They said he should be in right away."

She began to roll the pencil back and forth between her palms. "I hope he does. I feel sick and scared and I want to hear his voice again and maybe I won't feel so alone. I'm a coward and I can't help it."

"No," he said, "you're not a coward. You're afraid, but you're not a coward."

"Is there a difference?"

He nodded. "A lot of difference."

"I feel so alone. I never did feel like this before; like I was all by myself and there was nobody to care what happened to me. Always, before, there was Mama and Daddy there and my friends around me. I had lots of friends, and they had a going-away party for me the night before I left."

Friends and music and laughter for her to remember—and on the viewscreen Lotus Lake was going into the shadow.

"Is it the same with Gerry?" she asked. "I mean, if he should make a mistake, would he have to die for it, all alone and with no one to help him?"

"It's the same with all along the frontier; it will always be like that so long as there is a frontier."

"Gerry didn't tell us. He said the pay was good and he sent money home all the time because Daddy's little shop just brought in a bare living but he didn't tell us it was like this."

"He didn't tell you his work was dangerous?"

"Well—yes. He mentioned that, but we didn't understand. I always thought danger along the frontier was something that was a lot of fun; and exciting adventure, like the three-D shows." A wan smile touched her face for a moment. "Only it's not, is it? It's not the same at all, because when it's real you can't go home after the show is over."

"No," he said. "No, you can't."

Her glance flicked from the chronometer to the door of the air lock then down to the pad and pencil she still held. She shifted her position slightly to lay them on the bench beside her, moving one foot out a little. For the first time he saw that she was not wearing Vegan gypsy sandals but only cheap imitations; the expensive Vegan leather was some kind of grained plastic, the silver buckle was gilded iron, the jewels were coloured glass. *Daddy's little shop just brought in a bare living*——She must have left college in her second year, to take the course in linguistics that would enable her to make her own way and help her brother provide for her parents, earning what she could by part-time work after classes were over. Her personal possessions on the *Stardust* would be taken back to her parents—they would neither be of much value nor occupy much storage space for the return voyage.

"Isn't it——" She stopped, and he looked at her questioningly. "Isn't it cold in here?" she asked, almost apologetically. "Doesn't it seem cold to you?"

"Why, yes," he said. He saw by the main temperature gauge that the room was at precisely normal temperature. "Yes, it's colder than it should be."

"I wish Gerry would get back before it's too late. Do you really think he will, and you didn't say so just to make me feel better?"

"I think he will—they said he would be in pretty soon." On the viewscreen Lotus Lake had gone into the shadow but for the thin blue line of its western edge and it was apparent he had overestimated the time she would have in which to talk to her brother. Reluctantly, he said to her, "His camp will be out of radio range in a few minutes; he's on that part of Woden that's in the shadow"—he indicated the viewscreen—"and the turning of Woden will put him beyond contact. There may not be much time left when he comes in—not much time to talk to him before he fades out. I wish I could do something about it—I would call him right now if I could."

"Not even as much time as I will have to stay?"

"I'm afraid not."

"Then——" She straightened and looked toward the air lock with pale resolution. "Then I'll go when Gerry passes beyond range, I won't wait any longer after that—I won't have anything to wait for."

Again there was nothing he could say.

"Maybe I shouldn't wait at all. Maybe I'm selfish—maybe it would be better for Gerry if you just told him about it afterward."

There was an unconscious pleading for denial in the way she spoke and he said, "He wouldn't want you to do that, not to wait for him."

"It's already coming dark where he is, isn't it? There will be all the long night before him, and Mama and Daddy don't know yet that I won't ever be coming back like I promised them I would. I've caused everyone I love to be hurt, haven't I? I didn't want to—I didn't intend to."

"It wasn't your fault," he said. "It wasn't your fault at all. They'll know that. They'll understand."

"At first I was so afraid to die that I was a coward and thought only of myself. Now, I see how selfish I was. The terrible thing about dying like this is not that I'll be gone but that I'll never see them again; never be able to tell them that I didn't take them for granted; never be able to tell them I knew of the sacrifices they made to keep my life happier, that I knew all the things they did for me and that I loved them so much more than I ever told them. I've never told them any of those things. You don't tell them such things when you're young and your life is all before you—you're afraid of sounding sentimental and silly.

"But it's so different when you have to die—you wish you had told them while you could and you wish you could tell them you're sorry for all the little mean things you ever did or said to them. You wish you could tell them that you didn't really mean to ever hurt their feelings and for them only to remember that you always loved them far more than you ever let them know."

"You don't have to tell them that," he said. "They will know—they've always known it."

"Are you sure?" she asked. "How can you be sure? My people are strangers to you."

"Wherever you go, human nature and human hearts are the same."

"And they will know what I want them to know—that I love them?"

"They've always known it, in a way far better than you could ever put in words for them."

"I keep remembering the things they did for me, and it's the little things they did that seem to be the most important to me, now. Like Gerry—he sent me a bracelet of fire-rubies on my sixteenth birthday. It was beautiful—it must have cost him a month's pay. Yet, I remember him more for what he did the night my kitten got run over in the street. I was only six years old and he held me in his arms and wiped away my tears and told me not to cry, that Flossy was gone for just a little while, for just long enough to get herself a new fur coat and she would be on the foot of my bed the very next morning. I believed him and quit crying and went to sleep dreaming about my kitten coming back. When I woke up the next morning, there was Flossy on the foot of my bed in a brand-new white fur coat, just like he had said she would be.

"It wasn't until a long time later that Mama told me Gerry had got the petshop owner out of bed at four in the morning and, when the man got mad about it, Gerry told him he was either going to go down and sell him the white kitten right then or he'd break his neck."

"It's always the little things you remember people by; all the little things they did because they wanted to do them for you. You've done the same for Gerry and your father and mother; all kinds of things that you've forgotten about but they will never forget."

"I hope I have. I would like for them to remember me like that."

"They will."

"I wish——" She swallowed. "The way I'll die—I wish they wouldn't ever think of that. I've read how people look who have died in space—their insides all ruptured and exploded and their lungs out between their teeth and then, a few seconds later, they're all dry and shapeless and horribly ugly. I don't want them to ever think of me as something dead and horrible, like that."

"You're their own, their child and their sister. They could never think of you other than the way you want them to; the way you looked the last time they saw you."

"I'm still afraid," she said. "I can't help it, but I don't want Gerry to know it. If he gets back in time, I'm going to act like I'm not afraid at all and——"

The signal buzzer interrupted her, quick and imperative.

"Gerry!" She came to her feet. "It's Gerry, now!"

He spun the volume control knob and asked: "Gerry Cross?"

"Yes," her brother answered, an undertone of tenseness to his reply. "The bad news—what is it?"

She answered for him, standing close behind him and leaning down a little toward the communicator, her hand resting small and cold on his shoulder.

"Hello, Gerry." There was only a faint quiver to betray the careful casualness of her voice. "I wanted to see you——"

"Marilyn!" There was sudden and terrible apprehension in the way he spoke her name. "What are you doing on that EDS?"

"I wanted to see you," she said again. "I wanted to see you, so I hid on this ship——"

"You *hid* on it?"

"I'm a stowaway . . . I didn't know what it would mean——"

"Marilyn!" It was the cry of a man who calls hopeless and desperate to someone already and forever gone from him. "What have you done?"

"I . . . it's not——" Then her own composure broke and the cold little hand gripped his shoulder convulsively. "Don't, Gerry—I only wanted to see you; I didn't intend to hurt you. Please, Gerry, don't feel like that——"

Something warm and wet splashed on his wrist and he slid out of the chair, to help her into it and swing the microphone down to her level.

"Don't feel like that—— Don't let me go knowing you feel like that——"

The sob she tried to hold back choked in her throat and her brother spoke to her. "Don't cry, Marilyn." His voice was suddenly deep and infinitely gentle, with all the pain held out of it. "Don't cry, Sis—you mustn't do that. It's all right, Honey—everything is all right."

"I——" Her lower lip quivered and she bit into it. "I didn't want you to feel that way—I just wanted us to say good-bye because I have to go in a minute."

"Sure—sure. That's the way it will be, Sis. I didn't mean to sound the way I did." Then his voice changed to a tone of quick and urgent demand. "EDS—have you called the *Stardust?* Did you check with the computers?"

"I called the *Stardust* almost an hour ago. It can't turn back, there are no other cruisers within forty light-years, and there isn't enough fuel."

"Are you sure that the computers had the correct data—sure of everything?"

"Yes—do you think I could ever let it happen if I wasn't sure? I did everything I could do. If there was anything at all I could do now, I would do it."

"He tried to help me, Gerry." Her lower lip was no longer trembling and the short sleeves of her blouse were wet where she had dried her tears. "No one can help me and I'm not going to cry any more and everything will be all right with you and Daddy and Mama, won't it?"

"Sure—sure, it will. We'll make out fine."

Her brother's words were beginning to come in more faintly and he turned the volume control to maximum. "He's going out of range," he said to her. "He'll be gone within another minute."

"You're fading out, Gerry," she said. "You're going out of range. I wanted to tell you—but I can't, now. We must say good-bye so soon—but maybe I'll see you again. Maybe I'll come to you in your dreams with my hair in braids and crying because the kitten in my arms is dead; maybe I'll be the touch of a breeze that whispers to you as it goes by; maybe I'll be one of those gold-winged larks you told me about, singing my silly head off to you; maybe, at times, I'll be nothing you can see but you will know I'm there beside you. Think of me like that, Gerry; always like that and not—the other way."

Dimmed to a whisper by the turning of Woden, the answer came back:

"Always like that, Marilyn—always like that and never any other way."

"Our time is up, Gerry—I have to go, now. Good——" Her voice broke in mid-word and her mouth tried to twist into crying. She pressed her hand hard against it and when she spoke again the words came clear and true:

"Good-bye, Gerry."

Faint and ineffably poignant and tender, the last words came from the cold metal of the communicator.

"Good-bye, little sister——"

She sat motionless in the hush that followed, as though listening to the shadow-echoes of the words as they died away, then she turned away from the communicator toward the air lock, and he pulled down the black lever beside him. The inner door of the air lock slid swiftly open, to reveal the bare little cell that was waiting for her, and she walked to it.

She walked with her head up and the brown curls brushing her shoulders, with the white sandals stepping as sure and steady as the fractional gravity would permit and the gilded buckles twinkling with little lights of blue and red and crystal. He let her walk alone and made no move to help her, knowing she would not want it that way. She stepped into the air lock and turned to face him, only the pulse in her throat to betray the wild beating of her heart.

"I'm ready," she said.

He pushed the lever up and the door slid its quick barrier between them, inclosing her in black and utter darkness for her last moments of life. It clicked as it locked in place and he jerked down the red lever. There was a slight waver to the ship as the air gushed from the lock, a vibration to the wall as though something had bumped the outer door in passing, then there was nothing and the ship was dropping true and steady again. He shoved the red lever back to close the door on the empty air lock and turned away, to walk to the pilot's chair with the slow steps of a man old and weary.

Back in the pilot's chair he pressed the signal button of the normal-space transmitter. There was no response; he had expected none. Her brother would have to wait through the night until the turning of Woden permitted contact through Group One.

It was not yet time to resume deceleration and he waited while the ship dropped endlessly downward with him and the drives purred softly. He saw that the white hand of the supplies closet temperature was on zero. A cold equation had been balanced and he was alone on the ship. Something shapeless and ugly was hurrying ahead of him, going to Woden where its brother was waiting through the night, but the empty ship still lived for a little while with the presence of the girl who had not known about the forces that killed with neither hatred nor malice. It seemed, almost, that she still sat small and bewildered and frightened on the metal box beside him, her words echoing hauntingly clear in the void she had left behind her:

I didn't do anything to die for—I didn't do anything——

QUESTIONS FOR DISCUSSION: THE COLD EQUATIONS

1. Discuss whether the fact that the young woman passenger was a stowaway justified the decision to jettison her. Would it have been wrong to do so even if she had been a legal passenger? Explain which of the moral standards proposed in Chapter 1 best supports your answer.

2. In a critique of utilitarianism, the contemporary British philosopher Bernard Williams describes the following situation: A U.S. tourist, driving through a central American country ruled by a cruel dictator, stops in a village where twenty rebellious peasants are lined up against a wall, facing a firing squad. The commanding officer approaches the tourist and offers to spare nineteen of the rebels if the tourist takes the officer's revolver and shoots one of the rebels. Compared to the dilemma facing the pilot of the spaceship in "The Cold Equations," is the tourist's moral dilemma more, less, or equally difficult to resolve morally? Defend your position as you compare the two situations.

3

PHYSICIAN-ASSISTED SUICIDE AND EUTHANASIA

When, if ever, is it morally right to take human life? Of all our moral convictions, that of the sanctity of human life is the most deeply rooted in our nature and in our oldest traditions. If there are permissible exceptions to this principle, then it may seem doubtful that any moral principles are immune from exceptions. Yet occasions arise, such as the unbearable suffering of someone terminally ill, a desperately unwanted pregnancy resulting from a rape, or a terrorist massacre of innocent people, that seem to call for mercy killing, abortion, or capital punishment. Are there values that take precedence over human life in such circumstances, or is life so sacred that it must never be taken? If not, then perhaps nothing is really sacred. In that case, do we not slide down a slippery slope toward moral skepticism?

In our search for when, if ever, human life can justifiably be taken, we begin with the cases that seem most relevant: those in which the owners of the lives in question are suffering unbearably and want—indeed, beg for— ending them. In the ancient world suicide was not condemned until the rise of the Jewish, Christian, and Islamic religions, which have regarded suicide as a sin equal to or even worse than murder because it destroys what God has created, without divine permission and therefore contrary to divine will. As a result, suicide has been looked upon, even by many nonreligious people, as cowardly and shameful. Assisting in its commission, or killing the person who wishes to die, has been prohibited by law and has been morally condemned by custom, as well as by religious teaching.

The issue of what is sometimes described as "the right to die" has come to a head in recent years with the trials of Dr. Jack Kevorkian ("Dr. Death," as some call him). He has provided apparatus for patients to end their own lives and, most recently, administered a lethal injection to a patient, videotaping his action to test the law in Michigan against mercy killing. He was acquitted of the charge of murder when tried for assisting at suicide, but he was convicted at his last trial for performing the lethal action himself.

Although some nations, most notably the Netherlands, have legalized voluntary active euthanasia (mercy killing) under carefully controlled conditions, none of the United States has done so. However, the state of Oregon recently legalized physician-assisted suicide over the strenuous objections of the federal government as represented by Attorney General Ashcroft. What is sometimes called "passive euthanasia," meaning refraining from attempts to keep a dying person alive, has been generally accepted in recent years as permissible. Some groups still insist on a distinction between not starting such attempts (i.e., not turning on the life-saving equipment) and terminating them (turning the equipment off), but this distinction seems to be losing force.

Whether Dr. Kevorkian's step from assistance at suicide to active euthanasia is so important, morally, as to permit the former while prohibiting the latter, is one of the two burning issues discussed in the following essays. The other issue is whether both activities or neither one should be considered permissible. These questions are so intimately linked that it seems necessary to explore them together.

Dan Brock and Frances Kamm argue in defense of both activities, whereas Daniel Callahan and Sissela Bok argue against them. Interestingly, Brock and Callahan both argue that passive and active euthanasia, as well as assisted suicide, are morally equivalent; yet Brock concludes that all are morally permissible, whereas Callahan concludes that all are impermissible. Kamm, on the other hand, argues that they are not morally equivalent but that, depending on other factors, all three types of action may be morally permissible. Bok, on the other hand, avoids moralizing on the subject; she merely argues that assisted suicide and active euthanasia should be forbidden, on the grounds that they are too easily subject to abuse. (Passive euthanasia, such as not employing, or turning off, "heroic" measures like respirators and dialysis machines, is already generally accepted. Perhaps for that reason, Bok does not discuss it.)

THE MORAL JUSTIFIABILITY
OF ASSISTED SUICIDE

Dan W. Brock

There are two central and distinct moral issues about physician-assisted suicide. First, is physician-assisted suicide morally justified in any individual cases? Second, would it be ethically justified for public and legal policy to permit physician-assisted suicide? This chapter is concerned only with the first of these questions, and I shall argue the affirmative answer. . . . The affirmative case for a public policy permitting physician-assisted suicide is in my view more complex and less decisive, though nevertheless also sound. But my concern will be broader than the first question in one important respect. The argument that I shall make applies in nearly all essentials to voluntary active euthanasia as well as physician-assisted suicide, and I shall begin by indicating why I believe the two are not importantly different morally. (For brevity and unless explicitly indicated otherwise, I shall hereafter use "assisted suicide" to refer to physician-assisted suicide and "euthanasia" to refer to voluntary active euthanasia.)

In the recent bioethics literature some have endorsed assisted suicide but not euthanasia, even in individual cases and not only for public policy. Moreover, the policy proposals that in the last few years have been brought to legislatures or to the public in state referenda in nearly all cases have applied only to assisted suicide and not to euthanasia. Are they sufficiently different that the moral arguments that apply to one often do not apply to the other? First, what is the difference between assisted suicide and euthanasia? A paradigm case of assisted suicide is a patient's ending his or her life with a lethal dose of a medication requested of and provided by a physician for that purpose. A paradigm case of euthanasia is a physician's administering the lethal dose, often because the patient is unable to do so. The only difference that need exist between the two is the person who actually administers the lethal dose—the physician or the patient. In each, the physician plays an active and necessary causal role in providing the lethal dose. In each, the intent of the patient and physician is to pursue a course of action that will end in the patient's death.

In assisted suicide the patient acts last (for example, Janet Adkins pushed the button after Dr. Jack Kevorkian hooked her up to his suicide machine), whereas in euthanasia the physician acts last by performing the physical equivalent of pushing the button. In both cases, however, the choice rests fully with the patient in the sense that neither will take place without the patient's desire for them; of course, in each the physician must also be willing to play his or her role. In both the patient acts last in the sense of retaining the right to change his or her mind until the point at which the lethal process becomes irreversible. How could there be a substantial moral difference between the two based only on this small difference in the part played by the physician in the causal process resulting in death? Of course, it might be held that the moral difference is obvious and important—in euthanasia the physician kills the patient, whereas in assisted suicide the patient kills him- or herself. But this is misleading at best. In assisted suicide the physician and patient act together to kill the patient. To see this, suppose a physician supplied a lethal dose to a patient with the knowledge and intent that the patient will wrongfully administer it to another. We would have no difficulty in morality or the law recognizing this as a case of joint action to bring about another's death, or to kill, for which both are responsible. The physician is involved in killing in both assisted suicide and euthanasia. . . .

If there is no significant, intrinsic moral difference between assisted suicide and euthanasia, it is also difficult to see why public or legal policy should permit one but not the other; worries about abuse or about giving anyone dominion over the lives of others seem also to apply equally to either. Some argue that because in assisted suicide the patient must take the final physical act that results in his or her death, there is greater certainty of the patient's voluntary resolve to die than when the physician performs that act. In some cases this may be true, but there are also cases of euthanasia in which the voluntary resolve of the patient to die is not in significant doubt. However, I shall not pursue the policy issue here, but I shall take the arguments developed below about individual cases of physician-assisted suicide to apply both to assisted suicide and to euthanasia.

My concern here will be only with *voluntary* cases of assisted suicide or euthanasia, that is, with cases in which a clearly competent patient makes a fully voluntary and persistent request for assisted suicide or euthanasia. Perhaps the assumption of voluntariness is implicit in the very concept of physician-assisted suicide, either in the condition that the patient performs the final physical act of using the means to end his or her life or in the notion of the physician assisting the patient, but I have said that my argument applies to active euthanasia as well, and voluntariness is not implicit there. Involuntary euthanasia, in which a competent patient explicitly refuses or opposes receiving euthanasia, and nonvoluntary euthanasia, in which a patient is incompetent and unable to express his or her wishes about euthanasia, are both possible but will not be my concern here. Finally, I will be concerned with assisted suicide and euthanasia where the motive of those who perform them is to respect the wishes of the patient and to provide the patient with a "good death"; only in such cases is the physician's participation morally justified. . . .

THE CENTRAL ETHICAL ARGUMENT
FOR ASSISTED SUICIDE AND EUTHANASIA

The central ethical argument for assisted suicide and euthanasia is familiar. It is that the very same two fundamental ethical values supporting the consensus on patients' rights to decide about life-sustaining treatment also support the ethical permissibility of assisted suicide and euthanasia in some circumstances. And this implies that acceptance of assisted suicide and euthanasia is not as radical a moral departure from the current consensus and practice giving patients the right to decide to forgo life support, as is commonly supposed. These values are individual self-determination or autonomy and individual well-being. By self-determination, as it bears on assisted suicide and euthanasia, I mean people's interest in making important decisions about their lives for themselves according to their own values or conceptions of a good life and in being left free to act on those decisions. Self-determination is valuable because it permits people to form and to live in accordance with their own conception of a good life, at least within the bounds of justice and consistent with not preventing others from doing so as well. In exercising self-determination people exercise significant control over their lives and thereby take responsibility for their lives and for the kinds of persons they become. A central aspect of human dignity and the moral worth of persons lies in individuals' capacity to direct their lives in this way. The value of exercising self-determination presupposes some minimum of decision-making capacities or competence, which thus limits the scope of assisted suicide or euthanasia supported by self-determination; it does not apply, for example, in cases of serious dementia or treatable clinical depression that impair the individual's decision-making capacity.

Individual self-determination has special importance in choices about the time and manner of one's death, including assisted suicide and euthanasia. Most people are very concerned about the nature of the last stage of their lives. This reflects not just a fear of experiencing substantial pain or suffering or of being abandoned by loved ones when dying, but also a desire to retain dignity and control to the extent possible during this last period of life. Death is today increasingly preceded by a long period of significant physical and mental decline, due in part to the technological interventions of modern medicine designed to stave off death. Many people adjust to their disability and dependency and find meaning and value in new activities and ways. Others find the impairments and burdens in the last stage of their lives at some point sufficiently great to make life no longer worth living. For some patients near death, maintaining the quality of one's life, avoiding great pain or suffering, maintaining one's dignity, and ensuring that others remember us as we wish them to become of paramount importance and outweigh merely extending one's life. But there is no single, objectively correct answer for everyone regarding when, if at all, one's life when critically or terminally ill becomes, all things considered, a burden and unwanted. If self-determination is a fundamental value, then the great variability among people on this question makes it especially important that individuals control to the extent possible the manner, circumstances, and timing of their dying and death.

The other main value that supports assisted suicide and euthanasia is individual well-being. It might seem that protecting and promoting individual well-being must always conflict with a person's self-determination when the person requests assisted suicide or euthanasia, but it is important to understand why this is not so. Life itself is commonly understood to be a central good for persons, often valued for its own sake, as well as necessary for the pursuit of all other goods within a life. But when a competent patient decides to forgo all further life-sustaining treatment, then the patient, either explicitly or implicitly, commonly decides that the best life possible for him or her with treatment is of sufficiently poor quality that it is worse than no further life at all. Life is then no longer considered a benefit by the patient but has now become without value or meaning and a burden. The same judgment underlies a request for assisted suicide or euthanasia—continued life is then seen by the patient as no longer a benefit, but now a burden. Especially in the often severely compromised and debilitated states of many critically ill or dying patients, there is no objective standard but only the competent patient's judgment of whether continued life is no longer a benefit.

Of course, sometimes conditions such as clinical depression call into question whether the patient has made a competent choice, either to forgo life-sustaining treatment or to seek assisted suicide or euthanasia, and then the patient's choice need not be evidence that continued life is no longer a benefit for him or her. Just as with decisions about treatment, a determination of incompetence can warrant not honoring the patient's request for assisted suicide or euthanasia; in the case of treatment, we then transfer decisional authority to a surrogate, though in the case of assisted suicide or voluntary euthanasia a determination that the patient is incompetent to make that choice means that neither should take place. . . .

ASSISTED SUICIDE AND EUTHANASIA ARE DELIBERATE KILLING OF AN INNOCENT PERSON

In order to state the argument of the opponent of assisted suicide and euthanasia in its strongest form and to avoid unnecessary complexity in exposition, I shall focus in this section on euthanasia. The claim that any individual instance of euthanasia is a case of deliberate killing of an innocent person is, with only minor qualifications, correct. Unlike forgoing life-sustaining treatment, commonly understood as allowing to die, euthanasia is clearly killing, understood as depriving of life or causing the death of a living being. While providing morphine for pain relief at doses where the risk of respiratory depression and an earlier death may be a foreseen but unintended side effect of treating the patient's pain, in a case of euthanasia the patient's death is deliberate or intended even if in both the physician's ultimate end may be respecting the patient's wishes. If the deliberate killing of an innocent person is wrong, euthanasia would be nearly always impermissible.

In the context of medicine, the ethical prohibition against deliberately killing the innocent derives some of its plausibility from the belief that nothing in the currently accepted practice of medicine is deliberate killing. Thus, in commenting on the "It's Over Debbie" case in which a resident deliberately gave a patient a lethal dose of morphine, four prominent physicians and bioethicists, led by Willard Gaylin, could entitle their paper "Doctors Must Not Kill." The belief that doctors do not kill requires the corollary belief that forgoing life-sustaining treatment, whether by not starting or by stopping treatment, is allowing to die, not killing. Common though this view is, I shall argue that it is confused and mistaken. Typical cases of stopping life-sustaining treatment are killing, not allowing to die, although they are cases of ethically justified killing. But if so, that shows that an unqualified ethical prohibition of the deliberate killing of innocent persons is indefensible and must be revised.

Why is the common view mistaken that stopping life-sustaining treatment is allowing to die and not killing? Consider the case of a patient terminally ill with amytrophic lateral sclerosis disease (ALS, or Lou Gehrig's disease). She is completely respirator dependent with no hope of ever being weaned from the respirator. She is unquestionably competent but finds her condition intolerable and persistently requests to be removed from the respirator and allowed to die. Most people and physicians would likely agree that the patient's physician should respect the patient's wishes and remove her from the respirator, though this will certainly cause the patient's death. The common understanding is that the physician thereby allows the patient to die. But is that correct?

Suppose the patient has a greedy and hostile son who mistakenly believes both that his mother will never decide to stop her life-sustaining treatment and that even if she did her physician would not respect her wishes and remove her from the respirator. Afraid that his inheritance will be dissipated by a long and expensive hospitalization, he enters his mother's room while she is sedated, extubates her, and she dies. Shortly thereafter the medical staff discovers what he has done and confronts the son. He replies, "I didn't kill her, I merely allowed her to die. It was her ALS disease that caused her death." I think this would rightly be dismissed as transparent sophistry—the son went into his mother's room and deliberately killed her. But, of course, the son performed just the same physical actions, did just the same thing, with all the same consequences for the patient, that the physician would have done. If that is so, then doesn't the physician also kill the patient when he extubates her and stops the respirator?

I underline immediately that there are important ethical differences between what the physician and the greedy son do. First, the physician acts with the patient's consent, whereas the son does not. Second, the physician acts with a good motive—to respect the patient's wishes and self-determination—whereas the son acts with a bad motive—to protect his own inheritance. Third, the physician acts in a social role through which he is legally authorized to carry out the patient's decision to stop treatment, whereas the son has no such authorization. These and perhaps other ethically important differences show that what the physician did was morally justified, whereas what the son did was morally wrong. What they do *not* show, however, is that the son killed while the physician allowed to die. One can either kill or allow to die with or without consent, with a good or bad motive, within or outside a social role that legally authorizes one to do so.

The difference between killing and allowing to die that I have been implicitly appealing to here is roughly the difference between acts and omissions resulting in death. Both the physician and the greedy son act in a manner intended to cause death, do cause death, and so both kill; neither allows to die. One reason this conclusion is resisted is that on a different understanding of the distinction between killing and allowing to die, what the physician does is allow to die. In this account, the mother's ALS is a lethal disease whose normal progression is being held back or blocked by the life-sustaining respirator treatment. Removing this artificial intervention is then viewed as standing aside and allowing the patient to die of her underlying disease. I have argued elsewhere that this alternative account is deeply problematic, in part because it seems to have the unacceptable implication that what the greedy son also does is to allow to die, not kill. Here I want to note two other reasons why the conclusion that stopping life support is killing is resisted.

The first reason is that killing is often understood, especially within medicine, as unjustified or wrongful causing of death; in medicine it is thought to be done only accidentally or negligently. It is also increasingly widely accepted that a physician is ethically justified in stopping life support in a case like that of the ALS patient. But if both of these beliefs are correct, then what the physician does cannot be killing and so instead must be allowing to die. Killing patients is not, to put it flippantly, understood to be part of a physician's job description. What is mistaken in this line of reasoning is the assumption that all killings are *unjustified or wrongful* causings of death. Instead, some killings are ethically justified, including most instances of stopping life support.

Another reason for resisting the conclusion that stopping life support is often killing is that it is psychologically uncomfortable. Suppose the physician had stopped the ALS patient's respirator and had made the son's claim, "I didn't kill her, I merely allowed her to die. It was her ALS disease that caused her death." The clue to the psychological role here is how naturally the "merely" modifies "allowed her to die." The characterization as allowing to die is meant to shift felt responsibility away from the agent—the physician—and to the lethal disease process that the physician merely allowed to proceed to the patient's death. Other language common in death and dying contexts plays a similar role; "letting nature take its course" or "stopping prolonging the dying process" both seem to shift responsibility from the physician who stops life support to the fatal disease process. However psychologically helpful these conceptualizations may be in making the difficult responsibility of a physician's role in the patient's death bearable, they nevertheless are confusions. Both physicians and family members can instead be helped to understand that it is the patient's decision and consent to stopping treatment that limits their responsibility for the patient's death and which shifts that responsibility to the patient.

Many who accept this understanding of the difference between killing and allowing to die as the difference between acts and omissions resulting in death have gone on to argue that killing is not in itself morally different from allowing to die. In this account, very roughly, one kills when one performs an action that causes the death of a person (e.g., we are in a boat, you cannot swim, I push you overboard, and you drown), and one allows to die when one has the ability and opportunity to prevent the death of another, knows this, and omits doing so, with the result that the person dies (e.g., we are in a boat, you cannot swim, you fall overboard, I don't throw you an available life ring, and you drown). Those who see no moral difference between killing and allowing to die typically employ the strategy of comparing cases that differ in these and no other potentially morally important respects. This will allow people to consider whether the mere difference that one is a case of killing and the other of allowing to die matters morally, or whether instead it is other features that make most killings worse than most instances of allowing to die. Here is such a pair of cases.

> *Case 1.* A very gravely ill patient is brought to a hospital emergency room and sent up to the ICU. The patient begins to develop respiratory failure that is likely to require intubation very soon. At that point the patient's family members and long-time physician arrive at the ICU and inform the ICU staff that there had been extensive discussion about future care with the patient when he was unquestionably competent. Given his grave and terminal illness as well as his state of debilitation, the patient had firmly rejected being placed on a respirator under any circumstances, and the family and physician produce the patient's advance directive to that effect. The ICU staff do not intubate the patient, who dies of respiratory failure.

> *Case 2.* The same as Case 1 except that the family and physician are slightly delayed in traffic and arrive shortly after the patient has been intubated and placed on the respirator. The ICU staff extubate the patient, who dies of respiratory failure.

In Case 1 the patient is allowed to die, in Case 2 he is killed, but it is hard to see why what is done in Case 2 is significantly different morally than what is done in Case 1. It must be other factors that make most killings worse than most allowings to die, and if so, assisted suicide and euthanasia cannot be wrong simply because they are killing instead of allowing to die.

A RIGHTS APPROACH TO THE MORALITY OF KILLING

Suppose that both my arguments are mistaken. Suppose that killing is worse than allowing to die and that withdrawing life support is not killing, although assisted suicide and euthanasia are. Assisted suicide and euthanasia still need not for that reason be morally wrong. To see this, we need to determine the basic principle for the moral evaluation of killing persons. What is it that makes paradigm cases of wrongful killing wrongful? One very plausible answer is that killing denies the victim a very great good over whose possession he or she should have control—continued life or a future. Our continued life or future is typically the object of one of our strongest desires. It can be thought of as a dispositional or standing desire, which typically becomes an occurrent desire, occupying an important place in one's conscious desires and plans, when one's life is threatened. Moreover, continued life is a necessary condition for being able to pursue and achieve any of one's other plans and purposes; loss of life brings the frustration of all of these plans and purposes as well. In a nutshell, wrongful killing typically deprives a person of a great and valued good—his or her future and all that the person wanted and planned to do in that future. It is important to see that there is another distinct moral idea at work in this account of the wrongness of killing besides that killing typically deprives the victim of a very great good, on which nearly all other goods for that person depend. The other idea is that one's life is a good over which, at least within limits, a person him- or herself should retain control.

Sometimes these two moral ideas or values can be in conflict, as, for example, when an apparently competent patient makes an informed and voluntary choice to refuse life-sustaining treatment that would restore the patient to full function and a life that most people would consider a life well worth having. Here the patient is exercising his or her right of control over his or her life and what is done to his or her body to give up the apparently very great good of continued life. If we cannot come to understand why the patient reasonably does not value that continued life or cannot find serious impairments in the patient's decision making or cannot persuade the patient to accept the treatment, then we may be forced to decide which value is more important, preserving the good of the patient's life or respecting the patient's right of control over his or her own life, that is, his or her self-determination or autonomy.

Public policy, as expressed in the law, gives competent patients the right to refuse any treatment, including life-sustaining treatment, and thereby gives greater weight to respecting the patient's right of control or self-determination regarding his or her own life. The law's resolution of this conflict in favor of self-determination recognizes not only the deep place of that value in our moral, cultural, and legal traditions but also the circumstance that when a competent individual rejects life-sustaining treatment he or she either no longer finds continued life a good or finds the means of gaining it unacceptable (for example, when Jehovah's Witness patients reject life-sustaining blood products). Our moral and cultural traditions, however, do not speak with one voice about how these values should be weighed when they are in conflict. Reasonable people can and do disagree about how this conflict should be resolved when an apparently worthwhile life is being given up by a competent patient.

In a comparable case in which a person with an apparently worthwhile life sought assisted suicide or euthanasia, most physicians and most persons probably would refuse to take part. But that is not at all the typical case in which assisted suicide or euthanasia is sought; nor is it the kind of case in which I am arguing that they are morally permissible and justified. Instead, in the typical and relevant case others view the competent individual's decision as quite reasonable, that continued life is no longer a good because that life is so filled with suffering and bereft of possibilities for the activities and experiences that make life valuable and meaningful. In such cases, the morally great good of continued life and the respect owed that patient's self-determination are not in conflict because continued life is no longer a great good but is now reasonably judged by the patient to be a burden and without value. Some physicians who give great weight to patient self-determination might be willing to participate in assisted suicide even when they cannot accept the patient's judgment that his or her life is no longer worth living. But many others would be willing to participate in assisted suicide or euthanasia only if they either share or at least view as reasonable the patient's judgment that his or her life is no longer worth living. In such cases, no significant good for the patient need be sacrificed in order to respect the patient's self-determination.

A natural expression of my account of the wrongness of killing is that people have a moral right not to be killed. But the right not to be killed, like other rights, should be understood as waivable when the person makes a competent decision that continued life is no longer wanted or a good but is instead worse than no further life at all, and so wishes to die. In this rights view of the wrongness of killing, assisted suicide and euthanasia are properly understood as cases in which the person killed has waived his or her right not to be killed, thereby making the physician's action not a violation of that right.

This rights view of the wrongness of killing is not, of course, universally shared. Many people's moral views about killing have their origins in religious beliefs that human life comes from God and cannot be justifiably destroyed or taken away, either by the person whose life it is or by another. I noted earlier that I would be addressing only secular moral arguments regarding assisted suicide and euthanasia, and so will only reiterate two points made there. First, in a pluralistic society like our own with a strong commitment to freedom of religion, public policy should not be grounded in religious beliefs which many in that society reject. Second, if the position about the wrongness of killing rests on theological premises that many persons can and do reasonably reject, then those persons will have been given no reason why they should regard such killing as wrong.

The rejection of the rights view of the wrongness of killing, however, does not always have a religious basis. Some people believe it is always morally wrong deliberately to take an innocent human life—what is sometimes called a duty-based view on taking human life. The "innocence condition" may permit killing in self-defense or even in capital punishment under some interpretations, but not when a person seeks assisted suicide or euthanasia. If this moral prohibition does not derive from God, however, it is difficult to see what its moral basis can be. That basis can be neither that life is a very great good that should never be destroyed nor that one individual should never claim dominion over the life of another. As we have seen, sometimes the killing of an innocent person, in particular assisted suicide and euthanasia, does not conflict with but is instead supported by these two values. These are the moral values that support the rights account, not the duty account, of the morality of killing.

THE IMMORALITY OF ASSISTED SUICIDE

Daniel Callahan

What can be said about human suffering? This much at least: No one wants to suffer. No one wants a death marked by suffering. Only tyrants and those who are pathologically cruel want others to suffer. Medicine is dedicated to the relief of suffering, and we proclaim ourselves to be a society that will not knowingly countenance the relievable misery of any group. Suffering not only brings pain, physical and mental (just as pain can bring suffering), it can in its extreme forms seem to rob people altogether of their humanity.

Given so many shared convictions—our mutual agreement that human suffering should be avoided if possible and relieved when it occurs—how can anyone morally oppose physician-assisted suicide (PAS) to save someone from it? Even if one personally opposes it, how in a free and pluralistic society can one legitimately deny it to others, those with a different ethical view? What could be a more private matter than our own life and fate? Who am *I* morally to judge what is bearable or unbearable suffering in others, or to evaluate what others might do to relieve their suffering? Does not common sense, moreover, seem to indicate that if someone is going to die anyway, and do so with needlessly unbearable suffering, PAS offers a merciful way of averting that misery?

For many people, the answers to these now-familiar questions seem almost self-evident. The moral case in favor of PAS appears to draw so obviously upon a store of shared values, a pervasive consensus about freedom and the relief of suffering, that it is sometimes hard to understand why the matter should so trouble others. Is that a matter of prejudice and irrationality? Or moral insensitivity? Or religious dogmatism?

No. It is none of those things, though they may surely be present in some people opposed to PAS. On the contrary, the longstanding historical prohibition of PAS—cultural, medical, and religious—rests upon a solid and enduring insight: that it is dangerous and wrong to sanction and endorse suicide as a way of relieving suffering and equally hazardous to make physicians the helping agents of such an action. I contend that there is no such thing as a right to PAS and that even if some *believe* they have such a right, they should voluntarily waive its exercise because of its dangers to others (much as we should not exercise our legal right of free speech to make nasty and demeaning racist statements).

There are, conventionally, two general philosophical approaches to the morality of euthanasia and PAS. One of them tries to show that those actions are intrinsically wrong—wrong, that is, even if some or all of their consequences may be beneficial. The other approach attempts to demonstrate that the consequences of PAS, its actual results, would be harmful, either directly and immediately or because they would lead us down that famous slippery slope. This tidy kind of dichotomy in moral theory is not helpful. It is hard to imagine how we can ignore consequences in determining what is intrinsically wrong and no less difficult to determine what counts as good and bad consequences without some notion of what is intrinsically right and wrong. Each theory seems, in practice, to need the other even to make good sense.

This is not the place to take up any further that longstanding debate in moral philosophy. For the purposes of this essay, I will adopt what I characterize as an ecological approach to the moral questions. Think of PAS as a seemingly attractive flower that we contemplate planting in the meadow that is our society. Should we do this or not? To answer this question we need, first, to ask whether the plant will take root and flourish in its own right. Will it grow as expected? We must ask, second, what it will do to the other plants in the meadow. How will it affect their flourishing? We must, that is, ask a twofold question: is PAS good in its own terms, and what will be its meaning and implications for the society in which it is introduced?

On the whole, it is that latter question that will most interest me here, but I want at the outset to say something about the intrinsic rightness or wrongness of PAS. What kind of a plant is it that we want to introduce into our societal meadow: good or bad, beneficial or noxious? I believe that PAS is in and of itself noxious. While I am quite prepared to acknowledge that some people may, out of despair over their fate or their suffering, want to commit suicide and am no less prepared to suspend moral judgment about their particular act, it is a wholly different matter to socially endorse and legitimate suicide as an acceptable and routine, even if relatively rare, way of dealing with the problem of an unhappy life. Our common moral intuition that suicide is ordinarily an act of desperation, that it usually bespeaks some degree of treatable depression, and that it ought not to be encouraged, strikes me as entirely valid. It is a way to defend ourselves, and help others defend us, from the despair that life can bring our way; and it is generally recognized that we need to help each other cope with it, not succumb to it. To give a physician, moreover, the power to kill another, even with the permission of that person, or to assist someone to kill himself is to place too much power in the physician's hands, that of a right to take life as a means of eliminating despair.

EUTHANASIA AND PHYSICIAN-ASSISTED SUICIDE: ARE THEY MORALLY DIFFERENT?

Quite apart from that argument, however, do I not here confuse and conflate euthanasia and PAS? After all, in PAS the physician does not kill at all. It is the patient who is the direct cause and agent of death. The distinction between euthanasia and PAS is not morally significant. A physician who provides a patient with a deadly drug and instructions about its use to bring about death bears as much responsibility for the death as the patient himself. The doctor is knowingly a part, and a necessary part, of the causal chain leading to the death of the patient. In most jurisdictions, the law holds equally responsible those who are "accessory" to capital crimes: if I give one person the gun with which I know he intends to kill another person, then stand by while he does so, the law will hold me as responsible for the death as the person who pulled the trigger. The same reasoning applies here: doctors who kill directly by injection or give others the pills to kill themselves are fully blameworthy (or praiseworthy if one accepts such actions as ethically acceptable) for what occurs.

I contend, then, that it is wrong to give one person an absolute power over the life of another, whether this power is gained by force or by voluntary means, and whether it is achieved directly or by accessory means. Consenting adult killing, where the parties are in voluntary agreement, is a moral wrong, not mitigated by its voluntary nature nor excusable because of its possibly beneficial consequences. I concede one exception to a general rule against giving people the legal power to kill each other or help each other to die: when that is the only way of saving or protecting the lives of others. But even that exception must be looked at with care and a wary eye. Western societies have allowed one person to kill another under three general circumstances: in self-defense, when that is the only way to protect one's own life; in just warfare, when that is the only way to defend one's country or community; and in capital punishment, when that is believed to be the only way to protect the lives of others. In each case, it should be noted, there is now considerable controversy. The harms, deliberate and accidental, done in the name of capital punishment (unjust executions), just warfare (massacres of civilians and other atrocities), and self-defense (negligent homicides) are notorious. For just that reason, many nations have abolished capital punishment, have denied their citizens the right to own hand guns (even for self-defense), and have become skeptical about the idea of a "just" war (though not enough to make much difference).

Euthanasia and PAS would have the dubious benefit of adding one more socially tolerated reason for one person to kill another or to assist another to kill herself. Given the well-established and longstanding failures and the corruptions of the other accepted reasons why one person may be allowed to kill another, considerable doubt is in order about whether this newest entry into our repertoire of acceptable killing will improve our common lot. In sum, I believe PAS to be wrong in and of itself because of the excessive power it puts in the hands of physicians; and this perception of wrongness is strengthened by the collateral experience of many societies that abuse seems a natural and inevitable component of the exercise of similar powers over the lives of others in a variety of contexts.

Even if one grants that the potential for abuse is considerable, two responses are possible. One of them is that some degree of abuse is a corollary of any legislation for any purpose. Abuse-free legislation is not possible and thus cannot be advanced as a reason to avoid passing laws whose purpose is otherwise taken to be morally acceptable. As a general proposition, that is undoubtedly correct, but we have to ask just what *exactly* it would mean in *this* context to tolerate some degree of abuse. It would mean this: that we would tolerate the deliberate killing of someone (euthanasia) or the deliberate manipulation of someone to kill herself (PAS) to support the freedom of others to be killed or be assisted in killing themselves. We would, in short, be allowing some lives to be unjustly taken in order that others could take their own lives. That would be a most strange and wrongful way of advancing or supporting self-determination: my autonomy would be promoted at the price of the wrongful taking of the life of another.

The other response is that the meaning of our individual right to life is, in actuality, not a positive right to live but, instead, a right not to be killed by others against our will. It is, so to speak, a negative right, which we should be free to waive if we believe that to be in our interest and beneficial to our welfare. From this perspective, it is then argued that we ought to be free to allow a physician to kill us, by waiving our right not to be killed, or to ask a physician to assist us in committing suicide, where we choose to forego our life by our own hand.

It is hard to know what to make of this seemingly arbitrary stipulation of the meaning of a right to life. The basis of the entire modern movement for general welfare rights, whether the right to a job or food or health care, has been based on the assumption that we owe each other more than a mere abstention from killing or harming them. It has been an effort to lay out a framework of positive rights, drawing upon widely shared convictions that we have positive obligations to each other no less than negative, noninterference obligations. Is the right of women not to be raped merely a negative right, which they may waive if they choose? Is the right not to be enslaved no less a right that can be waived if we are made an attractive enough offer to buy our bodies? The cost, in short, of taking our right to life to be merely a right to noninterference, a right not to be killed, is to impoverish the notion of rights and to threaten the expanded range of mutual human obligations that have been advanced in modern times.

A TURNING POINT?

Let me turn to the social meaning and impact of PAS. I take the desire of some, even many, for the legalization and social legitimation of PAS to be profoundly emblematic of three important turning points in Western thought. The first I have already sketched and will not say more about: the acceptance of PAS would morally sanction what can only be called consenting adult killing, whether the killing of another (euthanasia) or the assisted killing of oneself (PAS).

The second turning point lies in the meaning and limits of self-determination. The acceptance of euthanasia would sanction a view of autonomy holding that individuals may, in the name of their own private view of the good life and the relief of suffering, call upon others—doctors—to help them pursue that life, even at the risk of harm to the common good. This works against the idea that the meaning and scope of our right to lead our own lives must be conditioned by and be compatible with the good of the community, which is more than an aggregate of self-directing individuals.

The third turning point is to be found in the claim being made upon the institution of medicine, that it should be prepared to make its skills available to individuals to help them achieve their private vision of the good life. This puts medicine in the business of promoting the individualistic pursuit of general human happiness and well-being. It would overturn the traditional belief that medicine should limit its domain to promoting and preserving human health and life, redirecting it instead to the relief of that suffering which stems from life itself, not merely from a sick body or mind.

At each of these three turning points, proponents of PAS push us in the wrong direction. Arguments in favor of PAS fall into four general categories, which I will take up in turn: (1) the moral claim of individual self-determination and well-being; (2) the supposed moral irrelevance of the difference between killing and allowing to die; (3) the alleged lack of evidence to show the likely harmful consequences of legalized euthanasia; and (4) the compatibility of euthanasia and medical practice.

SELF-DETERMINATION

Central to most arguments for PAS is the principle of self-determination. People are presumed to have a right to decide for themselves, according to their own beliefs about what makes life good, how they will conduct their lives. That is an important value, highly and correctly honored. But the question in the PAS context is: what does it mean and how far should it extend? If it were a question of suicide, where a person takes her own life without assistance from another, that principle might be pertinent, at least for debate. But assisted suicide is not that limited a matter. The self-determination in that case can only be effected by the moral and physical assistance of another. Assisted suicide is thereby no longer a matter only of self-determination but of a mutual, social decision between two people, the one to commit suicide and the other to technically facilitate it. Since, moreover, it is presently illegal in most jurisdictions, any change in the law will require the social sanction of a legislature or the courts; that would be a powerful act of legitimation—changing a longstanding set of convictions and laws—and not merely a neutral act of permissibility.

By what warrant, however, are we to make the moral move from my right of self-determination to some doctor's right to assist me—from *my* right to *his* right? From whence comes the doctor's moral license to help someone kill himself? Ought doctors to be able to help people kill themselves as long as a request to do so comes from those who are mentally competent? Is our right to life just like a piece of property, to be given away or alienated if the price is right (happiness, relief of suffering)? And then to be destroyed with our permission once alienated?

In answer to all those questions, I will say this: I have yet to hear a plausible argument why it should be permissible for us to put this kind of power in the hands of another, whether a doctor or anyone else. The idea that we can waive our right to life, then give to another the power to take that life or help us take it, requires a justification yet to be provided by anyone. To simply say that we have a right to delegate the sovereignty over our life to another begs the question. That question is whether someone ought to have the right to take the life of another or assist in its taking simply because someone is willing to hand over or to exercise his sovereignty in that way. Put another way, can one receive from another that kind of delegated right?

There are two possible rationales for such a transfer. One of them is that (a) the very notion of sovereignty over self, of full self-determination, allows us to do with our self what we will, including the transfer of that right to someone else to exercise it in our behalf. The other rationale is that (b) under some circumstances, it may be physically impossible to exercise our right of self-determination, thus requiring the assistance of another to make the right efficacious.

(a) *The sovereignty of the self.* I will consider the first rationale, that of our right to transfer to another our right of self-determination, by offering two analogies, situations where civilized societies have denied an absolute sovereignty of self. Slavery was long ago outlawed on the ground that one person should not have the right to own another, *even with the other's permission*. Why? Because it is a fundamental moral wrong for one person to give over his life and fate to another, whatever the good consequences, and no less a wrong for another person to have that kind of total, final power. Like slavery, dueling was long ago banned on similar grounds: even free, competent individuals should not have the power to kill each other, whatever their motives, whatever the circumstances. Consenting adult killing, like consenting adult slavery or degradation, is a strange route to human dignity.

There is another problem as well. If doctors, once sanctioned to carry out euthanasia or PAS, are to be themselves responsible moral agents—not simply hired hands with lethal injections or deadly pills at the ready—then they must have their own *independent* moral grounds to kill or assist those who request such services. What do I mean? As those who favor euthanasia are quick to point out, some people want it because their life has become so burdensome it no longer seems worth living. The doctor will have a difficulty at this point. The degree and intensity to which people suffer from their diseases and their dying, whether they find life more of a burden than a benefit, has little directly to do with the nature or extent of their actual physical condition. Physical and mental suffering are, by themselves, utterly poor predictors of a desire for suicide. Three people, moreover, can have the same grave medical condition, but only one will find the suffering unbearable. People suffer, but suffering is as much a function of the values of individuals as it is of the physical or psychological causes of that suffering. Inevitably in that circumstance, the doctor will in effect be treating the patient's values. To be responsible, the doctor would have to share those values. The doctor would have to decide, on her own, whether the patient's life was "no longer worth living."

But how could a doctor possibly know that or make such a judgment? Just because the patient said so? I raise this question because in Holland at a euthanasia conference, the Dutch doctors present agreed that there is no objective way of measuring or judging the claims of patients that their suffering is unbearable. And if it is difficult to measure suffering, how much more difficult to determine the value of a patient's statement that her life is not worth living?

However one might want to answer such questions, the need to ask them, to inquire into the physician's responsibility and grounds for medical and moral judgment, points out the social nature of the decision. Euthanasia and PAS are not private matters of self-determination. They are acts that require two people to make either act possible and a complicit society to make either act acceptable.

(b) *Inability to exercise self-determination.* I turn to the second rationale for a right of physicians to help another commit suicide, that of the physical inability of some patients to exercise their right of self-determination, as, for instance, with ALS or quadriplegia. Here the issue is somewhat different. Can it be said, first, that we have a right to commit suicide to such an extent that a physical inability to do so constitutes an impediment to the exercise of that right? Second, if we grant such a right, does that entail a corresponding right on the part of physicians to assist us in committing suicide?

Suicide is legal in the United States, in the sense that there is no law forbidding it. Does that fact entail that there is a right to suicide? Not necessarily. Many acts are permitted that are not understood to be rights; that is, we have no special claim to perform those acts, only the permission of society to perform them. We are free to use our power of vision and hearing, but there is no constitutional or other right to them. We are free to eat in restaurants rather than at home, but no one claims that there is a right to do so. Suicide seems to fall into this category. The permissiveness of society in not forbidding me to commit suicide does not translate into a positive right to do so; we cannot, that is, call upon the power of the state to help us commit suicide or to require others to honor our decision to do so. This conclusion follows whether the person committing suicide is physically capable of doing so or not; that is irrelevant. Suicide, then, falls into that gray zone of acts that are permitted by the state but not given the privileged place of an accepted right.

Given this situation, I conclude that no one can claim that another has an obligation to help her commit suicide. No one, that is, can claim that there is a right to commit suicide and thus an obligation on the part of someone to assist us in doing so. What if, however, a doctor is willing to assist, even if not obliged to do so? Ought such assistance be permitted if a person who desires to commit suicide is physically unable to carry it out? This question, however, cannot be answered apart from our overall moral evaluation of assisted suicide. I have argued that self-determination as a moral principle is not sufficient to make a *prima facie* case for physician-assisted suicide. As the case of voluntary slavery makes clear (or legal prohibitions against the sale of organs) we do not grant unlimited rights to people to do what they will to or with their bodies simply because they are their bodies. A right of self-determination does not, that is, entail that every way of exercising that right must be equally protected, much less assisted. To say, then, that those who are physically unable to commit suicide have a claim upon doctors to help them, or that doctors have an obligation to help them, or that they *may* help them— each of those claims begs the question; and that question is whether we ought (a) to extend the right of self-determination to encompass physician-assisted suicide or (b) at least permit it in the case of those who are physically unable to commit suicide.

We can answer neither of those questions solely in terms of a right to self-determination. The reason for that is evident: if there is no *prima facie* right of self-determination to commit suicide, there can be no right either to the help of another to do so; and this would be true even if we are unable to commit suicide on our own. The question before us is not whether there is a right to PAS but whether we want to permit it as social policy. Self-determination as a principle does not automatically entail that conclusion.

KILLING AND ALLOWING TO DIE

I have argued that there is *no essential moral difference* between the direct killing of a patient, euthanasia, and directly assisting a patient to kill himself (i.e., providing him the means to do so). Now it has been held by some that there is no moral distinction between killing a person and allowing that person to die by virtue of the termination of life-preserving treatment. Can it, therefore, be argued that there is also no moral difference between (a) directly killing a patient (euthanasia), (b) terminating life-saving treatment on a dying patient (allowing to die), and (c) assisting a dying person to kill herself (PAS)? Consider the case of a victim of ALS, dependent upon a respirator but able to control some hand movements, who considers the following choices: (a) being killed by a physician's injection; (b) having the respirator turned off; (c) and being given a pill in order to commit suicide. Are these equivalent moral actions, such that it is morally irrelevant whether the choice is (a), (b), or (c)?

The argument I want to make is that (a) and (c) are morally equivalent, but that (b) is not. I want, that is, to say that while euthanasia and PAS are moral equivalents—for it will be the action of another (a doctor) or of oneself aided by another (PAS) that is the physical *cause* of death—turning off the respirator is different. In the latter case it will be the underlying ALS that is the cause of death. We may want to make the moral judgment that it is wrong to turn off the respirator of someone suffering from ALS even if that patient is dying, but it would be a mistake to equate the morality of the physician's act in so doing with nature's act in ending life.

Since it has become all too common to conflate euthanasia, assisted suicide, and allowing to die, it is important to see why the distinction between killing and helping to kill another, on the one hand, and allowing to die, on the other, are morally different. Consider one broad implication of what the erasure of the distinction between these two categories implies: that death from disease has been banished, leaving only the actions of physicians in terminating treatment as the cause of death. Biology, which used to bring about death, has apparently been displaced by human agency; doctors end life, not nature.

What is the mistake here? It lies in confusing causality and culpability and in failing to note the way in which human societies have overlaid natural causes with moral rules and interpretations. Causality (by which I mean the direct physical causes of death) and culpability (by which I mean our attribution of moral responsibility to human actions) are confused under three circumstances.

They are confused, first, when the action of a physician in stopping treatment of a patient with an underlying lethal disease is construed as *causing* death. On the contrary, the physician's omission can only bring about death on the condition that the patient's disease will kill him in the absence of treatment. We may hold the physician morally responsible for the death if we have morally judged such actions wrongful omissions. But it confuses reality and moral judgment to see an omitted action as having the same causal status as one that directly kills. A lethal injection will kill both a healthy person and a sick person. A physician's omitted treatment, by contrast, will have no effect on a healthy person. Turn off the machine on me, a well person, and nothing will happen. The same action will only bring the life of a sick person to an end because of an underlying fatal disease.

Causality and culpability are confused, second, when we fail to note that judgments of moral responsibility and culpability are human constructs. By that I mean that we human beings, after moral reflection, have decided to call some actions right or wrong and to devise moral rules to deal with them. When physicians could do nothing to stop death, they were not held responsible for it. When, with medical progress, they began to have some power over death—but only its timing and circumstances, not its ultimate inevitability—moral rules were devised to set forth their obligations. Natural causes of death were not thereby banished. They were, instead, overlaid with a medical ethic designed to determine moral culpability in deploying medical power.

To confuse the judgments of this ethic with the physical causes of death—which is the connotation of the word *kill*—is to confuse nature and human action. People will, one way or another, die of some disease; death will have dominion over all of us. To say that a doctor "kills" a patient by allowing this to happen should only be understood as a moral judgment about the licitness of his omission, nothing more. We can, as a fashion of speech only, talk about a doctor killing a patient by omitting treatment he should have provided. It is a fashion of speech precisely because it is the underlying disease that brings death when treatment is omitted; that is its cause, not the physician's omission. It is a misuse of the word *killing* to use it when a doctor stops a treatment he believes will no longer benefit the patient—when, that is, he steps aside to allow an eventually inevitable death to occur now rather than later. The only deaths that human beings invented are those that come from direct killing—when, with a lethal injection, we both cause death and are morally responsible for it. In the case of omissions, we do not cause death even if we may be judged morally responsible for it.

This difference between causality and culpability also helps us see why a doctor who has omitted a treatment he should have provided has "killed" that patient while another doctor—performing precisely the same act of omission on another patient in different circumstances—does not kill her but only allows her to die. The difference is that we have come, by moral convention and conviction, to classify unauthorized or illegitimate omissions as acts of "killing." We call them "killing" in the expanded sense of the term: a culpable action that permits the real cause of death, the underlying disease, to proceed to its lethal conclusion. By contrast, the doctor who, at the patient's request, omits or terminates unwanted treatment does not kill at all. Her underlying disease, not his action, is the physical cause of death; and we have agreed to consider actions of that kind to be morally licit. He thus can truly be said to have "allowed" her to die.

If we fail to maintain the distinction between killing and allowing to die, moreover, there are some disturbing possibilities. The first would be to confirm many physicians in their already too-powerful belief that when patients die or when physicians stop treatment because of the futility of continuing it, they are somehow both morally and physically responsible for the deaths that follow. That notion needs to be abolished, not strengthened. It needlessly and wrongly burdens the physician, to whom should not be attributed the powers of the gods. The second possibility would be that in every case where a doctor judges medical treatment no longer effective in prolonging life, a quick and direct killing of the patient or assisting the patient to commit suicide would be seen as the next most reasonable step on grounds of both humaneness and economics. I do not see how that logic could easily be rejected.

CALCULATING THE CONSEQUENCES

I have tried to show that physician-assisted suicide and euthanasia are intrinsically wrong because of the excessive power they would put in the hands of physicians, a wrongness that is independent of the voluntary desire of a patient to give them such power. There are also a number of important consequentialist reasons for judging PAS to be morally wrong. Like all such reasons, they depend upon the unwanted events actually taking place; in that sense, consequentialist arguments rest on probabilities. If they are not likely to happen, then they lose their moral force as arguments. I need, then, to show (a) that a legalization of PAS and a social legitimization of the practice *could* have bad consequences and that (b) those consequences are highly certain to take place. In this case, it will be easier to show the possibility of bad consequences than their certainty of occurring. There has been little experience anywhere with PAS and thus there is nothing immediately at hand to draw upon to calculate directly the probabilities of different outcomes. Nonetheless, I believe we can imagine easily enough what some of the harmful consequences might be, and we can also reasonably extrapolate from the Dutch experience with euthanasia to indirectly calculate some probabilities of what is likely to happen with accepted PAS.

Three consequences seem fully plausible: the inevitability of some significant abuse of any law; the difficulty of precisely writing, then enforcing, any law; and the inherent slipperiness of the moral reasons for legalizing PAS in the first place, pushing us in dangerous directions.

Why is abuse inevitable? One reason is that almost all laws on delicate, controversial matters are to some extent abused. This happens because not everyone will agree with the law as written and will bend it or ignore it if they can get away with it. Yet even if it is likely that all or most laws will be abused to some extent, there are good reasons to think that laws attempting to regulate PAS will particularly invite abuse.

Here we have one major social experiment to draw upon, that of the effect of efforts in the Netherlands to regulate euthanasia and PAS. What can we learn about the success of regulatory efforts in the Netherlands, where euthanasia and PAS have been permitted by the courts when certain criteria have been met: a free choice, a considered and persistent request, unacceptable suffering, consultation with another physician, and accurate reporting on the cause of death?

What has been the Dutch experience? The best information on this subject comes from a survey commissioned by the Dutch government's Commission on Euthanasia appointed in January 1990. The survey, directed by Professor P. J. van der Maas, encompassed a sample of 406 physicians, and two other studies, which, when taken together, led to the following estimate. The official results showed that based on that sample, out of a total of 129,000 deaths, there were some 2,300 cases of voluntary ("free choice") euthanasia and 400 cases of assisted suicide. In addition and most strikingly, there were some 1,000 cases of intentional termination of life without explicit request, what the Dutch call "nonvoluntary euthanasia." In short, out of 3,300 euthanasia deaths, nearly one-third were nonvoluntary. Unfortunately, there is no analysis or discussion of the 400 PAS deaths, but if it is the case that such a large proportion of all euthanasia deaths are nonvoluntary, we can reasonably infer that at least some of the PAS cases probably involved some abuse of physician power as well, most likely the well-placed suggestion and insinuation or a casual attitude toward the patient's competence and psychological state.

Is the same result likely in the United States? Here one can only speculate, of course, but there is no special reason to believe a different, less damaging pattern would emerge here. The rationale advanced for the Dutch nonvoluntary cases, that of "necessity," or *force majuere*—that is, that euthanasia was the only ethically possible choice in some heartrending cases, whatever the law might say—could just as easily be advanced in this country. It would be no less difficult for physicians to claim, as they do in Holland, that the patients had at some time in the past said things to indicate they wanted euthanasia and that such statements should be sufficient. There is some plausibility to this contention, just as it is plausible in my judgment to terminate treatment on a dying patient who had at some time in the past informally told others or a doctor that he would not want treatment continued under certain conditions. Unfortunately, among the 1,000 estimated nonvoluntary cases in the Netherlands, there were some where the patient was competent and could have been asked but was not. Here it is apparently the case that the doctors take it upon themselves to judge when continued life is not tolerable, invoking past statements on occasion but, if they are lacking, simply making unilateral judgments even when consent (or nonconsent) would be possible. Could this happen in the United States? Why not?

Apart from those abuse problems, there is a more profound worry. There is no way, even in principle, to write or enforce a meaningful law that can guarantee effective procedural safeguards. The reason is obvious yet almost always overlooked: the euthanasia or PAS transaction will ordinarily take place within the boundaries of the private and confidential doctor-patient relationship. No one can possibly know what occurs in that context unless the doctor or the patient chooses to reveal it. In Holland, fewer than 50 percent of the physicians report their acts of euthanasia, and those who do not enjoy almost complete legal impunity. There is no reason why the situation should be any better elsewhere. Doctors will have their own reasons for keeping euthanasia secret, and some patients will have no less a motive for wanting it concealed.

I would mention, finally, that the moral logic of the motives for euthanasia and PAS contain within them the ingredients of abuse. The two standard motives for euthanasia and assisted suicide are said to be our right of self-determination and our claim upon the mercy of others, especially doctors, to relieve our suffering. These two motives are typically spliced together and presented as a single justification. Yet if they are considered independently—and there is no inherent reason why they must be linked—they reveal serious problems. It is said that a competent, adult person should have a right to euthanasia for the relief of suffering. But why must the person be suffering? Does not that stipulation already compromise the principle of self-determination? How can self-determination have any limits? Whatever the person's motives may be, why are they not sufficient? Those laws that would limit PAS to terminal illness or to insupportable chronic illness already arbitrarily limit self-determination. It would be easy to challenge that arbitrary limitation if we are to be consistent in supporting self-determination. And it would surely be reasonable for those who are handicapped or otherwise physically incapable of committing suicide to demand euthanasia on the grounds that the law did not afford them equal rights and equal protection. A legal acceptance of PAS, that is, would surely pave the way for a legal acceptance of euthanasia.

Consider next the person who is suffering but not competent, who is perhaps demented or mentally retarded. The standard argument would deny euthanasia to that person, as lacking the capacity for self-determination. But why? If a person is suffering but not competent, then it would seem grossly unfair to deny relief solely on the grounds of incompetence. Are the incompetent less entitled to relief from suffering than the competent? Will it only be affluent, middle-class people, mentally fit and savvy about the medical system, who can qualify? Do the incompetent suffer less because of their incompetence? It is precisely this kind of reasoning that has led Dutch doctors, in the name of "necessity," to carry out euthanasia on the incompetent in the absence of any permission.

Considered from these angles, there are no good moral reasons to limit euthanasia or PAS once the principle of taking life or helping another to take her life has been legitimated. If we really believe in self-determination, then any competent person should have a right to be killed by a doctor for any reason that suits him and no less to be assisted in suicide. If we believe in the relief of suffering, then it seems cruel and capricious to deny it to the incompetent. There is, in short, no reasonable or logical stopping point once the turn has been made down the road to euthanasia or PAS, which could soon turn into a convenient and commodious expressway.

EUTHANASIA AND THE PURPOSES OF MEDICINE

A fourth kind of argument one often hears both in the Netherlands and in this country is that euthanasia and assisted suicide are perfectly compatible with the aims of medicine. I would note at the very outset that a physician who participates in another person's suicide already abuses medicine. Apart from depression (the main statistical cause of suicide), people commit suicide because they find life empty, oppressive, or meaningless. Their judgment is a judgment about the value of continued life, not only about health (even if they are sick). Are doctors now to be given the right to make judgments about the kinds of life worth living and to give their blessing to suicide for those they judge wanting? What conceivable competence, technical or moral, could doctors claim to play such a role? Are we to medicalize suicide, turning judgments about its worth and value into one more clinical issue?

Yes, those are rhetorical questions, yet they bring us to the core of the problem of euthanasia, PAS, and medicine. The great temptation of modern medicine, not always resisted, is to move beyond the promotion and preservation of health into the boundless realm of general human happiness and well-being. The root problem of illness and morality is both medical and philosophical or religious. Why must I die? can be asked as a technical, biological question or as a question about the meaning of life. When medicine tries to respond to the latter, which it is always under pressure to do, it moves beyond its proper role. Medicine has no special insight into the meaning of life or the meaning of a life marked by suffering and death.

It is not medicine's place to lift from us the burden of that suffering which turns on the meaning we assign to the decay of the body and its eventual death. It is not medicine's place to determine when lives are not worth living or when the burden of life is too great to be borne. Doctors have no conceivable way of evaluating such claims on the part of patients, and they should have no right to act in response to them. Medicine should try to relieve human suffering, but only that suffering which is brought on by illness and dying as biological phenomena, not that suffering which comes from anguish or despair at the human condition.

Doctors ought to relieve those forms of suffering that medically accompany serious illness and the threat of death. They should relieve pain, do what they can to allay anxiety and uncertainty, and be a comforting presence. As sensitive human beings, doctors should be prepared to respond to patients who ask why they must die or die in pain. But here the doctor and the patient are at the same level. The doctor may have no better answer to those old questions than anyone else and certainly no special insight from his training as a physician. It would be terrible for physicians to forget this and to think that in a swift, lethal injection or in the provision of suicide pills, medicine has found its own technical answer to the riddle of life.

Physicians ought not to abandon their critically ill, suffering patients. They should accompany them to the end. But it is not abandonment for a physician to refuse to step over that line which separates the medical struggle against pain, suffering, and death from the active pursuit of death, to positively seek death as the answer to the problem of life. That is to fundamentally compromise the nature of medicine, to mistake its skill with the lethal tools of death as a warrant for the bringing of death to relieve a patient of the burden of life. But would this be true even in those cases where it was the earlier actions of the physician that perhaps brought on the pain and suffering of a critical or terminal illness? Do not physicians have a duty to relieve that suffering which was caused by their treatment?

This seems a false conclusion. If patients understand that doctors do not have a moral license to commit euthanasia or engage in PAS and also give their informed consent to treatment, they can hardly blame the physician if, despite good intentions, the treatment does not turn out well. Nor does it follow that because a doctor was a causal source of pain and suffering, doctors should be able to directly kill patients or help them kill themselves by way of reparation. Medicine is an uncertain art and a less than perfect science. There is no call for reparation when it fails, nor is unavoidable pain and suffering to be understood as a failure of medicine. Human bodies must fail and eventually die. It can hardly be made an obligation on the part of medicine to be held responsible for that biological state of affairs. Nor can it be a right of patients to claim that doctors must set the world right when it goes wrong.

A final word. It is not within the power of medicine—and probably never will be—to master life and death and to control nature. It *ought* never to be within the moral power of medicine to use its skills to bring about death, whether directly or indirectly. A medicine that took on that role would soon corrupt itself, inevitably falling into abuse and assuming a kind of power it ought not to have; and it would inevitably corrupt the rest of us as well, turning to medicine to relieve us of the weight and meaning of life. Medicine does not and cannot have that kind of wisdom, and it surely would not gain it by acting as our agent in death.

A RIGHT TO CHOOSE DEATH?

F. M. Kamm

Do people have a right to choose death? More particularly, are *euthanasia* and *physician-assisted suicide* morally permissible? To clarify terms: Euthanasia involves a death that is intended to benefit the person who dies, and requires a final act by some other person (for example, a doctor); physician-assisted suicide, which requires a final act by the patient, can also be undertaken for the good of that patient, and I will confine my attention to cases in which it is. The essential point is that both involve *intentionally* ending a human life: In voluntary euthanasia, the patient and doctor both intend the death; in physician-assisted suicide, the patient intends the death and the doctor may. But how, some ask, can we ever permit people to intentionally end human lives (even their own lives) without degrading human life? How, others ask, can we simply prevent people from deciding when to end their own lives without denying people the autonomy so essential to the value of a human life? As this pair of questions suggests, the debate about the right to choose death may appear to present a stand-off between people who endorse life's intrinsic value, and those who think life's value depends on the interests, judgments, and choices of the person whose life it is.

This picture of irreconcilable moral conflict is, I believe, too despairing about the powers of moral argument. To make headway, however, we may need to pay closer attention to the complexities of cases and the specific moral terrain they occupy: to think about people on medication, being treated by physicians, sometimes relying on technical means to stay alive, trying to decide how to live out what remains of their lives. I will explore this terrain in *moral,* not legal, terms: I will be asking you to consult your moral judgments about cases, and follow out the implications of those judgments. Though this moral argument bears on constitutional argument and on appropriate legislation, I will not propose laws or rules for judges, doctors, or hospital administrators to consult, or worry about slippery slopes created by legally hard cases. The moral landscape affords firmer footing, and does not, I will suggest, permit a blanket ban on euthanasia and physician-assisted suicide: Though both involve intentionally ending human lives, both are sometimes morally permissible. I will conclude by discussing a different argument for such permissibility offered by a distinguished group of moral philosophers in a recent *amicus* brief to the Supreme Court.

I. LOGICAL TROUBLES?

Before getting to the issue of moral permissibility, we need to overcome a preliminary hurdle. I said that euthanasia and physician-assisted suicide are intended to benefit the patient. Some may object that these ideas make no sense. How is it possible for death to benefit the person who dies? Death eliminates the person—how can we produce a benefit if we eliminate the potential beneficiary?

To see how, consider the parallel question about death as a harm: Can a person be harmed by her own death even though death means that she is no longer around to suffer the harm? Suppose Schubert's life would have included even greater musical achievement had he not died so young. Because musical achievement is an important good, Schubert had a less good life overall than he would have had if he lived longer. But living a less good life is a harm. By excluding those achievements, then, Schubert's death harmed him: it prevented the better life. Now come back to the original concern about how death might be a benefit. Suppose a person's life would go on containing only misery and pain with no compensating goods. That person will be better off living a shorter life containing fewer such uncompensated-for bad things rather than a longer one containing more of them. But living a better life is a benefit. By interfering with the important bads, the person's death benefits him: it prevents the worse life.

It is possible, in short, to benefit a person by ending his life. The concept of euthanasia is, therefore, at least not simply logically confused; similarly for the idea that physician-assisted suicide may be aimed at the good of the patient. But conceptual coherence does not imply moral permissibility. So let's turn now to the moral question: Is it ever morally permissible to benefit a person by hastening his death, even when he requests it?

II. A RIGHT TO CHOOSE

Suppose a doctor is treating a terminally ill patient in severe pain. Suppose, too, that the pain can only be managed with morphine, but that giving the morphine is certain to hasten the patient's death. With the patient's consent, the doctor may nevertheless give the morphine. Why so? Because, in this particular case, the greater good for the patient is relief of pain, and the lesser evil is loss of life: after all, the patient is terminally ill, and in severe pain, so life would end soon anyway and is not of very good quality. So the patient is overall benefited by having a shorter pain-free life rather than a longer, even more painful life. (Notice that this could be true even if the morphine put the patient in a deep unconscious state from which he never awoke, so that he never consciously experienced pain-free time.)

In giving morphine to produce pain relief, the doctor foresees with certainty (let's assume) that the patient will die soon. Still, death is a side-effect of the medication, not the doctor's goal or reason for giving it: the doctor, that is, is not *intending* the patient's death, and would give the medication even if he thought death would not result. (If I have a drink to soothe my nerves and foresee a hangover, it does not follow that I intend the hangover.) Because the intended death is not present, we don't yet have a case of euthanasia or physician-assisted suicide. At the same time, in giving morphine for pain relief, the doctor is not simply letting the patient die as the disease runs its course; he administers a drug which causes death. So I think this should be understood as a case of killing, even though the doctor does not intend the death. (In other cases we have no trouble seeing that it is possible to kill without intending death: consider a driver who runs someone over while speeding.)

Now suppose the morphine loses its power to reduce the intensity of the patient's pain, but that administering it would still shorten the patient's life and thus limit the duration of his pain. Suppose, too, that the patient requests the morphine; fully aware of its effects, he wants to take it so that it will end his pain by killing him. In short, we now have a case of *morphine for death* rather than *morphine for pain relief.* Is it still morally permissible to give the morphine? Some people say that we may not kill in this case. They do not deny that relief of pain is still the greater good and death the lesser evil: they know that the consequences are essentially the same as in the case of morphine for pain relief. The problem, they say, lies in a difference of intent. In the case of giving morphine for pain relief, we intend the pain relief, and merely foresee the death; but in the case of giving morphine for death, we intend the death (which is the lesser evil): we would not give the morphine if we did not expect the death. But some people think it is impermissible to act with the intent to produce an evil. They support what is called the *Doctrine of Double Effect,* according to which there is a large moral difference between acting with the foresight that one's conduct will have some evil consequence and acting with the intent to produce that same evil (even as part of or means to a greater good). So whereas killing the patient by giving morphine for pain relief is permissible, killing the patient by giving morphine for death is impermissible.

The distinction between intending an evil and merely foreseeing it sometimes makes a moral difference. But does it provide a reason to refrain from performing euthanasia or assisting in suicide? I think not. On many occasions already, doctors (with a patient's consent) *intend the lesser evil* to a person in order *to produce his own greater good.* For example, a doctor may intentionally amputate a healthy leg (the lesser evil) in order to get at and remove a cancerous tumor, thereby saving the patient's life (the greater good). Or, he may intentionally cause blindness in a patient if seeing would somehow, for example, destroy the patient's brain, or cause him to die. Furthermore, he may intentionally cause someone pain, thereby acting contrary to a duty to relieve suffering, if this helps to save the person's life. The duty to save life sometimes just outweighs the other duty. Why then is it impermissible for doctors to intend death when it is the lesser evil, in order to produce the greater good of no pain; why is it morally wrong to benefit the patient by giving her a shorter, less painful life rather than having her endure a longer, more painful one? Recall that in the case of morphine for pain relief, it was assumed that death would be the lesser evil and pain relief the greater good. That was one reason we could give the morphine. Why is it wrong, then, for doctors sometimes to act against a duty to preserve life in order to relieve pain, just as they could sometimes act against a duty not to intend pain in order to save a life?

To summarize, I have constructed a three-step argument for physician-assisted suicide and euthanasia. Assuming patient consent:

1. We may permissibly cause death as a side effect if it relieves pain, because sometimes death is a lesser evil and pain relief a greater good.

2. We may permissibly intend other lesser evils to the patient, for the sake of her greater good.

3. Therefore, when death is a lesser evil, it is sometimes permissible for us to intend death in order to stop pain.

Thus, suppose we accept that it is sometimes permissible to *knowingly* shorten a life by giving pain-relieving medication, and agree, too, that it is sometimes permissible for a doctor to *intend* a lesser evil in order to produce a greater good. How, then, can it be wrong to *intentionally* shorten a life when that will produce the greater good?

I don't expect that everyone will immediately find this argument compelling. I suspect that many—including some who are inclined to agree with the conclusion—will feel that death is different, so to speak. While they agree that we may intend pain, if it is a lesser evil, in order to save a life, they think it is impermissible to intentionally hasten death in order to relieve pain. I will address this concern later. But first I want to add another set of considerations that support euthanasia and physician-assisted suicide.

III. AN ARGUMENT FOR DUTY

According to the three-step argument, a doctor is *permitted* to give morphine for pain relief, even though he knows it will expedite the patient's death, if death is the lesser evil. But I think we can say more. Suppose, as I have stipulated, that giving morphine is the only way for a doctor to relieve a patient's suffering. A doctor, I assume, has a duty to relieve suffering. I conclude that the doctor has a *duty* to relieve suffering by giving the morphine, if the patient requests this. He cannot refuse to give the morphine on the ground that he will be a killer if he does.

If doctors have a duty to relieve pain, and even being a killer does not override this duty when the patient requests morphine for pain relief, then perhaps they also have a duty, not merely a permission, to kill their patients, or aid in their being killed, intending their deaths in order to relieve suffering. Now we have a new argument. Assuming patient consent:

1. There is a duty to treat pain even if it foreseeably makes one a killer, when death is the lesser evil and no pain is the greater good.

2. There is a duty to intend the other lesser evils (e.g., amputation) for a patient's own greater good.

3. There is a duty to kill the patient, or assist in his being killed, intending his death when this is the lesser evil and pain relief the greater good.

I think this argument, too, is compelling, but will concentrate here on the case for permissibility.

IV. IS KILLING SPECIAL?

As I indicated earlier, a natural rejoinder to the three-step argument for euthanasia and physician-assisted suicide is to emphasize that "death is different." But how precisely is it different, and why is the difference morally important?

Perhaps it will be said, simply, that the doctor who intends the death of his patient is *killing.* Even if intending a lesser evil for a greater good is often permissible, it might be condemned when it involves killing. Killing, it might be said, is not on a par with other lesser evils.

But this does not suffice to upset the three-step argument. For giving a lethal injection of morphine to relieve pain also involves killing, and we approve of giving the morphine. To be sure, a patient's right to life includes a right not to be killed. But that right gives us a protected option whether to live or die, an option with which others cannot legitimately interfere; it does not give one a duty to live. If a patient decides to die, he is waiving his right to live. By waiving his right, he releases others (perhaps a specific other person) from a duty not to kill him, at least insofar as that duty stems from his right to live. The duty not to kill him may also stem from their duty not to harm him, even if he so wishes; but I have stipulated that the doctor is to kill only when death is the lesser evil.

A more compelling version of the objection is, however, waiting in the wings. This one points not merely to the fact of killing, but to intentional killing. It claims that there is something distinctive about intending death, and that this distinction makes a large moral difference. In particular, acting with the intention to bring about death as a lesser evil requires that we treat ourselves or other persons as available to be used for achieving certain goods—in particular, the reduction of suffering. In euthanasia and physician-assisted suicide, we intentionally terminate a being with a rational nature—a being that judges, aims at goals, and evaluates how to act. We have no such intention to use a person as a mere means when we aim at such lesser evils as destruction of a leg. Indeed, one of the things that seems odd about killing someone only if he is capable of voluntarily deciding in a reasonable way to end his life is that one is thereby ensuring that what is destroyed is a reasoning, thinking being, and therefore a being of great worth. This will not be so if the person is unconscious or vegetative or otherwise no longer functioning as a rational being. Obviously, people take control of their lives and devote their rational natures to the pursuit of certain goals within those lives; but, it is claimed, when this is appropriate, they do not aim to interfere with or destroy their personhood but set it in one direction or another.

The idea that there are limits on what we may do to ourselves as persons derives from Immanuel Kant. In his moral writings, Kant said that rational humanity, as embodied in ourselves and others, is—and should be treated as—*an end in itself, and not a mere means* to happiness or other goals. The fact that one is a judging, aiming, evaluating rational agent has worth in itself. To have this value as a person is more like an honor to us (Kant called it "dignity") than a benefit that answers to some interest of ours. Thus my life may have worth, even if my life is not a benefit to me (and my death would benefit me) because goods *other than* being a person are outweighed by bads. The worth of my life is not measured solely by its worth to me in satisfying my desires, or its worth to others in satisfying theirs. According to Kant, then, it is wrong for others to treat me as a mere means for their ends, but equally wrong for me to treat myself as a mere means for my own ends: As others should respect my dignity as a person by not using me merely as a means for their purposes, I should have proper regard for my own dignity as a person, and not simply use myself as a means for my own purposes. But that is precisely what I do when I aim at my own death as a way to eliminate pain. So I ought not to pursue that aim, and therefore ought not to consent to a morphine injection aiming at death, or give one to a patient who has consented.

Before assessing this Kantian argument, I want to justify focusing it on intentional killing rather than other ways of intentionally contributing to a death. Consider a patient who intends his own death and therefore wants life support of any sort removed. Suppose, for the sake of argument, that we disapprove of this intention. Suppose, too, that we disapprove of a doctor's agreeing to remove treatment because he also intends this patient's death. But while we may disapprove of the intentions and conduct, acting on that disapproval would require us to *force* life support on the patient, and he has a right that we not do this. Our opposition to his intentions and the doctor's is trumped by our opposition to forced invasion of the patient. So we permit the patient and doctor to act—to remove treatment—intending death. Consider, in contrast, a patient who intends his own death and, therefore, requests a lethal injection or pills. Suppose, once more, that we disapprove of this intention. Acting on our opposition would require us to refrain from invading him with a lethal injection or refuse the pills. But it seems clear that the right not to be invaded with treatment against one's will is stronger than the right simply to be invaded (with a lethal injection) or given pills. So the fact that we must terminate treatment, even when the patient and doctor intend the patient's death, does not show that it is permissible to kill the patient or assist him in killing when he and his doctor intend his death. Correspondingly, an objection to intentional killing need not imply an objection to terminating treatment for someone who intends his own death.

I turn now to the Kantian-style argument against aiming at one's death (or aiming at another's death with his consent). In assessing this argument, we must distinguish three different ways in which one may treat a person as a mere means:

1. Calculating the worth of living on in a way which gives insufficient weight to the worth of being a person.

2. Treating the nonexistence of persons as a means to a goal (e.g., no pain).

3. Using persons in order to bring about their own end.

The first idea is that being a person has worth in itself and is not merely a means to an overall balance of other goods over evils in the person's life. On this interpretation, we treat persons as a mere means if we give inadequate weight in our decisions to the value of our existence as persons; if we do, then death may seem a lesser evil. But even when there are few goods in life besides the capacity to be a rational agent, the loss of life—and therefore the loss of that capacity—may still be a greater evil than pain.

Though I do not doubt that this idea has force, it can equally well be given as a reason for not terminating a course of treatment, even when one merely foresees one's death. Because this way of treating a person as a mere means does not distinguish the *morality of intending death* from the *morality of merely foreseeing death,* it cannot be used to explain why intentional killing in particular is impermissible.

It might be said that this observation should prompt us to rethink the permissibility of killing in, for example, the case of morphine for pain relief, where death is foreseeable but not intended. For it might be said that the concern to treat people as ends and not mere means can be met only by giving *overriding* weight to the value of rational humanity, and that this requires that we refrain from acting in ways that we foresee as leading to death, and not simply from intentional killing. This response seems unjustified. Suppose life involves such unbearable pain that one's whole life is focused on that pain. In such circumstances, one could, I believe, decline the honor of being a person. In so doing, we need not treat our life as mere means to a balance of good over evil. We might acknowledge the great (and normally overriding) value of being a person, and believe it is right to go on in life even if it has more pain than other goods besides rational agency: though we reject the thought that rational agency is merely a means to happiness, we allow that some bad conditions may overshadow its very great value.

What, then, about the second and third interpretations of the idea of using persons as mere means? To see the difference between them, consider an analogy: My radio is a device for getting good sounds and filtering out bad sounds. It is a means to a balance of good sounds over bad ones. Suppose it stops performing well, that it only produces static, but cannot be turned off. I can wait until its batteries run down and not replace them, or I can smash it now, thus using the radio itself to stop the noise it produces. Either way, I would see its death as I saw its life, as a means to a better balance of good over bad sounds. While I have always seen my radio as a mere means to an end, if I smash it, I use it as a means to its end (termination): This is sense (3). If I let the radio run down, intending its demise, but do not smash it— I see it wasting away and do not replace its parts—then I do not see it as a means to its own end, but I do see *its end as a means* to a better balance of sounds. This is sense (2).

Active suicide is analogous to smashing the radio: the person uses himself as a means to his own death. Some people find this complete taking control of one's life particularly morally inappropriate, perhaps because they think our bodies belong to God and that we have no right to achieve the goal of our own death by manipulating a "tool" that is not ours (or intending that others manipulate it). This objection is not present if—here we have sense (2)—we terminate medical assistance with the intention that the system run down, aiming at its death. For then we achieve the goal of death by interfering with what is ours (the medication), not God's. Here we have another reason why someone may object to killing but not to terminating treatment, even if accompanied by the intention that the system run down: unlike intentional killing, terminating treatment does not involve using persons to bring about their own end. Some say, though, that this way of using persons as means is also more objectionable than merely foreseeing the death. They say that if we terminate medical assistance, intending death, we do not merely treat our life as a means to greater good over bad, but treat *our death (the end of our life)* as a means to greater good over bad.

How much weight, then, should be placed on the second and third senses of "using a person as a means"? Should they really stand in our way? I believe not. It cannot be argued, at least in secular moral terms, that one's body belongs to someone else and that one cannot, therefore, use it as a means to achieve death. Notice also that if your body belonged to someone else, it isn't clear why you should be permitted to use it by administering morphine to stop your pain when you merely foresee that this will destroy the body. We aren't usually permitted to treat other people's property in this way either. Nor does it seem that treating one's death as available for one's purposes (i.e., being rid of pain) is necessarily a morally inappropriate attitude to take to oneself—so long as there is no failure to properly value the importance of just being a person. If this is right, then, at least sometimes, a patient would do no wrong in intending or causing his death. At least sometimes, a doctor who helped him by giving pills would also do no wrong merely because he killed, or assisted killing, aiming at death.

The strongest case for such conduct can be made, I believe, if the overriding aim is to end physical pain. The need to do this may be rare with modern techniques of pain control, but still the patient has a "disjunctive" right: either to adequate pain control or the assistance in suicide of a willing doctor. Psychological suffering which is a reaction to one's knowledge or beliefs about a state of affairs is a weaker case. The test I suggest here is: Would we give a drug to treat psychological suffering if we *foresaw* that it would rapidly kill as a side effect? If not, then giving pills to a patient intending that they kill him in order to end psychological suffering would not be permissible. This same test can be applied to other reasons that might be offered for seeking death by euthanasia or physician-assisted suicide. For example, would we allow a patient to use a drug that will rapidly cause death (rather than a safer one) if it will save him money? If not, then we may not perform euthanasia or physician-assisted suicide to stop the drain on his family finances. Would we give a demented patient a drug that unraveled the tangled neurons that caused his dementia but which we foresaw would rapidly kill him as a side effect? If not, then why should we be permitted to give him pills, intending his death? Of course, the application of this test may yield positive responses rather than negative ones to these questions.

V. A PHILOSOPHER'S BRIEF

I have argued that if it is permissible to treat someone in his best interests though we *foresee* that this treatment will rapidly cause death, it is permissible to kill or assist in killing someone *intending* his death when this is in his best interest. (Consent is required in both cases.) In their recent "philosophers' brief," Ronald Dworkin, Thomas Nagel, Robert Nozick, John Rawls, Thomas Scanlon, and Judith Jarvis Thomson also reject a blanket ban on physician-assisted suicide, but their strategy of argument (and some of their conclusions) differ from mine. They argue from the premise that it is permissible to omit or terminate treatment with the intention that the patient die to the conclusion that it is permissible to assist in the killing of the patient intending death. I think this approach neglects the moral force of the distinction between killing a person and letting her die.

Dworkin et al. wrote as *amici curiae* in the "assisted suicide cases" that the Supreme Court heard this past January (2001). The cases came on appeal from two circuit courts, which had both ruled that government cannot simply prohibit doctors from prescribing medication that would hasten the death of patients who request such medication. The philosophers urge the Supreme Court to uphold those decisions. One part of their argument builds on the Court's 1990 decision in *Cruzan v. Missouri,* in which the Court majority assumed (if only for the sake of argument) that patients have a constitutional right to refuse life-preserving treatment. According to Dworkin et al., the existence of a right to refuse treatment also implies a right to assistance in suicide: if, as *Cruzan* indicates, it is permissible for doctors to let a patient die (even when patient and doctor intend the patient's death), then it is permissible for doctors to assist in killing. In a preface to the philosophers' brief written after the Supreme Court heard oral argument on the case, Ronald Dworkin notes that several justices rejected this link between *Cruzan* and the assisted suicide cases. They sought to distinguish them by reference to a "common-sense distinction" between the moral significance of acts and omissions: assisting suicide is an act, and thus requires a compelling moral justification; in contrast, not providing treatment is an omission, a matter of "letting nature take its course," and can be justified more easily. Dworkin says that "the brief insists that such suggestions wholly misunderstand the 'common-sense' distinction, which is not between acts and omissions, but between acts or omissions that are designed to cause death and those that are not."

I agree that the *act/omission* distinction will not bear much moral weight in this setting: When a doctor removes treatment by pulling a plug, she acts, though she does not necessarily kill. If the doctor is terminating aid she (or an organization she is part of) started, then I think she does not kill the patient but lets him die. Consider an analogy: I am saving someone from drowning and decide to stop. Even if I have to push a button to make myself stop, I do not kill the person but let him die. When the doctor gives morphine to ease pain, foreseeing it also causes death, she also acts and even kills. But I part company with these philosophers when they argue that, once a patient has consented, we can always move from the permissibility of removing treatment while intending the patient's death to the permissibility of assisted suicide. Killing is not on a moral par with letting die. Let me explain by reference to some cases.

In the first, doctors act *against* their patients' wishes to live. Dworkin et al. agree that a doctor may permissibly deny an organ to a patient in order to give it to another, but *not* kill a patient to get his organ for another. This is not, they say, because of a moral difference between letting a patient die and killing him, but because the doctor merely foresees death in the first case, whereas he intends it in the second. If this showed, however, that killing made no moral difference, it would imply that it is permissible for a doctor, in order to transplant an organ into a patient, to use a chemical that he *foresees* will seep into the next room where another patient lies, killing that patient. For in this case, the doctor does not intend to kill the patient in the other room, but only foresees his death as a side-effect of the chemical. Presumably, though, transplanting with this effect is wrong because it is a killing, albeit foreseeable rather than intended. So in cases in which we merely foresee death, killing may be wrong, even if letting die is not.

Killing can also be a significant factor in cases where a patient does not want to die because letting die with the intention that death occur might be permissible even if killing with such intention is not. It is true, as the brief says, that a doctor who lets his patient die of infection against the patient's will, intending that he die so that his organs are available, has done something wrong, as has a doctor who kills the same sort of patient, intending him to die. In both cases, the doctors aim against the welfare of their patients and violate their rights. The first doctor violates a right to treatment; the second doctor violates a right against being killed. But this does not always imply, as Dworkin et al. think, that "a doctor violates his patient's rights whether the doctor acts or refrains from acting against the patient's wishes in a way that is designed to cause death." For example, suppose that someone does not want to die but it would be in his interest to die. If a treatment is experimental, or in general something to which the patient has no positive right, it may be permissible to deny it to him because death would be in his own best interest. I do not believe the patient acquires a right to have the experimental therapy merely because the doctor's reason for refusing it is that he aims at the patient's death. Still, it would be morally wrong to kill the patient if he did not want to die, even if it were in his interest to die.

Consider next the type of case in which the patient wants death. Here, the distinction between killing and letting die makes a moral difference when deciding on the scope of permissible refusal of treatment versus permissible assistance to killing. Dworkin et al. seem to suggest the scope should be the same, saying that if a doctor can turn off a respirator, he can prescribe pills. But a mentally competent patient may legally refuse treatment, intending to die, even when it is not in his best interest to do so and, on many occasions, even when he could be cured. Presumably, in many of these cases, he could also insist on terminating treatment, even if his intention is to die. Furthermore, even if the doctor in these cases improperly intends that the patient die, the treatment must be terminated. *This is because the alternative to letting the patient die is forcing treatment on him.* We think a competent patient's right not to be physically invaded against his will is typically stronger than our interest in his well-being (though this right is, to be sure, not absolute and can sometimes be overridden by considerations of public safety). But if he asks for assistance in killing himself when it is not in his interest to be killed, it might well be morally impermissible to kill him. Contrary to what Dworkin et al. say, therefore, a doctor might in some cases be permitted and even required to turn off a respirator but not permitted to give pills.

The alternative to letting die, then, has such a morally objectionable feature — forcing treatment which he has a right we not do — that even if we think the patient's and doctor's goals are wrong, we must terminate aid. In contrast, the alternative to assisted suicide may simply be leaving the patient alone; this often does not violate any of his rights against us, and so we can, and sometimes we should be required to, refuse to help because we disapprove of his goals. Many people — including the Supreme Court justices Dworkin et al. cite — might, then, reasonably distinguish refusing treatment and thus letting a patient die from assisting in a suicide. The move from *Cruzan*'s right to refuse treatment to the permissibility of assisted suicide is, therefore, not generally available. Still, my discussion here indicates that we may have other reasons to accept the fundamental moral conclusion: that assisted suicide (and euthanasia) are sometimes morally permissible.

PHYSICIAN-ASSISTED SUICIDE

Sissela Bok

> *There are governments that have taken it upon themselves to determine the justice and opportuneness of voluntary deaths. In our own Marseilles in the past there was kept, at public expense, some poison prepared with hemlock for those who wanted to hasten their deaths, which they could use after having first had the reasons for their enterprise approved by the Six Hundred, their Senate; and it was not lawful to lay hands upon oneself otherwise than by leave of the authorities and for legitimate reasons. This law also existed elsewhere.*
>
> MONTAIGNE, *ESSAYS* (1588)

Providing the means for suicide after judging the "justice and opportuneness of voluntary deaths" is far from unprecedented, as Montaigne's example shows. Since antiquity, doctors have at times told patients intent on ending their lives in what dosage poisons and various other preparations become lethal. Some have prescribed such preparations for these patients; others have simply left barbiturates or other medications at their bedside, specifying that they should be careful about not exceeding a certain dosage since this would bring about their death. Likewise, it is from doctors that commandos and spies going on missions have acquired poisons to carry along in case of capture by enemy forces.

While all such practices have a long history, the term "physician-assisted suicide" is a neologism, perhaps less than ten years old, employed in challenges to laws prohibiting doctors (as well as all others) from being direct accessories to suicide. By now, the term is more central to the U.S. debate over voluntary dying than "euthanasia" and "mercy killing." Depending on who is speaking, it has been used for activities as different as physicians prescribing pills for a patient and explaining what amounts would be needed to bring about death, and Dr. Jack Kevorkian's far more active part in constructing and operating the contraptions used for the "patholysis" that he has dramatized, photographed, and videotaped, with the patient executing the last step.

ASSISTANCE

In the term "physician-assisted suicide," unlike the terms "mercy killing" and "euthanasia," the element of killing other people that many have found so jarring in debates over euthanasia is absent. Instead, the primary moral focus of philosophers advocating legalization is on the liberty of persons to commit suicide if this is their considered choice. In addition, two further elements are inherent in the concept: the element of helpfulness or assistance and the singling out of physicians, not relatives or others, as providing such assistance. Both the emphasis on helpfulness and the restriction to physicians as alone permitted to offer such help have proved reassuring to many who remain wary of active euthanasia.

One view regarding how physicians should be authorized to render such assistance is laid out in the model statute proposed by Charles Baron and colleagues in 1996:

> Ending one's life in solitude can be a lonely and frightening undertaking, fraught with uncertainty, ambivalence, and opportunities for failure. We hope that the responsible physician will be present at the patient's death in order to reassure the patient and to make certain that the process is carried out effectively.

The proposed statute does not specify what the nature of this assistance might be in case the patient does not manage to bring about death unaided. But its authors would presumably disapprove of the suggestions that abound, in the popular literature, for further "assistance" by physicians or other bystanders to ensure success, as by placing a pillow over the face of the patient. Such actions, even though they may be viewed as merely helping to finish the act of suicide undertaken by the patient, clearly cross the line to euthanasia.

It is in part to avert the risks of such crossovers that others advocating physician-assisted suicide specify that physicians should be allowed to prescribe the medication needed by their patients, but not to be present at the suicide. In 1997, voters in Oregon approved, a second time, the Death with Dignity Act, which made physician-assisted suicide lawful so long as it conformed with certain specifications: that the patient be of sound mind, have less than six months left to live, and make a request both orally and in writing; and that two doctors agree that these conditions obtain and that the patient is not too depressed to make a judgment about seeking to die. In such cases, patients may obtain a lethal dose of drugs after a fifteen-day waiting period, and can proceed to commit suicide. Doctors may assist by prescribing the barbiturates but must not administer them or carry out any other lethal procedure, nor be present at the time of the suicide itself.

The voters of Oregon knew that the law already gives patients the rights to refuse treatment, resuscitation, and hospitalization, even if they can expect to die as a result, and that increasing numbers now also have access to the means of suicide and information about how to carry it out. Self-help suicide manuals abound. And the Internet has made such information still more easily accessible. But the movement to allow physicians to assist further in making suicide possible has gained in strength because these rights on the part of patients are not being observed, as evidenced by the SUPPORT study, and because of lingering concerns that patients may not be able to ascertain what is the dosage and method most likely to achieve a painless death in their particular case.

In part, too, the movement has gained adherents because it is perceived as a step on the way to extending the law in a number of ways: to cover persons who may not be able to prove—what is often impossible to pin down—that they have less than six months left to live or that they are not depressed; and to allow physicians to do much more in the way of assistance than the Oregon law now permits. Much of the public's fear of powerlessness at the end of life concerns two types of cases that could never satisfy the criteria established in the Oregon legislation or any others yet proposed for legalizing physician-assisted suicide. In the first category are patients who cannot obtain the requisite medication or administer it to themselves, perhaps because they are paralyzed or too weak to take the medication or unable to swallow. In the second are the many who are not presently suffering and who are not likely to die within six months, but who fear the ravages of a mentally incapacitating condition such as Alzheimer's disease that will rob them of the competence needed for any request for physician-assisted suicide to be granted. They fear what Seneca referred to in . . . , claiming that he would commit suicide if old age began to unseat his reason. Some do commit suicide while still able to do so, fearing such a fate; those who do not, however, know that the condition they anticipate will not permit them to be candidates for physician-assisted suicide as presently envisaged.

It turns out that the two fears are more present to the minds of persons not yet suffering from such conditions and to relatives of those who are, than to the patients themselves. New research is challenging the assumption that most seriously ill people prefer quality of life to quantity: as Dr. Christine Cassel points out, many people erroneously assume that "once you're 80 years old and have a number of chronic illnesses, your quality of life is impaired."

Finally, the movement for physician-assisted suicide has benefited from the conceptual straddling of the notion of "assistance" in "physician-assisted suicide." This poses no problem for those among the proponents of Oregon-style legislation who see no moral difference between suicide, physician-assisted suicide, and voluntary euthanasia—holders of view A—and who take permissive legislation regarding the second to open the door, in the long run, to acceptance also of the third. Many philosophers who support physician-assisted suicide hold voluntary euthanasia to be, likewise, morally acceptable. But for holders of view B, who distinguish, from a moral point of view, between suicide and killing others, this straddling is cause for concern. For them, there need be no inherent moral problem with what doctors have long done in prescribing barbiturates and cautioning patients about what would constitute a lethal dose, even as serious risks may flow from enacting physician-assisted suicide into law.

The risks are of two kinds. The first reflects caution with respect to a slippery slope, akin to that signaled in the debate over euthanasia. Once the law is changed to endorse physician-assisted suicide, there may be pressure to extend it to more active ministration; and it may seem wrong to leave patients to their own devices when it comes to killing themselves and possibly failing. There may also be pressure to extend the law to cover patients who are at present automatically excluded—those, for instance, who are not terminally ill but are suffering grievously, or those who are not fully competent. The experience in the Netherlands shows how difficult it is to enforce respect for criteria and safeguards set forth in official guidelines.

The second risk, also at issue in debates over euthanasia but increasingly prominent in the 1990s as proposals for legalizing physician-assisted suicide moved through the courts, concerns the role of physicians. What does instituting a public policy of authorizing them to carry out physician-assisted suicide mean for them as moral agents and for the integrity of their profession?

THE ROLE OF PHYSICIANS

It is understandable that if any group should be designated to carry out the steps mandated in proposed laws concerning assisted suicide, the choice would fall on physicians. They are bound to uphold professional standards and trained to maintain greater objectivity about persons who are suffering than is always possible for family members. And they are often more knowledgeable about the condition of the patients, about treatment alternatives, and about the effects of medications than other health professionals.

It is equally understandable, however, that the role of physicians in executing such social policies should be most sharply contested among physicians themselves. Even as many health professionals shield themselves from awareness of the suffering of patients at the end of life, as demonstrated by the SUPPORT and other studies, so others empathize intensely with such suffering. And the more physicians learn about how the inadequacies and inequities of medical care at the end of life raise the likelihood that patients will endure needless pain and suffering, the more they are brought to ask about their own responsibilities in providing those in greatest anguish a peaceful death.

Anyone raising the question of physician-assisted suicide among a group of doctors comes to recognize their conflicted response. All may recognize the anguish of individual sufferers pleading for release. There are reluctant proponents of physician-assisted suicide in the medical profession, but few outright enthusiasts. When it comes to singling out their own profession to carry out a *practice* of assisted suicide, both proponents and opponents share a sense of worried unease. The sense of apprehension in the health care community is heightened by a consideration that physicians rarely discuss in public: the levels of impairment within their own profession that could affect patients whose expressions of a desire to die would call for the most scrupulous and skilled examination. Alcoholism and dependency on other drugs afflict approximately 10 percent and 7 percent, respectively, of physicians; depression, fatigue, and overwork affect a number of health professionals with symptoms labeled "stress impairment syndrome"; between 6 and 20 percent of the cases reported to state physician health programs concern impairment due to mental illness. Many cases of incompetence or impairment are never reported. And a study of the more than 13,000 doctors in the United States who have been disciplined for serious incompetence or misconduct has found that most of them retain their licences and continue to treat patients. Little wonder that many conscientious physicians who could envisage engaging in physician-assisted suicide themselves are more guarded when it comes to legalizing such a practice on a statewide or society-wide scale.

The concern of health professionals, as of others who worry about legalizing physician-assisted suicide, is not just that there will be movement along some one slippery slope, but that the risks of slippage arise along a number of dimensions. These risks are in turn minimized, or even rejected as mere fictions, by advocates of physician-assisted suicide. But to the extent that advocates wish to wipe out the distinction between acts and omissions or between killing and letting die, they are driven to insist the more vigorously, instead, on the capacity of physicians or courts of law to enforce the voluntary/ nonvoluntary distinction with respect to who does and does not express a considered and well-founded desire to die.

Intellectuals are more prone than practitioners in most lines of work to fall into the trap of believing that they can devise a set of rules to guide participants in an inherently dangerous practice. They may take for granted that the rules once enacted into law will work in the intended fashion. Too often, experience shows that their faith turns out to be misplaced. At times, those to whom the rules are supposed to apply don't know of their existence. At other times, the rules are known but people do not obey them, or evade them by finding loopholes or ambiguities to avoid compliance.

There is every reason to look with wary eyes at any calls to put much faith in the power of "appropriate legal safeguards" to succeed in guarding the very rights of patients to refuse interventions that existing laws protect so poorly. In addition to doubts about how well the safeguards for legalized physician-assisted suicide will be made to work in practice, physicians are also concerned about how the already diminishing levels of trust between health professionals and consumers might be affected by a shift in the public's perception of them as capable of serving both life-giving and death-dealing purposes. They have direct experience of the pressures from a shifting health care system in which powerful incentives to reduce the costs of patient care are much more prominent than in the past. When treatments are already being withdrawn on financial grounds rather than patient needs, there may be temptations to accede too rapidly to requests for suicide assistance.

Most vulnerable at such times are the many Americans who have no health insurance, let alone a long-standing relationship with a personal physician such as those with whom most Dutch citizens can discuss their fears and problems at length before reaching a choice about whether or not to seek to die. Michael Walzer points out that patients at clinics and hospitals that serve minority populations are three times more likely to receive inadequate pain relief than those treated elsewhere; under such conditions, and with the growing numbers of Americans without any health insurance whatsoever, the vulnerable population

> is just too large for this particular social experiment. I don't mean that people would be assisted against their will (though there would probably be cases like that), but rather that the suffering that leads them to seek assistance in dying will often be avoidable suffering, and that it will be distributed, as it is now, in morally unacceptable ways.

A CRY FOR HELP?

Physicians are trained to respond to patient references to suicide as constituting cries for help. By analogy, might the debate about euthanasia and suicide constitute such an appeal on a society-wide scale? Just as revealing one's intention to commit suicide is often a cry for help on the part of persons not yet ready to die, despairing of securing humane attention and relief of suffering in any other way, so it may be that the debates about physician-assisted suicide also have overtones of a cry for help. They sound an alarm about the needless pain and suffering at the end of life that is now the lot of so many in our society, meant to call attention to what more adequate treatment would mean. Polls show that most people would prefer adequate palliative care and hospice care near the end of life to physician-assisted suicide, were these forms of treatment generally available. Instead, fewer than a fifth of terminally ill patients have access to them at present.

Among patients aware that they are being denied such care it is possible that some might even request physician-assisted suicide, not out of a considered desire to die but hoping to get priority in our troubled health care system. True, they would be taking a great risk; but some who felt they had little to lose might take the gamble. If physician-assisted suicide became lawful, with the provision that it be the last resort, nothing would bring more specialists and consultants to their bedside than such a request. After all, few who are terminally ill can count on psychiatric evaluation to consider whether they are clinically depressed, much less on therapy for such a condition. Nor do most receive the adequate pain relief or the visits from social workers explaining alternatives to suicide, which many stipulate ought to be explored before helping anyone to commit suicide.

Since the preliminary criteria that must be satisfied before physician-assisted suicide can be contemplated are intended to single out the few who will still choose death from the many who will change their minds once assured of optimal care, why shouldn't enterprising patients try to secure the best care available to them? Even some who waver in their desire to die may see a request for aid in dying as a chance to finally get the care and treatment they despaired of securing in any other way.

TREATMENT

What practical choices should we make, for ourselves and for our society, in addition to ensuring the most basic safeguards of patients against neglect and abuse? What forms of *treatment* should we seek out or wish to see as lawful at the end of life? Three senses of "treatment" interact so as to reflect ambiguities that help explain why a problem such as that of voluntary euthanasia can pull us in such radically different directions at once.

The therapeutic sense of the word, first of all, involves the application of remedies to patients with the object of effecting a cure, or to offer them support and comfort even if no cure seems possible and at the very least to mitigate suffering. The ambiguities here are well known, concerning whether the treatment is of the disease or the patient, whether it involves acting or abstaining from action, whether it represents treating for the sake of treatment, for the physician's protection, or for the patient's best interests, and how far it is legitimate to go to provide comfort and mitigate suffering at the end of life and still regard what is being done as carrying out treatment.

The second sense in which "treatment" is often used is that of expressive or aesthetic treatment. We can think of Shakespeare's treatment of King Lear or of Desdemona, to take two persons at the end of their lives, or of Molière's or William Carlos Williams's treatment of physicians in their dealings with patients. "Treatment" in this sense concerns how we portray individuals in literature, through case histories, or in media accounts. In medicine as in literature, this kind of treatment goes from the fullest kind of seeing—visual and moral—of human beings to the most perfunctory, even dehumanizing perception of them. And the ambiguities of the concept of treatment in this sense of portrayal, in medicine, are sometimes similar to those attaching to treatment as the administering of remedies, especially with respect to who or what is being treated, and whether we are seeing and conveying only the disease or the moral problem or also the human beings involved.

The third, and most general sense of "treatment" is the moral sense. It concerns how well or badly we treat ourselves and others, how we deal with one another, how we conduct ourselves toward one another. It is in this moral sense of the term that Immanuel Kant formulates his categorical imperative, enjoining us to act in such a way that we treat humanity, whether in our own person or in that of another, always at the same time as an end and never simply as a means. It is the moral sense of the term, as well, that is at issue in the different formulations of the golden rule, calling for us to do unto others as we would have them do unto us. References to "treatment" in this third sense often address, in fact, *mistreatment* of persons in a particular group, as when we speak of the treatment of women or of minorities or of persons who are weakened by illness and suffering.

The debates about voluntary euthanasia and physician-assisted suicide concern this sense of the word too. Some ask: How *can* you regard the inadequate treatment that dying persons often receive, the prolongation of death for so many, as anything but mistreatment? And others reply: How can *you* think of killing them as anything but the gravest mistreatment? The clash between the two views of what moral treatment is due patients near the end of life is rendered sharper still by the fact that two fundamental moral values are at issue: that of providing care for those in need and above all refraining from harming them, much less taking their lives. Health professionals have traditionally been enjoined to honor both of these values; the dispute arises when the two appear to be in irreconcilable conflict.

At the very least, those who differ on these points might agree that medical treatment should never be at war with moral treatment. Even though medical treatment is specialized and often differs, in that sense, from the more general forms of treatment human beings can expect of one another, medical treatment should never be so construed as to *go against* the basic moral precepts of how human beings should treat one another.

From this perspective, I continue to find great and needless risks in moving toward legalizing euthanasia or physician-assisted suicide. I also remain convinced that such measures will not deal in any way adequately with the needs of most persons at the end of life, least of all in societies without adequate health care insurance available to all. No society has yet worked out the hardest questions of how to help those patients who desire to die without endangering others who do not. There is a long way to go before we arrive at a social resolution of those questions that does not do damage to our institutions.

In part as a result of the momentum gained through the debates in different societies about suicide, euthanasia, and physician-assisted suicide, there has been increasing movement in the past few years toward providing greater access to palliative care when cure is no longer a possibility and to hospice care at the end of life. Our first priorities must be to reinforce the right of patients to such humane and respectful care; and to collaborate with the many on all sides of the debates who struggle to wipe out the worst and the most inhumane maltreatment and to improve and cultivate the best forms of medical *and* humane treatment at the end of life.

QUESTIONS FOR DISCUSSION
PHYSICIAN-ASSISTED SUICIDE AND EUTHANASIA

1. Catholic authorities have declared that a ship's captain who elects to "go down with the ship" is essentially committing suicide and that suicide is self-murder and therefore morally wrong. What of the aviator who flies his plane full of bombs into an enemy battleship, or the soldier who throws himself on a hand grenade to save others—are they committing suicide? Defend your position on this question.

2. In his powerful novel *Man's Fate,* the writer André Malraux describes a Chinese revolutionary who is captured with several others, all of whom are about to be thrown alive into a locomotive furnace. The revolutionary courageously gives his cyanide capsule to a boy who is trembling with fear at what awaits them. In this situation is the revolutionary assisting the boy at suicide, and if so, is he doing something morally wrong? Explain your position.

3. On what grounds does Dan Brock argue that assisted suicide, passive euthanasia (letting die), and active voluntary euthanasia (mercy killing) are morally equivalent, and therefore equally permissible? On what grounds does Daniel Callahan argue that they are morally equivalent, therefore equally impermissible?

4. How does Frances Kamm argue that passive euthanasia and assisted suicide are not morally equivalent to active euthanasia, so that the former are sometimes permissible when the latter is not?

5. Why does Sissela Bok think it is dangerous to legalize physician-assisted suicide? What evidence does she cite to support this conclusion?

6. How do Brock and Kamm on the one hand, and Callahan and Bok on the other, explain why doctors should or should not be entrusted with the task of ending, or helping to end, a patient's life?

SELECTED READINGS

BEAUCHAMPS, T., ed. *Intending Death: The Ethics of Suicide and Euthanasia.* Englewood Cliffs, NJ: Prentice-Hall, 1996.

BOK, SISSELA. *Physician Assisted Suicide.* NY: Cambridge University Press, 1998.

DIXON, NICHOLAS. "On the Difference between Physician Assisted Suicide and Euthanasia." *Hastings Center Report,* ____ 1998.

DWORKIN, GERALD. "Physician Assisted Suicide and Public Policy." *Philosophical Studies,* ____ 1998.

RACHELS, JAMES. "Active and Passive Euthanasia." *New England Journal of Medicine,* ____ 1975.

UHLMANN, M. M., ed. *Last Rights? Assisted Suicide and Euthanasia Debated.* Grand Rapids, MI: Eerdmans, 1998.

WEIR, R., ed. *Physician Assisted Suicide.* Indianapolis: Indiana University Press, 1997.

WELLMAN, CARL. "A Moral Right to Assisted Suicide." *American Philosophical Quarterly,* July 2001.

WOOLFREY, JOAN. "What Happens Now? Oregon and Physician Assisted Suicide." *Hastings Center Report,* ____ 1998.

See also articles on suicide and euthanasia in *The Catholic Encyclopedias; The Jewish Encyclopedia; The Encyclopedia of the Social Sciences;* and *The Encyclopedia of Religion and Ethics.*

4

ABORTION

Does the belief in the sanctity of human life apply to human embryos and fetuses? If so, does it rule out the permissibility of abortions under any circumstances and at any stage of development? Abortion and infanticide were regularly practiced in ancient times, when children were regarded as property of their parents, and the same is still true today in some areas of the world. However, the three great Western religions, Judaism, Christianity, and Islam, have been committed to the cherishing of human life as God's favorite creation, even though they have sanctioned capital punishment and killing in self-defense.

Theologians have differed throughout the ages as to when "human life," understood as a unique human individual, comes into existence. Some have proposed "quickening," the movements of the fetus in the womb, usually after four months; some, including St. Thomas Aquinas, have proposed ten days after conception; and in the last century and a half, the Roman Catholic Church has ruled that the very moment of conception is the beginning of individual human life. Orthodox Judaism, fundamentalist Islam, and some Protestant churches agree.

Contemporary philosophers have been debating whether only a full-fledged person, endowed with self-awareness, should be valued above all else, rather than the mere existence of a human fetus with the potentiality to develop into a person. In the first of the following selections, Philip Devine argues for the almost total prohibition of abortion, on the grounds that it is wrong to take an innocent human life. A fetus, he argues, is a member of the human species and potentially a person; for both reasons it has a right to life that may not be violated. Mary Anne Warren takes the diametrically opposed position, in favor of abortion on demand, on the grounds that a woman has a right to rid herself of an unwanted fetus that, not yet a person, does not have a person's right to life. The mother's right to dispose of her body as she sees fit overrides any doubtful right claimed for the fetus. Warren argues that a fetus is only potentially a person and that only actual persons have full moral rights. This holds also, she suggests, for newborn infants in the first month or so of postnatal existence; so that, in her view, infanticide is also morally permissible, although socially undesirable.

Paul Wilkes, a well-known essayist and a devout Catholic, wrestles with the Church's prohibition of abortion and arrives at a compromise between "pro-life" and "pro-choice" in his recent book, *A Good Enough Catholic* (1996). Abortion, he holds, is not always morally permissible or always morally impermissible. Rape, incest, serious genetic defects, and pregnancy that threatens the life of the mother justify abortion, but less serious reasons such as personal convenience do not. Wilkes does not say whether the morally impermissible cases should be prohibited by criminal law, but his discussion suggests that he does not regard law enforcement as sufficiently sensitive to decide such matters.

THE WRONGS OF ABORTION

Philip Devine

I shall assume here that infants are protected by the moral rule against homicide. From this assumption it seems to follow immediately that fetuses, and other instances of human life from conception onward, are also so protected, so that, unless justified or mitigated, abortion is murder. For there seem to be only two possible grounds for asserting the humanity of the infant: (1) The infant is a member of the human species (species principle). (2) The infant will, in due course, think, talk, love, and have a sense of justice (potentiality principle). And both (1) and (2) are true of fetuses, embryos, and zygotes, as well as of infants. A zygote is alive (it grows) and presumably is an instance of the species *homo sapiens* (of what other species might it be?), and it will, if nothing goes wrong, develop into the kind of creature which is universally conceded to be a person.

But a number of arguments still have to be answered before the humanity or personhood of the fetus can be asserted with confidence. All of them are reflected in, and lend plausibility to, Joel Feinberg's remark: "To assert that a single-cell zygote, or a tiny cluster of cells, as such, is a complete human being already possessed of all the rights of a developed person seems at least as counter-intuitive as the position into which some liberals [defenders of abortion] are forced, that newly born infants have no right to continue living." These arguments are (1) that if a fetus is a person because of its potential and its biological humanity, spermatazoa and ova must also be considered persons, which is absurd; (2) that personhood is something one acquires gradually, so that a fetus is only imperfectly a person; (3) that there is an adequately defensible dividing point between the human and the nonhuman, the personal and the nonpersonal, which enables us to defend abortion (or "early" abortion) without being committed to the defense of infanticide; and finally (4) that the opponent of abortion himself does not take seriously the humanity of the fetus, an argument *ad hominem*. Insofar as one relies on intuition to establish the wrongness of infanticide, one must come to terms with the contention that the assertion that a fetus is a person is itself counter-intuitive.

Michael Tooley argues that if it is seriously wrong to kill infants or fetuses because they potentially possess human traits, it must also be seriously wrong

Philip Devine. "The Wrongs of Abortion." Excerpted from "Fetuses and Human Vegetables" in *The Ethics of Homicide, Relativism, Nihilism, and God; Human Diversity and the Culture Wars* by Philip Devine. Copyright © 1976 Cornell University Press. Reprinted by permission. [Original notes have been omitted.]

to prevent systems of objects from developing into an organism possessing self-consciousness, so that artificial contraception will be just as wrong as infanticide. But only organisms can have a right to life, although something more like an organism than a mere concatenation of sperm and egg might have a right to something like life. And the same point can be reached if we speak not in terms of a right to life but of a moral rule against certain kinds of killing, for only an organism can be killed.

There is another, more complicated, argument against the contention that a spermatazoon and an ovum, not united, might be protected by the moral rule against homicide (or would be if infants and fetuses were). Since the moral rule against homicide is a rule that protects rights, it cannot obtain unless there is some specifiable individual whose rights would be violated were it breached. A sperm conjoined with an ovum in this way is not in any sense an individual; therefore it cannot have any rights. For this reason the prevention of such a combination's being fruitful cannot be a violation of the moral rule against homicide. An ejaculation contains many more spermatazoa than could possibly be united with ova, and it is difficult to see the sperm-plus-ovum combinations which do not prevail as somehow deprived of something on which they have a claim.

But it is hard to reject all rights-claims made on behalf of inchoate subjects. It is commonly held to be prima facie wrong to exterminate entire species of animals, and such a wrong could be committed without destroying any individual animal (e.g., by rendering all members of the species sterile). It seems that many of us want to accord to the species as such a right to continue in existence as a species. (Compare the notion that genocide, the destruction of an entire race or ethnic group, is a crime over and above, and indeed apart from, the destruction of individual members of such a group.) How seriously we take talk of the rights of species depends on how seriously we take the interests of species. It will not do to refuse to admit the existence of such interests on the grounds that "a whole collection, as such, cannot have beliefs, expectations, wants, or desires," since such conditions are not necessary to the existence of interests. We can easily view the perpetuation of a species through its characteristic mode of reproduction as an act, not only of the individual organisms that engage in reproductive activity, but also of the species itself, acting through its members. It is thus possible to attribute an aim of preserving itself to the species as a whole and to see this aim as frustrated when a species becomes extinct.

If so, it seems also that human beings have at least a general duty to procreate, to the extent that it would be wrong to encompass, or to adopt maxims which entail, the dying-out of the human species. (What I have in mind are those who hold that truly virtuous or enlightened persons will abstain from sexual activity or reproduction, a view which has the result that the human species will be continued by fools or sinners, if by anyone.) Thus, it seems, unrealized human possibilities do have some sort of claim on us. Still, the distinction between an individual organism and an unrealized possibility of such an organism is surely great enough to block any attempt to bring such unrealized possibilities within the scope of the moral rule against homicide.

One can reply similarly to the contention that, since every cell in the body is a potential person (by cloning), and no very great moral weight attaches to the cells in the body, no very great moral weight attaches to potential persons. But even with cloning, an ordinary human cell is not only a merely potential person: it is also a merely potential organism. Belief that creatures which are potentially personal are persons is not the same as believing that anything from which such a creature might arise is also a person. One might, in view of the possibility of cloning, argue that a one-celled zygote is only a potential organism, essentially no different from an ovum or an ordinary cell; but the embryo and the fetus are clearly actual organisms, even if they are supposed to be merely potential persons. Hence, if to be potentially personal is to be a person, they are actual persons as well.

Spermatozoa and ova might be said to be living individuals in a sense. But it is clear that a spermatozoon cannot be considered a member of the human species or a being potentially possessing the traits we regard as distinctively human in the way a fetus or infant can. A developed human being issuing from a sperm alone is a possibility far outside the normal powers of the spermatozoon in the way a developed human being issuing from a fetus or infant is not outside the normal powers of those creatures.

The case of the ovum is more complicated, since parthenogenesis, reproduction from ovum alone, takes place in at least some species. But, apart from considerations involving twinning and recombination (to be discussed below), fertilization still remains a relatively bright line available for distinguishing prehuman organic matter from the developing human organism. Finally, we must remember that sperm and ovum are biologically parts of *other* human individuals (the parents).

Perhaps, however, it is a mistake to look for a bright line between prehuman organic matter and a developing human being or person. Perhaps personhood is a quality the developing human creature acquires gradually. This suggestion will always have a considerable appeal to the moderate-minded. For it avoids the harshness, or seeming harshness, of those who would require great suffering on the part of the woman carrying a fetus for the sake of that fetus's rights, while avoiding also the crudity of those who regard abortion as of no greater moral significance than cutting one's toenails, having a tooth pulled, or swatting a fly. Moreover, that abortion is morally less desirable the closer it is to birth—and not simply because a late abortion is more likely to harm the woman—is one of the few intuitions widely shared on all sides of the abortion controversy, and thus not to be despised. That abortion should become harder and harder to justify as pregnancy proceeds, without being ever as hard to justify as is the killing of a person, is a suggestion which ought therefore to be given the most serious attention.

The gradualist suggestion raises a problem of quite general scope. Not only as regards the distinction between prehuman organic matter and a human person, but also as regards that between human beings and brute animals, and that between a dying person and a corpse, our thought is pulled in two different directions On the one hand, we find it natural to look for sharp, if not radical, breaks between different kinds of being, for evolutionary quanta so to speak. On the other hand, we are suspicious of sharp breaks and look for continuities at every point in nature. On a merely theoretical level, Kant's suggestion—that we regard the principle of continuity and the principle of speciation as regulative ideals or heuristic principles which, although contradictory if asserted together, are nonetheless useful in prompting the advance of knowledge; in other words, that we should look for both continuities and gaps—is most attractive. But it is of very little use to us here.

For what we are looking for is a way of making abortion decisions that offers some hope of rational agreement. And there seems to be no stable, non-arbitrary way of correlating stages of fetal development with justifying grounds. At the stage of development when the embryo most closely resembles a fish, the moderate on the abortion question will want to ascribe it stronger rights than he does fish, but weaker rights than he does full human beings. And the moderate, as I conceive him, regards an infant as a human person, though the difference between a human infant and an infant ape is not palpable. Turning to "indications," it is far from clear why incestuous conception, for instance, plays the kind of role it does in justifying abortion to many moderates.

There is a form of the moderate position which seems to escape this line of attack. Marvin Kohl defines and defends a "moderate feminist" view of abortion, according to which "a living potential human being has the prima facie right to life but . . . the actual right may be reasonably denied in cases of abortion on request." In other words, although the killing of a fetus requires justification, any reason which might prompt a woman to request an abortion is sufficient.

Kohl concedes that there is nothing in his view to prevent a woman from having an abortion for no reason at all, or more precisely, nothing in his view to permit Kohl to disapprove such abortions. But he sees no need for such a preventative. To suppose that a significant number of women will have frivolous abortions, thinks Kohl, is to be guilty of "the most deadly anti-women bias of all, namely: that unless women are carefully controlled they will kill their own progeny without reason because they are not fully rational creatures." In this way, Kohl combines a moderate assessment of the fetus with an avoidance of line-drawing. The issue of how much justification is required for killing a fetus is left to the good sense and discretion of the pregnant woman.

There are three answers to Kohl here: one qualitative, one quantitative, and one conceptual. The qualitative point is that while it is of course extremely unlikely that a woman will have an abortion for a lark, there is also evidence that women and couples (I do not know what Kohl considers a significant number) will sometimes request abortions for uncompelling reasons. There have been reports of women having abortions because the child turned out to be of the "wrong" sex, and because a one-in-twenty chance of a cleft lip was diagnosed. Quantitatively, where permissive attitudes toward abortion prevail, the number of abortions has been known to exceed the number of live births. To defend such results one has to abandon all pretense of moderation about abortion and contend that the fetus has no right to live, even a prima facie one, against its mother. For—and this is the conceptual point—there is a connection between the concept of a right and the maxim that no one shall be judge in his own cause. I should remark in conclusion that I do not regard either women or men as fully rational beings. A writer on ethics who denies the irrational (even perverse) side of the human make-up, including his own, is doomed to irrelevance. In any case, questions of sexual bias, however important they may be in other contexts, are of very little relevance here. For the unborn, at least as much as women, may be victims of prejudice.

Moreover, if personhood or humanity admits of degrees before birth, then it would seem that it must admit of degrees after birth as well. And even if we can manage to block such inferences as that kings are more persons than peasants, Greeks than barbarians, men than women (or women than men), or those with Ph.D.'s than those with M.A.'s, according to this theory we should still expect that adults will be considered more fully human than children. But few hold and fewer still teach that a ten-year-old child can be killed on lighter grounds than an adult. Indeed the killing of small children is often considered worse than the killing of adults. (Although a parent who kills his child is likely to receive a less severe sentence than someone who kills an adult, this remnant of the *patria potestas* is the result of excuse or mitigation rather than of justification.)

Some philosophers, it is true, might contend that there are degrees of humanity, but that full-fledged humanity is attained well before the age of ten. The question then is at what point full-fledged humanity is attained. Tooley's suggestion—twenty-four hours after birth—is clearly dictated by considerations of convenience rather than by the nature of the newborn. Some might say that first use of speech is a plausible criterion, but the development of linguistic capacities is a process, if anything is, not completed, if ever, until much later in a human being's development than his tenth birthday. If one wishes to fix a point after birth when someone becomes a full-fledged person, it could seem plausible to some thinkers to choose a point after the age of ten—when the nervous system is fully developed, at puberty, or at the conventional age of majority. In any case, the gradualist does not avoid the central problem—that of determining when we have a person in the full sense on our hands.

It has also been argued that a graduation from personhood into nonpersonhood can be observed at the end of life. But the consequences of such a view are scarcely tolerable. For what the analogy with abortion leads to is the killing of old people (1) without their consent, and (2) for the sake of relieving *others* of the burden they pose. Whatever our conclusion might be concerning voluntary euthanasia, and whatever difficulties there might be in fixing a precise moment of death, we cannot admit that anyone who is humanly conscious, or will or may regain human consciousness, is anything but a full-fledged person. This point can be restated in more technical terms as follows. The concept of a person is normally both open-textured and flexible in its application—a corporation for instance may be treated legally as a person for some purposes and not for others. But when the concept of a person is given one particular use, to mark out those creatures whose existence and interests are to be given special protection in the court of morality, there are special reasons weighing in the direction of clarity and rigidity. Whatever the extent to which the interest of a given person might legitimately be sacrificed for the good of the community, it seems intolerable that a creature should be regarded as not a person—and hence of next to no account in moral deliberation—simply because it is or appears to be in the interest of others to so regard that creature. At any rate, to proceed in such a manner would be to overthrow some of the most fundamental elements of our moral tradition.

The difference between early and late abortion is best accounted for, I believe, not by the more nearly human status of the mature fetus as compared with the younger one, but rather by the closer imaginative and emotional link between the mature fetus and a born child and hence between such a creature and an adult human than is the case for a young fetus or embryo. Hence, while whatever norms are appropriate to our treatment of fetuses might be applied with greater strictness to them when they are mature than when they are young, nonetheless the fundamental moral status of all fetuses might still be the same.

We might also be faced with a gray area, not an area in which the unborn creature is gradually becoming a person, but one in which its status as a person or as prehuman organic matter (like an ovum) is open to reasonable doubt. The question for interventions in such a gray area would be on which side—of excessive risk or excessive caution—we prefer to err, and the decision might well depend on which end of the gray area we were at, just as the justifiability of firing a gun at an unidentified animal depends on how likely it is that it is a human being rather than a dangerous beast, without its being necessary to invoke the possibility that it might be something in between. In such cases the doctrine called probabilism—that the agent is entitled to take the benefit of an honest doubt—and its rivals in the history of casuistry become of relevance. It would seem that one's decision must be based not only on the strength of the doubts in question, but also on the relative importance of the interests at stake, so that even a fairly small possibility that what one is doing is taking the life of a person requires interests of considerable importance to override it.

Germain Grisez takes a more stringent view of this issue. He argues that if someone kills an embryo, not knowing whether or not it is a person (but having some reason to suppose that it is), he is in no different a moral posture than someone who kills what he knows is a person. In his own words, "to be willing to kill what for all we know might be a person is to be willing to kill it if it is a person." And he observes of possibly or probably abortifacient methods of birth control: "If one is willing to get a desired result by killing, and does not know whether he is killing or not, he might as well know that he is killing." (This last case is an extremely complex one, since several layers of doubt may be superimposed upon one another: whether the method chosen results in the destruction of zygotes, whether there is a moral distinction between the prevention of implantation and the outright killing of the zygote, and whether the zygote is a human person within the meaning of the moral rule against homicide. This last doubt is itself complex, having factual, conceptual, and moral elements difficult or impossible to disentangle from one another.)

It does seem to me, however, that there is some difference, although not a large one or one it is desirable to emphasize, even between someone who says, "I know I am killing a person" and someone who says, "I may be killing a person, and I'd just as soon not find out whether I am." The latter might, after all, find out what he is doing despite himself, and stop doing it. But someone who says, "I may be killing a person, but I'm not satisfied that I am, and if you satisfy me, I'll stop" is in neither of these positions. (He may still be *wrong*, of course.) . . .

A final objection to the claim that abortion is homicide is the argument *ad hominem.* Ralph B. Potter, Jr., phrases this objection:

> Neither the church nor the state nor the family actually carries out the practices logically entailed by the affirmation that the fetus is fully human. The church does not baptize the outpouring spontaneously aborted soon after conception. Extreme unction is not given. Funeral rites are not performed. The state calculates age from date of birth, not of conception, and does not require a death or a burial or a birth certificate nor even a report of the demise of a fetus aborted early in pregnancy. Convicted abortionists are not subjected to penalties for murder. The intensity of grief felt within a family over a miscarriage is typically less than that experienced upon the loss of an infant, an older child, or an adult.

But alongside the indications of a less than personal status for the fetus in our laws and customs listed by defenders of abortion, there have been many indications of fetal personhood. Since Potter mentions baptism, it is worth remarking that the Roman Catholic Church ordains the baptism of embryos of whatever degree of maturity, although problems of feasibility naturally arise in cases close to conception because the nascent organism is so small. And Protestants who do not baptize fetuses need not be expressing a lesser evaluation of unborn life, but only a non-Catholic baptismal theology. (Certainly many Protestants have condemned abortion, as have many non-Christians, who of course do not baptize anyone.)

There have been many indications that the fetus has been considered a person in the law of torts and the law of property. One might also notice the holding of a New York court that a fetus is a patient for the purposes of the doctor-patient testimonial privilege, as well as the traditional reluctance to execute a pregnant woman and the accompanying feeling that the killing of a pregnant woman is a peculiarly reprehensible act. And men and women sometimes feel significant grief over the loss of an unborn child. Even contemporary sensibility has little difficulty personalizing a fetus—calling it a "baby," and using the pronouns "he" and "she"—in the context, say, of instruction in the facts of reproduction or in the techniques of prenatal care. Finally, the existence of inherited norms forbidding abortion itself testifies to a recognition of fetal rights.

Some (although hardly all) of the above features of our laws and customs might be explained in other terms. A fetus might be treated as a person with a condition subsequent, in other words as having rights (now), subject to the rebuttable expectation that it will mature. So artificial a concept—while no doubt acceptable in law—should not be introduced into morality without very compelling justification. A few might tend to think of a fetus as a person when its interests and those of its mother work together (for instance in the getting of food stamps), while doubting its status only when the mother herself desires to be rid of her child. But it is difficult to see how this could be justified.

Moreover, the practices that seem to point away from fetal personhood can be explained in other ways. To the extent that funeral practices are designed to deal with a severed relationship, they are not necessary when no such relationship has been established. The same can be said of the rule of inheritance cited by Joel Feinberg as counting against fetal personhood: "A posthumous child . . . may inherit; but if he dies in the womb, or is stillborn, his inheritance fails to take effect, and no one can claim through him, though it would have been different if he lived for an hour after birth." It can be explained in part as a special rule of intestate succession designed (*inter alia*) to guarantee that spurious or doubtful pregnancy will not confuse inheritance. The disposition of its property is in any case a matter of indifference to a dead fetus. Finally, the reluctance of the courts to treat the fetus as a human person in criminal-law contexts other than abortion requested by a pregnant woman can be explained as reflecting an unwillingness of courts to read criminal statutes more broadly than their language requires.

Nor is it necessary that the opponent of abortion insist that abortion be treated, legally or socially, as murder. The difficult situation pregnancy often poses for a woman, and the difficulty many people feel in regarding the fetus as a human person—in particular the understandable difficulty some women have in regarding the fetus as a person separate from themselves—suffice to mitigate abortion to a moral analogue of (voluntary) manslaughter. Another analogy is the special offense of infanticide which exists in a number of jurisdictions. On the other hand, while these mitigating circumstances are quite powerful when the well-being of another human being—the mother—is at stake, the opponent of abortion need have no hesitation in regarding as murder (and demanding the severest punishment for) the killing of embryos where what is at stake is only scientific curiosity—for instance when embryos conceived *in vitro* are disposed of, or when embryos are conceived *in vitro* with the intent that they should be so disposed of if they survive.

When conventional morality is ambiguous, the rational course is to resolve its ambiguities in the most coherent way possible. And the result of so doing is to ascribe a right to live to the fetus or embryo from the sixth week of gestation at the very latest, since this is the latest point at which the possibility of arousing sympathy might be said to begin. It should be added that, where there is even some probability that the life at stake in a decision is that of a human person, some morally persuasive reason, even if not so grave a one as is required to warrant what is clearly homicide, is required if that life is to be rightly taken.

THE RIGHT TO ABORTION

Mary Anne Warren

We will be concerned with both the moral status of abortion, which for our purposes we may define as the act which a woman performs in voluntarily terminating, or allowing another person to terminate, her pregnancy, and the legal status which is appropriate for this act. I will argue that, while it is not possible to produce a satisfactory defense of a woman's right to obtain an abortion without showing that a fetus is not a human being, in the morally relevant sense of that term, we ought not to conclude that the difficulties involved in determining whether or not a fetus is human make it impossible to produce any satisfactory solution to the problem of the moral status of abortion. For it is possible to show that, on the basis of intuitions which we may expect even the opponents of abortion to share, a fetus is not a person, and hence not the sort of entity to which it is proper to ascribe full moral rights.

Of course, while some philosophers would deny the possibility of any such proof, others will deny that there is any need for it, since the moral permissibility of abortion appears to them to be too obvious to require proof. But the inadequacy of this attitude should be evident from the fact that both the friends and the foes of abortion consider their position to be morally self-evident. Because proabortionists have never adequately come to grips with the conceptual issues surrounding abortion, most if not all, of the arguments which they advance in opposition to laws restricting access to abortion fail to refute or even weaken the traditional antiabortion argument, i.e., that a fetus is a human being, and therefore abortion is murder.

These arguments are typically of one of two sorts. Either they point to the terrible side effects of the restrictive laws, e.g., the deaths due to illegal abortions, and the fact that it is poor women who suffer the most as a result of these laws, or else they state that to deny a woman access to abortion is to deprive her of her right to control her own body. Unfortunately, however, the fact that restricting access to abortion has tragic side effects does not, in itself, show that the restrictions are unjustified, since murder is wrong regardless of the consequences of prohibiting it; and the appeal to the right to control one's body, which is generally construed as a property right, is at best a rather feeble argument for the permissibility of abortion. Mere ownership does not give me the right to kill innocent people whom I find on my property, and indeed I am apt to be held responsible if such people injure themselves while on my property. It is equally unclear that I have any moral right to expel an innocent person from my property when I know that doing so will result in his death.

Furthermore, it is probably inappropriate to describe a woman's body as her property, since it seems natural to hold that a person is something distinct from her property, but not from her body. Even those who would object to the identification of a person with his body, or with the conjunction of his body and his mind, must admit that it would be very odd to describe, say, breaking a leg, as damaging one's property, and much more appropriate to describe it as injuring one*self*. Thus it is probably a mistake to argue that the right to obtain an abortion is in any way derived from the right to own and regulate property.

But however we wish to construe the right to abortion, we cannot hope to convince those who consider abortion a form of murder of the existence of any such right unless we are able to produce a clear and convincing refutation of the traditional antiabortion argument, and this has not, to my knowledge, been done. With respect to the two most vital issues which that argument involves, i.e., the humanity of the fetus and its implication for the moral status of abortion, confusion has prevailed on both sides of the dispute.

Thus, both proabortionists and antiabortionists have tended to abstract the question of whether abortion is wrong to that of whether it is wrong to destroy a fetus, just as though the rights of another person were not necessarily involved. This mistaken abstraction has led to the almost universal assumption that if a fetus is a human being, with a right to life, then it follows immediately that abortion is wrong (except perhaps when necessary to save the woman's life), and that it ought to be prohibited. It has also been generally assumed that unless the question about the status of the fetus is answered, the moral status of abortion cannot possibly be determined.

Two recent papers, one by B. A. Brody, and one by Judith Thomson, have attempted to settle the question of whether abortion ought to be prohibited apart from the question of whether or not the fetus is human. Brody examines the possibility that the following two statements are compatible: (1) that abortion is the taking of innocent human life, and therefore wrong; and (2) that nevertheless it ought not to be prohibited by law, at least under the present circumstances. Not surprisingly, Brody finds it impossible to reconcile these two statements, since, as he rightly argues, none of the unfortunate side effects of the prohibition of abortion is bad enough to justify legalizing the *wrongful* taking of human life. He is mistaken, however, in concluding that the incompatibility of (1) and (2), in itself, shows that "the legal problem about abortion cannot be resolved independently of the status of the fetus problem."

What Brody fails to realize is that (1) embodies the questionable assumption that if a fetus is a human being, then of course abortion is morally wrong, and that an attack on *this* assumption is more promising, as a way of reconciling the humanity of the fetus with the claim that laws prohibiting abortion are unjustified, than is an attack on the assumption that if abortion is the wrongful killing of innocent human beings then it ought to be prohibited. He thus overlooks the possibility that a fetus may have a right to life and abortion still be morally permissible, in that the right of a woman to terminate an unwanted pregnancy might override the right of the fetus to be kept alive. The immorality of abortion is no more demonstrated by the humanity of the fetus, in itself, than the immorality of killing in self-defense is demonstrated by the fact that the assailant is a human being. Neither is it demonstrated by the *innocence* of the fetus, since there may be situations in which the killing of innocent human beings is justified.

It is perhaps not surprising that Brody fails to spot this assumption, since it has been accepted with little or no argument by nearly everyone who has written on the morality of abortion. John Noonan is correct in saying that "the fundamental question in the long history of abortion is, How do you determine the humanity of a being?" He summarizes his own antiabortion argument, which is a version of the official position of the Catholic Church, as follows:

> . . . it is wrong to kill humans, however poor, weak, defenseless, and lacking in opportunity to develop their potential they may be. It is therefore morally wrong to kill Biafrans. Similarly, it is morally wrong to kill embryos.

Noonan bases his claim that fetuses are human upon what he calls the theologians' criterion of humanity: that whoever is conceived of human being is human. But although he argues at length for the appropriateness of this criterion, he never questions the assumption that if a fetus is human then abortion is wrong for exactly the same reason that murder is wrong.

Judith Thomson is, in fact, the only writer I am aware of who has seriously questioned this assumption; she has argued that, even if we grant the antiabortionist his claim that a fetus is a human being, with the same right to life as any other human being, we can still demonstrate that, in at least some and perhaps most cases, a woman is under no moral obligation to complete an unwanted pregnancy. Her argument is worth examining, since if it holds up it may enable us to establish the moral permissibility of abortion without becoming involved in problems about what entitles an entity to be considered human, and accorded full moral rights. To be able to do this would be a great gain in the power and simplicity of the proabortion position, since, although I will argue that these problems can be solved at least as decisively as can any other moral problem, we should certainly be pleased to be able to avoid having to solve them as part of the justification of abortion.

On the other hand, even if Thomson's argument does not hold up, her insight, i.e., that it requires *argument* to show that if fetuses are human then abortion is properly classified as murder, is an extremely valuable one. The assumption she attacks is particularly invidious, for it amounts to the decision that it is appropriate, in deciding the moral status of abortion, to leave the rights of the pregnant woman out of consideration entirely, except possibly when her life is threatened. Obviously, this will not do; determining what moral rights, if any, a fetus possesses is only the first step in determining the moral status of abortion. Step two, which is at least equally essential, is finding a just solution to the conflict between whatever rights the fetus may have, and the rights of the woman who is unwillingly pregnant. While the historical error has been to pay far too little attention to the second step, Ms. Thomson's suggestion is that if we look at the second step first we may find that a woman has a right to obtain an abortion *regardless* of what rights the fetus has.

Our own inquiry will also have two stages. In Section I, we will consider whether or not it is possible to establish that abortion is morally permissible even on the assumption that a fetus is an entity with a full-fledged right to life. I will argue that in fact this cannot be established, at least not with the conclusiveness which is essential to our hopes of convincing those who are skeptical about the morality of abortion, and that we therefore cannot avoid dealing with the question of whether or not a fetus really does have the same right to life as a (more fully developed) human being.

In Section II, I will propose an answer to this question, namely, that a fetus cannot be considered a member of the moral community, the set of beings with full and equal moral rights, for the simple reason that it is not a person, and that it is personhood, and not genetic humanity, i.e., humanity as defined by Noonan, which is the basis for membership in this community. I will argue that a fetus, whatever its stage of development, satisfies none of the basic criteria of personhood, and is not even enough *like* a person to be accorded even some of the same rights on the basis of this resemblance. Nor, as we will see, is a fetus's *potential* personhood a threat to the morality of abortion, since, whatever the rights of potential people may be, they are invariably overridden in any conflict with the moral rights of actual people.

I

We turn now to Professor Thomson's case for the claim that even if a fetus has full moral rights, abortion is still morally permissible, at least sometimes, and for some reasons other than to save the woman's life. Her argument is based upon a clever, but I think faulty, analogy. She asks us to picture ourselves waking up one day, in bed with a famous violinist. Imagine that you have been kidnapped, and your bloodstream hooked up to that of the violinist, who happens to have an ailment which will certainly kill him unless he is permitted to share your kidneys for a period of nine months. No one else can save him, since you alone have the right type of blood. He will be unconscious all that time, and you will have to stay in bed with him, but after the nine months are over he may be unplugged, completely cured, that is provided that you have cooperated.

Now then, she continues, what are your obligations in this situation? The antiabortionist, if he is consistent, will have to say that you are obligated to stay in bed with the violinist: for all people have a right to life, and violinists are people, and therefore it would be murder for you to disconnect yourself from him and let him die. But this is outrageous, and so there must be something wrong with the same argument when it is applied to abortion. It would certainly be commendable to you to agree to save the violinist, but it is absurd to suggest that your refusal to do so would be murder. His right to life does not obligate you to do whatever is required to keep him alive; nor does it justify anyone else in forcing you to do so. A law which required you to stay in bed with a violinist would clearly be an unjust law, since it is no proper function of the law to force unwilling people to make huge sacrifices for the sake of other people toward whom they have no such prior obligation.

Thomson concludes that, if this analogy is an apt one, then we can grant the antiabortionist his claim that a fetus is a human being, and still hold that it is at least sometimes the case that a pregnant woman has the right to refuse to be a Good Samaritan towards a fetus, i.e., to obtain an abortion. For there is a great gap between the claim that *x* has a right to life, and the claim that *y* is obligated to do whatever is necessary to keep *x* alive, let alone that he ought to be forced to do so. It is *y*'s duty to keep *x* alive only if he has some-how contracted a *special* obligation to do so; and a woman who is unwillingly pregnant, e.g., who was raped, has done nothing which obligates her to make the enormous sacrifice which is necessary to preserve the conceptus.

This argument is initially quite plausible, and in the extreme case of preg-nancy due to rape it is probably conclusive. Difficulties arise, however, when we try to specify more exactly the range of cases in which abortion is clearly justifiable even on the assumption that the fetus is human. Professor Thomson considers it a virtue of her argument that it does not enable us to conclude that abortion is *always* permissible. It would, she says, be "indecent" for a woman in her seventh month to obtain an abortion just to avoid having to postpone a trip to Europe. On the other hand, her argument enables us to see that "a sick and desperately frightened schoolgirl pregnant due to rape may *of course* choose abortion, and that any law which rules this out is an insane law." So far, so good; but what are we to say about the woman who becomes pregnant not through rape but as a result of her own carelessness, or because of con-traceptive failure, or who gets pregnant intentionally and then changes her mind about wanting a child? With respect to such cases, the violinist analogy is of much less use to the defender of the woman's right to obtain an abortion.

Indeed, the choice of a pregnancy due to rape, as an example of a case in which abortion is permissible even if a fetus is considered a human being, is extremely significant; for it is only in the case of pregnancy due to rape that the woman's situation is adequately analogous to the violinist case for our intuitions about the latter to transfer convincingly. The crucial difference between a pregnancy due to rape and the *normal* case of an unwanted preg-nancy is that in the normal case we cannot claim that the woman is in no way responsible for her predicament; she could have remained chaste, or taken her pills more faithfully, or abstained on dangerous days, and so on. If, on the other hand, you are kidnapped by strangers, and hooked up to a strange vio-linist, then you are free of any shred of responsibility for the situation, on the basis of which it could be argued that you are obligated to keep the vio-linist alive. Only when her pregnancy is due to rape is a woman clearly just as nonresponsible.

Consequently, there is room for the antiabortionist to argue that in the normal case of unwanted pregnancy a woman has, by her own actions, assumed responsibility for the fetus. For if *x* behaves in a way which he could have avoided, and which he knows involves, let us say, a 1 percent chance of bringing into existence a human being, with a right to life, and does so knowing that if this should happen then that human being will perish unless *x* does certain things to keep him alive, then it is by no means clear that when it does happen *x* is free of any obligation to what he knew in advance would be required to keep that human being alive.

The plausibility of such an argument is enough to show that the Thomson analogy can provide a clear and persuasive defense of a woman's right to obtain an abortion only with respect to those cases in which the woman is in no way responsible for her pregnancy, e.g., where it is due to rape. In all other cases, we would almost certainly conclude that it was necessary to look carefully at the particular circumstances in order to determine the extent of the woman's responsibility, and hence the extent of her obligation. This is an extremely unsatisfactory outcome, from the viewpoint of the opponents of restrictive abortion laws, most of whom are convinced that a woman has a right to obtain an abortion regardless of how and why she got pregnant.

Of course a supporter of the violinist analogy might point out that it is absurd to suggest that forgetting her pill one day might be sufficient to obligate a woman to complete an unwanted pregnancy. And indeed it *is* absurd to suggest this. As we will see, the moral right to obtain an abortion is not in the least dependent upon the extent to which the woman is responsible for her pregnancy. But unfortunately, once we allow the assumption that a fetus has full moral rights, we cannot avoid taking this absurd suggestion seriously. Perhaps we can make this point more clear by altering the violinist story just enough to make it more analogous to a normal unwanted pregnancy and less to a pregnancy due to rape, and then seeing whether it is still obvious that you are not obligated to stay in bed with the fellow.

Suppose, then, that violinists are peculiarly prone to the sort of illness the only cure for which is the use of someone else's bloodstream for nine months, and that because of this there has been formed a society of music lovers who agree that whenever a violinist is stricken they will draw lots and the loser will, by some means, be made the one and only person capable of saving him. Now then, would you be obligated to cooperate in curing the violinist if you had voluntarily joined this society, knowing the possible consequences, and then your name had been drawn and you had been kidnapped? Admittedly, you did not promise ahead of time that you would, but you did deliberately place yourself in a position in which it might happen that a human life would be lost if you did not. Surely this is at least a prima facie reason for supposing that you have an obligation to stay in bed with the violinist. Suppose that you had gotten your name drawn deliberately; surely *that* would be quite a strong reason for thinking that you had such an obligation.

It might be suggested that there is one important disanalogy between the modified violinist case and the case of an unwanted pregnancy, which makes the woman's responsibility significantly less, namely, the fact that the fetus *comes into existence* as the result of the woman's actions. This fact might give her a right to refuse to keep it alive, whereas she would not have had this right had it existed previously, independently, and then as a result of her actions become dependent upon her for its survival.

My own intuition, however, is that *x* has no more right to bring into existence, either deliberately or as a foreseeable result of actions he could have avoided, a being with full moral rights *(y)*, and then refuse to do what he knew beforehand would be required to keep that being alive, than he has to enter into an agreement with an existing person, whereby he may be called upon to save that person's life, and then refuse to do so when so called upon. Thus, *x*'s responsibility for *y*'s existence does not seem to lessen his obligation to keep *y* alive, if he is also responsible for *y*'s being in a situation in which only he can save him.

Whether or not this intuition is entirely correct, it brings us back once again to the conclusion that once we allow the assumption that a fetus has full moral rights it becomes an extremely complex and difficult question whether and when abortion is justifiable. Thus the Thomson analogy cannot help us produce a clear and persuasive proof of the moral permissibility of abortion. Nor will the opponents of the restrictive laws thank us for anything less; for their conviction (for the most part) is that abortion is obviously *not* a morally serious and extremely unfortunate, even though sometimes justified act, comparable to killing in self-defense or to letting the violinist die, but rather is closer to being a morally neutral act, like cutting one's hair.

The basis of this conviction, I believe, is the realization that a fetus is not a person, and thus does not have a full-fledged right to life. Perhaps the reason why this claim has been so inadequately defended is that it seems self-evident to those who accept it. And so it is, insofar as it follows from what I take to be perfectly obvious claims about the nature of personhood, and about the proper grounds for ascribing moral rights, claims which ought, indeed, to be obvious to both the friends and foes of abortion. Nevertheless, it is worth examining these claims, and showing how they demonstrate the moral innocuousness of abortion, since this apparently has not been adequately done before.

II

The question which we must answer in order to produce a satisfactory solution to the problem of the moral status of abortion is this: How are we to define the moral community, the set of beings with full and equal moral rights, such that we can decide whether a human fetus is a member of this community or not? What sort of entity, exactly, has the inalienable rights to life, liberty, and the pursuit of happiness? Jefferson attributed these rights to all *men,* and it may or may not be fair to suggest that he intended to attribute them *only* to men. Perhaps he ought to have attributed them to all human beings. If so, then we arrive, first, at Noonan's problem of defining what makes a being human, and, second, at the equally vital question which Noonan does not consider, namely, What reason is there for identifying the moral community with the set of all human beings, in whatever way we have chosen to define that term?

1. On the Definition of "Human"

One reason why this vital second question is so frequently overlooked in the debate over the moral status of abortion is that the term "human" has two distinct, but not often distinguished, senses. This fact results in a slide of meaning, which serves to conceal the fallaciousness of the traditional argument that since (1) it is wrong to kill innocent human beings, and (2) fetuses are innocent human beings, then (3) it is wrong to kill fetuses. For if "human" is used in the same sense in both (1) and (2) then, whichever of the two senses is meant, one of these premises is question-begging. And if it is used in two different senses then of course the conclusion doesn't follow.

Thus, (1) is a self-evident moral truth, and avoids begging the question about abortion, only if "human being" is used to mean something like "a full-fledged member of the moral community." (It may or may not also be meant to refer exclusively to members of the species *Homo sapiens*.) We may call this the *moral* sense of "human." It is not to be confused with what we will call the *genetic* sense, i.e., the sense in which *any* member of the species is a human being, and no member of any other species could be. If (1) is acceptable only if the moral sense is intended, (2) is non–question-begging only if what is intended is the genetic sense.

In "Deciding Who Is Human," Noonan argues for the classification of fetuses with human beings by pointing to the presence of the full genetic code, and the potential capacity for rational thought. It is clear that what he needs to show, for his version of the traditional argument to be valid, is that fetuses are human in the moral sense, the sense in which it is analytically true that all human beings have full moral rights. But, in the absence of any argument showing that whatever is genetically human is also morally human, and he gives none, nothing more than genetic humanity can be demonstrated by the presence of the human genetic code. And, as we will see, the *potential* capacity for rational thought can at most show that an entity has the potential for *becoming* human in the moral sense.

2. Defining the Moral Community

Can it be established that genetic humanity is sufficient for moral humanity? I think that there are very good reasons for not defining the moral community in this way. I would like to suggest an alternative way of defining the moral community, which I will argue for only to the extent of explaining why it is, or should be, self-evident. The suggestion is simply that the moral community consists of all and only *people,* rather than all and only human beings; and probably the best way of demonstrating its self-evidence is by considering the concept of personhood, to see what sorts of entity are and are not persons, and what the decision that a being is or is not a person implies about its moral rights.

What characteristics entitle an entity to be considered a person? This is obviously not the place to attempt a complete analysis of the concept of personhood, but we do not need such a fully adequate analysis just to determine whether and why a fetus is or isn't a person. All we need is a rough and approximate list of the most basic criteria of personhood, and some idea of which, or how many, of these an entity must satisfy in order to properly be considered a person.

In searching for such criteria, it is useful to look beyond the set of people with whom we are acquainted, and ask how we would decide whether a totally alien being was a person or not. (For we have no right to assume that genetic humanity is necessary for personhood.) Imagine a space traveler who lands on an unknown planet and encounters a race of beings utterly unlike any he has ever seen or heard of. If he wants to be sure of behaving morally toward these beings, he has to somehow decide whether they are people, and hence have full moral rights, or whether they are the sort of thing which he need not feel guilty about treating as, for example, a source of food.

How should he go about making this decision? If he has some anthropological background, he might look for such things as religion, art, and the manufacturing of tools, weapons, or shelters, since these factors have been used to distinguish our human from our prehuman ancestors, in what seems to be closer to the moral than the genetic sense of "human." And no doubt he would be right to consider the presence of such factors as good evidence that the alien beings were people, and morally human. It would, however, be overly anthropocentric of him to take the absence of these things as adequate evidence that they were not, since we can imagine people who have progressed beyond, or evolved without ever developing, these cultural characteristics.

I suggest that the traits which are most central to the concept of personhood, or humanity in the moral sense, are, very roughly, the following:

1. consciousness (of objects and events external and/or internal to the being), and in particular the capacity to feel pain;
2. reasoning (the *developed* capacity to solve new and relatively complex problems);
3. self-motivated activity (activity which is relatively independent of either genetic or direct external control);
4. the capacity to communicate, by whatever means, messages of an indefinite variety of types, that is, not just with an indefinite number of possible contents, but on indefinitely many possible topics;
5. the presence of self-concepts, and self-awareness, either individual or racial, or both.

Admittedly, there are apt to be a great many problems involved in formulating precise definitions of these criteria, let alone in developing universally valid behavioral criteria for deciding when they apply. But I will assume that both we and our explorer know approximately what (1)-(5) mean, and that he is also able to determine whether or not they apply. How, then, should he use his findings to decide whether or not the alien beings are people? We needn't suppose that an entity must have *all* of these attributes to be properly considered a person; (1) and (2) alone may well be sufficient for personhood, and quite probably (1)-(3) are sufficient. Neither do we need to insist that any one of these criteria is *necessary* for personhood, although once again (1) and (2) look like fairly good candidates for necessary conditions, as does (3), if "activity" is construed so as to include the activity of reasoning.

All we need to claim, to demonstrate that a fetus is not a person, is that any being which satisfies *none* of (1)-(5) is certainly not a person. I consider this claim to be so obvious that I think anyone who denied it, and claimed that a being which satisfied none of (1)-(5) was a person all the same, would thereby demonstrate that he had no notion at all of what a person is—perhaps because he had confused the concept of a person with that of genetic humanity. If the opponents of abortion were to deny the appropriateness of these five criteria, I do not know what further arguments would convince them. We would probably have to admit that our conceptual schemes were indeed irreconcilably different, and that our dispute could not be settled objectively.

I do not expect this to happen, however, since I think that the concept of a person is one which is very nearly universal (to people), and that it is common to both proabortionists and antiabortionists, even though neither group has fully realized the relevance of this concept to the resolution of their dispute. Furthermore, I think that on reflection even the antiabortionists ought to agree not only that (1)-(5) are central to the concept of personhood, but also that it is a part of this concept that all and only people have full moral rights. The concept of a person is in part a moral concept; once we have admitted that *x* is a person, we have recognized, even if we have not agreed to respect, *x*'s right to be treated as a member of the moral community. It is true that the claim that *x* is a *human being* is more commonly voiced as part of an appeal to treat *x* decently than is the claim that *x* is a person, but this is either because "human being" is here used in the sense which implies personhood, or because the genetic and moral senses of "human" have been confused.

Now if (1)-(5) are indeed the primary criteria of personhood, then it is clear that genetic humanity is neither necessary nor sufficient for establishing that an entity is a person. Some human beings are not people, and there may well be people who are not human beings. A man or woman whose consciousness has been permanently obliterated but who remains alive is a human being which is no longer a person; defective human beings, with no appreciable mental capacity, are not and presumably never will be people; and a fetus is a human being which is not yet a person, and which therefore cannot coherently be said to have full moral rights. Citizens of the next century should be prepared to recognize highly advanced, self-aware robots or computers, should such be developed, and intelligent inhabitants of other worlds, should such be found, as people in the fullest sense, and to respect their moral rights. But to ascribe full moral rights to an entity which is not a person is as absurd as to ascribe moral obligations and responsibilities to such an entity.

3. Fetal Development and the Right to Life

Two problems arise in the application of these suggestions for the definition of the moral community to the determination of the precise moral status of a human fetus. Given that the paradigm example of a person is a normal adult human being, then (1) How like this paradigm, in particular how far advanced since conception, does a human being need to be before it begins to have a right to life by virtue, not of being fully a person as of yet, but of being *like* a person? and (2) To what extent, if any, does the fact that a fetus has the *potential* for becoming a person endow it with some of the same rights? Each of these questions requires some comment.

In answering the first question, we need not attempt a detailed consideration of the moral rights of organisms which are not developed enough, aware enough, intelligent enough, etc., to be considered people, but which resemble people in some respects. It does seem reasonable to suggest that the more like a person, in the relevant respects, a being is, the stronger is the case for regarding it as having a right to life, and indeed the stronger its right to life is. Thus we ought to take seriously the suggestion that, insofar as "the human individual develops biologically in a continuous fashion . . . the rights of a human person might develop in the same way." But we must keep in mind that the attributes which are relevant in determining whether or not an entity is enough like a person to be regarded as having some of the same moral rights are no different from those which are relevant in determining whether or not it is fully a person—i.e., are no different from (1)-(5)—and that being genetically human, or having recognizably human facial and other physical features, or detectable brain activity, or the capacity to survive outside the uterus, are simply not among these relevant attributes.

Thus it is clear that even though a seven- or eight-month fetus has features which make it apt to arouse in us almost the same powerful protective instinct as is commonly aroused by a small infant, nevertheless it is not significantly more personlike than is a very small embryo. It is *somewhat* more personlike; it can apparently feel and respond to pain, and it may even have a rudimentary form of consciousness, insofar as its brain is quite active. Nevertheless, it seems safe to say that it is not fully conscious, in the way that an infant of a few months is, and that it cannot reason, or communicate messages of indefinitely many sorts, does not engage in self-motivated activity, and has no self-awareness. Thus, in the *relevant* respects, a fetus, even a fully developed one, is considerably less personlike than is the average mature mammal, indeed the average fish. And I think that a rational person must conclude that if the right to life of a fetus is to be based upon its resemblance to a person, then it cannot be said to have any more right to life than, let us say, a newborn guppy (which also seems to be capable of feeling pain), and that a right of that magnitude could never override a woman's right to obtain an abortion, at any stage of her pregnancy.

There may, of course, be other arguments in favor of placing legal limits upon the stage of pregnancy in which an abortion may be performed. Given the relative safety of the new techniques of artificially inducing labor during the third trimester, the danger to the woman's life or health is no longer such an argument. Neither is the fact that people tend to respond to the thought of abortion in the later stages of pregnancy with emotional repulsion, since mere emotional responses cannot take the place of moral reasoning in determining what ought to be permitted. Nor, finally, is the frequently heard argument that legalizing abortion, especially late in the pregnancy, may erode the level of respect for human life, leading, perhaps to an increase in unjustified euthanasia and other crimes. For this threat, if it is a threat, can be better met by educating people to the kinds of moral distinctions which we are making here than by limiting access to abortion (which limitation may, in its disregard for the rights of women, be just as damaging to the level of respect for human rights).

Thus, since the fact that even a fully developed fetus is not personlike enough to have any significant right to life on the basis of its personlikeness shows that no legal restrictions upon the stage of pregnancy in which an abortion may be performed can be justified on the grounds that we should protect the rights of the older fetus; and since there is no other apparent justification for such restrictions, we may conclude that they are entirely unjustified. Whether or not it would be *indecent* (whatever that means) for a woman in her seventh month to obtain an abortion just to avoid having to postpone a trip to Europe, it would not, in itself, be *immoral,* and therefore it ought to be permitted.

4. Potential Personhood and the Right to Life

We have seen that a fetus does not resemble a person in any way which can support the claim that it has even some of the same rights. But what about its *potential,* the fact that if nurtured and allowed to develop naturally it will very probably become a person? Doesn't that alone give it at least some right to life? It is hard to deny that the fact that an entity is a potential person is a strong prima facie reason for not destroying it; but we need not conclude from this that a potential person has a right to life, by virtue of that potential. It may be that our feeling that it is better, other things being equal, not to destroy a potential person is better explained by the fact that potential people are still (felt to be) an invaluable resource, not to be lightly squandered. Surely, if every speck of dust were a potential person, we would be much less apt to conclude that every potential person has a right to become actual.

Still, we do not need to insist that a potential person has no right to life whatever. There may well be something immoral, and not just imprudent, about wantonly destroying potential people, when doing so isn't necessary to protect anyone's rights. But even if a potential person does have some prima facie right to life, such a right could not possibly outweigh the right of a woman to obtain an abortion, since the rights of any actual person invariably outweigh those of any potential person, whenever the two conflict. Since this may not be immediately obvious in the case of a human fetus, let us look at another case.

Suppose that our space explorer falls into the hands of an alien culture, whose scientists decide to create a few hundred thousand or more human beings, by breaking his body into its component cells, and using these to create fully developed human beings, with, of course, his genetic code. We may imagine that each of these newly created men will have all of the original man's abilities, skills, knowledge, and so on, and also have an individual self-concept, in short that each of them will be a bona fide (though hardly unique) person. Imagine that the whole project will take only seconds, and that its chances of success are extremely high, and that our explorer knows all of this, and also knows that these people will be treated fairly. I maintain that in such a situation he would have every right to escape if he could, and thus to deprive all of these potential people of their potential lives; for his right to life outweighs all of theirs together, in spite of the fact that they are all genetically human, all innocent, and all have a very high probability of becoming people very soon, if only he refrains from acting.

Indeed, I think he would have a right to escape even if it were not his life which the alien scientists planned to take, but only a year of his freedom, or indeed, only a day. Nor would he be obligated to stay if he had gotten captured (thus bringing all these people-potentials into existence) because of his own carelessness, or even if he had done so deliberately, knowing the consequences. Regardless of how he got captured, he is not morally obligated to remain in captivity for *any* period of time for the sake of permitting any number of potential people to come into actuality, so great is the margin by which one actual person's right to liberty outweighs whatever right to life even a hundred thousand potential people have. And it seems reasonable to conclude that the rights of a woman will outweigh by a similar margin whatever right to life a fetus may have by virtue of its potential personhood.

Thus, neither a fetus's resemblance to a person, nor its potential for becoming a person provides any basis whatever for the claim that it has any significant right to life. Consequently, a woman's right to protect her health, happiness, freedom, and even her life, by terminating an unwanted pregnancy, will always override whatever right to life it may be appropriate to ascribe to a fetus, even a fully developed one. And thus, in the absence of any overwhelming social need for every possible child, the laws which restrict the right to obtain an abortion, or limit the period of pregnancy during which an abortion may be performed, are a wholly unjustified violation of a woman's most basic moral and constitutional rights.

POSTSCRIPT ON INFANTICIDE

Since the publication of this article, many people have written to point out that my argument appears to justify not only abortion, but infanticide as well. For a new-born infant is not significantly more person-like than an advanced fetus, and consequently it would seem that if the destruction of the latter is permissible so too must be that of the former. Inasmuch as most people, regardless of how they feel about the morality of abortion, consider infanticide a form of murder, this might appear to represent a serious flaw in my argument.

Now, if I am right in holding that it is only people who have a full-fledged right to life, and who can be murdered, and if the criteria of personhood are as I have described them, then it obviously follows that killing a new-born infant isn't murder. It does *not* follow, however, that infanticide is permissible, for two reasons. In the first place, it would be wrong, at least in this country and in this period of history, and other things being equal, to kill a new-born infant, because even if its parents do not want it and would not suffer from its destruction, there are other people who would like to have it, and would, in all probability, be deprived of a great deal of pleasure by its destruction. Thus, infanticide is wrong for reasons analogous to those which make it wrong to wantonly destroy natural resources, or great works of art.

Secondly, most people, at least in this country, value infants and would much prefer that they be preserved, even if foster parents are not immediately available. Most of us would rather be taxed to support orphanages than allow unwanted infants to be destroyed. So long as there are people who want an infant preserved, and who are willing and able to provide the means of caring for it, under reasonably humane conditions, it is, *ceteris parabis,* wrong to destroy it.

But, it might be replied, if this argument shows that infanticide is wrong, at least at this time and in this country, doesn't it also show that abortion is wrong? After all, many people value fetuses, are disturbed by their destruction, and would much prefer that they be preserved, even at some cost to themselves. Furthermore, as a potential source of pleasure to some foster family, a fetus is just as valuable as an infant. There is, however, a crucial difference between the two cases: so long as the fetus is unborn, its preservation, contrary to the wishes of the pregnant woman, violates her rights to freedom, happiness, and self-determination. Her rights override the rights of those who would like the fetus preserved, just as if someone's life or limb is threatened by a wild animal, his right to protect himself by destroying the animal overrides the rights of those who would prefer that the animal not be harmed.

The minute the infant is born, however, its preservation no longer violates any of its mother's rights, even if she wants it destroyed, because she is free to put it up for adoption. Consequently, while the moment of birth does not mark any sharp discontinuity in the degree to which an infant possesses the right to life, it does mark the end of its mother's to determine its fate. Indeed, if abortion could be performed without killing the fetus, she would never possess the right to have the fetus destroyed, for the same reasons that she has no right to have an infant destroyed.

On the other hand, it follows from my argument that when an unwanted or defective infant is born into a society which cannot afford and/or is not willing to care for it, then its destruction is permissible. This conclusion will, no doubt, strike many people as heartless and immoral; but remember that the very existence of people who feel this way, and who are willing and able to provide care for unwanted infants, is reason enough to conclude that they should be preserved.

THE MORAL DILEMMA OF ABORTION

Paul Wilkes

Non-Catholics may not realize that even the sound of this word—abortion—sends chills through Catholics. Those of us who went through Catholic schools remember that whenever it was mentioned—which was not often, for the weight of the word was so great and its impact so onerous—it was uttered in a hushed tone, as if even its use would contaminate the speaker. It is a word that drips with evil and death. Little wonder that the debate over the legality and morality of abortion is especially charged for Catholics.

Pro-life; pro-choice. The battle lines have been drawn, with each side seemingly unwilling to listen to the other. We'll work our way through this very difficult issue, but let us start with one area of agreement.

No one is *pro*-abortion.

No one—not the woman (or more often young girl) who has an abortion, not her mate, not the members of her family, and not her friends—looks upon abortion as something good. It might be considered necessary, or looked upon as the lesser of two evils; but it is never *good.* Of course, I was raised Catholic; but I seriously doubt that any girl or woman has ever walked blissfully into an abortion clinic, undergone an abortion, and walked out feeling simply wonderful. Relieved, perhaps; but there is often a profound sense of sadness, often a sadness that is never quite erased.

Abortion is a terribly serious act, and no thinking person can go through it and not be affected. In the earliest states, tiny cells are being preempted in their ingenious scheme of combining, mutating, and growing as they seek to form a new life. As a pregnancy continues, a definable physical form is being removed from the only place that can sustain it. So it is understandable that the Catholic Church—and indeed every major religion—has historically taken a firm stand against abortion. And it is understandable that there is a continuing moral repugnance against abortion in the population at large.

For the Good Enough Catholic to make a sensible and moral judgment on this confusing and often immediate dilemma, it's necessary to trace the historical development of the church's thinking and teaching on abortion. We need to know how the understanding of the conception and development of life, and the perceived presence of a soul within that life, has evolved over the centuries.

THE MYSTERY OF NEW LIFE

Some maintain that the church's stand on abortion has been consistent down through the centuries. That is hardly the case. For centuries, the church based its doctrine on Aristotle's *De generatione animalium,* which maintained (wrongly, it turns out) that each male seed contained a life, needing only the nutrition of the womb to thrive. A distinction was later made in the early church between a formed and unformed fetus—although such terms were being used at a time when precious little was actually known about the reproductive system. Both St. Jerome (d. 420) and St. Augustine, two of the earliest writers on this issue, taught that abortion was homicide and grievously sinful, but only when the bodily elements had come together to form a fetus. The ideas of the "unensouled fetus" and the "ensouled fetus" differentiated between what was considered only matter, and matter infused with an immortal soul. In 1713, a decree of the Holy Office actually forbade the baptism of a spontaneously aborted (that is, miscarried) fetus if there was no reasonable foundation that it was "animated by a rational soul." Thus it is apparent that the church has not always considered these early forms of life capable of having a soul.

As more was discovered about reproduction—including, in 1827, the presence of the ovum, or egg—Catholic teaching changed in response. The distinction between the ensouled and unensouled fetus was removed from Catholic canon law in 1869. Faced with a continuing stream of revolutionary scientific information, the church, perhaps in frustration, finally opted out of the abortion debate. A new understanding was proclaimed: The soul was infused at the very moment of conception, the church pronounced (although we now know conception is not accomplished in a moment at all); doing anything to frustrate that process of conception, or the attendant growth of a fetus, was akin to murder.

While no one was able to prove or disprove the precise moment at which the soul was actually infused, the church invoked a traditional posture of Catholic moral theology—that one may never act in the presence of doubt. Of course, doubt is present in many of life's decisions; but here the church stood firm upon its authority, claiming that human life was too precious to be tampered with in the face of uncertainty. Vatican II's *Gaudium et Spes* condemned abortion as an "abominable crime." Indeed, the church has stood firm on all reproductive matters, not only condemning artificial birth control, but opposing as well any pregnancy terminated—from RU-486, the so-called morning after pill, to outright abortion—regardless of the circumstances of conception.

There has, of course, been considerable debate on these points. From a purely biological point of view, Catholic thinkers and moral theologians have pointed out that, first of all, conception is not an instantaneous occurrence; it takes place over a period of days. Fertilization itself takes twenty-four hours. Furthermore, in the earliest days of a pregnancy, the zygote can still be subdivided; twins are not formed until about the fourteenth day. As a soul cannot be subdivided, how is it possible that there be a soul present at that juncture? Human cells are present, but they lack the structure of a human organism. True human life is only recognizable at about three weeks, and primitive brain function does not begin until about the eighth week.

Regardless of these biological facts, the Catholic Church has not only stood firm—forbidding Catholics, under pain of mortal sin, from advocating or having an abortion—but has mounted an unprecedented public campaign to ban abortions in America and the rest of the world. In consequence, abortion has been a sadly divisive issue in the church, pitting good people against good people. Certain Catholic theologians and politicians have been banned from speaking at Catholic institutions, threatened with excommunication, and reviled for their willingness to even discuss the issue openly. The staunchest pro-life and pro-choice advocates demand 100 percent acceptance of their point of view, leaving no room for debate or compromise. For the most committed, the only legitimate objective is converting the other side—and, indeed, the whole public debate—to their way of thinking.

This bold effort by the Catholic Church to influence both public opinion and the law has not only been divisive, it has been counterproductive. The church's unyielding call to make abortions illegal has actually increased public support for a woman's right to choose whether or not she will have an abortion. It appears that the church can no longer use its moral authority as a bully pulpit when addressing an increasingly independently minded laity.

It is not that the Good Enough Catholic can't easily see both sides of the abortion debate. Wanton murder of fetuses is a sickening prospect. But dissent against "ossification of doctrines" and "temptations of ideologies"— words of the eminent theologian Bernard Haring—must also be heard. For the Good Enough Catholic, there is an enormous personal, physical, and moral range between the termination of a pregnancy that risks killing the mother, or bringing forth a severely malformed baby, and a pregnancy that will yield a child of a gender other than what the parents had hoped for. It might be helpful to discuss some of the different situations that present themselves.

First, consider tubal pregnancy or a pregnancy at the onset of serious disease—say, a cancer of the uterus, which, if not removed, may be fatal to the pregnant woman. More and more Catholic theologians—as well as Catholics at large—no longer hold the unyielding view that a woman should face devastating physical harm or possible death rather than have her pregnancy terminated. They see this as clearly a case of choosing the lesser of two evils— in this instance, sacrificing the fetus in order to save the woman's life.

Then come a second tier of problem pregnancies, those resulting from rape or incest. These are not conceptions resulting from mutual love, or anything resembling mutual passion. There was no intent of procreation; there was neither consent nor any semblance of intimacy. These are pregnancies that constitute perhaps the starkest invasion of a woman's body. For not only is such a pregnancy an unspeakable burden for a woman or young girl to carry, but how can she be expected to love and nurture a child that is the product of such a heinous act? Is this not too much to ask of that woman, and too great a burden to inflict upon that child?

In both of these situations, it's important not to scurry to our ideological corners simply to proclaim that we know what is the "right" course of action. Rather, the position of the Good Enough Catholic is to look at all the circumstances. Even in cases where a woman appears likely to die if her pregnancy continues, or has become pregnant after a brutal rape, it is never possible to categorically say this pregnancy must end or that one must continue. This is a time for prayer, for seeking God's guidance; it is a time to ask for the gift of discernment . . . to make a good decision.

As Good Enough Catholics—conflicted and imperfect as we are—we struggle for the faith that God will provide an answer if we are both bold enough and humble enough to ask him. For God's grace is more encompassing than human or scientific knowledge, more wise than volumes of moral theology, more profound than our deepest thoughts. God is a loving father who wishes us to be happy; he gives us the wisdom to find our way through the worst times in our lives. He cares deeply about us, regardless of the decisions we make. We are never outside the love or grace of God; and we can make even the most agonizing decisions in our lives certain of his acceptance.

THE EDUCATION OF ONE CATHOLIC

A more difficult decision, one that presents itself far more frequently, is that of an unintended pregnancy—one where no force has been used, and the woman's life is not in danger. Most often, a young (statistically, the average age is 18.6), unmarried woman is involved. Viewed in the abstract—given our individual pro-life or pro-choice orientation—such decisions might seem easy to make. But for many of us, myself included, it is a much different situation when actually faced with a real person and a real pregnancy.

I grew up at a time when abortions were virtually unheard of (not that they weren't happening), and I could never imagine being part of such a heinous act. But then, like many people in the 1970s, I began to examine my once-categorical opposition to abortion as I saw how unwanted pregnancies visited heartache and grinding poverty upon poor families, both in developing nations and here in the United States. Even so, mine were all theoretical judgments—until one afternoon in Brooklyn, when a teary-eyed girl walked through the front door of the makeshift social service center and soup kitchen where I was volunteering at the time.

Alycia, a fifteen-year-old Puerto Rican girl, sobbed as she told me she was pregnant. I knew Alycia well; she was a bright, determined girl who had hoped to go on to college and break the cycle of poverty into which she had been born. I knew that if she had this child her life would instead more likely follow the well-worn path already trod by her mother and so many of her young friends. All of them were single mothers, poor, and living on the margins of society.

Alycia was despondent. What should she do? What could she do?

I was amazed with the quickness of my advice, which I offered to her the next day. By the end of the next week, I was driving her and her young boyfriend to an abortion clinic. I felt I was doing her a great service. I had rescued her; I had been the supportive parent she needed, and lacked, at a crucial juncture in her life.

I thought about that categorical decision many years later in a dark sonogram room, as a technician passed an electronic wand over my wife's slightly swollen stomach. On the screen were the shadowy outlines of our first child—then only a months-old fetus, but an unmistakable human being nonetheless, with legs and fingers and eye sockets. My mind went back to Alycia. And suddenly I wasn't so sure I had helped her.

Did I present Alycia with other possibilities—like adoption—and offer to help her through the months of her pregnancy? Exactly how pregnant was she? What did that fetus look like? Was it as developed as the child I was seeing on the screen? What became of Alycia? Did that abortion change her life—and, if so, for better or worse? Did she go on to college—or on to a string of unwanted pregnancies by men she would never marry? Where was she today?

My position on abortion had slowly moved from the traditional Catholic stance inculcated by seventeen years of Catholic education to one I had considered both compassionate and realistic, and certainly enlightened. But in that sonogram room, it was suddenly wrenched back to a point somewhere in between. No, I could never go back to the unbending stance of my church; but neither would I ever again be able to so blithely assist another person in terminating a pregnancy.

I'm sure my experience is hardly unique. Many Catholics are struggling to find an approach to the abortion issue that is both moral and sensible. Knowing the sheer biology of reproduction, I would venture a guess that a good many Good Enough Catholics would not have grave difficulty accepting the use of a "morning after" contraceptive like RU-486, which stops the development of what is then a small gathering of cells. Others will see as reasonable the termination of a pregnancy that threatens the mother's life, or would result in a profoundly deformed infant whose life was not sustainable. And still others would advocate ending a pregnancy that resulted from rape or incest.

Beyond these, however, there remains the rest of the problem of unwanted pregnancies, the vast majority—and these require considerably more contemplation and divine guidance.

The Good Enough Catholic can be bold enough to ask, along with today's moral theologians, ethicists, and pregnant women who wrestle with these difficult issues: Does God seek every life, regardless of the circumstances and the human cost? A person can, with the highest of moral standards, see this as a life-and-death, black-and-white, question; or, with equally high moral standards, see a continuum colored by vastly varying circumstances.

In addition to birth, we must also consider the life thereafter. There are some 1.5 million abortions each year in the United States. For whatever reasons—the highest or the most base—they are unwanted children. Would we be condemning these infants to a world of unremitting financial or emotional poverty, or to living in homes surrounded by outright pathology? Can we keep alive, by the brilliance of modern medical science, fetuses and infants who will never think or live as anything resembling a human being? For ethicist Father Robert Springer, it comes down to this question: "How great a value must be present to countervail the sacrifice of life?" Or as Father Brian Jordan, who has counseled many poor and indigent women in his Maryland parish, has concluded: "I'm pro-life. But I'm also pro-person. You have to listen to every story."

QUESTIONS FOR DISCUSSION
ABORTION

1. Do the insane and the mentally retarded have the same rights as normal people? Do they have as much right to live as anyone else? Do fetuses have the same rights? Defend your response to each of these questions.

2. Many Catholic theologians cite the "principle of double effect" as the justification for therapeutic abortions only, despite the fetal right to live. According to this principle, it is permissible to abort a fetus that threatens the mother's life, because the "primary" effect intended is only to save the mother, even knowing that the fetus will die. Discuss this principle. Is it consistent with the Catholic doctrine of "natural law"? The first rule of that doctrine is: Evil may not be done that good come of it. Explain your position clearly.

3. Discuss the two principles proposed by Philip Devine that, he maintains, rule out all but therapeutic abortions. Do you agree with both principles? Explain why or why not. Is his conclusion valid? Defend your response.

4. On what grounds does Mary Anne Warren reject the claim that the mother's body is her property and that therefore she may expel any intruder from it? What principle does Warren offer in its place to justify abortion? Do you agree with Warren? Explain why or why not.

5. What reason does Warren give for rejecting the pro-life identification of the concept of a human being with the concept of a person? What, for her, is the difference, and how does it apply to abortion?

6. What reason does Paul Wilkes cite from modern embryology to reject the claim that the embryo has a human soul as soon as conception has occurred? Is he right that "a soul cannot be subdivided"?

SELECTED READINGS

BAIRD, S. *The Ethics of Abortion*. Buffalo: Prometheus, 1989.

CAIRD, R. "Infanticide and the Liberal View on Abortion." *Bioethics,* _____ 2000.

CALLAHAN, D., and S. CALLAHAN. *Abortion: Understanding Differences*. New York: Plenum, 1984.

DEVINE, PHILIP. *The Ethics of Homicide*. Ithaca, NY: Cornell University Press, 1978.

GALLAGHER, K. "Abortion and Choice." *Public Affairs Quarterly,* _____ 1993.

HARMAN, ELIZABETH. "Creation Ethics: The Moral Status of Early Fetuses." *Philosophy and Public Affairs,* Fall 1999.

JAGGAR, A. "Abortion and a Woman's Right to Decide." *Philosophical Forum,* _____ 1973.

KAMM, F. *Creation and Abortion*. New York: Oxford University Press, 1992.

NOONAN, J., ed. *The Morality of Abortion*. Cambridge, MA: Harvard University Press, 1970.

PIUS XI. *Casti Connubi.* London: Catholic Truth Society, 1931.

REIMAN, J. *Abortion and the Ways We Value Life.* Lanham, MD: Rowman and Little-field, 1999.

THOMSON, J. J. "A Defense of Abortion: A Compromise View." *Philosophy and Public Affairs,* _____ 1975.

5

CAPITAL PUNISHMENT

Is capital punishment a vestige of primitive brutality, or is it a just and necessary means of protecting society? We have been admonished "Thou shalt not kill" ever since Moses ascended Mount Sinai, and yet strong objections to legal execution were not voiced before the eighteenth century. The Judeo-Christian emphasis on mercy and the sanctity of human life somehow had little effect on penal institutions prior to the Enlightenment, perhaps because of humankind's religious preoccupation with salvation in the next world, and consequent disregard for diminishing suffering in this world. Indeed, it was difficult to reconcile the belief in an omnipotent Lawgiver, fearfully punishing those who broke His commandments, with opposition to executions by church and state, which were considered His agents on earth.

Anticlerical writers of the eighteenth and early nineteenth centuries were the first to denounce cruel and excessive punishments. Beccaria, Voltaire, Diderot, and even Robespierre demanded a humane and reasonable penal system. Russia under Catherine the Great, in 1750, was the first nation to abolish the death penalty for all crimes except treason. During the nineteenth century, utilitarian freethinkers, joined by some religious groups, agitated successfully to reduce the number of crimes punishable by death from two hundred to only two—murder and treason. In the last century many American states abolished capital punishment altogether, although some later reinstated it. The general worldwide trend of the last two centuries has been toward eliminating it, although grounds remain, as we shall see, for retaining it for unusually vicious crimes. The execution by the state of Israel of the Nazi mass-murderer Rudolph Eichmann was a particularly challenging test for those who oppose capital punishment.

In the first selection in this chapter, Louis Pojman defends the death penalty for premeditated murder on the grounds that it is needed by society to deter would-be killers from murdering innocent victims. He acknowledges statistical evidence that the death sentence has no greater deterrent value than life imprisonment, but he argues that there is also statistical evidence for the opposite conclusion, thus leaving the issue statistically undecided. In light of this, Pojman suggests (citing an argument first offered by Ernest van den Haag), there is a risk either way: without capital punishment, there is a possibility that some murders that would have been deterred will in fact not be deterred; with capital punishment, there is a risk that the executions of those convicted of murder will fail to prevent any subsequent murders. Thus, we must choose between risking the lives of innocent victims and risking the lives of convicted murderers. Pojman argues that the latter risk is more reasonable than the former.

Jeffrey Reiman offers a strong rebuttal to Pojman's argument, maintaining, as Jeremy Bentham pointed out long ago, that the likelihood of punishment is a stronger deterrent than its severity; and because the death penalty is far less likely to be enforced than imprisonment, if the latter fails to deter a murderer, the former will fail as well. Reiman further maintains that a more humane penal system has a civilizing effect on a society insofar as the government thereby sets a better example for its citizens.

Supreme Court justice Blackmun's 1994 dissenting opinion in the *Callins v. Collins case* holds that the requirement of the Supreme Court in its *Furman v. Georgia* decision of 1972, that "the death penalty must be imposed fairly and with reasonable consistency," has not been met by the way that the states have imposed the death sentence, and probably cannot be met at all, so that capital punishment is unconstitutional according to the Supreme Court's own earlier ruling. Justice Scalia, in a concurring opinion, replies to Blackmun that the Fifth Amendment of the Constitution provides for capital punishment, so it cannot be contrary to the Constitution. However, he grants Blackmun that the *Furman v. Georgia* decision of 1972 was muddled, requiring incompatible conditions for the death sentence, and thus, as far as Scalia was concerned, should be disregarded.

THE WISDOM OF
CAPITAL PUNISHMENT

Louis P. Pojman

The utilitarian argument for capital punishment is that it deters would-be offenders from committing first degree murder. Thorstein Sellin's study of comparing states with and without capital punishment concludes that the death penalty is not a better deterrent of homicides than imprisonment. On the other hand, Isaac Ehrlich's study, the most thorough study to date, takes into account the problems of complex sociological data in terms of race, heredity, regional lines, standards of housing, education, opportunities, cultural patterns, intelligence, and so forth, and concludes that the death penalty does deter. His simultaneous equation regression model suggests that over the period 1933–1969 "an additional execution per year . . . may have resulted on the average in 7 or 8 fewer murders." It should be noted that Ehrlich began his study as an abolitionist, but his data forced him to change his position. However, Ehrlich's study has been criticized, largely for technical reasons, so that his conclusion that we have significant statistical evidence that the death penalty deters better than prison sentences is not conclusive. The problems seem to be that there are simply too many variables to control in comparing demographic patterns (culture, heredity, poverty, education, religion, and general environmental factors) and that the death penalty isn't carried out frequently enough to have the effect that it might have under circumstances of greater use. One criticism of Ehrlich's work is that if he had omitted the years 1962 to 1969, he would have had significantly different results. David Baldus and James Cole contend that Ehrlich omitted salient variables, such as the rate of migration from rural to urban areas. On the other hand, Stephen Layson's study in 1985 corroborates Ehrlich's conclusion, except that Layson's work indicates that each time the death penalty is applied, the murder rate is reduced by about eighteen murders. A consensus is wanting, so that at present we must conclude that we lack strong statistical evidence that capital punishment deters. But this should not be construed as evidence against the deterrence thesis. There is no such evidence for nondeterrence either. The statistics available are simply inconclusive either way.

Precisely on the basis of this inconclusivity with regard to the evidence, some abolitionists, for example, Stephen Nathanson, argue that deterrence cannot be the moral basis for capital punishment. "The death penalty can be justified as analogous to defensive killing only if it can be shown that it does save lives. Since that has not been shown, one cannot appeal to this protective function as providing a moral basis for executing murderers." I think Nathanson is wrong about this. There is some nonstatistical evidence based on common sense that gives credence to the hypothesis that the threat of the death penalty deters and that it does so better than long prison sentences. I will discuss the commonsense case below, but first I want to present an argument for the deterrent effect of capital punishment that is agnostic as to whether the death penalty deters better than lesser punishments.

Ernest van den Haag has set forth what he calls the Best Bet Argument. He argues that even though we don't know for certain whether the death penalty deters or prevents other murders, we should bet that it does. Indeed, due to our ignorance, any social policy we take is a gamble. Not to choose capital punishment for first-degree murder is as much a bet that capital punishment doesn't deter as choosing the policy is a bet that it does. There is a significant difference in the betting, however, in that to bet against capital punishment is to bet against the innocent and for the murderer, while to bet for it is to bet against the murderer and for the innocent.

The point is this: We are accountable for what we let happen, as well as for what we actually do. If I fail to bring up my children properly, so that they are a menace to society, I am to some extent responsible for their bad behavior. I could have caused it to be somewhat better. If I have good evidence that a bomb will blow up the building you are working in and fail to notify you (assuming I can), I am partly responsible for your death, if and when the bomb explodes. So we are responsible for what we omit doing, as well as for what we do. Purposefully to refrain from a lesser evil which we know will allow a greater evil to occur is to be at least partially responsible for the greater evil. This responsibility for our omissions underlies van den Haag's argument, to which we now return.

Suppose that we choose a policy of capital punishment for capital crimes. In this case we are betting that the death of some murderers will be more than compensated for by the lives of some innocents not being murdered (either by these murderers or others who would have murdered). If we're right, we have saved the lives of the innocent. If we're wrong, unfortunately, we've sacrificed the lives of some murderers. But say we choose not to have a social policy of capital punishment. If capital punishment doesn't work as a deterrent, we've come out ahead, but if it does work, then we've missed an opportunity to save innocent lives. If we value the saving of innocent lives more highly than the loss of the guilty, then to bet on a policy of capital punishment turns out to be rational. The reasoning goes like this. Let "CP" stand for "capital punishment":

THE WAGER

	CP works	CP doesn't work
We bet on CP	a. We win: Some murderers die & innocents are saved.	b. We lose: Some murderers die for no purpose.
We bet against CP	c. We lose: Murderers live & innocents needlessly die.	d. We win: Murderers live & some lives of others are unaffected.

Suppose that we estimate that the utility value of a murderer's life is 5, while the value of an innocent's life is 10. (Although we cannot give lives exact numerical values, we can make rough comparative estimates of value—e.g. Mother Teresa's life is more valuable than Adolf Hitler's; all things being equal, the life of an innocent person has at least twice the value of a murderer's life. My own sense is that the murderer has forfeited most, if not all, of his worth, but if I had to put a ratio to it, it would be 1,000 to 1.) Given van den Haag's figures, the sums work out this way:

A murderer saved	+5
A murderer executed	−5
An innocent saved	+10
An innocent murdered	−10

Suppose that for each execution only two innocent lives are spared. Then the outcomes (correlating to the above wager table) read as follows:

a. −5 + 20 = +15
b. −5
c. +5 − 20 = −15
d. +5

If all the possibilities are roughly equal, we can sum their outcomes like this:
If we bet on capital punishment, (a) and (b) obtain = +10.
If we bet against capital punishment (c) and (d) obtain = −10.
So to execute convicted murderers turns out to be a good bet. To abolish the death penalty for convicted murderers would be a bad bet. We unnecessarily put the innocent at risk.

Even if we value the utility of an innocent life only slightly more than that of a murderer, it is still rational to execute convicted murderers. As van den Haag writes, "Though we have no proof of the positive deterrence of the penalty, we also have no proof of zero or negative effectiveness. I believe we have no right to risk additional future victims of murder for the sake of sparing convicted murderers; on the contrary, our moral obligation is to risk the possible ineffectiveness of executions."

A Critique of the Best Bet Argument

The abolitionist David Conway has constructed an instructive, imaginary dialogue about van den Haag's argument in which an opponent (O) objects to this line of reasoning, contending that the gambling metaphor regarding capital punishment (C.P.) is misleading, for it seems to devalue the lives of the guilty. We ought not to gamble with human lives. The issue is between the *possibility* of saving some lives (if deterrence works) and the *certainty* of sacrificing some lives (whether or not it works). Conway's proponent (P) for van den Haag's argument counters that gambling can be interpreted as doing a cost-benefit analysis with regard to saving lives. Here is a segment of Conway's dialogue:

P: [T]here are other circumstances in which we must gamble with lives in this way. Suppose you were almost, but not quite certain that a madman was about to set off all the bombs in the Western hemisphere. On [your] principle [that we ought not gamble with human life], you would not be justified in shooting him, even if it were the only possible way to stop him.
O: Yes, I suppose that I must grant you that. But perhaps my suppositions that gambling is taking the risk and that gambling with human lives is wrong, taken together, at least partially account for my intuitive revulsion with van den Haag's argument.
P: That may be. But so far, your intuitions have come to nothing in producing a genuine objection to the argument. I might add that I cannot even agree with your intuition that not gambling is taking the sure thing. Don't we sometimes disapprove of the person who refuses to take out life insurance or automobile insurance on the grounds that he is unwisely gambling that he will not die prematurely or be responsible for a highway accident? And he is taking the sure thing, keeping the premium money in his pocket. So, in common sense terms, failure to take a wise bet is sometimes "gambling."
O: You are right again. . . . But that does not change my views about C.P. Once the bet is clarified, it should be clear that you are asking us to risk too much, to actually take a human life on far too small a chance of saving others. It is just a rotten bet.
P: But it is not. As I have said, the life of each murderer is clearly worth much less than the life of an innocent, and, besides, each criminal life lost may save many innocents.

The opponent remains troubled by the notion of evaluating human worth, but finally admits that he is willing to grant that the life of the innocent is worth somewhat more than that of the murderer. Yet he goes on to give his fundamental objection:

O: The basic problem with your wager is simply that we have no reason to think that C.P. does work, and in the absence of such reason, the probability that it does is virtually zero. In general, you're confused about the evidence. First, you say C.P. deters. Then you are confronted with evidence such as: State A and State B have virtually identical capital crime rates but State A hasn't had C.P. for one hundred years. You reply, for instance, that this could be because State A has more Quakers, who are peace-loving folk and so help to keep the crime rate down. And, you say, with C.P. and all those Quakers, State A perhaps could have had an even lower crime rate. Since we do not know about all such variables, the evidence is "inconclusive." Here "inconclusive" can only mean that while the evidence does not indicate that C.P. deters, it also does not demonstrate that it does not.

The next thing we see is your proponents saying that we just do not know whether C.P. deters or not, since the evidence is "inconclusive." But for this to follow, "inconclusive" must mean something like "tends to point both ways." The only studies available, on your own account, fail to supply any evidence at all that it *does* deter. From this, we cannot get "inconclusive" in the latter sense; we can't say that "we just don't know" whether it deters, we can only conclude, "we have no reason to think it does." Its status as a deterrent is no different from, e.g., prolonged tickling of murderers' feet. It could deter, but why think it does? . . .

P: So you demand that we have definite, unequivocal evidence and very high probability that C.P. deters before it could be said to be justifiable.

O: No, I never said that . . . I think the "Best-Bet Argument" shows that the demand is too strong. Given the possible gains and losses, if there is even a strong possibility that it works, I do not think it would be irrational to give it another try. But we should do so in full cognizance of the betting situation. We would be taking lives on the chance that there will be more than compensating saving of lives. And, I also think that it is damned difficult to show that there is even a strong possibility that C.P. deters.

There are several things to say about Conway's dialogue. Like his opponent, you may object that this kind of quantifying of human life is entirely inappropriate. But if you had to choose between saving an innocent person and saving one who had just committed cold-blooded murder, which would you choose? We generally judge that conscientiously moral people are more worthy than viciously immoral ones, that the innocent are more worthy of aid than those who are guilty of squandering aid. Van den Haag's argument only formalizes these comparisons and applies them to the practice of capital punishment. Some humans are worth more than others, and some have forfeited their right not to be killed, whereas most people have not. Our practices should take this into account.

Secondly, you may still have doubts about the validity of putting a value on human life. But ask yourself, "What gives humans value?" or "What gives their lives value?" From a religious perspective they may have intrinsic value, but they still may forfeit a right to life by committing murder. But if you accept a secular point of view, isn't it some quality like moral integrity or contribution to the community that at least partly gives us worth? If so, then the murderer has lost a good bit of whatever value his life had. Kant, who set forth the idea that persons have intrinsic worth based on their ability to reason, held that we could forfeit that worth ("obliterate it") through immoral acts, so that the death penalty might well be appropriate.

Thirdly, if we had evidence that there was a 50 percent chance that executing a murderer would bring back the innocent victim, wouldn't you vote for the execution? I would vote for it if there was *virtually any chance* at all. But how different is that bet from the one that says there is a good chance that executing a person convicted of first-degree murder will prevent the murders of other innocent people? If the death penalty does deter, and we have evidence that it does, then we are partly responsible for the deaths of additional innocents by not inflicting that penalty.

Finally, the opponent is wrong in arguing that we have no evidence at all about the deterrent effect of capital punishment, so that it is tantamount to the evidence that tickling murderers' feet deters. We have evidence, though not statistical proof, based on commonsense experience, which makes the case for deterrence even stronger than the Best Bet argument. I now turn to the Argument from Anecdotal Evidence, a commonsense argument.

The Argument from Anecdotal Evidence

Abolitionists like Stephen Nathanson argue that because the statistical evidence in favor of the deterrent effect of capital punishment is indecisive, we have no basis for concluding that it is a better deterrent than long prison sentences. If I understand these opponents, their argument presents us with an exclusive disjunct: Either we must have conclusive statistical evidence (i.e., a proof) for the deterrent effect of the death penalty, or we have no grounds for supposing that the death penalty deters. Many people accept this argument. Just this morning a colleague said to me, "There is no statistical evidence that the death penalty deters," as if to dismiss the argument from deterrence altogether. This is premature judgment, for the argument commits the fallacy of supposing that only two opposites are possible. There is a middle position that holds that while we cannot prove conclusively that the death penalty deters, the weight of evidence supports its deterrence. Furthermore, I think there are too many variables to hold constant for us to prove via statistics the deterrence hypothesis, and even if the requisite statistics were available, we could question whether they were cases of mere correlation versus causation. On the other hand, commonsense or anecdotal evidence may provide insight into the psychology of human motivation, providing evidence that fear of the death penalty deters some types of would-be criminals from committing murder. Granted, people are sometimes deceived about their motivation. But usually they are not deceived, and, as a rule, we should presume they know their motives until we have evidence to the contrary. The general commonsense argument goes like this:

1. What people (including potential criminals) fear more will have a greater deterrent effect on them.
2. People (including potential criminals) fear death more than they do any other humane punishment.
3. The death penalty is a humane punishment.
4. Therefore, people (including criminals) will be deterred more by the death penalty than by any other humane punishment.

Since the purpose of this argument is to show that the death penalty very likely deters more than long-term prison sentences, I am assuming it is *humane,* that is, acceptable to the moral sensitivities of the majority in our society. Torture might deter even more, but it is not considered humane. I will say more about the significance of humaneness with regard to the death penalty below.

Common sense informs us that most people would prefer to remain out of jail, that the threat of public humiliation is enough to deter some people, that a sentence of twenty years will deter most people more than a sentence of two years, that a life sentence will deter most would-be criminals more than a sentence of twenty years. I think that we have commonsense evidence that the death penalty is a better deterrent than prison sentences. For one thing, as Richard Herrnstein and James Q. Wilson have argued in *Crime and Human Nature,* a great deal of crime is committed on a cost-benefit schema, wherein the criminal engages in some form of risk assessment as to his or her chances of getting caught and punished in some manner. If he or she estimates the punishment mild, the crime becomes inversely attractive, and vice versa. The fact that those who are condemned to death do everything in their power to get their sentences postponed or reduced to long-term prison sentences, in a way lifers do not, shows that they fear death more than life in prison.

The point is this: Imprisonment constitutes one evil, the loss of freedom, but the death penalty imposes a more severe loss, that of life itself. If you lock me up, I may work for a parole or pardon, I may learn to live stoically with diminished freedom, and I can plan for the day when my freedom has been restored. But if I believe that my crime may lead to death, or loss of freedom followed by death, then I have more to fear than mere imprisonment. I am faced with a great evil plus an even greater evil. I fear death more than imprisonment because it alone takes from me all future possibility.

I am not claiming that the fear of legal punishment is all that keeps us from criminal behavior. Moral character, habit, fear of being shamed, peer pressure, fear of authority, or the fear of divine retribution may have a greater influence on some people. However, many people will be deterred from crime, including murder, by the threat of severe punishment. The abolitionist points out that many would-be murderers simply do not believe they will be caught. Perhaps this is true for some. While the fantastic egoist has delusions of getting away with his crime, many would-be criminals are not so bold or delusionary.

Former Prosecuting Attorney for the State of Florida, Richard Gernstein has set forth the commonsense case for deterrence. First of all, he claims, the death penalty certainly deters the murderer from any further murders, including those he or she might commit within the prison where he is confined. Secondly, statistics cannot tell us how many potential criminals have refrained from taking another's life through fear of the death penalty. He quotes Judge Hyman Barshay of New York: "The death penalty is a warning, just like a lighthouse throwing its beams out to sea. We hear about shipwrecks, but we do not hear about the ships the lighthouse guides safely on their way. We do not have proof of the number of ships its saves, but we do not tear the lighthouse down."

Some of the commonsense evidence is anecdotal as the following quotation shows. British member of Parliament Arthur Lewis explains how he was converted from an abolitionist to a supporter of the death penalty:

> One reason that has stuck in my mind, and which has proved [deterrence] to me beyond question, is that there was once a professional burglar in [my] constituency who consistently boasted of the fact that he had spent about one-third of his life in prison. . . . He said to me "I am a professional burglar. Before we go out on a job we plan it down to every detail. Before we go into the boozer to have a drink we say 'Don't forget, no shooters' — shooters being guns." He adds "We did our job and didn't have shooters because at that time there was capital punishment. Our wives, girlfriends and our mums said, 'Whatever you do, do not carry a shooter because if you are caught you might be topped [executed].' If you do away with capital punishment they will all be carrying shooters."

It is difficult to know how widespread this reasoning is. My own experience corroborates this testimony. Growing up in the infamous Cicero, Illinois, home of Al Capone and the Mafia, I had friends who went into crime, mainly burglary and larceny. It was common knowledge that one stopped short of killing in the act of robbery. A prison sentence could be dealt with — especially with a good lawyer — but being convicted of murder, which at that time included a reasonable chance of being electrocuted, was an altogether different matter. No doubt exists in my mind that the threat of the electric chair saved the lives of some of those who were robbed in my town. No doubt some crimes are committed in the heat of passion or by the temporarily (or permanently) insane, but some are committed through a process of risk assessment. Burglars, kidnappers, traitors and vindictive people will sometimes be restrained by the threat of death. We simply don't know how much capital punishment deters, but this sort of commonsense, anecdotal evidence must be taken into account in assessing the institution of capital punishment.

John Stuart Mill admitted that capital punishment does not inspire terror in hardened criminals, but it may well make an impression on prospective murderers. "As for what is called the failure of the death punishment, who is able to judge of that? We partly know who those are whom it has not deterred; but who is there who knows whom it has deterred, or how many human beings it has saved who would have lived to be murderers if that awful association had not been thrown round the idea of murder from their earliest infancy." Mill's points are well taken: (1) Not everyone will be deterred by the death penalty, but some will; (2) The potential criminal need not consciously calculate a cost-benefit analysis regarding his crime to be deterred by the threat. The idea of the threat may have become a subconscious datum "from their earliest infancy." The repeated announcement and regular exercise of capital punishment may have deep causal influence.

Gernstein quotes the British Royal Commission on Capital Punishment (1949–53), which concluded that there was evidence that the death penalty has some deterrent effect on normal human beings. Some of its evidence in favor of the deterrence effect includes:

1. "Criminals who have committed an offense punishable by life imprisonment, when faced with capture, refrained from killing their captor though by killing, escape seemed probable. When asked why they refrained from

the homicide, quick responses indicated a willingness to serve life sentence, but not risk the death penalty."

2. "Criminals about to commit certain offenses refrained from carrying deadly weapons. Upon apprehension, answers to questions concerning absence of such weapons indicated a desire to avoid more serious punishment by carrying a deadly weapon, and also to avoid use of the weapon which could result in imposition of the death penalty."

3. "Victims have been removed from a capital punishment state to a noncapital punishment state to allow the murderer opportunity for homicide without threat to his own life. This in itself demonstrates that the death penalty is considered by some would-be-killers."

Gernstein then quotes former District Attorney of New York, Frank S. Hogan, representing himself and his associates:

> We are satisfied from our experience that the deterrent effect is both real and substantial . . . for example, from time to time accomplices in felony murder state with apparent truthfulness that in the planning of the felony they strongly urged the killer not to resort to violence. From the context of these utterances, it is apparent that they were led to these warnings to the killer by fear of the death penalty which they realized might follow the taking of life. Moreover, victims of hold-ups have occasionally reported that one of the robbers expressed a desire to kill them and was dissuaded from so doing by a confederate. Once again, we think it not unreasonable to suggest that fear of the death penalty played a role in some of these intercessions.
>
> On a number of occasions, defendants being questioned in connection with homicide have shown a striking terror of the death penalty. While these persons have in fact perpetrated homicide, we think that their terror of the death penalty must be symptomatic of the attitude of many others of their type, as a result of which many lives have been spared.

It seems likely that the death penalty does not deter as much as it could due to its inconsistent and rare use. For example, out of an estimated 23,370 cases of murder, nonnegligent manslaughter, and rape in 1949, there were only 119 executions carried out in the United States. In 1953, only 62 executions out of 7,000 cases for those crimes took place. Few executions were carried out in the 1960s and none at all from 1967 to 1977. Gernstein points out that at that rate a criminal's chances of escaping execution are better than 100 to 1. Actually, since Gernstein's report, the figures have become even more weighted against the chances of the death sentence. In 1993, there were 24,526 cases of murder and nonnegligent manslaughter and only 56 executions; and in 1994, there were 23,305 cases of murder and nonnegligent manslaughter and only 31 executions—for a ratio of better than 750 to 1 in favor of the criminal. The average length of stay for a prisoner executed in 1994 was ten years and two months. If potential murderers perceived the death penalty as a highly probable outcome of murder, would they not be more reluctant to kill? Gernstein notes:

> The commissioner of police of London, England, in his evidence before the Royal Commission on Capital Punishment, told of a gang of armed robbers

who continued operations after one of their members was sentenced to death and his sentence commuted to penal servitude, but the same gang disbanded and disappeared when, on a later occasion, two others were convicted of murder and hanged.

Gernstein sums up his data: "Surely it is a commonsense argument, based on what is known of human nature, that the death penalty has a deterrent effect particularly for certain kinds of murderers. Furthermore, as the Royal Commission opined the death penalty helps to educate the conscience of the whole community, and it arouses among many people a quasi-religious sense of awe. In the mind of the public there remains a strong association between murder and the penalty of death. Certainly one of the factors which restrains some people from murder is fear of punishment and surely, since people fear death more than anything else, the death penalty is the most effective deterrent."

I should also point out that, given the retributivist argument for the death penalty, based on desert, the retentionist does not have to prove that the death penalty deters *better* than long prison sentences, but if the death penalty is deemed at least as effective as its major alternative, it would be justified. If evidence existed that life imprisonment were a *more effective* deterrent, the retentionist might be hard pressed to defend it on retributivist lines alone. My view is that the desert argument plus the commonsense evidence — being bolstered by the Best Bet Argument — strongly supports retention of the death penalty.

It is noteworthy that prominent abolitionists, such as Charles Black, Hugo Adam Bedau, Ramsey Clark, and Henry Schwartzchild, have admitted to Ernest van den Haag that even if every execution were to deter a hundred murders, they would oppose it, from which van den Haag concludes "to these abolitionist leaders, the life of every murderer is more valuable than the lives of a hundred prospective victims, for these abolitionists would spare the murderer, even if doing so will cost a hundred future victims their lives." Black and Bedau said they would favor abolishing the death penalty even if they knew that doing so would increase the homicide rate 1,000 percent. This response of abolitionists is puzzling, since one of Bedau's arguments against the death penalty is that it doesn't bring back the dead. "We cannot do anything for the dead victims of crime. (How many of those who oppose the death penalty would continue to do so if, *mirabile dictu,* executing the murderer might bring the victim back to life?)" Apparently, he would support the death penalty if it brought a dead victim back to life, but not if it prevented a hundred innocent victims from being murdered.

If the Best Bet Argument is sound, or if the death penalty does deter would-be murderers, as common sense suggests, then we should support some uses of the death penalty. It should be used for those who commit first-degree murder, for whom no mitigating factors are present, and especially for those who murder police officers, prison guards, and political leaders. Many states rightly favor it for those who murder while committing another crime, e.g., burglary or rape. It should also be used for treason and terrorist bombings.

THE FOLLY OF CAPITAL PUNISHMENT

Jeffrey Reiman

Common Sense and the Deterrent Effect of the Death Penalty

Conceding that it has not been proven that the death penalty deters more murders than life imprisonment, Ernest van den Haag has argued that neither has it been proven that the death penalty does not deter more murders. Thus, his argument goes, we must follow common sense, which teaches that the higher the cost of something, the fewer the people who will choose it. Therefore, at least some potential murderers who would not be deterred by life imprisonment will be deterred by the death penalty. Van den Haag continues:

> [O]ur experience shows that the greater the threatened penalty, the more it deters. . . .
>
> Life in prison is still life, however unpleasant. In contrast, the death penalty does not just threaten to make life unpleasant—it threatens to take life altogether. This difference is perceived by those affected. We find that when they have the choice between life in prison and execution, 99% of all prisoners under sentence of death prefer life in prison. . . .
>
> From this unquestioned fact a reasonable conclusion can be drawn in favor of the superior deterrent effect of the death penalty. Those who have the choice in practice . . . fear death more than they fear life in prison. . . . If they do, it follows that the threat of the death penalty, all other things equal, is likely to deter more than the threat of life in prison. One is most deterred by what one fears most. From which it follows that whatever statistics fail, or do not fail, to show, the death penalty is likely to be more deterrent than any other.

Those of us who recognize how commonsensical it was, and still is, to believe that the sun moves around the earth will be less willing than van den Haag to follow common sense here, especially when it comes to doing something awful to our fellows. Moreover, there are good reasons for doubting common sense on this matter. Here are three.

1. From the fact that one penalty is more feared than another, it does not follow that the more feared penalty will deter more than the less feared, un-

282

less we know that the less feared penalty is not fearful enough to deter everyone who can be deterred—and this is just what we don't know with regard to the death penalty. This point is crucial because it shows that *the common-sense argument includes a premise that cannot be based on common sense,* namely, that the deterrence impact of a penalty rises without limit in proportion to the fearfulness of the penalty. All that common sense could possibly indicate is that deterrence impact increases with fearfulness of penalty *within a certain normally experienced range.* Since few of us ever face a choice between risking death and risking lifetime confinement, common sense has no resources for determining whether this difference in fearfulness is still within the range that increases deterrence. To figure that out, we will have to turn to social science—as a matter of common sense! And when we do, we find that most of the research we have on the comparative deterrent impact of execution versus life imprisonment suggests that there is no difference in deterrent impact between the death penalty and life imprisonment.

Since it seems to me that whoever would be deterred by a given likelihood of death would be deterred by an *equal* likelihood of life behind bars, I suspect that the commonsense argument only seems plausible because we evaluate it while unconsciously assuming that potential criminals will face larger likelihoods of death sentences than of life sentences. If the likelihoods were equal, it seems to me that where life imprisonment were improbable enough to make it too distant a possibility to worry much about, a similar low probability of death would have the same effect. After all, we are undeterred by small likelihoods of death every time we walk the streets. And if life imprisonment were sufficiently probable to pose a real deterrent threat, it would pose as much of a deterrent threat as death. And then it seems that any lengthy prison sentence—say, twenty years—dependably imposed and not softened by parole, would do the same.

2. In light of the fact that the number of privately owned guns in America is substantially larger than the number of households in America, as well as the fact that about twelve hundred suspected felons are killed or wounded by the police in the line of duty every year, it must be granted that anyone contemplating committing a crime already faces a substantial risk of ending up dead as a result. It's hard to see why anyone *who is not already deterred by this* would be deterred by the addition of the more distant risk of death after apprehension, conviction, and appeal.

3. Van den Haag has maintained that deterrence works not only by means of cost-benefit calculations made by potential criminals, but also by the lesson about the wrongfulness of murder that is slowly learned in a society that subjects murderers to the ultimate punishment. If, however, I am correct in claiming that the refusal to execute even those who deserve it has a civilizing effect, then the refusal to execute also teaches a lesson about the wrongfulness of murder. My claim here is admittedly speculative, but no more so than van den Haag's to the contrary. And my view has the added virtue of accounting for the failure of research to show an increased deterrent effect from executions, *without having to deny the plausibility of van den Haag's*

commonsense argument that at least some additional potential murderers will be deterred by the prospect of the death penalty. If there is a deterrent effect from *not executing,* then it is understandable that while executions will deter some murderers, this effect will be balanced out by the weakening of the deterrent effect of not executing, such that no net reduction in murders will result. This, by the way, also disposes of van den Haag's argument that, in the absence of knowledge one way or the other on the deterrent effect of executions, we should execute murderers rather than risk the lives of innocent people whose murders might have been deterred if we had executed. If there is a deterrent effect of not executing, it follows that we risk innocent lives either way. And if this is so, it seems that the only reasonable course of action is to refrain from imposing what we know is a horrible fate.

I conclude then that we have no good reason to think that we need the death penalty to protect innocent people from murder. Life in prison (or, at least, a lengthy prison term without parole) dependably meted out, will do as well.

PAIN AND CIVILIZATION

The arguments of the previous section prove that, though the death penalty is a just punishment for murder, no injustice is done to actual or potential victims if we refrain from imposing the death penalty. In this section, I shall show that, in addition, there are good moral reasons for refraining.

The argument that I gave for the justice of the death penalty for murderers proves the justice of beating assaulters, raping rapists, and torturing torturers. Nonetheless, I take it that it would not be right for us to beat assaulters, rape rapists, or torture torturers, *even though it were their just deserts*—and even if this were the only way to make them suffer as much as they made their victims suffer. Calling for the abolition of the death penalty, though it be just, then, amounts to urging that we as a society place execution in the same category of sanction as beating, raping, and torturing and treat it as something it would also not be right for us to do to offenders, *even if it were their just deserts.*

To argue for placing execution in this category, I must show what would be gained therefrom. To show that, I shall indicate what we gain from placing torture in this category and argue that a similar gain is to be had from doing the same with execution. I select torture because I think the reasons for placing it in this category are, due to the extremity of torture, most easily seen— but what I say here applies with appropriate modification to other severe physical punishments, such as beating and raping. First, and most evident, placing torture in this category broadcasts the message that we as a society judge torturing so horrible a thing to do to a person that we refuse to do it even when it is deserved. Note that such a judgment does not commit us to an absolute prohibition on torturing. No matter how horrible we judge something to be, we may still be justified in doing it if it is necessary to prevent something even worse. Leaving this aside for the moment, what is gained by broadcasting the public judgment that torture is too horrible to inflict even if deserved?

1. The Advancement of Civilization and the Modern State

I think that the answer to the question just posed lies in what we understand as civilization. In *The Genealogy of Morals,* Friedrich Nietzsche says that in early times "pain did not hurt as much as it does today." The truth in this intriguing remark is that progress in civilization is characterized by a lower tolerance for one's own pain and that suffered by others. And this is appropriate, since, via growth in knowledge, civilization brings increased power to prevent or reduce pain, and, via growth in the ability to communicate and interact with more and more people, civilization extends the circle of people with whom we empathize. If civilization is characterized by lower tolerance for our own pain and that of others, then publicly refusing to do horrible things to our fellows both signals the level of our civilization *and, by our example, continues the work of civilizing.* This gesture is all the more powerful if we refuse to do horrible things to those who deserve them. I contend, then, that the more horrible things we are able to include in the category of what we will not do, the more civilized we are and the more civilizing. Thus we gain from including torture in this category, and, if execution is especially horrible, we gain still more by including it.

But notice, it is not just any refraining from horrible punishments that is likely to produce this gain. It is important to keep in mind that I am talking about modern states, with their extreme visibility, their moral authority (tattered of late but not destroyed), and their capacity to represent millions, even hundreds of millions, of citizens. It is when modern states refrain from imposing grave harms on those who deserve them that a powerful message about the repugnant nature of such harms is broadcast. It is this message that I contend contributes to civilization by increasing people's repugnance for such harmful acts generally. And, I believe that, because of modern states' unique position—their size, visibility, and moral authority, modern states have a duty to act in ways that advance civilization.

Needless to say, the content, direction, and even the worth of civilization are hotly contested issues, and I shall not be able to win those contests in this brief space. At a minimum, however, I take it that civilization involves the taming of the natural environment and of the human animals in it, and that the overall trend in human history is toward increasing this taming, though the trend is by no means unbroken or without reverses. On these grounds, we can say that growth in civilization generally marks human history, that a reduction in the horrible things we tolerate doing to our fellows (even when they deserve them) is part of this growth, and that, once the work of civilization is taken on consciously, it includes carrying forward and expanding this reduction. It might be objected that this view of civilization is ethnocentric, distinct to citizens of modern Western states but not shared, say, by hardy nomadic tribes. My response is that, while I do not believe the view is limited in this way, if it is, then so be it. I am, after all, addressing the citizens of a modern Western state and urging that they advance civilization by refraining from imposing the death penalty. What other guide should these citizens use than their own understanding of what constitutes civilization?

Some evidence for the larger reach of my claim about civilization and punishment is found in what Émile Durkheim identified, nearly a century ago, as "two laws which seem . . . to prevail in the evolution of the apparatus of punishment." The first, the *law of quantitative change,* Durkheim formulates thusly:

> The intensity of punishment is the greater the more closely societies approximate to a less developed type—and the more the central power assumes an absolute character.

And the second, which Durkheim refers to as the *law of qualitative change,* is this:

> Deprivations of liberty, and of liberty alone, varying in time according to the seriousness of the crime, tend to become more and more the normal means of social control.

Several things should be noted about these laws. First of all, they are not two separate laws. As Durkheim understands them, the second exemplifies the trend toward moderation of punishment referred to in the first. Second, the first law really refers to two distinct trends, which usually coincide but do not always. Moderation of punishment accompanies both the movement from less to more advanced types of society and the movement from more to less absolute rule. Normally these go hand in hand, but where they do not, the effect of one trend may offset the effect of the other. Thus, a primitive society without absolute rule may have milder punishments than an equally primitive, but more absolutist, society. This complication need not trouble us, since the claim I am making refers to the first trend, namely, that punishments tend to become milder as societies become more advanced; and that this is a trend in history is not refuted by the fact that it is accompanied by other trends and even occasionally offset by them. Finally, and most important for our purposes, Durkheim's claim that punishment becomes less intense as societies become more advanced is a generalization that he supports with an impressive array of evidence from historical societies from pre-Christian times to the time in which he wrote—and this supports my claim that reduction in the horrible things we do to our fellows is in fact part of the advance of civilization.

Against this it might be argued that there are many trends in history, some good, some bad, and some mixed, and thus that the mere existence of some historical trend is not a sufficient reason to continue it. Thus, for example, history is marked generally by growth in population, but we are not for that reason called upon to continue the work of civilization by continually increasing our population. What this suggests is that in order to identify something as part of the work of civilizing, we must show not only that it generally advances over the course of history, but that its advance is, on some independent grounds, clearly an advance for the human species—that is, either an unmitigated gain or at least consistently a net gain. And this implies that even trends we might generally regard as advances may in some cases bring losses with them, such that when they did, it would not be appropriate for us to lend our efforts to continuing them. Of such trends, we can say that they are advances in civilization except when their gains are outweighed by the losses they bring—and that we are called upon to further these trends only when their gains are not outweighed in this way. It is clear, in this light, that increasing population is a mixed blessing at best, bringing both gains and losses. Consequently, population increase is not always an advance in civilization that we should further, though at times it may be.

What can be said of reducing the horrible things that we do to our fellows even when deserved? First of all, given our attitude toward suffering and pain, it seems clearly a gain. Is it, however, an unmitigated gain? Would such a reduction ever amount to a loss? It seems to me that there are two conditions under which it would be a loss, namely, if the reduction made our lives more dangerous, or if not doing what is justly deserved were a loss in itself. As for the former, as I have already indicated, I accept that if some horrible punishment is necessary to deter equally or more horrible acts, then we might have to impose the punishment. (After all, in self-defense, we accept the imposition by the defender of harms equal to those threatened by his attacker.) Thus my claim is that reduction in the horrible things we do to our fellows is an advance in civilization *as long as our lives are not thereby made more dangerous* and that it is only then that we are called upon to extend that reduction as part of the work of civilization. Assuming, then, that we suffer no increased danger by refraining from doing horrible things to our fellows when they justly deserve them, does such refraining to do what is justly deserved amount to a loss?

The answer to this must be that refraining to do what is justly deserved is a loss only where it amounts to doing an injustice. But such refraining to do what is just is not doing what is unjust, unless what we do instead falls below the bottom end of the range of just punishments. Otherwise, it would be unjust to refrain from torturing torturers, raping rapists, or beating assaulters. If there is no injustice in refraining from torturing torturers, then there is no injustice in refraining from doing horrible things to our fellows generally, when they deserve them, as long as what we do instead is compatible with believing that they do nonetheless deserve those horrible things. Thus, if such refraining does not make our lives more dangerous, then it is no loss, and, given our vulnerability to pain, it is a gain. Consequently, reduction in the horrible things we do to our fellows, when those things are not necessary to our protection, is an advance in civilization.

2. The Horribleness of the Death Penalty

To complete the argument, however, I must show that execution is horrible enough to warrant its inclusion alongside torture. Against this it will be said that execution is not especially horrible, since it only hastens a fate that is inevitable for all of us. I think that this view overlooks important differences in the manner in which people reach their inevitable ends. I contend that execution is especially horrible, and it is so in a way similar to (though not identical with) the way in which torture is especially horrible. I believe we view torture as especially awful because of two of its features, which also characterize execution: intense pain and the spectacle of one person being completely subject to the power of another. This latter is separate from the issue of pain, since it is something that offends us about unpainful things, such as slavery (even voluntarily entered) and prostitution (even voluntarily chosen as an occupation). Execution shares this separate feature, since killing a bound and defenseless human being enacts the total subjugation of that person to his fellows.

Execution, even by physically painless means, is characterized not only by the spectacle of subjugation, but also by a special and intense psychological pain that distinguishes it from the loss of life that awaits us all. Interesting in this regard is the fact that, although we are not terribly squeamish about the loss of life itself, allowing it in war, in self-defense, as a necessary cost of progress, and so on, we are, as the extraordinary hesitance of our courts testifies, quite reluctant to execute. I think this is because execution involves the most psychologically painful features of death. We normally regard death from human causes as worse than death from natural causes, since a humanly caused shortening of life lacks the consolation of unavoidability. And we normally regard death whose coming is foreseen by its victim as worse than sudden death because a foreseen death adds to the loss of life the terrible consciousness of that impending loss. As a humanly caused death whose advent is foreseen by its victim, an execution combines the worst of both. Indeed, it was on just such grounds that Albert Camus regarded the death penalty as itself a kind of torture: "As a general rule, a man is undone by waiting for capital punishment well before he dies. Two deaths are inflicted on him, the first being worse than the second, whereas he killed but once. Compared to such torture, the penalty of retaliation seems like a civilized law."

Thus far, by analogy with torture, I have argued that execution should be avoided because of how horrible it is to the one executed. But there are reasons of another sort that follow from the analogy with torture. Torture is to be avoided not only because of what it says about what we are willing to do to our fellows, but also because of what it says about us who are willing to do it. To torture someone is an awful spectacle not only because of the intensity of pain imposed, but also because of what is required to be able to impose such pain on one's fellows. The tortured body cringes, using its full exertion to escape the pain imposed upon it—it literally begs for relief with its muscles as it does with its cries. To torture someone is to demonstrate a capacity to resist this begging, and that, in turn, demonstrates a kind of hard-heartedness that a society ought not to parade.

This is true not only of torture, but of all severe corporal punishment. Indeed, I think this constitutes part of the answer to the puzzling question of why we refrain from punishments like whipping, even when the alternative (some months in jail versus some lashes) seems more costly to the offender. Imprisonment is painful to be sure, but it is a reflective pain, one that comes with comparing what is to what might have been and that can be temporarily ignored by thinking about other things. But physical pain has an urgency that holds body and mind in a fierce grip. Of physical pain, as Orwell's Winston Smith recognized, "you could only wish one thing: that it should stop." By refraining from torture in particular and corporal punishment in general, we both refuse to put a fellow human being in this grip and refuse to show our ability to resist this wish. The death penalty is the last corporal punishment used officially in the Western world. It is corporal not only because it is administered via the body, but also because the pain of foreseen, humanly administered death strikes its victim with the urgency that characterizes intense physical pain, causing even hardened criminals to cry, faint, and lose control of their bodily functions. There is something to be gained by refusing to endorse the hardness of heart necessary to impose such a fate.

By placing execution alongside torture in the category of things we will not do to our fellow human beings even when they deserve them, our state broadcasts the message that totally subjugating a person to the power of others and confronting him with the advent of his own humanly administered demise is too horrible to be done by civilized human beings to their fellows even when they have earned it: too horrible to do, and too horrible to be capable of doing. And I contend that the state's broadcasting this message loud and clear would, in the long run, contribute to the general detestation of murder and be, to the extent to which it worked itself into the hearts and minds of the populace, a deterrent. In short, refusing to execute murderers though they deserve it both reflects and continues the taming of the human species that we call civilization—and it should, over time, contribute to reducing the incidence of murder. Thus, I take it that the abolition of the death penalty, though that penalty is a just punishment for murder, is part of the civilizing mission of modern states.

Notice, before moving on, that I have not here argued that the death penalty is *inhumane*. Inhumane punishments are normally thought to be incompatible with respecting the person of the offender and thus forbidden except perhaps under the most extreme circumstances. Speaking of the death penalty, Kant wrote that "the death of the criminal must be kept entirely free of any maltreatment that would make an abomination of the humanity residing in the person suffering it." Torture almost surely and maybe even execution are inhumane, but I have argued only that they are horrible, that is, that they are punishments that cause their recipients extreme pain, physical and/or psychological. I have tried to show the ways in which the death penalty, even imposed without physical pain, is still a horrible punishment in that it causes extreme psychological suffering often to the point of loss of physical control. I then urged that it would be good for the state to avoid doing such things to people, not simply because it is always morally preferable to impose less pain rather than more, but also because the state—

by virtue of its size, high visibility, and moral authority—is able to have impact on citizens beyond the immediate act it authorizes.

In particular, I have suggested that the state, by the vivid example of its unwillingness to execute even those—*especially those*—who deserve it, would contribute to the process of civilizing humankind, which I take in part to include reducing our tolerance for pain imposed on our fellows. I have called this an advance in civilization for two reasons: first, because history shows that the harshness of punishments seems generally to decline over time, and second, because it seems good to reduce our willingness to impose pain on our fellows. The first condition here is empirical, a matter of what history actually records. And while I think that the elimination of ear cropping, branding, drawing and quartering, and boiling in oil, as well as the practice of throwing members of unpopular religions to the lions for public entertainment, all suggest that the taming that I have in mind is the general trend of history, there are exceptions, of course. The Nazis, for example, tortured their enemies with awful ferocity. But most would recognize Nazism as a step backward in civilization. So, my claim is a broad empirical claim, much in the vein of Richard Rorty's recent suggestion that, in the West, there has been a tendency to want to reduce or eliminate cruelty. But it is equally a moral claim. I have argued that even stable historical trends do not count as advances in civilization unless they are also, on independent grounds, good.

In sum, my argument is that, though the death penalty is just punishment for some murders, execution is a horrible thing to do to our fellows, and, if the state can avoid execution without thereby doing injustice to actual or potential victims of murder, then, in addition to whatever is good about causing less pain, the state would also, by its example, contribute to a general reduction in people's tolerance for doing painful things to one another, a reduction that I think is an advance in civilization. And I think that modern states are morally bound to promote the advance of civilization because they are uniquely positioned to do so and because of the goodness that must characterize a trend if it is to count as an advance in civilization.

Recall that I argued . . . that offenders deserve the least amount of punishment that imposes on them harm equivalent to the harm they caused their victims *and* the harm they caused to society by taking unfair advantage of the law-abiding *and* that will effectively deter rational people from committing such crimes in the future. If we take these conjuncts separately, it should be clear from the previous section's argument that the deterrence component can be satisfied with life in prison or some lengthy prison term. Since I take the fairness component to be the same in any crime, it will not in itself add more than a small increment to any particular punishment. Consequently, it, too, should be satisfied if we impose a lengthy prison term on murderers. As for the first component, the *lex talionis* indicates that the murderer justly deserves to die, and nothing I have argued alters this conclusion. However, I have also argued that retribution can be satisfied without executing murderers, so long as they are punished in some other suitably severe way. It follows that, though the death penalty is justly deserved punishment for some murderers, all the rationales for punishment will be satisfied if murderers are sentenced to life in prison or at least to a substantial prison term, such as twenty years without parole. I have argued . . . that refraining from executing murderers will contribute to the advance of civilization and may, in the long run, reduce the incidence of murder. In sum, there are no moral reasons against, and some very good ones for, abolishing the death penalty. All of this has been based on the idea that the death penalty is just punishment for murder in principle. Additional reasons for abolishing the death penalty appear when we look at it in practice.

CALLINS V. COLLINS—DISSENTING
Supreme Court Justice H. Blackmun

[*Callins* v. *Collins,* Director, Texas Department of Criminal Justice, Institutional Division. The petition for a writ of certiorari is denied.

Justice Blackmun, dissenting.]

On February 23, 1994, at approximately 1:00 A.M., Bruce Edwin Callins will be executed by the State of Texas. Intravenous tubes attached to his arms will carry the instrument of death, a toxic fluid designed specifically for the purpose of killing human beings. The witnesses, standing a few feet away, will behold Callins, no longer a defendant, an appellant, or a petitioner, but a man, strapped to a gurney, and seconds away from extinction.

Within days, or perhaps hours, the memory of Callins will begin to fade. The wheels of justice will churn again, and somewhere, another jury or another judge will have the unenviable task of determining whether some human being is to live or die. We hope, of course, that the defendant whose life is at risk will be represented by competent counsel—someone who is inspired by the awareness that a less-than-vigorous defense truly could have fatal consequences for the defendant. We hope that the attorney will investigate all aspects of the case, follow all evidentiary and procedural rules, and appear before a judge who is still committed to the protection of defendants' rights—even now, as the prospect of meaningful judicial oversight has diminished. In the same vein, we hope that the prosecution, in urging the penalty of death, will have exercised its discretion wisely, free from bias, prejudice, or political motive, and will be humbled, rather than emboldened, by the awesome authority conferred by the State.

But even if we can feel confident that these actors will fulfill their roles to the best of their human ability, our collective conscience will remain uneasy. Twenty years have passed since this Court declared that the death penalty must be imposed fairly, and with reasonable consistency, or not at all, see *Furman* v. *Georgia* . . . (1972), and, despite the effort of the States and courts to devise legal formulas and procedural rules to meet this daunting challenge, the death penalty remains fraught with arbitrariness, discrimination, caprice, and mistake. This is not to say that the problems with the death penalty today are identical to those that were present twenty years ago. Rather, the problems that were pursued down one hole with procedural rules and verbal formulas have come to the surface somewhere else, just as virulent and pernicious as they were in their original form. Experience has taught us that the constitutional goal of eliminating arbitrariness and discrimination from the administration of death . . . can never be achieved without compromising an equally essential component of fundamental fairness—individualized sentencing. See *Lockett* v. *Ohio* . . . (1978).

It is tempting, when faced with conflicting constitutional commands, to sacrifice one for the other or to assume that an acceptable balance between them already has been struck. In the context of the death penalty, however, such jurisprudential maneuvers are wholly inappropriate. The death penalty must be imposed "fairly, and with reasonable consistency, or not at all." *Eddings* v. *Oklahoma* . . . (1982).

To be fair, a capital sentencing scheme must treat each person convicted of a capital offense with that "degree of respect due the uniqueness of the individual." *Lockett* v. *Ohio.* . . . That means affording the sentencer the power and discretion to grant mercy in a particular case, and providing avenues for the consideration of any and all relevant mitigating evidence that would justify a sentence less than death. Reasonable consistency, on the other hand, requires that the death penalty be inflicted evenhandedly, in accordance with reason and objective standards, rather than by whim, caprice, or prejudice. Finally, because human error is inevitable, and because our criminal justice system is less than perfect, searching appellate review of death sentences and their underlying convictions is a prerequisite to a constitutional death penalty scheme.

On their face, these goals of individual fairness, reasonable consistency, and absence of error appear to be attainable: Courts are in the very business of erecting procedural devices from which fair, equitable, and reliable outcomes are presumed to flow. Yet, in the death penalty area, this Court, in my view, has engaged in a futile effort to balance these constitutional demands, and now is retreating not only from the *Furman* promise of consistency and rationality, but from the requirement of individualized sentencing as well. Having virtually conceded that both fairness and rationality cannot be achieved in the administration of the death penalty, see *McCleskey* v. *Kemp* . . . (1987), the Court has chosen to deregulate the entire enterprise, replacing, it would seem, substantive constitutional requirement with mere aesthetics, and abdicating its statutorily and constitutionally imposed duty to provide meaningful judicial oversight to the administration of death by the States.

From this day forward, I no longer shall tinker with the machinery of death. For more than twenty years I have endeavored—indeed, I have struggled—along with a majority of this Court, to develop procedural and substantive rules that would lend more than the mere appearance of fairness to the death penalty endeavor. Rather than continue to coddle the Court's delusion that the desired level of fairness has been achieved and the need for regulation eviscerated, I feel morally and intellectually obligated simply to concede that the death penalty experiment has failed. It is virtually self-evident to me now that no combination of procedural rules or substantive regulations ever can save the death penalty from its inherent constitutional deficiencies. The basic question—does the system accurately and consistently determine which defendants "deserve" to die—cannot be answered in the affirmative. It is not simply that this Court has allowed vague aggravating circumstances to be employed, see, e.g., *Arave* v. *Creech* . . . (1993), relevant mitigating evidence to be disregarded, see, e.g., *Johnson* v. *Texas* . . . and vital judicial review to be blocked, see, e.g., *Coleman* v. *Thompson.* The problem is that the inevitability of factual, legal, and moral error gives us a system that we know must wrongly kill some defendants, a system that fails to deliver the fair, consistent, and reliable sentences of death required by the Constitution.

In 1971, in an opinion which has proved partly prophetic, . . . Justice Harlan, writing for the Court, observed:

> Those who have come to grips with the hard task of actually attempting to draft means of channeling capital sentencing discretion have confirmed the lesson taught by the history recounted above. To identify before the fact those characteristics of criminal homicides and their perpetrators which call for the death penalty, and to express these characteristics in language which can be fairly understood and applied by the sentencing authority, appear to be tasks which are beyond present human ability. . . . For a court to attempt to catalog the appropriate factors in this elusive area could inhibit rather than expand the scope of consideration, for no list of circumstances would ever be really complete. *McGautha* v. *California* . . . (1971)

In *McGautha,* the petitioner argued that a statute which left the penalty of death entirely in the jury's discretion, without any standards to go for its imposition, violated the Fourteenth Amendment. Although the Court did not deny that serious risks were associated with a sentencer's unbounded discretion, the Court found no remedy in the Constitution for the inevitable failings of human judgment.

A year later, the Court reversed its course completely in *Furman* v. *Georgia* . . . (1972). . . . The concurring Justices argued that the glaring inequities in the administration of death, the standardless discretion wielded by judges and juries, and the pervasive racial and economic discrimination, rendered the death penalty, at least as administered, "cruel and unusual" within the meaning of the Eighth Amendment. Justice White explained that, out of the hundreds of people convicted of murder every year, only a handful were sent to their deaths, and that there was "no meaningful basis for distinguishing the few cases in which [the death penalty] is imposed from the many cases in which it is not." . . . If any discernible basis could be identified for the selection of those few who were chosen to die, it was "the constitutionally impermissible basis of race." Ib., at 310 (Stewart, J., concurring).

I dissented in *Furman.* Despite my intellectual, moral, and personal objections to the death penalty, I refrained from joining the majority because I found objectionable the Court's abrupt change of position in the single year that had passed since *McGautha.* While I agreed that the Eighth Amendment's prohibition against cruel and unusual punishments "may acquire meaning as public opinion becomes enlightened by a humane justice," . . . I objected to the "suddenness of the Court's perception of progress in the human attitude since decisions of only a short while ago." . . . Four years after *Furman* was decided, I concurred in the judgment in *Gregg* v. *Georgia,* . . . (1976), and its companion cases which upheld death sentences rendered under statutes passed after *Furman* was decided. . . .

There is little doubt now that *Furman's* essential holding was correct. Although most of the public seems to desire, and the Constitution appears to permit, the penalty of death, it surely is beyond dispute that if the death penalty cannot be administered consistently and rationally, it may not be administered at all. *Eddings* v. *Oklahoma.* . . . I never have quarreled with this principle; in my mind, the real meaning of *Furman's* diverse concurring opinions did not emerge until some years after *Furman* was decided. See *Gregg* v. *Georgia.* . . . ("*Furman* mandates that where discretion is afforded a sentencing body on a matter so grave as the determination of whether a human life should be taken or spared, that discretion must be suitably directed and limited so as to minimize the risk of wholly arbitrary and capricious action"). Since *Gregg,* I faithfully have adhered to the *Furman* holding and have come to believe that it is indispensable to the Court's Eighth Amendment jurisprudence.

Delivering on the *Furman* promise, however, has proved to be another matter. *Furman* aspired to eliminate the vestiges of racism and the effects of poverty in capital sentencing; it deplored the "wanton" and "random" infliction of death by a government with constitutionally limited power. *Furman* demanded that the sentencer's discretion be directed and limited by procedural rules and objective standards in order to minimize the risk of arbitrary and capricious sentences of death.

In the years following *Furman,* serious efforts were made to comply with its mandate. State legislatures and appellate courts struggled to provide judges and juries with sensible and objective guidelines for determining who should live and who should die. Some States attempted to define who is "deserving" of the death penalty through the use of carefully chosen adjectives, reserving the death penalty for those who commit crimes that are "especially heinous, atrocious, or cruel," . . . or "wantonly vile, horrible or inhuman." . . . Other States enacted mandatory death penalty statutes, reading *Furman* as an invitation to eliminate sentencer discretion altogether. . . . Still other States specified aggravating and mitigating factors that were to be considered by the sentencer and weighed against one another in a calculated and rational manner. . . .

Unfortunately, all this experimentation and ingenuity yielded little of what *Furman* demanded. It soon became apparent that discretion could not be eliminated from capital sentencing without threatening the fundamental fairness due a defendant when life is at stake. Just as contemporary society was no longer tolerant of the random or discriminatory infliction of the penalty of death . . . , evolving standards of decency required due consideration of the uniqueness of each individual defendant when imposing society's ultimate penalty. . . .

This development in the American conscience would have presented no constitutional dilemma if fairness to the individual could be achieved without sacrificing the consistency and rationality promised in *Furman*. But over the past two decades, efforts to balance these competing constitutional commands have been to no avail. Experience has shown that the consistency and rationality promised in *Furman* are inversely related to the fairness owed the individual when considering a sentence of death. A step toward consistency is a step away from fairness.

There is a heightened need for fairness in the administration of death. This unique level of fairness is born of the appreciation that death truly is different from all other punishments a society inflicts upon its citizens. "Death, in its finality, differs more from life imprisonment than a 100-year prison term differs from one of only a year or two." Woodson [1958]. . . . Because of the qualitative difference of the death penalty, "there is a corresponding difference in the need for reliability in the determination that death is the appropriate punishment in a specific case." Ibid. In *Woodson,* a decision striking down mandatory death penalty statutes as unconstitutional, a plurality of the Court explained: "A process that accords no significance to relevant facets of the character and record of the individual offender or the circumstances of the particular offense excludes from consideration in fixing the ultimate punishment of death the possibility of compassionate or mitigating factors stemming from the diverse frailties of humankind." . . .

While the risk of mistake in the determination of the appropriate penalty may be tolerated in other areas of the criminal law, "in capital cases the fundamental respect for humanity underlying the Eighth Amendment . . . requires consideration of the character and record of the individual offender and the circumstances of the particular offense as a constitutionally indispensable part of the process of inflicting the penalty of death." Ibid. Thus, although individualized sentencing in capital cases was not considered essential at the time the Constitution was adopted, *Woodson* recognized that American standards of decency could no longer tolerate a capital sentencing process that failed to afford a defendant individualized consideration in the determination whether he or she should live or die. . . .

The Court elaborated on the principle of individualized sentencing in *Lockett* v. *Ohio* . . . (1978). In that case, a plurality acknowledged that strict restraints on sentencer discretion are necessary to achieve the consistency and rationality promised in *Furman,* but held that, in the end, the sentencer must retain unbridled discretion to afford mercy. Any process or procedure that prevents the sentencer from considering "as a mitigating factor, any aspect of a defendant's character or record and any circumstances of the offense that the defendant proffers as a basis for a sentence less than death," creates the constitutionally intolerable risk that "the death penalty will be imposed in spite of factors which may call for a less severe penalty." . . . See also *Sumner* v. *Shuman* . . . (1987) (invalidating a mandatory death penalty statute reserving the death penalty for life-term inmates convicted of murder). The Court's duty under the Constitution therefore is to "develop a system of capital punishment at once consistent and principled but also humane and sensible to the uniqueness of the individual." *Eddings* v. *Oklahoma*.

I believe the *Woodson-Lockett* line of cases to be fundamentally sound and rooted in American standards of decency that have evolved over time. The notion of prohibiting a sentencer from exercising its discretion "to dispense mercy on the basis of factors too intangible to write into a statute," *Gregg* . . . is offensive to our sense of fundamental fairness and respect for the uniqueness of the individual. In *California* v. *Brown* . . . (1987), I said in dissent:

> The sentencer's ability to respond with mercy towards a defendant has always struck me as a particularly valuable aspect of the capital sentencing procedure. . . . [W]e adhere so strongly to our belief that a sentencer should have the opportunity to spare a capital defendant's life on account of compassion for the individual because, recognizing that the capital sentencing decision must be made in the context of "contemporary values," *Gregg* v. *Georgia* . . . we see in the sentencer's expression of mercy a distinctive feature of our society that we deeply value. . . .

Yet, as several Members of the Court have recognized, there is real "tension" between the need for fairness to the individual and the consistency promised in *Furman.* . . . On the one hand, discretion in capital sentencing must be "controlled by clear and objective standards so as to produce nondiscriminatory [and reasoned] application." *Gregg.* . . . On the other hand, the Constitution also requires that the sentencer be able to consider "any relevant mitigating evidence regarding the defendant's character or background, and the circumstances of the particular offense." *California* v. *Brown.* . . . (1987). The power to consider mitigating evidence that would warrant a sentence less than death is meaningless unless the sentencer has the discretion and authority to dispense mercy based on that evidence. Thus, the Constitution, by requiring a heightened degree of fairness to the individual, and also a greater degree of equality and rationality in the administration of death, demands sentencer discretion that is at once generously expanded and severely restricted.

This dilemma was laid bare in *Penry* v. *Lynaugh* . . . (1989). The defendant in *Penry* challenged the Texas death penalty statute, arguing that it failed to allow the sentencing jury to give full mitigating effect to his evidence of mental retardation and history of child abuse. The Texas statute required the jury, during the penalty phase, to answer three "special issues"; if the jury unanimously answered "yes" to each issue, the trial court was obligated to sentence the defendant to death. . . . Only one of the three issues—whether the defendant posed a "continuing threat to society"—was related to the evidence Penry offered in mitigation. But Penry's evidence of mental retardation and child abuse was a two-edged sword as it related to that special issue: "it diminish[ed] his blameworthiness for his crime even as it indicate[d] that there [was] a probability that he [would] be dangerous in the future." . . . The Court therefore reversed Penry's death sentence, explaining that a reasonable juror could have believed that the statute prohibited a sentence less than death based upon his mitigating evidence.

After *Penry*, the paradox underlying the Court's post-*Furman* jurisprudence was undeniable. Texas had complied with Furman by severely limiting the sentencer's discretion, but those very limitations rendered Penry's death sentence unconstitutional.

The theory underlying *Penry* and *Lockett* is that an appropriate balance can be struck between the *Furman* promise of consistency and the *Lockett* requirement of individualized sentencing if the death penalty is conceptualized as consisting of two distinct stages. In the first stage of capital sentencing, the demands of *Furman* are met by "narrowing" the class of death-eligible offenders according to objective, fact-bound characteristics of the defendant or the circumstances of the offense. Once the pool of death-eligible defendants has been reduced, the sentencer retains the discretion to consider whatever relevant mitigating evidence the defendant chooses to offer. See *Graham* v. *Collins* . . . (arguing that providing full discretion to the sentencer is not inconsistent with *Furman* and may actually help to protect against arbitrary and capricious sentencing).

Over time, I have come to conclude that even this approach is unacceptable: It simply reduces, rather than eliminates, the number of people subject to arbitrary sentencing. It is the decision to sentence a defendant to death—not merely the decision to make a defendant eligible for death—that may not be arbitrary. While one might hope that providing the sentencer with as much relevant mitigating evidence as possible will lead to more rational and consistent sentences, experience has taught otherwise. It seems that the decision whether a human being should live or die is so inherently subjective—rife with all of life's understandings, experiences, prejudices, and passions—that it inevitably defies the rationality and consistency required by the Constitution.

The arbitrariness inherent in the sentencer's discretion to afford mercy is exacerbated by the problem of race. Even under the most sophisticated death penalty statutes, race continues to play a major role in determining who shall live and who shall die. Perhaps it should not be surprising that the biases and prejudices that infect society generally would influence the determination of who is sentenced to death, even within the narrower pool of death-eligible defendants selected according to objective standards. No matter how narrowly the pool of death-eligible defendants is drawn according to objective standards, *Furman's* promise still will go unfulfilled so long as the sentencer is free to exercise unbridled discretion within the smaller group and thereby to discriminate. "'The power to be lenient [also] is the power to discriminate.'" *McCleskey* v. *Kemp* . . . (1973).

A renowned example of racism infecting a capital-sentencing scheme is documented in *McCleskey* v. *Kemp* . . . (1987). Warren McCleskey, an African-American, argued that the Georgia capital-sentencing scheme was administered in a racially discriminatory manner, in violation of the Eighth and Fourteenth Amendments. In support of his claim, he proffered a highly reliable statistical study (the Baldus study) which indicated that, "after taking into account some 230 nonracial factors that might legitimately influence a sentencer, the jury more likely than not would have spared McCleskey's life had his victim been black." . . . The Baldus study further demonstrated that blacks who kill whites are sentenced to death "at nearly twenty-two times the rate of blacks who kill blacks, and more than seven times the rate of whites who kill blacks." . . .

Despite this staggering evidence of racial prejudice infecting Georgia's capital-sentencing scheme, the majority turned its back on McCleskey's claims, apparently troubled by the fact that Georgia had instituted more procedural and substantive safeguards than most other states since *Furman,* but was still unable to stamp out the virus of racism. . . .

In the years since *McCleskey,* I have come to wonder whether there was truth in the majority's suggestion that discrimination and arbitrariness could not be purged from the administration of capital punishment without sacrificing the equally essential component of fairness—individualized sentencing. Viewed in this way, the consistency promised in *Furman* and the fairness to the individual demanded in *Lockett* are not only inversely related, but irreconcilable in the context of capital punishment. Any statute or procedure that could effectively eliminate arbitrariness from the administration of death would also restrict the sentencer's discretion to such an extent that the sentencer would be unable to give full consideration to the unique characteristics of each defendant and the circumstances of the offense. By the same token, any statute or procedure that would provide the sentencer with sufficient discretion to consider fully and act upon the unique circumstances of each defendant would "thro[w] open the back door to arbitrary and irrational sentencing." . . . All efforts to strike an appropriate balance between these conflicting constitutional commands are futile because there is a heightened need for both in the administration of death.

CALLINS V. COLLINS—CONCURRING

Supreme Court Justice A. Scalia

[*Callins* v. *Collins,* Director, Texas Department of Criminal Justice, Institutional Division. The petition for a writ of certiorari is denied.

Justice Scalia, concurring.]

Justice Blackmun dissents from the denial of certiorari in this case with statement explaining why the death penalty "as currently administered," . . . is contrary to the Constitution of the United States. That explanation often refers to "intellectual, moral, and personal" perceptions, but never to the text and tradition of the Constitution. It is the latter rather than the former that ought to control. The Fifth Amendment provides that "[n]o person shall be held to answer for a capital . . . crime, unless on a presentment or indictment of a Grand Jury, . . . nor be deprived of life . . . without due process of law." This clearly permits the death penalty to be imposed, and establishes beyond doubt that the death penalty is not one of the "cruel and unusual punishments" prohibited by the Eighth Amendment.

As Justice Blackmun describes, however, over the years since 1972 this Court has attached to the imposition of the death penalty two quite incompatible sets of commands: the sentencer's discretion to impose death must be closely confined, see *Furman* v. *Georgia* . . . (1972) . . . but the sentencer's discretion not to impose death (to extend mercy) must be unlimited, see *Eddings* v. *Oklahoma* . . . (1982); *Lockett* v. *Ohio* . . . (1978). These commands were invented without benefit of any textual or historical support; they are the product of just such "intellectual, moral, and personal" perceptions as Justice Blackmun expresses today, some of which (viz., those that have been "perceived" simultaneously by five members of the Court) have been made part of what is called "the Court's Eighth Amendment jurisprudence."

Though Justice Blackmun joins those of us who have acknowledged the incompatibility of the Court's *Furman* and *Lockett-Eddings* lines of jurisprudence . . . he unfortunately draws the wrong conclusion from the acknowledgment. He says:

Supreme Court Justice A. Scalia. "Callins vs. Collins Concurring." Reproduced with permission from *The United States Law Week,* February 22, 1994, 62, U.S.L.W. 3546. Copyright © 1994 by The Bureau of National Affairs, Inc. (800-372-1033). www.bna.com.

300

> [T]he proper course when faced with irreconcilable constitutional commands is not to ignore one or the other, nor to pretend that the dilemma does not exist, but to admit the futility of the effort to harmonize them. This means accepting the fact that the death penalty cannot be administered in accord with our Constitution.

Surely a different conclusion commends itself—to wit, that at least one of these judicially announced irreconcilable commands which cause the Constitution to prohibit what its text explicitly permits must be wrong.

Convictions in opposition to the death penalty are often passionate and deeply held. That would be no excuse for reading them into a Constitution that does not contain them, even if they represented the convictions of a majority of Americans. Much less is there any excuse for using that course to thrust a minority's views upon the people. Justice Blackmun begins his statement by describing with poignancy the death of a convicted murderer by lethal injection. He chooses, as the case in which to make that statement, one of the less brutal of the murders that regularly come before us—the murder of a man ripped by a bullet suddenly and unexpectedly, with no opportunity to prepare himself and his affairs, and left to bleed to death on the floor of a tavern. The death-by-injection which Justice Blackmun describes looks pretty desirable next to that. It looks even better next to some of the other cases currently before us which Justice Blackmun did not select as the vehicle for his accouncement that the death penalty is always unconstitutional—for example, the case of the 11-year-old girl raped by four men and then killed by stuffing her panties down her throat. See *McCollum* v. *North Carolina,* No. 93-7200, cert. now pending before the Court. How enable a quiet death by lethal injection compared with that! If the people conclude that such more brutal deaths may be deterred by capital punishment; indeed, if they merely conclude that justice requires such brutal deaths to be avenged by capital punishment; the creation of false, untextual and unhistorical contradictions within "the Court's Eighth Amendment jurisprudence" should not prevent them.

QUESTIONS FOR DISCUSSION
CAPITAL PUNISHMENT

1. Pojman mentions two different statistical studies, one apparently showing that capital punishment has no greater deterrent value than life imprisonment, the other apparently showing that it does. Assuming uncertainty about which study is correct, how does Pojman, quoting Ernest van den Haag, argue that it is more reasonable to gamble on the death penalty rather than against it?

2. Pojman argues that because "it seems likely that the death penalty as such does not deter as much as it could due to its inconsistent and rare use, . . . if potential murderers perceived the death penalty as a highly probable outcome of murder, would they not be more reluctant to kill?" Explain the implications of this argument. Is Pojman recommending a considerable increase in the number of death sentences meted out?

3. What is Reiman's answer to the van den Haag–Pojman "common sense argument" that because many people fear death more than life, the death penalty must have at least a bit more deterrent effect than life imprisonment? Do you agree with Reiman? Defend your position.

4. What is Reiman's analogy between capital punishment and torture? Why does he think that both policies retard the advance of civilization? Why, according to him, is capital punishment a worse policy for democracies than for tyrannies?

5. On what grounds does Justice Blackmun argue that the death penalty is contrary to the American Constitution? Do you agree? Explain why or why not.

6. How does Justice Scalia reply to Blackmun's constitutional argument against the death penalty? Do you agree with Scalia? Defend your position.

SELECTED READINGS

BEDAU, H. A., ed. *The Death Penalty in America.* New York: Oxford University Press, 1997.

———. *Death Is Different.* Boston: Northeastern University Press, 1987.

CAMUS, A. *Reflections on the Guillotine.* Trans. R. Howard. Michigan City: Fridtjof-Karla, 1959.

DEVINE, P. "Capital Punishment and the Sanctity of Life." *Midwest Studies in Philosophy,* 2000.

EHRLICH, I. "The Deterrent Effect of Capital Punishment, a Question of Life and Death." *American Economic Review,* June 1975.

KOESTLER, A., and C. ROLPH. *Hanged by the Neck.* Baltimore: Penguin, 1961.

LEISER, B. "Capital Punishment and Retributive Justice: A Reasoned Response to Crime." *Free Inquiry,* Summer 2001.

NATHANSON, S. *An Eye for an Eye.* Totowa, NJ: Rowman and Littlefield, 1987.

SELLIN, T. "The Death Penalty." In *The Death Penalty in America,* ed. H. Bedau. New York: Anchor, 1967.

PART THREE

THE GOOD SOCIETY

The issues addressed in Part III involve conditions for a good society: How much each person should sacrifice for the benefit of others (Chapter 6), what to do about the devastation of our natural environment (Chapter 7), to what extent individual privacy and freedom of action can be limited by government (Chapter 8), whether groups previously victimized by discrimination should be provided with compensatory advantages (Chapter 9), whether animals have rights that humans should respect (Chapter 10), the extent to which genetic engineering should be limited and publicly controlled (Chapter 11), whether greater cultural diversity should be imposed on public education (Chapter 12), and whether terrorist tactics are ever morally justifiable (Chapter 13).

As an introduction to these issues, the selection that follows from Aldous Huxley's literary masterpiece *Brave New World* (1934) highlights the dangers of surrendering too much power to a highly intelligent and technologically sophisticated dictatorship, no matter how benevolent its despotism may be. The book was, no doubt, inspired by the so-called "great experiment" of Soviet Communism, which was hailed by many thoughtful people as a society whose ruling elite exercised total power over the citizenry in order—according to their own (initially) sincere beliefs—to create the social and economic conditions for lasting prosperity and general felicity. Yet in many ways the book appears to be a parody of Plato's ancient masterpiece *The Republic,* which describes a utopia in which the wisest and best educated rule over the citizenry for the citizens' best interests and, to that end, deny themselves the very satisfactions they try to provide for their subjects. In effect, Huxley's dystopia (bad society) is the deliberate inversion both of Plato's utopia (ideal society) and, prophetically, the Soviet "great experiment." In the succeeding chapters of this book, the social policies debated are viewed by one side as utopian and by the other side as dystopian. In evaluating the arguments for each policy, every reader must decide to which vision it more properly belongs.

from BRAVE NEW WORLD

Aldous Huxley

The room into which the three were ushered was the Controller's study.

"His fordship will be down in a moment." The Gamma butler left them to themselves.

Helmholtz laughed aloud.

"It's more like a caffeine-solution party than a trial," he said, and let himself fall into the most luxurious of the pneumatic arm-chairs. "Cheer up, Bernard," he added, catching sight of his friend's green unhappy face. But Bernard would not be cheered; without answering, without even looking at Helmholtz, he went and sat down on the most uncomfortable chair in the room, carefully chosen in the obscure hope of somehow deprecating the wrath of the higher powers.

The Savage meanwhile wandered restlessly round the room, peering with a vague superficial inquisitiveness at the books in the shelves, at the sound-track rolls and reading machine bobbins in their numbered pigeon-holes. On the table under the window lay a massive volume bound in limp black leather-surrogate, and stamped with large golden T's. He picked it up and opened it. MY LIFE AND WORK, BY OUR FORD. The book had been published at Detroit by the Society for the Propagation of Fordian Knowledge. Idly he turned the pages, read a sentence here, a paragraph there, and had just come to the conclusion that the book didn't interest him, when the door opened, and the Resident World Controller for Western Europe walked briskly into the room.

Mustapha Mond shook hands with all three of them; but it was to the Savage that he addressed himself. "So you don't much like civilization, Mr. Savage," he said.

The Savage looked at him. He had been prepared to lie, to bluster, to remain sullenly unresponsive; but, reassured by the good-humoured intelligence of the Controller's face, he decided to tell the truth, straightforwardly. "No." He shook his head.

Bernard started and looked horrified. What would the Controller think? To be labelled as the friend of a man who said that he didn't like civilization—said it openly and, of all people, to the Controller—it was terrible. "But, John," he began. A look from Mustapha Mond reduced him to an abject silence.

"Of course," the Savage went on to admit, "there are some very nice things. All that music in the air, for instance . . ."

"Sometimes a thousand twangling instruments will hum about my ears and sometimes voices."

The Savage's face lit up with a sudden pleasure. "Have you read it too?" he asked. "I thought nobody knew about that book here, in England."

"Almost nobody. I'm one of the very few. It's prohibited, you see. But as I make the laws here, I can also break them. With impunity, Mr. Marx," he added, turning to Bernard. "Which I'm afraid you *can't* do."

Bernard sank into a yet more hopeless misery.

"But why is it prohibited?" asked the Savage. In the excitement of meeting a man who had read Shakespeare he had momentarily forgotten everything else.

The Controller shrugged his shoulders. "Because it's old; that's the chief reason. We haven't any use for old things here."

"Even when they're beautiful?"

"Particularly when they're beautiful. Beauty's attractive, and we don't want people to be attracted by old things. We want them to like the new ones."

"But the new ones are so stupid and horrible. Those plays, where there's nothing but helicopters flying about and you *feel* the people kissing." He made a grimace. "Goats and monkeys!" Only in Othello's word could he find an adequate vehicle for his contempt and hatred.

"Nice tame animals, anyhow," the Controller murmured parenthetically.

"Why don't you let them see *Othello* instead?"

"I've told you; it's old. Besides, they couldn't understand it."

Yes, that was true. He remembered how Helmholtz had laughed at *Romeo and Juliet.* "Well then," he said, after a pause, "something new that's like *Othello,* and that they could understand."

"That's what we've all been wanting to write," said Helmholtz, breaking a long silence.

"And it's what you never will write," said the Controller. "Because, if it were really like *Othello* nobody could understand it, however new it might be. And if it were new, it couldn't possibly be like *Othello.*"

"Why not?"

"Yes, why not?" Helmholtz repeated. He too was forgetting the unpleasant realities of the situation. Green with anxiety and apprehension, only Bernard remembered them; the others ignored him. "Why not?"

"Because our world is not the same as Othello's world. You can't make flivvers without steel—and you can't make tragedies without social instability. The world's stable now. People are happy; they get what they want, and they never want what they can't get. They're well off; they're safe; they're never ill; they're not afraid of death; they're blissfully ignorant of passion and old age; they're plagued with no mothers or fathers; they've got no wives, or children, or lovers to feel strongly about; they're so conditioned that they practically can't help behaving as they ought to behave. And if anything should go wrong, there's *soma.* Which you go and chuck out of the window in the name of liberty, Mr. Savage. *Liberty!*" He laughed. "Expecting Deltas to know what liberty is! And now expecting them to understand *Othello!* My good boy!"

The Savage was silent for a little. "All the same," he insisted obstinately, "*Othello*'s good, *Othello*'s better than those feelies."

"Of course it is," the Controller agreed. "But that's the price we have to pay for stability. You've got to choose between happiness and what people used to call high art. We've sacrificed the high art. We have the feelies and the scent organ instead."

"But they don't mean anything."

"They mean themselves; they mean a lot of agreeable sensations to the audience."

"But they're . . . they're told by an idiot."

The Controller laughed. "You're not being very polite to your friend, Mr. Watson. One of our most distinguished Emotional Engineers . . ."

"But he's right," said Helmholtz gloomily. "Because it *is* idiotic. Writing when there's nothing to say . . ."

"Precisely. But that requires the most enormous ingenuity. You're making flivvers out of the absolute minimum of steel—works of art out of practically nothing but pure sensation."

The Savage shook his head. "It all seems to me quite horrible."

"Of course it does. Actual happiness always looks pretty squalid in comparison with the over-compensations for misery. And, of course, stability isn't nearly so spectacular as instability. And being contented has none of the glamour of a good fight against misfortune, none of the picturesqueness of a struggle with temptation, or a fatal overthrow by passion or doubt. Happiness is never grand."

"I suppose not," said the Savage after a silence. "But need it be quite so bad as those twins?" He passed his hand over his eyes as though he were trying to wipe away the remembered image of those long rows of identical midgets at the assembling tables, those queued-up twin-herds at the entrance to the Brentford monorail station, those human maggots swarming round Linda's bed of death, the endlessly repeated face of his assailants. He looked at his bandaged left hand and shuddered. "Horrible!"

"But how useful! I see you don't like our Bokanovsky Groups; but, I assure you, they're the foundation on which everything else is built. They're the gyroscope that stabilizes the rocket plane of state on its unswerving course." The deep voice thrillingly vibrated; the gesticulating hand implied all space and the onrush of the irresistible machine. Mustapha Mond's oratory was almost up to synthetic standards.

"I was wondering," said the Savage, "why you had them at all—seeing that you can get whatever you want out of those bottles. Why don't you make everybody an Alpha Double Plus while you're about it?"

Mustapha Mond laughed. "Because we have no wish to have our throats cut," he answered. "We believe in happiness and stability. A society of Alphas couldn't fail to be unstable and miserable. Imagine a factory staffed by Alphas—that is to say by separate and unrelated individuals of good heredity and conditioned so as to be capable (within limits) of making a free choice and assuming responsibilities. Imagine it!" he repeated.

The Savage tried to imagine it, not very successfully.

"It's an absurdity. An Alpha-decanted, Alpha-conditioned man would go mad if he had to do Epsilon Semi-Moron work—go mad, or start smashing things up. Alphas can be completely socialized—but only on condition that you make them do Alpha work. Only an Epsilon can be expected to make Epsilon sacrifices, for the good reason that for him they aren't sacrifices; they're the line of least resistance. His conditioning has laid down rails along which he's got to run. He can't help himself; he's foredoomed. Even after decanting, he's still inside a bottle—an invisible bottle of infantile and embryonic fixations. Each one of us, of course," the Controller meditatively continued, "goes through life inside a bottle. But if we happen to be Alphas, our bottles are, relatively speaking, enormous. We should suffer acutely if we were confined in a narrower space. You cannot pour upper-caste champagne-surrogate into lower-caste bottles. It's obvious theoretically. But it has also been proved in actual practice. The result of the Cyprus experiment was convincing."

"What was that?" asked the Savage.

Mustapha Mond smiled. "Well, you can call it an experiment in rebottling if you like. It began in A.F. 473. The Controllers had the island of Cyprus cleared of all its existing inhabitants and re-colonized with a specially prepared batch of twenty-two thousand Alphas. All agricultural and industrial equipment was handed over to them and they were left to manage their own affairs. The result exactly fulfilled all the theoretical predictions. The land wasn't properly worked; there were strikes in all the factories; the laws were set at naught, orders disobeyed; all the people detailed for a spell of low-grade work were perpetually intriguing for high-grade jobs, and all the people with high-grade jobs were counter-intriguing at all costs to stay where they were. Within six years they were having a first-class civil war. When nineteen out of the twenty-two thousand had been killed, the survivors unanimously petitioned the World Controllers to resume the government of the island. Which they did. And that was the end of the only society of Alphas that the world has ever seen."

The Savage sighed, profoundly.

"The optimum population," said Mustapha Mond, "is modelled on the iceberg—eight-ninths below the water line, one-ninth above."

"And they're happy below the water line?"

"Happier than above it. Happier than your friend here, for example." He pointed.

"In spite of that awful work?"

"Awful? *They* don't find it so. On the contrary, they like it. It's light, it's childishly simple. No strain on the mind or the muscles. Seven and a half hours of mild, unexhausting labour, and then the *soma* ration and games and unrestricted copulation and the feelies. What more can they ask for? True," he added, "they might ask for shorter hours. And of course we could give them shorter hours. Technically, it would be perfectly simple to reduce all lower-caste working hours to three or four a day. But would they be any the happier for that? No, they wouldn't. The experiment was tried, more than a century and a half ago. The whole of Ireland was put on to the four-hour day. What was the result? Unrest and a large increase in the consumption of *soma;* that was all. Those three and a half hours of extra leisure were so far from being a source of happiness, that people felt constrained to take a holiday from them. The Inventions Office is stuffed with plans for labour-saving processes. Thousands of them." Mustapha Mond made a lavish gesture. "And why don't we put them into execution? For the sake of the labourers; it would be sheer cruelty to afflict them with excessive leisure. It's the same with agriculture. We could synthesize every morsel of food, if we wanted to. But we don't. We prefer to keep a third of the population on the land. For their own sakes—because it takes *longer* to get food out of the land than out of a factory. Besides, we have our stability to think of. We don't want to change. Every change is a menace to stability. That's another reason why we're so chary of applying new inventions. Every discovery in pure science is potentially subversive; even science must sometimes be treated as a possible enemy. Yes, even science."

Science? The Savage frowned. He knew the word. But what it exactly signified he could not say. Shakespeare and the old men of the pueblo had never mentioned science, and from Linda he had only gathered the vaguest hints: science was something you made helicopters with, something that caused you to laugh at the Corn Dances, something that prevented you from being wrinkled and losing your teeth. He made a desperate effort to take the Controller's meaning.

"Yes," Mustapha Mond was saying, "that's another item in the cost of stability. It isn't only art that's incompatible with happiness; it's also science. Science is dangerous; we have to keep it most carefully chained and muzzled."

"What?" said Helmholtz, in astonishment. "But we're always saying that science is everything. It's a hypnopædic platitude."

"Three times a week between thirteen and seventeen," put in Bernard.

"And all the science propaganda we do at the College . . ."

"Yes; but what sort of science?" asked Mustapha Mond sarcastically. "You've had no scientific training, so you can't judge. I was a pretty good physicist in my time. Too good—good enough to realize that all our science is just a cookery book, with an orthodox theory of cooking that nobody's allowed to question, and a list of recipes that mustn't be added to except by special permission from the head cook. I'm the head cook now. But I was an inquisitive young scullion once. I started doing a bit of cooking on my own. Unorthodox cooking, illicit cooking. A bit of real science, in fact." He was silent.

"What happened?" asked Helmholtz Watson.

The Controller sighed. "Very nearly what's going to happen to you young men. I was on the point of being sent to an island."

The words galvanized Bernard into violent and unseemly activity. "Send *me* to an island?" He jumped up, ran across the room, and stood gesticulating in front of the Controller. "You can't send *me*. I haven't done anything. It was the others. I swear it was the others." He pointed accusingly to Helmholtz and the Savage. "Oh, please don't send me to Iceland. I promise I'll do what I ought to do. Give me another chance. Please give me another chance." The tears began to flow. "I tell you, it's their fault," he sobbed. "And not to Iceland. Oh please, your fordship, please . . ." And in a paroxysm of abjection he threw himself on his knees before the Controller. Mustapha Mond tried to make him get up; but Bernard persisted in his grovelling; the stream of words poured out inexhaustibly. In the end the Controller had to ring for his fourth secretary.

"Bring three men," he ordered, "and take Mr. Marx into a bedroom. Give him a good *soma* vaporization and then put him to bed and leave him."

The fourth secretary went out and returned with three green-uniformed twin footmen. Still shouting and sobbing, Bernard was carried out.

"One would think he was going to have his throat cut," said the Controller, as the door closed. "Whereas, if he had the smallest sense, he'd understand that his punishment is really a reward. He's being sent to an island. That's to say, he's being sent to a place where he'll meet the most interesting set of men and women to be found anywhere in the world. All the people who, for one reason or another, have got too self-consciously individual to fit into community-life. All the people who aren't satisfied with orthodoxy, who've got independent ideas of their own. Every one, in a word, who's any one. I almost envy you, Mr. Watson."

Helmholtz laughed. "Then why aren't you on an island yourself?"

"Because, finally, I preferred this," the Controller answered. "I was given the choice; to be sent to an island, where I could have got on with my pure science, or to be taken on to the Controllers' Council with the prospect of succeeding in due course to an actual Controllership. I chose this and let the science go." After a little silence, "Sometimes," he added, "I rather regret the science. Happiness is a hard master—particularly other people's happiness. A much harder master, if one isn't conditioned to accept it unquestioningly, than truth." He sighed, fell silent again, then continued in a brisker tone, "Well, duty's duty. One can't consult one's own preference. I'm interested in truth, I like science. But truth's a menace, science is a public danger. As dangerous as it's been beneficent. It has given us the stablest equilibrium in history. China's was hopelessly insecure by comparison; even the primitive matriarchies weren't steadier than we are. Thanks, I repeat, to science. But we can't allow science to undo its own good work. That's why we so carefully limit the scope of its researches—that's why I almost got sent to an island. We don't allow it to deal with any but the most immediate problems of the moment. All other enquiries are most sedulously discouraged. It's curious," he went on after a little pause, "to read what people in the time of Our Ford used to write about scientific progress. They seemed to have imagined that it could be allowed to go on indefinitely, regardless of everything else. Knowledge was the highest good, truth the supreme value; all the rest was secondary and subordinate. True, ideas were beginning to change even then.

Our Ford himself did a great deal to shift the emphasis from truth and beauty to comfort and happiness. Mass production demanded the shift. Universal happiness keeps the wheels steadily turning; truth and beauty can't. And, of course, whenever the masses seized political power, then it was happiness rather than truth and beauty that mattered. Still, in spite of everything, unrestricted scientific research was still permitted. People still went on talking about truth and beauty as though they were the sovereign goods. Right up to the time of the Nine Years' War. *That* made them change their tune all right. What's the point of truth or beauty or knowledge when the anthrax bombs are popping all around you? That was when science first began to be controlled—after the Nine Years' War. People were ready to have even their appetites controlled then. Anything for a quiet life. We've gone on controlling ever since. It hasn't been very good for truth, of course. But it's been very good for happiness. One can't have something for nothing. Happiness has got to be paid for. You're paying for it, Mr. Watson—paying because you happen to be too much interested in beauty. I was too much interested in truth; I paid too."

"But *you* didn't go to an island," said the Savage, breaking a long silence.

The Controller smiled. "That's how I paid. By choosing to serve happiness. Other people's—not mine. It's lucky," he added, after a pause, "that there are such a lot of islands in the world. I don't know what we should do without them. Put you all in the lethal chamber, I suppose. By the way, Mr. Watson, would you like a tropical climate? The Marquesas, for example; or Samoa? Or something rather more bracing?"

Helmholtz rose from his pneumatic chair. "I should like a thoroughly bad climate," he answered. "I believe one would write better if the climate were bad. If there were a lot of wind and storms, for example . . ."

The Controller nodded his approbation. "I like your spirit, Mr. Watson. I like it very much indeed. As much as I officially disapprove of it." He smiled. "What about the Falkland Islands?"

"Yes, I think that will do," Helmholtz answered. "And now, if you don't mind, I'll go and see how poor Bernard's getting on."

"Art, science—you seem to have paid a fairly high price for your happiness," said the Savage, when they were alone. "Anything else?"

"Well, religion, of course," replied the Controller. "There used to be something called God—before the Nine Years' War. But I was forgetting; you know all about God, I suppose."

"Well . . ." The Savage hesitated. He would have liked to say something about solitude, about night, about the mesa lying pale under the moon, about the precipice, the plunge into shadowy darkness, about death. He would have liked to speak; but there were no words. Not even in Shakespeare.

The Controller, meanwhile, had crossed to the other side of the room and was unlocking a large safe set into the wall between the bookshelves. The heavy door swung open. Rummaging in the darkness within, "It's a subject," he said, "that has always had a great interest for me." He pulled out a thick black volume. "You've never read this, for example."

The Savage took it. *"The Holy Bible, containing the Old and New Testaments,"* he read aloud from the title-page.

"Nor this." It was a small book and had lost its cover.

"The Imitation of Christ."

"Nor this." He handed out another volume.

"The Varieties of Religious Experience. By William James."

"And I've got plenty more," Mustapha Mond continued, resuming his seat. "A whole collection of pornographic old books. God in the safe and Ford on the shelves." He pointed with a laugh to his avowed library—to the shelves of books, the rack full of reading-machine bobbins and sound-track rolls.

"But if you know about God, why don't you tell them?" asked the Savage indignantly. "Why don't you give them these books about God?"

"For the same reason as we don't give them *Othello:* they're old; they're about God hundreds of years ago. Not about God now."

"But God doesn't change."

"Men do, though."

"What difference does that make?"

"All the difference in the world," said Mustapha Mond. He got up again and walked to the safe. "There was a man called Cardinal Newman," he said. "A cardinal," he exclaimed parenthetically, "was a kind of Arch-Community-Songster."

"'I Pandulph, of fair Milan, cardinal.' I've read about them in Shakespeare."

"Of course you have. Well, as I was saying, there was a man called Cardinal Newman. Ah, here's the book." He pulled it out. "And while I'm about it I'll take this one too. It's by a man called Maine de Biran. He was a philosopher, if you know what that was."

"A man who dreams of fewer things than there are in heaven and earth," said the Savage promptly.

"Quite so. I'll read you one of the things he *did* dream of in a moment. Meanwhile, listen to what this old Arch-Community-Songster said." He opened the book at the place marked by a slip of paper and began to read. "'We are not our own any more than what we possess is our own. We did not make ourselves, we cannot be supreme over ourselves. We are not our own masters. We are God's property. Is it not our happiness thus to view the matter? Is it any happiness or any comfort, to consider that we *are* our own? It may be thought so by the young and prosperous. These may think it a great thing to have everything, as they suppose, their own way—to depend on no one—to have to think of nothing out of sight, to be without the irksomeness of continual acknowledgment, continual prayer, continual reference of what they do to the will of another. But as time goes on, they, as all men, will find that independence was not made for man—that it is an unnatural state—will do for a while, but will not carry us on safely to the end . . .'" Mustapha Mond paused, put down the first book and, picking up the other, turned over the pages. "Take this, for example," he said, and in his deep voice once more began to read: "'A man grows old; he feels in himself that radical sense of weakness, of listlessness, of discomfort, which accompanies the advance of age; and, feeling thus, imagines himself merely sick, lulling his fears with the notion that this distressing condition is due to some particular cause, from which, as from an illness, he hopes to recover. Vain imaginings! That sickness is old age; and a horrible disease it is. They say that it is the fear of death and of what comes after death that makes men turn to religion as they advance in years. But my own experience has given me the conviction that, quite apart from any such terrors or imaginings, the religious sentiment tends to develop as we grow older; to develop because, as the passions grow calm, as the fancy and sensibilities are less excited and less excitable, our reason becomes less troubled in its working, less obscured by the images, desires and distractions, in which it used to be absorbed; whereupon God emerges as from behind a cloud; our soul feels, sees, turns towards the source of all light; turns naturally and inevitably; for now that all that gave to the world of sensations its life and charms has begun to leak away from us, now that phenomenal existence is no more bolstered up by impressions from within or from without, we feel the need to lean on something that abides, something that will never play us false—a reality, an absolute and everlasting truth. Yes, we inevitably turn to God; for this religious sentiment is of its nature so pure, so delightful to the soul that experiences it, that it makes up to us for all our other losses.'" Mustapha Mond shut the book and leaned back in his chair. "One of the numerous things in heaven and earth that these philosophers didn't dream about was this" (he waved his hand), "us, the modern world. 'You can only be independent of God while you've got youth and prosperity; independence won't take you safely to the end.' Well, we've now got youth and prosperity right up to the end. What follows? Evidently, that we can be independent of God. 'The religious sentiment will compensate us for all our losses.' But there aren't any losses for us to compensate; religious sentiment is superfluous. And why should we go hunting for a substitute for youthful desires, when youthful desires never fail? A substitute for distractions, when we go on enjoying all the old fooleries to the very last? What need have we of repose when our minds and bodies continue to delight in activity? of consolation, when we have *soma?* of something immovable, when there is the social order?"

"Then you think there is no God?"

"No, I think there quite probably is one."

"Then why? . . ."

Mustapha Mond checked him. "But he manifests himself in different ways to different men. In premodern times he manifested himself as the being that's described in these books. Now . . ."

"How does he manifest himself now?" asked the Savage.

"Well, he manifests himself as an absence; as though he weren't there at all."

"That's your fault."

"Call it the fault of civilization. God isn't compatible with machinery and scientific medicine and universal happiness. You must make your choice. Our civilization has chosen machinery and medicine and happiness. That's why I have to keep these books locked up in the safe. They're smut. People would be shocked if . . ."

The Savage interrupted him. "But isn't it *natural* to feel there's a God?"

"You might as well ask if it's natural to do up one's trousers with zippers," said the Controller sarcastically. "You remind me of another of those old fellows called Bradley. He defined philosophy as the finding of bad reason for what one believes by instinct. As if one believed anything by instinct! One believes things because one has been conditioned to believe them. Finding bad reasons for what one believes for other bad reasons—that's philosophy. People believe in God because they've been conditioned to believe in God."

"But all the same," insisted the Savage, "it is natural to believe in God when you're alone—quite alone, in the night, thinking about death . . ."

"But people never are alone now," said Mustapha Mond. "We make them hate solitude; and we arrange their lives so that it's almost impossible for them ever to have it."

The Savage nodded gloomily. At Malpais he had suffered because they had shut him out from the communal activities of the pueblo, in civilized London he was suffering because he could never escape from those communal activities, never be quietly alone.

"Do you remember that bit in *King Lear*?" said the Savage at last. "'The gods are just and of our pleasant vices make instruments to plague us; the dark and vicious place where thee he got cost him his eyes,' and Edmund answers—you remember, he's wounded, he's dying—'Thou hast spoken right; 'tis true. The wheel has come full circle; I am here.' What about that now? Doesn't there seem to be a God managing things, punishing, rewarding?"

"Well, does there?" questioned the Controller in his turn. "You can indulge in any number of pleasant vices with a freemartin and run no risks of having your eyes put out by your son's mistress. 'The wheel has come full circle; I am here.' But where would Edmund be nowadays? Sitting in a pneumatic chair, with his arm round a girl's waist, sucking away at his sex-hormone chewing-gum and looking at the feelies. The gods are just. No doubt. But their code of law is dictated, in the last resort, by the people who organize society; Providence takes its cue from men."

"Are you sure?" asked the Savage. "Are you quite sure that the Edmund in that pneumatic chair hasn't been just as heavily punished as the Edmund who's wounded and bleeding to death? The gods are just. Haven't they used his pleasant vices as an instrument to degrade him?"

"Degrade him from what position? As a happy, hard-working, goods-consuming citizen he's perfect. Of course, if you choose some other standard than ours, then perhaps you might say he was degraded. But you've got to stick to one set of postulates. You can't play Electro-magnetic Golf according to the rules of Centrifugal Bumble-puppy."

"But value dwells not in particular will," said the Savage. "It holds his estimate and dignity as well wherein 'tis precious of itself as in the prizer."

"Come, come," protested Mustapha Mond, "that's going rather far, isn't it?"

"If you allowed yourselves to think of God, you wouldn't allow yourselves to be degraded by pleasant vices. You'd have a reason for bearing things patiently, for doing things with courage. I've seen it with the Indians."

"I'm sure you have," said Mustapha Mond. "But then we aren't Indians. There isn't any need for a civilized man to bear anything that's seriously unpleasant. And as for doing things—Ford forbid that he should get the idea into his head. It would upset the whole social order if men started doing things on their own."

"What about self-denial, then? If you had a God, you'd have a reason for self-denial."

"But industrial civilization is only possible when there's no self-denial. Self-indulgence up to the very limits imposed by hygiene and economics. Otherwise the wheels stop turning."

"You'd have a reason for chastity!" said the Savage, blushing a little as he spoke the words.

"But chastity means passion, chastity means neurasthenia. And passion and neurasthenia mean instability. And instability means the end of civilization. You can't have a lasting civilization without plenty of pleasant vices."

"But God's the reason for everything noble and fine and heroic. If you had a God . . ."

"My dear young friend," said Mustapha Mond, "civilization has absolutely no need of nobility or heroism. These things are symptoms of political inefficiency. In a properly organized society like ours, nobody has any opportunities for being noble or heroic. Conditions have got to be thoroughly unstable before the occasion can arise. Where there are wars, where there are divided allegiances, where there are temptations to be resisted, objects of love to be fought for or defended—there, obviously, nobility and heroism have some sense. But there aren't any wars nowadays. The greatest care is taken to prevent you from loving any one too much. There's no such thing as a divided allegiance; you're so conditioned that you can't help doing what you ought to do. And what you ought to do is on the whole so pleasant, so many of the natural impulses are allowed free play, that there really aren't any temptations to resist. And if ever, by some unlucky chance, anything unpleasant should somehow happen, why, there's always *soma* to give you a holiday from the facts. And there's always *soma* to calm your anger, to reconcile you to your enemies, to make you patient and long-suffering. In the past you could only accomplish these things by making a great effort and after years of hard moral training. Now, you swallow two or three half-gramme tablets, and there you are. Anybody can be virtuous now. You can carry at least half your mortality about in a bottle. Christianity without tears—that's what *soma* is."

"But the tears are necessary. Don't you remember what Othello said? 'If after every tempest came such calms, may the winds blow till they have wakened death.' There's a story one of the old Indians used to tell us, about the Girl of Mátaski. The young men who wanted to marry her had to do a morning's hoeing in her garden. It seemed easy; but there were flies and mosqui-toes, magic ones. Most of the young men simply couldn't stand the biting and stinging. But the one that could—he got the girl."

"Charming! But in civilized countries," said the Controller, "you can have girls without hoeing for them; and there aren't any flies or mosquitoes to sting you. We got rid of them all centuries ago."

The Savage nodded, frowning. "You got rid of them. Yes, that's just like you. Getting rid of everything unpleasant instead of learning to put up with it. Whether 'tis better in the mind to suffer the slings and arrows of out-rageous fortune, or to take arms against a sea of troubles and by opposing end them . . . But you don't do either. Neither suffer nor oppose. You just abolish the slings and arrows. It's too easy."

He was suddenly silent, thinking of his mother. In her room on the thirty-seventh floor, Linda had floated in a sea of singing lights and perfumed caresses—floated away, out of space, out of time, out of the prison of her memories, her habits, her aged and bloated body. And Tomakin, ex-Director of Hatcheries and Conditioning, Tomakin was still on holiday—on holiday from humiliation and pain, in a world where he could not hear those words, that derisive laughter, could not see that hideous face, feel those moist and flabby arms round his neck, in a beautiful world . . .

"What you need," the Savage went on, "is something *with* tears for a change. Nothing costs enough here."

("Twelve and a half million dollars," Henry Foster had protested when the Savage told him that. "Twelve and a half million—that's what the new Conditioning Centre cost. Not a cent less.")

"Exposing what is mortal and unsure to all that fortune, death and dan-ger dare, even for an egg-shell. Isn't there something in that?" he asked, look-ing up at Mustapha Mond. "Quite apart from God—though of course God would be a reason for it. Isn't there something in living dangerously?"

"There's a great deal in it," the Controller replied. "Men and women must have their adrenals stimulated from time to time."

"What?" questioned the Savage, uncomprehending.

"It's one of the conditions of perfect health. That's why we've made the V.P.S. treatments compulsory."

"V.P.S.?"

"Violent Passion Surrogate. Regularly once a month. We flood the whole system with adrenin. It's the complete physiological equivalent of fear and rage. All the tonic effects of murdering Desdemona and being murdered by Othello, without any of the inconveniences."

"But I like the inconveniences."

"We don't," said the Controller. "We prefer to do things comfortably."

"But I don't want comfort. I want God, I want poetry, I want real dan-ger, I want freedom, I want goodness. I want sin."

"In fact," said Mustapha Mond, "you're claiming the right to be unhappy."

"All right then," said the Savage defiantly, "I'm claiming the right to be unhappy."

"Not to mention the right to grow old and ugly and impotent; the right to have syphilis and cancer; the right to have too little to eat; the right to be lousy; the right to live in constant apprehension of what may happen tomorrow; the right to catch typhoid; the right to be tortured by unspeakable pains of every kind." There was a long silence.

"I claim them all," said the Savage at last.

Mustapha Mond shrugged his shoulders. "You're welcome," he said.

QUESTIONS FOR DISCUSSION: BRAVE NEW WORLD

1. Is Mustapha Mond right in claiming that as long as the people he governs are satisfied (with the help of the "feelies" and the tranquilizing "soma") there is no reason to grant them the freedom that will only result in conflict and chaos? In defending your response, consider whether a happy slave is better off than a person who is free but miserable. What does it mean to be "better off"?

2. The society of *Brave New World* is eugenically controlled to produce precise numbers of children of different intellectual levels, the highest level consisting of "Alphas" and the lowest of "Epsilons." Mustapha Mond defends this system on the grounds that people of different levels are required to do different jobs. For example, "An . . . Alpha-conditioned man would go mad if he had to do Epsilon Semi-Moron work. . . . Only an Epsilon can be expected to make Epsilon sacrifices, for the good reason that for him they aren't sacrifices." Compare this ideal for society with the Marxist ideal of every citizen sharing every type of work, from pure thinking to manual labor. Which ideal is more attainable? To which is our present society closer, and toward which are we advancing? Explain your answers.

6

FAMINE RELIEF

One of the most poignant dilemmas that confronts people in affluent societies is what to do about the poverty and suffering in many areas of the world, including the affluent societies' own ghettos. To what extent should the well-off contribute money, food, clothing, and medicine to alleviate the misery of the less fortunate? Peter Singer argues persuasively that we have as strong a moral obligation to contribute to famine relief whatever we can spare above our bare necessities as we have to refrain from theft and murder. Garrett Hardin argues, to the contrary, that we are morally obligated *not* to give such assistance, on the grounds that the foreseeable consequences of such largesse would be greater suffering in the long run due to overpopulation and failure to improve methods of food production in the areas that need help.

Singer's plea for maximum aid to the less fortunate is derived from his utilitarian moral theory. The fundamental principle that should govern our actions, he holds, is this: "If it is in our power to prevent something bad from happening, without thereby sacrificing anything of comparable moral importance, we ought to do it." This principle defines what is sometimes called "negative utilitarianism" (in contrast with John Stuart Mill's more positive "greatest happiness" principle: that we ought always to act so as to bring about the greatest happiness of the greatest number). The duty to alleviate suffering seems to most people considerably more compelling than the alleged duty to promote happiness, because our best efforts to make even oneself happy—and still less, another person—are so frequently unsuccessful.

One might expect a utilitarian moralist to be less demanding of self-sacrifice than a religious absolutist like Robert Adams or a rational absolutist (deontologist) like Immanuel Kant (see Chapter 1). For the utilitarian requires us to calculate benefits in a detached and unsentimental way, rather than be moved by sympathy at the sight of desperate poverty. The rather coldly tough-minded argument of Hardin against famine relief seems more in accord with the popular image of utilitarian counsel, of the kind engendered by political economists who talk of cost-benefit analysis and game theoretical strategies, than does Singer's appeal to moral duty, an appeal that people usually associate with missionary zeal. But Singer holds that both the Christian ideal of charity and the Kantian notion of a meritorious duty to help others in need fail to make such assistance as obligatory as refraining from criminal assault. Singer argues that it is commonly but mistakenly believed that although helping others is praiseworthy, failure to do so is not serious enough to warrant moral condemnation. Singer and most utilitarians hold that failing to save life is as culpable as actively taking life.

Hardin does not quarrel with this negative utilitarian outlook, but he maintains, on the basis of the same principle, that we should allow people in underdeveloped areas of the world to suffer and die of hunger and disease in order to prevent overpopulation and excessive dependence on foreign aid, which would cause more suffering in the long run.

Singer acknowledges this concern but warns us not to conclude that we need to do nothing to alleviate poverty and famine. Rather, he insists we should do all we can, both to provide food and medicine, and also to provide technical assistance at population control and more productive methods of farming.

Raziel Abelson offers a position midway between Singer's view that we have a moral duty to contribute all we have above the basic necessities and Hardin's view that we owe the disadvantaged no more than technical assistance. Abelson defends what he calls the "common sense moral principle" that our duty to assist others varies in strength in proportion to the emotional closeness between them and us. This entails, he argues, an order of precedence such that one should give more and prior assistance to one's immediate family, then to friends and neighbors, and last to strangers in other lands, on the grounds that positive duties to assist involve priorities, unlike negative duties not to harm. The latter, he holds, are owed equally to all human beings—and, he suggests but does not insist, perhaps to all sentient beings.

Rich and poor

Peter Singer

This is the background situation, the situation that prevails on our planet all the time. It does not make headlines: People died from malnutrition and related diseases yesterday, and more will die tomorrow. The occasional droughts, cyclones, earthquakes, and floods that take the lives of tens of thousands in one place and at one time are more newsworthy. They add greatly to the total amount of human suffering; but it is wrong to assume that when there are no major calamities reported, all is well.

The problem is not that the world cannot produce enough to feed and shelter its people. People in the poor countries consume, on average, 180 kilos of grain a year, while North Americans average around 900 kilos. The difference is caused by the fact that in the rich countries we feed most of our grain to animals, converting it into meat, milk, and eggs. Because this is a highly inefficient process, people in rich countries are responsible for the consumption of far more food than those in poor countries who eat few animal products. If we stopped feeding animals on grains and soybeans, the amount of food saved would—if distributed to those who need it—be more than enough to end hunger throughout the world.

These facts about animal food do not mean that we can easily solve the world food problem by cutting down on animal products, but they show that the problem is essentially one of distribution rather than production. The world does produce enough food. Moreover, the poorer nations themselves could produce far more if they made more use of improved agricultural techniques.

So why are people hungry? Poor people cannot afford to buy grain grown by farmers in the richer nations. Poor farmers cannot afford to buy improved seeds, or fertilizers, or the machinery needed for drilling wells and pumping water. Only by transferring some of the wealth of the rich nations to the poor can the situation be changed.

That this wealth exists is clear. Against the picture of absolute poverty that McNamara has painted, one might pose a picture of "absolute affluence." Those who are absolutely affluent are not necessarily affluent by comparison with their neighbors, but they are affluent by any reasonable definition of human needs. This means that they have more income than they need to provide themselves adequately with all the basic necessities of life. After

321

buying (either directly or through their taxes) food, shelter, clothing, basic health services, and education, the absolutely affluent are still able to spend money on luxuries. The absolutely affluent choose their food for the pleasures of the palate, not to stop hunger; they buy new clothes to look good, not to keep warm; they move house to be in a better neighborhood or have a play-room for the children, not to keep out the rain; and after all this there is still money to spend on stereo systems, video-cameras, and overseas holidays.

At this stage I am making no ethical judgments about absolute affluence, merely pointing out that it exists. Its defining characteristic is a significant amount of income above the level necessary to provide for the basic human needs of oneself and one's dependents. By this standard, the majority of citizens of Western Europe, North America, Japan, Australia, New Zealand, and the oil-rich Middle Eastern states are all absolutely affluent. To quote McNamara once more:

> "The average citizen of a developed country enjoys wealth beyond the wildest dreams of the one billion . . . in countries with per capita incomes under $200." These, therefore, are the countries—and individuals—who have wealth that they could, without threatening their own basic welfare, transfer to the absolutely poor.

At present, very little is being transferred. Only Sweden, the Netherlands, Norway, and some of the oil-exporting Arab states have reached the modest target, set by the United Nations, of 0.7 per cent of gross national product (GNP). Britain gives 0.31 per cent of its GNP in official development assis-tance and a small additional amount in unofficial aid from voluntary organi-zations. The total comes to about £2 per month per person, and compares with 5.5 per cent of GNP spent on alcohol, and 3 per cent on tobacco. Other, even wealthier nations, give little more: Germany gives 0.41 per cent and Japan 0.32 per cent. The United States gives a mere 0.15 per cent of its GNP.

THE MORAL EQUIVALENT OF MURDER?

If these are the facts, we cannot avoid concluding that by not giving more than we do, people in rich countries are allowing those in poor countries to suffer from absolute poverty, with consequent malnutrition, ill health, and death. This is not a conclusion that applies only to governments. It applies to each absolutely affluent individual, for each of us has the opportunity to do something about the situation; for instance, to give our time or money to voluntary organizations like Oxfam, Care, War on Want, Freedom from Hunger, Community Aid Abroad, and so on. If, then, allowing someone to die is not intrinsically different from killing someone, it would seem that we are all murderers.

Is this verdict too harsh? Many will reject it as self-evidently absurd. They would sooner take it as showing that allowing to die cannot be equivalent to killing than as showing that living in an affluent style without contributing to an overseas aid agency is ethically equivalent to going over to Ethiopia and shooting a few peasants. And no doubt, put as bluntly as that, the verdict is too harsh.

There are several significant differences between spending money on luxuries instead of using it to save lives, and deliberately shooting people.

First, the motivation will normally be different. Those who deliberately shoot others go out of their way to kill; they presumably want their victims dead, from malice, sadism, or some equally unpleasant motive. A person who buys a new stereo system presumably wants to enhance her enjoyment of music—not in itself a terrible thing. At worst, spending money on luxuries instead of giving it away indicates selfishness and indifference to the sufferings of others, characteristics that may be undesirable but are not comparable with actual malice or similar motives. Second, it is not difficult for most of us to act in accordance with a rule against killing people: it is, on the other hand, very difficult to obey a rule that commands us to save all the lives we can. To live a comfortable, or even luxurious life it is not necessary to kill anyone; but it is necessary to allow some to die whom we might have saved, for the money that we need to live comfortably could have been given away. Thus the duty to avoid killing is much easier to discharge completely than the duty to save. Saving every life we could would mean cutting our standard of living down to the bare essentials needed to keep us alive. To discharge this duty completely would require a degree of moral heroism utterly different from that required by mere avoidance of killing.

A third difference is the greater certainty of the outcome of shooting when compared with not giving aid. If I point a loaded gun at someone at close range and pull the trigger, it is virtually certain that the person will be killed; whereas the money that I could give might be spent on a project that turns out to be unsuccessful and helps no one.

Fourth, when people are shot there are identifiable individuals who have been harmed. We can point to them and to their grieving families. When I buy my stereo system, I cannot know who my money would have saved if I had given it away. In a time of famine I may see dead bodies and grieving families on television reports, and I might not doubt that my money would have saved some of them; even then it is impossible to point to a body and say that had I not bought the stereo, that person would have survived.

Fifth, it might be said that the plight of the hungry is not my doing, and so I cannot be held responsible for it. The starving would have been starving if I had never existed. If I kill, however, I am responsible for my victims' deaths, for those people would not have died if I had not killed them.

These differences need not shake our previous conclusion that there is no intrinsic difference between killing and allowing to die. They are extrinsic differences, that is, differences normally but not necessarily associated with the distinction between killing and allowing to die. We can imagine cases in which someone allows another to die for malicious or sadistic reasons; we can imagine a world in which there are so few people needing assistance, and they are so easy to assist, that our duty not to allow people to die is as easily discharged as our duty not to kill; we can imagine situations in which the outcome of not helping is as sure as shooting; we can imagine cases in which we can identify the person we allow to die. We can even imagine a case of allowing to die in which, if I had not existed, the person would not have died—for instance, a case in which if I had not been in a position to help (though I don't help) someone else would have been in my position and would have helped. . . .

(That an ethic that put saving all one possibly can on the same footing as not killing would be an ethic for saints or heroes should not lead us to assume that the alternative must be an ethic that makes it obligatory not to kill, but puts us under no obligation to save anyone. There are positions in between these extremes, as we shall soon see.)

Here is a summary of the five differences that normally exist between killing and allowing to die, in the context of absolute poverty and overseas aid. The lack of an identifiable victim is of no moral significance, though it may play an important role in explaining our attitudes. The idea that we are directly responsible for those we kill, but not for those we do not help, depends on a questionable notion of responsibility and may need to be based on a controversial theory of rights. Differences in certainty and motivation are ethically significant, and show that not aiding the poor is not to be condemned as murdering them; it could, however, be on a par with killing someone as a result of reckless driving, which is serious enough. Finally the difficulty of completely discharging the duty of saving all one possibly can makes it inappropriate to blame those who fall short of this target as we blame those who kill; but this does not show that the act itself is less serious. Nor does it indicate anything about those who, far from saving all they possibly can, make no effort to save anyone.

These conclusions suggest a new approach. Instead of attempting to deal with the contrast between affluence and poverty by comparing not saving with deliberate killing, let us consider afresh whether we have an obligation to assist those whose lives are in danger, and if so, how this obligation applies to the present world situation.

THE OBLIGATION TO ASSIST

The Argument for an Obligation to Assist

The path from the library at my university to the humanities lecture theatre passes a shallow ornamental pond. Suppose that on my way to give a lecture I notice that a small child has fallen in and is in danger of drowning. Would anyone deny that I ought to wade in and pull the child out? This will mean getting my clothes muddy and either canceling my lecture or delaying it until I can find something dry to change into; but compared with the avoidable death of a child this is insignificant.

A plausible principle that would support the judgment that I ought to pull the child out is this: if it is in our power to prevent something very bad from happening, without thereby sacrificing anything of comparable moral significance, we ought to do it. This principle seems uncontroversial. It will obviously win the assent of consequentialists; but non-consequentialists should accept it too, because the injunction to prevent what is bad applies only when nothing comparably significant is at stake. Thus the principle cannot lead to the kinds of actions of which non-consequentialists strongly disapprove—serious violations of individual rights, injustice, broken promises, and so on. If non-consequentialists regard any of these as comparable in moral significance to the bad thing that is to be prevented, they will automatically regard the principle as not applying in those cases in which the bad thing can only be prevented by violating rights, doing injustice, breaking promises, or whatever else is at stake. Most non-consequentialists hold that we ought to prevent what is bad and promote what is good. Their dispute with consequentialists lies in their insistence that this is not the sole ultimate ethical principle: that it is an ethical principle is not denied by any plausible ethical theory.

Nevertheless the uncontroversial appearance of the principle that we ought to prevent what is bad when we can do so without sacrificing anything of comparable moral significance is deceptive. If it were taken seriously and acted upon, our lives and our world would be fundamentally changed. For the principle applies, not just to rare situations in which one can save a child from a pond, but to the everyday situation in which we can assist those living in absolute poverty. In saying this I assume that absolute poverty, with its hunger and malnutrition, lack of shelter, illiteracy, disease, high infant mortality, and low life expectancy, is a bad thing. And I assume that it is within the power of the affluent to reduce absolute poverty, without sacrificing anything of comparable moral significance. If these two assumptions and the principle we have been discussing are correct, we have an obligation to help those in absolute poverty that is no less strong than our obligation to rescue a drowning child from a pond. Not to help would be wrong, whether or not it is intrinsically equivalent to killing. Helping is not, as conventionally thought, a charitable act that it is praiseworthy to do, but not wrong to omit; it is something that everyone ought to do.

This is the argument for an obligation to assist. Set out more formally, it would look like this.

First premise: If we can prevent something bad without sacrificing anything of comparable significance, we ought to do it.

Second premise: Absolute poverty is bad.

Third premise: There is some absolute poverty we can prevent without sacrificing anything of comparable moral significance.

Conclusion: We ought to prevent some absolute poverty.

The first premise is the substantive moral premise on which the argument rests, and I have tried to show that it can be accepted by people who hold a variety of ethical positions.

The second premise is unlikely to be challenged. Absolute poverty is, as McNamara put it, "beneath any reasonable definition of human decency" and it would be hard to find a plausible ethical view that did not regard it as a bad thing.

The third premise is more controversial, even though it is cautiously framed. It claims only that some absolute poverty can be prevented without the sacrifice of anything of comparable moral significance. It thus avoids the objection that any aid I can give is just "drops in the ocean" for the point is not whether my personal contribution will make any noticeable impression on world poverty as a whole (of course it won't) but whether it will prevent some poverty. This is all the argument needs to sustain its conclusion, since the second premise says that any absolute poverty is bad, and not merely the total amount of absolute poverty. If without sacrificing anything of comparable moral significance we can provide just one family with the means to raise itself out of absolute poverty, the third premise is vindicated.

I have left the notion of moral significance unexamined in order to show that the argument does not depend on any specific values or ethical principles. I think the third premise is true for most people living in industrialized nations, on any defensible view of what is morally significant. Our affluence means that we have income we can dispose of without giving up the basic necessities of life, and we can use this income to reduce absolute poverty. Just how much we will think ourselves obliged to give up will depend on what we consider to be of comparable moral significance to the poverty we could prevent: stylish clothes, expensive dinners, a sophisticated stereo system, overseas holidays, a (second?) car, a larger house, private schools for our children, and so on. For a utilitarian, none of these is likely to be of comparable significance to the reduction of absolute poverty; and those who are not utilitarians surely must, if they subscribe to the principle of universalizability, accept that at least some of these things are of far less moral significance than the absolute poverty that could be prevented by the money they cost. So the third premise seems to be true on any plausible ethical view—although the precise amount of absolute poverty that can be prevented before anything of moral significance is sacrificed will vary according to the ethical view one accepts.

Objections to the Argument

Taking care of our own. Anyone who has worked to increase overseas aid will have come across the argument that we should look after those near us, our families, and then the poor in our own country, before we think about poverty in distant places.

No doubt we do instinctively prefer to help those who are close to us. Few could stand by and watch a child drown; many can ignore a famine in Africa. But the question is not what we usually do, but what we ought to do, and it is difficult to see any sound moral justification for the view that distance, or community membership, makes a crucial difference to our obligations.

Consider, for instance, racial affinities. Should people of European origin help poor Europeans before helping poor Africans? Most of us would reject such a suggestion out of hand, and our discussion of the principle of equal consideration of interests in Chapter 2 [of *Practical Ethics*] has shown why we should reject it: people's need for food has nothing to do with their race, and if Africans need food more than Europeans, it would be a violation of the principle of equal consideration to give preference to Europeans.

The same point applies to citizenship or nationhood. Every affluent nation has some relatively poor citizens, but absolute poverty is limited largely to the poor nations. Those living on the streets of Calcutta, or in the drought-prone Sahel region of Africa, are experiencing poverty unknown in the West. Under these circumstances it would be wrong to decide that only those fortunate enough to be citizens of our own community will share our abundance. We feel obligations of kinship more strongly than those of citizenship. Which parents could give away their last bowl of rice if their own children were starving? To do so would seem unnatural, contrary to our nature as biologically evolved beings—although whether it would be wrong is another question altogether. In any case, we are not faced with that situation, but with one in which our own children are well-fed, well-clothed, well-educated, and would now like new bikes, a stereo set, or their own car. In these circumstances any special obligations we might have to our children have been fulfilled, and the needs of strangers make a stronger claim upon us.

The element of truth in the view that we should first take care of our own, lies in the advantage of a recognized system of responsibilities. When families and local communities look after their own poorer members, ties of affection and personal relationships achieve ends that would otherwise require a large, impersonal bureaucracy. Hence it would be absurd to propose that from now on we all regard ourselves as equally responsible for the welfare of everyone in the world; but the argument for an obligation to assist does not propose that. It applies only when some are in absolute poverty, and others can help without sacrificing anything of comparable moral significance. To allow one's own kin to sink into absolute poverty would be to sacrifice something of comparable significance; and before that point had been reached, the breakdown of the system of family and community responsibility would be a factor to weigh the balance in favor of a small degree of preference for family and community. This small degree of preference is, however, decisively outweighed by existing discrepancies in wealth and property.

Property myths. Do people have a right to private property, a right that contradicts the view that they are under an obligation to give some of their wealth away to those in absolute poverty? According to some theories of rights (for instance, Robert Nozick's), provided one has acquired one's property without the use of unjust means like force and fraud, one may be entitled to enormous wealth while others starve. This individualistic conception of rights is in contrast to other views, like the early Christian doctrine to be found in the works of Thomas Aquinas, which holds that since property exists for the satisfaction of human needs, "whatever a man has in superabundance is owed, of natural right, to the poor for their sustenance." A socialist would also, of course, see wealth as belonging to the community rather than the individual, while utilitarians, whether socialist or not, would be prepared to override property rights to prevent great evils.

Does the argument for an obligation to assist others therefore presuppose one of these other theories of property rights, and not an individualistic theory like Nozick's? Not necessarily. A theory of property rights can insist on our *right* to retain wealth without pronouncing on whether the rich *ought* to give to the poor. Nozick, for example, rejects the use of compulsory means like taxation to redistribute income, but suggests that we can achieve the ends we deem morally desirable by voluntary means. So Nozick would reject the claim that rich people have an "obligation" to give to the poor, in so far as this implies that the poor have a right to our aid, but might accept that giving is something we ought to do and failing to give, though within one's rights, is wrong—for there is more to an ethical life than respecting the rights of others.

The argument for an obligation to assist can survive, with only minor modifications, even if we accept an individualistic theory of property rights. In any case, however, I do not think we should accept such a theory. It leaves too much to chance to be an acceptable ethical view. For instance, those whose forefathers happened to inhabit some sandy wastes around the Persian Gulf are now fabulously wealthy, because oil lay under those sands; while those whose forefathers settled on better land south of the Sahara live in absolute poverty, because of drought and bad harvests. Can this distribution be acceptable from an impartial point of view? If we imagine ourselves about to begin life as a citizen of either Bahrain or Chad—but we do not know which—would we accept the principle that citizens of Bahrain are under no obligation to assist people living in Chad?

Population and the ethics of triage. Perhaps the most serious objection to the argument that we have an obligation to assist is that since the major cause of absolute poverty is overpopulation, helping those now in poverty will only ensure that yet more people are born to live in poverty in the future.

In its most extreme form, this objection is taken to show that we should adopt a policy of "triage." The term comes from medical policies adopted in wartime. With too few doctors to cope with all the casualties, the wounded were divided into three categories: those who would probably survive without medical assistance, those who might survive if they received assistance, but otherwise probably would not, and those who even with medical assistance probably would not survive. Only those in the middle category were given medical assistance. The idea, of course, was to use limited medical resources as effectively as possible. For those in the first category, medical treatment was not strictly necessary; for those in the third category, it was likely to be useless. It has been suggested that we should apply the same policies to countries, according to their prospects of becoming self-sustaining. We would not aid countries that even without our help will soon be able to feed their populations. We would not aid countries that, even with our help, will not be able to limit their population to a level they can feed. We would aid those countries where our help might make the difference between success and failure in bringing food and population into balance. Advocates of this theory are understandably reluctant to give a complete list of the countries they would place into the "hopeless" category; Bangladesh has been cited as an example, and so have some of the countries of the Sahel region of Africa. Adopting the policy of triage would, then, mean cutting off assistance to these countries and allowing famine, disease, and natural disasters to reduce the population of those countries to the level at which they can provide adequately for all. In support of this view Garrett Hardin has offered a metaphor: we in the rich nations are like the occupants of a crowded lifeboat adrift in a sea full of drowning people. If we try to save the drowning by bringing them aboard, our boat will be overloaded and we shall all drown. Since it is better that some survive than none, we should leave the others to drown. In the world today, according to Hardin, "lifeboat ethics" apply. The rich should leave the poor to starve, for otherwise the poor will drag the rich down with them.

Against this view, some writers have argued that overpopulation is a myth. The world produces ample food to feed its population, and could, according to some estimates, feed ten times as many. People are hungry not because there are too many but because of inequitable land distribution, the manipulation of third world economies by the developed nations, wastage of food in the West, and so on. Putting aside the controversial issue of the extent to which food production might one day be increased, it is true, as we have already seen, that the world now produces enough to feed its inhabitants—the amount lost by being fed to animals itself being enough to meet existing grain shortages. Nevertheless population growth cannot be ignored. Bangladesh could, with land reform and using better techniques, feed its present population of 115 million; but by the year 2000, according to United Nations Population Division estimates, its population will be 150 million. The enormous effort that will have to go into feeding an extra 35 million people, all added to the population within a decade, means that Bangladesh must develop at full speed to stay where it is. Other low-income countries are in similar situations. By the end of the century, Ethiopia's population is expected to rise from 49 to 66 million; Somalia's from 7 to 9 million, India's from 853 to 1041 million, Zaire's from 35 to 49 million.

What will happen if the world population continues to grow? It cannot do so indefinitely. It will be checked by a decline in birth rates or a rise in death rates. Those who advocate triage are proposing that we allow the population growth of some countries to be checked by a rise in death rates—that is, by increased malnutrition, and related diseases; by widespread famines; by increased infant mortality; and by epidemics of infectious diseases.

The consequences of triage on this scale are so horrible that we are inclined to reject it without further argument. How could we sit by our television sets, watching millions starve while we do nothing? Would not that be the end of all notions of human equality and respect for human life? . . .

Don't people have a right to our assistance, irrespective of the consequences? Anyone whose initial reaction to triage was not one of repugnance would be an unpleasant sort of person. Yet initial reactions based on strong feelings are not always reliable guides. Advocates of triage are rightly concerned with the long-term consequences of our actions. They say that helping the poor and starving now merely ensures more poor and starving in the future. When our capacity to help is finally unable to cope—as one day it must be—the suffering will be greater than it would be if we stopped helping now. If this is correct, there is nothing we can do to prevent absolute starvation and poverty, in the long run, and so we have no obligation to assist. Nor does it seem reasonable to hold that under these circumstances people have a right to our assistance. If we do accept such a right, irrespective of the consequences, we are saying that, in Hardin's metaphor, we should continue to haul the drowning into our lifeboat until the boat sinks and we all drown. If triage is to be rejected it must be tackled on its own ground, within the framework of consequentialist ethics. Here it is vulnerable. Any consequentialist ethics must take probability of outcome into account. A course of action that will certainly produce some benefit is to be preferred to an alternative course that may lead to a slightly larger benefit, but is equally likely to result in no benefit at all. Only if the greater magnitude of the uncertain benefit outweighs its uncertainty should we choose it. Better one certain unit of benefit than a 10 percent chance of five units; but better a 50 per cent chance of three units than a single certain unit. The same principle applies when we are trying to avoid evils.

The policy of triage involves a certain, very great evil: population control by famine and disease. Tens of millions would die slowly. Hundreds of millions would continue to live in absolute poverty, at the very margin of existence. Against this prospect, advocates of the policy place a possible evil that is greater still: the same process of famine and disease, taking place in, say, fifty years' time, when the world's population may be three times its present level, and the number who will die from famine, or struggle on in absolute poverty, will be that much greater. The question is: how probable is this forecast that continued assistance now will lead to greater disasters in the future?

Forecasts of population growth are notoriously fallible, and theories about the factors that affect it remain speculative. One theory, at least as plausible as any other, is that countries pass through a "demographic transition" as their standard of living rises. When people are very poor and have no access to modern medicine their fertility is high, but population is kept in check by high death rates. The introduction of sanitation, modern medical techniques, and other improvements reduces the death rate, but initially has little effect on the birth rate. Then population grows rapidly. Some poor countries, especially in sub-Saharan Africa, are now in this phase. If standards of living continue to rise, however, couples begin to realize that to have the same number of children surviving to maturity as in the past, they do not need to give birth to as many children as their parents did. The need for children to provide economic support in old age diminishes. Improved education and the emancipation and employment of women also reduce the birth-rate, and so population growth begins to level off. Most rich nations have reached this stage, and their populations are growing only very slowly, if at all. If this theory is right, there is an alternative to the disasters accepted as inevitable by supporters of triage. We can assist poor countries to raise the living standards of the poorest members of their population. We can encourage the governments of these countries to enact land reform measures, improve education, and liberate women from a purely child-bearing role. We can also help other countries to make contraception and sterilization widely available. There is a fair chance that these measures will hasten the onset of the demographic transition and bring population growth down to a manageable level.

THE ERROR OF FAMINE RELIEF

Garrett Hardin

Environmentalists use the metaphor of the earth as a "spaceship" in trying to persuade countries, industries and people to stop wasting and polluting our natural resources. Since we all share life on this planet, they argue, no single person or institution has the right to destroy, waste, or use more than a fair share of its resources.

But does everyone on earth have an equal right to an equal share of its resources? The spaceship metaphor can be dangerous when used by misguided idealists to justify suicidal policies for sharing our resources through uncontrolled immigration and foreign aid. In their enthusiastic but unrealistic generosity, they confuse the ethics of a spaceship with those of a lifeboat.

A true spaceship would have to be under the control of a captain, since no ship could possibly survive if its course were determined by committee. Spaceship Earth certainly has no captain; the United Nations is merely a toothless tiger, with little power to enforce any policy upon its bickering members.

If we divide the world crudely into rich nations and poor nations, two thirds of them are desperately poor, and only one third comparatively rich, with the United States the wealthiest of all. Metaphorically each rich nation can be seen as a lifeboat full of comparatively rich people. In the ocean outside each lifeboat swim the poor of the world, who would like to get in, or at least to share some of the wealth. What should the lifeboat passengers do?

First, we must recognize the limited capacity of any lifeboat. For example, a nation's land has a limited capacity to support a population and as the current energy crisis has shown us, in some ways we have already exceeded the carrying capacity of our land.

ADRIFT IN A MORAL SEA

So here we sit, say fifty people in our lifeboat. To be generous, let us assume it has room for ten more, making a total capacity of sixty. Suppose the fifty of us in the lifeboat see 100 others swimming in the water outside, begging for admission to our boat or for handouts. We have several options: we may be tempted to live by the Christian ideal of being "our brother's keeper," or by the Marxist ideal of "to each according to his needs." Since the needs of all in the water

---

are the same, and since they can all be seen as "our brothers," we could take them all into our boat, making a total of 150 in a boat designed for sixty. The boat swamps, everyone drowns. Complete justice, complete catastrophe.

Since the boat has an unused excess capacity of ten more passengers, we could admit just ten more to it. But which ten do we let in? How do we choose? Do we pick the best ten, the neediest ten, "first come, first served"? And what do we say to the ninety we exclude? If we do let an extra ten into our lifeboat, we will have lost our "safety factor," an engineering principle of critical importance. For example, if we don't leave room for excess capacity as a safety factor in our country's agriculture, a new plant disease or a bad change in the weather could have disastrous consequences.

Suppose we decide to preserve our small safety factor and admit no more to the lifeboat. Our survival is then possible, although we shall have to be constantly on guard against boarding parties.

While this last solution clearly offers the only means of our survival, it is morally abhorrent to many people. Some say they feel guilty about their good luck. My reply is simple: "Get out and yield your place to others." This may solve the problem of the guilt-ridden person's conscience, but it does not change the ethics of the lifeboat. The needy person to whom the guilt-ridden person yields his place will not himself feel guilty about this good luck. If he did, he would not climb aboard. The net result of conscience-stricken people giving up their unjustly held seats is the elimination of that sort of conscience from the lifeboat.

This is the basic metaphor within which we must work out our solutions. Let us now enrich the image, step by step, with substantive additions from the real world, a world that must solve real and pressing problems of over-population and hunger.

The harsh ethics of the lifeboat become even harsher when we consider the reproductive differences between the rich nations and the poor nations. The people inside the lifeboats are doubling in numbers every eighty-seven years; those swimming around outside are doubling, on the average, every thirty-five years, more than twice as fast as the rich. And since the world's resources are dwindling, the difference in prosperity between the rich and the poor can only increase.

As of 1973, the United States had a population of 210 million people, who were increasing by 0.8 percent per year. Outside our lifeboat, let us imagine another 210 million people (say the combined populations of Colombia, Ecuador, Venezuela, Morocco, Pakistan, Thailand and the Philippines), who are increasing at a rate of 3.3 percent per year. Put differently, the doubling time for this aggregate population is twenty-one years, compared to eighty-seven years of the United States.

MULTIPLYING THE RICH AND THE POOR

Now suppose the United States agreed to pool its resources with those seven countries, with everyone receiving an equal share. Initially the ratio of

Americans to non-Americans in this model would be one-to-one. But consider what the ratio would be after eighty-seven years, by which time the Americans would have doubled to a population of 420 million. By then, doubling every twenty-one years, the other group would have swollen to 3.54 billion. Each American would have to share the available resources with more than eight people.

But, one could argue, this discussion assumes that current population trends will continue, and they may not. Quite so. Most likely the rate of population increase will decline much faster in the United States than it will in the other countries and there does not seem to be much we can do about it. In sharing with "each according to his needs," we must recognize that needs are determined by population size, which is determined by the rate of reproduction, which at present is regarded as a sovereign right of every nation, poor or not. This being so, the philanthropic load created by the sharing ethic of the spaceship can only increase.

THE TRAGEDY OF THE COMMONS

The fundamental error of spaceship ethics, and the sharing it requires, is that it leads to what I call "the tragedy of the commons." Under a system of private property, the men who own property recognize their responsibility to care for it, for if they don't they will eventually suffer. A farmer, for instance, will allow no more cattle in a pasture than its carrying capacity justifies. If he overloads it, erosion sets in, weeds take over, and he loses the use of the pasture.

If a pasture becomes a commons open to all, the right of each to use it may not be matched by a corresponding responsibility to protect it. Asking everyone to use it with discretion will hardly do, for the considerate herdsman who refrains from overloading the commons suffers more than a selfish one who says his needs are greater. If everyone would restrain himself, all would be well; but it takes only one less than everyone to ruin a system of voluntary restraint. In a crowded world of less than perfect human beings, mutual ruin is inevitable if there are no controls. This is the tragedy of the commons.

One of the major tasks of education today should be the creation of such an acute awareness of the dangers of the commons that people will recognize its many varieties. For example, the air and water have become polluted because they are treated as commons. Further growth in the population or per capita conversion of natural resources into pollutants will only make the problem worse. The same holds true for the fish of the oceans. Fishing fleets have nearly disappeared in many parts of the world, technological improvements in the art of fishing are hastening the day of complete ruin. Only the replacement of the system of the commons with a responsible system of control will save the land, air, water and oceanic fisheries.

THE WORLD FOOD BANK

In recent years there has been a push to create a new commons called a World Food Bank, an international depository of food reserves to which nations would contribute according to their abilities and from which they would draw according to their needs. This humanitarian proposal has received support from many liberal international groups, and from such prominent citizens as Margaret Mead, U.N. Secretary General Kurt Waldheim, and senators Edward Kennedy and George McGovern.

A world food bank appeals powerfully to our humanitarian impulses. But before we rush ahead with such a plan, let us recognize where the greatest political push comes from, lest we be disillusioned later. Our experience with the "Food for Peace program," or Public Law 480, gives us the answer. This program moved billions of dollars worth of U.S. surplus grain to food-short, population-long countries during the past two decades. But when P.L. 480 first became law, a headline in the business magazine *Forbes* revealed the real power behind it: "Feeding the World's Hungry Millions: How It will Mean Billions for U.S. Business."

And indeed it did. In the years 1960 to 1970, U.S. taxpayers spent a total of $7.9 billion on the Food for Peace program. Between 1948 and 1970, they also paid an additional $50 billion for other economic-aid programs, some of which went for food and food-producing machinery and technology. Though all U.S. taxpayers were forced to contribute to the cost of P.L. 480, certain special interest groups gained handsomely under the program. Farmers did not have to contribute the grain; the Government, or rather the taxpayers, bought it from them at full market prices. The increased demand raised prices of farm products generally. The manufacturers of farm machinery, fertilizers and pesticides benefited by the farmers' extra efforts to grow more food. Grain elevators profited from storing the surplus until it could be shipped. Railroads made money hauling it to ports, and shipping lines profited from carrying it overseas. The implementation of P.L. 480 required the creation of a vast Government bureaucracy, which then acquired its own vested interest in continuing the program regardless of its merits.

EXTRACTING DOLLARS

Those who proposed and defended the Food for Peace program in public rarely mentioned its importance to any of these special interests. The public emphasis was always on its humanitarian effects. The combination of silent selfish interests and highly humanitarian apologists made a powerful and successful lobby for extracting money from taxpayers. We can expect the same lobby to push now for the creation of a World Food Bank.

However great the potential benefit to selfish interests, it should not be a decisive argument against a truly humanitarian program. We must ask if such a program would actually do more good than harm, not only momentarily but also in the long run. Those who propose the food bank usually refer to a current "emergency" or "crisis" in terms of world food supply. But what is an emergency? Although they may be infrequent and sudden, everyone knows that emergencies will occur from time to time. A well-run family, company, organization or country prepares for the likelihood of accidents and emergencies. It expects them, it budgets for them, it saves for them.

LEARNING THE HARD WAY

What happens if some organizations or countries budget for accidents and others do not? If each country is solely responsible for its own well-being, poorly managed ones will suffer. But they can learn from experience. They may mend their ways, and learn to budget for infrequent but certain emergencies. For example, the weather varies from year to year, and periodic crop failures are certain. A wise and competent government saves out of the production of the good years in anticipation of bad years to come. Joseph taught this policy to Pharaoh in Egypt more than 2,000 years ago. Yet the great majority of the governments in the world today do not follow such a policy. They lack either the wisdom or the competence, or both. Should those nations that do manage to put something aside be forced to come to the rescue each time an emergency occurs among the poor nations?

"But it isn't their fault!" some kindhearted liberals argue. "How can we blame the poor people who are caught in an emergency? Why must they suffer for the sins of their governments?" The concept of blame is simply not relevant here. The real question is, what are the operational consequences of establishing a world food bank? If it is open to every country every time a need develops, slovenly rulers will not be motivated to take Joseph's advice. Someone will always come to their aid. Some countries will deposit food in the world food bank, and others will withdraw it. There will be almost no overlap. As a result of such solutions to food shortage emergencies, the poor countries will not learn to mend their ways, and will suffer progressively greater emergencies as their populations grow.

POPULATION CONTROL THE CRUDE WAY

On the average, poor countries undergo a 2.5 percent increase in population each year; rich countries, about 0.8 percent. Only rich countries have anything in the way of food reserves set aside, and even they do not have as much as they should. Poor countries have none. If poor countries received no food from the outside, the rate of their population growth would be periodically checked by crop failures and famines. But if they can always draw on a world food bank in time of need, their population can continue to grow unchecked, and so will their "need" for aid. In the short run, a world food bank may diminish that need, but in the long run it actually increases the need without limit.

Without some system of worldwide food sharing, the proportion of people in the rich and poor nations might eventually stabilize. The overpopulated poor countries would decrease in numbers, while the rich countries that had room for more people would increase. But with a well-meaning system of sharing, such as a world food bank, the growth differential between the rich and the poor countries will not only persist, it will increase. Because of the higher rate of population growth in the poor countries of the world, 88 percent of today's children are born poor, and only 12 percent rich. Year by year the ratio becomes worse, as the fast-reproducing poor outnumber the slow-reproducing rich.

A world food bank is thus a commons in disguise. People will have more motivation to draw from it than to add to any common store. The less provident and less able will multiply at the expense of the abler and more provident, bringing eventual ruin upon all who share in the commons. Besides, any system of "sharing" that amounts to foreign aid from the rich nations to the poor nations will carry the taint of charity, which will contribute little to the world peace so devoutly desired by those who support the idea of a world food bank.

As past U.S. foreign-aid programs have amply and depressingly demonstrated, international charity frequently inspires mistrust and antagonism rather than gratitude on the part of the recipient nation.

CHINESE FISH AND MIRACLE RICE

The modern approach to foreign aid stresses the export of technology and advice, rather than money and food. As an ancient Chinese proverb goes: "Give a man a fish and he will eat for a day; teach him how to fish and he will eat for the rest of his days." Acting on this advice, the Rockefeller and Ford Foundations have financed a number of programs for improving agriculture in the hungry nations. Known as the "Green Revolution," these programs have led to the development of "miracle rice" and "miracle wheat," new strains that offer bigger harvests and greater resistance to crop damage. Norman Borlaug, the Nobel Prize winning agronomist who, supported by the Rockefeller Foundation, developed "miracle wheat," is one of the most prominent advocates of a world food bank.

Whether or not the Green Revolution can increase food production as much as its champions claim is a debatable but possibly irrelevant point. Those who support this well-intended humanitarian effort should first consider some of the fundamentals of human ecology. Ironically, one man who did was the late Alan Gregg, a vice president of the Rockefeller Foundation. Two decades ago he expressed strong doubts about the wisdom of such attempts to increase food production. He likened the growth and spread of humanity over the surface of the earth to the spread of cancer in the human body, remarking that "cancerous growths demand food; but, as far as I know, they have never been cured by getting it."

OVERLOADING THE ENVIRONMENT

Every human born constitutes a draft on all aspects of the environment: food, air, water, forests, beaches, wildlife, scenery, and solitude. Food can, perhaps, be significantly increased to meet a growing demand. But what about clean beaches, unspoiled forests, and solitude? If we satisfy a growing population's need for food, we necessarily decrease its per capita supply of the other resources needed by men.

India, for example, now has a population of 600 million, which increases by 15 million each year. This population already puts a huge load on a relatively impoverished environment. The country's forests are now only a small fraction of what they were three centuries ago, and floods and erosion continually destroy the insufficient farmland that remains. Every one of the 15 million new lives added to India's population puts an additional burden on the environment, and increases the economic and social costs of crowding. However humanitarian our intent, every Indian life saved through medical or nutritional assistance from abroad diminishes the quality of life for those who remain, and for subsequent generations. If rich countries make it possible, through foreign aid, for 600 million Indians to swell to 1.2 billion in a mere twenty-eight years, as their current growth rate threatens, will future generations of Indians thank us for hastening the destruction of their environment? Will our good intentions be sufficient excuse for the consequences of our actions?

My final example of a commons in action is one for which the public has the least desire for rational discussion—immigration. Anyone who publicly questions the wisdom of current U.S. immigration policy is promptly charged with bigotry, prejudice, ethnocentrism, chauvinism, isolationism or selfishness. Rather than encounter such accusations, one would rather talk about other matters, leaving immigration policy to wallow in the crosscurrents of special interests that take no account of the good of the whole, or the interests of posterity.

Perhaps we still feel guilty about things we said in the past. Two generations ago the popular press frequently referred to Dagos, Wops, Polacks, Chinks, and Krauts in articles about how America was being "overrun" by foreigners of supposedly inferior genetic stock. But because the implied inferiority of foreigners was used then as justification for keeping them out, people now assume that restrictive policies could only be based on such misguided notions. There are other grounds.

A NATION OF IMMIGRANTS

Just consider the numbers involved. Our Government acknowledges a net inflow of 400,000 immigrants a year. While we have no hard data on the extent of illegal entries, educated guesses put the figure at about 600,000 a year. Since the natural increase (excess of births over deaths) of the resident population now runs about 1.7 million per year, the yearly gain from immigration amounts to at least 19 percent of the total annual increase, and may be as much as 37 percent if we include the estimate for illegal immigrants. Considering the growing use of birth control devices, the potential effect of educational campaigns by such organizations as Planned Parenthood Federation of America and Zero Population Growth, and the influence of inflation and the housing shortage, the fertility rate of American women may decline so much that immigration could account for all the yearly increase in population. Should we not at least ask if that is what we want?

For the sake of those who worry about whether the "quality" of the average immigrant compares favorably with the quality of the average resident, let us assume that immigrants and nativeborn citizens are of exactly equal quality, however one defines that term. We will focus here only on quantity; and since our conclusions will depend on nothing else, all charges of bigotry and chauvinism become irrelevant.

IMMIGRATION VS. FOOD SUPPLY

World food banks *move food to the people,* hastening the exhaustion of the environment of the poor countries. Unrestricted immigration, on the other hand, *moves people to the food,* thus speeding up the destruction of the environment of the rich countries. We can easily understand why poor people should want to make this latter transfer, but why should rich hosts encourage it?

As in the case of foreign-aid programs, immigration receives support from selfish interests and humanitarian impulses. The primary selfish interest in unimpeded immigration is the desire of employers for cheap labor, particularly in industries and trades that offer degrading work. In the past, one wave of foreigners after another was brought into the United States to work at wretched jobs for wretched wages. In recent years the Cubans, Puerto Ricans and Mexicans have had this dubious honor. The interests of the employers of cheap labor mesh well with the guilty silence of the country's liberal intelligentsia. White Anglo-Saxon Protestants are particularly reluctant to call for a closing of the doors to immigration for fear of being called bigots.

But not all countries have such reluctant leadership. Most educated Hawaiians, for example, are keenly aware of the limits of their environment, particularly in terms of population growth. There is only so much room on the islands, and the islanders know it. To Hawaiians, immigrants from the other forty-nine states present as great a threat as those from other nations. At a recent meeting of Hawaiian government officials in Honolulu, I had the ironic delight of hearing a speaker, who like most of his audience was of Japanese ancestry, ask how the country might practically and constitutionally close its doors to further immigration. One member of the audience countered: "How can we shut the doors now? We have many friends and relatives in Japan we'd like to bring here some day so that they can enjoy Hawaii too." The Japanese-American speaker smiled sympathetically and answered: "Yes, but we have children now, and someday we'll have grandchildren too. We can bring people here from Japan only by giving away some of the land that we hope to pass on to our grandchildren some day. What right do we have to do that?"

At this point, I can hear U.S. liberals asking: "How can you justify slamming the door once you're inside? You say that immigrants should be kept out. But aren't we all immigrants, or the descendents of immigrants? If we insist on staying, must we not admit all others?" Our craving for intellectual order leads us to seek and prefer symmetrical rules and morals: a single rule for me and everybody else; the same rule yesterday, today, and tomorrow. Justice, we feel, should not change with time and place.

We Americans of non-Indian ancestry can look upon ourselves as the descendants of thieves who are guilty morally, if not legally, of stealing this land from its Indian owners. Should we then give back the land to the now living American descendants of those Indians? However morally or logically sound this proposal may be, I, for one, am unwilling to live by it and I know no one else who is. Besides, the logical consequence would be absurd. Suppose that, intoxicated with a sense of pure justice, we should decide to turn our land over to the Indians. Since all our wealth has also been derived from the land, wouldn't we be morally obligated to give that back to the Indians too?

PURE JUSTICE VS. REALITY

Clearly, the concept of pure justice produces an infinite regression to absurdity. Centuries ago, wise men invented statutes of limitations to justify the rejection of such pure justice, in the interest of preventing continual disorder. The law zealously defends property rights, but only relatively recent property rights. Drawing a line after an arbitrary time has elapsed may be unjust, but the alternatives are worse.

We are all the descendants of thieves, and the world's resources are inequitably distributed. But we must begin the journey to tomorrow from the point where we are today. We cannot remake the past. We cannot safely divide the wealth equitably among all peoples so long as people reproduce at different rates. To do so would guarantee that our grandchildren, and everyone else's grandchildren, would have only a ruined world to inhabit.

To be generous with one's own possessions is quite different from being generous with those of posterity. We should call this point to the attention of those who, from a commendable love of justice and equality, would institute a system of the commons, either in the form of a world food bank, or of unrestricted immigration. We must convince them if we wish to save at least some parts of the world from environmental ruin.

Without a true world government to control reproduction and the use of available resources, the sharing ethic of the spaceship is impossible. For the foreseeable future, our survival demands that we govern our actions by the ethics of a lifeboat, harsh though they may be. Posterity will be satisfied with nothing less.

A MIDDLE VIEW

Raziel Abelson

I want to defend what Derek Parfit has aptly named "agent centered ethics," as encapsulated in the common sense principle that one's duties to assist others vary in strength and rank of precedence in inverse proportion to the emotional distance of the beneficiaries of one's actions from oneself as the center of concern. That is, the closer others are to oneself emotionally—normally, although not necessarily, this means, first, one's spouse and children, then one's parents and siblings, then other relatives, then friends, then neighbors and colleagues, then compatriots, then strangers, then later generations— the more assistance we owe them. On this principle, some egoistic thinkers, such as Bernard Mandeville and Ayn Rand, maintain that we owe primary consideration to ourselves, but I doubt if this follows, for the reason that, as obligatee, one has the option of declining first consideration, for example, one may offer an older person one's seat on a crowded bus. Self-sacrifice is never blameworthy because one is always free to forgive oneself any debt one owes to oneself. In brief, when obligator and obligatee are the same person, the latter may always release the former from obligation. The concept of duty to oneself is pragmatically vacuous. . . .

I should qualify the above principle to exclude the special duties we incur in our social roles and professions, such as doctor to patient, lawyer to client, public official to constituent, cleric to parishioner, etc., which have their own criteria of priority. I am not sure just how these special duties stack up against the more personal ones toward family and friends. Many people seem to consider them equal to, or even stronger than, the strongest personal duties, such as family duties. ("It's my job," drawls the sheriff, as he shoots his outlaw brother.)

The American legal profession, in refusing, recently, to modify its notorious principle of "zealous advocacy" (do anything for your client as long as it isn't provably illegal), seems to give professional duties priority over all others—even the strict negative duties not unjustly to harm others; and the incrimination, in 1974, of 28 out of 31 White House lawyers in the Watergate scandal showed that this is the common attitude of the legal profession (bearing in mind, of course, that the Nixon lawyers had no inkling that their illegal acts would be found out).

Common sense morality is unfortunately not clear on the relation between personal and professional duties, although it is, I believe, clear enough to all but lawyers that strict negative duties take precedence over all positive duties, including professional ones. For example, it is generally understood that a doctor may not waylay a passerby and remove his vital organs in order to save one or more patients. Most professionals seem to favor their professional over their personal duties, but their spouses and children often complain of the injustice of this (to them) perverse favoritism. Here there would seem to be a genuine option with respect to order of precedence. Which comes first may well depend on the agent's way of life and personal relationships. It seems fair to say that the professional who puts family first ought to warn her clients, and the one who puts clients first ought to warn her family, because these matters are not governed by custom or tradition, nor are they deducible from any more fundamental moral principles.

Utilitarian do-gooders are the modern heirs of early Christianity, with its sermon-on-the-mount exhortation to love even one's enemies. For utilitarians the supreme moral principle that should guide our actions is universal beneficence: Do as much good for as many sentient creatures as you possibly can; in the jargon of game theoretical economics, maximize net expectable utility.

If this principle were consistently followed by most people, human life would be radically altered and probably not for the better. Family, professional, and community ties that now motivate most of our actions would have little influence on our conduct. Parents would pay no more attention to their children than to all sentient beings capable of being affected by them, regardless of age, geography or even species, which means, in effect, that they wouldn't care much for anyone. Nor would doctors attend assiduously to their patients, nor friends to friends, etc. Ideally, everyone would receive less than one five billionth of attention from anyone else, or even less if we take into account, as many utilitarians say we should, of all future people, and all present and future animals. In any case the impact of one person's actions on any other person would be negligible.

Derek Parfit, to his great credit, perceived this problem for utilitarian theory, and therefore proposed a compromise between the principle of universal beneficence and the commonsense principle of agent-centered precedence formulated above. He proposed that in bringing up children we train them to develop non-utilitarian agent-centered habits of favoring their own children, friends, clients, etc., much if not all of the time. He recognized that personal and professional ties are the glue that holds society together. Nevertheless, he maintains, universal beneficence is theoretically a morally superior principle to agent-centeredness, which, although useful for achieving maximum social benefit, motivates conduct that is justifiable on practical grounds, but immoral on theoretical grounds. His argument employs various forms of the notorious Prisoner's Dilemma (a situation in which cooperative behavior is much riskier than selfish behavior) to prove that equal concern for the interests of others will, in many competitive situations, produce better outcomes than agent-centered priorities even though the latter engender indispensable social habits. He may very well be right about that, but it hardly proves the superiority of universal beneficence to our agent-centered principle of emotional closeness. One would have to prove that most predicaments in life are Prisoner's Dilemma situations in which everyone taking the risk of subjugating personal interest to the needs of others will produce the best outcome for all, but such a proof is unlikely to be forthcoming.

I know of very few other efforts to provide a rational justification for the principle of universal beneficence. There is Jeremy Bentham's very dubious claim that his "greatest happiness principle" (universal beneficence) is inescapable—it is our nature to obey it; we only fail to apply it properly. And there is Henry Sidgwick's intuitionist contention that it is self-evident. Finally, there is Peter Singer's argument that the universality of ethical judgment entails universal beneficence. Before examining Singer's view I cannot refrain from remarking the extraordinary paucity of argumentative support for so important a claim that attempts to deconstruct common sense morality. One would expect that those who call for revolutionary overthrow of traditional values would be willing to shoulder the burden of proof rather than shifting it, as so many do, to common sense morality. I think I know the reason for this, and I will explain it later on—here, briefly, I will just say that it has to do with the common confusion between positive and negative duties. But more of this later.

In his justly renowned book *Practical Ethics,* Peter Singer writes:

> In accepting that ethical judgments must be made from a universal point of view, I am accepting that my own interests cannot, simply because they are my interests, count more than the interest of anyone else. Thus my very natural concern that my own interests be looked after must, when I think ethically, be extended to the interests of others. . . . In place of my own interests, I now have to take account of the interests of all those affected by my decision. This requires me to weigh up all these interests and adopt the course of action most likely to maximize the interests of those affected.

Singer's argument commits a *non-sequitur* in leaping, without benefit of a logical bridge, from the universality of justifying reasons to the universality of the beneficiaries of action, that is, from the rather banal fact that anyone's interest is as good a reason to act as anyone else's interest, to the conclusion that only actions aimed at fulfilling all relevant interests are justified. Granting Singer that if my interest justifies my action, then your interest equally justifies your doing the same thing, it in no way follows that I ought to aim at your interest, or you at mine. It is one thing to claim that, since my interest in my children's welfare justifies my working overtime to benefit them, therefore anyone is justified in working overtime to benefit his or her children, but quite another thing to claim that everyone should work overtime to benefit all children. Universality of beneficence hardly follows from universality of grounds of justification. . . .

Since Singer's argument fails to provide a rational ground for the utilitarian principle of universal benevolence, my task of defending the commonsense moral priorities may seem to be completed. But I want to do more, namely, to counter, in advance, any attempt to undermine agent-centered morality in favor of the pied piper of universal beneficence. To achieve this wider goal, I shall help myself to Singer's own line of reasoning, but turn it in the reverse direction.

In preparation for this new task, more should be said about the differences only briefly mentioned, between positive duties to assist, and negative duties not to harm, a distinction that utilitarians scorn as passionately as they scorn agent-centeredness. The philosopher who deserves the credit for recognizing the importance of this distinction was Immanuel Kant, who called the former duties "meritorious duties of imperfect obligation" (meaning that we need not always act on them) and the latter, "strict duties of perfect obligation" (meaning that we must always obey them). Now the point I want to make is that only positive duties to assist (Kant's meritorious duties) are subject to agent-centered ordering of precedence based on emotional closeness. Obligations not to harm are everywhere equal. We have no more right to defraud strangers than to defraud our friends. This seems to me the deep truth of Kantian moral theory. This is not to deny that it is less bad, say, to break someone's leg than to kill him, but to do so would be no less wrong, no less a violation of one's moral duty. Utilitarians hold that we should always aim at the greater good, or at least, at the lesser evil. I doubt this, but even if it were true, it would still not be the case that we have a moral duty to do so. We can sympathize with Odysseus, in Sophocles' drama *Philoctetes,* for stealing the golden bow in order to win the Trojan War, but the play would not nearly be so dramatic if it were clear that he had a moral duty to do it. Shelley Kagan has argued persuasively that not benefiting is, in fact, causing harm, which, if true, would make the distinction between positive and negative duties illusory. This is a deep issue that I cannot settle here, but I beg the reader, for the sake of developing the main theme of this discussion, to assume with me and most people that the positive duties to assist can be clearly distinguished from the negative duties not to harm. My claim is that the former involve an order of precedence as to whom to help first, whom next, and how much of one's limited assets to expend. The question then arises as to the ordering principle, or criterion, of ranking. I submit that mankind has evolved the criterion of emotional closeness so that, as we develop from infancy, we learn to apply this criterion in deciding whom to help when. What makes it morally imperative that we do so is that we tacitly commit ourselves to honoring this criterion by the expectations we engender in others. If for some transcendent reason, we find it necessary to act otherwise (say, in some catastrophic situation like the attack on the World Trade Center), we owe it to those who depend on us to warn them, if possible. Commitments are not etched in stone. With suitable warning, and sometimes with subsequent compensation, or, at least, apologies, they can be temporarily disregarded.

Singer, it will be recalled, argued that morality entails concern for the interests of everyone—in brief, universal beneficence. But we have seen that morality entails only the universality of justifying reasons (i.e., what is a morally good reason for one is a morally good reason for all), not the universality of the targets of benevolent action. We are now in position to see that, in fact, the universality of moral reasons entails the non-universality of who is to benefit, if anyone (there need not, as has been noted, always be a beneficiary of the fulfillment of a moral duty, as in the case of repaying a loan to a compulsive gambler).

If, under conditions C, a person P ought to perform an action A, there are then six possibilities with respect to who will benefit or suffer: 1. Everyone benefits and none suffer, 2. some benefit and none suffer, 3. some benefit and some suffer, 4. none benefit and some suffer, 5. none benefit and none suffer, 6. none benefit and everyone suffers. From a utilitarian standpoint we can disregard (5) as morally irrelevant, and we can pretty well disregard (1) and (6) as utopian dream and dystopian nightmare. Even (2) and (4) are so rare as to be safely ignored, leaving (3) as the only statistically meaningful outcome. Needless to say, this *ensures* non-universality of beneficence.

Perhaps this is making too much of an issue of universality. Utilitarians might well protest that, of course, few actions can be expected to benefit all interested parties, so that literal universality of beneficence is not a realistic goal of action. Singer tells us that "we must weigh up the interests of all those affected" and such weighing implies that some may be harmed, so long as the benefits outweigh the harms. Thus, it might be argued, utilitarianism's appeal is to impartiality toward the beneficiaries and/or victims of action, not universality. What counts is not that all benefit, but that most benefit (whether this should mean the greatest number of beneficiaries, or the greatest amount of benefit when added up, is a matter of dispute among utilitarians, but it need not concern us here). The main point is that no order of precedence, no discrimination among possible beneficiaries, is, morally, in order. Thus, if one's actions help more sinners than saints, more Nazis than Jews, or more child molesters than children, so be it, that is what one ought to do. It is hardly necessary to remark that this conclusion is morally preposterous. . . .

Any attempt to argue that we should be impartial toward the beneficiaries of our actions undermines the universality of justifying reasons from which Singer has tried to deduce the principle of universal beneficence. For we are to look as kindly on those who cannot morally justify their actions by good reasons as on those who can. Impartiality toward beneficiaries entails impartiality toward reasons for action, since beneficiaries are also agents who act for good and bad reasons, and impartiality toward the moral worth of their reasons makes mincemeat of moral judgment.

The view I have outlined in defense of the moral priorities for helping others, priorities that have evolved over millennia of human experience, should not be confused with the morality of self-interest argued for by rugged individualists from Bernard Mandeville to Ayn Rand. I have not meant to deny that we all have duties to assist strangers as well as intimates and to contribute what we reasonably can to the reduction of poverty and malnutrition throughout the world. Quite to the contrary: The evolution of our moral responsibilities has clearly been in the direction of tacit commitments toward wider circles of responsibility from family to clan, to tribe, to ethnic group, to nation, to humankind, perhaps, ultimately, to all sentient creatures, and I celebrate this moral progress. I mean only to defend the commonsense priorities based on emotional distance from beneficiaries that utilitarian ethics necessarily undermines, despite the special efforts of sensitive utilitarians like Parfit and Singer to soften the sting. Parfit explicitly recognizes the social value of giving special care and attention to one's children and parents, but, acknowledging its inconsistency with his general doctrine of impartiality, he relegates it to an oxymoronic limbo of "moral immorality." Why we should prefer limbo to heaven he does not further explain. Singer makes the same point at greater length yet also with greater vagueness, as follows:

> The element of truth in the view that we should first take care of our own, lies in the advantage of a recognized system of responsibilities. When families and local communities look after their poorer members, ties of affection and personal relationships achieve ends that would otherwise require a large, impersonal bureaucracy. Hence it would be absurd to propose that from now on we all regard ourselves as equally responsible for the welfare of everyone in the world, but the argument for an obligation to assist does not propose that. It applies only when some are in absolute poverty and others can help without sacrificing anything of comparable moral significance, and before family and community responsibility would be a factor to weigh the balance in favor of a small degree of preference for family and community. This small degree of preference is, however, decisively outweighed by existing discrepancies in wealth and property.

Why "the argument for an obligation to assist . . . applies only when some are in absolute poverty" needs explaining, given the universality initially claimed for the principle with which he began: "If it is in our power to prevent something bad from happening . . ." etc. Surely absolute poverty and resulting starvation are not the only bad thing that it is in our power to prevent by sacrificing all luxuries. We could also help to overcome illiteracy, poor sanitation, dietary imbalance, overcrowded housing, air and water pollution and many other social ills while depriving ourselves and our families of such luxuries as higher education, vacations, cultural activities such as visits to museums, operas, plays, music and art lessons for ourselves and our children, and so on. Granting Singer that we ought to make some sacrifices for charitable purposes (as in fact, most people do), the question remains: How much? How small should be the "small degree of preference" for ourselves, our children, our relatives and friends proposed by Singer; and why, *on his own view,* should the assertion of equal responsibility for everyone be considered "absurd"? The proposal of a "small degree of preference" looks like a bone thrown to moral common sense to protect utilitarian ethics from precisely the absurdity that Singer's concession attempts to avoid. Nevertheless, the concession is welcome. But the next question is—What is its moral ground, if not the criterion of emotional closeness, which provides a measure of how large or small our degrees of preference should be?

I conclude from all these considerations, that the commonsense principle that our positive duties to assist vary in strength and priority with the degree of emotional closeness between us and our beneficiaries is the only reasonable game in town.

QUESTIONS FOR DISCUSSION
FAMINE RELIEF

1. Does Singer's proposed principle of charitable giving—that we should give as much as possible "without sacrificing anything of comparable moral significance"—require that a middle-class parent forgo music lessons and summer camp for her own children? Defend your response.

2. Is Singer right that we are morally obliged to give more when others are likely to give too little? Would the fact that some give more influence others to give less, or would it influence others to give more? Explain.

3. Discuss Singer's argument that not saving lives by maximum contribution is tantamount to mass murder. How does he reply to the five arguments against this claim? Does he think there is a moral difference between killing and letting die? Do you agree? Why or why not?

4. Is Hardin right that "lifeboat ethics" requires different rules of conduct from ordinary ethics? Which general moral theory of those presented in Chapter 1 seems to support Hardin's claim best, and which theory most strongly rejects it? Which theory best supports Singer's view? Explain your response.

5. What forms of assistance does Hardin maintain should be given by affluent nations to disadvantaged nations? To what extent does Singer agree?

6. Is the priority claimed by Abelson for one's duties to family and friends allowed for by Singer's concession that "it would be absurd to propose that from now on we all regard ourselves as equally responsible for the welfare of everyone in the world"? How does Abelson propose to assign different degrees of responsibility for intimates and for strangers?

SELECTED READINGS

BITTNER, R. "Morality and World Hunger." *Metaphilosophy,* January 2001.

DENUYL, D. "The Right to Welfare and the Virtue of Charity." *Social Philosophy and Policy,* ___ 1993.

KENT, G. *The Political Economy of Hunger.* New York: Praeger, 1984.

KUNKEL, J. "The Rich Get Richer and the Poor Starve: Is There an Ethical Alternative?" In *Philosophical Perspectives on Power and Domination,* ed. L. D. Kaplan. Amsterdam: Rodopi, 1997.

LUCAS, G., and T. OGLETREE, eds. *Lifeboat Ethics.* New York: Harper & Row, 1976.

SINGER, P. "Famine, Affluence and Morality." *Philosophy and Public Affairs,* ___ 1972.

———. *How Are We to Live?* New York: Cambridge University Press, 1993.

TYDINGS, J. *Born to Starve.* New York: Morrow, 1970.

UNGER, P. *Living High and Letting Die.* New York: Oxford University Press, 1996.

7

ENVIRONMENTAL ETHICS

In his influential book *Earth in the Balance,* former vice president Al Gore presents a powerful case for greatly increasing both governmental and personal efforts to reduce pollution and to clean up the natural environment—oceans and rivers, the forests, the atmosphere—and preserve underground resources essential to continued animal and plant life, without which human civilization would come to an end. Gore details the disappearance of hundreds of thousands of plant and animal species, and of ever larger portions of the rain forests that produce oxygen and facilitate essential rainfall, and the global warming that threatens to melt the polar caps, thereby producing destructive tidal waves and murderous droughts. He blames the population explosion of the last century and the consequent excessive use of natural resources and polluting technology, such as gasoline-driven vehicles, as the main causes of this ever increasing threat to life on earth.

Gore does not specify precisely what steps should be taken to reverse, or at least slow down, this fateful trend; but as vice president he supported the Kyoto international treaty of 1996 to reduce carbon emissions by specified amounts, and he argues for voluntary restraint on the use of energy and natural resources.

Wallace Kaufman severely criticizes environmentalist organizations for reckless exaggerations and false alarms based, according to him, on scientifically unsound statistical studies. He denies that forests are rapidly disappearing, that air and water pollution and global warming are becoming a serious threat to life on earth. Against the statistical studies cited by Al Gore and others, Kaufman counters with contrary statistical studies. He even maintains that organic food products are more toxic than those sprayed with insecticides, and that the disbenefits of recycling exceed its benefits.

How can we non-experts decide who is right in this controversy where both sides appeal to expert evidence and testimony for opposite conclusions? Bearing in mind that in such complex and heated disputes both sides tend to exaggerate their opponents' errors and their own merits, we should perhaps look for a middle ground between the most extreme claims on both sides. Nevertheless, in consideration of the drastic consequences if the warnings of environmentalists happen to be right, one might have reason to tilt more toward the environmentalists than toward their critics who advise inaction, merely on the grounds that humankind can afford (1) excessive precautions against catastrophe should environmentalists be wrong, more than (2) insufficient precautions should they happen to be right.

The need for environmental protection

Al Gore

. . . some of the most disturbing images of environmental destruction can be found exactly halfway between the North and South poles—precisely at the equator in Brazil—where billowing clouds of smoke regularly blacken the sky above the immense but now threatened Amazon rain forest. Acre by acre, the rain forest is being burned to create fast pasture for fast-food beef; as I learned when I went there in early 1989, the fires are set earlier and earlier in the dry season now, with more than one Tennessee's worth of rain forest being slashed and burned each year. According to our guide, the biologist Tom Lovejoy, there are more different species of birds in each square mile of the Amazon than exist in all of North America—which means we are silencing thousands of songs we have never even heard.

But for most of us the Amazon is a distant place, and we scarcely notice the disappearance of these and other vulnerable species. We ignore these losses at our peril, however. They're like the proverbial miners' canaries, silent alarms whose message in this case is that living species of animals and plants are now vanishing around the world *one thousand times faster* than at any time in the past 65 million years.

To be sure, the deaths of some of the larger and more spectacular animal species now under siege do occasionally capture our attention. I have also visited another place along the equator, East Africa, where I encountered the grotesquely horrible image of a dead elephant, its head mutilated by poachers who had dug out its valuable tusks with chain saws. Clearly, we need to change our purely aesthetic consideration of ivory, since its source is now so threatened. To me, its translucent whiteness seems different now, like evidence of the ghostly presence of a troubled spirit, a beautiful but chill apparition, inspiring both wonder and dread.

A similar apparition lies just beneath the ocean. While scuba diving in the Caribbean, I have seen and touched the white bones of a dead coral reef. All over the earth, coral reefs have suddenly started to "bleach" as warmer ocean temperatures put unaccustomed stress on the tiny organisms that normally live in the skin of the coral and give the reef its natural coloration. As these organisms—nicknamed "zooks"—leave the membrane of the coral, the coral itself becomes transparent, allowing its white limestone skeleton to shine through—hence its bleached appearance. In the past, bleaching was almost always an occasional and temporary phenomenon, but repeated episodes can exhaust the coral. In the last few years, scientists have been shocked at the sudden occurrence of extensive worldwide bleaching episodes from which increasing numbers of coral reefs have failed to recover. Though dead, they shine more brightly than before, haunted perhaps by the same ghost that gives spectral light to an elephant's tusk.

But one doesn't have to travel around the world to witness humankind's assault on the earth. Images that signal the distress of our global environment are now commonly seen almost anywhere. A few miles from the Capitol, for example, I encountered another startling image of nature out of place. Driving in the Arlington, Virginia, neighborhood where my family and I live when the Senate is in session, I stepped on the brake to avoid hitting a large pheasant walking across the street. It darted between the parked cars, across the sidewalk, and into a neighbor's backyard. Then it was gone. But this apparition of wildness persisted in my memory as a puzzle: Why would a pheasant, let alone such a large and beautiful mature specimen, be out for a walk in my neighborhood? Was it a much wilder place than I had noticed? Were pheasants, like the trendy Vietnamese potbellied pigs, becoming the latest fashion in unusual pets? I didn't solve the mystery until weeks later, when I remembered that about three miles away, along the edge of the river, developers were bulldozing the last hundred acres of untouched forest in the entire area. As the woods fell to make way for more concrete, more buildings, parking lots, and streets, the wild things that lived there were forced to flee. Most of the deer were hit by cars; other creatures—like the pheasant that darted into my neighbor's backyard—made it a little farther.

Ironically, before I understood the mystery, I felt vaguely comforted to imagine that perhaps this urban environment, so similar to the one in which many Americans live, was not so hostile to wild things after all. I briefly supposed that, like the resourceful raccoons and possums and squirrels and pigeons, all of whom have adapted to life in the suburbs, creatures as wild as pheasants might have a fighting chance. Now I remember that pheasant when I take my children to the zoo and see an elephant or a rhinoceros. They too inspire wonder and sadness. They too remind me that we are creating a world that is hostile to wildness, that seems to prefer concrete to natural landscapes. We are encountering these creatures on a path we have paved—one that ultimately leads to their extinction.

On some nights, in high northern latitudes, the sky itself offers another ghostly image that signals the loss of ecological balance now in progress. If the sky is clear after sunset—and if you are watching from a place where pollution hasn't blotted out the night sky altogether—you can sometimes see a strange kind of cloud high in the sky. This "noctilucent cloud" occasionally appears when the earth is first cloaked in the evening darkness; shimmering above us with a translucent whiteness, these clouds seem quite unnatural. And they should: noctilucent clouds have begun to appear more often because of a huge buildup of methane gas in the atmosphere. (Also called natural gas, methane is released from landfills, from coal mines and rice paddies, from billions of termites that swarm through the freshly cut forestland, from the burning of biomass and from a variety of other human activities.) Even though noctilucent clouds were sometimes seen in the past, all this extra methane carries more water vapor into the upper atmosphere, where it condenses at much higher altitudes to form more clouds that the sun's rays still strike long after sunset has brought the beginning of night to the surface far beneath them.

What should we feel toward these ghosts in the sky? Simple wonder or the mix of emotions we feel at the zoo? Perhaps we should feel awe for our own power: just as men tear tusks from elephants' heads in such quantity as to threaten the beast with extinction, we are ripping matter from its place in the earth in such volume as to upset the balance between daylight and darkness. In the process, we are once again adding to the threat of global warming, because methane has been one of the fastest-growing greenhouse gases, and is third only to carbon dioxide and water vapor in total volume, changing the chemistry of the upper atmosphere. But, without even considering that threat, shouldn't it startle us that we have now put these clouds in the evening sky which glisten with a spectral light? Or have our eyes adjusted so completely to the bright lights of civilization that we can't see these clouds for what they are—a physical manifestation of the violent collision between human civilization and the earth?

Even though it is sometimes hard to see their meaning, we have by now all witnessed surprising experiences that signal the damage from our assault on the environment—whether it's the new frequency of days when the temperature exceeds 100 degrees, the new speed with which the sun burns our skin, or the new constancy of public debate over what to do with growing mountains of waste. But our response to these signals is puzzling. Why haven't we launched a massive effort to save our environment? To come at the question another way: Why do some images startle us into immediate action and focus our attention on ways to respond effectively? And why do other images, though sometimes equally dramatic, produce instead a kind of paralysis, focusing our attention not on ways to respond but rather on some convenient, less painful distraction?

In a roundabout way, my visit to the North Pole caused me to think about these questions from a different perspective and gave them a new urgency. On the submarine, I had several opportunities to look through the periscope at the translucent bottom of the ice pack at the North Pole. The sight was not a little claustrophobic, and at one point I suddenly thought of the three whales that had become trapped under the ice of the Beaufort Sea a couple of years earlier. Television networks from four continents came to capture their poignant struggle for air and in the process so magnified the emotions felt around the world that soon scientists and rescue workers flocked to the scene. After several elaborate schemes failed, a huge icebreaker from the Soviet Union cut a path through the ice for the two surviving whales. Along with millions of others, I had been delighted to see them go free, but there on the submarine it occurred to me that if we are causing 100 extinctions each day—and many scientists believe we are—approximately 2,000 living species had disappeared from the earth during the whales' ordeal. They disappeared forever—unnoticed.

Similarly, when a little girl named Jessica McClure fell into a well in Texas, her ordeal and subsequent rescue by a legion of heroic men and women attracted hundreds of television cameras and journalists who sent the story into the homes and minds of hundreds of millions of people. Here, too, our response seems skewed: during the three days of Jessica's ordeal, more than 100,000 boys and girls her age or younger died of preventable causes—mostly starvation and diarrhea—due to failures of both crops and politics. As they struggled for life, none of these children looked into a collection of television cameras, anxious to send word of their plight to a waiting world. They died virtually unnoticed. Why?

Perhaps one part of the answer lies in the perceived difficulty of an effective response. If the problem portrayed in the image is one whose solution appears to involve more effort or sacrifice than we can readily imagine, or if even maximum effort by any one individual would fail to prevent the tragedy, we are tempted to sever the link between stimulus and moral response. Then, once a response is deemed impossible, the image that briefly caused us to consider responding becomes not just startling but painful. At that point, we begin to react not to the image but to the pain it now produces, thus severing a more basic link in our relationship to the world: the link between our senses and our emotions. Our eyes glaze over as our hearts close. We look but we don't see. We hear but refuse to listen.

Still, there are so many distressing images of environmental destruction that sometimes it seems impossible to know how to absorb or comprehend them. Before considering the threats themselves, it may be helpful to classify them and thus begin to organize our thoughts and feelings so that we may be able to respond appropriately.

A useful system comes from the military, which frequently places a conflict in one of three different categories, according to the theater in which it takes place. There are "local" skirmishes, "regional" battles, and "strategic" conflicts. This third category is reserved for struggles that can threaten a nation's survival and must be understood in a global context.

Environmental threats can be considered in the same way. For example, most instances of water pollution, air pollution, and illegal waste dumping are essentially local in nature. Problems like acid rain, the contamination of underground aquifers, and large oil spills are fundamentally regional. In both of these categories, there may be so many similar instances of particular local and regional problems occurring simultaneously all over the world that the pattern appears to be global, but the problems themselves are still not truly strategic because the operation of the global environment is not affected and the survival of civilization is not at stake.

However, a new class of environmental problems does affect the global ecological system, and these threats are fundamentally strategic. The 600 percent increase in the amount of chlorine in the atmosphere during the last forty years has taken place not just in those countries producing the chlorofluorocarbons responsible but in the air above every country, above Antarctica, above the North Pole and the Pacific Ocean—all the way from the surface of the earth to the top of the sky. The increased levels of chlorine disrupt the global process by which the earth regulates the amount of ultraviolet radiation from the sun that is allowed through the atmosphere to the surface; and if we let chlorine levels continue to increase, the radiation levels will also increase—to the point that all animals and plant life will face a new threat to their survival.

Global warming is also a strategic threat. The concentration of carbon dioxide and other heat-absorbing molecules has increased by almost 25 percent since World War II, posing a worldwide threat to the earth's ability to regulate the amount of heat from the sun retained in the atmosphere. This increase in heat seriously threatens the global climate equilibrium that determines the pattern of winds, rainfall, surface temperatures, ocean currents, and sea level. These in turn determine the distribution of vegetative and animal life on land and sea and have a great effect on the location and pattern of human societies.

In other words, the entire relationship between humankind and the earth has been transformed because our civilization is suddenly capable of affecting the entire global environment, not just a particular area. All of us know that human civilization has usually had a large impact on the environment; to mention just one example, there is evidence that even in prehistoric times, vast areas were sometimes intentionally burned by people in their search for food. And in our own time we have reshaped a large part of the earth's surface with concrete in our cities and carefully tended rice paddies, pastures, wheatfields, and other croplands in the countryside. But these changes, while sometimes appearing to be pervasive, have, until recently, been relatively trivial factors in the global ecological system. Indeed, until our lifetime, it was always safe to assume that nothing we did or could do would have any lasting effect on the global environment. But it is precisely that assumption which must now be discarded so that we can think strategically about our new relationship to the environment.

Human civilization is now the dominant cause of change in the global environment. Yet we resist this truth and find it hard to imagine that our effect on the earth must now be measured by the same yardstick used to calculate the strength of the moon's pull on the oceans or the force of the wind against the mountains. And if we are now capable of changing something so basic as the relationship between the earth and the sun, surely we must acknowledge a new responsibility to use that power wisely and with appropriate restraint. So far, however, we seem oblivious of the fragility of the earth's natural systems.

This century has witnessed dramatic changes in two key factors that define the physical reality of our relationship to the earth: a sudden and startling surge in human population, with the addition of one China's worth of people every ten years, and a sudden acceleration of the scientific and technological revolution, which has allowed an almost unimaginable magnification of our power to affect the world around us by burning, cutting, digging, moving, and transforming the physical matter that makes up the earth.

The surge in population is both a cause of the changed relationship and one of the clearest illustrations of how startling the change has been, especially when viewed in a historical context. From the emergence of modern humans 200,000 years ago until Julius Caesar's time, fewer than 250 million people walked on the face of the earth. When Christopher Columbus set sail for the New World 1,500 years later, there were approximately 500 million people on earth. By the time Thomas Jefferson wrote the Declaration of Independence in 1776, the number had doubled again, to 1 billion. By midway through this century, at the end of World War II, the number had risen to just above 2 billion people.

In other words, from the beginning of humanity's appearance on earth to 1945, it took more than ten thousand generations to reach a world population of 2 billion people. Now, in the course of one human lifetime—mine—the world population will increase from 2 to more than 9 billion, and it is already more than halfway there.

Like the population explosion, the scientific and technological revolution began to pick up speed slowly during the eighteenth century. And this ongoing revolution has also suddenly accelerated exponentially. For example, it is now an axiom in many fields of science that more new and important discoveries have taken place in the last ten years than in the entire previous history of science. While no single discovery has had the kind of effect on our relationship to the earth that nuclear weapons have had on our relationship to warfare, it is nevertheless true that taken together, they have completely transformed our cumulative ability to exploit the earth for sustenance—making the consequences of unrestrained exploitation every bit as unthinkable as the consequences of unrestrained nuclear war.

Now that our relationship to the earth has changed so utterly, we have to see that change and understand its implications. Our challenge is to recognize that the startling images of environmental destruction now occurring all over the world have much more in common than their ability to shock and awaken us. They are symptoms of an underlying problem broader in scope and more serious than any we have ever faced. Global warming, ozone depletion, the loss of living species, deforestation—they all have a common cause: the new relationship between human civilization and the earth's natural balance.

There are actually two aspects to this challenge. The first is to realize that our power to harm the earth can indeed have global and even permanent effects. The second is to realize that the only way to understand our new role as a co-architect of nature is to see ourselves as part of a complex system that does not operate according to the same simple rules of cause and effect we are used to. The problem is not our effect *on* the environment so much as our relationship *with* the environment. As a result, any solution to the problem will require a careful assessment of that relationship as well as the complex interrelationship among factors within civilization and between them and the major natural components of the earth's ecological system.

There is only one precedent for this kind of challenge to our thinking, and again it is military. The invention of nuclear weapons and the subsequent development by the United States and the Soviet Union of many thousands of strategic nuclear weapons forced a slow and painful recognition that the new power thus acquired forever changed not only the relationship between the two superpowers but also the relationship of humankind to the institution of warfare itself. The consequences of all-out war between nations armed with nuclear weapons suddenly included the possibility of the destruction of both nations—completely and simultaneously. That sobering realization led to a careful reassessment of every aspect of our mutual relationship to the prospect of such a war. As early as 1946 one strategist concluded that strategic bombing with missiles "may well tear away the veil of illusion that has so long obscured the reality of the change in warfare—from a fight to a process of destruction."

Nevertheless, during the earlier stages of the nuclear arms race, each of the superpowers assumed that its actions would have a simple and direct effect on the thinking of the other. For decades, each new advance in weaponry was deployed by one side for the purpose of inspiring fear in the other. But each such deployment led to an effort by the other to leapfrog the first one with a more advanced deployment of its own. Slowly, it has become apparent that the problem of the nuclear arms race is not primarily caused by technology. It is complicated by technology, true; but it arises out of the relationship between the superpowers and is based on an obsolete understanding of what war is all about.

The eventual solution to the arms race will be found, not in a new deployment by one side or the other of some ultimate weapon or in a decision by either side to disarm unilaterally, but rather in new understandings and in a mutual transformation of the relationship itself. This transformation will involve changes in the technology of weaponry and the denial of nuclear technology to rogue states. But the key changes will be in the way we think about the institution of warfare and about the relationship between states.

The strategic nature of the threat now posed *by* human civilization to the global environment and the strategic nature of the threat *to* human civilization now posed by changes in the global environment present us with a similar set of challenges and false hopes. Some argue that a new ultimate technology, whether nuclear power or genetic engineering, will solve the problem. Others hold that only a drastic reduction of our reliance on technology can improve the conditions of life—a simplistic notion at best. But the real solution will be found in reinventing and finally healing the relationship between civilization and the earth. This can only be accomplished by undertaking a careful reassessment of all the factors that led to the relatively recent dramatic change in the relationship. The transformation of the way we relate to the earth will of course involve new technologies, but the key changes will involve new ways of thinking about the relationship itself.

THE EXCESSES OF ENVIRONMENTALISM

Wallace Kaufman

Popular horse-racing tabloids are much more scientific than the environmental press. People who write the racing sheets know the uncertainty and risk in their predictions. News on the environment features experts who claim to be almost entirely certain about their predictions. Claiming to be certain, especially about a future disaster, can sell books and raise funds. Even when the writers are not sure of the facts, they will place a heavy bet, usually with someone else's money. In the case of developing countries, they will even wager someone else's comfort or life span.

The purpose of environmental journalism is not to convey the truth about nature or the impact of civilization. Rather, its goal is to sell the myths of the movement. The environmental movement appeals for converts in much the same way that Pascal argued for people to believe in God. Although the seventeenth-century French philosopher doubted the existence of God, he proposed that a prudent person should bet on the Almighty. After all, he argued, if there is a God, the believer has everything to gain and the nonbeliever, everything to lose. But if God does not exist, the believer and nonbeliever go to the same fate.

The environmental movement's grip on the media relies on information that trickles down from a point where great generalities are manufactured. At the grass-roots level, anecdotal information provides the "proof." Global warming is a fine example of the environmental trickle-down theory. In the 1980s, when computer models predicted that as carbon dioxide levels rise, the atmosphere will warm, anecdotes poured in about local heat waves and droughts. When the summers of 1987 and 1988 brought unusually high heat, Al Gore, then a senator, joined environmental groups everywhere in suggesting that this could be global warming in action. However, not a single credible scientist believed that the North American summers proved anything—except that if you don't like the weather, wait a few years.

In 1984, environmentalists seized a huge media opportunity when Lester Brown's Worldwatch Institute published its first annual state of the world report. Nobody else was publishing such material. Brown began the first volume with a flood of highly selective tables and charts and highly biased analysis.

In a vacuum of other readable reports, *State of the World* became a popular reference book for journalists, especially those sympathetic to the environmental movement. Each year's report often sells more than 100,000 copies (more than many best-sellers).

In 1986, *Time* magazine wrote that "Brown's presumptuous 263 page volume may be studied more intently by more people in more countries than Reagan's [state of the union] address." The MacArthur Foundation, always ready to finance apostles of the apocalypse, awarded Brown a $250,000 "genius grant." The Worldwatch Institute's budget is well over $1 million a year, almost entirely slated for generating information for the environmental movement. But to read the annual reports three to five years after they appear, the figures and predictions become useless, or are exposed by later events as simply fraudulent. For example, Brown's 1989 report touched off a huge campaign to stop logging in the Amazon by citing fuzzy satellite data combined with guesses about the number of fires burning. He warned readers that "satellite data show that 8 million hectares [20 million acres] were cleared in 1987 alone, 5 to 6 million more than were thought to have been cleared annually in the early eighties." Brown never revealed that his figures were based on a Brazilian study that has been refuted by many competent scientists. By 1990, improved interpretations would slash Brown's estimate by an area the size of Zimbabwe. In 1993, better data led scientists to estimate that the rate of annual clearing was actually 2.1 million hectares between 1978 and 1989, falling to 1.4 million hectares between 1989 and 1990. In his 1989 report, Brown had claimed almost 400 percent more deforestation than actually existed. Despite his reliance on questionable data, the popular press continues to give Brown's predictions and annual reports reverent coverage.

The environmental movement has been a blessing to the media. Scientists have traditionally remained too cautious and modest to provide the excitement the media needs to get readers, listeners, and viewers. Environmentalists, using the language of science, seem to provide the easy answers and the drama. Einstein once compared the pursuit of atomic physics to following the tracks of a great beast across the universe. Scientists are still following such tracks, but with less hope of seeing the beast. They have realized that nature and the universe are far too complex to be fully understood by the human mind. From a religious point of view, this may be the same as admitting we will never see the face of God. Through the environmental movement, however, the popular press, radio, and television are always seeing the face of God. For them, scientific uncertainty seldom exists, or if it does, it is kept in the back closet like a crazy relative.

Environmental groups will sacrifice even their own goals to remain politically correct. One of the most difficult stories for the environmental movement is the fate of the elephant in Africa. The worldwide ban on elephant ivory is supposed to save the elephant. Ironically, however, those countries that enforce the ban continue to lose elephants to poachers, while in Zimbabwe and Botswana, where ivory harvesting is legal, elephant herds have been increasing. This is because local people want to protect a valuable source of income, an entirely rational response. However, fundraisers for World Wildlife Fund International (WWF) convinced the fund's experts not to use this information, since maintaining the ban is better for fundraising. England's Prince Philip, WWF's president, wrote in a confidential memo:

> The awkward problem for WWF is the massive popular support for a total trade ban regardless of its chances of success or its consequences. The ban is a typical "knee-jerk" reaction by the "greens" and it is not going to be easy to get rational measures adopted for the control of poaching and for limiting demand to sustainable supply.

At the next higher level of environmental hysteria are public radio and television. Financed primarily by large foundations, environmental coverage is often quite different from higher-quality scientific programs. The prestigious show "Frontline," for instance, launched a frontal attack on agricultural chemicals to celebrate the thirtieth anniversary of Rachel Carson's *The Silent Spring*. To demonstrate the dangers of farm chemicals, the earnest Bill Moyers cited the "McFarland cancer cluster" in California. In fact, no epidemiologists have been able to link those cancers to farm chemicals. Every farmer knows the dangers of heavy doses of pesticides, and farmers and farm children generally enjoy lower cancer rates than the rest of the population, a fact that "Frontline" could not or would not use. If small doses of agricultural pesticides do cause health problems, the problems should appear in farm families first.

Few news or documentary pieces ever report important advances in technological management of environmental quality. For example, in the same period that the Carson anniversary show pretended to be competent science reporting, "Frontline" turned down several proposals by accomplished producers for a show on new methods for assessing the risks from toxic chemicals.

When scientific uncertainty cannot be avoided, everybody finds a way to take advantage of it. For many political conservatives, it becomes the reason to do nothing until science fills in all but the tiniest gaps. Environmentalists, however, will fill in large gaps with conjecture and often with outright fiction. If in the contest of evidence they find themselves surrounded and in short supply of facts, they will dig in waiting for new supplies. Air pollution has been an excellent example. No one likes dirty air except perhaps cigarette smokers. But getting people to look beyond the costs and start a quick clean-up requires certainty of imminent disaster.

In the 1970s, people such as the astronomer Carl Sagan and the climatologist Stephen Schneider warned that atmospheric pollution would cause global cooling. In an essay entitled "Eco-Catastrophe!" in Friends of the Earth's 1970 *Environmental Handbook,* Paul Ehrlich looked into the future and imagined a 1977 issue of *Science* magazine announcing "that incident solar radiation had been so reduced by worldwide air pollution that serious effects on the world's vegetation could be expected." To reach this wrong conclusion, the doomsayers filled in huge gaps in climate research with pure guesswork.

The evidence in 1993 for global warming may have been more sophisticated than the 1970 evidence for global cooling, but it was hardly more decisive. Global warming exists only in theory and in the realm of quite limited computer models. No competent scientist claims to have measured on a thermometer, or any other meter, an actual increase in average global temperature. The best data we have on the overall global temperature come from NASA's satellites. An analysis provided by NASA and the Earth System Science Lab at the University of Alabama demonstrates that from 1979 to 1993 there was no significant trend toward either cooler or warmer temperatures. From 1988 to 1991, when Al Gore was writing his book, global temperatures were warmer than average. From 1984 to 1987, and in 1992 and 1994, they were cooler than average. Nevertheless, environmental groups and politicians have filled in the uncertainty gap with information that wins financial support and votes. Perhaps by the time these words are published, the gap will have narrowed, and Ehrlich will finally have bet on a winning prediction. But for now, his bet is on winning rhetoric.

In the meantime, the "certainty" of global warming provides the focal point for Bill McKibben's *The End of Nature* and Al Gore's *Earth in the Balance*. Even after Gore's election he continued to exploit false evidence for global warming. In 1993, he asked an environmental conference in Kentucky if it were just a coincidence that carbon dioxide has gone up along with temperatures in the last fifteen years.

Dominating media attention is more important for the environmental movement than getting the story straight. The Conservation Fund's 1989 survey of environmental organizations in forty-nine states makes the point. The fund asked each organization for its most important strategies. In their responses, nothing approached the importance of using the media to change public opinion. Seventy-two percent of the environmental leaders rated the media strategy as "very important" or "most important." Monitoring government agencies came in a distant second, with 51 percent rating it "very high." When the fund asked about the highest priority within the organization, only 3 percent said "hiring professional researchers." So where do they get their most valuable information? Among the possible sources proposed as extremely useful by the fund, more than half of the environmental leaders chose talking to other environmental leaders. Only 18 percent listed "discussions with leading thinkers in conservation history," and 24 percent chose "a fellowship in natural resource management." When evaluating newly hired staff, 57 percent of the environmental leaders surveyed rated their employees as excellent in interpersonal communication, but when it came to scientific knowledge, only 22 percent gave their own staff members an excellent rating. Fewer than half of the environmental leaders had a bachelor's degree in one of the sciences.

The Sierra Club's 1970 *Ecotactics* laid down the guidelines for the movement's domination of the media. It was called "advocacy journalism" and its intent was to "destroy the dangerous anonymity afforded by objectivity or 'balance.'" The chapter "Getting into Print" ends by noting with approval that "at the meeting of the U.S. Student Press Association in Boulder, just before Woodstock, student editors began realizing the necessity of politicizing their papers."

Advocacy journalism on environmental issues has since spread to most major television and print outlets. When the Smithsonian Institution sponsored a conference for media people in 1989—called "Global Environment: Are We Overreacting?"—the answer was built into the program. Panels were loaded with speakers like Ehrlich and Brown. There was no dissent.

At the conference, the *Wall Street Journal* editorial writer David Brooks reported that Charles Alexander of *Time* said, "As the science editor of *Time* I would freely admit that on this issue we have crossed the boundary from news reporting to advocacy." NBC's Andrea Mitchell agreed: "Clearly the networks have made that decision now, where you'd have to call it advocacy." The *Washington Post* executive editor Ben Bradlee, noting that C-Span was taping the conference, warned about the dangers of being so public about the media abandoning objective reporting. He did not object to the practice, but he was concerned about how it results in "a whole kooky constituency to respond to, which you can waste a lot of time on."

Environmental journalism runs the gamut from sleazy to brilliant, but the advocacy journalism promoted in the 1970s has taken over environmental magazines and newsletters. It has become the main source of information for school books and curricula, college courses on environmental issues, and citizen action groups.

Some writers and professors have legitimized advocacy journalism by claiming that objectivity does not exist. Perfection in any discipline, as Plato observed over 2,000 years ago, does not exist in the human world, only shadows of perfection. Yet the impossibility of purely objective reporting is a miserable excuse for not trying. Besides, if writers and environmentalists insist on undermining science by mocking *its* objectivity, they could destroy the only means we have for understanding what we want to save and whether our efforts are succeeding:

> Those who manipulate science as a tool of persuasion do not respect the sanctity of science. Nor do they respect the sanctity of an individual's right to self-determination. Their belief is that when given the truth people do not have the ability to make the "correct" decisions, so they must be lied to instead. Only the environmentalist manipulators of science have the ability to come to "correct" decisions.

Well-reasoned and fairly argued writing exists, but it is generally ignored or picked over for partisan goodies as if it were nothing more than flea market trash and treasure.

The controversy over dioxin is a particularly good example of how advocates get locked into one point of view and then refuse to adapt to contradictory evidence. Dioxin, a by-product of pesticides, herbicides, and other industrial products, first became famous when the U.S. military sprayed massive amounts of Agent Orange on the forests of Vietnam to expose guerrillas in hiding. Many veterans blamed later health problems on the dioxin in Agent Orange. This became proof for the environmentalists' bias against synthetic chemicals, and they rushed to celebrate.

However, epidemiological studies turned up no direct link, or even a pattern of illnesses, that could be caused by dioxin. Studies of people exposed to dioxin after a chemical plant explosion in Seveso, Italy, in 1976 also showed no pattern, except pregnant women deliberately aborting their babies in fear of predicted birth defects. The lack of evidence did not deter environmental journalists at the time. Luckily for them, their fabrications were recently given substance by a newly emerging number of soft-tissue cancers in the exposed populations.

Despite such chance rescues, endless hollow claims of disaster in the 1970s and 1980s have invited a conservative backlash. Environmentalists have been wrong so many times that conservatives have stopped listening. They glibly dismissed the discoveries in 1992 that dioxin-like chemicals bind to important sites within animal cells (including human cells). There the chemicals exert their influence by slightly depressing the immune system and changing the growth pattern of embryonic cells and sexual development. Many conservatives assume that toxic chemicals are just a liberal bogeyman. The conservative mistake has been to discount any prediction of environmental disaster solely because an environmentalist makes it. . . .

CREATING THE EVENTS THAT CREATE THE NEWS

When the environmental movement cannot write its own news, it knows that dramatic action can dominate the media. A well-crafted image, along with quotable sound bites, often stays with the reader longer than the journalism that surrounds it. If the 1970s counterculture achieved real expertise in any field, it was the creation of the "media event."

The first big media events in the television age were staged by the civil rights movement. These sit-ins and marches were actual events in which victims of social injustices went face to face with their opponents at schools, swimming pools, restaurants, hotels, movie theaters, and parks. In contrast, most counterculture protests in the 1970s were symbolic or ritualistic media events.

The biggest media event of the environmental movement came in 1992, when it orchestrated the agenda for the star-studded Earth Summit in Rio de Janeiro. The summit was officially planned by the United Nations as the Conference on Environment and Development, but the meetings and background papers that determined the course of the summit were dominated by activists and politicians rather than scientists.

The goal was to create a conference of such great import that world leaders could not refuse to come. Interior Secretary Bruce Babbitt understood the process: "Gradually the process took on a life of its own, making it impossible for political leaders to ignore." More than one hundred presidents, prime ministers, and other high officials came, legitimizing the politicization of science and guaranteeing enormous media exposure. Environmental activists made sure the media had a veritable circus of symbolic entertainments.

The assumptions of the summit mirrored those of the environmental movement. Global warming, along with the guilt of the rich, was accepted as the cause of the problems of the poor. The official document issued after the summit says, "The poor are often the victims of environmental stresses caused by actions of the rich." Poor nations and rich environmentalists agreed that the first step toward a solution is for the industrialized countries to transfer a large portion of their wealth to poor nations.

The giant media event memorialized its success in *Agenda 21*, edited by the lawyer Daniel Sitarz, another of the huge volumes that the movement produces periodically as a comprehensive guide for public opinion. At the beginning of the modern environmental movement, the document was the Club of Rome's computer fantasy, *The Limits to Growth*, with its clumsy computer models projecting past trends into the future as if nothing could ever change. In 1980, the big shocker was Gerald Barney's *Global 2000 Report to the President*, which predicted worldwide catastrophe by the end of the century. President Carter made the report a centerpiece of environmental diplomacy. *Time* and *Newsweek* ran full-page articles. Four years later, a meticulous exposé of the report's cooked numbers, shaky sources, and bad science, *The Resourceful Earth*, edited by the economists Julian Simon and Herman Kahn, received little attention. In our society, messengers bearing bad news become heroes and heroines. Messengers bearing good news are ignored.

As environmentalists began their massive public relations campaign for the Rio summit, many scientists recognized that propaganda was again about to be passed off as science. They saw that committees meeting to prepare the summit's agenda had few scientists, and those who were included were seldom specialists in the area being discussed. The chemist Michel Salomon helped organize a group of scientists to warn world leaders and opinion makers that the Rio summit would have noble motives, eloquent speeches, and a distinct antiscientific bias.

Salomon and other scientists staged an event of their own to demonstrate how scientists approach such problems as global warming, ozone thinning, and hazardous chemicals. In April, some fifty scientists from different disciplines gathered in Heidelberg to discuss the management of hazardous substances. Discussion inevitably turned to the upcoming Rio conference.

The scientists adopted the Heidelberg Appeal to Heads of States and Governments. The statement, eventually signed by more than eight hundred scientists, including sixty-two Nobel Prize winners, endorsed the summit's concern for the poor and its call for science to address social problems. However, the scientists warned "authorities in charge of our planet's destiny against decisions which are supported by pseudo-scientific arguments or false and non-relevant data." The Heidelberg Appeal names no names, calls for no money, and predicts no catastrophes. Its signers were not asked by the press to comment on the Rio summit or to appear on the news and talk shows reporting on summit events and conclusions.

CHILDREN AND EDUCATION

If environmental groups talk about any one reason for saving the planet, that reason is children, the future generations. The long-term dimension of their advocacy journalism is advocacy education.

Advocacy education about the environment takes two paths. One is political vaccination, which assumes that children should be given truth, so that when they begin to learn how to ask questions and do scientific experiments, they will already know the answers. The second is "keep 'em primitive." In other words, don't let them lose those childhood fantasies. Encourage them to talk to trees and to think of animals as their equals who just never learned to speak human language.

The political vaccination takes the form of a catechism. While the environmental movement is too sophisticated to require rote memorization of something like "two legs bad, four legs good" (the slogan of the ruling pigs in Orwell's *Animal Farm*), several "truths" appear over and over in children's lessons, television, and books. They include:

1) Recycling is always good.
2) Forests are disappearing, development is the bad guy.
3) Global warming threatens life on earth.
4) Greed causes environmental problems.
5) Nature is always right.
6) Primitive people were smarter managers of nature than we are.

Putting aside the question of truth, I wonder how kind or smart it is to scare the hell out of little kids. Four of these six messages are scary. Even if all of these messages were true, telling children about dangers they cannot avoid is a form of child abuse. At times, we do not even tell adult hospital patients all the bad news about their illness.

Even religious people who threaten children with burning in hell are at least talking about another world, one for which they have not yet booked a ticket. We may teach children the Ten Commandments and expect them to accept those rules before they can fully understand the reasons, but at least a child can intuitively understand such maxims as "Thou shall not murder" and "Thou shall honor thy father and mother." Children know pain hurts. And they understand that someone besides themselves must run the household. Our society has no serious quarrel with the Ten Commandments. But the commandments and truths of environmental education are subject to a lot of qualifications. Consider how some of them are taught and what the facts are.

Recycling

"Thou shall recycle" could stand a lot of important qualifiers that young children cannot understand and older children seldom get the chance to consider. From teachers' guides to EPA's education program, students of all ages are taught recycling as a commandment, not as an option for solving environmental problems. In fact, recycling frequently costs more than it saves, and while it usually preserves resources, it sometimes wastes them. For example, the use of reusable cloth diapers may save trees, but it also wastes energy through both production and repeated washing. Further, cleaning requires lots of water and detergents. The local sewage plant must increase its capacity and chemical use. Recycling paper also saves trees, but the chemicals necessary to remove ink and stains create more pollutants than the chemicals used to process new wood.

Both children and adults hear over and over again that we are running out of landfill space. The popular children's book *Fifty Simple Things Kids Can Do to Save the Earth* has sold almost a million copies and claims that "we are making so much garbage that in many places there is not enough room to bury it all." But most garbage does not pollute. It consists of paper, yard clippings, stumps, dirt, concrete, tin, aluminum, and plastic. We are not running out of space at all. The problem is more economic and psychological. Who wants to live near a dump? And how much will we have to pay to haul garbage to a dump site?

Environmental education does not teach thinking; rather, it teaches obedience to unelected, uncriticized authority. This is the kind of education that should be reserved for basic religious and social values such as the Ten Commandments and civil rights, concepts about which there can be little doubt. John Javna, the author of *Fifty Simple Things,* estimates that children send him 10,000 letters a year. Javna told the *Wall Street Journal* that "he detects an almost religious fervor."

Forests Are Disappearing

Popular books and movies such as *Fern Gully* tell kids that the bad guys are aiming to clear every last tree from the face of the earth and there are only a few left. The message about the spotted owl forests of the Northwest is that it is now or never to save the last old-growth rain forests north of the tropics. Everywhere else developers are also paving over paradise and forests are vanishing. Almost all of these claims are highly exaggerated or simply false.

About redwoods and old growth, we hear only that the last 10 percent is about to be cut. The last 10 percent of what? Untouchable national parks contain millions of acres, including 109,000 in Redwood, 403,000 in Sequoia, 2.2 million in Yellowstone, almost a million in Olympic, and 235,000 in Mount Rainier. Washington State claims 2.5 million acres of public park, forest, and other land locked away as officially protected wilderness. Oregon has 2 million. The proper questions about old growth are how much should we preserve, where, and why?

From Pennsylvania to Maine, we now have more forests than we had fifty years ago, and the tree cover is increasing. A large part of the reason for this increase is that we have replaced the horse on farms and roads with tractors, autos, buses, and trucks. Every horse and mule used for power required some two to three acres of cleared pasture land. Even in Europe, where children are told that air pollution has created "forest death" or *waldsterben,* scientists have found what journalists and textbook writers do not want to hear—forests are expanding. A Finnish study of Europe's trees found that between 1971 and 1990, growth increased by 30 percent and would probably continue to increase.

The point is not to say pollution is harmless. It could already be weakening forests. The point is that in the real world, nature is a very complex and interesting system. In the world of eco-education, nature is simple and human beings are simple-minded saints and devils. We are not educating children to solve real problems.

Plastics Are Bad for the Environment

When I was working with my Episcopal diocese on environmental issues, I asked why everyone was so dead set against Styrofoam cups. The ready answer: because they are plastic, made with harmful chemicals, and use up landfill space. *Fifty Simple Things* encourages kids to "stamp out Styrofoam" because "using Styrofoam means using up precious resources . . . and adding more garbage to our world."

What educators should be doing is teaching students how to analyze choices between plastics and, say, paper. That's science, not propaganda. When *Science* reported such an analysis, the chemist Martin Hocking considered the energy used in production, the landscape impact of getting the raw materials, air pollution, recycling costs, and greenhouse gases. Among other things, he found the following:

- Foam cups require a sixth of the amount of nonrecycled chemicals in production.
- "The paper cup consumes about 12 times as much steam, 36 times as much electricity, and twice as much cooling water."
- The greenhouse gas effect of a foam cup's pentane is less than that of the methane released by a landfilled paper cup.

A more appropriate message to children about this subject might be that substituting synthetics for natural products is a strategy that sometimes saves more than it destroys. We are fortunate to have choices.

Pesticides Are Unnecessary and Deadly

Many chemicals used to kill bugs, fungi, and weeds can also kill or harm people, especially in large doses. If one day we can grow crops without them, it will be because we have genetically engineered plants to produce their own internal pesticides.

Although organic gardening has contributed to a reduction in the use of pesticides, not a single study shows that its methods could produce food to feed the world. Children need to know that in large quantities pesticides are poisonous, but that they are necessary in safe quantities. They also need to understand that plants produce natural pesticides, many of which cause cancer in high doses. The choice is not between a chemical-free organic world and a toxic world. The choice is between the skillful use of chemicals and costly fear.

One of the older examples of this nonsense is that cedar wood is nature's safe way to prevent moths from eating wool clothes. First, cedar does not prevent moths from eating clothes unless the cedar makes a box or closet that can be tightly sealed against the entry of moths. Metal would do just as well, although perhaps moth larvae already in the clothes are weakened by the cedar aroma. Second, as far as I know, the aromatic chemicals in cedar are no more kindly to humans than the compounds in moth balls. Red cedar smells nice, but whenever I cut it or sand it, I am seized by violent sneezing, stuffed sinuses, and running eyes. Do I really want to spend one-third of each day sleeping in a room where the closet gives off a constant low-level stream of such powerful chemicals?

Corporations Destroy, Environmentalists Save

The greatest purveyor of this idea is the movies, and its most successful practitioner for children is Steven Spielberg, the director who never grew up and accepted the complexity of the world in which children must eventually live.

In *Jurassic Park,* the message is not that people can be corrupted, but that science and industry are corrupt by definition: science, because it has no heart, corporations, because their purpose is to make money. In the movie, Spielberg turns scientists against their own profession, a most persuasive trick. The paleobotanist played by Laura Dern tells the park's designer, "You can't control nature!" The hip mathematician spouting one-liners about chaos theory says that science is "a violent, penetrative act." In other words, scientists rape nature just like other bad guys.

Carrying on in the tradition of Rousseau, Wordsworth, and Thoreau, environmental movie makers have paired the industry's early sentimentalism about nature (à la *Bambi*) with stereotyped symbols of evil—scientists, businessmen, and lawyers.

Children must be taught to recognize evil, of course. Great religious literature has done this quite well. The difference between Hollywood environmentalism and the Koran, the Talmud, or the Bible is that the sacred books do not teach that particular professions (other than prostitution and thievery) are evil. A rich man may have great difficulty entering heaven, but not because he is inherently evil. Discussing the power of the movie industry, the English professor Carol Muske Dukes said:

> Whether the next generation uses Big Science to our ultimate benefit or detriment may well come down to one question: Which applied science has a better chance of manipulating our images of the future, gene-splicing or big-screen special effects? Think fast. You have exactly three minutes before the planet blows up.

It is hard to judge the consequences of simple-minded environmentalism on education and what students will do in a few years when they become voters, governors, legislators, and presidents. Lenin is supposed to have said, "Give us the child for eight years and it will be a Bolshevik forever." But perhaps he was no wiser about children than about the wonders of communism. When reality eventually erodes the last supports of false idols, they often collapse in harmless dust.

It is one thing to present recycling and organically grown foods as interesting new choices, and something else entirely to present them as proven solutions that eight-year-olds must accept on faith. Most environmental educators with wide influence leave no doubt that they are promoting "truths" rather than curiosity or science.

Mike Weilbacher, a Philadelphia news broadcaster, rejoices that the annual Earth Day sets the tone for America's environmental education: "It is a day of extremes, for mourning and dancing, for educating and advocating, for dressing as a timber wolf and lecturing on global warming. . . . *But mostly, it is a day for kids* [emphasis added]." Weilbacher calls Earth Day "the new children's crusade."

Environmentalism has not yet come under the ban against teaching religion in school, but maybe it should. Earth Day is a good idea, but it has been dedicated to propaganda rather than thinking. It has done what its opponents consistently have failed to do—interest the American public in environmental issues. Naturally, its creators have taken possession of its contents. The former Wisconsin senator Gaylord Nelson, who helped invent Earth Day, says, "Every kid in 12th grade has now been through some kind of Earth Day experience, and they're getting formalized education in increasing numbers."

The young Harvard student who organized the first Earth Day for Nelson was Dennis Hayes, who continues to take part in it. Hayes notes that the environmental movement pays a lot of attention to charismatic animals such as bears, wolves, pandas, and whales, "but there is no more charismatic megafauna than your eight-year-old daughter. Hell, there's nothing someone my age wants more than to be a hero to your child."

Like the consumer product advertisers whom environmentalists despise, they themselves know that the way to sell ideas and products is through children. Hayes says, "Watch out for these kids; they may be the fourth wave, washing in on the rising tide of environmentalism, pulled by the gravity of Earth Day."

QUESTIONS FOR DISCUSSION
Environmental Ethics

1. Do future generations have claim rights against us? Do nonexisting beings have any rights at all; that is, do we have any moral obligations toward them? Why or why not? If we do, how strong are those obligations, and how do they compare to the obligations, discussed in the previous chapter, to relieve the sufferings of people who live now?

2. What evidence does Al Gore cite to prove that global warming is a serious problem? What evidence does Wallace Kaufman cite in opposition? Which argument is more persuasive, and why?

3. Does Kaufman agree with Gore that the forests are disappearing, thus reducing the needed oxygen they generate and extinguishing many species of birds? What counterevidence does he offer?

4. What is Kaufman's argument against the value of recycling waste? Why does he think organic produce, which does not employ insecticides, does more harm than good?

5. Even if Kaufman has stronger evidence against environmentalist policies than Gore has in favor of them, is there good reason to "play it safe" by adopting some of these policies on the grounds that (1) if not adopting them can possibly result in the disasters prophesized by environmentalists, it will be too late to change, whereas (2) if they are adopted and prove unnecessary, we will be free to abandon them? Or does the fact that the threatened catastrophes will harm only our descendants weigh heavily against paying the high price such policies will cost? Defend your response.

SELECTED READINGS

BAIER, K. "Justice and Procreation." *Journal of Social Philosophy,* ____ 1991.

BARRY, B., and R. SIKORA. *Obligations to Future Generations.* Philadelphia: Temple University Press, 1978.

COOPER, D., and J. PALMER. *The Environment in Question.* New York: Routledge, 1992.

DESHALIT, A. "Community and the Rights of Future Generations." *Journal of Applied Philosophy,* ____ 1992.

MARSHALL, P. "Thinking for Tomorrow." *Journal of Applied Philosophy,* ____ 1993.

PARFIT, D. *Reasons and Persons.* New York: Oxford University Press, 1987.

PARTRIDGE, E., ed. *Responsibilities to Future Generations.* Buffalo: Prometheus, 1981.

RAWLS, J. *A Theory of Justice,* section 44. Cambridge, MA: Harvard University Press, 1971.

SCHERER, D., ed. *Upstream, Downstream: Issues in Environmental Ethics.* Philadelphia: Temple University Press, 1990.

8

PRIVACY AND ITS LIMITS

One of the most bitterly disputed issues of political philosophy is where to draw the line between government power and individual liberty. What may society legitimately require of its members, and what must it leave to their personal initiative? In his classic work, *On Liberty*, John Stuart Mill draws that line in a clear and simple way that has influenced many people. He distinguishes the "private domain" of individual liberty, where, except for vital emergencies, the state should never interfere, from the "public domain," which is the proper domain of governmental regulation. He defines the private domain as all those personal actions that directly and seriously affect only the person who performs them, and the public domain as all activities that seriously affect other people. Over the latter area, he asserts, "society has jurisdiction . . . and the question whether the general welfare will or will not be promoted by interfering with it becomes open to discussion."

As Gerald Dworkin points out in the second selection in this chapter, Mill offers two main arguments for his division between these two domains: a utilitarian argument consistent with his general ethical theory, and a deontological argument that appeals to a right of privacy and personal autonomy. The utilitarian argument, although plausible, is of course open to refutation, because it depends on all sorts of variable factors whether an interference in the private domain works out for the better or for the worse. (For example, at present many people are arguing heatedly over whether the U.S. government is justified in secretly monitoring telephone calls and e-mail in its effort to uncover terrorist plots.) Mill argues that it is to the long-run benefit of society that its members be entrusted to make their own decisions and even to make their own mistakes, from which they can learn to do better. Moreover, each individual knows what is in his or her own interest better than any government officials and therefore will, on the whole, make better decisions affecting only himself than those imposed by the government.

Mill's deontological argument is that a person has an unimpeachable right to act in accordance with his own conception of what is best for him, because that is what it means to be an autonomous person rather than a slave. The one exception Mill allows to noninterference in the private domain is that the state may forbid a citizen to indenture himself or herself to servitude, which destroys the very autonomy that defines the private domain. Aside from this exception, any interference by the state on the grounds that it is protecting people from harming themselves is denounced as paternalism—treating adults as if they were children.

Gerald Dworkin agrees with Mill's utilitarian argument that *in general* it is best for society to grant its members autonomy of action that is clearly not harmful to others, but he argues that many exceptions can and should be made to this general rule—many more than the one acknowledged by Mill. As for the second, more stringent argument based on the right of privacy, the wealth of exceptions Dworkin points to shows, he claims, that this deontological position of Mill is mistaken and, indeed, inconsistent with Mill's utilitarian ethics. Dworkin offers a list of paternalistic laws—such as requiring motorcycle helmets, prohibiting the sale of harmful drugs, protecting the consumer from fraudulent advertising, and compelling workers to save through Social Security—that he considers justified limitations on individual liberty.

David Richards defends the more thoroughly libertarian position of Mill against the paternalistic view of Dworkin, with particular reference to what most people believe is justified interference in the private domain: the prohibition of drugs deemed to be dangerous and addictive. Richards, following Mill, considers this "war on drugs" to be seriously mistaken. He notes that not all dangerous drugs are forbidden (e.g., tobacco and alcohol). Which drugs are and which are not prohibited by law seems to depend more on successful bribery of officials and on majority social habits than on how dangerous they are to one's health. In any case, if people want to take great risks (e.g., free-fall parachuting, rock climbing, bungee jumping, or using drugs) for the sake of enhanced perception, or amusement, or curiosity, they should have that freedom in a democratic society that respects privacy and individual autonomy.

THE PRIVATE DOMAIN

John Stuart Mill

What, then, is the rightful limit to the sovereignty of the individual over him-self? Where does the authority of society begin? How much of human life should be assigned to individuality, and how much to society?

Each will receive its proper share if each has that which more particu-larly concerns it. To individuality should belong the part of life in which it is chiefly the individual that is interested; to society, the part which chiefly in-terests society.

Though society is not founded on a contract, and though no good pur-pose is answered by inventing a contract in order to deduce social obliga-tions from it, everyone who receives the protection of society owes a return for the benefit, and the fact of living in society renders it indispensable that each should be bound to observe a certain line of conduct toward the rest. This conduct consists, first, in not injuring the interests of one another, or rather certain interests which, either by express legal provision or by tacit understanding, ought to be considered as rights; and secondly, in each per-son's bearing his share (to be fixed on some equitable principle) of the labors and sacrifices incurred for defending the society or its members from injury and molestation. These conditions society is justified in enforcing at all costs to those who endeavor to withhold fulfillment. Nor is this all that society may do. The acts of an individual may be hurtful to others or want-ing in due consideration for their welfare, without going to the length of vi-olating any of their constituted rights. The offender may then be justly punished by opinion, though not by law. As soon as any part of a person's conduct affects prejudicially the interests of others, society has jurisdiction over it, and the question whether the general welfare will or will not be pro-moted by interfering with it becomes open to discussion. But there is no room for entertaining any such question when a person's conduct affects the interests of no persons besides himself, or needs not affect them unless they like (all the persons concerned being of full age and the ordinary amount of understanding). In all such cases, there should be perfect freedom, legal and social, to do the action and stand the consequences.

It would be a great misunderstanding of this doctrine to suppose that it is one of selfish indifference which pretends that human beings have no busi-ness with each other's conduct in life, and that they should not concern them-selves about the well-doing or well-being of one another, unless their own interest is involved. Instead of any diminution, there is need of a great increase of disinterested exertion to promote the good of others. But disinterested

From *On Liberty*, first published in 1859.

benevolence can find other instruments to persuade people to their good than whips and scourges, either of the literal or the metaphysical sort. I am the last person to undervalue the self-regarding virtues; they are only second in importance, if even second, to the social. It is equally the business of education to cultivate both. But even education works by conviction and persuasion as well as by compulsion, and it is by the former only that, when the period of education is passed, the self-regarding virtues should be inculcated. Human beings owe to each other help to distinguish the better from the worse, and encouragement to choose the former and avoid the latter. They should be forever stimulating each other to increased exercise of their higher faculties and increased direction of their feelings and aims toward wise instead of foolish, elevating instead of degrading, objects and contemplations. But neither one person, nor any number of persons, is warranted in saying to another human creature of ripe years that he shall not do with his life for his own benefit what he chooses to do with it. He is the person most interested in his own well-being: the interest which any other person, except in cases of strong personal attachment, can have in it is trifling compared with that which he himself has; the interest which society has in him individually (except as to his conduct to others) is fractional and altogether indirect, while with respect to his own feelings and circumstances the most ordinary man or woman has means of knowledge immeasurably surpassing those that can be possessed by anyone else. The interference of society to overrule his judgment and purposes in what only regards himself must be grounded on general presumptions which may be altogether wrong and, even if right, are as likely as not to be misapplied to individual cases, by persons no better acquainted with the circumstances of such cases than those who look at them merely from without. In this department, therefore, of human affairs, individuality has its proper field of action. In the conduct of human beings toward one another it is necessary that general rules should for the most part be observed in order that people may know what they have to expect; but in each person's own concerns his individual spontaneity is entitled to free exercise. Considerations to aid his judgment, exhortations to strengthen his will may be offered to him, even obtruded on him, by others; but he himself is the final judge. All errors which he is likely to commit against advice and warning are far outweighed by the evil of allowing others to constrain him to what they deem his good.

I do not mean that the feelings with which a person is regarded by others ought not to be in any way affected by his self-regarding qualities or deficiencies. This is neither possible nor desirable. If he is eminent in any of the qualities which conduce to his own good, he is, so far, a proper object of admiration. He is so much the nearer to the ideal perfection of human nature. If he is grossly deficient in those qualities, a sentiment the opposite of admiration will follow. There is a degree of folly, and a degree of what may be called (though the phrase is not unobjectionable) lowness or depravation of taste, which, though it cannot justify doing harm to the person who manifests it, renders him necessarily and properly a subject of distaste, or, in extreme cases, even of contempt: a person could not have the opposite qualities in due strength without entertaining these feelings. Though doing no wrong to anyone, a person may so act as to compel us to judge him, and feel to him, as a fool or as a being of an inferior order; and since this judgment and feeling are a fact which he would prefer to avoid, it is doing him a service to warn him of it beforehand, as of any other disagreeable consequence to which he exposes himself. It would be well, indeed, if this good office were much more freely rendered than the common notions of politeness at present permit, and if one person could honestly point out to another that he thinks him in fault, without being considered unmannerly or presuming. We have a right, also, in various ways, to act upon our unfavorable opinion of anyone, not to the oppression of his individuality, but in the exercise of ours. We are not bound, for example, to seek his society; we have a right to avoid it (though not to parade the avoidance), for we have a right to choose the society most acceptable to us. We have a right, and it may be our duty, to caution others against him if we think his example or conversation likely to have a pernicious effect on those with whom he associates. We may give others a preference over him in optional good offices, except those which tend to his improvement. In these various modes a person may suffer very severe penalties at the hands of others for faults which directly concern only himself; but he suffers these penalties only in so far as they are the natural and, as it were, the spontaneous consequences of the faults themselves, not because they are purposely inflicted on him for the sake of punishment. A person who shows rashness, obstinacy, self-conceit—who cannot live within moderate means; who cannot restrain himself from hurtful indulgence; who pursues animal pleasures at the expense of those of feeling and intellect—must expect to be lowered in the opinion of others, and to have a less share of their favorable sentiments; but of this he has no right to complain unless he has merited their favor by special excellence in his social relations and has thus established a title to their good offices, which is not affected by his demerits toward himself.

What I contend for is that the inconveniences which are strictly inseparable from the unfavorable judgment of others are the only ones to which a person should ever be subjected for that portion of his conduct and character which concerns his own good, but which does not affect the interest of others in their relations with him. Acts injurious to others require a totally different treatment. Encroachment on their rights; infliction on them of any loss or damage not justified by his own rights; falsehood or duplicity in dealing with them; unfair or ungenerous use of advantages over them; even selfish abstinence from defending them against injury—these are fit objects of moral reprobation and, in grave cases, of moral retribution and punishment. And not only these acts, but the dispositions which lead to them, are properly immoral and fit subjects of disapprobation which may rise to abhorrence. Cruelty of disposition; malice and ill-nature; that most antisocial and odious of all passions, envy; dissimulation and insincerity, irascibility on insufficient cause, and resentment disproportionate to the provocation; the love of domineering over others; the desire to engross more than one's share of advantages (the *pleonexia* of the Greeks); the pride which derives gratification from the abasement of others; the egotism which thinks self and its concerns more important than everything else, and decides all doubtful questions in its own favor—these are moral vices and constitute a bad and odious moral character; unlike the self-regarding faults previously mentioned, which are not properly immoralities and, to whatever pitch they may be carried, do not constitute wickedness. They may be proofs of any amount of folly or want of personal dignity and self-respect, but they are only a subject of moral reprobation when they involve a breach of duty to others, for whose sake the individual is bound to have care for himself. What are called duties to ourselves are not socially obligatory unless circumstances render them at the same time duties to others. The term duty to oneself, when it means anything more than prudence, means self-respect or self-development, and for none of these is anyone accountable to his fellow creatures, because for none of them is it for the good of mankind that he be held accountable to them.

The distinction between the loss of consideration which a person may rightly incur by defect of prudence or of personal dignity, and the reprobation which is due to him for an offense against the rights of others, is not a merely nominal distinction. It makes a vast difference both in our feelings and in our conduct toward him whether he displeases us in things in which we think we have a right to control him or in things in which we know that we have not. If he displeases us, we may express our distaste, and we may stand aloof from a person as well as from a thing that displeases us; but we shall not therefore feel called on to make his life uncomfortable. We shall reflect that he already bears, or will bear, the whole penalty of his error; if he spoils his life by mismanagement, we shall not, for that reason, desire to spoil it still further; instead of wishing to punish him, we shall rather endeavor to alleviate his punishment by showing him how he may avoid or cure the evils his conduct tends to bring upon him. He may be to us an object of pity, perhaps of dislike, but not of anger or resentment; we shall not treat him like an enemy of society; the worst we shall think ourselves justified in doing is leaving him to himself, if we do not interfere benevolently by showing interest or concern for him. It is far otherwise if he has infringed the rules necessary for the protection of his fellow creatures, individually or collectively. The evil consequences of his acts do not then fall on himself, but on others; and society, as the protector of all its members, must retaliate on him, must inflict pain on him for the express purpose of punishment, and must take care that it be sufficiently severe. In the one case, he is an offender at our bar, and we are called on not only to sit in judgment on him, but, in one shape or another, to execute our own sentence; in the other case, it is not our part to inflict any suffering on him, except what may incidentally follow from our using the same liberty in the regulation of our own affairs which we allow to him in his.

The distinction here pointed out between the part of a person's life which concerns only himself and that which concerns others, many persons will refuse to admit. How (it may be asked) can any part of the conduct of a member of society be a matter of indifference to the other members? No person is an entirely isolated being; it is impossible for a person to do anything seriously or permanently hurtful to himself without mischief reaching at least to his near connections, and often far beyond them. If he injures his property, he does harm to those who directly or indirectly derived support from it, and usually diminishes, by a greater or less amount, the general resources of the community. If he deteriorates his bodily or mental faculties, he not only brings evil upon all who depended on him for any portion of their happiness, but disqualifies himself for rendering the services which he owes to his fellow creatures generally, perhaps becomes a burden on their affection or benevolence; and if such conduct were very frequent hardly any offense that is committed would detract more from the general sum of good. Finally, if by his vices or follies a person does no direct harm to others, he is nevertheless (it may be said) injurious by his example, and ought to be compelled to control himself for the sake of those whom the sight or knowledge of his conduct might corrupt or mislead.

And even (it will be added) if the consequences of misconduct could be confined to the vicious or thoughtless individual, ought society to abandon to their own guidance those who are manifestly unfit for it? If protection against themselves is confessedly due to children and persons under age, is not society equally bound to afford it to persons of mature years who are equally incapable of self-government? If gambling, or drunkenness, or incontinence, or idleness, or uncleanliness are as injurious to happiness, and as great a hindrance to improvement, as many or most of the acts prohibited by law, why (it may be asked) should not law, as far as is consistent with practicability and social convenience, endeavor to repress these also? And as a supplement to the unavoidable imperfections of law, ought not opinion at least to organize a powerful police against these vices and visit rigidly with social penalties those who are known to practice them? There is no question here (it may be said) about restricting individuality, or impeding the trial of new and original experiments in living. The only things it is sought to prevent are things which have been tried and condemned from the beginning of the world until now—things which experience has shown not to be useful or suitable to any person's individuality. There must be some length of time and amount of experience after which a moral or prudential truth may be regarded as established; and it is merely desired to prevent generation after generation from falling over the same precipice which has been fatal to their predecessors.

I fully admit that the mischief which a person does to himself may seriously affect, both through their sympathies and their interests, those nearly connected with him and, in a minor degree, society at large. When, by conduct of this sort, a person is led to violate a distinct and assignable obligation to any other person or persons, the case is taken out of the self-regarding class and becomes amenable to moral disapprobation in the proper sense of the term. If, for example, a man, through intemperance or extravagance, becomes unable to pay his debts, or, having undertaken the moral responsibility of a family, becomes from the same cause incapable of supporting or educating them, he is deservedly reprobated and might be justly punished; but it is for the breach of duty to his family or creditors, not for the extravagance. If the resources which ought to have been devoted to them had been diverted from them for the most prudent investment, the moral culpability would have been the same. George Barnwell murdered his uncle to get money for his mistress, but if he had done it to set himself up in business, he would equally have been hanged. Again, in the frequent case of a man who causes grief to his family by addiction to bad habits, he deserves reproach for his unkindness or ingratitude; but so he may for cultivating habits not in themselves vicious, if they are painful to those with whom he passes his life, or who from personal ties are dependent on him for their comfort. Whoever fails in the consideration generally due to the interests and feelings of others, not being compelled by some more imperative duty, or justified by allowable self-preference, is a subject of moral disapprobation for that failure, but not for the cause of it, nor for the errors, merely personal to himself, which may have remotely led to it. In like manner, when a person disables himself, by conduct purely self-regarding, from the performance of some definite duty incumbent on him to the public, he is guilty of a social offense. No person ought to be punished simply for being drunk; but a soldier or a policeman should be punished for being drunk on duty. Whenever, in short, there is a definite damage, or a definite risk of damage, either to an individual or to the public, the case is taken out of the province of liberty and placed in that of morality or law. . . .

But the strongest of all the arguments against the interference of the public with purely personal conduct is that, when it does interfere, the odds are that it interferes wrongly and in the wrong place. On questions of social morality, of duty to others, the opinion of the public, that is, of an overruling majority, though often wrong, is likely to be still oftener right, because on such questions they are only required to judge of their own interests, of the manner in which some mode of conduct, if allowed to be practiced, would affect themselves. But the opinion of a similar majority, imposed as a law on the minority, on questions of self-regarding conduct is quite as likely to be wrong as right, for in these cases public opinion means, at the best, some people's opinion of what is good or bad for other people, while very often it does not even mean that—the public, with the most perfect indifference, passing over the pleasure or convenience of those whose conduct they censure and considering only their own preference. There are many who consider as an injury to themselves any conduct which they have a distaste for, and resent it as an outrage to their feelings; as a religious bigot, when charged with disregarding the religious feelings of others, has been known to retort that they disregard his feelings by persisting in their abominable worship or creed. But there is not parity between the feeling of a person for his own opinion and the feeling of another who is offended at his holding it, no more than between the desire of a thief to take a purse and the desire of the right owner to keep it. And a person's taste is as much his own peculiar concern as his opinion or his purse. It is easy for anyone to imagine

an ideal public which leaves the freedom and choice of individuals in all uncertain matters undisturbed and only requires them to abstain from modes
of conduct which universal experience has condemned. But where has there
been seen a public which set any such limit to its censorship? Or when does
the public trouble itself about universal experience? In its interferences with
personal conduct it is seldom thinking of anything but the enormity of acting or feeling differently from itself; and this standard of judgment, thinly disguised, is held up to mankind as the dictate of religion and philosophy by
nine-tenths of all moralists and speculative writers. These teach that things
are right because they are right; because we feel them to be so. They tell us
to search in our own minds and hearts for laws of conduct binding on ourselves and on all others. What can the poor public do but apply these instructions and make their own personal feelings of good and evil, if they are
tolerably unanimous in them, obligatory on all the world?

The evil here pointed out is not one which exists only in theory; and it
may perhaps be expected that I should specify the instances in which the
public of this age and country improperly invests its own preferences with
the character of moral laws. I am not writing an essay on the aberrations of
existing moral feeling. That is too weighty a subject to be discussed parenthetically, and by way of illustration. Yet examples are necessary to show that
the principle I maintain is of serious and practical moment, and that I am not
endeavoring to erect a barrier against imaginary evils. And it is not difficult
to show, by abundant instances, that to extend the bounds of what may be
called moral police until it encroaches on the most unquestionably legitimate liberty of the individual is one of the most universal of all human
propensities.

As a first instance, consider the antipathies which men cherish on no
better grounds than that persons whose religious opinions are different from
theirs do not practice their religious observances, especially their religious
abstinences. To cite a rather trivial example, nothing in the creed or practice
of Christians does more to envenom the hatred of Mohammedans against
them than the fact of their eating pork. There are few acts which Christians
and Europeans regard with more unaffected disgust than Mussulmans regard
this particular mode of satisfying hunger. It is in the first place, an offense
against their religion; but this circumstance by no means explains either the
degree or the kind of their repugnance; for wine also is forbidden by their
religion, and to partake of it is by all Mussulmans accounted wrong, but not
disgusting. Their aversion to the flesh of the "unclean beast" is, on the contrary, of that peculiar character, resembling an instinctive antipathy, which
the idea of uncleanness, when once it thoroughly sinks into the feelings,
seems always to excite even in those whose personal habits are anything but
scrupulously clean, and of which the sentiment of religious impurity, so intense in the Hindus, is a remarkable example. Suppose now that in a people
of whom the majority were Mussulmans, that majority should insist upon
not permitting pork to be eaten within the limits of the country. This would
be nothing new in Mohammedan countries. Would it be a legitimate exercise

of the moral authority of public opinion, and if not, why not? The practice is really revolting to such a public. They also sincerely think that it is forbidden and abhorred by the Deity. Neither could the prohibition be censured as religious persecution. It might be religious in its origin, but it would not be persecution for religion, since nobody's religion makes it a duty to eat pork. The only tenable ground of condemnation would be that with the personal tastes and self-regarding concerns of individuals the public has no business to interfere.

To come somewhat nearer home: the majority of Spaniards consider it a gross impiety, offensive in the highest degree to the Supreme Being, to worship him in any other manner than the Roman Catholic; and no other public worship is lawful on Spanish soil. The people of all southern Europe look upon a married clergy as not only irreligious, but unchaste, indecent, gross, disgusting. What do Protestants think of these perfectly sincere feelings, and of the attempt to enforce them against non-Catholics? Yet, if mankind are justified in interfering with each other's liberty in things which do not concern the interests of others, on what principle is it possible consistently to exclude these cases? Or who can blame people for desiring to suppress what they regard as a scandal in the sight of God and man? No stronger case can be shown for prohibiting anything which is regarded as a personal immorality than is made out for suppressing these practices in the eyes of those who regard them as impieties; and unless we are willing to adopt the logic of persecutors, and to say that we may persecute others because we are right, and that they must not persecute us because they are wrong, we must beware of admitting a principle of which we should resent as a gross injustice the application to ourselves.

The preceding instances may be objected to, although unreasonably, as drawn from contingencies impossible among us—opinion, in this country, not being likely to enforce abstinence from meats or to interfere with people for worshipping and for either marrying or not marrying, according to their creed or inclination. The next example, however, shall be taken from an interference with liberty which we have by no means passed all danger of. Wherever the Puritans have been sufficiently powerful, as in New England, and in Great Britain at the time of the Commonwealth, they have endeavored, with considerable success, to put down all public, and nearly all private, amusements: especially music, dancing, public games, or other assemblages for purposes of diversion, and the theater. There are still in this country large bodies of persons by whose notions of morality and religion these recreations are condemned; and those persons belonging chiefly to the middle class, who are the ascendant power in the present social and political condition of the kingdom, it is by no means impossible that persons of these sentiments may at some time or other command a majority in Parliament. How will the remaining portion of the community like to have the amusements that shall be permitted to them regulated by the religious and moral sentiments of the stricter Calvinists and Methodists? Would they not, with considerable peremptoriness, desire these intrusively pious members of society to mind their own business? This is precisely what should be said to every government and every public who have the pretension that no person shall enjoy any pleasure which they think wrong. But if the principle of the pretension be admitted, no one can reasonably object to its being acted on in the sense of the majority, or other preponderating power in the country; and all persons must be ready to conform to the idea of a Christian commonwealth as understood by the early settlers in New England, if a religious profession similar to theirs should ever succeed in regaining its lost ground, as religions supposed to be declining have so often been known to do.

To imagine another contingency, perhaps more likely to be realized than the one last mentioned. There is confessedly a strong tendency in the modern world toward a democratic constitution of society, accompanied or not by popular political institutions. It is affirmed that in the country where this tendency is most completely realized—where both society and the government are most democratic: the United States—the feeling of the majority, to whom any appearance of a more showy or costly style of living than they can hope to rival is disagreeable, operates as a tolerably effectual sumptuary law, and that in many parts of the Union it is really difficult for a person possessing a very large income to find any mode of spending it which will not incur popular disapprobation. Though such statements as these are doubtless much exaggerated as a representation of existing facts, the state of things they describe is not only a conceivable and possible, but a probable result of democratic feeling combined with the notion that the public has a right to a veto on the manner in which individuals shall spend their incomes. We have only further to suppose a considerable diffusion of Socialist opinions, and it may become infamous in the eyes of the majority to possess more property than some very small amount, or any income not earned by manual labor. Opinions similar in principle to these already prevail widely among the artisan class and weigh oppressively on those who are amenable to the opinion chiefly of that class, namely, its own members. It is known that the bad workmen who form the majority of the operatives in many branches of industry are decidedly of the opinion that bad workmen ought to receive the same wages as good, and that no one ought to be allowed, through piecework or otherwise, to earn by superior skill or industry more than others can without it. And they employ a moral police, which occasionally becomes a physical one, to deter skillful workmen from receiving, and employers from giving, a larger remuneration for a more useful service. If the public have any jurisdiction over private concerns, I cannot see that these people are in fault, or that any individual's particular public can be blamed for asserting the same authority over his individual conduct which the general public asserts over people in general.

But, without dwelling upon suppositious cases, there are, in our own day, gross usurpations upon the liberty of private life actually practiced, and still greater ones threatened with some expectation of success, and opinions propounded which assert an unlimited right in the public not only to prohibit by law everything which it thinks wrong, but, in order to get at what it thinks wrong, to prohibit a number of things which it admits to be innocent.

Under the name of preventing intemperance, the people of one English colony, and of nearly half the United States, have been interdicted by law from making any use whatever of fermented drinks, except for medical purposes, for prohibition of their sale is in fact, as it is intended to be, prohibition of their use. And though the impracticability of executing the law has caused its repeal in several of the States which had adopted it, including the one from which it derives its name, an attempt has notwithstanding been commenced, and is prosecuted with considerable zeal by many of the professed philanthropists, to agitate for a similar law in this country. The association, or "Alliance," as it terms itself, which has been formed for this purpose, has acquired some notoriety through the publicity given to a correspondence between its secretary and one of the very few English public men who hold that a politician's opinion ought to be founded on principles. Lord Stanley's share in this correspondence is calculated to strengthen the hopes already built on him by those who know how rare such qualities as are manifested in some of his public appearances unhappily are among those who figure in political life. The organ of the Alliance, who would "deeply deplore the recognition of any principle which could be wrested to justify bigotry and persecution," undertakes to point out the "broad and impassable barrier" which divides such principles from those of the association. "All matters relating to thought, opinion, conscience, appear to me," he says, "to be without the sphere of legislation; all pertaining to social act, habit, relation, subject only to a discretionary power vested in the State itself, and not in the individual, to be within it." No mention is made of a third class, different from either of these, viz., acts and habits which are not social, but individual; although it is to this class, surely, that the act of drinking fermented liquors belongs. Selling fermented liquors, however, is trading, and trading is a social act. But the infringement complained of is not on the liberty of the seller, but on that of the buyer and consumer; since the State might just as well forbid him to drink wine as purposely make it impossible for him to obtain it. The secretary, however, says, "I claim, as a citizen, a right to legislate whenever my social rights are invaded by the social act of another." And now for the definition of these "social rights": "If anything invades my social rights, certainly the traffic in strong drink does. It destroys my primary right of security by constantly creating and stimulating social disorder. It invades my right of equality by deriving a profit from the creation of a misery I am taxed to support. It impedes my right to free moral and intellectual development by surrounding my path with dangers and by weakening and demoralizing society, from which I have a right to claim mutual aid and intercourse." A theory of "social rights" the like of which probably never before found its way into distinct language: being nothing short of this—that it is the absolute social right of every individual that every other individual shall act in every respect exactly as he ought; that whosoever fails thereof in the smallest particular violates my social right and entitles me to demand from the legislature the removal of the grievance. So monstrous a principle is far more dangerous than any single interference with liberty; there is no violation of liberty which it would not justify; it acknowledges no right to any freedom whatever, except perhaps to that of holding opinions in secret, without ever disclosing them; for the moment an opinion which I consider noxious passes anyone's lips, it invades all the "social rights" attributed to me by the Alliance. The doctrine ascribes to all mankind a vested interest in each other's moral, intellectual, and even physical perfection, to be defined by each claimant according to his own standard.

Another important example of illegitimate interference with the rightful liberty of the individual, not simply threatened, but long since carried into triumphant effect, is Sabbatarian legislation. Without doubt, abstinence on one day in the week, so far as the exigencies of life permit, from the usual daily occupation, though in no respect religiously binding on any except Jews, is a highly beneficial custom. And inasmuch as this custom cannot be observed without a general consent to that effect among the industrious classes, therefore, in so far as some persons by working may impose the same necessity on others, it may be allowable and right that the law should guarantee to each the observance by others of the custom, by suspending the greater operations of industry on a particular day. But this justification, grounded on the direct interest which others have in each individual's ob-servance of the practice, does not apply to the self-chosen occupations in which a person may think fit to employ his leisure, nor does it hold good, in the smallest degree, for legal restrictions on amusements. It is true that the amusement of some is the day's work of others; but the pleasure, not to say the useful recreation, of many is worth the labor of a few, provided the oc-cupation is freely chosen and can be freely resigned. The operatives are per-fectly right in thinking that if all worked on Sunday, seven days' work would have to be given for six days' wages; but so long as the great mass of em-ployments are suspended, the small number who for the enjoyment of oth-ers must still work to obtain a proportional increase of earnings . . . are not obliged to follow these occupations if they prefer leisure to emolument. If a further remedy is sought, it might be found in the establishment by cus-tom of a holiday on some other day of the week for those particular classes of persons. The only ground, therefore, on which restrictions on Sunday amusements can be defended must be that they are religiously wrong—a motive of legislation which can never be too earnestly protested against. *"Deorum injuriae Diis curae."* It remains to be proved that society or any of its officers holds a commission from on high to avenge any supposed offense to Omnipotence which is not also a wrong to our fellow creatures. The no-tion that it is one man's duty that another should be religious was the foun-dation of all the religious persecutions ever perpetrated, and, if admitted, would fully justify them. Though the feeling which breaks out in the re-peated attempts to stop railway traveling on Sunday, in the resistance to the opening of museums, and the like, has not the cruelty of the old persecutors, the state of mind indicated by it is fundamentally the same. It is a determination not to tolerate others in doing what is permitted by their religion, because it is not permitted by the persecutor's religion. It is a belief that God not only abominates the act of the misbeliever, but will not hold us guiltless if we leave him unmolested.

PATERNALISM

Gerald Dworkin

> *Neither one person, nor any number of persons, is warranted in saying to another human creature of ripe years, that he shall not do with his life for his own benefit what he chooses to do with it.*
>
> —MILL

> *I do not want to go along with a volunteer basis. I think a fellow should be compelled to become better and not let him use his discretion whether he wants to get smarter, more healthy or more honest.*
>
> —GENERAL HERSHEY

I take as my starting point the "one very simple principle" proclaimed by Mill in *On Liberty* . . . "That principle is, that the sole end for which mankind are warranted, individually or collectively, in interfering with the liberty of action of any of their number, is self-protection. That the only purpose for which power can be rightfully exercised over any member of a civilized community, against his will, is to prevent harm to others. He cannot rightfully be compelled to do or forbear because it will be better for him to do so, because it will make him happier, because, in the opinion of others, to do so would be wise, or even right."

This principle is neither "one" nor "very simple." It is at least two principles; one asserting that self-protection or the prevention of harm to others is sometimes a sufficient warrant and the other claiming that the individual's own good is *never* a sufficient warrant for the exercise of compulsion either by the society as a whole or by its individual members. I assume that no one, with the possible exception of extreme pacifists or anarchists, questions the correctness of the first half of the principle. This essay is an examination of the negative claim embodied in Mill's principle—the objection to paternalistic interferences with a man's liberty.

I

By paternalism I shall understand roughly the interference with a person's liberty of action justified by reasons referring exclusively to the welfare, good, happiness, needs, interests or values of the person being coerced. One

---

385

is always well-advised to illustrate one's definitions by examples but it is not easy to find "pure" examples of paternalistic interferences. For almost any piece of legislation is justified by several different kinds of reasons and even if historically a piece of legislation can be shown to have been introduced for purely paternalistic motives, it may be that advocates of the legislation with an anti-paternalistic outlook can find sufficient reasons justifying the legislation without appealing to the reasons which were originally adduced to support it. Thus, for example, it may be that the original legislation requiring motorcyclists to wear safety helmets was introduced for purely paternalistic reasons. But the Rhode Island Supreme Court recently upheld such legislation on the grounds that it was "not persuaded that the legislature is powerless to prohibit individuals from pursuing a course of conduct which could conceivably result in their becoming public charges," thus clearly introducing reasons of a quite different kind. Now I regard this decision as being based on reasoning of a very dubious nature but it illustrates the kind of problem one has in finding examples. The following is a list of the kinds of interferences I have in mind as being paternalistic.

II

1. Laws requiring motorcyclists to wear safety helmets when operating their machines.
2. Laws forbidding persons from swimming at a public beach when lifeguards are not on duty.
3. Laws making suicide a criminal offense.
4. Laws making it illegal for women and children to work at certain types of jobs.
5. Laws regulating certain kinds of sexual conduct, e.g. homosexuality among consenting adults in private.
6. Laws regulating the use of certain drugs which may have harmful consequences to the user but do not lead to antisocial conduct.
7. Laws requiring a license to engage in certain professions with those not receiving a license subject to fine or jail sentence if they do engage in the practice.
8. Laws compelling people to spend a specified fraction of their income on the purchase of retirement annuities (Social Security).
9. Laws forbidding various forms of gambling (often justified on the grounds that the poor are more likely to throw away their money on such activities than the rich who can afford to).
10. Laws regulating the maximum rates of interest for loans.
11. Laws against duelling.

In addition to laws which attach criminal or civil penalties to certain kinds of action there are laws, rules, regulations, decrees which make it either difficult or impossible for people to carry out their plans and which are also justified on paternalistic grounds. Examples of this are:

1. Laws regulating the types of contracts which will be upheld as valid by the courts, e.g. (an example of Mill's to which I shall return) no man may make a valid contract for perpetual involuntary servitude.

2. Not allowing assumption of risk as a defense to an action based on the violation of a safety statute.

3. Not allowing as a defense to a charge of murder or assault the consent of the victim.

4. Requiring members of certain religious sects to have compulsory blood transfusions. This is made possible by not allowing the patient to have recourse to civil suits for assault and battery and by means of injunctions.

5. Civil commitment procedures when these are specifically justified on the basis of preventing the person being committed from harming himself. The D.C. Hospitalization of the Mentally Ill Act provides for involuntary hospitalization of a person who "is mentally ill, and because of that illness, is likely to injure himself or others if allowed to remain at liberty." The term injure in this context applies to unintentional as well as intentional injuries.

All of my examples are of existing restrictions on the liberty of individuals. Obviously one can think of interferences which have not been imposed. Thus one might ban the sale of cigarettes, or require that people wear safety-belts in automobiles (as opposed to merely having them installed), enforcing this by not allowing motorists to sue for injuries even when caused by other drivers if the motorist was not wearing a seatbelt at the time of the accident.

I shall not be concerned with activities which though defended on paternalistic grounds are not interferences with the liberty of persons, e.g. the giving of subsidies in kind rather than in cash on the grounds that the recipients would not spend the money on the goods which they really need, or not including a $1,000 deductible provision in a basic protection automobile insurance plan on the ground that the people who would elect it could least afford it. Nor shall I be concerned with measures such as "truth-in-advertising" acts and Pure Food and Drug legislation which are often attacked as paternalistic but which should not be considered so. In these cases all that is provided—it is true by the use of compulsion—is information which it is presumed that rational persons are interested in having in order to make wise decisions. There is no interference with the liberty of the consumer unless one wants to stretch a point beyond good sense and say that his liberty to apply for a loan without knowing the true rate of interest is diminished. It is true that sometimes there is sentiment for going further than providing information, for example when laws against usurious interest are passed preventing those who might wish to contract loans at high rates of interest from doing so, and these measures may correctly be considered paternalistic.

III

Bearing these examples in mind, let me return to a characterization of paternalism. I said earlier that I meant by the term, roughly, interference with a person's liberty for his own good. But, as some of the examples show, the class of persons whose good is involved is not always identical with the class of persons whose freedom is restricted. Thus, in the case of professional licensing it is the practitioner who is directly interfered with but it is the would-be patient whose interests are presumably being served. Not allowing the consent of the victim to be a defense to certain types of crime primarily affects the would-be aggressor but it is the interests of the willing victim that we are trying to protect. Sometimes a person may fall into both classes as would be the case if we banned the manufacture and sale of cigarettes and a given manufacturer happened to be a smoker as well.

Thus we may first divide paternalistic interferences into "pure" and "impure" cases. In "pure" paternalism the class of persons whose freedom is restricted is identical with the class of persons whose benefit is intended to be promoted by such restrictions. Examples: the making of suicide a crime, requiring passengers in automobiles to wear seatbelts, requiring a Christian Scientist to receive a blood transfusion. In the case of "impure" paternalism in trying to protect the welfare of a class of persons we find that the only way to do so will involve restricting the freedom of other persons besides those who are benefited. Now it might be thought that there are no cases of "impure" paternalism since any case could always be justified on nonpaternalistic grounds, i.e. in terms of preventing harm to others. Thus we might ban cigarette manufacturers from continuing to manufacture their product on the grounds that we are preventing them from causing illness to others in the same way that we prevent other manufacturers from releasing pollutants into the atmosphere, thereby causing danger to the members of the community. The difference is, however, that in the former but not the latter case the harm is of such a nature that it could be avoided by those individuals affected if they so chose. The incurring of the harm requires, so to speak, the active cooperation of the victim. It would be mistaken theoretically and hypocritical in practice to assert that our interference in such cases is just like our interference in standard cases of protecting others from harm. At the very least someone interfered with in this way can reply that no one is complaining about his activities. It may be that impure paternalism requires arguments or reasons of a stronger kind in order to be justified, since there are persons who are losing a portion of their liberty and they do not even have the solace of having it be done "in their own interest." Of course in some sense, if paternalistic justifications are ever correct, then we are protecting others, we are preventing some from injuring others, but it is important to see the differences between this and the standard case.

Paternalism then will always involve limitations on the liberty of some individuals in their own interest but it may also extend to interferences with the liberty of parties whose interests are not in question.

IV

Finally, by way of some more preliminary analysis, I want to distinguish paternalistic interference with liberty from a related type with which it is often confused. Consider, for example, legislation which forbids employees to work more than, say, 40 hours per week. It is sometimes argued that such legislation is paternalistic for if employees desired such a restriction on their hours of work they could agree among themselves to impose it voluntarily. But because they do not the society imposes its own conception of their best interests upon them by the use of coercion. Hence this is paternalism.

Now it may be that some legislation of this nature is, in fact, paternalistically motivated. I am not denying that. All I want to point out is that there is another possible way of justifying such measures which is not paternalistic in nature. It is not paternalistic because, as Mill puts it in a similar context, such measures are "required not to overrule the judgment of individuals respecting their own interest, but to give effect to that judgment: they being unable to give effect to it except by concert, which concert again cannot be effectual unless it receives validity and sanction from the law." (*Principles of Political Economy*).

The line of reasoning here is a familiar one first found in Hobbes and developed with great sophistication by contemporary economists in the last decade or so. There are restrictions which are in the interests of a class of persons taken collectively but are such that the immediate interest of each individual is furthered by his violating the rule when others adhere to it. In such cases the individuals involved may need the use of compulsion to give effect to their collective judgment of their own interest by guaranteeing each individual compliance by the others. In these cases compulsion is not used to achieve some benefit which is not recognized to be a benefit by those concerned, but rather because it is the only feasible means of achieving some benefit which *is* recognized as such by all concerned. This way of viewing matters provides us with another characterization of paternalism in general. Paternalism might be thought of as the use of coercion to achieve a good which is not recognized as such by those persons for whom the good is intended. Again while this formulation captures the heart of the matter—it is surely what Mill is objecting to in *On Liberty*—the matter is not always quite like that. For example, when we force motorcyclists to wear helmets we are trying to promote a good—the protection of the person from injury—which is surely recognized by most of the individuals concerned. It is not that a cyclist doesn't value his bodily integrity; rather, as a supporter of such legislation would put it, he either places, perhaps irrationally, another value or good (freedom from wearing a helmet) above that of physical well-being, or, perhaps, while recognizing the danger in the abstract, he either does not fully appreciate it or he underestimates the likelihood of its occurring. But now we are approaching the question of possible justifications of paternalistic measures and the rest of this essay will be devoted to that question.

V

I shall begin for dialectical purposes by discussing Mill's objections to paternalism and then go on to discuss more positive proposals.

An initial feature that strikes one is the absolute nature of Mill's prohibitions against paternalism. It is so unlike the carefully qualified admonitions of Mill and his fellow Utilitarians on other moral issues. He speaks of self-protection as the *sole* end warranting coercion, of the individual's own goals as *never* being a sufficient warrant. Contrast this with his discussion of the prohibition against lying in *Utilitarianism:*

> Yet that even this rule, sacred as it is, admits of possible exception, is acknowledged by all moralists, the chief of which is where the withholding of some fact . . . would save an individual . . . from great and unmerited evil.

The same tentativeness is present when he deals with justice:

> It is confessedly unjust to break faith with any one: to violate an engagement, either express or implied, or disappoint expectations raised by our own conduct, at least if we have raised these expectations knowingly and voluntarily. Like all the other obligations of justice already spoken of, this one is not regarded as absolute, but as capable of being overruled by a stronger obligation of justice on the other side.

This anomaly calls for some explanation. The structure of Mill's argument is as follows:

1. Since restraint is an evil the burden of proof is on those who propose such restraint.
2. Since the conduct which is being considered is purely self-regarding, the normal appeal to the protection of the interests of others is not available.
3. Therefore we have to consider whether reasons involving reference to the individual's own good, happiness, welfare, or interests are sufficient to overcome the burden of justification.
4. We either cannot advance the interests of the individual by compulsion, or the attempt to do so involves evils which outweigh the good done.
5. Hence the promotion of the individual's own interests does not provide a sufficient warrant for the use of compulsion.

Clearly the operative premise here is (4), and it is bolstered by claims about the status of the individual as judge and appraiser of his welfare, interests, needs, etc.:

> With respect to his own feelings and circumstances, the most ordinary man or woman has means of knowledge immeasurably surpassing those that can be possessed by anyone else.
>
> He is the man most interested in his own well-being: the interest which any other person, except in cases of strong personal attachment, can have in it is trifling, compared to that which he himself has.

These claims are used to support the following generalizations concerning the utility of compulsion for paternalistic purposes:

> The interferences of society to overrule his judgment and purposes in what only regards himself must be grounded on general presumptions; which may be altogether wrong, and even if right, are as likely as not to be mis-applied to individual cases.
>
> But the strongest of all the arguments against the interference of the public with purely personal conduct is that when it does interfere, the odds are that it interferes wrongly and in the wrong place.
>
> All errors which the individual is likely to commit against advice and warning are far outweighed by the evil of allowing others to constrain him to what they deem his good.

Performing the utilitarian calculation by balancing the advantages and disadvantages we find that: "Mankind are greater gainers by suffering each other to live as seems good to themselves, than by compelling each other to live as seems good to the rest." Ergo, (4).

This classical case of a utilitarian argument with all the premises spelled out is not the only line of reasoning present in Mill's discussion. There are asides, and more than asides, which look quite different and I shall deal with them later. But this is clearly the main channel of Mill's thought and it is one which has been subjected to vigorous attack from the moment it appeared—most often by fellow Utilitarians. The link that they have usually seized on is, as Fitzjames Stephen put it in *Liberty, Equality, Fraternity,* the absence of proof that the "mass of adults are so well acquainted with their own inter-ests and so much disposed to pursue them that no compulsion or restraint put upon them by any others for the purpose of promoting their interest can really promote them." Even so sympathetic a critic as H. L. A. Hart is forced to the conclusion that:

> In Chapter 5 of his essay [On Liberty] Mill carried his protests against pa-ternalism to lengths that may now appear to us as fantastic. . . . No doubt if we no longer sympathise with this criticism this is due, in part, to a general decline in the belief that individuals know their own interest best.
>
> Mill endows the average individual with "too much of the psychology of a middle-aged man whose desires are relatively fixed, not liable to be artifi-cially stimulated by external influences; who knows what he wants and what gives him satisfaction or happiness; and who pursues these things when he can."

Now it is interesting to note that Mill himself was aware of some of the limitations on the doctrine that the individual is the best judge of his own interests. In his discussion of government intervention in general (even where the intervention does not interfere with liberty but provides alternative institutions to those of the market), after making claims which are parallel to those just discussed, e.g. "People understand their own business and their own interests better, and care for them more, than the government does, or can be expected to do," he goes on to an intelligent discussion of the "very large and conspicuous exceptions" to the maxim that:

> Most persons take a juster and more intelligent view of their own interest, and of the means of promoting it than can either be prescribed to them by a general enactment of the legislature, or pointed out in the particular case by a public functionary.

Thus there are things

> of which the utility does not consist in ministering to inclinations, nor in serving the daily uses of life, and the want of which is least felt where the need is greatest. This is peculiarly true of those things which are chiefly useful as tending to raise the character of human beings. The uncultivated cannot be competent judges of cultivation. Those who most need to be made wiser and better, usually desire it least, and, if they desired it, would be incapable of finding the way to it by their own lights.
>
>   . . . A second exception to the doctrine that individuals are the best judges of their own interest, is when an individual attempts to decide irrevocably now what will be best for his interest at some future and distant time. The presumption in favor of individual judgment is only legitimate, where the judgment is grounded on actual, and especially on present, personal experience; not where it is formed antecedently to experience, and not suffered to be reversed even after experience has condemned it.

The upshot of these exceptions is that Mill does not declare that there should never be government interference with the economy but rather that

> . . . in every instance, the burden of making out a strong case should be thrown not on those who resist but on those who recommend government interference. Letting alone, in short, should be the general practice: every departure from it, unless required by some great good, is a certain evil.

In short, we get a presumption, not an absolute prohibition. The question is why doesn't the argument against paternalism go the same way?

I suggest that the answer lies in seeing that in addition to a purely utilitarian argument Mill uses another as well. As a Utilitarian, Mill has to show, in Fitzjames Stephen's words, that: "Self-protection apart, no good object can be attained by any compulsion which is not in itself a greater evil than the absence of the object which the compulsion obtains." To show this is impossible; one reason being that it isn't true. Preventing a man from selling himself into slavery (a paternalistic measure which Mill himself accepts as legitimate), or from taking heroin, or from driving a car without wearing seatbelts may constitute a lesser evil than allowing him to do any of these things. A consistent Utilitarian can only argue against paternalism on the grounds that it (as a matter of fact) does not maximize the good. It is always a contingent question that may be refuted by the evidence. But there is also a noncontingent argument which runs through *On Liberty.* When Mill states that "there is a part of the life of every person who has come to years of discretion, within which the individuality of that person ought to reign uncontrolled either by any other person or by the public collectively," he is saying something about what it means to be a person, an autonomous agent. It is because coercing a person for his own good denies this status as an independent entity that Mill objects to it so strongly and in such absolute terms. To be able to choose is a good that is independent of the wisdom of what is chosen. A man's "mode of laying out his existence is the best, not because it is the best in itself, but because it is his own mode." It is the privilege and proper condition of a human being, arrived at the maturity of his faculties, to use and interpret experience in his own way.

As further evidence of this line of reasoning in Mill, consider the one exception to his prohibition against paternalism.

> In this and most civilised countries, for example, an engagement by which a person should sell himself, or allow himself to be sold, as a slave, would be null and void; neither enforced by law nor by opinion. The ground for thus limiting his power of voluntarily disposing of his own lot in life, is apparent, and is very clearly seen in this extreme case. The reason for not interfering, unless for the sake of others, with a person's voluntary acts, is consideration for his own liberty. His voluntary choice is evidence that what he so chooses is desirable, or at least endurable, to him, and his good is on the whole best provided for by allowing him to take his own means of pursuing it. But by selling himself for a slave, he abdicates his liberty; he foregoes any future use of it beyond that single act. He therefore defeats, in his own case, the very purpose which is the justification of allowing him to dispose of himself. He is no longer free; but is thenceforth in a position which has no longer the presumption in its favour, that would be afforded by his voluntarily remaining in it. The principle of freedom cannot require that he should be free not to be free. It is not freedom to be allowed to alienate his freedom.

Now leaving aside the fudging on the meaning of freedom in the last line it is clear that part of this argument is incorrect. While it is true that *future* choices of the slave are not reasons for thinking that what he chooses then is desirable for him, what is at issue is limiting his immediate choice; and since this choice is made freely, the individual may be correct in thinking that his interests are best provided for by entering such a contract. But the main consideration for not allowing such a contract is the need to preserve the liberty of the person to make future choices. This gives us a principle— a very narrow one—by which to justify some paternalistic interferences. Paternalism is justified only to preserve a wider range of freedom for the individual in question. How far this principle could be extended, whether it can justify all the cases in which we are inclined upon reflection to think paternalistic measures justified, remains to be discussed. What I have tried to show so far is that there are two strains of argument in Mill—one a straight-forward Utilitarian mode of reasoning and one which relies not on the goods which free choice leads to but on the absolute value of the choice itself. The first cannot establish any absolute prohibition but at most a presumption and indeed a fairly weak one given some fairly plausible assumptions about human psychology; the second, while a stronger line of argument, seems to me to allow on its own grounds a wider range of paternalism than might be suspected. I turn now to a consideration of these matters.

VI

We might begin looking for principles governing the acceptable use of paternalistic power in cases where it is generally agreed that it is legitimate. Even Mill intends his principles to be applicable only to mature individuals, not those in what he calls "non-age." What is it that justifies us in interfering with children? The fact that they lack some of the emotional and cognitive capacities required in order to make fully rational decisions. It is an empirical question to just what extent children have an adequate conception of their own present and future interests but there is not much doubt that there are many deficiencies. For example, it is very difficult for a child to defer gratification for any considerable period of time. Given these deficiencies and given the very real and permanent dangers that may befall the child it becomes not only permissible but even a duty of the parent to restrict the child's freedom in various ways. There is however an important moral limitation on the exercise of such parental power which is provided by the notion of the child eventually coming to see the correctness of his parent's interventions. Parental paternalism may be thought of as a wager by the parent on the child's subsequent recognition of the wisdom of the restrictions. There is an emphasis on what could be called future-oriented consent—on what the child will come to welcome, rather than on what he does welcome.

The essence of this idea has been incorporated by idealist philosophers into various types of "real-will" theory as applied to fully adult persons. Extensions of paternalism are argued for by claiming that in various respects, chronologically mature individuals share the same deficiencies in knowledge, capacity to think rationally, and the ability to carry out decisions that children possess. Hence in interfering with such people we are in effect doing what they would do if they were fully rational. Hence we are not really opposing their will, hence we are not really interfering with their freedom. The dangers of this move have been sufficiently exposed by Berlin in his *Two Concepts of Freedom*. I see no gain in theoretical clarity nor in practical advantage in trying to pass over the real nature of the interferences with liberty that we impose on others. Still the basic notion of consent is important and seems to me the only acceptable way of trying to delimit an area of justified paternalism.

Let me start by considering a case where the consent is not hypothetical in nature. Under certain conditions it is rational for an individual to agree that others should force him to act in ways which, at the time of action, the individual may not see as desirable. If, for example, a man knows that he is subject to breaking his resolves when temptation is present, he may ask a friend to refuse to entertain his requests at some later stage.

A classical example is given in the Odyssey when Odysseus commands his men to tie him to the mast and refuse all future orders to be set free, because he knows the power of the Sirens to enchant men with their songs. Here we are on relatively sound ground in later refusing Odysseus' request to be set free. He may even claim to have changed his mind but since it is *just* such changes that he wished to guard against we are entitled to ignore them.

A process analogous to this may take place on a social rather than individual basis. An electorate may mandate its representatives to pass legislation which when it comes time to "pay the price" may be unpalatable. I may believe that a tax increase is necessary to halt inflation though I may resent the lower pay check each month. However in both this case and that of Odysseus the measure to be enforced is specifically requested by the party involved and at some point in time there is genuine consent and agreement on the part of those persons whose liberty is infringed. Such is not the case of the paternalistic measures we have been speaking about. What must be involved here is not consent to specific measures but rather consent to a system of government, run by elected representatives, with an understanding that they may act to safeguard our interests in certain limited ways.

I suggest that since we are all aware of our irrational propensities, deficiencies in cognitive and emotional capacities, and avoidable and unavoidable ignorance it is rational and prudent for us to in effect take out "social insurance policies." We may argue for and against proposed paternalistic measures in terms of what fully rational individuals would accept as forms of protection. Now clearly, since the initial agreement is not about specific measures we are dealing with a more-or-less blank check and therefore there have to be carefully defined limits. What I am looking for are certain kinds of conditions which make it plausible to suppose that rational men could reach agreement to limit their liberty even when other men's interests are not affected.

Of course as in any kind of agreement schema there are great difficulties in deciding what rational individuals would or would not accept. Particularly in sensitive areas of personal liberty, there is always a danger of the dispute over agreement and rationality being a disguised version of evaluative and normative disagreement.

Let me suggest types of situations in which it seems plausible to suppose that fully rational individuals would agree to having paternalistic restrictions imposed upon them. It is reasonable to suppose that there are "goods" such as health which any person would want to have in order to pursue his own good—no matter how that good is conceived. This is an argument used in connection with compulsory education for children but it seems to me that it can be extended to other goods which have this character. Then one could agree that the attainment of such goods should be promoted even when not recognized to be such, at the moment, by the individuals concerned.

An immediate difficulty arises from the fact that men are always faced with competing goods and that there may be reasons why even a value such as health—or indeed life—may be overridden by competing values. Thus the problem with the Christian Scientist and blood transfusions. It may be more important for him to reject "impure substances" than to go on living. The difficult problem that must be faced is whether one can give sense to the notion of a person irrationally attaching weights to competing values.

Consider a person who knows the statistical data on the probability of being injured when not wearing seatbelts in an automobile and knows the types and gravity of the various injuries. He also insists that the inconvenience attached to fastening the belt every time he gets in and out of the car outweighs for him the possible risks to himself. I am inclined in this case to think that such a weighing is irrational. Given his life-plans, which we are assuming are those of the average person, his interests and commitments already undertaken, I think it is safe to predict that we can find inconsistencies in his calculations at some point. I am assuming that this is not a man who for some conscious or unconscious reasons is trying to injure himself nor is he a man who just likes to "live dangerously." I am assuming that he is like us in all the relevant respects but just puts an enormously high negative value on inconvenience—one which does not seem comprehensible or reasonable.

It is always possible, of course, to assimilate this person to creatures like myself. I, also, neglect to fasten my seatbelt and I concede such behavior is not rational but not because I weigh the inconvenience differently from those who fasten their belts. It is just that having made (roughly) the same calculation as everybody else I ignore it in my actions. [Note: a much better case of weakness of the will than those usually given in ethics texts.] A plausible explanation for this deplorable habit is that although I know in some intellectual sense what the probabilities and risks are I do not fully appreciate them in an emotionally genuine manner.

We have two distinct types of situation in which a man acts in a non-rational fashion. In one case he attaches incorrect weights to some of his values; in the other he neglects to act in accordance with his actual preferences and desires. Clearly there is a stronger and more persuasive argument for paternalism in the latter situation. Here we are really not—by assumption—imposing a good on another person. But why may we not extend our interference to what we might call evaluative delusions? After all, in the case of cognitive delusions we are prepared, often, to act against the expressed will of the person involved. If a man believes that when he jumps out the window he will float upwards—Robert Nozick's example—would not we detain him, forcibly if necessary? The reply will be that this man doesn't wish to be injured and if we could convince him that he is mistaken as to the consequences of his action he would not wish to perform the action. But part of what is involved in claiming that the man who doesn't fasten his seatbelts is attaching an incorrect weight to the inconvenience of fastening them is that if he were to be involved in an accident and severely injured he would look back and admit that the inconvenience wasn't as bad as all that. So there is a sense in which if I could convince him of the consequences of his action he also would not wish to continue his present course of action. Now the notion of consequences being used here is covering a lot of ground. In one case it's being used to indicate what will or can happen as a result of a course of action and in the other it's making a prediction about the future evaluation of the consequences—in the first sense—of a course of action. And whatever the difference between facts and values—whether it be hard and fast or soft and slow—we are genuinely more reluctant to consent to interferences where evaluative differences are the issue. Let me now consider another factor which comes into play in some of these situations which may make an important difference in our willingness to consent to paternalistic restrictions.

Some of the decisions we make are of such a character that they produce changes which are in one or another way irreversible. Situations are created in which it is difficult or impossible to return to anything like the initial stage at which the decision was made. In particular, some of these changes will make it impossible to continue to make reasoned choices in the future. I am thinking specifically of decisions which involve taking drugs that are physically or psychologically addictive and those which are destructive of one's mental and physical capacities.

I suggest we think of the imposition of paternalistic interferences in situations of this kind as being a kind of insurance policy which we take out against making decisions which are far-reaching, potentially dangerous and irreversible. Each of these factors is important. Clearly there are many decisions we make that are relatively irreversible. In deciding to learn to play chess I could predict in view of my general interest in games that some portion of my free time was going to be preempted and that it would not be easy to give up the game once I acquired a certain competence. But my whole life-style was not going to be jeopardized in an extreme manner. Further it might be argued that even with addictive drugs such as heroin one's normal life plans would not be seriously interfered with if an inexpensive and adequate supply were readily available. So this type of argument might have a much narrower scope than appears to be the case at first.

A second class of cases concerns decisions which are made under extreme psychological and sociological pressures. I am not thinking here of the making of the decision as being something one is pressured into—e.g. a good reason for making duelling illegal is that unless this is done many people might have to manifest their courage and integrity in ways in which they would rather not do so—but rather of decisions, such as that to commit suicide, which are usually made at a point where the individual is not thinking clearly and calmly about the nature of his decision. In addition, of course, this comes under the previous heading of all-too-irrevocable decisions. Now there are practical steps which a society could take if it wanted to decrease the possibility of suicide—for example not paying social security benefits to the survivors or, as religious institutions do, not allowing persons to be buried with the same status as natural deaths. I think we may count these as interferences with the liberty of persons to attempt suicide and the question is whether they are justifiable.

Using my argument schema the question is whether rational individuals would consent to such limitations. I see no reason for them to consent to an absolute prohibition but I do think it is reasonable for them to agree to some kind of enforced waiting period. Since we are all aware of the possibility of temporary states, such as great fear or depression, that are inimical to the making of well-informed and rational decisions, it would be prudent for all of us if there were some kind of institutional arrangement whereby we were restrained from making a decision which is so irreversible. What this would be like in practice is difficult to envisage and it may be that if no practical arrangements were feasible we would have to conclude that there should be no restriction at all on this kind of action. But we might have a "cooling off" period, in much the same way that we now require couples who file for divorce to go through a waiting period. Or, more farfetched, we might imagine a Suicide Board composed of a psychologist and another member picked by the applicant. The Board would be required to meet and talk with the person proposing to take his life, though its approval would not be required.

A third class of decisions—these classes are not supposed to be disjointed—involves dangers which are either not sufficiently understood or appreciated correctly by the persons involved. Let me illustrate, using the example of cigarette smoking, a number of possible cases.

1. A man may not know the facts—e.g. smoking between 1 and 2 packs a day shortens life expectancy 6.2 years, the costs and pain of the illness caused by smoking, etc.

2. A man may know the facts, wish to stop smoking, but not have the requisite willpower.

3. A man may know the facts but not have them play the correct role in his calculation because, say, he discounts the danger psychologically since it is remote in time and/or inflates the attractiveness of other consequences of his decisions which he regards as beneficial.

In case 1 what is called for is education, the posting of warnings, etc. In case 2 there is no theoretical problem. We are not imposing a good on someone who rejects it. We are simply using coercion to enable people to carry out their own goals. (Note: There obviously is a difficulty in that only a subclass of the individuals affected wish to be prevented from doing what they are doing.) In case 3 there is a sense in which we are imposing a good on someone in that given his current appraisal of the facts he doesn't wish to be restricted. But in another sense we are not imposing a good since what is being claimed—and what must be shown or at least argued for—is that an accurate accounting on his part would lead him to reject his current course of action. Now we all know that such cases exist, that we are prone to disregarding dangers that are only possibilities, that immediate pleasures are often magnified and distorted.

If in addition the dangers are severe and far-reaching, we could agree to allow the state a certain degree of power to intervene in such situations. The difficulty is in specifying in advance, even vaguely, the class of cases in which intervention will be legitimate.

A related difficulty is that of drawing a line so that it is not the case that all ultrahazardous activities are ruled out, e.g. mountain climbing, bullfighting, sports-car racing, etc. There are some risks—even very great ones—which a person is entitled to take with his life.

A good deal depends on the nature of the deprivation—e.g. does it prevent the person from engaging in the activity completely or merely limit his participation—and how important to the nature of the activity is the absence of restriction when this is weighed against the role that the activity plays in the life of the person. In the case of automobile seatbelts, for example, the restriction is trivial in nature, interferes not at all with the use or enjoyment of the activity, and does, I am assuming, considerably reduce a high risk of serious injury. Whereas, for example, making mountain climbing illegal completely prevents a person from engaging in an activity which may play an important role in his life and his conception of the person he is.

In general, the easiest cases to handle are those which can be argued about in the terms which Mill thought to be so important—a concern not just for the happiness or welfare, in some broad sense, of the individual but rather a concern for the autonomy and freedom of the person. I suggest that we would be most likely to consent to paternalism in those instances in which it preserves and enhances for the individual his ability to rationally consider and carry out his own decisions.

I have suggested in this essay a number of types of situations in which it seems plausible that rational men would agree to granting the legislative powers of a society the right to impose restrictions on what Mill calls "self-regarding" conduct. However, rational men knowing something about the resources of ignorance, ill-will and stupidity available to the lawmakers of a society—a good case in point is the history of drug legislation in the United States—will be concerned to limit such intervention to a minimum. I suggest in closing two principles designed to achieve this end.

In all cases of paternalistic legislation there must be a heavy and clear burden of proof placed on the authorities to demonstrate the exact nature of the harmful effects (or beneficial consequences) to be avoided (or achieved) and the probability of their occurrence. The burden of proof here is twofold—what lawyers distinguish as the burden of going forward and the burden of persuasion. That the authorities have the burden of going forward means that it is up to them to raise the question and bring forward evidence of the evils to be avoided. Unlike the case of new drugs where the manufacturer must produce some evidence that the drug has been tested and found not harmful, no citizen has to show with respect to self-regarding conduct that it is not harmful or promotes his best interests. In addition the nature and cogency of the evidence for the harmfulness of the course of action must be set at a high level. To paraphrase a formulation of the burden of proof for criminal proceedings—better 10 men ruin themselves than one man be unjustly deprived of liberty.

Finally, I suggest a principle of the least restrictive alternative. If there is an alternative way of accomplishing the desired end without restricting liberty although it may involve great expense, inconvenience, etc., the society must adopt it.

SEX, DRUGS, AND PRIVACY

David A. J. Richards

It is initially important to distinguish two kinds of paternalism: interference on the basis of facts unknown to the agent, in order to save the agent from harms that he would wish to avoid, and interference on the basis of values that the agent does not himself share. Paternalism of the first kind, as applied in such laws as those securing the purity of drugs, is unobjectionable. Paternalism of the second kind, which underlies many laws currently criminalizing drug use, is not only objectionable, it is a violation of human rights.

On this basis, no good argument can be made that paternalistic considerations justify the kind of interference in choices to use drugs that is involved in the current criminalization of many forms of drug use. Indeed, in many cases, such choices seem all *too* rational.

Drug use serves many disparate purposes: therapeutic care and cure, the relief of pain or anxiety, the stimulation or depression of mood or levels of arousal, the exploration of imaginative experience for creative, aesthetic, religious, therapeutic, recreational, or other purposes, and sheer recreative pleasure. These purposes are not irrational. To the contrary, the pursuit of them may enable the person better to achieve his ends in general, or to explore aspects of experience or attitudes to living which he may reasonably wish to incorporate into his theory of ends. There is almost no form of drug use which, in a suitably supportive context and setting, may not advance important human goods, including the capacity of some poor and deprived people to work more comfortably, to endure adverse climatic and environmental circumstances, and in general to meet more robustly and pleasurably the demands on their lives. Some religions, like some artists, have centered themselves on drug use, finding in drugs a matrix of religious and imaginative experience in which to explore and sometimes realize their higher-order interests in giving life intelligible meaning and coherence. Some persons today find in the triumph of technological society the *reductio ad absurdum* of certain dynamics of Western culture and identify drug use as one organon for cultivating a saner and more balanced metaphysical orientation that expresses their most authentic and reasonable interests. Some find even in "addictive" drugs a way of life with more interest, challenge, and self-respect than the available alternatives. It is dogmatic to assert that these and other people do not, through drug use, more rationally advance their ends.

Sometimes the paternalistic argument is made that certain forms of drug use, even if carefully regulated, may result in certain clear harms to the user. For example, heroin use may lead to addiction, to impotence, to certain organic disorders, and sometimes, despite all proper precautions, to death. As long as any such irreparable harm to the person is in prospect, it is argued, paternalistic interference is justified. Even if certain of these alleged harms, for example, addiction, are morally problematic and question-begging, others, such as death, are not. The first requirement of just paternalism, however, is that judgments of irrationality must rest on a neutral theory of the good consistent with the agent's own higher-order interests in rationality and freedom. Even intentionally ending one's own life cannot, in all circumstances, be supposed irrational under this criterion. If intentional killing is not always irrational, neither, a fortiori, is drug use, in which the user makes trade-offs between valued forms of activity and higher risks of death that reasonable persons sometimes embrace. Certainly, the right of persons to engage in many high-risk occupations and activities is uncontroversial. Part of respect for human rights is the recognition of the right of persons, as free and rational beings, to determine the meanings of their own lives and projects, including the frame of such plans at the boundaries of life and death. The values that some persons place on drug use can be accorded no less respect. Certainly, drug use does not enable a person to realize more than is implicit in the interests and ambitions brought to the drug experience, but that indicates not the frivolity or pointlessness of the experience, but its potential seriousness for the kinds of spiritual exploration and risk-taking by independent-minded and rational persons that should be centrally protected in a free society.

At most, paternalistic concern for forms of irreparable harm might dictate appropriate forms of regulation to insure that drugs are available only to mature persons who understand, critically evaluate and voluntarily accept the risks. To minimize pointless risks, such regulations might insure that certain drugs, LSD, for example, are taken only under appropriate supervision. In general, however, there is no ground of just paternalism for an absolute prohibition of such drugs.

The radical vision of autonomy and mutual concern and respect is a vision of persons, as such, having human rights to create their own lives on terms fair to all. To view individuals in this way is to affirm basic intrinsic limits on the degree to which, even benevolently, one person may control the life of another. Within ethical constraints expressive of mutual concern and respect for autonomy, people are, in this conception, free to adopt a number of disparate and irreconcilable visions of the good life. Indeed, the adoption of different kinds of life plans, within these constraints, affords the moral good of different experiments in living by which people can more rationally assess such basic life choices. The invocation of inadequate moral and paternalistic arguments of the kind discussed violates these considerations of human rights, confusing unreflective personal ideology with the moral reasoning that alone can justify the deprivation of liberty by criminal penalty.

DRUG USE AND CONSTITUTIONAL PRIVACY

I have thus far set forth a number of negative arguments to show why various moral arguments condemning drug use are mistaken. The remainder of the chapter will consider the affirmative case for allowing forms of drug use, that is, for the existence of rights of the person that include the right to use drugs. In this way, the scope and limits of this right can be clarified, and its relation to the personal ideals secure from state intervention can be addressed.

. . . The constitutional right to privacy may be interpreted, consistent with the human rights perspective embodied in the Constitution, as subjecting the scope of the criminal law to constitutional assessment and criticism in terms of the autonomy-based interpretation of treating persons as equals. The United States is a constitutional democracy committed to the conception of human rights as an unwritten constitution, in terms of which the meaning of constitutional guaranties is to be construed. It is wholly natural and historically consistent with constitutional commitments to regard the autonomy-based interpretation of treating persons as equals as the regulative ideal in terms of which the public morality, which the criminal law expresses, is to be interpreted. Sometimes this thought has been expressed, as a rough first approximation, in terms of the harm principle, the principle that the state may impose criminal sanctions only on conduct which harms others. The present account has tried to reformulate the thought in terms of the autonomy-based interpretation of treating persons as equals, and has tried to show how this conception imposes specific constraints on the kinds of principles that may permissibly be enforced by the public morality. The traditional idea of "harm," for example, appears in the account, but is interpreted in terms of the rights of the person, in contrast to Mill's utilitarian reformulation.

A corollary of this way of thinking is that, when the scope of the criminal law exceeds such moral constraints, it violates human rights. The constitutional right to privacy expresses a form of this moral criticism of unjust overcriminalization, and may be understood as a convergence of three viewpoints. These include, first, the view that the traditional moral argument for criminalization is critically deficient, and, indeed, demonstrably fails to respect human rights. A second element is an antipaternalistic feature. The still extant force of the invalid traditional moral arguments distorts the capacity to see that certain traditionally condemned life choices may be rationally undertaken. Paternalistic interference is tolerated and even encouraged, when, in fact, such interference cannot be justified. Third, there is a strong autonomy-based liberty interest in protecting human dignity from the invasions of moralism and paternalism.

In light of this convergence of factors, it is natural to expect that the constitutional right to privacy would have been aggressively invoked to invalidate prohibitions on drug use, as it was in sexual and, more recently, right-to-die contexts. In fact, aside from a free exercise of religion case not directly relevant to constitutional privacy issues, in only one notable case, *Ravin v. State,* has a court unequivocally pursued such a privacy argument to strike down prohibitions of marijuana use in the home. Even the *Ravin* court, however, refused to attach the right to drug use in itself, finding the privacy right to arise out of the home context instead. In short, American courts seem disinclined to pursue privacy arguments in contexts of drug use because they fail to identify drug use as a basic life choice.

In my view, this judgment cannot withstand critical examination. In order to understand why decisions to use drugs are embraced by the constitutional right to privacy, it is necessary to draw together earlier observations regarding the idea of human rights, the values of dignity and moral personality that it encompasses and should protect, the unjust moral argument that often underlies prohibitions of drug use, and the necessary implications of these ideas and values for the protection of certain forms of drug use. Even if decisions to use drugs were, in fact, rarely or never made or acted on, the right to so decide is, for reasons now to be explained, fundamental.

I have interpreted the human rights perspective in terms of the autonomy-based interpretation of treating persons as equals, which includes respect for the higher-order interests of persons in freedom and rationality. One central component must be respect for the capacity of persons—beings capable of critical self-consciousness—to regulate and interpret their experiences in terms of their own standards of reasonable argument and evidence. Thus, both historically and as a matter of moral principle, respect for independent religious conscience and for principles of religious toleration have been at the heart of evolving ideas of human rights. Historically, respect for religious belief has expressed what is today regarded as the deeper principle of respect for individual conscience, the right of persons independently to evaluate and control their own experience.

Commitment to this basic moral principle requires a neutral respect for evaluative independence. But this principle is, as we have seen, violated by the moral perfectionism that has dominated the American approach to drug control. Indeed, this moral perfectionism attacks the very foundations of evaluative independence; for it seeks to inculcate through law a kind and quality of subjective human experience modeled after a religious ideal of rigid self-control dedicated selflessly to the good of others. In the place of independent control over and evaluation of one's own experience, we have a reigning orthodoxy. Majoritarian legislatures seek to enforce a kind of secularized version of the religious technology of self-mastery. The state, consistent with the autonomy-based interpretation of treating persons as equals, has no just role adjudicating among or preferring, let alone enforcing, one such technology over another. Such a use of state power is precisely the form of content-based control over ways of life, thought, and experience against which constitutional morality rebels. Indeed, the enforcement of perfectionist ideals expresses precisely the contempt for autonomous evaluative independence and self-control that should trigger appropriate constitutional attack and remedy.

It may be objected that drug experience is not the kind of subjective experience protected by constitutional principles of toleration. This is not an argument; rather it is an expression of the long American tradition of the public morality. This tradition cannot, as has been shown, be sustained. It is based on untenable forms of moral argument and is, on examination, inconsistent with deeper constitutional values to which all espouse fundamental allegiance. It fails to observe constitutional constraints on the kind of harm that may be the object of criminal penalties; indeed, ideologically, it seeks supremacy for its own model of self-mastery through the criminal law in the way that constitutional morality clearly forbids. In short, since this common sense of public morality cannot be sustained, higher-order interests in freedom and rationality would identify respect for choices to use drugs as an aspect of personal dignity that is worthy of protection under the constitutional right to privacy, and call for its implementation by courts and legislatures.

A fair-minded respect for this right will assure respect for the pluralistic cultures and ways of life which different patterns of drug use embody and which have been heretofore lacking in America's cultural life. Patterns of drug use are implicitly ideological: alcohol use, for example, is often associated with cultural patterns in which aggressiveness plays a central role; use of marijuana, in contrast, is associated with more peaceful and inward ways of life. Respect for the right of drug use would preserve individual and subcultural experience and experiment from a majoritarian cultural hegemony, rooted in a crude and callously manipulative utilitarianism. There is no good reason why this utilitarian ideology has been permitted to go unchallenged as the governing American ideal in matters of drug policy; it trivializes our values into simplistic subservience to technological civilization and fails to take seriously American ideals of human rights and their implications for a pluralism of spiritual perspectives.

We may summarize the implications of this right to use drugs in terms of the background moral principles, expressive of the autonomy-based interpretation of treating persons as equals, which define its limits. The principle of autonomy in matters of drugs does not apply to persons presumably lacking rational capacities, such as young children, nor does it validate the use of particular drugs in circumstances where they would lead to the infliction on others of serious bodily harm. There is no objection, for example, to the prohibition of drugs whose use demonstrably leads to violence, or to limitations of drug use in certain contexts, such as before driving. In addition, the liberty of drug use includes the right of others to avoid involvement in the drug experience. There would be no objection, therefore, to reasonable regulations of the time, manner, and place of drug use, or of the obtrusive solicitation of drug use.

Finally, it is important to remind ourselves, yet again, that there are limits to an argument grounded in human rights of the kind here presented. To say that a person has a human right to do an act is to make a political and legal claim that certain conduct must be protected by the state from forms of coercive prohibition. To assert the existence of such a right is not to assert that it should be exercised. The latter question is an issue of personal morality. Its disposition may turn on considerations that have no proper place in questions of political and legal morality.

To say, therefore, that people have a human right to use drugs is not to conclude that everyone should exercise this right. For example, a person might justifiably invoke certain perfectionist ideals in declining to use drugs. These ideals might include religious dedications or purely secular conceptions that the control and cultivation of aspects of personal competence and subjectivity are inconsistent with drug use. Certainly, such ideals cannot justifiably be invoked to qualify our general rights of autonomy, for self-respect and fulfillment do not require conformity to such ideals. Even as personal moral ideas, however, perfectionist notions may be criticized as inhumanly rigid, masochistically manipulative, directed at questionable moral aims, and insensitive to the values of spontaneity and humanely varied experience. Nonetheless, an individual may justifiably espouse a moral ideal, regulate his or her life accordingly, and criticize others for not observing as humane an ideal in their personal lives. However, legal enforcement of such an ideal wrongly imposes a personal ideal upon persons who may find it unfulfilling or even oppressive and exploitative.

QUESTIONS FOR DISCUSSION
PRIVACY AND ITS LIMITS

1. What does Mill mean by the "private domain"? Does his rule against governmental interference in the private domain apply to parental mistreatment? to wife-beating? Explain your response.

2. Explain Mill's two main arguments against paternalistic legislation. Which argument seems to you more persuasive? Why?

3. In its historic *Roe v. Wade* decision legalizing abortion, the U.S. Supreme Court claimed that the Constitution guarantees a "right of privacy" that protects a woman's decision to terminate her pregnancy in the first two trimesters. Critics have denied that any such right is implied by the Constitution. Research the court decisions on this question, and construct an argument in support of one side or the other.

4. According to Gerald Dworkin, Mill recognizes two important exceptions to his anti-paternalism. Identify these. What additional exceptions does Dworkin propose? Do you agree? Why?

5. Which of Mill's two main arguments does Dworkin reject? On what grounds?

6. Which of Mill's two main arguments does David Richards support and employ in his criticism of anti-drug legislation? Is it the one that, in replying to Question Two, you regard as the more persuasive?

7. Are enforced savings through Social Security taxation and laws requiring seatbelt use objectionable cases of paternalistic legislation, or can they be justified on nonpaternalistic grounds? Take a position on this, and defend it.

SELECTED READINGS

ANGEL, C. "The Right to Privacy." *Journal of Information Ethics,* Fall 2000.

CAPRON, A. "Privacy: Dead and Gone?" *Hastings Center Report,* _____ 1992.

DECEW, J. *In Pursuit of Privacy.* Ithaca: Cornell University Press, 1997.

INNESS, J. *Privacy, Intimacy and Isolation.* New York: Oxford University Press, 1992.

JOHNSON, J. "A Theory of the Nature and Value of Privacy." *Public Affairs Quarterly,* _____ 1992.

KLEINIG, J. *Paternalism.* Totowa, NJ: Rowman and Littlefield, 1984.

MACHAN, T. "The Right to Privacy vs. Uniformitarianism." *Journal of Social Philosophy,* _____ 1992.

PAUL, E., F. MILLER, and J. PAUL, eds. *The Right to Privacy.* New York: Cambridge University Press, 2000.

RICHARDS, DAVID A. J. *Sex, Drugs, Death and the Law.* Totowa, NJ: Rowman and Littlefield, 1982.

SHOEMAN, F. *Privacy and Social Freedom.* New York: Cambridge University Press, 1992.

9

AFFIRMATIVE ACTION

For the last few decades, beginning with the historic Supreme Court decision of 1954 ordering racial integration "with all deliberate speed," the United States has been engaged in a mighty effort to solve what the sociologist Gunnar Myrdal called "The American Dilemma": the conflict between the commitment to equality of rights on which the nation was founded, and its history of mistreatment of native Americans, blacks, and other minorities.

It is not easy to undo the effects of centuries of injustice. The very attempt is bound to cause new injustices and considerable resentment on the part of the victims. The slaughter of the native Americans by the white settlers, and the importation of black African slaves, followed by centuries of exploitation of their descendants, have finally come to be recognized as unworthy of a nation that prides itself on its belief in freedom, democracy, and the "brotherhood of man." The question remains as to how best to undo the effects of past evils. The 1960s was a time of political struggles over de jure desegregation of schools, theaters, swimming pools, restaurants, and housing. In the 1970s strenuous efforts were made to achieve de facto desegregation by means of compulsory busing of school children. Movements then arose demanding similar amelioration of the condition of women, the disabled, and other disadvantaged groups.

The governmental policy for rectifying past injustices that has aroused the most controversy in recent years is the policy called "affirmative action" by its supporters and "reverse discrimination" by its critics. The present chapter examines this policy. Its avowed purpose has been to improve the racial, ethnic, and gender balance in prestigious and lucrative professions by giving preference to members of disadvantaged groups in admissions, hiring, and promotions. The federal government has formulated guidelines for colleges, professional schools, business, and government bureaus and has utilized its power of financial subsidies to enforce compliance. This policy has encountered considerable resistance by conservatives and even by many liberals, for it threatens the entrenched prerogatives of the middle-class intelligentsia—the very social group that, in the past, has led movements for greater social and economic equality and for the recognition of universal human rights.

The issue of affirmative action is particularly divisive because it seems to require abandonment, or at least modification, of two principles that have long been thought essential to social justice: equal opportunity, and selection according to merit. Throughout the first half of the twentieth century, social reformers were demanding that Jews, blacks, and women be granted equal opportunities to compete for prestigious social positions and that such positions be awarded according to merit, without regard to race, gender, or ethnic origin. Affirmative action seems to require that selections no longer be color blind or gender blind, but rather employ racial, gender, and ethnic criteria in addition to that of merit. It is hard for old-fashioned liberals and libertarians to swallow this new medicine. Hard or not, does social justice require that they do so?

Lisa Newton says no. She maintains that it is contrary to the liberal tradition of supporting equal opportunity for all and equal treatment under the law to favor one group over others for social benefits and honors. She warns that anyone may regard himself or herself as belonging to some particular minority group and on that grounds claim compensation for past discrimination, so that, once the precedent is set for acknowledging such claims, society will become a battleground of all sorts of groups competing for special consideration. Fair adjudication of such claims, Newton argues, is impossible when laws defining the precise rights of citizens cannot be cited as objective grounds for granting compensation. How much compensation to award, to which groups, becomes a "free for all" decided by political muscle rather than by impartial adjudication, and the democratic ideal of the "rule of law" is seriously undermined.

Newton grants that the moral ideal of equality is wider than that of political justice, understood as equality under the law, but she maintains that it cannot be realized by preferential treatment of minorities because that would be inconsistent with political justice. The proper way to realize this wider moral equality, she holds, is to establish and enforce better laws that will ensure equal treatment of all citizens.

Ronald Dworkin answers yes to our initial question. The goal of affirmative action is, he maintains, to compensate members of disadvantaged groups for the deprivations from which they have suffered, by offering them or their descendants special opportunities to improve their conditions of life. He concedes that such a policy will frustrate the interests of those candidates for prestigious positions who might otherwise have won out in various competitions. However, he points out, they are not thereby being punished or deprived of their rights, because no one has a right to a privileged social position—a privilege is not the same thing as a right. He denies that such positions have in the past been awarded solely, or even mainly, on merit, as compared with regional balance, parentage, and so-called "character and fitness" (meaning personality traits thought likely to serve the profession and the community). Few who now denounce affirmative action, he maintains, have ever complained about the use of these non-merit criteria.

In any case, he argues, the purpose of establishing any criteria for the awarding of social privileges is to benefit society, so that any criteria that fulfill this purpose are justified, and proportional representation of all minorities does so par excellence.

Charles Murray acknowledges that the strategy called "affirmative action" for overcoming the injustices of racism, a strategy initiated by President Lyndon Johnson in the mid-1960s, was well intentioned and, for a limited period, socially beneficial. However, according to Murray, the original goal of ensuring more equal opportunity for minorities by breaking down barriers of discrimination changed, a few years later, into a reverse kind of discrimination by means of preferential quotas for minority candidates for prestigious schools and high offices. He cites a number of cases that, he claims, show that this strategy of "affirmative racism" is, in the long run, harmful to the minority candidates given this preferential treatment as well as to the majority victims, because it gives people the impression that even the most worthy minority candidates lack the ability to succeed without special help.

Gertrude Ezorsky replies to this and other criticisms of affirmative action (referred to in her selection as "AA") by denying that it is a form of inverse racism and maintaining that it is a necessary compensation for centuries of mistreatment of African Americans. In the long run, she argues, overcoming the effects of past racism will benefit both blacks and whites by improving social harmony. In response to the frequent complaint that preferential treatment violates the valuable rule that competence should be the criterion for admission to high positions, she points out that many criteria other than competence—such as personal contacts, veteran status, and "irrelevant subjective standards"—have often been used for such admissions and promotions.

If Dworkin and Ezorsky are right in denying that affirmative action violates anyone's rights, claiming that at worst it merely withholds merited privileges, then the soundness of the policy becomes a matter of whether, in the long run, it is likely to do more good than harm. Clearly, it is divisive. Its implementation has already engendered resistance and resentment among many citizens. Yet almost any innovative social policy is bound to provoke resentment on the part of those who must pay its costs. The crucial question, therefore, is whether we are more likely in the long run to achieve social harmony by paying no attention to differences of race, sex, and ethnic origin (the liberal ideal of the past) or by taking note of such factors where they constitute serious disadvantages, and compensating for those disadvantages (as is done in handicap sports events such as golf and horseracing). Perhaps only further experience can provide a clear answer.

THE INJUSTICE
OF AFFIRMATIVE ACTION

Lisa H. Newton

I have heard it argued that "simple justice" requires that we favor women and blacks in employment and educational opportunities, since women and blacks were "unjustly" excluded from such opportunities for so many years in the not so distant past. It is a strange argument, an example of a possible implication of a true proposition advanced to dispute the proposition itself, like an octopus absent-mindedly slicing off his head with a stray tentacle. A fatal confusion underlies this argument, a confusion fundamentally relevant to our understanding of the notion of the rule of law.

Two senses of justice and equality are involved in this confusion. The root notion of justice, progenitor of the other, is the one that Aristotle (*Nichomachean Ethics* 5. 6; *Politics* 1.2; 3. 1) assumes to be the foundation and proper virtue of the political association. It is the condition which free men establish among themselves when they "share a common life in order that their association bring them self-sufficiency"—the regulation of their relationship by law, and the establishment, by law, of equality before the law. Rule of law is the name and pattern of this justice; its equality stands against the inequalities—of wealth, talent, etc.—otherwise obtaining among its participants, who by virtue of that equality are called "citizens." It is an achievement—complete, or, more frequently, partial—of certain people in certain concrete situations. It is fragile and easily disrupted by powerful individuals who discover that the blind equality of rule of law is inconvenient for their interests. Despite its obvious instability, Aristotle assumed that the establishment of justice in this sense, the creation of citizenship, was a permanent possibility for men and that the resultant association of citizens was the natural home of the species. At levels below the political association, this rule-governed equality is easily found; it is exemplified by any group of children agreeing together to play a game. At the level of the political association, the attainment of this justice is more difficult, simply because the stakes are so much higher for each participant. The equality of citizenship is not something that happens of its own accord, and without the expenditure of a fair amount of effort it will collapse into the rule of a powerful few over an apathetic many. But at least it has been achieved, at some times in some places;

Lisa H. Newton. "The Injustice of Affirmative Action." Original title, "Reverse Discrimination as Unjustified" from *Ethics* 83:4 (1973): 308–12. Copyright © 1973. Reprinted by permission of the University of Chicago Press and the author.

it is always worth trying to achieve, and eminently worth trying to maintain, wherever and to whatever degree it has been brought into being.

Aristotle's parochialism is notorious; he really did not imagine that persons other than Greeks could associate freely in justice, and the only form of association he had in mind was the Greek *polis*. With the decline of the *polis* and the shift in the center of political thought, his notion of justice underwent a sea change. To be exact, it ceased to represent a political type and became a moral ideal: the ideal of equality as we know it. This ideal demands that all men be included in citizenship—that one Law govern all equally, that all men regard all other men as fellow citizens, with the same guarantees, rights, and protections. Briefly, it demands that the circle of citizenship achieved by any group be extended to include the entire human race. Properly understood, its effect on our associations can be excellent: it congratulates us on our achievement of rule of law as a process of government but refuses to let us remain complacent until we have expanded the associations to include others within the ambit of the rules, as often and as far as possible. While one man is a slave, none of us may feel truly free. We are constantly prodded by this ideal to look for possible unjustifiable discrimination, for inequalities not absolutely required for the functioning of the society and advantageous to all. And after twenty centuries of pressure, not at all constant, from this ideal, it might be said that some progress has been made. To take the cases in point for this problem, we are now prepared to assert, as Aristotle would never have been, the equality of sexes and of persons of different colors. The ambit of American citizenship, once restricted to white males of property, has been extended to include all adult free men, then all adult males including ex-slaves, then all women. The process of acquisition of full citizenship was for these groups a sporadic trail of half-measures, even now not complete; the steps on the road to full equality are marked by legislation and judicial decisions which are only recently concluded and still often not enforced. But the fact that we can now discuss the possibility of favoring such groups in hiring shows that over the area that concerns us, at least, full equality is presupposed as a basis for discussion. To that extent, they are full citizens, fully protected by the law of the land.

It is important for my argument that the moral ideal of equality be recognized as logically distinct from the condition (or virtue) of justice in the political sense. Justice in this sense exists *among* a citizenry, irrespective of the number of the populace included in that citizenry. Further, the moral ideal is parasitic upon the political virtue, for "equality" is unspecified—it means nothing until we are told in what respect that equality is to be realized. In a political context, "equality" is specified as "equal rights"—equal access to the public realm, public goods and offices, equal treatment under the law—in brief, the equality of citizenship. If citizenship is not a possibility, political equality is unintelligible. The ideal emerges as a generalization of the real condition and refers back to that condition for its content.

Now, if justice (Aristotle's justice in the political sense) is equal treatment under law for all citizens, what is injustice? Clearly, injustice is the violation of that equality, discriminating for or against a group of citizens, favoring them with special immunities and privileges or depriving them of those guaranteed to the others. When the southern employer refuses to hire blacks in white-collar jobs, when Wall Street will only hire women as secretaries with new titles, when Mississippi high schools routinely flunk all black boys above ninth grade, we have examples of injustice, and we work to restore the equality of the public realm by ensuring that equal opportunity will be provided in such cases in the future. But of course, when the employers and the schools *favor* women and blacks, the same injustice is done. Just as the previous discrimination did, this reverse discrimination violates the public equality which defines citizenship and destroys the rule of law for the areas in which these favors are granted. To the extent that we adopt a program of discrimination, reverse or otherwise, justice in the political sense is destroyed, and none of us, specifically affected or not, is a citizen, a bearer of rights—we are all petitioners for favors. And to the same extent, the ideal of equality is undermined, for it has content only where justice obtains, and by destroying justice we render the ideal meaningless. It is, then, an ironic paradox, if not a contradiction in terms, to assert that the ideal of equality justifies the violation of justice; it is as if one should argue, with William Buckley, that an ideal of humanity can justify the destruction of the human race.

Logically, the conclusion is simple enough: all discrimination is wrong *prima facie* because it violates justice, and that goes for reverse discrimination too. No violation of justice among the citizens may be justified (may overcome the *prima facie* objection) by appeal to the ideal of equality, for that ideal is logically dependent upon the notion of justice. Reverse discrimination, then, which attempts no other justification than an appeal to equality, is wrong. But let us try to make the conclusion more plausible by suggesting some of the implications of the suggested practice of reverse discrimination in employment and education. My argument will be that the problems raised there are insoluble, not only in practice but in principle.

We may argue, if we like, about what "discrimination" consists of. Do I discriminate against blacks if I admit none to my school when none of the black applicants are qualified by the tests I always give? How far must I go to root out cultural bias from my application forms and tests before I can say that I have not discriminated against those of different cultures? Can I assume that women are not strong enough to be roughnecks on my oil rigs, or must I test them individually? But this controversy, the most popular and well-argued aspect of the issue, is not as fatal as two others which cannot be avoided: if we are regarding the blacks as a "minority" victimized by discrimination, what is a "minority"? And for any group—blacks, women, whatever—that has been discriminated against, what amount of reverse discrimination wipes out the initial discrimination? Let us grant as true that women and blacks were discriminated against, even when laws forbade such discrimination, and grant for the sake of argument that a history of discrimination must be wiped out by reverse discrimination. What follows?

First, are there other groups which have been discriminated against? For they should have the same right of restitution. What about American Indians, Chicanos, Appalachian Mountain whites, Puerto Ricans, Jews, Cajuns, and Orientals? And if these are to be included, the principle according to which we specify a "minority" is simply the criterion of "ethnic (sub) group," and we're stuck with every hyphenated American in the lower-middle class clamoring for special privileges for *his* group—and with equal justification. For be it noted, when we run down the Harvard roster, we find not only a scarcity of blacks (in comparison with the proportion in the population) but an even more striking scarcity of those second-, third-, and fourth-generation ethnics who make up the loudest voice of Middle America. Shouldn't they demand *their* share? And eventually, the WASPs will have to form their own lobby, for they too are a minority. The point is simply this: there is no "majority" in America who will not mind giving up just a bit of their rights to make room for a favored minority. There are only other minorities, each of which is discriminated against by the favoring. The initial injustice is then repeated dozens of times, and if each minority is granted the same right of restitution as the others, an entire area of rule governance is dissolved into a pushing and shoving match between self-interested groups. Each works to catch the public eye and political popularity by whatever means of advertising and power politics lend themselves to the effort, to capitalize as much as possible on temporary popularity until the restless mob picks another group to feel sorry for. Hardly an edifying spectacle, and in the long run no one can benefit: the pie is no larger—it's just that instead of setting up and enforcing rules for getting a piece, we've turned the contest into a free-for-all, requiring much more effort for no larger a reward. It would be in the interest of all the participants to reestablish an objective rule to govern the process, carefully enforced and the same for all.

Second, supposing that we do manage to agree in general that women and blacks (and all the others) have some right of restitution, some right to a privileged place in the structure of opportunities for a while, how will we know when that while is up? How much privilege is enough? When will the guilt be gone, the price paid, the balance restored? What recompense is right for centuries of exclusion? What criterion tells us when we are done? Our experience with the Civil Rights movement shows us that agreement on these terms cannot be presupposed: a process that appears to some to be going at a mad gallop into a black takeover appears to the rest of us to be at a standstill. Should a practice of reverse discrimination be adopted, we may safely predict that just as some of us begin to see "a satisfactory start toward righting the balance," others of us will see that we "have already gone too far in the other direction" and will suggest that the discrimination ought to be reversed again. And such disagreement is inevitable, for the point is that we could not *possibly* have any criteria for evaluating the kind of recompense we have in mind. The context presumed by any discussion of restitution is the context of rule of law: law sets the rights of men and simultaneously sets the method for remedying the violation of those rights. You may exact suffering from others and/or damage payments for yourself if and only if the others have violated your rights; the suffering you have endured is not sufficient reason for them to suffer. And remedial rights exist only where there is law: primary human rights are useful guides to legislation but cannot stand as reasons for awarding remedies for injuries sustained. But then, the context presupposed by any discussion of restitution is the context of preexistent full citizenship. No remedial rights could exist for the excluded; neither in law nor in logic does there exist a right to *sue* for a standing to sue.

From these two considerations, then, the difficulties with reverse discrimination become evident. Restitution for a disadvantaged group whose rights under the law have been violated is possible by legal means, but restitution for a disadvantaged group whose grievance is that there was no law to protect them simply is not. First, outside of the area of justice defined by the law, no sense can be made of "the group's rights," for no law recognizes that group or the individuals in it, qua members, as bearers of rights (hence *any* group can constitute itself as a disadvantaged minority in some sense and demand similar restitution). Second, outside of the area of protection of law, no sense can be made of the violation of rights (hence the amount of the recompense cannot be decided by any objective criterion). For both reasons, the practice of reverse discrimination undermines the foundation of the very ideal in whose name it is advocated; it destroys justice, law, equality, and citizenship itself, and replaces them with power struggles and popularity contests.

THE JUSTICE OF AFFIRMATIVE ACTION

Ronald Dworkin

I

In 1945 a black man named Sweatt applied to the University of Texas Law School, but was refused admission because state law provided that only whites could attend. The Supreme Court declared that this law violated Sweatt's rights under the Fourteenth Amendment to the United States Constitution, which provides that no state shall deny any man the equal protection of its laws. In 1971 a Jew named DeFunis applied to the University of Washington Law School; he was rejected although his test scores and college grades were such that he would have been admitted if he had been a black or a Filipino or a Chicano or an American Indian. DeFunis asked the Supreme Court to declare that the Washington practice, which required less exacting standards of minority groups, violated his rights under the Fourteenth Amendment.

The Washington Law School's admission procedures were complex. Applications were divided into two groups. The majority—those not from the designated minority groups—were first screened so as to eliminate all applicants whose predicted average, which is a function of college grades and aptitude test scores, fell below a certain level. Majority applicants who survived this initial cut were then placed in categories that received progressively more careful consideration. Minority-group applications, on the other hand, were not screened; each received the most careful consideration by a special committee consisting of a black professor of law and a white professor who had taught in programs to aid black law students. Most of the minority applicants who were accepted in the year in which DeFunis was rejected had predicted averages below the cutoff level, and the law school conceded that any minority applicant with his average would certainly have been accepted.

The *DeFunis* case split those political action groups that have traditionally supported liberal causes. The B'nai B'rith Anti-Defamation League and the AFL-CIO, for example, filed briefs as amici curiae in support of DeFunis's claim, while the American Hebrew Women's Council, the UAW, and the UMWA filed briefs against it.

These splits among old allies demonstrate both the practical and the philosophical importance of the case. In the past liberals held, within one set of attitudes, three propositions: that racial classification is an evil in itself; that every person has a right to an educational opportunity commensurate with his abilities; and that affirmative state action is proper to remedy the serious inequalities of American society. In the last decade, however, the opinion has grown that these three liberal propositions are in fact not compatible, because the most effective programs of state action are those that give a competitive advantage to minority racial groups.

That opinion has, of course, been challenged. Some educators argue that benign quotas are ineffective, even self-defeating, because preferential treatment will reinforce the sense of inferiority that many blacks already have. Others make a more general objection. They argue that any racial discrimination, even for the purpose of benefiting minorities, will in fact harm those minorities, because prejudice is fostered whenever racial distinctions are tolerated for any purpose whatever. But these are complex and controversial empirical judgments, and it is far too early, as wise critics concede, to decide whether preferential treatment does more harm or good. Nor is it the business of judges, particularly in constitutional cases, to overthrow decisions of other officials because the judges disagree about the efficiency of social policies. This empirical criticism is therefore reinforced by the moral argument that even if reverse discrimination does benefit minorities and does reduce prejudice in the long run, it is nevertheless wrong because distinctions of race are inherently unjust. They are unjust because they violate the rights of individual members of groups not so favored, who may thereby lose a place, as DeFunis did.

DeFunis presented this moral argument, in the form of a constitutional claim, to the courts. The Supreme Court did not, in the end, decide whether the argument was good or bad. DeFunis had been admitted to the law school after one lower court had decided in his favor, and the law school said that he would be allowed to graduate however the case was finally decided. The Court therefore held that the case was moot and dismissed the appeal on that ground. But Justice Douglas disagreed with this neutral disposition of the case; he wrote a dissenting opinion in which he argued that the Court should have upheld DeFunis's claim on the merits. Many universities and colleges have taken Justice Douglas's opinion as handwriting on the wall, and have changed their practices in anticipation of a later Court decision in which his opinion prevails. In fact, his opinion pointed out that law schools might achieve much the same result by a more sophisticated policy than Washington used. A school might stipulate, for example, that applicants from all races and groups would be considered together, but that the aptitude tests of certain minority applicants would be graded differently, or given less weight in overall predicted average, because experience had shown that standard examinations were for different reasons a poorer test of the actual ability of these applicants. But if this technique is used deliberately to achieve the same result, it is devious, and it remains to ask why the candid program used by the University of Washington was either unjust or unconstitutional.

II

DeFunis plainly has no constitutional right that the state provide him a legal education of a certain quality. His rights would not be violated if his state did not have a law school at all, or if it had a law school with so few places that he could not win one on intellectual merit. Nor does he have a right to insist that intelligence be the exclusive test of admission. Law schools do rely heavily on intellectual tests for admission. That seems proper, however, not because applicants have a right to be judged in that way, but because it is reasonable to think that the community as a whole is better off if its lawyers are intelligent. That is, intellectual standards are justified, not because they reward the clever, but because they seem to serve a useful social policy.

Law schools sometimes serve that policy better, moreover, by supplementing intelligence tests with other sorts of standards: they sometimes prefer industrious applicants, for example, to those who are brighter but lazier. They also serve special policies for which intelligence is not relevant. The Washington Law School, for example, gave special preference not only to minority applicants but also to veterans who had been at the school before entering the military, and neither DeFunis nor any of the briefs submitted in his behalf complained of that preference.

DeFunis does not have an absolute right to a law school place, nor does he have a right that only intelligence be used as a standard for admission. He says he nevertheless has a right that race *not* be used as a standard, no matter how well a racial classification might work to promote the general welfare or to reduce social and economic inequality. He does not claim, however, that he has this right as a distinct and independent political right that is specifically protected by the Constitution, as is his right to freedom of speech and religion. The Constitution does not condemn racial classification directly, as it does condemn censorship or the establishment of a state religion. DeFunis claims that his right that race not be used as a criterion of admission follows from the more abstract right of equality that is protected by the Fourteenth Amendment, which provides that no state shall deny to any person the equal protection of the law.

But the legal arguments made on both sides show that neither the text of the Constitution nor the prior decisions of the Supreme Court decisively settle the question whether, as a matter of law, the Equal Protection Clause makes all racial classifications unconstitutional. The Clause makes the concept of equality a test of legislation, but it does not stipulate any particular conception of that concept. Those who wrote the clause intended to attack certain consequences of slavery and racial prejudice, but it is unlikely that they intended to outlaw all racial classifications, or that they expected such a prohibition to be the result of what they wrote. They outlawed whatever policies would violate equality, but left it to others to decide, from time to time, what that means. There cannot be a good legal argument in favor of DeFunis, therefore, unless there is a good moral argument that all racial classifications, even those that make society as a whole more equal, are inherently offensive to an individual's right to equal protection for himself.

There is nothing paradoxical, of course, in the ideal that an individual's right to equal protection may sometimes conflict with an otherwise desirable social policy, including the policy of making the community more equal overall. Suppose a law school were to charge a few middle-class students, selected by lot, double tuition in order to increase the scholarship fund for poor students. It would be serving a desirable policy—equality of opportunity—by means that violated the right of the students selected by lot to be treated equally with other students who could also afford the increased fees. It is, in fact, part of the importance of DeFunis's case that it forces us to acknowledge the distinction between equality as a policy and equality as a right, a distinction that political theory has virtually ignored. He argues that the Washington Law School violated his individual right to equality for the sake of a policy of greater equality overall, in the same way that double tuition for arbitrarily chosen students would violate their rights for the same purpose.

We must therefore concentrate our attention on that claim. We must try to define the central concept on which it turns, which is the concept of an individual right to equality made a constitutional right by the Equal Protection Clause. What rights to equality do citizens have as individuals which might defeat programs aimed at important economic and social policies, including the social policy of improving equality overall?

There are two different sorts of rights they may be said to have. The first is the right to *equal treatment,* which is the right to an equal distribution of some opportunity or resource or burden. Every citizen, for example, has a right to an equal vote in a democracy; that is the nerve of the Supreme Court's decision that one person must have one vote even if a different and more complex arrangement would better secure the collective welfare. The second is the right to *treatment as an equal,* which is the right, not to receive the same distribution of some burden or benefit, but to be treated with the same respect and concern as anyone else. If I have two children, and one is dying from a disease that is making the other uncomfortable, I do not show equal concern if I flip a coin to decide which should have the remaining dose of a drug. This example shows that the right to treatment as an equal is fundamental, and the right to equal treatment, derivative. In some circumstances the right to treatment as an equal will entail a right to equal treatment, but not, by any means, in all circumstances.

DeFunis does not have a right to equal treatment in the assignment of law school places; he does not have a right to a place just because others are given places. Individuals may have a right to equal treatment in elementary education, because someone who is denied elementary education is unlikely to lead a useful life. But legal education is not so vital that everyone has an equal right to it.

DeFunis does have the second sort of right—a right to treatment as an equal in the decision as to which admissions standards should be used. That is, he has a right that his interests be treated as fully and sympathetically as the interests of any others when the law school decides whether to count race as a pertinent criterion for admission. But we must be careful not to overstate what that means.

Suppose an applicant complains that his right to be treated as an equal is violated by tests that place the less intelligent candidates at a disadvantage against the more intelligent. A law school might properly reply in the following way. Any standard will place certain candidates at a disadvantage as against others, but an admission policy may nevertheless be justified if it seems reasonable to expect that the overall gain to the community exceeds the overall loss, and if no other policy that does not provide a comparable disadvantage would produce even roughly the same gain. An individual's right to be treated as an equal means that his potential loss must be treated as a matter of concern, but that loss may nevertheless be outweighed by the gain to the community as a whole. If it is, then the less intelligent applicant cannot claim that he is cheated of his right to be treated as an equal just because he suffers a disadvantage others do not.

Washington may make the same reply to DeFunis. Any admissions policy must put some applicants at a disadvantage, and a policy of preference for minority applicants can reasonably be supposed to benefit the community as a whole, even when the loss to candidates such as DeFunis is taken into account. If there are more black lawyers, they will help to provide better legal services to the black community, and so reduce social tensions. It might well improve the quality of legal education for all students, moreover, to have a greater number of blacks as classroom discussants of social problems. Further, if blacks are seen as successful law students, then other blacks who do meet the usual intellectual standards might be encouraged to apply and that, in turn, would raise the intellectual quality of the bar. In any case, preferential admissions of blacks should decrease the difference in wealth and power that now exists between different racial groups, and so make the community more equal overall. It is, as I said, controversial whether a preferential admissions program will in fact promote these various policies, but it cannot be said to be implausible that it will. The disadvantage to applicants such as DeFunis is, on that hypothesis, a cost that must be paid for a greater gain; it is in that way like the disadvantage to less intelligent students that is the cost of ordinary admissions policies.

We now see the difference between DeFunis's case and the case we imagined, in which a law school charged students selected at random higher fees. The special disadvantage to these students was not necessary to achieve the gain in scholarship funds, because the same gain would have been achieved by a more equal distribution of the cost amongst all the students who could afford it. That is not true of DeFunis. He did suffer from the Washington policy more than those majority applicants who were accepted. But that discrimination was not arbitrary; it was a consequence of the meritocratic standards he approves. DeFunis's argument therefore fails. The Equal Protection Clause gives constitutional standing to the right to be treated as an equal, but he cannot find, in that right, any support for his claim that the clause makes all racial classification illegal.

III

If we dismiss DeFunis's claim in this straightforward way, however, we are left with this puzzle. How can so many able lawyers, who supported his claim both in morality and law, have made that mistake? These lawyers all agree that intelligence is a proper criterion for admission to law schools. They do not suppose that anyone's constitutional right to be treated as an equal is compromised by that criterion. Why do they deny that race, in the circumstances of this decade, may also be a proper criterion?

They fear, perhaps, that racial criteria will be misused; that such criteria will serve as an excuse for prejudice against the minorities that are not favored, such as Jews. But that cannot explain their opposition. Any criteria may be misused, and in any case they think that racial criteria are wrong in principle and not simply open to abuse.

Why? The answer lies in their belief that, in theory as well as in practice, *DeFunis* and *Sweatt* must stand or fall together. They believe that it is illogical for liberals to condemn Texas for raising a color barrier against Sweatt, and then applaud Washington for raising a color barrier against DeFunis. The difference between these two cases, they suppose, must be only the subjective preference of liberals for certain minorities now in fashion. If there is something wrong with racial classifications, then it must be something that is wrong with racial classifications as such, not just classifications that work against those groups currently in favor. That is the inarticulate premise behind the slogan, relied on by defendants of DeFunis, that the Constitution is colorblind. That slogan means, of course, just the opposite of what it says: it means that the Constitution is so sensitive to color that it makes any institutional racial classification invalid as a matter of law.

It is of the greatest importance, therefore, to test the assumption that *Sweatt* and *DeFunis* must stand or fall together. If that assumption is sound, then the straightforward argument against DeFunis must be fallacious after all, for no argument could convince us that segregation of the sort practiced against Sweatt is justifiable or constitutional. Superficially, moreover, the arguments against DeFunis do indeed seem available against Sweatt, because we can construct an argument that Texas might have used to show that segregation benefits the collective welfare, so that the special disadvantage to blacks is a cost that must be paid to achieve an overall gain.

Suppose the Texas admissions committee, though composed of men and women who themselves held no prejudice, decided that the Texas economy demanded more white lawyers than they could educate, but could find no use for black lawyers at all. That might have been, after all, a realistic assessment of the commercial market for lawyers in Texas just after World War II. Corporate law firms needed lawyers to serve booming business but could not afford to hire black lawyers, however skillful, because the firms' practices would be destroyed if they did. It was no doubt true that the black community in Texas had great need of skillful lawyers, and would have preferred to use black lawyers if they were available. But the committee might well have thought that the commercial needs of the state as a whole outweighed that special need.

Or suppose the committee judged, no doubt accurately, that alumni gifts to the law school would fall off drastically if it admitted a black student. The committee might deplore that fact, but nevertheless believe that the consequent collective damage would be greater than the damage to black candidates excluded by the racial restriction.

It may be said that these hypothetical arguments are disingenuous, because any policy of excluding blacks would in fact be supported by a prejudice against blacks as such, and arguments of the sort just described would be accepted by men who do not have the prejudices the objection assumes. It therefore does not follow from the fact that the admissions officers were prejudiced that, if they were, then they would have rejected these arguments if they had not been. . . .

IV

So these familiar arguments that might distinguish the two cases are unconvincing. That seems to confirm that *Sweatt* and *DeFunis* must be treated alike, and therefore that racial classification must be outlawed altogether. But fortunately a more successful ground of distinction can be found to support our initial sense that the cases are in fact very different. This distinction does not rely, as these unconvincing arguments do, on features peculiar to issues of race or segregation, or even on features peculiar to issues of educational opportunity. It relies instead on further analysis of the idea, which was central to my argument against *DeFunis,* that in certain circumstances a policy which puts many individuals at a disadvantage is nevertheless justified because it makes the community as a whole better off.

Any institution which uses that idea to justify a discriminatory policy faces a series of theoretical and practical difficulties. There are, in the first place, two distinct senses in which a community may be said to be better off as a whole, in spite of the fact that certain of its members are worse off, and any justification must specify which sense is meant. It may be better off in a *utilitarian* sense, that is, because the average or collective level of welfare in the community is improved even though the welfare of some individuals falls. Or it may be better off in an *ideal* sense, that is, because it is more just, or in some other way closer to an ideal society, whether or not average welfare is improved. The University of Washington might use either utilitarian or ideal arguments to justify its racial classification. It might argue, for example, that increasing the number of black lawyers reduces racial tensions, which improves the welfare of almost everyone in the community. That is a utilitarian argument. Or it might argue that, whatever effect minority preference will have on average welfare, it will make the community more equal and therefore more just. That is an ideal, not a utilitarian, argument.

The University of Texas, on the other hand, cannot make an ideal argument for segregation. It cannot claim that segregation makes the community more just whether it improves the average welfare or not. The arguments it makes to defend segregation must therefore all be utilitarian arguments. The arguments I invented, like the argument that white lawyers could do more than black lawyers to improve commercial efficiency in Texas, are utilitarian, since commercial efficiency makes the community better off only if it improves average welfare.

Utilitarian arguments encounter a special difficulty that ideal arguments do not. What is meant by average or collective welfare? How can the welfare of an individual be measured, even in principle, and how can gains in the welfare of different individuals be added and then compared with losses, so as to justify the claim that gains outweigh losses overall? The utilitarian argument that segregation improves average welfare presupposes that such calculations can be made. But how?

Jeremy Bentham, who believed that only utilitarian arguments could justify political decisions, gave the following answer. He said that the effect of a policy on an individual's welfare could be determined by discovering the amount of pleasure or pain the policy brought him, and that the effect of the policy on the collective welfare could be calculated by adding together all the pleasure and subtracting all of the pain it brought to everyone. But, as Bentham's critics insisted, it is doubtful whether there exists a simple psychological state of pleasure common to all those who benefit from a policy or of pain common to all those who lose by it; in any case it would be impossible to identify, measure, and add the different pleasures and pains felt by vast numbers of people.

Philosophers and economists who find utilitarian arguments attractive, but who reject Bentham's psychological utilitarianism, propose a different concept of individual and overall welfare. They suppose that whenever an institution or an official must decide upon a policy, the members of the community will each prefer the consequences of one decision to the consequences of others. DeFunis, for example, prefers the consequences of the standard admissions policy to the policy of minority preference Washington used, while the blacks in some urban ghetto might each prefer the consequences of the latter policy to the former. If it can be discovered what each individual prefers, and how intensely, then it might be shown that a particular policy would satisfy on balance more preferences, taking into account their intensity, than alternative policies. On this concept of welfare, a policy makes the community better off in a utilitarian sense if it satisfies the collection of preferences better than alternative policies would, even though it dissatisfies the preferences of some.

Of course, a law school does not have available any means of making accurate judgments about the preferences of all those whom its admissions policies will affect. It may nevertheless make judgments which, though speculative, cannot be dismissed as implausible. It is, for example, plausible to think that in postwar Texas, the preferences of the people were overall in favor of the consequences of segregation in law schools, even if the intensity of the competing preference for integration, and not simply the number of those holding that preference, is taken into account. The officials of the Texas law school might have relied upon voting behavior, newspaper editorials, and simply their own sense of their community in reaching that decision. Though they might have been wrong, we cannot now say, even with the benefit of hind-sight, that they were.

So even if Bentham's psychological utilitarianism is rejected, law schools may appeal to preference utilitarianism to provide at least a rough and specu-lative justification for admissions policies that put some classes of applicants at a disadvantage. But once it is made clear that these utilitarian arguments are based on judgments about the actual preferences of members of the com-munity, a fresh and much more serious difficulty emerges.

The utilitarian argument, that a policy is justified if it satisfies more pref-erences overall, seems at first sight to be an egalitarian argument. It seems to observe strict impartiality. If the community has only enough medicine to treat some of those who are sick, the argument seems to recommend that those who are sickest be treated first. If the community can afford a swim-ming pool or a new theater, but not both, and more people want the pool, then it recommends that the community build the pool, unless those who want the theater can show that their preferences are so much more intense that they have more weight in spite of the numbers. One sick man is not to be preferred to another because he is worthier of official concern: the tastes of the theater audience are not to be preferred because they are more ad-mirable. In Bentham's phrase, each man is to count as one and no man is to count as more than one.

These simple examples suggest that the utilitarian argument not only re-spects, but embodies, the right of each citizen to be treated as the equal of any other. The chance that each individual's preferences have to succeed, in the competition for social policy, will depend upon how important his pref-erence is to him, and how many others share it, compared to the intensity and number of competing preferences. His chance will not be affected by the esteem or contempt of either officials or fellow citizens, and he will there-fore not be subservient or beholden to them.

But if we examine the range of preferences that individuals in fact have, we shall see that the apparent egalitarian character of a utilitarian argument is often deceptive. Preference utilitarianism asks officials to attempt to sat-isfy people's preferences so far as this is possible. But the preferences of an individual for the consequences of a particular policy may be seen to reflect, on further analysis, either a *personal* preference for his own enjoyment of some goods or opportunities, or an *external* preference for the assignment of goods and opportunities to others, or both. A white law school candidate might have a personal preference for the consequences of segregation, for example, because the policy improves his own chances of success, or an ex-ternal preference for those consequences because he has contempt for blacks and disapproves social situations in which the races mix.

The distinction between personal and external preferences is of great importance for this reason. If a utilitarian argument counts external prefer-ences along with personal preferences, then the egalitarian character of that argument is corrupted, because the chance that anyone's preferences have to succeed will then depend, not only on the demands that the personal preferences of others make on scarce resources, but on the respect or affection they have for him or for his way of life. If external preferences tip the balance, then the fact that a policy makes the community better off in a utilitarian sense would *not* provide a justification compatible with the right of those it disadvantages to be treated as equals.

This corruption of utilitarianism is plain when some people have external preferences because they hold political theories that are themselves contrary to utilitarianism. Suppose many citizens, who are not themselves sick, are racists in political theory, and therefore prefer that scarce medicine be given to a white man who needs it rather than a black man who needs it more. If utilitarianism counts these political preferences at face value, then it will be, from the standpoint of personal preferences, self-defeating, because the distribution of medicine will then not be, from that standpoint, utilitarian at all. In any case, self-defeating or not, the distribution will not be egalitarian in the sense defined. Blacks will suffer, to a degree that depends upon the strength of the racist preference, from the fact that others think them less worthy of respect and concern.

There is a similar corruption when the external preferences that are counted are altruistic or moralistic. Suppose many citizens, who themselves do not swim, prefer the pool to the theater because they approve of sports and admire athletes, or because they think that the theater is immoral and ought to be repressed. If the altruistic preferences are counted, so as to reinforce the personal preferences of swimmers, the result will be a form of double counting: each swimmer will have the benefit not only of his own preference, but also of the preference of someone else who takes pleasure in his success. If the moralistic preferences are counted, the effect will be the same: actors and audiences will suffer because their preferences are held in lower respect by citizens whose personal preferences are not themselves engaged.

In these examples, external preferences are independent of personal preferences. But of course political, altruistic, and moralistic preferences are often not independent, but grafted on to the personal preferences they reinforce. If I am white and sick, I may also hold a racist political theory. If I want a swimming pool for my own enjoyment I may also be altruistic in favor of my fellow athlete, or I may also think that the theater is immoral. The consequences of counting these external preferences will be as grave for equality as if they were independent of personal preference, because those against whom the external preferences run might be unable or unwilling to develop reciprocal external preferences that would right the balance.

External preferences therefore present a great difficulty for utilitarianism. That theory owes much of its popularity to the assumption that it embodies the right of citizens to be treated as equals. But if external preferences are counted in overall preferences, then this assumption is jeopardized. That is, in itself, an important and neglected point in political theory; it bears, for example, on the liberal thesis, first made prominent by Mill, that the government has no right to enforce popular morality by law. It is often said that this liberal thesis is inconsistent with utilitarianism, because if the preferences of the majority that homosexuality should be repressed, for example, are sufficiently strong, utilitarianism must give way to their wishes. But the preference against homosexuality is an external preference, and the present argument provides a general reason why utilitarians should not count external preferences of any form. If utilitarianism is suitably reconstituted so as to count only personal preferences, then the liberal thesis is a consequence, not an enemy, of that theory.

It is not always possible, however, to reconstitute a utilitarian argument so as to count only personal preferences. Sometimes personal and external preferences are so inextricably tied together, and so mutually dependent, that no practical test for measuring preferences will be able to discriminate the personal and external elements in any individual's overall preference. That is especially true when preferences are affected by prejudice. Consider, for example, the associational preference of a white law student for white classmates. This may be said to be a personal preference for an association with one kind of colleague rather than another. But it is a personal preference that is parasitic upon external preferences: except in very rare cases a white student prefers the company of other whites because he has racist social and political convictions, or because he has contempt for blacks as a group. If these associational preferences are counted in a utilitarian argument used to justify segregation, then the egalitarian character of the argument is destroyed just as if the underlying external preferences were counted directly. Blacks would be denied their right to be treated as equals because the chance that their preferences would prevail in the design of admissions policy would be crippled by the low esteem in which others hold them. In any community in which prejudice against a particular minority is strong, then the personal preferences upon which a utilitarian argument must fix will be saturated with that prejudice; it follows that in such a community no utilitarian argument purporting to justify a disadvantage to the minority can be fair.

This final difficulty is therefore fatal to Texas' utilitarian arguments in favor of segregation. The preferences that might support any such argument are either distinctly external, like the preferences of the community at large for racial separation, or are inextricably combined with and dependent upon external preferences, like the associational preferences of white students for white classmates and white lawyers for white colleagues. These external preferences are so widespread that they must corrupt any such argument. Texas' claim, that segregation makes the community better off in a utilitarian sense, is therefore incompatible with Sweatt's right to treatment as an equal guaranteed by the Equal Protection Clause.

It does not matter, to this conclusion, whether external preferences figure in the justification of a fundamental policy, or in the justification of derivative policies designed to advance a more fundamental policy. Suppose Texas justifies segregation by pointing to the apparently neutral economic policy of increasing community wealth, which satisfies the personal preferences of everyone for better homes, food, and recreation. If the argument that segregation will improve community wealth depends upon the fact of external preference; if the argument notices, for example, that because of prejudice industry will run more efficiently if factories are segregated; then the argument has the consequence that the black man's personal preferences are defeated by what others think of him. Utilitarian arguments that justify a disadvantage to members of a race against whom prejudice runs will always be unfair arguments, unless it can be shown that the same disadvantage would have been justified in the absence of the prejudice. If the prejudice is widespread and pervasive, as in fact it is in the case of blacks, that can never be shown. The preferences on which any economic argument justifying segregation must be based will be so intertwined with prejudice that they cannot be disentangled to the degree necessary to make any such contrary-to-fact hypothesis plausible.

We now have an explanation that shows why any form of segregation that disadvantages blacks is, in the United States, an automatic insult to them, and why such segregation offends their right to be treated as equals. The argument confirms our sense that utilitarian arguments purporting to justify segregation are not simply wrong in detail but displaced in principle. This objection to utilitarian arguments is not, however, limited to race or even prejudice. There are other cases in which counting external preferences would offend the rights of citizens to be treated as equals, and it is worth briefly noticing these, if only to protect the argument against the charge that it is constructed ad hoc for the racial case. I might have a moralistic preference against professional women, or an altruistic preference for virtuous men. It would be unfair for any law school to count preferences like these in deciding whom to admit to law schools; unfair because these preferences, like racial prejudices, make the success of the personal preferences of an applicant depend on the esteem and approval, rather than on the competing personal preferences, of others.

The same objection does not hold, however, against a utilitarian argument used to justify admission based on intelligence. That policy need not rely, directly or indirectly, on any community sense that intelligent lawyers are intrinsically more worthy of respect. It relies instead upon the law school's own judgment, right or wrong, that intelligent lawyers are more effective in satisfying personal preferences of others, such as the preference for wealth or winning law suits. It is true that law firms and clients prefer the services of intelligent lawyers; that fact might make us suspicious of any utilitarian argument that is said not to depend upon that preference, just as we are suspicious of any argument justifying segregation that is said not to depend upon prejudice. But the widespread preference for intelligent lawyers is, by and large, not parasitic on external preferences: law firms and clients prefer intelligent lawyers because they also hold the opinion that such lawyers will be more effective in serving their personal preferences. Instrumental preferences, of that character, do not themselves figure in utilitarian arguments, though a law school may accept, on its own responsibility, the instrumental hypothesis upon which such preferences depend.

V

We therefore have the distinctions in hand necessary to distinguish *DeFunis* from *Sweatt.* The arguments for an admissions program that discriminates against blacks are all utilitarian arguments, and they are all utilitarian arguments that rely upon external preferences in such a way as to offend the constitutional right of blacks to be treated as equals. The arguments for an admissions program that discriminates in favor of blacks are both utilitarian and ideal. Some of the utilitarian arguments do rely, at least indirectly, on external preferences, such as the preference of certain blacks for lawyers of their own race; but the utilitarian arguments that do not rely on such preferences are strong and may be sufficient. The ideal arguments do not rely upon preferences at all, but on the independent argument that a more equal society is a better society even if its citizens prefer inequality. That argument does not deny anyone's right to be treated as an equal himself.

We are therefore left, in *DeFunis,* with the simple and straightforward argument with which we began. Racial criteria are not necessarily the right standards for deciding which applicants should be accepted by law schools. But neither are intellectual criteria, nor indeed, any other set of criteria. The fairness—and constitutionality—of any admissions program must be tested in the same way. It is justified if it serves a proper policy that respects the right of all members of the community to be treated as equals, but not otherwise. The criteria used by schools that refused to consider blacks failed that test, but the criteria used by the University of Washington Law School do not.

We are all rightly suspicious of racial classifications. They have been used to deny, rather than to respect, the right of equality, and we are all conscious of the consequent injustice. But if we misunderstand the nature of that injustice because we do not make the simple distinctions that are necessary to understand it, then we are in danger of more injustice still. It may be that preferential admissions programs will not, in fact, make a more equal society, because they may not have the effects their advocates believe they will. That strategic question should be at the center of debate about these programs. But we must not corrupt the debate by supposing that these programs are unfair even if they do work. We must take care not to use the Equal Protection Clause to cheat ourselves of equality.

AFFIRMATIVE RACISM

Charles Murray

A few years ago, I got into an argument with a lawyer friend who is a partner in a New York firm. I was being the conservative, arguing that preferential treatment of blacks was immoral; he was being the liberal, urging that it was the only way to bring blacks to full equality. In the middle of all this he abruptly said, "But you know, let's face it. We must have hired at least ten blacks in the last few years, and none of them has really worked out." He then returned to his case for still stronger affirmative action, while I wondered what it had been like for those ten blacks. And if he could make a remark like that so casually, what remarks would he be able to make some years down the road, if by that time it had been fifty blacks who hadn't "really worked out"?

My friend's comment was an outcropping of a new racism that is emerging to take its place alongside the old. It grows out of preferential treatment for blacks, and it is not just the much-publicized reactions, for example, of the white policemen or firemen who are passed over for promotion because of an affirmative action court order. The new racism that is potentially most damaging is located among the white elites—educated, affluent, and occupying the positions in education, business, and government from which this country is run. It currently focuses on blacks; whether it will eventually extend to include Hispanics and other minorities remains to be seen.

The new racists do not think blacks are inferior. They are typically long-time supporters of civil rights. But they exhibit the classic behavioral symptom of racism: they treat blacks differently from whites, because of their race. The results can be as concretely bad and unjust as any that the old racism produces. Sometimes the effect is that blacks are refused an education they otherwise could have gotten. Sometimes blacks are shunted into dead-end jobs. Always, blacks are denied the right to compete as equals.

The new racists also exhibit another characteristic of racism: they *think* about blacks differently from the way they think about whites. Their global view of blacks and civil rights is impeccable. Blacks must be enabled to achieve full equality. They are still unequal, through no fault of their own (it is the fault of racism, it is the fault of inadequate opportunity, it is the legacy of history). But the new racists' local view is that the blacks they run across professionally are not, on the average, up to the white standard. Among the new racists, lawyers have gotten used to the idea that the brief a black colleague turns in will be a little less well-rehearsed and argued than the one they would have done. Businessmen expect that a black colleague will not read a balance sheet as subtly as they do. Teachers expect black students to wind up toward the bottom of the class.

The new racists also tend to think of blacks as a commodity. The office must have a sufficient supply of blacks, who must be treated with special delicacy. The personnel problems this creates are more difficult than most because whites barely admit to themselves what's going on.

What follows is a foray into very poorly mapped territory. I will present a few numbers that explain much about how the process gets started. But the ways that the numbers get translated into behavior are even more important. The cases I present are composites constructed from my own observations and taken from firsthand accounts. All are based on real events and real people, stripped of their particularities. But the individual cases are not intended as evidence, because I cannot tell you how often they happen. They have not been the kind of thing that social scientists or journalists have wanted to count. I am writing this because so many people, both white and black, to whom I tell such stories know immediately what I am talking about. It is apparent that a problem exists. How significant is it? What follows is as much an attempt to elicit evidence as to present it.

As in so many of the crusades of the 1960s, the nation began with a good idea. It was called "affirmative action," initiated by Lyndon Johnson through Executive Order 11246 in September 1965. It was an attractive label and a natural corrective to past racism: actively seek out black candidates for jobs, college, or promotions, without treating them differently in the actual decision to hire, admit, or promote. The term originally evoked both the letter and the spirit of the order.

Then, gradually, affirmative action came to mean something quite different. In 1970 a federal court established the legitimacy of quotas as a means of implementing Johnson's executive order. In 1971 the Supreme Court ruled that an employer could not use minimum credentials as a prerequisite for hiring if the credential acted as a "built-in headwind" for minority groups—even when there was no discriminatory intent and even when the hiring procedures were "fair in form." In 1972 the Equal Employment Opportunity Commission acquired broad, independent enforcement powers.

Thus by the early 1970s it had become generally recognized that a good-faith effort to recruit qualified blacks was not enough—especially if one's school depended on federal grants or one's business depended on federal contracts. Even for businesses and schools not directly dependent on the government, the simplest way to withstand an accusation of violating Title VII of the Civil Rights Act of 1964 was to make sure not that they had just interviewed enough minority candidates, but that they had actually hired or admitted enough of them. Employers and admissions committees arrived at a rule of thumb: if the blacks who are available happen to be the best candidates, fine; if not, the best available black candidates will be given some sort of edge in the selection process. Sometimes the edge will be small; sometimes it will be predetermined that a black candidate is essential, and the edge will be very large.

Perhaps the first crucial place where the edge applies is in admission to college. Consider the cases of the following three students: John, William, and Carol, 17 years old and applying to college, are all equal on paper. Each has a score of 520 in the mathematics section of the Scholastic Aptitude Test, which puts them in the top third—at the 67th percentile—of all students who took the test. (Figures are based on 1983 data.)

John is white. A score of 520 gets him into the state university. Against the advice of his high school counselor, he applies to a prestigious school, Ivy U., where his application is rejected in the first cut—its average white applicant has math scores in the high 600s.

William is black, from a middle-class family who sent him to good schools. His score of 520 puts him at the 95th percentile of all blacks who took the test. William's high school counselor points out that he could probably get into Ivy U. William applies and is admitted—Ivy U. uses separate standards for admission of whites and blacks, and William is among the top blacks who applied.

Carol is black, educated at an inner-city school, and her score of 520 represents an extraordinary achievement in the face of terrible schooling. An alumnus of Ivy U. who regularly looks for promising inner-city candidates finds her, recruits her, and sends her off with a full scholarship to Ivy U.

When American universities embarked on policies of preferential admissions by race, they had the Carols in mind. They had good reason to be optimistic that preferential treatment would work—for many years, the best universities had been weighting the test scores of applicants from small-town public schools when they were compared against those of applicants from the top private schools, and had been giving special breaks to students from distant states to ensure geographic distribution. The differences in preparation tended to even out after the first year or so. Blacks were being brought into a long-standing and successful tradition of preferential treatment.

In the case of blacks, however, preferential treatment ran up against a large black-white gap in academic performance combined with ambitious goals for proportional representation. This gap had been the hardest for whites to confront. But though it is not necessary or even plausible to believe that such differences are innate, it is necessary to recognize openly that the differences exist. By pretending they don't, we begin the process whereby both the real differences and the racial factor are exaggerated.

The black-white gap that applies most directly to this discussion is the one that separates blacks and whites who go to college. In 1983, for example, the mean Scholastic Aptitude Test score for all blacks who took the examination was more than 100 points below the white score on both the verbal and the math sections. Statistically, it is an extremely wide gap. To convert the gap into more concrete terms, think of it this way: in 1983, the same Scholastic Aptitude Test math score that put a black at the 50th percentile of all blacks who took the test put him at the 16th percentile of all whites who took the test.

These results clearly mean we ought to be making an all-out effort to improve elementary and secondary education for blacks. But that doesn't help much now, when an academic discrepancy of this magnitude is fed into a preferential admissions process. As universities scramble to make sure they are admitting enough blacks, the results feed the new racism. Here's how it works:

In 1983, only 66 black students nationwide scored above 700 in the verbal section of the Scholastic Aptitude Test, and only 205 scored above 700 in the mathematics section. This handful of students cannot begin to meet the demand for blacks with such scores. For example, Harvard, Yale, and Princeton have in recent years been bringing an aggregate of about 270 blacks into each entering class. If the black students entering these schools had the same distribution of scores as that of the freshman class as a whole, then every black student in the nation with a verbal score in the 700s, and roughly 70 percent of the ones with a math score in the 700s, would be in their freshman classes.

The main problem is not that a few schools monopolize the very top black applicants, but that these same schools have much larger implicit quotas than they can fill with those applicants. They fill out the rest with the next students in line—students who would not have gotten into these schools if they were not black, who otherwise would have been showing up in the classrooms of the nation's less glamorous colleges and universities. But the size of the black pool does not expand appreciably at the next levels. The number of blacks scoring in the 600s on the math section in 1983, for example, was 1,531. Meanwhile, 31,704 nonblack students in 1983 scored in the 700s on the math section and 121,640 scored in the 600s. The prestige schools cannot begin to absorb these numbers of other highly qualified freshmen, and they are perforce spread widely throughout the system.

At schools that draw most broadly from the student population, such as the large state universities, the effects of this skimming produce a situation that confirms the old racists in everything they want most to believe. There are plenty of outstanding students in such student bodies (at the University of Colorado, for example, 6 percent of the freshmen in 1981 had math scores in the 700s and 28 percent had scores in the 600s), but the skimming process combined with the very small raw numbers means that almost none of them are black. What students and instructors see in their day-to-day experience in the classroom is a disproportionate number of blacks who are below the white average, relatively few blacks who are at the white average, and virtually none who are in the first rank. The image that the white student carries away is that blacks are less able than whites.

I am not exalting the SAT as an infallible measure of academic ability, or pointing to test scores to try to convince anyone that blacks are performing below the level of whites. I am simply using them to explain what instructors and students already notice, and talk about, among themselves.

They do not talk openly about such matters. One characteristic of the new racism is that whites deny in public but acknowledge in private that there are significant differences in black and white academic performance. Another is that they dismiss the importance of tests when black scores are at issue, blaming cultural bias and saying that test scores are not good predictors of college performance. At the same time, they watch anxiously over their own children's test scores.

The differences in academic performance do not disappear by the end of college. Far from narrowing, the gap separating black and white academic achievement appears to get larger. Various studies, most recently at Harvard, have found that during the 1970s blacks did worse in college (as measured by grade point average) than their test scores would have predicted. Moreover, the black-white gap in the Graduate Record Examination is larger than the gap in the Scholastic Aptitude Test. The gap between black and white freshmen is a bit less than one standard deviation (the technical measure for comparing scores). Black and white seniors who take the Graduate Record Examination reveal a gap of about one and a quarter standard deviations.

Why should the gap grow wider? Perhaps it is an illusion—for example, perhaps a disproportionate number of the best black students never take the examination. But there are also reasons for suspecting that in fact blacks get a worse education in college than whites do. Here are a few of the hypotheses that deserve full exploration.

Take the situation of William—a slightly above-average student who, because he is black, gets into a highly competitive school. William studies very hard during the first year. He nonetheless gets mediocre grades. He has a choice. He can continue to study hard to continue to get mediocre grades, and be seen by his classmates as a black who cannot do very well. Or he can explicitly refuse to engage in the academic game. He decides to opt out, and his performance gets worse as time goes on. He emerges from college with a poor education and is further behind the whites than he was as a freshman.

If large numbers of other black students at the institution are in the same situation as William, the result can be group pressure not to compete academically. (At Harvard, it is said, the current term among black students for a black who studies like a white is "incognegro.") The response is not hard to understand. If one subpopulation of students is conspicuously behind another population and is visibly identifiable, then the population that is behind must come up with a good excuse for doing poorly. "Not wanting to do better" is as good as any.

But there is another crucial reason why blacks might not close the gap with whites during college: they are not taught as well as whites are. Racist teachers impeding the progress of students? Perhaps, but most college faculty members I know tend to bend over backward to be "fair" to black students—and that may be the problem. I suggest that inferior instruction is more likely to be a manifestation of the new racism than the old.

Consider the case of Carol, with outstanding abilities but deprived of decent prior schooling: she struggles the first year, but she gets by. Her academic skills still show the aftereffects of her inferior preparation. Her instructors diplomatically point out the more flagrant mistakes, but they ignore minor lapses, and never push her in the aggressive way they push white students who have her intellectual capacity. Some of them are being patronizing (she is doing quite well, considering). Others are being prudent: teachers who criticize black students can find themselves being called racists in the classroom, in the campus newspaper, or in complaints to the administration.

The same process continues in graduate school. Indeed, because there are even fewer blacks in graduate schools than in undergraduate schools, the pressures to get black students through to the degree, no matter what, can be still greater. But apart from the differences in preparation and ability that have accumulated by the end of schooling, the process whereby we foster the appearance of black inferiority continues. Let's assume that William did not give up during college. He goes to business school, where he gets his Masters degree. He signs up for interviews with the corporate recruiters. There are 100 persons in his class, and William is ranked near the middle. But of the 5 blacks in his class, he ranks first (remember that he was at the 95th percentile of blacks taking the Scholastic Aptitude Test). He is hired on his first interview by his first-choice company, which also attracted the very best of the white students. He is hired alongside 5 of the top-ranking white members of the class.

William's situation as one of 5 blacks in a class of 100 illustrates the proportions that prevail in business schools, and business schools are by no means one of the more extreme examples. The pool of black candidates for any given profession is a small fraction of the white pool. This works out to a 20-to-1 edge in business; it is even greater in most of the other professions. The result, when many hiring institutions are competing, is that a major gap between the abilities of new black and white employees in any given workplace is highly likely. Everyone needs to hire a few blacks, and the edge that "being black" confers in the hiring decision warps the sequence of hiring in such a way that a scarce resource (the blacks with a given set of qualifications) is exhausted at an artificially high rate, producing a widening gap in comparison with the remaining whites from which an employer can choose.

The more aggressively affirmative action is enforced, the greater the imbalance. In general, the first companies to hire can pursue strategies that minimize or even eliminate the difference in ability between the new black and white employees. IBM and Park Avenue law firms can do very well, just as Harvard does quite well in attracting the top black students. But the more effectively they pursue these strategies, the more quickly they strip the population of the best black candidates.

To this point I have been discussing problems that are more or less driven by realities we have very little hope of manipulating in the short term except by discarding the laws regarding preferential treatment. People do differ in acquired abilities. Currently, acquired abilities in the white and black populations are distributed differently. Schools and firms do form a rough hierarchy when they draw from these distributions. The results follow ineluctably. The dangers they represent are not a matter of statistical probabilities, but of day-to-day human reactions we see around us.

The damage caused by these mechanistic forces should be much less in the world of work than in the schools, however. Schools deal in a relatively narrow domain of skills, and "talent" tends to be assigned specific meanings and specific measures. Workplaces deal in highly complex sets of skills, and "talent" consists of all sorts of combinations of qualities. A successful career depends in large part upon finding jobs that elicit and develop one's strengths.

At this point the young black professional must sidestep a new series of traps laid by whites who need to be ostentatiously nonracist. Let's say that William goes to work for the XYZ Corporation, where he is assigned with another management trainee (white) to a department where much of the time is spent preparing proposals for government contracts. The white trainee is assigned a variety of scut work—proofreading drafts, calculating the costs of minor items in the bid, making photocopies, taking notes at conferences. William gets more dignified work. He is assigned portions of the draft to write (which are later rewritten by more experienced staff), sits in on planning sessions, and even goes to Washington as a highly visible part of the team to present the bid. As time goes on, the white trainee learns a great deal about how the company operates, and is seen as a go-getting young member of the team. William is perceived to be a bright enough fellow, but not much of a detail man and not really much of a self-starter.

Even if a black is hired under terms that put him on a par with his white peers, the subtler forms of differential treatment work against him. Particularly for any corporation that does business with the government, the new employee has a specific immediate value purely because he is black. There are a variety of requirements to be met and rituals to be observed for which a black face is helpful. These have very little to do with the long-term career interests of the new employee; on the contrary, they often lead to a dead end as head of the minority-relations section of the personnel department.

Added to this is another problem that has nothing to do with the government. When the old racism was at fault (as it often still is), the newly hired black employee was excluded from the socialization process because the whites did not want him to become part of the group. When the new racism is at fault, it is because many whites are embarrassed to treat black employees as badly as they are willing to treat whites. Hence another reason that whites get on-the-job training that blacks do not: much of the early training of an employee is intertwined with menial assignments and mild hazing. Blacks who are put through these routines often see themselves as racially abused (and when a black is involved, old-racist responses may well have crept in). But even if the black is not unhappy about the process, the whites are afraid that he is, and so protect him from it. There are many variations, all having the same effect: the black is denied an apprenticeship that the white has no way of escaping. Without serving the apprenticeship, there is no way of becoming part of the team.

Carol suffers a slightly different fate. She and a white woman are hired as reporters by a major newspaper. They both work hard, but after a few months there is no denying it; neither one of them can write. The white woman is let go. Carol is kept on, because the paper cannot afford to have any fewer blacks than it already has. She is kept busy with reportorial work, even though they have to work around the writing problem. She is told not to worry—there's lots more to being a journalist than writing.

It is the mascot syndrome. A white performing at a comparable level would be fired. The black is kept on, perhaps to avoid complications with the Equal Employment Opportunity Commission (it can be very expensive to fire a black), perhaps out of a more diffuse wish not to appear discriminatory. Everybody pretends that nothing is wrong—but the black's career is at a dead end. The irony, of course, is that the white who gets fired and has to try something else has been forced into accepting a chance of making a success in some other line of work whereas the black is seduced into *not* taking the same chance.

Sometimes differential treatment takes an even more pernicious form: the conspiracy to promote a problem out of existence. As part of keeping Carol busy, the newspaper gives her some administrative responsibilities. They do not amount to much. But she has an impressive title on a prominent newspaper and she is black—a potent combination. She gets an offer from a lesser paper in another part of the country to take a senior editorial post. Her current employer is happy to be rid of an awkward situation and sends along glowing references. She gets a job that she is unequipped to handle—only this time, she is in a highly visible position, and within a few weeks the deficiencies that were covered up at the old job have become the subject of jokes all over the office. Most of the jokes are openly racist.

It is important to pause and remember who Carol is: an extremely bright young woman, not (in other circumstances) a likely object of condescension. But being bright is no protection. Whites can usually count on the market to help us recognize egregious career mistakes and to prevent us from being promoted too far from a career line that fits our strengths, and too far above our level of readiness. One of the most prevalent characteristics of white differential treatment of blacks has been to exempt blacks from these market considerations, substituting for them a market premium attached to race.

The most obvious consequence of preferential treatment is that every black professional, no matter how able, is tainted. Every black who is hired by a white-run organization that hires blacks preferentially has to put up with the knowledge that many of his co-workers believe he was hired because of his race; and he has to put up with the suspicion in his own mind that they might be right.

Whites are curiously reluctant to consider this a real problem—it is an abstraction, I am told, much less important than the problem that blacks face in getting a job in the first place. But black professionals talk about it, and they tell stories of mental breakdowns; of people who had to leave the job altogether; of long-term professional paralysis. What white would want to be put in such a situation? Of course it would be a constant humiliation to be resented by some of your co-workers and condescended to by others. Of course it would affect your perceptions of yourself and your self-confidence. No system that produces such side effects—as preferential treatment *must* do—can be defended unless it is producing some extremely important benefits.

And that brings us to the decisive question. If the alternative were no job at all, as it was for so many blacks for so long, the resentment and condescension are part of the price of getting blacks into the positions they deserve. But is that the alternative today? If the institutions of this country were left to their own devices now, to what extent would they refuse to admit, hire, and promote people because they were black? To what extent are American institutions kept from being racist by the government's intervention?

It is another one of those questions that are seldom investigated aggressively, and I have no evidence. Let me suggest a hypothesis that bears looking into: that the signal event in the struggle for black equality during the last thirty years, the one with real impact, was not the Civil Rights Act of 1964 or Executive Order 11246 or any other governmental act. It was the civil rights movement itself. It raised to a pitch of acute and lasting discomfort the racial consciousness of the generations of white Americans who are now running the country. I will not argue that the old racism is dead at any level of society. I will argue, however, that in the typical corporation or in the typical admissions office, there is an abiding desire to be not-racist. This need not be construed as brotherly love. Guilt will do as well. But the civil rights movement did its job. I suggest that the laws and the court decisions and the continuing intellectual respectability behind preferential treatment are now holding many doors open to qualified blacks that would otherwise be closed.

Suppose for a moment that I am right. Suppose that, for practical purposes, racism would not get in the way of blacks if preferential treatment were abandoned. How, in my most optimistic view, would the world look different?

There would be fewer blacks at Harvard and Yale; but they would all be fully competitive with the whites who were there. White students at the state university would encounter a cross-section of blacks who span the full range of ability, including the top levels, just as whites do. College remedial courses would no longer be disproportionately black. Whites rejected by the school they wanted would quit assuming they were kept out because a less-qualified black was admitted in their place. Blacks in big corporations would no longer be shunted off to personnel-relations positions, but would be left on the main-line tracks toward becoming comptrollers and sales managers and chief executive officers. Whites would quit assuming that black colleagues had been hired because they were black. Blacks would quit worrying that they had been hired because they were black.

Would blacks still lag behind? As a population, yes, for a time, and the nation should be mounting a far more effective program to improve elementary and secondary education for blacks than it has mounted in the last few decades. But in years past virtually every ethnic group in America has at one time or another lagged behind as a population, and has eventually caught up. In the process of catching up, the ones who breached the barriers were evidence of the success of that group. Now blacks who breach the barriers tend to be seen as evidence of the inferiority of that group.

And that is the evil of preferential treatment. It perpetuates an impression of inferiority. The system segments whites and blacks who come in contact with each other so as to maximize the likelihood that whites have the advantage in experience and ability. The system then encourages both whites and blacks to behave in ways that create self-fulfilling prophecies even when no real differences exist.

It is here that the new racism links up with the old. The old racism has always openly held that blacks are permanently less competent than whites. The new racism tacitly accepts that, in the course of overcoming the legacy of the old racism, blacks are temporarily less competent than whites. It is an extremely fine distinction. As time goes on, fine distinctions tend to be lost. Preferential treatment is providing persuasive evidence for the old racists, and we can already hear it *sotto voce:* "We gave you your chance, we let you educate them and push them into jobs they couldn't have gotten on their own and coddle them every way you could. And see: they still aren't as good as whites, and you are beginning to admit it yourselves." Sooner or later this message is going to be heard by a white elite that needs to excuse its failure to achieve black equality.

The only happy aspect of the new racism is that the corrective—to get rid of the policies encouraging preferential treatment—is so natural. Deliberate preferential treatment by race has sat as uneasily with America's equal-opportunity ideal during the post-1965 period as it did during the days of legalized segregation. We had to construct tortuous rationalizations when we permitted blacks to be kept on the back of the bus—and the rationalizations to justify sending blacks to the head of the line have been just as tortuous. Both kinds of rationalization say that sometimes it is all right to treat people of different races in different ways. For years, we have instinctively sensed this was wrong in principle but intellectualized our support for it as an expedient. I submit that our instincts were right. There is no such thing as good racial discrimination.

A REPLY TO CRITICS
OF AFFIRMATIVE ACTION

Gertrude Ezorsky

[Affirmative Action's] benefits to blacks can be viewed from both a forward-looking and a backward-looking moral perspective. From a forward-looking perspective, the purpose of AA is to reduce institutional racism, thereby moving blacks toward the goal of occupational integration. When that goal is achieved, millions of blacks will no longer be unfairly barred by the effects of their racist history from employment benefits. Moreover, such integration will significantly dissipate invidious racist attitudes. As I have suggested earlier, individuals socialized in a world where blacks are assimilated throughout the hierarchy of employment will no longer readily assume that they belong at the bottom.

From a backward-looking perspective, blacks have a moral claim to compensation for past injury. The paramount injustice perpetrated against blacks— enslavement—requires such compensation. If the effects of that murderous institution had been dissipated over time, the claim to compensation now would certainly be weaker. From the post-Reconstruction period to the present, however, racist practices have continued to transmit and reinforce the consequences of slavery. Today blacks still predominate in those occupations that in a slave society would be reserved for slaves.

Such ongoing racism has not been the work only of private parties. The racism of government practices encouraged race discrimination by landlords who blocked the escape of blacks from ghettos, and by employers and unions who refused to hire, promote, or train them, as well as widespread communication of an insulting stereotype of blacks, derogatory to their ability and character. During the first two thirds of this century, racism was in many respects official public policy. That policy included: legally compulsory segregation into inferior private and publicly owned facilities such as schools, which—as recognized in *Brown* v. *Board of Education of Topeka* (1954)—violated the constitutional rights of black children; court-upheld racially restrictive covenants in the transfer of private residences; antimiscegenation laws that resembled the prohibition of marriage by persons with venereal diseases; race discrimination in government practices such as public employment, voting registration procedures, federal assistance to business persons and farmers, and allocation of state and municipal services to black neighborhoods (e.g., police protection, sanitation, and educational resources); manifest racial bias in the courts; and pervasive police brutality against black people.

The practices of the Federal Housing Authority exemplified governmental racism. For decades after its inception in 1934, the FHA, which insured mortgage loans, enshrined racial segregation as public policy. The agency set itself up as the protector of all-white neighborhoods, especially in the suburbs. According to urban planner Charles Abrams, the FHA's racial policies could "well have been culled from the Nuremberg Laws." Today white suburban youths continue to benefit from the past racist practices of this government agency. Not only will they inherit homes purchased with the FHA assistance, denied to blacks; they also enjoy racially privileged access to the expanding employment opportunities in all-white suburbs. In 1973, legal scholar Boris I. Bittker summed up governmental misconduct against blacks: "More than any other form of official misconduct, racial discrimination against blacks was systematic, unrelenting, authorized at the highest governmental levels, and practiced by large segments of the population." The role of government in practicing, protecting, and providing sanction for racism by private parties suffices to demonstrate the moral legitimacy of legally required compensation to blacks.

This past of pervasive racism—public and private—follows blacks into the labor market, as we have seen. They are also especially vulnerable to recessionary layoffs because they possess far smaller reserves of money and property to sustain them during periods of joblessness. Such vulnerability also affects many newly middle-class blacks who, lacking inherited or accumulated assets, are—as the saying goes—two paychecks away from poverty.

Are AA measures, such as preferential treatment in employment, an appropriate method of compensation for blacks? In fact, federal and state governments recognized the appropriateness of employment preference as an instrument of compensation to veterans long before the adoption of AA measures. This court-sanctioned policy has affected the employment of millions of workers, and in some states where veteran preference is practiced, nonveterans have practically no chance to obtain the best positions.

What are the specific claims of those who find moral fault with such programs? First, concerning the compensatory rationale for AA, some analysts argue that compensation for blacks is counterproductive. Others claim that better-off blacks do not deserve the compensation of preferential treatment, especially where whites excluded by such preference are themselves disadvantaged. Second, AA trammels the rights of others—of employers who have a right to hire whomever they please, or of white candidates who are wrongfully excluded by preferential treatment. Finally, some critics suggest that blacks themselves may be morally injured by racial preference, which allegedly damages their self-respect.

COMPENSATION AS COUNTERPRODUCTIVE?

Shelby Steele, a professor of English, criticizes the compensatory claim for AA, according to which AA is "something 'owed,' as reparation": "Suffering can be endured and overcome, it cannot be repaid. To think otherwise is to prolong the suffering." But if compensation should be withheld from blacks because suffering cannot be repaid, then for the same reason compensation should also be withheld from veterans, Holocaust survivors, and victims of industrial accidents. Members of these groups do not complain that compensation prolongs their "suffering"; on the contrary, they have often insisted on their right to such benefits. I see no reason for assuming that compensation per se injures its recipients.

AFFLUENT BLACKS AS UNDESERVING

The philosopher William Blackstone criticizes the compensatory rationale for preferential treatment for affluent blacks:

> There is no invariable connection between a person's being black . . . and suffering from past invidious discrimination. . . . There are many blacks and other minority group members who are highly advantaged, who are sons and daughters of well-educated, affluent lawyers, doctors and industrialists. A policy of reverse discrimination would mean that such highly advantaged individuals would receive preferential treatment over the sons and daughters of disadvantaged whites or disadvantaged members of other minorities. I submit that such a situation is not social justice.

Blackstone offers two arguments: (1) Black persons born into better-off black families have not suffered discrimination; hence, he suggests, they do not deserve compensation. (2) Preference that benefits these blacks at the expense of disadvantaged non-blacks is unjust.

First, it is false that blacks born into better-off families have not been injured by discrimination. Because racist treatment of blacks in business and professions reduced family income, it hurt their sons and daughters. Among the racist injuries these black parents suffered were the racially discriminatory policies of federal agencies in allocation of business loans, low-interest mortgages, agrarian price supports, and government contracts. They also were victimized by racist exclusion from practice in white law firms and hospitals and by legally imposed or encouraged residential and school segregation that impaired their education and isolated them from white business contacts. Because of such invidious discrimination, black professionals and entrepreneurs could do far less for their children than their white counterparts. Moreover, the sons and daughters of black lawyers, doctors, and business persons have themselves suffered the experience of living in a segregated, pervasively racist society.

Laurence Thomas, a black university professor of philosophy, attests to the humiliating distrust that he and other well-placed black academics endure today in public places. Fears that affect blacks of all classes are described by Don Jackson, a black police sergeant who, while investigating reports of police racism in 1989, was stopped by white police officers, one of whom shoved Jackson's head through a window during the arrest.

> The feeling that no matter how hard you worked you could always be reduced to the status of a "field nigger" haunts the lives of black Americans at every economic stratum. . . . It has long been the role of the police to see that the plantation mentality is passed from one generation of blacks to another. . . . The black American finds that the most prominent reminder of his second-class citizenship are the police. . . . A variety of stringent laws were enacted and enforced to stamp the imprint of inequality on the mind of the black American. . . . No one has enforced these rules with more zeal than the police. Operating free of constitutional limitations, the police have long been the greatest nemesis of blacks, irrespective of whether they are complying with the law or not. We have learned that there are cars we are not supposed to drive, streets we are not supposed to walk. We may still be stopped and asked "Where are you going, boy?" Whether we're in a Mercedes or a Volkswagen.

Even if one assumes that the economically better-off blacks are less deserving of compensation, it hardly follows that they do not deserve any compensation. As Bernard Boxill observes in *Blacks and Social Justice:* "Because I have lost only one leg, I may be less deserving of compensation than another who has lost two legs, but it does not follow that I deserve no compensation."

It is true that where preference has been extended to blacks—as with craft workers, professionals, blue- and white-collar employees, teachers, police, and firefighters—some excluded whites may be financially less well off than the blacks who gained. This shift fails to show that these blacks were not victimized by invidious discrimination for which they should be compensated. Also, compensatory employment preference is sometimes given to veterans who are more affluent than the nonveterans who are thereby excluded from jobs. Indeed, some veterans gained, on the whole, from military life: placed in noncombat units, they often learned a valuable skill. Yet no one proposes that for this reason veteran preference be abandoned.

UNQUALIFIED BLACKS AS UNAFFECTED BY AA

Thomas Nagel, a philosopher who endorses preferential treatment, nevertheless faults the compensatory justification for such preference, claiming that blacks who benefit from it are probably not the ones who suffered most from discrimination; "those who don't have the qualifications even to be considered" do not gain from preferential policies.

Of course, AA preference does not help blacks obtain very desirable employment if they lack the qualifications even to be considered for such positions. But preferential treatment in diverse areas of the public and private sector has benefited not only highly skilled persons but also poorly educated workers. It is also true that blacks who lack the qualifications even to be considered for *any* employment will not gain from AA preference. As I indicated in my critique of William J. Wilson, AA cannot help those so destroyed as to be incapable of any work or on-the-job training, who require other compensatory race-specific rehabilitation programs. But AA employment programs should not perform the function of these programs. The claim that unemployable blacks are most deserving does not imply that employable blacks fail to deserve any—or even a great deal of—compensation.

Granted, we do not know whether the particular blacks who benefit from preference at each level in the hierarchy of employment are the very same individuals who, absent a racist past, would have qualified at that level by customary standards. Justified group compensation, however, does not require satisfaction of such rigid criteria. Veterans who enjoy hiring, promotion, and seniority preference are surely not the very same individuals who, absent their military service, would have qualified for the positions they gained by such preference.

Unlike job preference for veterans, AA racial preference in employment contributes to eradication of a future evil. It is an instrument for ending occupational segregation of blacks, a legacy of their enslavement.

THE RIGHTS OF EMPLOYERS

According to libertarian philosophers, laws that require any type of AA in the workplace—indeed, those merely requiring passive nondiscrimination—violate the rights of private employers. The philosopher Robert Nozick suggests that the right of employers to hire is relevantly similar to the right of individuals to marry. Just as individuals should be free to marry whomever they please, so private entrepreneurs should be free to employ whomever they please, and government should not interfere with employers in their hiring decisions.

But surely the freedom to choose one's spouse and the freedom to select one's employees are relevantly different. Individuals denied such freedom of choice in marriage are forced to give their bodies to their spouses. They are subject to rape—a destructive, brutal, and degrading intrusion. Marital choices belong to the deeply personal sphere where indeed government should keep out. State intervention in employment is another matter. To require that an auto plant hire some black machinists falls outside the sphere of the deeply personal; it is not, like rape, a destructive, brutal, and degrading personal intrusion. I conclude that the analogy between freedom to marry and freedom to hire fails.

THE RIGHTS OF WHITE CANDIDATES

According to some philosophers, while the social goal of preferential treatment may be desirable, the moral cost is too high. The burden it imposes on adversely affected whites violates their right to equal treatment. They are unfairly singled out for sacrifice. Thomas Nagel states that "the most important argument against preferential treatment is that it subordinates the individual's right to equal treatment to broader social aims."

Some proponents of preferential treatment reject the charge of unfairness because, as they see the matter, whites have either been responsible for immoral racist practices or have gained from them. According to this claim, all whites *deserve* to pay the cost of preferential treatment (hereafter, the desert claim). I do not accept the desert claim; indeed, I suggest that the criticism of racial preference as unfair to adversely affected whites is not without merit. The relevant point is not that such preference be abandoned but rather that it be implemented differently.

According to the desert claim, whites either have been responsible for racism or have passively benefited from it. Let us examine the responsibility claim first.

Certainly no one has demonstrated that all whites, or even a majority, are responsible for racism. How then shall the culpable whites be identified? Many employers and unions have certainly engaged in either overt racism or avoidable neutral practices that obviously excluded blacks. Perhaps they should pay the cost of discrimination remedies by, for example, continuing to pay blacks laid off by race-neutral seniority? But, on the other hand, some employers and union officials were not responsible for racist injury to blacks, and they do not deserve to pay the cost of a remedy for racism.

Similar problems arise when we attempt to identify those who passively benefited from racist practices. Let us assume that such beneficiaries do bear a measure of culpability for racism. How can we mark them out?

The salient fact is that white workers have *both* gained and lost from racism. On the one hand, the benefits to white workers from racism—overt and institutional—are undeniable. As a group, they have been first in line for hiring, training, promotion, and desirable job assignment, but last in line for seniority-based layoff. As white, they have also benefited from housing discrimination in areas where jobs could be had and from the racist impact of selection based on personal connections, seniority, and qualifications. Indeed many white candidates fail to realize that their superior qualifications may be due to their having attended predominantly white schools.

On the other hand, white workers have also lost because of racism. As a divisive force, racism harms labor, both black and white. Since blacks have more reason to fear management reprisal, they are less unwilling to work under excessive strain or for lower wages. This attitude, although quite understandable, makes it more difficult for labor, white as well as black, to attain better working conditions. I give two illustrations:

In the early 1970s a speedup was established in an auto factory whereby jobs performed by a unit of whites were assigned to a smaller group of blacks. The heavier work load then became the norm for everyone. White workers who complained were told that if they couldn't do the job, there were people who would.

In 1969, an AT&T vice president informed the assembled presidents of all Bell companies: "We must have access to an ample supply of people who will work at comparatively low rates of pay. . . . That means lots of black people." He explained that, of the persons available to work for "as little as four to five thousand a year," two-thirds were black.

The willingness of blacks to accept lower wages and adverse working conditions reduces labor's bargaining power generally with management.

Racism also has inhibited the formation of trade unions. In the South, racism, because it impedes union organization, contributed to the low wage level of both white and black workers. Also some northern employers, attracted by cheaper labor costs, moved their plants—with their jobs—to the South. A labor historian summed up the divisive effect of racism: "Hiring black laborers . . . fit[s] conveniently into the anti-union efforts of many industrialists. . . . A labor force divided along ethnic and racial lines poses great difficulties for union organizers; by importing blacks, a cheap work force could be gained and unionization efforts weakened at the same time."

On the whole, some white workers have lost and some have gained from racism. But to disentangle the two groups is a practical impossibility; the blameworthy cannot be marked off from the innocent. . . .

PREFERENTIAL TREATMENT AND BLACK SELF-RESPECT

Some commentators suggest that preferential treatment may be morally injurious to black persons. Thus Midge Decter and the economist Thomas Sowell worry that preference damages the self-respect of blacks.

Does preference really injure the self-respect of those it benefits? Traditional preference extended to personal connections has occasioned no such visible injury to self-respect. Career counselors who advise job seekers to develop influential contacts exhibit no fear that their clients will think less well of themselves; indeed, job candidates who secure powerful connections count themselves *fortunate.*

It might be objected that blacks (or any persons) who gain their positions through preferential treatment ought to respect themselves less. But this claim assumes that these blacks do not deserve such treatment. I believe that, because the overwhelming majority of blacks has been grievously wronged by racism, they deserve to be compensated for such injury and that black beneficiaries of employment preference—like veterans compensated by employment preference—have no good reason to feel unworthy.

Moreover, telling blacks—the descendants of slaves—that they ought to feel unworthy of their preferential positions can become self-fulfilling prophecy. Where are the black persons whose spirit and self-confidence have not already suffered because of the palpable barriers to attending white schools, living in white neighborhoods, and enjoying relations of friendship and intimacy with white people? Those blacks who, despite all the obstacles of overt and institutional racism, have become basically qualified for their positions should be respected for that achievement. Justice Marshall reminds us that the history of blacks differs from that of other ethnic groups. It includes not only slavery but also its aftermath, in which as a people they were marked inferior by our laws, a mark that has endured. Opportunities created by preferential treatment should symbolize an acknowledgment of such injustice and a commitment to create a future free of racism.

QUESTIONS FOR DISCUSSION
AFFIRMATIVE ACTION

1. What two senses of "justice" does Lisa Newton distinguish between? Why, according to her, is the political sense the only one relevant to the issue of affirmative action? Do you agree? Explain your response.

2. Why, according to Newton, does the attempt to compensate the victims of past discrimination that was, at that time, legal, undermine the ideal of equality before the law?

3. What is Ronald Dworkin's distinction between treating people equally and treating them as equals? Which is morally obligatory?

4. Is affirmative action for women as necessary as affirmative action for minorities? Take a position on this issue, and defend your stance.

5. State three arguments of Charles Murray against affirmative action, and summarize Gertrude Ezorsky's rebuttal to each argument.

6. Affirmative action programs have sometimes generated resentment and backlash among people who have felt victimized by them. Is this a reason to oppose such programs, or is it further evidence of the need for them? Develop an argument for one side or the other.

7. Are quotas essential to effective affirmative action? Why or why not?

SELECTED READINGS

COHEN, M., T. NAGEL, and T. SCANLON, eds. *Equality and Preferential Treatment.* Princeton: Princeton University Press, 1977.

CORLETT, J. "Racism and Affirmative Action." *Journal of Social Philosophy,* _____ 1993.

EZORSKY, G. *Reason and Justice.* Ithaca: Cornell University Press, 1991.

GROSS, B., ed. *Reverse Discrimination.* Buffalo: Prometheus, 1977.

HARWOOD, S. "Affirmative Action Is Justified." *Contemporary Philosophy,* _____ 1990.

HILL, T. "The Message of Affirmative Action." *Social Philosophy and Policy,* _____ 1991.

NEWTON, L. "Corruptions of Thought, Word and Deed." *Contemporary Philosophy,* _____ 1991.

ROSENFELD, M. *Affirmative Action and Justice.* New Haven: Yale University Press, 1991.

TAYLOR, B. *Affirmative Action at Work.* Pittsburgh: University of Pittsburgh Press, 1991.

10

DO ANIMALS HAVE RIGHTS?

The rights of human fetuses, severely defective infants, the insane or mentally retarded, and future generations are matters of controversy. So are the right of nonhuman animals, but in this case many people deny that the concept of moral rights applies at all (thus people often speak of "human rights," as if they were the only general rights we need worry about). What then of the salient differences between (1) nonhuman mammals, birds, and fish, and (2) human beings? Are those differences morally relevant? Tom Regan says no, Ruth Cigman says yes, and Christina Hoff says—sometimes.

Regan proposes that the social goal of animal liberation be added to the goals of black, Hispanic, women's, and gay liberation, on the grounds that refusing to do so is unfair discrimination akin to other modes of injustice. The fact that nonhuman animals are mentally inferior to most (but not all) humans does not, he argues, justify regarding them as property to be made use of as one wishes. If intellectual inferiority had such consequences, most of the human race would be in trouble. Regan holds that animals suffer as intensely as humans and have the same right not to be tortured or killed for the amusement or benefit of others.

Powerfully rebutting the traditional Cartesian reasons for doubting that nonhuman animals have any degree of consciousness (Descartes claimed that animals are unconscious automata to which the concept of a mental state such as pain does not even apply), Regan insists that their lack of linguistic and related mental skills such as reasoning ability has no bearing on their right not to have pain, mutilation, or death inflicted on them. He denounces animal experimentation for scientific as well as for commercial purposes and the cruel "factory farming" of animals, as well as the slaughtering of them for food. All animals, he claims, have the same right to be treated with respect and humane consideration as have the members of our own species.

Cigman grants that it is morally wrong to mistreat animals by inflicting unnecessary pain on them, as in hunting, nonvital laboratory experimentation, and factory farming; but she denies that in doing so we violate their rights, on the grounds that a creature with no concept of itself as an enduring subject of experience (see Mary Anne Warren's essay on abortion in Chapter 4) does not have a right to life or any other rights. Cigman concedes that causing "gratuitous" suffering of animals is cruel and immoral, but she grants that "gratuitous" is vague enough to be subject to varying interpretations. She sees no reason why humans owe all animals equal concern or treatment, thus no reason why species discrimination should be likened to racial discrimination; and she holds that the suffering of nonhuman animals, while regrettable, is less intense and therefore less serious than that of human beings.

Christina Hoff does not go as far as Ruth Cigman in denying any rights to nonhuman animals or in considering them to be less capable of intense suffering. She grants that they have the right not to be killed for mere sport, nor to be treated cruelly; but she holds that their rights are weaker than those of humans, so that animal experiments for important scientific purposes and raising them for slaughter are not moral wrongs, on the grounds that "human lives are of far greater worth than animal lives." What the relation is between the worth of a life and the right to life is an interesting question that Hoff does not address.

ANIMALS HAVE RIGHTS

Tom Regan

A common argument against recognition of the rights of farm animals takes the following form. Since these animals would not exist except for the economic interest the farmer has in raising them, his economic interests should determine how they ought to be treated. If, then, the intensive rearing of farm animals serves the farmer's economic interests, factory farming is justified. The harm done to these animals is, as it were, the price they pay for having that share of existence that falls their way because of the decisions and interests of the farmer.

This argument assumes that those agents who are causally responsible for bringing about a given individual's existence are sovereigns over that individual, once that individual exists, the treatment due that individual to be determined by the interests of those who arrange for his or her existence in the first place. This assumption lacks any claim to credibility. My son would not now exist except for the past decisions and acts of my wife and myself. In that sense, he "owes" his existence to us. But it does not follow from this that, once he has come to be, we, his parents, are thereby entitled to do just anything to him we like. Once he has himself become the subject-of-a-life that fares better or worse for him, logically independently of us, there are strict moral restrictions, grounded in the recognition of his inherent value, that we must respect if we are to treat him as justice requires. We are not his moral sovereigns. The case of farm animals does not differ in any morally relevant way. Once any given animal has become the subject-of-a-life that fares better or worse for her, the same principles of just treatment apply. If the farmer were to protest that it was not for the purpose of just treatment that he brought the animal into existence in the first place, we would be entitled to reply that that makes no moral difference. Once he has such an animal in his care, his past motives and intentions for arranging for the animal to come to be simply do not override the right of the animal to treatment consistent with, and required by, the respect to which she is due. . . .

To treat farm animals as renewable resources is to fail to treat them with the respect they are due as possessors of inherent value. It is, then, to treat them unjustly, and this finding makes all the moral difference in the world when, as we are supposing, the farmer claims that he is "within his rights"

---

in raising these animals for human consumption. He *would* be "within his rights," given the liberty principle, *only if* those who are harmed by what he does (namely, the animals he raises) *were treated with respect*. But they are not treated with respect, and cannot be, so long as they are treated as if they are renewable resources. This is why, on the rights view, farmers who raise animals for human consumption are engaged in an unjust practice. Morally, they *exceed* their rights. Morally, this practice ought to cease, and consumers ought to cease to support it. Even if it were true, which it is not, that consumers would be made worse-off relative to the condition of farm animals if they stopped buying meat, it would not follow that consumers "act within *their* rights" when, by choosing to buy meat, they choose to support the practice that allows and requires this treatment. Consumers would be acting within their rights only if this practice treated animals with the respect they are due. Since, for the reasons given, the current practice of raising farm animals for human consumption fails to treat these animals with respect, those who support this practice by buying meat exceed their rights. Their purchase makes them a party to the perpetuation of an unjust practice. Vegetarianism is not supererogatory; it is obligatory.

Here it will be protested that it is not just the economic interests of the farmers, meat packers, wholesalers, and the like, that are at stake; the economy of the nation is directly tied to the maintenance and growth of the meat industry. To cease purchasing the products of this industry would bring about economic calamity, affecting the welfare of millions upon millions of people, many of whom, through no fault of their own, and without having voluntarily run the risks associated with participation in the meat industry, will be made worse-off. It is in order to avoid this catastrophe that we ought to continue to buy meat.

The rights view denies this defense of support of the meat industry. Just as the benefits others obtain as a result of an unjust institution or practice is no moral defense of that practice or institution, so the harms others might face as a result of the dissolution of this practice or institution is no defense of allowing it to continue. Put alternatively, no one has a right to be protected against being harmed if the protection in question involves violating the rights of others. Since, for reasons given in the preceding, the practice of raising farm animals, as presently conducted, routinely treats these animals in ways that are contrary to the respect they are due as a matter of strict justice, that practice violates the rights of these animals. As such, no one, neither those directly involved in the meat industry nor those who would be affected by its collapse, has a right to be protected against being harmed by allowing that industry to continue. In this sense and for these reasons, the rights view implies that justice *must* be done, though the (economic) heavens fall.

It is, of course, extremely unlikely that the economic heavens will fall. We are not likely to awake tomorrow to discover that, overnight, everyone has been converted to vegetarianism, a development that precipitates the total and instantaneous collapse of the meat industry and the economic gloom such a collapse conceivably might bring. The scenario sketched two paragraphs back, therefore, is most improbable. The dissolution of the meat industry, as we know it, will come incrementally, not all at once, and the economy of the nation and the world will have time to adjust to the change in dietary life-styles. Nevertheless, the essential moral point remains. No one has a right to be protected by the continuation of an unjust practice, one that violates the rights of others. And this is true whether one actively participates in this practice or, though not an active participant, benefits from it and would be harmed by its discontinuance. Vegetarians who would be harmed by the total and instantaneous collapse of the meat industry would have no more right to complain of the "injustice" done to them than would meat-eaters. Since no injustice would be done to them, were that industry to dissolve, even "the veggies" could have no grounds for complaint. . . .

The dissolution of commercial animal farming as we know it obviously requires more than our individual commitment to vegetarianism. To refuse on principle to buy the products of the meat industry is to do what is right, but it is not to do enough. To recognize the rights of animals is to recognize the related duty to defend them against those who violate their rights, and to discharge this duty requires more than our individual abstention. It requires acting to bring about those changes that are necessary if the rights of these animals are not to be violated. Fundamentally, then, it requires a commitment to contribute to the revolution in our culture's thought about, and in its accepted treatment of, farm animals. Mill's words are again apposite. Recall his observing that, when an individual has a valid claim, and thus a right, to something, "society" ought to defend that individual in the possession of that right, "either by the force of law or by that of education or opinion." Our challenge, then, may be conceived in these terms: to help *to educate* those who presently support the animal industry to the implications of their support; to help *to forge the opinion* that this industry, as we know it, violates the rights of farm animals; and to work to bring *the force of law,* if necessary, to bear on this industry to effect the necessary changes. That is no small challenge, to be sure, but to reach the goal of justice for these animals requires nothing less. Merely to content oneself with personal abstention is to become part of the problem rather than part of the solution.

WHY HUNTING AND TRAPPING ARE WRONG

Since animals can pose innocent threats and because we are sometimes justified in overriding their rights when they do, one cannot assume that all hunting or trapping must be wrong. If rabid foxes have bitten some children and are known to be in the neighboring woods, and if the circumstances of their lives assure future attacks if nothing is done, then the rights view sanctions nullifying the threat posed by these animals. When we turn from cases where we protect ourselves against the innocent threats wild animals pose, to the activities of hunting and trapping, whether for commercial profit or "sport," the rights view takes a dim view indeed. Standard justifications of the "sport" of hunting—that those who engage in it get exercise, take plea-sure in communion with nature, enjoy the camaraderie of their friends, or take satisfaction in a shot well aimed—are lame, given the rights view. All these pleasures are obtainable by engaging in activities that do not result in killing any animal (walking through the woods with friends and a camera substitutes nicely), and the aggregate of the pleasures hunters derive from hunting could only override the rights of these animals if we viewed them as mere receptacles, which, on the rights view, they are not. . . .

Scientific Research

One can imagine someone accepting the arguments advanced against toxic-ity tests on animals but putting his foot down when it comes to scientific re-search. To deny science use of animals in research is, it might be said, to bring scientific and allied medical progress to a halt, and that is reason enough to oppose it. The claim that progress would be "brought to a halt" is an exag-geration certainly. It is not an exaggeration to claim that, given its present dominant tendency, the rights view requires massive redirection of scientific research. The dominant tendency involves routinely harming animals. It should come as no surprise that the rights view has principled objections to its continuation.

A recent statement of the case for unrestricted use of animals in neuro-biological research contrasts sharply with the rights view and will serve as an introduction to the critical assessment of using animals in basic research. The situation, as characterized by C. R. Gallistel, a psychologist at the Uni-versity of Pennsylvania, is as follows: "Behavioral neurobiology tries to estab-lish the manner in which the nervous system mediates behavioral phenomena. It does so by studying the behavioral consequences of one or more of the fol-lowing procedures: (a) destruction of a part of the nervous system, (b) stimu-lation of a part, (c) administration of drugs that alter neural functioning. These three techniques are as old as the discipline. A recent addition is (d) the recording of electrical activity. All four cause the animal at least temporary distress. In the past they have frequently caused intense pain, and they oc-casionally do so now. Also, they often impair an animal's proper functioning, sometimes transiently, sometimes permanently." The animals subjected to these procedures are, in a word, harmed. When it comes to advancing our knowledge in neurobiology, however, "there is no way to establish the rela-tion between the nervous system and behavior without some experimental surgery," where by "experimental surgery" Gallistel evidently means to in-clude the four procedures just outlined. The issue, then, in Gallistel's mind, is not whether to allow such surgery or not; it is whether any restrictions should be placed on the use made of animals. Gallistel thinks not.

In defense of unrestricted use of animals in research, Gallistel claims that "most experiments conducted by neurobiologists, *like scientific experiments generally,* may be seen in retrospect to have been a waste of time, in the sense that they did not prove or yield any new insight." But, claims Gallistel, "there is no way of discriminating in advance the waste-of-time experiments from the illuminating ones with anything approaching certainty." The logical upshot, so Gallistel believes, is that "restricting research on living animals is certain to restrict the progress in our understanding of the nervous system and behavior. Therefore," he concludes, "one should advocate such restrictions only if one believes that the moral value of this scientific knowledge and of the many human and humane benefits that flow from it cannot outweigh the suffering of a rat," something that, writing autobiographically, Gallistel finds "an affront to my ethical sensibility."

Even those unpersuaded by the rights view ought to challenge Gallistel's argument at every point. Is it true, as he claims, "that there is *no* way to establish the relation between the nervous system and behavior without some experimental surgery"? Can we learn nothing whatever about this connection from, say, clinical observation of those who have been injured? Again, is it true that *we can never say in advance* that a given proposal has been drawn up by an incompetent researcher who doesn't know what he is looking for and wouldn't recognize it if he found it? What could be the grounds for peer review of research proposals if Gallistel's views were accepted? Why not draw straws instead? Those stirrings in the scientific community, away from unrestricted use of animals toward the refinement of one's protocol (thereby eliminating so-called unnecessary experiments) and reduction in the number of animals used, will find no support from the no-holds-barred approach Gallistel advocates. Since there is, in his view, no way to separate the scientific wheat from the chaff in advance of experimenting, why worry about refinement? Why worry about reduction?

These matters aside, the rights view rejects Gallistel's approach at a more fundamental level. On the rights view, we cannot justify harming a single rat *merely* by aggregating "the many human and humane benefits" that flow from doing it, since, as stated, this is to assume that the rat has value only as a receptacle, which, on the rights view, is not true. Moreover, the benefits argument that Gallistel deploys is deficient. Not even a single rat is to be treated as if that animal's value were reducible to his *possible utility* relative to the interests of others, which is what we would be doing if we intentionally harmed the rat on the grounds that this *just might* "prove" something, *just might* "yield" a "new insight," *just might* produce "benefits" for others.

It bears emphasizing that the rights view's critique of the use of animals in research is unlike some that find favor in the literature on this matter. Some object on methodological grounds, arguing that the results of such research offer very little hope of benefits for humanity because of the by-now well-established difficulty of extrapolating results from animals tests to the species *Homo sapiens;* others challenge the necessity of a variety of experiments, cases where animals have been cut, blinded, deformed, mutilated, shocked into "learned helplessness," and so on, all in the name of research. Neither of these critical approaches, though each has clear validity as far as it goes, gets to the moral heart of the matter. It is not that the methodology is suspect (though it is), nor that a great deal of research is, Gallistel's opinion to the contrary notwithstanding, known to be a waste of time before it is undertaken. The point to note is that both these challenges *invite the continuation of research on animals,* the latter because it would rule out only that research known to be a waste of time before it is conducted, and the former because it gives researchers a blank check to continue animal experiments in the hope of overcoming the deficiencies in the present methodology. If we are seriously to challenge the use of animals in research, we must challenge the *practice* itself, not only individual instances of it or merely the liabilities in its present methodology.

The rights view issues such a challenge. Routine use of animals in research assumes that their value is reducible to their possible utility relative to the interests of others. The rights view rejects this view of animals and their value, as it rejects the justice of institutions that treat them as renewable resources. They, like us, have a value of their own, logically independently of their utility for others and of their being the object of anyone else's interests. To treat them in ways that respect their value, therefore, requires that we *not* sanction practices that institutionalize treating them as if their value was reducible to their possible utility relative to our interests. Scientific research, when it involves routinely harming animals in the name of possible "human and humane benefits," violates this requirement of respectful treatment. Animals are not to be treated as mere receptacles or as renewable resources. Thus does the practice of scientific research on animals violate their rights. Thus ought it to cease, according to the rights view. It is not enough first conscientiously to look for nonanimal alternatives and then, having failed to find any, to resort to using animals. Though that approach is laudable as far as it goes, and though taking it would mark significant progress, it does not go far enough. It assumes that it is all right to allow practices that use animals as if their value were reducible to their possible utility relative to the interests of others, provided that we have done our best not to do so. The rights view's position would have us go further in terms of "doing our best." *The best we can do in terms of not using animals is not to use them.* Their inherent value does not disappear just because we have failed to find a way to avoid harming them in pursuit of our chosen goals. Their value is independent of these goals and their possible utility in achieving them.

A variant of the lifeboat case discussed earlier is likely to surface at this point, if not before. Let us suppose that the lifeboat contains four normal adults and a dog. Provisions are plentiful this time, and there is more than enough room. Only now suppose the humans have a degenerative brain disease, while the dog is healthy. Also on board, so it happens, is a new medicine that just might be the long-awaited cure of the disease the humans have. The medicine has not been tested. However, it is known to contain some potentially fatal compounds. The means exist to give the degenerative disease to the dog. In these dire circumstances, would it be all right to do this and then to administer the medicine to the animal to assess its curative properties?

Quite possibly most people would give an affirmative reply, at least initially—but not those who subscribe to the rights view. Animals are not to be treated as if their value were reducible *merely* to their possible utility relative to human interests, which is what the survivors would be doing if they made the healthy animal (who, after all, stands to gain nothing and lose everything) run their risks in their stead.

Some might seize upon this verdict of the rights view as a basis for urging what they regard as a fatal objection: since most people think it would be all right to give the medicine to the dog, since the rights view allows appeals to what most people think as a basis for testing alternative moral principles and theories, and since what most people think in this case conflicts with the verdict of the rights view, it follows, some may think, that the practice of using animals in harmful research is justifiable.

Three replies must suffice. First, just because most people think the dog should be treated as described, assuming that most do so, it does not follow that most people think well in this case. Our prereflective intuitions, as was explained in an earlier chapter, must be tested reflectively to determine how well they stand up under the conscientious attempt to reach an ideal moral judgment. Without making this attempt, those who are content to appeal to "what most people think" have no rational basis to assume that what most people think in any given case is not based on their shared ignorance, their shared prejudices, or their shared irrationality. *Merely* to appeal to "what most people think," in other words, is not decisive in this, or in any other, moral context.

Second, even in those cases where a given belief continues to be held by most people *after* they have made a conscientious effort to remove the insidious effects of ignorance, prejudice, and the like, the possibility still remains that the belief in question stands in need of revision or abandonment. For if a given belief cannot be squared with moral principles that themselves pass the relevant tests for assessing their validity (namely, scope, precision, consistency, and conformity with a host of other intuitions that stand up on reflection), one must come to doubt the rational grounds of that belief and others like it in the relevant respects. Again, then, *merely* to announce that, after having given the matter one's conscientious attention, one still thinks that the dog should be treated as described in the lifeboat case, is not to mount a serious challenge to the rights view or its verdict in this case. A serious challenge can be raised only if, in addition to citing one's belief in this case, one also adduces the general principles that would support it and shows that these principles are equal or superior to the rights view when these principles are themselves subjected to the tests of scope, precision, and the like.

But third—and here we echo earlier observations—the justice of policies or practices are not guaranteed by generalizing on one's judgment in exceptional cases; and lifeboat cases, as was mentioned earlier, are exceptional cases. To make the danger of generalizing on such cases clearer, imagine that the lifeboat contains four exceptional and one average human. Suppose the four are preeminent scientists, each on the verge of making discoveries that portend enormous health benefits for humanity. The fifth man delivers Twinkies to retail stores in Brooklyn. The four scientists have the degenerative brain disease. The Twinkies deliveryman does not. Would it be permissible to give the disease to him and then test for the drug's efficacy by administering it to him first? No doubt many people would be inclined to reply affirmatively (though not, again, those who subscribe to the rights view). Even among those who think the deliveryman should serve as the proverbial guinea pig in these exceptional circumstances, however, none with the slightest egalitarian tendencies would be willing to generalize on the basis of this unusual case and favor a policy or practice of doing research on average humans so that humans who are very bright or who make large social contributions might benefit. Such a practice leaves the bad taste of perfectionism in our mouths. The rights view categorically rejects perfectionism as a basis for assessing the justice of practices involving humans, whether in science or elsewhere. And so should we all. But just as perfectionism is not an equitable basis for assessing the justice of practices involving humans, so it is an unacceptable basis for assessing the justice of practices involving animals. And it is implicit allegiance to perfectionism that would tempt one to sanction the harmful use of animals in research, their "lesser" value being "sacrificed" for the "greater" value of humanity. Grounded in the recognition of the equal inherent value of all those who have inherent value, the rights view denies that a distinction between lesser and greater should be made where the perfectionist defense of the use of animals in research requires it. Thus does it deplore the continuation of this practice.

The rights view does not oppose using what is learned from conscientious efforts to treat a sick animal (or human) to facilitate and improve the treatment tendered other animals (or humans). In *this* respect, the rights view raises no objection to the "many human and humane benefits" that flow from medical science and the research with which it is allied. What the rights view opposes are practices that cause intentional harm to laboratory animals (for example, by means of burns, shock, amputation, poisoning, surgery, starvation, and sensory deprivation) preparatory to "looking for something that just might yield some human or humane benefit." Whatever benefits happen to accrue from such a practice are irrelevant to assessing its tragic injustice. Lab animals are not our tasters; we are not their kings.

The tired charge of being antiscientific is likely to fill the air once more. It is a moral smokescreen. The rights view is not against research on animals, if this research does not harm these animals or put them at risk of harm. It is apt to remark, however, that this objective will not be accomplished merely by ensuring that test animals are anaesthetized, or given postoperative drugs to ease their suffering, or kept in clean cages with ample food and water, and so forth. For it is not only the pain and suffering that matters—though they certainly matter—but it is the *harm* done to the animals, including the diminished welfare opportunities they endure as a result of the deprivations caused by the surgery, *and* their untimely death. It is unclear whether a *benign* use of animals in research is possible or, if possible, whether scientists could be persuaded to practice it. That being so, and given the serious risks run by relying on a steady supply of human volunteers, research should take the direction away from the use of any moral agent or patient. If nonanimal alternatives are available, they should be used; if they are not available, they should be sought. That is the moral challenge to research, given the rights view, and it is those scientists who protest that this "can't be done," in advance of the scientific commitment to try—not those who call for the exploration—who exhibit a lack of commitment to, and belief in, the scientific enterprise—who are, that is, antiscientific at the deepest level. Like Galileo's contemporaries, who would not look through the telescope because they had already convinced themselves of what they would see and thus saw no need to look, those scientists who have convinced themselves that there can't be viable scientific alternatives to the use of whole animals in research (or toxicity tests, etc.) are captives of mental habits that true science abhors.

The rights view, then, is far from being antiscientific. On the contrary, as is true in the case of toxicity tests, so also in the case of research: it calls upon scientists *to do science* as they redirect the traditional practice of their several disciplines away from reliance on "animal models" toward the development and use of nonanimal alternatives. All that the rights view prohibits is science that violates individual rights. If that means that there are some things we cannot learn, then so be it. There are also some things we cannot learn by using humans, if we respect their rights. The rights view merely requires moral consistency in this regard.

The rights view's position regarding the use of animals in research cannot be fairly criticized on the grounds that it is antihumanity. The implications of this view in this regard are those that a rational human being should expect, especially when we recall that nature neither respects nor violates our rights. Only moral agents do; indeed, only moral agents *can.* And nature is not a moral agent. We have, then, no basic right against nature not to be harmed by those natural diseases we are heir to. And neither do we have any basic right against humanity in this regard. What we do have, at this point in time at least, is a right to fair treatment on the part of those who have voluntarily decided to offer treatment for these maladies, a right that will not tolerate the preferential treatment of some (e.g., Caucasians) to the detriment of others (e.g., Native Americans). The right to fair treatment of our naturally caused maladies (and the same applies to mental and physical illnesses brought on by human causes, e.g. pollutants) is an *acquired right* we have against those moral agents who acquire the duty to offer fair treatment because they voluntarily assume a role within the medical profession. But those in this profession, as well as those who do research in the hope that they might improve health care, are not morally authorized to override the *basic rights* of others in the process—rights others have, that is, independently of their place in any institutional arrangement and independently of any voluntary act on the part of anyone. And yet that is what is annually done to literally millions of animals whose services, so to speak, are enlisted in the name of scientific research, including that research allied with medical science. For this research treats these animals as if their value is reducible to their possible utility relative to the interests of others. Thus does it routinely violate their basic right to respectful treatment. Though those of us who today are to be counted among the beneficiaries of the human benefits obtained from this research in the past might stand to lose some future benefits, at least in the short run, if this research is stopped, the rights view will not be satisfied with anything less than its total abolition. Even granting that we face greater prima facie harm than laboratory animals presently endure if future harmful research on these animals is stopped, and even granting that the number of humans and other animals who stand to benefit from allowing this practice to continue exceeds the number of animals used in it, this practice remains wrong because unjust.

ANIMALS DO NOT HAVE RIGHTS
Ruth Cigman

It has been argued that "speciesism"—unjust and discriminatory attitudes towards species other than our own—is a vice analogous to sexism and racism. Opposition to this phenomenon embraces two kinds of claims, one of them reasonable, the other by no means so. The weak claim, which I accept, is that we should treat many animals better than we do, and take whatever steps are necessary to oppose certain cruel practices toward them. The stronger claim is that, as women and blacks should have rights equal to those of men and whites, animals should have rights equal to those of persons, because difference of species does not constitute a morally relevant difference.

My view is that the stronger claim is sentimental and confused. Most important, it seriously misrepresents features of human experience such as attitudes to life and the misfortune of death. I shall attack it by exploring the relationship between (a) the kinds of obligations we have towards a creature (person, animal), and the correlative rights to which he or she is entitled; and (b) the kinds of misfortunes of which that creature may be a subject (or victim). In particular, I shall be concerned with the complex relationship between the right to life and the capacity to be a subject of the misfortune of death. This relationship is significant where human lives are concerned; it does not, I believe, carry over to the lives of other species. My claim will be that death is not, and cannot be, a misfortune for any creature other than a human; this is a reason for denying nonhumans the right to life and therefore for embracing a form of speciesism. I shall then consider some implications for vegetarianism.

I. SPECIES INEQUALITY

The phenomenon of speciesism must be described with care. One anti-speciesist has described it as the belief that it is justifiable "to treat a member of another species in a way in which it would be wrong to treat our own." This definition isn't quite right; nor does it parallel the definitions of racism and sexism. A school which received an application from a parent for admission of her child and pet monkey would be quite justified in accepting the child and rejecting the monkey, however dull the child and bright the monkey; just as a dramatic director would be justified in turning down the most talented actress in the world in favor of an inferior actor, to fill the role of King Lear. Neither school nor director would be guilty of the "ism" in question. The vice abhorred by anti-speciesists is not the denial that animals and persons are in all respects identical (whatever this would mean), and therefore entitled to identical treatment; it is rather a much more plausible claim about the possession across species (many, not all) of certain morally relevant *capacities*. Specifically, speciesism may be seen as a failure to acknowledge the equal capacities of persons and animals to *suffer*, and (it is claimed) the moral equality which is a corollary of this fact.

As such, speciesism bears at least a superficial resemblance to sexism and racism, the error of which consists in part in a failure to understand what Bernard Williams has called the "useful tautology" that all human beings are human beings. This phrase serves to remind anyone who believes that blacks or women are inherently inferior that these are not merely members of a certain species, but are also *human* or *persons*. The emphasis on these terms suggests certain capacities and related vulnerabilities which are more or less universally possessed by persons, and one is made to think of such truths as: all persons are able to suffer physical and mental pain, and to experience, and be frustrated in, affection for others. These truths give rise to certain moral claims which may be irrationally obscured by incidental characteristics such as skin color and sex.

Some anti-speciesists (notably Jeremy Bentham and, more recently, Peter Singer) have attacked speciesism along similar lines. Species equality, they argue, is typically overlooked by virtue of morally insignificant features such as the number of legs a creature possesses, or the inability to talk. Equal capacity to suffer is the only reasonable ground for moral equality; it has been shown, moreover, that many species are in possession of nervous systems of comparable complexity to those of humans, and that they therefore suffer pain of comparable intensity.

However the equal capacity to suffer physical pain is only part of what the antisexist or antiracist is getting at by emphasizing the humanity or personhood of all human beings. Implicit in this claim (the tautological status of which is, of course, more apparent than real) is an allusion to a *range* of vulnerabilities, or misfortunes, of which persons are able to be subjects, and by virtue of which they possess equal rights. Among these is the misfortune of death. Nothing that is said by the anti-speciesist about the suffering of physical pain suggests that animals are subject to the same range of misfortunes as persons, still less that death is a misfortune for an animal. Even if we grant that the equal capacity of persons and animals to suffer physical pain somehow yields equal rights not to be recipients of physical cruelty, it is far from clear why this should entail moral equality, that is, equality over a range of fundamental rights.

I want to suggest that a right to X entails the right to be protected from certain actions which will result in the misfortune, or possible misfortune, of not-X. A condition for being the subject of a right is therefore the *capacity* to be a subject of the corresponding misfortune. The relationship between capacity and desire in this context must be examined: for example, a creature may be a subject of the misfortune of death even if he or she doesn't *desire* not to die, so long as it is the case that he or she has the *capacity* to desire not to die. My suggestion is that, when we fill in the concept of desiring not to die in a way which is relevant to the misfortune of death and the right to life, we shall have to withhold this from animals.

I turn to these problems in subsequent sections. To conclude the present section, I want to clarify the distinction between the right to be protected from cruelty and the right to be protected from death with reference to a provocative example of Robert Nozick. Nozick asks us to imagine the following: someone derives a special, unsubstitutable pleasure from swinging a baseball bat, in circumstances where the regretted but unavoidable corollary of this act is the smashing of a cow's skull. We must consider whether the extra pleasure derived from this act, compared with a similar and harmless alternative act, could possibly justify the act morally. Nozick says that it cannot, thereby suggesting that the purely hedonistic justification for the (analogous) activity of meat-eating (and by implication, comparable activities which involve animal suffering and deaths) is inadequate.

What exactly does this example show? Its plausibility rests upon the suggested identification between, on the one hand, meat-eating and whimsical bat-swinging; and on the other, cow-skull–smashing and the taking of animal lives. The first pair are analogically but questionably related; it is arguable that meat-eating is unjustly viewed as a whimsical, essentially eccentric satisfaction. This is a relatively unimportant point which I shall set aside for now. The second identification is more serious, since it is hardly analogical (we are to assume that smashing the cow's skull is fatal), yet more liable to obscure the problem at hand. In particular, it obscures two claims which I want to distinguish:

(1) We have an obligation not to inflict gratuitous suffering on animals (or to refrain from gratuitous cruelty to animals).

(2) We have an obligation not to kill animals, [not even] quickly and painlessly.

Claim (1) is, I take it, sufficiently vague to be self-evidently true, or at any rate, not hard to defend. I shall not attempt to do this, but I shall suggest that, while there is room for many divergences of opinion over what counts as "gratuitous" suffering or cruelty, these will generally, and reasonably, fall within an area embraced by whimsical satisfaction and the protection of fundamental human interests (life, health) as, respectively, inadequate and adequate justifications for causing animal suffering. (I shall return to this topic later in connection with vegetarianism.) Claim (2), which is more interesting, I believe to be false. If so, the moral justification for meat-eating would appear to depend above all upon the *manner* in which animals are killed. The force of Nozick's example then rests upon the question (setting aside for now the problematic analogy between meat-eating and whimsical bat-swinging) whether or not skull-smashing is a quick and painless death for a cow. I don't know whether it is or not, but I shall proceed with the assumption that it is *possible* to kill a cow quickly and painlessly. The moral significance of such a death may then be considered.

II. ANIMAL MISFORTUNE AND HUMAN MISFORTUNE

Of what kinds of misfortunes are animals subjects? A claim which may be rejected at the start is this: it is impossible to know exactly how much animals suffer, or what counts as a misfortune *for them;* it is therefore a form of speciesist arrogance to assume that their misfortunes are worthy of less concern than our own. Against this it must be said that the evidence we have that animals suffer *at all* is the same as the evidence which enables us to judge the nature and extent of this suffering. No philosopher has suggested this more powerfully than Wittgenstein, in his remarks about the deeply misunderstood relationship between behavior and the "inner life." It is worth quoting some of these:

> . . . only of a living human being and what resembles (behaves like) a living human being can one say: it has sensations; it sees; is blind; hears; is deaf; is conscious or unconscious.

Look at a stone and imagine it having sensations. One says to oneself: How could one so much as get the idea of ascribing a *sensation to a thing?* One might as well ascribe it to a number!—And now look at a wriggling fly and at once these difficulties vanish and pain seems to get a foothold here, where before everything was so to speak, too smooth for it.

> One can imagine an animal, angry, frightened, unhappy, happy, startled. But hopeful? And why not?
> A dog believes his master is at the door. But can he also believe his master will come the day after tomorrow?—And *what* can he not do here?

Wittgenstein is not merely concerned in these passages with the difficulty of *imagining* the truth of certain mental descriptions (for example, "This dog is hopeful"; "This stone has sensations"). Maybe one *can* (or thinks one can—it may be hard to distinguish these) imagine these being true; what one cannot do is sensibly *consider* the possibility that they may be true, for to do this (Wittgenstein suggests) would be to remove the concept of hope from the context in which it has sense—where human beings talk and behave in ways which reveal their sense of the future, of alternative prospects, of concern for themselves and others, and so on. These form part of the structure, so to speak, of hope; it does not make sense to ascribe hope to a creature which manifests no awareness of future possibilities. Wittgenstein's choice of example may be questioned here; I think there do exist a small number of animals which may express hope in their behavior. But the point is sound; the mental experience which is sensibly attributed to a creature is commensurate with the complexity and nature of its behavioral expression. A wriggling fly may be supposed to feel pain; here, though, hope definitely fails to find a foothold.

If this is correct, two further conclusions must be drawn: (1) The "useful tautology" discussed earlier does not merely suggest certain vulnerabilities to which more or less everyone is subject; it also suggests, I think, certain complexities of experience surrounding these vulnerabilities, which are not attributable to animals. I have in mind, for example, the fear of death, or of contracting a fatal disease; the desire for respect or esteem from others; the desire to lead a fulfilling life (for one's life to have a "point," or "meaning"); the desire to achieve certain goals and resolve certain problems; and, finally, corresponding fears and desires on behalf of others. (2) These thoughts or experiences suggest a reason why persons deserve greater moral concern than animals. The capacity to talk does not *itself* provide such a reason; rather this capacity is related to, and is a condition for, the capacity to suffer complex and severe misfortunes, which animals are logically unable to suffer. Among these are the kinds of misfortunes which we call "tragic." It is with great strain that we say of an animal that he suffers a tragedy, even, I think, when he is destined for a premature death. The failure of Bentham and others to recognize this results from a crude conception of what it is to suffer a misfortune. . . .

III. DEATH AS A MISFORTUNE

. . . Thomas Nagel defends an Aristotelian conception of misfortune. This is as far from Bentham as one can imagine; Aristotle, we must remember, even included amongst a person's misfortunes the misfortunes of his or her descendants for an indefinite period of time beyond his or her death. It is very much in the Aristotelian spirit that Nagel says:

> It . . . seems to me worth exploring the position that most good and ill fortune has as its subject a person identified by his history and his possibilities, rather than merely by his categorical state of the moment. . . .

Nagel has in mind misfortunes such as deterioration to a "vegetable-like" condition, and betrayal in cases where the subject is ignorant that he has been betrayed. That these are not *experienced* as misfortunes does not prevent their being described as such. So it is also, Nagel suggests, with death, which is a misfortune for a clearly identified subject (contrary to Lucretius' argument) because it closes certain possibilities which would otherwise have been open to him or her. Nagel concludes that death is indeed a severe misfortune, even a tragedy, for most of us; for the experience of leading a life generally includes a sense of open-ended possibility which appears fortuitously circumscribed by the prospect of death at age eighty or so.

The concept of misfortune as something which befalls a subject "identified by his history and his possibilities" is unquestionably one which we possess. Yet this is rather vague, and should be considered briefly. Nagel appears to think that one's "history and possibilities" *may* be independent of one's desires, and that betrayal may be a misfortune for a person even though he is indifferent to whether he has ever been betrayed. Again, if desires are of negligible importance in deciding whether someone is the subject of a misfortune, an aborted fetus must, it seems to me, be seen as the victim of a terrible misfortune, being denied a possible life. This does not seem quite right—at least it is not obviously right. This is because what counts as a misfortune often depends not merely upon one's possibilities, but upon how these are viewed, how they are related to one's desires. (It is possible that Nagel had something like this in mind when he talked of a person's "history.") That this qualification is necessary is shown by the fact that most of us have many "possibilities" the nonfulfillment of which may wrongly be regarded as our misfortune, if our desires are ignored. It is very irritating, for example, to see parents bemoan their child's failure to become a concert pianist or a doctor because, despite his or her desire to do something else, this was a "possibility." One could in this way become the victim of all sorts of misfortunes, viewed differently by various anxious devotees, while leading a life with which one is perfectly content.

In the face of this, one may experience a kind of existentialist indignation, expressible in the words: "I am free to choose what counts as a misfortune *for me.*" Yet this isn't right either, and it brings out an important truth in Nagel's position. The concept of misfortune, like the concept of happiness, is partially normative; both concepts, that is, stand in some complex relation to a conception of goodness. This is shown by the fact that it is *sometimes* correct to say that a person who claims to be happy is, in fact not happy and even to see him as the subject of a misfortune if, for example, he falls wildly short of the way we think it is *good* for a person to be. Suppose, for example, he has come to take pleasure in evil, or in an idle, pointless pursuit such as spending every spare moment enjoying pleasurable sensations by operating electrodes. He may be in some sense contented, but he is surely not happy (though he may not be *un*happy either), and is justly described as unfortunate.

The normative concept of misfortune is strongly Aristotelian in its rejection of the idea that the subject's testimony upon his or her own experience is a sufficient criterion of misfortune. It may be argued that death is a misfortune in precisely this sense; that since death is so clearly not in one's best interests, it is a condition for which we reasonably pity others, irrespective of whether or not they feared it. If this is so, the death of an animal must be a great misfortune also; for a dead animal certainly falls short of the way we think it is "good" for animals to be.

I find this unconvincing, however, for it seems to me that death is not a misfortune merely because it is a bad condition to be in, relative to being alive, healthy, and so on; rather it is a misfortune because life is something most of us value, and want to experience for as long as possible. We usually pity a person who has just died for one of two reasons: because that person valued life and wanted to live; or because he or she did *not* value life, and failed to see death as a misfortune. I shall say more about the first reason in a moment. The second reason sheds an interesting complexion on the normative concept of a misfortune. For it suggests that what is unfortunate about the evil or idle person discussed above is that, like the person who did not value life, he does not have the right kinds of *desires or values,* and that we think it in some sense *possible* that he might have had these. The misfortune is not, then, simply his falling short of how we think it good to be; it is also, and I think fundamentally, his failing to desire to be this way. An animal cannot be the subject of a misfortune in this way. He can be better or worse in relation to some conception of what it is to be a good animal; but he cannot be an object of pity because he does not *want* to match up to this conception. It does not make sense to say of an animal, as we say of a person, "It's unfortunate for him that he didn't mind dying." For what this suggests in the case of a person is a condition of depressiveness, or indifference towards life, and a failure to appreciate the richness and interest of life for a creature as complex and sensitive as a person. It follows from the Wittgensteinian argument above that these emotions, and this failure, are not possible for an animal.

The concept of something's being a misfortune *for* X is not adequately captured by identifying a discrepancy between X's "history and possibilities" and X's actual condition, the alleged misfortune. X's misfortune must either be something which X did not want; or it must be something that X *should not* have wanted, because it so obviously conflicted with his interests. Without these qualifications, many conditions could be wrongly considered "X's misfortune," for example, X's failing to be a concert pianist, even though she succeeded in being the teacher she wanted to be. Also, there would be no reason to restrict subjects of misfortune in this sense to persons: an accident could be a misfortune *for my car,* or for the tree which was hit by it. We would of course beg the question unforgivably if we excluded the latter possibility merely by confining the possible subjects of misfortune to persons.

To be a possible subject of misfortunes which are not merely unpleasant experiences, one must be able to desire and value certain things. The kind of misfortune which is in question here is death, and to discover whether this is a misfortune for an animal, we must ask whether, or in what sense, animals don't want to die. Of course, in some sense this is true of virtually all animals, which manifest acute fear when their lives are threatened. Yet blindly clinging on to life is not the same as wanting to live because one *values* life. This is the kind of desire for life of which persons are capable. It is this which gives sense to the claim that death is a misfortune, even a tragedy, for a person. Bernard Williams (in a reply to Nagel) argues a view like this.

Williams introduces the useful concept of a categorical desire. This is a desire which does not merely presuppose being alive (like the desire to eat when one is hungry), but rather answers the question whether one wants to remain alive. It may answer this question affirmatively or not. Williams discusses what he calls a rational forward-looking desire for suicide: this desire is categorical because it resolves (negatively), rather than assumes, the question of one's continued existence. Alternatively one may resolve this question affirmatively with a desire, for example, to raise children or write a book. Such desires give one reason to go on living, they give life so-called point or meaning. Most persons have some such desires throughout substantial periods of their lives.

A person who possesses categorical desires of the second sort is, Williams suggests, vulnerable to the misfortune of death in a way which neither Lucretius nor Nagel grasps. "To want something," says Williams, "is to that extent to have a reason for resisting what excludes having that thing; and death certainly does that, for a very large range of things that one wants." A subject of categorical desires, therefore, "has reason to regard possible death as a misfortune to be avoided, and we, looking at things from his point of view, would have reason to regard his actual death as a misfortune." The fear of death need not grow out of a confused conception of death as a state which is somehow suffered, as Lucretius claims; it may be the entirely rational corollary of the desire to do certain things with one's life. Furthermore we often pity a person who has died on exactly the ground that death prevents the satisfaction of certain desires, and not merely—as Nagel suggests—that death closes certain possibilities that the subject may or may not have wanted to realize.

It will be obvious from the earlier discussion that I reject the suggestion that a categorical desire, or anything of this nature, is attributable to animals. For consider what would have to be the case if this were so. First, animals would have to possess essentially the same conceptions of life and death as persons do. The subject of a categorical desire must either understand death as a condition which closes a possible future forever, and leaves behind one a world in which one has no part as an agent or conscious being of any sort; or he must grasp, and then reject, this conception of death, in favor of a belief in immortality. Either way, the radical and exclusive nature of the transition from life to death must be understood—it must at least be appreciated why people think in these terms—so that the full significance of the idea that "X is a reason for living" may be grasped.

One can only understand life and death in these ways if one possesses the related concepts of long-term future possibilities, of life itself as an object of value, of consciousness, agency and their annihilation, and of tragedy and similar misfortunes. It is only by an imaginative leap that possession of these concepts seems attributable to animals as well as to persons; this leap is all the more tempting, and therefore all the more dangerous, because it is not *obviously* absurd. It is certainly the case, for example, that some animals experience emotions of a relatively sophisticated nature, and that these emotions involve a kind of recognition of such things as human misfortune, impending danger to another, potential loss, and so on. I see no reason to withhold the ascription of sympathy, anxiety, even grief, to some animals; I only want to deny (what may be suggested by an anti-speciesist) that these emotions, and the range of awareness which they presuppose, give us a way into legitimately ascribing to animals an understanding of the finality, and potentially tragic significance, of death. Such understanding is necessary for a subject of categorical desires.

IV. MISFORTUNES AND RIGHTS

If my argument is correct, animals lack the very capacity which is necessary for the right to life: the capacity to have categorical desires. This capacity is necessary for a creature to be a possible subject of the misfortune of death, and *this* possibility is presupposed by the right to life; otherwise the right to life would be a right to be protected from something which could not conceivably be a misfortune, which does not make sense. I want to suggest, furthermore, that the capacity to be a subject of the misfortune of death is *sufficient* for possession of the right to life. I shall try to clarify this last point with reference to an article by Michael Tooley.

Tooley points out that the concepts of a person and human being are usefully prized apart by employing the former as a purely moral concept, entailing the right to life, and the latter to denote membership of the species homo sapiens. The question may then be raised whether all human beings should be regarded as persons (how about fetuses and even newborn infants?), and whether some *non*humans shouldn't be regarded as persons. The distinction is a valuable one, but its usefulness depends upon the discovery of criteria for personhood in this purely moral sense. Tooley suggests that possession of the concept of self as a continuing subject of experiences, and knowledge that one is such a self, are necessary and sufficient for personhood. His claim seems to be that the right to life is entailed by the *desire* for life as a continuing "self," which is present, or explicably absent (for example, through insanity or indoctrination) in most persons. He argues (rather as I have done) that such a desire presupposes a degree of conceptual sophistication which not all humans (for example, fetuses and newborn infants) possess.

Despite resemblances to my own position, there are important differences. For Tooley, a right to *X* is essentially an obligation on the part of others to respect the subject's *desire* for *X;* this is so, it seems, irrespective of whether or not the desire is reasonable or rational, good or evil. However it is most implausible to suggest that the right to life depends on the desire to live; one reason is that one does not forgo this right by *relinquishing* the desire to live. More generally, rights are independent of desires, for people may have desires without corresponding rights (for example, the desire to steal), and rights without corresponding desires (for example, the right to become an American citizen).

The connection between rights and misfortunes is a much more fruitful one. Not all possible misfortunes are matched by rights, though I believe the converse is true. Yet it seems reasonable to suggest that the reason why most human beings (biological concept) have the right to life is related to the fact that death is regarded as possibly a grave misfortune for a human being. The fact that most people desperately do not *want* to die is not what makes death a misfortune, or gives us the right to life; it is rather that this desire is an aspect of a rich understanding of what is not, so to speak, in our "interests" as human beings. Human beings have, we feel, the capacity clearly to recognize what is so appalling about death—its finality and inexorable quality for a self-conscious being—and this recognition is part of what makes death appalling. This, combined with the fact that death is something from which we can to some extent be protected, is part of the reason why we ascribe to human beings the right to life. . . .

I have suggested, by contrast, that no nonhuman is even a candidate for the right to life. This should be qualified at this point with the distinction between those nonhumans (for example, mice) of which it might be said that this is a logical impossibility, given the primitiveness of their behavior; and those nonhumans of which this cannot quite be said. Chimpanzees and dolphins, for example, are often cited as potential or actual language-users, and it is not *absurd* to suggest that these might turn out to qualify as persons in the purely moral sense. I have serious doubts about this possibility, as I think anyone must who understands the conceptual complexity surrounding our awareness of death, but it is not to be denied that where a small number of unusually sophisticated animals are concerned, the final answer may lie with a critical empirical investigation.

V. IMPLICATIONS FOR VEGETARIANISM

Finally, we must consider the implications of my argument for the practice of meat-eating. This has been a background concern until now: I have been mainly concerned with correcting a certain picture of animals, and the claims they legitimately make upon us. I concluded that animals are deserving of some moral concern, but not as much as persons; that their sufferings, not their (quick and painless) deaths, are morally significant. It remains to be seen just how this affects the vegetarianism issue; I shall close with some suggestions on this point.

My argument, if successful, has pulled the carpet from under the vegetarian ideology which seeks to protect animals from human jaws on the grounds of equal rights. This may reasonably be seen as a disappointing victory for someone who is trying to decide whether or not to eat meat; all it does is remove one argument for *not* eating meat. What is missing, it seems, is some criterion for deciding what kinds of human interests justify causing animals to suffer, or even to die a quick and painless death. With respect to the former, I have already said that certain human interests may outweigh the wrongness of causing animals to suffer; it must now be added that, despite our conclusion that animals are not in any significant sense victims of the misfortune of death, the act of *causing* the quick and painless death of an animal is not necessarily morally neutral. I shall try to clarify these points now in connection with Nozick's example, to which I promised to return.

This example is intended to show that human pleasure inadequately justifies cruelty to animals. The question then arises whether meat-eating is, as the example assumes, reasonably seen as a kind of personal whim, a trivial pleasure with as little justificatory force as the eccentric satisfaction of swinging a baseball bat. If indeed this is the case, it is hard to see how meat-eating justifies either the painful or painless killing of animals. The bat-swinger whose special pleasure had as a (regretted) corollary the instantaneous killing of one, or let us say thirty, animals would, I feel, need to call upon something more than his eccentric pleasure to justify the act. Why this is so is not easy to say. It could of course be the case that the animals in question are valued by someone, or by other animals, and that this would bring us back to a verdict of gratuitous cruelty. Setting this possibility aside, we have to consider the intuition that whimsical bat-swinging, causing instantaneous animal deaths, is, if not a major misdemeanor, pointlessly destructive, perhaps in a way that is akin to the destroying of trees or certain artifacts. It is possible in this way to drive a slim wedge between the moral significance of (or appropriateness of moral concern towards) animal deaths on the one hand, and on the other the acts which bring these about.

The decision to eat or not to eat meat is, I suggest, profitably undertaken with this kind of example in mind. If meat-eating has more justificatory force than whimsical bat-swinging, we need to know what this is; it seems likely that, even if it were proved that meat is nutritively substitutable, a case could be made for according to meat-eating more weight as a reason for action than whimsical bat-swinging. After all, insofar as meat-eating is found pleasurable, this pleasure is generally rooted in certain attitudes and traditions of long standing, which many are understandably reluctant to give up. It would of course be conservative in the extreme to give *much* weight to these considerations; the question is whether they carry sufficient weight to justify what I have presented as the morally tolerable, though not insignificant, activity of killing animals quickly and painlessly. My own view is that some such considerations, combined with the contingent fact that the nutritional value of meat is by no means proven to be negligible, successfully justify this activity, though the more usual phenomenon of causing animals to suffer as they are prepared for death is another matter. As long as such suffering persists, and to the extent that one is confident that meat is nutritionally dispensable, vegetarianism may well be the correct course. It is important only to see that this issue cannot be settled in advance, but must be the consequence of many empirical and moral considerations.

Immoral and Moral Uses of Animals

Christina Hoff

One can do something wrong to a tree, but it makes no sense to speak of wronging it. Can one wrong an animal? Many philosophers think not, and many research scientists adopt the attitude that the use of laboratory animals raises no serious moral questions. It is understandable that they should do so. Moral neutrality toward the objects of one's research is conducive to scientific practice. Scientists naturally wish to concentrate on their research and thus tend not to confront the problems that may arise in the choice of techniques. In support of this attitude of indifference, they could cite philosophers who point to features peculiar to human life, by virtue of which painful experimentation on unwilling human beings is rightly to be judged morally reprehensible and that on animals not. What are these features?

Rationality and the ability to communicate meaningfully with others are the most commonly mentioned differentiating characteristics. Philosophers as diverse as Aristotle, Aquinas, Descartes, and Kant point to man's deliberative capacities as the source of his moral preeminence. Animals, because they are irrational, have been denied standing. The trouble is that not all human beings are rational. Mentally retarded or severely brain-damaged human beings are sometimes much less intelligent than lower primates that have been successfully taught to employ primitive languages and make simple, logical inferences beyond the capacity of the normal three-year-old child. The view that rationality is the qualifying condition for moral status has the awkward consequence of leaving unexplained our perceived obligations to nonrational humanity.

Some philosophers have therefore argued that man's privileged moral status is owed to his capacity for suffering. To be plausible, this way of explaining man's position as the only being who can be wronged must discount the apparent suffering of mammals and other highly organized creatures. It is sometimes assumed that the subjective experience of pain is quite different for animals and human beings. Descartes, for example, maintains that animals are machines: he speaks of tropisms of avoidance and desire rather than pleasure and pain. Although it is true that human beings can suffer in ways that animals cannot, the idea that animals and human beings experience physical pain differently is physiologically incoherent. We know that animals feel pain because of their behavioral reactions (including writhing, screaming, facial contortions, and desperate efforts to escape the source of pain), the evidence of their nervous systems, and the evolutionary value of pain. (By "animals" I mean mammals, birds, and other organisms of comparable evolutionary complexity.)

There are other sources of human suffering besides pain, but they too are not peculiarly human. One has only to consult the reports of naturalists or go to the zoo or own a pet to learn that the higher animals, at least, can suffer from loneliness, jealousy, boredom, frustration, rage, and terror. If, indeed, the capacity to suffer is the morally relevant characteristic, then the facts determine that animals, along with all human beings, are the proper subjects of moral consideration.

There is, however, another common way of defending human privilege. It is sometimes asserted that "just being human" is a sufficient basis for a protected moral status, that sheer membership in the species confers exclusive moral rights. Each human life, no matter how impoverished, has a depth and meaning that transcends that of even the most gifted dolphin or chimpanzee. One may speak of this as the humanistic principle. Cicero was one of its earliest exponents: "Honor every human being because he is a human being." Kant called it the Principle of Personality and placed it at the foundation of his moral theory. The principle appears evident to us because it is embodied in the attitudes and institutions of most civilized communities. Although this accounts for its intuitive appeal, it is hardly an adequate reason to accept it. Without further argument the humanistic principle is arbitrary. What must be adduced is an acceptable criterion for awarding special rights. But when we proffer a criterion based, say, on the capacity to reason or to suffer, it is clearly inadequate either because it is satisfied by some but not all members of the species *Homo sapiens,* or because it is satisfied by them all—and many other animals as well.

Another type of argument for denying equal consideration to animals goes back at least to Aristotle. I refer to the view that man's tyranny over animals is natural because his superiority as an animal determines for him the dominant position in the natural scale of things. To suggest that man give up his dominance over animals is to suggest that he deny his nature. The argument assumes that "denial of nature" is ethically incoherent. But conformity with nature is not an adequate condition for ethical standards. Being moral does not appear to be a question of abiding by the so-called laws of nature; just as often it seems to require us to disregard what is "natural" in favor of what is compassionate. We avoid slavery and child labor, not because we have discovered that they are unnatural, but because we have discovered that slaves and children have their own desires and interests and they engage our sympathy. Social Darwinism was an ethical theory that sought to deduce moral rules from the "facts" of nature. Wealthy 19th-century industrialists welcomed a theory that seemed to justify inhumane labor practices by reference to the "natural order of things." It has become clear that these so-called "laws" of nature cannot provide an adequate basis for a moral theory, if only because they may be cited to support almost any conceivable theory.

It is fair to say that no one has yet given good reasons to accept a moral perspective that grants a privileged moral status to all and only human beings. A crucial moral judgment is made when one decides that a given course of action with respect to a certain class of beings does not fall within the range of moral consideration. Historically, mistakes at this level have proved dangerous: they leave the agent free to perpetrate heinous acts that are not regarded as either moral or immoral and are therefore unchecked by normal inhibition. The exclusion of animals from the moral domain may well be a similar and equally benighted error. It is, in any case, arbitrary and unfounded in good moral argument.

Whatever belongs to the moral domain can be wronged. But if one rejects the doctrine that membership in the moral domain necessarily coincides with membership in the human species, then one must state a satisfactory condition for moral recognition. Bentham offers an intuitively acceptable starting point. "The question is not, Can they *reason?*, nor, Can they *talk?* but Can they *suffer?*" The capacity to suffer confers a minimal prima facie moral status on any creature, for it seems reasonable that one who is wantonly cruel to a sentient creature wrongs that creature. Animals too can be wronged; the practical consequences of such a moral position are, however, not as clear as they may seem. We must consider what we may and may not do to them.

I begin with a word about the comparative worthiness of human and animal life. Although animals are entitled to moral consideration, it does not follow that animals and human beings are always equal before the moral law. Distinctions must still be made. One may acknowledge that animals have rights without committing oneself to a radical egalitarianism that awards to animals complete parity with human beings. If hunting animals for sport is wrong, hunting human beings for the same purpose is worse, and such a distinction is not inconsistent with recognizing that animals have moral status. Although some proponents of animal rights would deny it, there are morally critical differences between animals and human beings. Animals share with human beings a common interest in avoiding pain, but the complexities of normal human life clearly provide a relevant basis for assigning to human beings a far more serious right to life itself. When we kill a human being, we take away his physical existence (eating, sleeping, and feeling pleasure and pain), but we deprive him of other things as well. His projects, his friendships, and his sense of himself as a human being are also terminated. To kill a human being is not only to take away his life, but to impugn the special meaning of his life. In contrast, an animal's needs and desires are restricted to his place in time and space. He lives "the life of the moment." Human lives develop and unfold; they have a direction. Animal lives do not. Accordingly, I suggest the following differential principle of life worthiness: Human lives are generally worthier than animal lives, and the right to life of a human being generally supersedes the right to life of an animal.

This differential principle rejects the Cartesian thesis, which totally dismisses animals from moral consideration, and it is consistent with two other principles that I have been tacitly defending: animals are moral subjects with claims to considerations that should not be ignored; and an animal's experience of pain is similar to a human being's experience of pain.

In the light of these principles I shall try to determine what general policies we ought to adopt in regulating the use of animals in experimental science. I am limiting myself to the moral questions arising in the specific area of painful or fatal animal experimentation, but some of the discussion will apply to other areas of human interaction with animals. Space does not allow discussion of killing animals for educational purposes.

Scientists who perform experiments on animals rarely see the need to justify them, but when they do they almost always stress the seriousness of the research. Although it may be regrettable that animals are harmed, their suffering is seen as an unavoidable casualty of scientific progress. The moral philosopher must still ask: is the price in animal misery worth it?

That the ends do not always justify the means is a truism, and when the means involve the painful treatment of unwilling innocents, serious questions arise. Although it is notoriously difficult to formulate the conditions that justify the consequences, it is plausible that desired ends are not likely to justify onerous means in the following situations: when those who suffer the means are not identical with those who are expected to enjoy the ends; when there is grave doubt that the justifying ends will be brought about by the onerous means; and when the ends can be achieved by less onerous means.

When a competent surgeon causes pain he does not run afoul of these conditions. On the other hand, social policies that entail mass misery on the basis of tenuous sociopolitical assumptions of great future benefits do run afoul of the last two conditions and often of the first as well. The use of laboratory animals often fails to satisfy these conditions of consequential justification; the first is ignored most frequently (I shall argue that this can often be justified), but scientists often violate the others as well when they carry out painful or fatal experiments with animals that are poorly designed or could have been just as well executed without intact living animals.

We can be somewhat more specific in formulating guidelines for animal experimentation if we consider the equality of animals and human beings with respect to pain. Because there are no sound biologic reasons for the idea that human pain is intrinsically more intense than animal pain, animals and men may be said to be equals with respect to pain. Equality in this case is a measure of their shared interest in avoiding harm and discomfort. The evil of pain, unlike the value of life, is unaffected by the identity of the individual sufferer.

Animals and human beings, however, do differ in their experience of the aftereffects of pain. When an injury leaves the subject cosmetically disfigured, for example, a human being may suffer from a continuing sense of shame and bitterness, but for the animal the trauma is confined to the momentary pain.

Even the permanent impairment of faculties has more serious and lasting aftereffects on human beings than on animals. It can be argued that a person who is stricken by blindness suffers his loss more keenly than an animal similarly stricken.

More important than the subjective experience of privation is the objective diminishment of a valuable being whose scope of activity and future experience have been severely curtailed. In terms of physical privation animals and human beings do not differ, but the measure of loss must be counted far greater in human beings. To sum up: human beings and animals have a parity with respect to the trauma of a painful episode but not with respect to the consequences of the trauma. Yet when an experiment involves permanent impairment or death for the subject and thus considerations of differential life worthiness make it wrong to use most human beings, the pain imposed on the animals should still be counted as intrinsically bad, as if human beings had been made to suffer it, regardless of the aftereffects.

Although I believe that the general inferiority of animal lives to human life is relevant to the formation of public policy, I cannot accept the view that their relative inferiority licenses harming animals except for very serious purposes in rather special circumstances. However, the special circumstances are not necessarily extraordinary. Many experiments, although not as many as is generally supposed, are medically important and needed. The researcher who is working to control cancer and other fatal and crippling diseases may be able to satisfy the conditions that justify the use of laboratory animals. Because I believe that normal human lives are of far greater worth than animal lives, I accept a policy in which those who suffer the means are not those who may enjoy the ends, which violates the first of the conditions of consequential justification mentioned above, by permitting the infliction of pain on animals to save human lives or to contribute substantially to their welfare. However, when researchers intend to harm an animal, they need more than a quick appeal to the worthiness of human life. They ought to be able to show that the resulting benefits are outstandingly compensatory; if the scientist cannot make a good case for the experiment, it should be proscribed. (On the other hand, if suffering is the main consideration in judging the admissibility of experiments with animals, then nonpainful experiments, even fatal ones, may be under fewer constraints than painful, nonfatal experiments. Although this idea may seem paradoxical, it is in accord with the common moral intuition that condones those who put a kitten "to sleep" while condemning those who torment one.) The implementation of this policy raises questions that cannot be dealt with here. Yet one might expect that research proposals involving painful animal experimentation should be reviewed by a panel of experts, perhaps composed of two scientists in the field of the experiment and a scientifically knowledgeable philosopher versed in medical ethics.

In closing, I wish to indicate how I would deal with a possible objection. It may appear that my criteria of life worthiness place human idiots on a par with animals. On what grounds could I prohibit the painful or fatal experimental use of human subjects whose capacity does not differ from that of many animals? I would be prepared to rethink or even abandon a position that could not distinguish between animal and human experimentation. Fortunately, this distinction can be made.

I oppose painful or fatal experimentation on defective, nonconsenting human beings not because I believe that any person, just because he is human, has a privileged moral status, but because I do not believe that we can safely permit anyone to decide which human beings fall short of worthiness. Judgments of this kind and the creation of institutions for making them are fraught with danger and open to grave abuse. It is never necessary to show that an animal's life is not as valuable as that of a normal human being, but just such an initial judgment of exclusion would have to be made for idiots. Because there is no way to circumvent this problem, experiments on human beings are precluded and practically wrong. There are other arguments against experimenting on mentally feeble human beings, but this one seems to me to be the strongest and to be sufficient to support the view that whereas animal experimentation is justifiable, no dangerous or harmful experiments involving unwilling human subjects could be.

Accordingly, I have reached the following conclusions concerning the painful exploitation of animals for human rewards. Animals should not be used in painful experiments when substantial benefits are not expected to result. Even when the objective is important, there is a presumption against the use of animals in painful and dangerous experiments that are expected to yield tenuous results of doubtful value. Animals but not human beings may be used in painful and dangerous experiments that are to yield vital benefits for human beings (or other animals).

Vast numbers of animals are currently being used in all kinds of scientific experiments, many of which entail animal misery. Some of these studies, unfortunately, do not contribute to medical science, and some do not even require the use of intact animals. Even the most conservative corrective measures in the implementation of a reasonable and morally responsible policy would have dramatic practical consequences.

QUESTIONS FOR DISCUSSION
Do Animals Have Rights?

1. Why, for Tom Regan, is it wrong to treat domestic animals as "renewable resources"? Does it follow that we cannot own them? Explain your response.
2. If animals were no longer raised for food, most domestic types, such as chickens, pigs, and beef cows, would probably become extinct. Is this a sound argument against vegetarianism? Explain why or why not.
3. If strict laws were passed mandating good treatment of animals and prohibiting hunting and experimentation for trivial reasons such as cosmetic research, would that satisfy Tom Regan's concerns? Would it satisfy Christina Hoff's? How about yours? Defend your response.
4. Discuss Regan's arguments that animals have rights against humans—which rights are they? What are Ruth Cigman's main counterarguments? Does she deny that we have any duties toward animals?
5. Compare Cigman's denial of animal rights with Mary Anne Warren's denial of fetal rights in Chapter 4. Are their arguments similar? In what ways?
6. Does every duty or obligation owed by A to B entail that B has a right against A? In brief, do all moral duties entail rights? Can you think of any duties that do not entail corresponding rights? Identify and explain.
7. Why, according to Cigman, is death a misfortune for a human but not for a nonhuman animal? Does Christina Hoff agree, in part or completely? Do you? Compare your own response with Cigman's and Hoff's.

SELECTED READINGS

BERNSTEIN, M. "Speciesism and Loyalty." *Behaviorism and Philosophy,* _____ 1991.

FINK, C. "The Moderate View on Animal Ethics." *Between the Species,* _____ 1991.

FULDA, J. "Reply to an Objection to Animal Rights." *Journal of Value Inquiry,* _____ 1992.

HARGROVE, E., ed. *The Animal Rights/Environmental Debate.* Albany: State University of New York Press, 1992.

LEAHY, M. *Against Liberation.* New York: Routledge, 1991.

MILLER, H., and W. WILLIAMS, eds. *Ethics and Animals.* Clifton, NJ: Humanities Press, 1983.

NELSON, J. "Autonomy and the Moral Status of Animals." *Between the Species,* _____ 1992.

ORLANS, F., T. BEAUCHAMPS, et al. *The Human Use of Animals.* New York: Oxford University Press, 1997.

REGAN, T. *The Case for Animal Rights.* Berkeley: University of California Press, 1983.

ROLLIN, B. *Animal Rights and Human Morality.* Buffalo: Prometheus, 1992.

SINGER, P. *Animal Liberation,* 2nd ed. New York: Avon, 1990.

11

IS GENETIC ENGINEERING GOOD OR BAD?

Microbiology and genetics have been rivaling computer science in the dizzying pace of their advances and in their impact on human life. Unlike computer science, whose discoveries and applications, whether for good or ill, seem entirely within human control, the two most exciting uses of genetic engineering have raised serious doubts as to their ultimate consequences for humankind. Recombining bacteria and cloning are processes whereby new forms of life are created by science and technology; these "advances" evoke religious fears about human presumption of the work of God and divinely governed nature, as well as the fears of scientists themselves about the unpredictability of the forces unleashed by their experiments.

Not since the development of nuclear power and thermonuclear weapons six decades ago have philosophers and scientists so sharply differed on the advisability of new directions of scientific research. Not long ago, in response to the recommendations of a presidential commission of inquiry into the use of stem cells in medical research aimed at finding cures for genetic diseases such as Parkinson's, Alzheimer's, and Lou Gehrig's diseases, President Bush prohibited federal support for medical research that involves the cloning of human embryos for this worthy purpose.

Robert Sinsheimer warns against the use of genetic engineering to combine genetic materials so as to create new life forms, such as recombinant bacteria, that can produce great medical and agricultural benefits but can also have catastrophic consequences if improperly handled or inadequately understood. The degree of probability of these harmful consequences, he argues, is impossible to estimate and therefore constitutes a risk that may prove too great to be acceptable, thus too high a price to pay for the hoped-for benefits. Sinsheimer, himself a research biologist, describes in technical detail the processes involved in genetic engineering and also the kinds of things that can go wrong, such as an epidemic of new cancer-producing viruses, or even the radical and undesirable transformation of human personality. He advises us not to stop genetic experimentation but to go more slowly and cautiously than his more adventurous colleagues would like.

The philosopher of science Stephen Stich argues, to the contrary, that the likely benefits of such research far exceed the possible harms. In defending the scientific program of genetic engineering, he nevertheless decries what he considers mistaken claims concerning it: that scientific inquiry should never be limited, and that this kind of research should be entirely prohibited. He grants that some investigations made in the name of science should not be allowed, for example, those that invade privacy or those that involve performing dangerous experiments on children. But the main argument of opponents like Sinsheimer, that recombinant DNA might possibly result in intended or unintended disasters, is, according to Stich, not a good reason to ban such research because, on such grounds, most scientific inquiry would be equally ruled out. The issue for him is how to compare the risks versus the potential benefits, and he believes that such comparison weighs in favor of continued genetic engineering.

The next two writers, Hilary Putnam and John Harris, disagree on the advisability of human cloning. This is a topic that has been heatedly debated by philosophers, scientists, and theologians since 1997, when, after many unsuccessful attempts, scientists in Scotland succeeded in cloning a sheep that they named Dolly.

Putnam maintains that our moral convictions need to be held together by what he calls a "moral image"; when applied to the issue of parental cloning of children, he asserts that such cloning would violate our common moral image of a family, in which the values of diversity and autonomy take precedence over the narcissistic satisfaction of parents who want their children to be just like themselves, or those who want their children to obey and serve them like slaves. Cloning to produce "designer children" would, Putnam argues, promote these generally recognized vices of family life.

Harris replies to Putnam by agreeing with Putnam's application to family life of Kant's principle that one must not use another as a mere means to one's own ends; but then Harris points out that this should not mean that we should never choose friends, hire employees, or adopt children who will best suit our purposes, so long as we act to suit their purposes as well. Harris agrees that diversity and autonomy are worthy family values, but he argues that these values are not seriously endangered by allowing parents to design their own children, and that freedom of choice is also an important value — one that is enhanced by allowing parents to choose the children they desire.

TOO DANGEROUS

Robert Sinsheimer

The essence of engineering is design and, thus, the essence of genetic engineering, as distinct from applied genetics, is the introduction of human design into the formulation of new genes and new genetic combinations. These methods thus supplement the older methods which rely upon the intelligent selection and perpetuation of those chance genetic combinations which arise in the natural breeding process.

The possibility of genetic engineering derives from major advances in DNA technology—in the means of synthesizing, analyzing, transposing and generally manipulating the basic genetic substance of life. Three major advances have all neatly combined to permit this striking accomplishment: these are (1) the discovery of means for the cleavage of DNA at highly specific sites; (2) the development of simple and generally applicable methods for the joining of DNA molecules; and (3) the discovery of effective techniques for the introduction of DNA into previously refractory organisms.

The art of DNA cleavage and degradation languished in a crude and unsatisfactory state until the discovery and more recent application of enzymes known as restriction endonucleases. These enzymes protect the host cells against invasion by foreign genomes by specifically severing the intruding DNA strands. For the purposes of genetic engineering, restriction enzymes provide a reservoir of means to cleave DNA molecules reproducibly at a limited number of sites by recognizing specific tracts of DNA ranging from four to eight nucleotides in length.

Unfortunately the . . . probabilities that some of these strains could persist in the intestines, the probabilities that the modified plasmids might be transferred to other strains, better adapted to intestinal life, the probabilities that the genome of an oncogenic virus could escape, could be taken up, could transform a host cell, are all largely unknown.

Following the call for a moratorium a conference was held at Asilomar at the end of . . . February [1975] to assess these problems. While it proved possible to rank various types of proposed experiments with respect to potential hazard, for the reasons already stated it proved impossible to establish, on any secure basis, the absolute magnitude of hazard. Various distinguished scientists differed very widely, but sincerely, in their estimates. Historical

Robert Sinsheimer. "Too Dangerous." Excerpted from "Troubled Dawn for Genetic Engineering" in *The Weekly Review of Science and Technology,* vol. 68, October 16, 1975. Reprinted by permission of Reed Elsevier.

experience indicated that simple reliance upon the physical containment of these new organisms could not be completely effective.

In the end a broad, but not universal, consensus was reached which recommended that the seemingly more dangerous experiments be deferred until means of "biological containment" could be developed to supplement physical containment. By biological containment is meant the crippling of all vehicles—cells or viruses—intended to carry the recombinant genomes through the insertion of a variety of genetic defects so as to reduce very greatly the likelihood that the organisms could survive outside of a protective, carefully supplemented laboratory culture.

This seems a sensible and responsible compromise. However, several of the less prominent aspects of the Asilomar conference also deserve much thought. The lens of Asilomar was focused sharply upon the potential biological and medical hazard of this new research, but other issues drifted in and out of the field of discussion. There was, for instance, no specific consideration of the wisdom of diverting appreciable research funds and talent to this field, in lieu of others. An indirect discussion of this question was perhaps implicit in the description of the significance and scientific potential of research in this field presented by those who were impatient of any delay.

Indeed the eagerness of the researchers to get on with the work in this field was most evident. To a scientist this was exhilarating. Obviously these new techniques open many previously closed doorways leading to the potential resolution of long-standing and important problems. I think also there is a certain romance in this joining together of DNA molecules that diverged billions of years ago and have pursued separate paths through all of these millenia. Personally I feel confident one could easily justify this new research direction. But a sociologist of science might see other undercurrents in this impetuous eagerness, and the bright scientific promise should not blind us to the realities of other concerns.

Rights are not found in nature. Rights are conferred within a human society and for each there is expected a corresponding responsibility. Inevitably at some boundaries different rights come into conflict, and the exercise of a right should not destroy the society that conferred it. We recognize this in other fields. Freedom of the press is a right but it is subject to restraints, such as libel and obscenity and, perhaps more dubiously, national security. The right to experiment on human beings is obviously constrained. Similarly, would we wish to claim the right of individual scientists to be free to create novel self-perpetuating organisms likely to spread about the planet in an uncontrollable manner for better or worse? I think not.

This does not mean we cannot advance our science or that we must doubt its ultimate beneficence. It simply means that we must be able to look at what we do in a mature way.

There was, at Asilomar, no explicit consideration of the potential broader social or ethical implications of initiating this line of research—of its role, as a possible prelude to longer-range, broader-scale genetic engineering of the flora and fauna of the planet, including, ultimately, man. It is not yet clear how these techniques may be applied to higher organisms but we should not underestimate scientific ingenuity. Indeed the oncogenic viruses may provide a key; and mitochondria may serve as analogues for plasmids.

CONTROLLED EVOLUTION?

How far will we want to develop genetic engineering? Do we want to assume the basic responsibility for life on this planet—to develop new living forms for our own purpose? Shall we take into our own hands our own future evolution? These are profound issues which involve science but also transcend science. They deserve our most serious and continuing thought. I can here mention only a very few of the more salient considerations.

Clearly the advent of genetic engineering, even merely in the microbial world, brings new responsibilities to accompany the new potentials. It is always thus when we introduce the element of human design. The distant yet much discussed application of genetic engineering to mankind would place this equation at the center of all future human history. It would in the end make human design responsible for human nature. It is a responsibility to give pause, especially if one recognizes that the prerequisite for responsibility is the ability to forecast, to make reliable estimates of the consequence.

Can we really forecast the consequence for mankind, for human society, of any major change in the human gene pool? The more I have reflected on this, the more I have come to doubt it. I do not refer here to the alleviation of individual genetic defects—or, if you will, to the occasional introduction of a genetic clone—but more broadly to the genetic redefinition of man. Our social structures have evolved so as to be more or less well adapted to the array of talents and personalities emergent by chance from the existing gene pool and developed through our cultural agencies. In our social endeavours we have, biologically, remained cradled in that web of evolutionary nature which bore us and which has undoubtedly provided a most valuable safety net as we have in our fumbling way created and tried our varied cultural forms.

To introduce a sudden major discontinuity in the human gene pool might well create a major mismatch between our social order and our individual capacities. Even a minor perturbation such as a marked change in the sex ratio from its present near equality could shake our social structures— or consider the impact of a major change in the human life span. Can we really predict the results of such a perturbation? And if we cannot foresee the consequence, do we go ahead?

It is difficult for a scientist to conceive that there are certain matters best left unknown, at least for a time. But science is the major organ of inquiry for a society—and perhaps a society, like an organism, must follow a developmental program in which the genetic information is revealed in an orderly sequence.

The dawn of genetic engineering is troubled. In part this is the spirit of the time—the very idea of progress through science is in question. People seriously wonder if through our cleverness we may not blunder into worse dilemmas than we seek to solve. They are concerned not only for the vagrant lethal virus or the escaped mutant deadly microbe, but also for the awful potential that we might inadvertently so arm the anarchic in our society as to shatter its bonds or conversely so arm the tyrannical in our society as to forever imprison liberty.

WORTH THE RISK

Stephen P. Stich

The debate over recombinant DNA research is a unique event, perhaps a turning point, in the history of science. For the first time in modern history there has been widespread public discussion about whether and how a promising though potentially dangerous line of research shall be pursued. At root the debate is a moral debate and, like most such debates, requires proper assessment of the facts at crucial stages in the argument. A good deal of the controversy over recombinant DNA research arises because some of the facts simply are not yet known. There are many empirical questions we would like to have answered before coming to a decision—questions about the reliability of proposed containment facilities, about the viability of enfeebled strains of *E. coli,* about the ways in which pathogenic organisms do their unwelcome work, and much more. But all decisions cannot wait until the facts are available; some must be made now. It is to be expected that people with different hunches about what the facts will turn out to be will urge different decisions on how recombinant DNA research should be regulated. However, differing expectations about the facts have not been the only fuel for controversy. A significant part of the current debate can be traced to differences over moral principles. Also, unfortunately, there has been much unnecessary debate generated by careless moral reasoning and a failure to attend to the logical structure of some of the moral arguments that have been advanced.

In order to help sharpen our perception of the moral issues underlying the controversy over recombinant DNA research, I shall start by clearing away some frivolous arguments that have deflected attention from more serious issues. We may then examine the problems involved in deciding whether the potential benefits of recombinant DNA research justify pursuing it despite the risks that it poses.

I. THREE BAD ARGUMENTS

My focus in this section will be on three untenable arguments, each of which has surfaced with considerable frequency in the public debate over recombinant DNA research.

The first argument on my list concludes that recombinant DNA research should not be controlled or restricted. The central premise of the argument is that scientists should have full and unqualified freedom to pursue whatever inquiries they may choose to pursue. This claim was stated repeatedly in petitions and letters to the editor during the height of the public debate over recombinant DNA research in the University of Michigan community. The general moral principle which is the central premise of the argument plainly does entail that investigators using recombinant DNA technology should be allowed to pursue their research as they see fit. However, we need only consider a few examples to see that the principle invoked in this "freedom of inquiry" argument is utterly indefensible. No matter how sincere a researcher's interest may be in investigating the conjugal behavior of American university professors, few would be willing to grant him the right to pursue his research in my bedroom without my consent. No matter how interested a researcher may be in investigating the effects of massive doses of bomb-grade plutonium on preschool children, it is hard to imagine that anyone thinks he should be allowed to do so. Yet the "free inquiry" principle, if accepted, would allow both of these projects and countless other Dr. Strangelove projects as well. So plainly the simplistic "free inquiry" principle is indefensible. It would, however, be a mistake to conclude that freedom of inquiry ought not to be protected. A better conclusion is that the right of free inquiry is a qualified right and must sometimes yield to conflicting rights and to the demands of conflicting moral principles. Articulating an explicit and properly qualified principle of free inquiry is a task of no small difficulty. We will touch on this topic again toward the end of Section II.

The second argument I want to examine aims at establishing just the opposite conclusion from the first. The particular moral judgment being defended is that there should be a total ban on recombinant DNA research. The argument begins with the observation that even in so-called low-risk recombinant DNA experiments there is at least a possibility of catastrophic consequences. We are, after all, dealing with a relatively new and unexplored technology. Thus it is at least possible that a bacterial culture whose genetic makeup has been altered in the course of a recombinant DNA experiment may exhibit completely unexpected pathogenic characteristics. Indeed, it is not impossible that we could find ourselves confronted with a killer strain of, say, *E. coli* and, worse, a strain against which humans can marshal no natural defense. Now if this is possible—if we cannot say with assurance that the probability of it happening is zero—then, the argument continues, all recombinant DNA research should be halted. For the negative utility of the imagined catastrophe is so enormous, resulting as it would in the destruction of our society and perhaps even of our species, that no work which could possibly lead to this result would be worth the risk.

The argument just sketched, which might be called the "doomsday scenario" argument, begins with a premise which no informed person would be inclined to deny. It is indeed *possible* that even a low-risk recombinant DNA experiment might lead to totally catastrophic results. No ironclad guarantee can be offered that this will not happen. And while the probability of such an unanticipated catastrophe is surely not large, there is no serious argument that the probability is zero. Still, I think the argument is a sophistry. To go from the undeniable premise that recombinant DNA research might possibly result in unthinkable catastrophe to the conclusion that such research should be banned requires a moral principle stating that *all* endeavors that might possibly result in such a catastrophe should be prohibited. Once the principle has been stated, it is hard to believe that anyone would take it at all seriously. For the principle entails that, along with recombinant DNA research, almost all scientific research and many other commonplace activities having little to do with science should be prohibited. It is, after all, at least logically possible that the next new compound synthesized in an ongoing chemical research program will turn out to be an uncontainable carcinogen many orders of magnitude more dangerous than aerosol plutonium. And, to vary the example, there is a non-zero probability that experiments in artificial pollination will produce a weed that will, a decade from now, ruin the world's food grain harvest.

I cannot resist noting that the principle invoked in the doomsday scenario argument is not new. Pascal used an entirely parallel argument to show that it is in our own best interests to believe in God. For though the probability of God's existence may be very low, if He nonetheless should happen to exist, the disutility that would accrue to the disbeliever would be catastrophic — an eternity in hell. But, as introductory philosophy students should all know, Pascal's argument only looks persuasive if we take our options to be just two: Christianity or atheism. A third possibility is belief in a jealous non-Christian God who will see to our damnation if and only if we *are* Christians. The probability of such a deity existing is again very small, but non-zero. So Pascal's argument is of no help in deciding whether or not to accept Christianity. For we may be damned if we do and damned if we don't.

I mention Pascal's difficulty because there is a direct parallel in the doomsday scenario argument against recombinant DNA research. Just as there is a non-zero probability that unforeseen consequences of recombinant DNA research will lead to disaster, so there is a non-zero probability that unforeseen consequences of *failing* to pursue the research will lead to disaster. There may, for example, come a time when, because of natural or man-induced climatic change, the capacity to alter quickly the genetic constitution of agricultural plants will be necessary to forestall catastrophic famine. And if we fail to pursue recombinant DNA research now, our lack of knowledge in the future may have consequences as dire as any foreseen in the doomsday scenario argument.

The third argument I want to consider provides a striking illustration of how important it is, in normative thinking, to make clear the moral *principles* being invoked. The argument I have in mind begins with a factual claim about recombinant DNA research and concludes that stringent restrictions, perhaps even a moratorium, should be imposed. However, advocates of the argument are generally silent on the normative principle(s) linking premise and conclusion.

The gap thus created can be filled in a variety of ways, resulting in very different arguments. The empirical observation that begins the argument is that recombinant DNA methods enable scientists to move genes back and forth across natural barriers, "particularly the most fundamental such barrier, that which divides prokaryotes from eukaryotes. The results will be essentially new organisms, self-perpetuating and hence permanent." Because of this, it is concluded that severe restrictions are in order. Plainly this argument is an enthymeme; a central premise has been left unstated. What sort of moral principle is being tacitly assumed?

The principle that comes first to mind is simply that natural barriers should not be breached, or perhaps that "essentially new organisms" should not be created. The principle has an almost theological ring to it, and perhaps there are some people who would be prepared to defend it on theological grounds. But short of a theological argument, it is hard to see why anyone would hold the view that breaching natural barriers or creating new organisms is *intrinsically* wrong. For if a person were to advocate such a principle, he would have to condemn the creation of new bacterial strains capable of, say, synthesizing human clotting factor or insulin, *even if* creating a new organism generated *no unwelcome side effects.*

There is quite a different way of unraveling the "natural barriers" argument which avoids appeal to the dubious principles just discussed. As an alternative, this second reading of the argument ties premise to conclusion with a second factual claim and a quite different normative premise. The added factual claim is that at present our knowledge of the consequences of creating new forms of life is severely limited; thus we cannot know with any assurance that the probability of disastrous consequences is very low. The moral principle needed to mesh with the two factual premises would be something such as the following:

> If we do not know with considerable assurance that the probability of an activity leading to disastrous consequences is very low, then we should not allow the activity to continue.

Now this principle, unlike those marshaled in the first interpretation of the natural barriers argument, is not lightly dismissed. It is, to be sure, a conservative principle, and it has the odd feature of focusing entirely on the dangers an activity poses while ignoring its potential benefits. Still, the principle may have a certain attraction in light of recent history, which has increasingly been marked by catastrophes attributable to technology's unanticipated side effects. I will not attempt a full scale evaluation of this principle just now. For the principle raises, albeit in a rather extreme way, the question of how risks and benefits are to be weighed against each other. In my opinion, that is the really crucial moral question raised by recombinant DNA research. It is a question which bristles with problems. In Section II I shall take a look at some of these problems and make a few tentative steps toward some solutions. While picking our way through the problems we will have another opportunity to examine the principle just cited.

II. RISKS AND BENEFITS

At first glance it might be thought that the issue of risks and benefits is quite straightforward, at least in principle. What we want to know is whether the potential benefits of recombinant DNA research justify the risks involved. To find out we need only determine the probabilities of the various dangers and benefits. And while some of the empirical facts—the probabilities—may require considerable ingenuity and effort to uncover, the assessment poses no particularly difficult normative or conceptual problems. Unfortunately, this sanguine view does not survive much more than a first glance. A closer look at the task of balancing the risks and benefits of recombinant DNA research reveals a quagmire of sticky conceptual problems and simmering moral disputes. In the next few pages I will try to catalogue and comment on some of these moral disputes. I wish I could also promise solutions to all of them, but to do so would be false advertising. . . .

Weighing Harms and Benefits

A second cluster of problems that confronts us in assessing the risks and benefits of recombinant DNA research turns on the assignment of a measure of desirability to the various possible outcomes. Suppose that we have a list of the various harms and benefits that might possibly result from pursuing recombinant DNA research. The list will include such "benefits" as development of an inexpensive way to synthesize human clotting factor and development of a strain of nitrogen-fixing wheat; and such "harms" as release of a new antibiotic-resistant strain of pathogenic bacteria and release of a strain of *E. coli* carrying tumor viruses capable of causing cancer in man.

Plainly, it is possible that pursuing a given policy will result in more than one benefit and in more than one harm. Now if we are to assess the potential impact of various policies or courses of action, we must assign some index of desirability to the possible *total outcomes* of each policy, outcomes which may well include a mix of benefits and harms. To do this we must confront a tangle of normative problems that are as vexing and difficult as any we are likely to face. We must *compare* the moral desirabilities of various harms and benefits. The task is particularly troublesome when the harms and benefits to be compared are of different kinds. Thus, for example, some of the attractive potential benefits of recombinant DNA research are economic: we may learn to recover small amounts of valuable metals in an economically feasible way, or we may be able to synthesize insulin and other drugs inexpensively. By contrast, many of the risks of recombinant DNA research are risks to human life or health. So if we are to take the idea of cost-benefit analysis seriously, we must at some point decide how human lives are to be weighed against economic benefits.

There are those who contend that the need to make such decisions indicates the moral bankruptcy of attempting to employ risk-benefit analyses when human lives are at stake. On the critics' view, we cannot reckon the possible loss of a human life as just another negative outcome, albeit a grave and heavily weighted one. To do so, it is urged, is morally repugnant and reflects a callous lack of respect for the sacredness of human life.

On my view, this sort of critique of the very idea of using risk-benefit analyses is ultimately untenable. It is simply a fact about the human condition, lamentable as it is inescapable, that in many human activities we run the risk of inadvertently causing the death of a human being. We run such a risk each time we drive a car, allow a dam to be built, or allow a plane to take off. Moreover, in making social and individual decisions, we cannot escape weighing economic consequences against the risk to human life. A building code in the Midwest will typically mandate fewer precautions against earthquakes than a building code in certain parts of California. Yet earthquakes are not impossible in the Midwest. If we elect not to require precautions, then surely a major reason must be that it would simply be too expensive. In this judgment, as in countless others, there is no escaping the need to balance economic costs against possible loss of life. To deny that we must and do balance economic costs against risks to human life is to assume the posture of a moral ostrich.

I have been urging the point that it is not *morally objectionable* to try to balance economic concerns against risks to human life. But if such judgments are unobjectionable, indeed necessary, they also surely are among the most difficult any of us has to face. It is hard to imagine a morally sensitive person not feeling extremely uncomfortable when confronted with the need to put a dollar value on human lives. It might be thought that the moral dilemmas engendered by the need to balance such radically different costs and benefits pose insuperable practical obstacles for a rational resolution of the recombinant DNA debate. But here, as in the case of problems with probabilities, I am more sanguine. For while some of the risks and potential benefits of recombinant DNA research are all but morally incommensurable, the most salient risks and benefits are easier to compare. The major risks, as we have noted, are to human life and health. However, the major potential benefits are *also* to human life and health. The potential economic benefits of recombinant DNA research pale in significance when set against the potential for major breakthroughs in our understanding and ability to treat a broad range of conditions, from birth defects to cancer. Those of us, and I confess I am among them, who despair of deciding how lives and economic benefits are to be compared can nonetheless hope to settle our views about recombinant DNA research by comparing the potential risks to life and health with the potential benefits to life and health. Here we are comparing plainly commensurable outcomes. If the balance turns out to be favorable, then we need not worry about factoring in potential economic benefits.

There is a certain irony in the fact that we may well be able to ignore economic factors entirely in coming to a decision about recombinant DNA research. For I suspect that a good deal of the apprehension about recombinant DNA research on the part of the public at large is rooted in the fear that (once again) economic benefits will be weighed much too heavily and potential damage to health and the environment will be weighed much too lightly.

The fear is hardly an irrational one. In case after well-publicized case, we have seen the squalid consequences of decisions in which private or corporate gain took precedence over clear and serious threats to health and to the environment. It is the profit motive that led a giant chemical firm to conceal the deadly consequences of the chemical which now threatens to poison the James River and perhaps all of Chesapeake Bay. For the same reason, the citizens of Duluth drank water laced with a known carcinogen. And the ozone layer that protects us all was eroded while regulatory agencies and legislators fussed over the loss of profits in the spray deodorant industry. Yet while public opinion about recombinant DNA research is colored by a growing awareness of these incidents and dozens of others, the case of recombinant DNA is fundamentally different in a crucial respect. The important projected benefits which must be set against the risks of recombinant DNA research are not economic at all, they are medical and environmental. . . .

III. LONG TERM RISKS

Thus far in our discussion of risks and benefits, the risks that have occupied us have been what might be termed "short-term" risks, such as the release of a new pathogen. The negative effects of these events, though they might be long-lasting indeed, would be upon us relatively quickly. However, some of those who are concerned about recombinant DNA research think there are longer-term dangers that are at least as worrisome. The dangers they have in mind stem not from the accidental release of harmful substances in the course of recombinant DNA research, but rather from the unwise use of the *knowledge* we will likely gain in pursuing the research. The scenarios most often proposed are nightmarish variations on the theme of human genetic engineering. With the knowledge we acquire, it is conjectured, some future tyrant may have people built to order, perhaps creating a whole class of people who willingly and cheaply do the society's dirty or dangerous work, as in Huxley's *Brave New World.* Though the proposed scenarios clearly are science fiction, they are not to be lightly dismissed. For if the technology they conjure is not demonstrably achievable, neither is it demonstrably impossible. And if only a bit of the science fiction turns to fact, the dangers could be beyond reckoning.

Granting that potential misuse of the knowledge gained in recombinant DNA research is a legitimate topic of concern, how ought we to guard ourselves against this misuse? One common proposal is to try to prevent the acquisition of such knowledge by banning or curtailing recombinant DNA research now. Let us cast this proposal in the form of an explicit moral argument. The conclusion is that recombinant DNA research should be curtailed, and the reason given for the conclusion is that such research could possibly produce knowledge which might be misused with disastrous consequences. To complete the argument we need a moral principle, and the one which seems to be needed is something such as this:

> If a line of research can lead to the discovery of knowledge which might be disastrously misused, then that line of research should be curtailed.

Once it has been made explicit, I think relatively few people would be willing to endorse this principle. For recombinant DNA research is hardly alone in potentially leading to knowledge that might be disastrously abused. Indeed, it is hard to think of an area of scientific research that could *not* lead to the discovery of potentially dangerous knowledge. So if the principle is accepted it would entail that almost all scientific research should be curtailed or abandoned.

It might be thought that we could avoid the extreme consequences just cited by retreating to a more moderate moral principle. The moderate principle would urge only that we should curtail those areas of research where the probability of producing dangerous knowledge is comparatively high. Unfortunately, this more moderate principle is of little help in avoiding the unwelcome consequences of the stronger principle. The problem is that the history of science is simply too unpredictable to enable us to say with any assurance which lines of research will produce which sorts of knowledge or technology. There is a convenient illustration of the point in the recent history of molecular genetics. The idea of recombining DNA molecules is one which has been around for some time. However, early efforts proved unsuccessful. As it happened, the crucial step in making recombinant DNA technology possible was provided by research on restriction enzymes, research that was undertaken with no thought of recombinant DNA technology. Indeed, until it was realized that restriction enzymes provided the key to recombining DNA molecules, the research on restriction enzymes was regarded as a rather unexciting (and certainly uncontroversial) scientific backwater. In an entirely analogous way, crucial pieces of information that may one day enable us to manipulate the human genome may come from just about any branch of molecular biology. To guard against the discovery of that knowledge we should have to curtail not only recombinant DNA research but all of molecular biology.

Before concluding, we would do well to note that there is a profound pessimism reflected in the attitude of those who would stop recombinant DNA research because it might lead to knowledge that could be abused. It is, after all, granted on all sides that the knowledge resulting from recombinant DNA research will have both good and evil potential uses. So it would seem the sensible strategy would be to try to prevent the improper uses of this knowledge rather than trying to prevent the knowledge from ever being uncovered. Those who would take the more extreme step of trying to stop the knowledge from being uncovered presumably feel that its improper use is all but inevitable, that our political and social institutions are incapable of preventing morally abhorrent applications of the knowledge while encouraging beneficial applications. On my view, this pessimism is unwarranted; indeed, it is all but inconsistent. The historical record gives us no reason to believe that what is technologically possible will be done, no matter what the moral price. Indeed, in the area of human genetic manipulation, the record points in quite the *opposite* direction. We have long known that the same techniques that work so successfully in animal breeding can be applied to humans as well. Yet there is no evidence of a "technological imperative" impelling our society to breed people as we breed dairy cattle, simply because we know that it can be done. Finally, it is odd that those who express no confidence in the ability of our institutions to forestall such monstrous applications of technology are not equally pessimistic about the ability of the same institutions to impose an effective ban on the uncovering of dangerous knowledge. If our institutions are incapable of restraining the application of technology when those applications would be plainly morally abhorrent, one would think they would be even more impotent in attempting to restrain a line of research which promises major gains in human welfare.

AGAINST CLONING PEOPLE

Hilary Putnam

When Ian Wilmut and his co-workers at the Roslin Institute in Edinburgh announced early in 1997 that a sheep "Dolly" had been successfully cloned, there was an amazing spontaneous reaction. People all around the world felt that something morally problematic was threatening to happen. I say "threatening to happen," because most of the concern centres not on the cloning of sheep, guinea pigs, etc., but on the likelihood that sooner or later someone will clone a human being. And I say "spontaneous reaction" because this is probably not a case in which a moral principle that had been formulated either by traditional ethical sources, religious or secular, was clearly violated or would be violated if we succeeded in cloning people, or someone would be deprived (if the feared possibility materializes) of what is already recognized to be a human right. Of course, some proposed uses of cloning do violate the great Kantian maxim against treating another person solely as a means—for example, cloning a human being solely so that the clone could be a kidney donor or a bone-marrow donor; but these are probably not the cases that came immediately to people's minds. I will argue that cloning humans (if and when that happens) may, indeed, violate human dignity even when the purpose is not as blatantly instrumental as producing an organ donor; but I don't think the spontaneous reaction I described resulted from a considered view as to how this would be the case.

The reaction was the sort of reaction that gives rise to a morality rather than the product of a worked through reflection. Such reflections can be the source of moral insight, but they can also lead to disastrous moral error. I do not conclude from the fact that a ban on, or restriction of, or condemnation of the practice is not easily derived from already codified moral doctrines that it should be presumed that cloning presents no moral problems; on the contrary, I shall argue that it poses extremely grave problems. What I want to do is say why the issue is a grave one—for I believe that the spontaneous reaction is justified—and to begin the kind of reflection that I believe we need to engage in, the kind of dialogue that we need to have, to make clearer to ourselves just what issues are at stake.

The scenario with which I shall be concerned—concerned with because it is, I believe, precisely the sequence of events that people fear may transpire—is the scenario in which (1) we learn how to clone people; and (2) the "technology" becomes widely employed, not just by infertile couples, but by ordinary fertile people who simply wish to have a child "just like" so-and-so. Why do so many of us view this scenario with horror?

Although this will be my central question, it must be mentioned that, quite apart from the spontaneous horror I described, there are additional grounds, including some obvious utilitarian grounds, for being worried about the possible misuse of cloning technology. (And anyone who relies on "market mechanisms" or "consumer sovereignty" by themselves to prevent misuse of anything must have his head in the sand.) For one thing, even techniques of "bioengineering" that seem utterly benign, such as the techniques that have so spectacularly increased the yields of certain crops, have the side-effect, when used as widely as they are being used now, of drastically reducing the genetic diversity of our food grains, and thus increasing the probability of a disaster of global proportions should a disease strike these "high-yield" crops. If cloning should be used not just to produce animals for the production of medically useful drugs, but to produce "twins" of, say, some sheep with especially fine wool, or some cow with especially high milk-yield or beef, and the practice should catch on in a big way, the resulting loss of genetic diversity might well be even more serious. And if cloning ever became a really popular way of having babies, then the question of the result of the practice on human genetic diversity would also have to be considered. But, although these issues are obvious and serious, it is not my purpose to address them further at this time, for I do not believe that *they* are what lies behind the spontaneous reaction to which I alluded.

THE FAMILY AS A MORAL IMAGE

When I say that I want to engage in a reflection that will help us become clearer about the cloning issue, I do not mean that I want in this chapter to propose a specific set of principles or a methodology for deciding whether cloning people could ever be justified (or deciding when it would be justified). In a book I published a decade ago, I argued that moral philosophers who confine themselves to talk about rights, or virtues, or duties, are making a mistake: that what we need first and foremost is a moral image of the world. A moral image, in the sense in which I use the term, is not a declaration that this or that is a virtue or a right; it is rather a picture of how our virtues and ideals hang together with one another, and what they have to do with the position we are in. I illustrated what I meant by the notion of a moral image by showing that we can get a richer appreciation of the Kantian project in ethics if we see the detailed principles that Kant argued for as flowing from such a moral image (one that I find extremely attractive): an image of human equality. I claimed that the respect in which human beings are equal, according to Kant, is that we have to think for ourselves concerning the question of how one ought to live, and that we have to do this without knowing of a human *telos*, or having a clear notion of human flourishing. I argued that this notion of equality, unlike earlier ones, is incompatible with totalitarianism and authoritarianism. But although I find this image very appealing, I argued that it is not sufficient, and I spoke of us needing a plurality of moral images. Commenting on this, Ruth Anna Putnam has written:

> I think that this reference to pluralism must be understood in a twofold way. On the one hand, the image of autonomous choosers is too sparse, it needs to be filled out in various ways, we need a richly textured yet coherent image. On the other hand, we need to recognize that people with different moral images may lead equally good lives. I do not say, of course, that all moral images are equally good, there are quite atrocious moral images: I am saying that there are alternative moral images by which people have led good lives, and that we can learn from their images as they can learn from ours. One of our very deep failings is, I suspect, a tendency to have moral images that are too sparse.

One more remark about moral images before I return to our primary topic. In stressing the importance of moral images I do not mean to suggest that in some way moral images are a foundation from which moral principles, lists of rights and virtues, etc., are to be derived. I have never been a foundationalist, in ethics or in philosophy of science or in any other area of philosophy. One can raise the question of justification with respect to a moral image of the world (or a part or aspect of the world or of life) just as we can raise it about any particular and partial value. As I put it in *The Many Faces of Realism:* "the notion of a value, the notion of a moral image, the notion of a standard, the notion of a need, are so intertwined that none of them can provide a 'foundation' for ethics." Thus Ruth Anna Putnam has observed:

> It follows, it seems to me, that when he says that a moral philosophy requires a moral image he must not be understood to say that a moral philosophy requires a foundation, or an ultimate justification for whatever values it espouses, a foundation that can only be provided by a moral image. Rather we must understand him to say, and with this I agree, that without a moral image any moral philosophy is incomplete.

What I want to do now is to describe some moral images of the family, moral images which turn out to influence how we think not just about the family but about communal life in general.

That we do use images derived from family life in structuring our whole way of looking at society and our whole way of seeing our moral responsibilities to one another is not difficult to see. I became keenly aware of this many years ago as the result of a conversation with my now late mother-in-law, Marie Hall. In her youth, Marie had lived a committed and dangerous life, being active in the anti-Hitler underground in Nazi Germany for two years before escaping the country and eventually making her way to the United States, and she continued to show an admirable commitment to a host of good causes until she died (she lived to be 86). I admired her and loved her and adored her not just for her commitment but also for the vitality and humour that accompanied everything she did, and I constantly "pumped" her about her attitudes and activities during various periods in her life. On one occasion I asked her why she was inspired to make such efforts and run such risks for a better world, in spite of all the setbacks. I was amazed when she answered by saying simply "all men are brothers." She meant it. For her, "all men are brothers" was not a cliché; it was an image that informed and inspired her whole life. It was at that moment that I understood the role that a moral image can play.

The particular image that inspired Marie Hall, the image of us as all brothers (and sisters), played a huge role in the French Revolution and after. The great slogan "Liberty, Equality, Fraternity" listed, perhaps for the first time, fraternity as an ideal on a par with equality and liberty. And to this day union members and members of the oppressed groups frequently refer to one another as brothers and sisters. Of course, we all known that "in real life" siblings frequently do not get along. Yet we do have images of what ideal family relations should be, and it is clear that these images are enormously powerful and can move large numbers of people to do both wonderful and (as the French Revolution also illustrates) terrible things.

The use of the image of an ideal family as a metaphor for what society should be is not confined to the West. Confucian thought, for example, has an elaborate picture of an ideal harmonious (and also hierarchically ordered) family which it consciously uses as a guiding metaphor in thinking about what an ideal society would be. What I want to turn to now is the following questions: what should our image of an ideal family be, and what bearing does that have on whether we do or don't view the "cloning scenario" with horror?

MORAL IMAGES OF THE FAMILY

I began this chapter by describing a "scenario" that is, I claimed, evoked by the prospect of cloning people. In that scenario, first, we learn how to clone people: and secondly, the "technology" becomes widely employed, not only by infertile couples, but by ordinary fertile people who simply wish to have a child "just like" so-and-so. I want now to see how our evaluation of this scenario will be evaluated from the standpoint of different possible (or immoral) images of the family.

Let us begin with an image that we would not regard as a moral image at all. Imagine that one's children come to be viewed simply as parts of one's "lifestyle." Just as one has the right to choose one's furniture to express one's personality, or to suit one's personal predilections, or (even if one does not wish to admit it) "to keep up with the Joneses," so, let us imagine that it becomes the accepted pattern of thought and behaviour to "choose" one's children (by choosing whom one will "clone" them from, from among the available relatives, or friends, or, if one has lots of money, persons who are willing to be cloned for cash). In the Brave New World I am asking us to imagine, one can have, so to speak, "designer children" as well as "designer clothes." Every narcissistic motive is allowed free reign.

What horrifies us about this scenario is that, in it, one's children are viewed simply as objects, as if they were commodities like a television set or a new carpet. Here what I referred to as the Kantian maxim against treating another person only as a means is clearly violated.

In a recent article, Richard Lewontin, a great evolutionary biologist and an outspoken radical, argued that it is hypocritical to worry about this as long as we allow capitalist production relations to exist.

> We would all agree that it is morally repugnant to use human beings as mere instruments of our deliberate ends. Or would we? That's what I do when I call in the plumber. The very words "employment" and "employee" are descriptions of an objectified relationship in which human beings are "things to be valued according to externally imposed standards."

But Lewontin is confused as to what the Kantian maxim means. Even when someone is one's employee, there is a difference between treating that someone as a mere thing and recognizing his or her humanity. That is why there are criteria of civilized behaviour with respect to employees but not with respect to screwdrivers. An excellent discussion of what these criteria require of one and how they are related to the Kantian principle can be found in Agnes Heller's *A Philosophy of Morals*.

Let me now describe the moral image I want to recommend, and then consider some alternatives which are not as blatantly narcissistic as the one in which children are treated simply as adjuncts to one's so-called lifestyle. First of all, if our image is to be a moral image at all, it should conform to the Kantain maxim. In an ideal family, the members regard one another as "ends in their own right," as human beings whose projects and whose happiness are important in themselves, and not simply as they conduce to the satisfaction of the parents' (or anyone else's) goals. Moreover, it should be inspired by the Kantian moral image I described at the outset, the image which assigns inestimable value to our capacity to *think for ourselves in moral matters*. Here, perhaps, one should think not only of Kant but also of Hegel, who, in *The Philosophy of Right,* argues that the task of good parents is precisely to *prepare children for autonomy.* The good parent, in this image, looks forward to having children who will live independently of the parents, not just in a physical or an economic sense, but in the sense of thinking for themselves, even if that means that they will inevitably disagree with the parent on some matters, and may disagree on matters that both parents and child regard as important. . . . I note that although the Confucian image of the good family to which I referred earlier would agree that all the members of a good family should value one another as ends and not as mere means, the valorization of autonomy is foreign to classical Confucianism, with one exception: having the capacity to stand up for the right, when the alternative is clearly evil, is valued in the Confucian tradition. What is missing is the value of independent thinking about what morality requires of one. (Contemporary Neo-Confucian thinkers are struggling with the problem of incorporating such Enlightenment values as autonomy and equality (including gender equality as well as equality between younger and older siblings) into a broadly Confucian framework, with interesting results.)

If one does accept the values I have described, and incorporates them into one's moral image of the family, then, I think, there is one further value that is important (and very natural) to add, and that is the value of willingness to accept diversity. As things stand now (I speak as the parent of four children and a grandparent as well), the amazing thing about one's children is that they come into one's life as different—very different—people seemingly from the moment of birth. In any other relationship, one can choose to some extent the traits of one's associates, but with one's children (and one's parents) one can only accept what God gives one to accept. And, paradoxically, that is one of the most valuable things about the love between parent and child: that, at its best, it involves the capacity to love what is very different from one's self. Of course, the love of a spouse or partner also involves that capacity, but in that case loving someone with those differences from oneself is subject to choice; one has no choice in the case of one's children.

But why should we value diversity in this way? One important reason, I believe, is precisely that our moral image of a good family strongly conditions our moral image of a good society. Consider the Nazi posters showing "good" Nazi families. Every single individual, adult or child, male or female, is blond; no one is too fat or too thin, all the males are muscular, etc.! The refusal to tolerate ethnic diversity in the society is reflected in the image of the family as utterly homogeneous in these ways.

I am not claiming that a positive valuation of diversity *follows from* a positive valuation of autonomy. On the contrary. There have been societies which valued autonomy and moral independence while devaluing diversity to the extent of believing in their own "racial superiority" and engaging in widespread sterilization of those who were seen as "unfit." I am thinking of the social-democratic Scandinavian countries which passed sterilization laws in the 1930s "with hardly any secular or religious protest." Here is Daniel Kevles's description: "Eugenics doctrines were articulated by physicians, mental-health professionals and scientists, notably biologists who were pursuing the new discipline of genetics. They were widely popularized in books, lectures, articles to the educated public of the day, and were bolstered by the research that poured out of institutes for the study of eugenics or 'race biology' that were established in a number of countries, including Denmark, Sweden and the United States." The experts raised the spectre of social "degeneration" insisting that "feeble-minded" people—to use the broad-brush term then commonly applied to persons believed to be mentally retarded—were responsible for a wide range of social problems and were proliferating at a rate that threatened social resources and stability. Feeble-minded women were held to be driven by a heedless sexuality, the product of biologically grounded flaws in their moral character that led them to prostitution and illegitimacy. Such biological analyses of social behaviour found a receptive audience among middle-class men and women, many of whom were sexually prudish and apprehensive about the discordant trends of modern urban, industrial society, including the growing demands for women's rights and sexual tolerance.

The Scandinavian region's population was relatively homogenous, predominately Lutheran in religion, and Nordic in what it took to be its racial identity. In this era, differences of ethnicity or nationality were often classified as racial distinctions. Swedish analysts found that the racial purity of their country might eventually be undermined, if only because so many Nordics were emigrating, Swedish speakers in Finland feared the proliferation of Finnish speakers, holding them to be fundamentally Mongols and as such a threat to national quality.

Our moral image of the family should reflect our tolerant and pluralistic values, not our narcissistic and xenophobic ones. And that means that we should welcome rather than deplore the fact that our children are not us and not designed by us, but radically Other.

Am I suggesting, then, that moral images of the family which depict the members of the ideal family as all alike, either physically or spiritually, may lead to the abominations that the eugenics movement contributed to? The answer is, "very easily." But my reasons for recommending an image of the family which rejects the whole idea of trying to pre-design one's offspring, by cloning or otherwise, are not, in the main, consequentialist ones. What I have been claiming is that the unpredictability and diversity of our progeny is an intrinsic value and that a moral image of the family that reflects it coheres with the moral images of society that underlay our democratic aspirations. Marie Hall was willing to risk her very life in Hitler's Germany for the principle that "all men are brothers." She did not mean that "all men are identical twins."

In closing, since this is a lecture devoted to human rights, I suppose that I should mention human rights at least once. If "rights" talk has not figured in my discussion, it is because, as explained, I believe that our conception of rights, values, duties, etc., needs to cohere with a moral image which is capable of inspiring us. But perhaps one novel human right is suggested by the present discussion: the "right" of each newborn child to be a complete surprise to its parents!

WHY NOT CLONE?

John Harris

The birth of Dolly, the world famous cloned sheep, has had an extraordinary impact on many dimensions of our lives, both intellectual and real. It has fuelled debate in a number of fora: genetic, scientific, political, moral, journalistic, and literary. It has also given rise to a number of myths, not least among which is the myth that Dolly presents a danger to humanity, the human genepool, genetic diversity, the ecosystem, the world as we know it, and the survival of the human species.

Dolly, or the technology by which she was created, raises a number of questions about human rights and how we are to understand the idea of respect for these rights and for human dignity. It is these questions that are the subject of this lecture. Cloning of the sort used to create Dolly has raised three main sets of questions which are vitally relevant to all who are interested in human rights and human freedoms and I shall try to say something about each of these.

First, the birth of Dolly provoked a hysterical reaction, the burden of which was that she represented an attack on human dignity and on human rights and values of unprecedented urgency and severity. Secondly, the legislative and regulatory response to this hysteria itself raised huge questions of vital significance to all concerned with upholding human rights. Finally, whatever one might *feel* about Dolly and the possibility of human equivalents, our freedom to act on these feelings may, as I shall argue, be circumscribed by other values that we hold, such as the conception of human rights to which most democratic societies are committed and which is presupposed by democracy itself. Thus, far from outlawing Dolly and her kind, it may actually be required of us, if not to welcome a human Dolly, at least to afford her, and her would-be creators, tolerance and respect. This tripartite family of concerns generates three specific questions which I shall try to answer in what follows. They are:

1. Does the creation of Dolly constitute an attack on human rights and dignity?

2. Does the legislative response to Dolly constitute an attack on human rights and dignity?

3. Are human Dollys protected by existing conventions on, and assumptions concerning, human rights?

I. DOES THE CREATION OF DOLLY CONSTITUTE AN ATTACK ON HUMAN RIGHTS AND DIGNITY?

When Dolly's birth was reported in *Nature* on 27 February 1997, the hysteria to which I have referred was immediately unleashed. The President of the United States called immediately for an investigation into the ethics of such procedures and announced a moratorium on public spending on human cloning. Clinton's investigation has now reported and, commenting recently, President Clinton said "there is virtually unanimous consensus in the scientific and medical communities that attempting to use these cloning techniques to actually clone a human being is untested and unsafe and morally unacceptable." Recently, Members of the European Parliament (MEPs) demanded that each EU member state "enact binding legislation prohibiting all research on human cloning and providing criminal sanctions for any breach." . . .

Even commentators from whom a more considered approach might have been expected were panicked into instant reaction. Dr Hiroshi Nakajima, Director General of the World Health Organization, said: "WHO considers the use of cloning for the replication of human individuals to be ethically unacceptable as it would violate some of the basic principles which govern medically assisted procreation. These include respect for the dignity of the human being and protection of the security of human genetic material." WHO followed up the line taken by Nakajima with a resolution of the Fiftieth World Health Assembly which saw fit to affirm "that the use of cloning for the replication of human individuals is ethically unacceptable and contrary to human integrity and morality." Federico Mayor of UNESCO, equally quick off the mark, commented that "Human beings must not be cloned under any circumstances." Finally, on 3 December 1997, UNESCO published a so-called *Universal Declaration of the Human Genome and Human Rights,* Article 11 of which announced: "Practices which are contrary to human dignity, such as reproductive cloning of human beings, shall not be permitted." In a staggeringly complacent preface Federico Mayor states: "The uncontested merit of this text resides in the balance it strikes between safeguarding respect for human rights and fundamental freedoms and the need to ensure freedom of research." However, Mayor is more than a little misleading when he reports in the Preface to the *Universal Declaration* that it "was adopted unanimously and by acclamation." We know that the statement defining cloning as "contrary to human dignity" was a late addition by UNESCO to the text originally produced by UNESCO's International Bioethics Committee. Moreover, one of the members of that committee, the distinguished molecular geneticist Michel Revel, who was also Israel's representative to the General Conference of UNESCO, has reported that "several delegations proposed not to rush in condemning any particular technique, including cloning."

More recently, Mayor has again expressed his objections to human cloning. He believes opposition to a ban on reproductive cloning "is based on two main types of argument. One defends individual 'rights' to clone, the second scientific freedom." I should state at once that my opposition to the ban is based on neither of these. It is, to be sure, based on freedom, but not on scientific freedom. I believe, and I shall return to this argument in the final section of this paper, that human liberty may not be abridged without good cause being shown. It is the argument of this paper that no one, not even UNESCO, has shown anything approaching good cause.

The European Parliament also rushed through a resolution on cloning (Paragraph B of) the preamble of which asserted,

> [T]he cloning of human beings . . . cannot under any circumstances be justified or tolerated by any society, because it is a serious violation of fundamental human rights and is contrary to the principle of equality of human beings as it permits a eugenic and racist selection of the human race, it offends against human dignity and it requires experimentation on humans.

And which went on to claim (in Clause 1) that "each individual has a right to his or her own genetic identity and that human cloning is, and must continue to be, prohibited."

These statements are almost entirely devoid of argument and rationale. There are vague references to "human rights" or "basic principles" with little or no attempt to explain what these principles are, or to indicate how they might apply to cloning. The WHO statement, for example, refers to the basic principles which govern human reproduction and singles out "respect for the dignity of the human being" and "protection of the security of genetic material." How is the security of genetic material compromised? Is it less secure when inserted with precision by scientists, or when spread around with the characteristic negligence of the average human male? Those of mischievous disposition might be tempted to ask whether the sin of Onan was not perhaps to compromise the security of his genetic material?

Human Dignity

The idea and ideal of human dignity have been much invoked in these debates. Typical of appeals to human dignity was that contained in the World Health Organization statement on cloning issued on 11 March 1997: "WHO considers the use of cloning for the replication of human individuals to be ethically unacceptable as it would violate some of the basic principles which govern medically assisted procreation. These include respect for the dignity of the human being." Appeals to human dignity are, of course, universally attractive; they are the political equivalents of motherhood and apple pie. Like motherhood, if not apple pie, they are also comprehensively vague. A first question to ask when the idea of human dignity is invoked is: whose dignity is attacked and how? If it is the duplication of a large part of the human genome that is supposed to constitute the attack on human dignity, or where the issue of "genetic identity" is invoked, we might legitimately ask whether and how the dignity of a natural twin is threatened by the existence of her sister and what follows as to the permissibility of natural monozygotic twinning? However, the notion of human dignity is often linked to Kantian ethics and it is this link I wish to examine more closely here.

A typical example, and one that attempts to provide some basis for objections to cloning based on human dignity, is that provided by Axel Kahn (a distinguished molecular biologist who helped draft the French National Ethics Committee's report on cloning). Kahn invokes this principle in his commentary in *Nature* where he states:

> The creation of human clones solely for spare cell lines would, from a philosophical point of view, be in obvious contradiction to the principle expressed by Emmanuel Kant: that of human dignity. This principle demands that an individual—and I would extend this to read human life—should never be thought of as a means, but always also as an end.

The Kantian principle, invoked without any qualification or gloss, is seldom helpful in medical or bio-science contexts. As I have argued in response to Kahn elsewhere, his formulation of it would surely outlaw, amongst other things, blood transfusions. The beneficiary of blood donation neither knows nor usually cares about the anonymous donor(s) and uses the blood and its donor(s) exclusively as a means to her own ends; the donor figures in the life of the recipient of blood exclusively as a means. The blood in the bottle has, after all, less identity, and is less connected with the individual from which it emanated, than chicken "nuggets" on the supermarket shelf. An abortion performed exclusively to save the life of the mother would also, presumably, be outlawed by Kahn's understanding of Kant's principle.

Instrumentalization

This idea of using individuals as a means to the purposes of others is, particularly in the European context, sometimes termed "instrumentalization." The "Opinion of the group of advisers on the ethical implications of biotechnology to the European Commission," for example, in its statement on "Ethical aspects of cloning techniques" uses this idea repeatedly. For example, referring to reproductive human cloning (in paragraph 2.6) it states: "Considerations of Instrumentalization and eugenics render any such acts ethically unacceptable."

Making sense of the idea of "instrumentalization" is not easy! If someone wants to have children in order to continue their genetic line do they act instrumentally? Where, as is standard practice in IVF, spare embryos are created, are these embryos created instrumentally? Kahn has considered these objections but he has not done so adequately. He reminds us, rightly, that Kant's famous principle states: "respect for human dignity requires that an individual is *never* used . . . *exclusively* as a means" and suggests that I have ignored the crucial use of the term "exclusively." I did not of course, and I'm happy with Kahn's reformulation of the principle. It is not that Kant's principle does not have powerful intuitive force, but that it is so vague and so open to selective interpretation and its scope for application is consequently so limited, that its utility as one of the "fundamental principles of modern bioethical thought," as Kahn describes it, is virtually nil.

Kahn himself rightly points out that debates concerning the moral status of the human embryo are debates about whether embryos fall within the scope of Kant's or indeed any other moral principles concerning persons; so the principle itself is not illuminating in this context. Applied to the creation of individuals who are, or will become, autonomous, it has limited application. True the Kantian principle rules out slavery, but so do a range of other principles based on autonomy and rights. If you are interested in the ethics of creating people then, so long as existence is in the created individual's own best interests, and the individual will have the capacity for autonomy, then the motives for which the individual was created are either morally irrelevant or subordinate to other moral considerations. So that even where, for example, a child is engendered exclusively to provide "a son and heir" (as so often occurs in many cultures) it is unclear how or whether Kant's principle applies. Either other motives are also attributed to the parent to square parental purposes with Kant, or the child's eventual autonomy, and its clear and substantial interest in or benefit from existence, take precedence over the comparatively trivial issue of parental motives. Either way the "fundamental principle of modern bioethical thought" is unhelpful.

. . . The distinguished American philosopher Hilary Putnam reiterates the Kantian imperative employed by Axel Kahn. Putnam imagines a scenario in which cloning is widely used by ordinary people so that they can have children "just like so-and-so." Putnam claims that "what horrifies us about this scenario is that, in it, one's children are viewed simply as objects, as if they were commodities like a television set or a new carpet. Here what I referred to as the Kantian maxim against treating another person only as a means is *clearly* violated."

Criticizing Richard Lewontin, Putnam suggests that Lewontin, and by implication the arguments defended in this lecture, are confused over the meaning of the Kantian principle he has invoked. Lewontin had pointed out, surely correctly, that almost all commercial relations people have with one another are basically instrumental. Putnam attempts to remedy the alleged confusion with this illustration: "Even when someone is one's employee, there is a difference between treating that someone as a mere thing and recognizing his or her humanity. That is why there are criteria of civilized behaviour with respect to employees but not with respect to screwdrivers."

Putnam is of course right to say that we do indeed have "criteria of civilized behaviour" with respect to children. This is what distinguishes not only our (humankind's) attitude to children generally, but each parent's attitude to his or her own child in particular, from "criteria of civilized behaviour" towards screwdrivers. There is no evidence for, and indeed no plausibility in, the supposition that if people choose to use a cloned genome in order to create *their own children,* that these children will not be loved for themselves, let alone not treated in a civilized way. We have noted that many people have children for a purpose; to continue their genes, to provide a son and heir, to create "a sister for Bill," to provide for support in old age, "because I've always wanted a child to look after," because our tribe or our ethnic group is threatened with extinction, etc. When, if ever, is it plausible to say that they are having children *exclusively* for such purposes?

Kant's maxim provides a plausible account of what's wrong with slavery, for example, and, if another were needed, it provides one of many objections to Nazi practices. Where it conspicuously fails to be of any help is when people use, or even think of, others *partially* in instrumental terms, as happens in employment, family relations, sexual relations, and almost any human context. As I have argued, it is almost never plausible to think that people, whose motives and intentions are almost always mixed and complex, could definitively be said to be treating others "exclusively" as a means, unless, as with the Nazis, they treated them as slaves or literally as things.

It is therefore strange that Kahn, Putnam, and others invoke the Kantian principle with such dramatic assurance, or how anyone could think that it applies to the ethics of human cloning. It comes down to this: either the ethics of human cloning turn on the creation or use of human embryos, in which case as Kahn himself says "in reality the debate is about the status of the human embryo" and Kant's principle must wait upon the outcome of that debate. Or it is about the ethics of producing clones who will become autonomous human persons. In this latter case, the ethics of their creation are, from a Kantian perspective, not dissimilar to other forms of assisted reproduction, or, as I have suggested, to the ethics of the conduct of parents concerned *exclusively* with producing an heir, or preserving their genes or, as is sometimes alleged, making themselves eligible for public housing. Debates about whether these are *exclusive* intentions can never be neatly resolved and are, in my view, ultimately sterile and unhelpful.

Putnam supplements his use of the Kantian principle with an interesting idea, that of a "moral image." Putnam accepts that such images are plural and diverse and that "people with different moral images may lead equally good moral lives." For Putnam any moral image must incorporate the Kantian principle which he believes is itself inspired by a moral image of autonomy, "our capacity to think for ourselves in moral matters." He then recommends an image of the family in which "the good parent . . . looks forward to having children who will live independently of the parents not just in a physical or an economic sense, but in the sense of thinking for themselves." This moral image has also to incorporate a "willingness to accept diversity." He then asks and answers a very important question:

> But why should we value diversity in this way? One important reason, I believe, is precisely that our moral image of a good family strongly conditions our moral image of a good society. Consider the Nazi posters showing "good" Nazi families. Every single individual, adult or child, male or female, is blond; no one is too fat or too thin, all the males are muscular, etc.! The refusal to tolerate ethnic diversity in the society is reflected in the image of the family as utterly homogeneous in these ways.

Putnam continues:

> Our moral image of the family should reflect our tolerant and pluralistic values, not our narcissistic and xenophobic ones. And that means that we should welcome rather than deplore the fact that our children are not us and not designed by us, but radically Other.
>
> Am I suggesting then, that moral images of the family which depict the members of the ideal family as all alike, either physically or spiritually, may lead to the abominations that the eugenics movement contributed to? The answer is, "very easily."

And concludes "But perhaps one novel human right is suggested by the present discussion: the 'right' of each newborn child to be a complete surprise to its parents!"

I am in great sympathy with much of this, indeed I have argued along the same lines myself. For example, in discussing the practice of race matching in adoption I commented:

> Why do so many people firmly believe that children should be like their parents, particularly in terms of their general colour and racial characteristics? It is difficult not to view this desire, and attempts to implement it, as a form of "ethnic cleansing." It smacks very much of the pressure that so many societies and cultures have put upon their members not to "marry out" or, to put it more bluntly, not to mate with somebody of another tribe or race.

It is perhaps timely to press the question: why do we assume that the desire for a different-race child is racially motivated in some discreditable way, whereas the desire for a same-race child is not? If we are going to suspect people's motives, the desire for a child of the same race is surely as likely to be discreditable. It is, after all, societies which exclude different races that are assumed to be racist, not societies which welcome and celebrate diversity. Why should this not be true of families?

The problem I have is with Putnam's interpretation of what follows from the attractive image that he presents. First, it does not follow from the fact that something is inconsistent with a moral image, that it should be banned, or controlled, nor does it follow that those who would be deviants may be punished. Not only is Putnam right to say that there are many equally good moral images, there are also many equally good interpretations of the same moral image. I accept Putnam's image but, unlike Putnam, I conclude that parents should therefore have free choice in designing their children. As I have argued at length elsewhere in the context of parents using reproductive technology, to choose children's phenotypic traits:

> Some people have objected that to choose the skin colour or racial features of children (insofar as these can be chosen—which is not very far) is an illicit form of parental preference. The phrase "designer children" is often used pejoratively to describe the children of parents who are more concerned with fashion and pleasing themselves, than with valuing children for the children's own sake. However, we should remember that choosing a same race or same race-mix child is also designing the child that you will

have. This is no less an exercise of parental preference than is the case of choosing a different race or race mix, or, for that matter, colour.

The best way both to avoid totalitarianism and to escape the possibility of racial (or gender) prejudice, either individual or social, dictating what sort of children people have, is to permit free parental choice in these matters. And to do so whether that choice is exercised by choice of procreational partner or by choice of gametes or embryo, or by genetic engineering. Such choices are, for the most part, likely to be as diverse as are the people making them.

And, of course, the reference to genetic engineering in the above passage includes the idea of cloning. As I have suggested, I accept the high value that Putnam places on a willingness to accept diversity, and on families which embody this image of diversity (few and far between as they are). I also accept the connection of such images with the sorts of society they are likely to produce. Unlike Putnam, however, I conclude from this that we should accept diversity in family foundation including the use of cloning.

I am not, of course, insisting that it is clear that I am right and Putnam wrong about how to interpret the value of autonomy and diversity. What I do claim, however, is that the same, or at any rate similar, moral images are guiding both approaches. In such a case, tolerance of diversity seems to require that decent people be permitted to follow their own moral images in their own way, and while we may take different views about the use of cloning, neither should foreclose the other's options.

. . . The problems with Putnam's view are: how to make his image yield the conclusions he wants on the subject of cloning and not other equally compatible conclusions of the sort that I would draw; whether the moral image of the family is sufficient, and sufficiently determinate, to license the limitation on the autonomy of those who wish to use cloning; and whether his conclusions, and the way he interprets his moral image, license, and indeed encourage something else?

With respect to the last of these problems we should note that most societies accept and use images not very unlike those in the Nazi posters. An "ideal" or idealized family, in adverts, for example, or in a "sitcom," would be likely to display the same homogeneity. As would an "ideal" or a "typical" Jewish family or an ideal or typical African-American family. As I have suggested, we don't normally think that people founding such families are doing anything wrong when they decline to marry or procreate outside their ethnic group. If we take seriously Putnam's Parthian shot, and support a "right of each new-born child to be a *complete* surprise to its parents," we should perhaps ask what would really surprise the parents of our imagined Jewish or African-American family? The answer would surely be that they would be genuinely surprised if their children turned out to be pure Aryan types straight from the Nazi posters! And the wicked pleasure that the reverse would cause, of a Nazi family giving birth to a Jewish or African (looking) child, is surely justification in itself. Should we use genetic manipulation to ensure that each family, like most good societies, is ethnically and culturally diverse, and that parents are always surprised by their offspring from the moment of birth, or even before? The more serious point here is that parents will, of course, always and inevitably be surprised by their children. If they use cloning techniques for reproduction they may be less surprised by their children's physical appearance, but they will, for sure, be surprised by their children's dispositions, desires, traits, and so on—the more so if they expected them to be identical with those of the nucleus donor.

Moreover, and this should not be forgotten, if parents have chosen their nucleus donor wisely, they may be less surprised by one thing: they should be less unpleasantly surprised by genetic diseases and defects, for they will not only know much about the nucleus donor, but will have had opportunities to carry out genetic tests before creating the clone. A moral image that limits these unpleasant and often catastrophic surprises is one we all should have constantly before us.

QUESTIONS FOR DISCUSSION
IS GENETIC ENGINEERING GOOD OR BAD?

1. Why does Robert Sinsheimer think there should be a moratorium on experiments at recombining microorganisms by splicing DNA molecules? What reasons does Stephen Stich give in opposition to a moratorium? Compare the two viewpoints.

2. Sinsheimer warns against scientists "creating new life forms" by means of genetic engineering. Can you think of more ordinary ways that people create new life forms? Does doing so by genetic engineering make an important difference? Explain your response.

3. What does Stephen Stich mean by "the principle that natural barriers should not be breached?" When, according to Stich, is it permissible to break this rule?

4. On what grounds does Stich argue that the probability of an epidemic resulting from the experimental recombining of microorganisms is lower than the probability of social benefits such as the production of vaccines and other useful medications? Do you agree? Defend your position.

5. What do you think Hilary Putnam means by a "moral image"? What does he seem to regard as a good moral image of a family, in virtue of which it would be wrong to "design" one's children?

6. What is the Kantian principle to which Putnam and others appeal in opposing the cloning of humans; and on what grounds does John Harris claim that this principle, "invoked without any qualification or gloss, is seldom helpful in medical or bio-science contexts"?

7. Discuss the difference between the conclusions Putnam draws from the value of autonomy and diversity, and the conclusions drawn by Harris from the same concepts.

SELECTED READINGS

BABU, M. "Human Cloning: An Ethically Negative Feat in Genetic Engineering." *Philosophy and Social Action,* _____ 1998.

BURGESS, J. "Is Genetic Engineering Wrong, 'per se'?" *Journal of Value Inquiry,* _____ 1998.

HUMBER, J., ed. *Human Cloning.* Totawa, NJ: Humana Press, 1998.

JACKSON, D., and S. STICH, eds. *The Recombinant DNA Debate.* Englewood Cliffs, NJ: Prentice Hall, 1979.

LUCASSEN, E. "The Ethics of Genetic Engineering." *Journal of Applied Philosophy,* _____ 1996.

MCGEE, G., ed. *The Human Cloning Debate.* Berkeley: Berkeley Hills Books, 1998.

REISS, M., and R. STRAUGHAN. *Improving Nature?* New York: Cambridge University Press, 1996.

510

RESNICK, D. "Genetic Engineering and Social Justice: A Rawlsian Approach." *Social Theory and Practice,* _____ 1997.

ROLLIN, B. "Keeping Up with the Cloneses—Issues in Human Cloning." *Journal of Ethics,* _____ 1999.

RUSE, M., and A. SHEPPARD, eds. *Cloning: Responsible or Technomadness?* Amherst, MA: Prometheus, 2001.

WOLF, S. "Ban Cloning? Why NBAC Is Wrong," *Hastings Center Report,* _____ 1997.

12

MULTICULTURALISM AND POLITICAL CORRECTNESS

The issues addressed in this chapter are of concern mainly to the academic intelligentsia—most notably, college teachers, students, and administrators—and also to public officials, clerics, and magazine and book editors. The issues have to do with whether traditional standards of what should be studied in schools, of what merits subsidization and publication as "classics," of what is regarded as essential to a "liberal education," and of what deserves to be frequently discussed in the media, are reasonably sound or are too dependent on outmoded prejudices and should be thoroughly revised to reflect more diverse cultures and traditions, as well as new political and social attitudes. Satisfaction with the traditional standards might be called "cultural conservatism," and insistence on more diversity is often called either "cultural radicalism" or, by many of its critics, "political correctness."

Lawrence Foster, after summarizing the main criticisms of the movement for multiculturalism (or cultural diversity), defends the enhancement of college curricula by adding courses and parts of survey courses in subjects that go far outside of the curricula that used to constitute a liberal arts education. He responds to what he calls the metaphysical criticism that the multicultural movement is based on the so-called postmodernist denial of any objective reality, and the epistemological denial of objective truth, by arguing that the movement insists only that reality and truth are describable in different ways and in culturally diverse conceptual structures, but not that they do not exist at all. There can be—and in fact is—more than one objective reality, he maintains.

Further, he claims, the recognition of this relativity of knowledge, and the consequent effort to view things from different cultural perspectives, promotes tolerance and mutual appreciation among different cultures, helping to break down the barriers of suspicion that breed wars.

Foster defends curricula that replace tried and true classics, like Kant's ethical works, with more contemporary and "relevant" works such as the writing of Martin Luther King, thus placing timeliness above philosophical depth and reducing the attention given to the products of Western civilization in favor of equal attention to the achievements of African, Asian, and Latin American nations, in order to promote world harmony.

The Canadian philosopher Jan Narveson strongly disagrees. He denounces the imposition of political considerations on the search for knowledge in academia by which he defines political correctness. Science, art, and philosophy, he insists, should be completely free of political pressures; therefore curricula should not be revised for such purposes as the achievement of greater world harmony or the improvement of race relations. In contrast with Foster, Narveson identifies multiculturalism with postmodernism and its denial of objective truth. These views, he claims, pursue an impossible and undesirable kind of equality by rejecting the "canon," or list of the greatest works, of Western civilization that are thought necessary for a liberal education, in order to give equal place to works of inferior quality.

IN SUPPORT OF MULTICULTURALISM

Lawrence Foster

The furor over multiculturalism has produced some powerful charges. Advocates of multiculturalism have been attacked for denigrating Western values, politicizing education, promoting nihilism and a self-defeating relativism, and even for denying an objective reality. If that were not a sufficient indictment, multiculturalists have also been vilified for rejecting the traditional search for truth, for maintaining that all standards are arbitrary and that anything goes, for failing to acknowledge the excellence or superiority of certain works, and for crushing dissent in order to promote unanimity of thought.

The charges are serious, the issues important. I examine and defend in this paper the case for the introduction of multiculturalist perspectives into the curriculum. Unlike other defenses, mine focuses on the epistemological/ metaphysical underpinnings for multiculturalism at the risk of downplaying the political dimension. I do this not because I believe that the political issues are secondary, but rather because the important epistemological/metaphysical issues have either been ignored or misconstrued by both critics and defenders of multiculturalism. In the end, I expect to have shown that epistemological relativism and metaphysical pluralism are defensible and plausible positions, that they don't lead to the self-defeating view that all standards are arbitrary and that anything goes, that the pursuit of truth is only one among many important goals of education and the various fields of inquiry—and probably not the most important—that relativism doesn't lead to subjectivism, and that these conclusions provide substantial support for the development of robust multicultural curricula.

Consider some of the specific charges. Roger Kimball, a vehement critic of multiculturalism, claims that the "multiculturalist imperative explicitly denies the intellectual and moral foundations of Western culture—preeminently its commitment to rationality and the ideal of objectivity." Dinesh D'Souza, no more sympathetic to multiculturalists, attributes to one well-known advocate the view that "there is no knowledge, no standard, no choice that is objective." Further, D'Souza contends, these critics of the canon, as multiculturalists have come to be known, even attack the very idea of truth. "It is the pursuit of truth itself that the modern critics spurn; more precisely by reducing all truth to the level of opinion, they deny the legitimacy of distinctions between truth and error. Yet, what is the goal of liberal education if not the ongoing search for truth? If education cannot help to separate truth from falsehood, beauty from vulgarity, right from wrong, then what can it teach us?"

Although Kimball and D'Souza emphatically reject these alleged multiculturalist claims, they lack the resources to produce any (rational) arguments against them. They are in part joined, however, by John Searle, a philosopher who clearly is better equipped to deal with such philosophical issues as the nature of truth, rationality, objective reality, and related notions. Searle notes approvingly that Kimball in his book *Tenured Radicals* attacks multiculturalists ("the cultural left") for not believing in "an objective and disinterested search for truth." And Searle further endorses Kimball's charge that these cultural leftists also (erroneously) reject the notion of an objective reality and the correspondence theory of truth; "they reject the idea that true statements are ever made true by virtue of the fact that there is an independently existing set of objects and features of the world to which such statements correspond."

Kimball and D'Souza are concerned with the political implications of the denial of an independently existing reality and objective truths and standards because, if anything goes, "it become[s] perfectly legitimate for teachers . . . to impose their politically preferred ideas on students." Searle has an additional concern, and it is an intellectual one. He believes that the rejection of an independent reality or of objective facts rests on a confusion between epistemology and ontology, "between how we know and what it is that we know when we know. . . . All investigations are relative to investigators. But it does not follow, nor is it indeed true, that all the matters investigated are relative to investigators. Real human investigators have to discover, e.g., that water is made of hydrogen and oxygen, but the fact that water is made of hydrogen and oxygen is not relative to any investigators." Searle further contends that any denial of metaphysical realism, the view that there exists a reality independent of our representations of it, removes "the rational restraints that are supposed to shape discourse, when that discourse aims at something beyond itself. . . . Without metaphysical realism, anything is permissible."

Multiculturalists, then, in rejecting metaphysical realism, are guilty of having adopted a view that is intellectually indefensible and has dangerous political/pedagogical implications. Searle goes on to produce an argument in support of his contention that the rejection of metaphysical realism is mistaken. He contends that the very denial of metaphysical realism presupposes a public language, but communication in a public language presupposes a world of independently existing objects. Hence, one cannot deny metaphysical realism without presupposing it. By adopting an indefensible metaphysical view, multiculturalists are left without one of the major intellectual supports for their curricular views—or so Searle argues.

The world is plastic.   —WILLIAM JAMES, QUOTING SCHILLER

Truths are many, and some truths conflict. This is not the alleged truism that the one and only ready-made real world has many true descriptions, but rather it is the contention that among the many true descriptions, some are in conflict. This conflict requires resolution in something other than the one ready-made, independently existing, real world. As James noted, "The world stands really malleable." The implications of this insight for multiculturalism are far-reaching.

Is the earth in motion? What about the sun? We assume, of course, a stationary earth in our everyday world when we take it as true that Jones, paralyzed by fear, did not move. But in other contexts we take it as true that the earth moves (and that the sun is stationary). Yet it is also true that the sun moves relative to the (stationary) stars of our Milky Way galaxy, which in turn moves relative to other galaxies. So, the earth moves, and it doesn't move. There are correct versions in which it moves and correct ones in which it doesn't. And the question "Does the earth really move in the one ready-made, independently existing, real world?" suddenly has a hollow ring.

This relativity of truth extends beyond the world of common sense and science to that of mathematics. If we ask what points are, *really,* we are asking the wrong question. A statement such as "Every point is made up of a pair of intersecting lines and nothing else" is true in one correct framework or system and false in another. It is true, for example, in a (correct) system in which points are defined as pairs of intersecting lines, and false in another (correct) system in which points are taken as primitives or, as in Whitehead's system, defined in terms of sets of sets of volumes.

Examples of such conflicting truths can be multiplied endlessly. Such hard-core astronomical facts as those concerning the regular occurrence of the vernal equinox or the summer and winter solstices depend upon our choice of systems or calendars. Systems or calendars that yielded irregularities here, but regularities, say, in the phases of the moon, could satisfy other goals and be equally serviceable and correct. And whether, as Kepler claimed, the planets move in elliptical orbits about the sun and carve out equal areas in equal amounts of time, depends, in part, upon our choice of a system of time. Our goals, values, and interests enter into such choices, but they do not always dictate a unique choice. Equally serviceable and correct systems can be devised and may conflict. The world stands really malleable.

The multiplicity of truths, with some in conflict, suggests that the traditional idea, proposed by D'Souza and others, that one of the purposes of education is the search for truth needs to be changed to the search for truths. But this is a rather innocuous amendment. More radical is the idea that in the search for truths we will come upon or, more accurately, help to create conflicting ones. And from this an even more radical conclusion follows. Because from a contradiction any statement whatsoever follows—an intolerable conclusion—we need to find ways to remove the conflict. But this requires an appeal to the notion that the conflicting truths are true in different worlds or world versions. Conflict is eliminated; worlds or correct world versions are multiplied. Worlds, rather than *the* world, are malleable. Metaphysical pluralism or, better, irrealism results. The antimulticulturalist assumption of a single, ready-made objective reality succumbs to conflicting truths and malleable worlds.

What then went wrong with Searle's argument? Recall Searle's contention that the very existence of a public language presupposes an independently existing reality to which the expressions in the language refer. That a public language presupposes the existence of public objects is surely a plausible claim. But that these public objects are what they are independent of our developing of concepts and categories is surely less obvious and less defensible. Indeed, even Searle's own example of a hard-core fact that supposedly is not relative to investigators is suspect. For the fact that water is made of two parts hydrogen and one part oxygen depends, in part, upon our counting as water the stuff that flows in seas and sewers but not the stuff that flows in our veins. And to return to Kepler, whether it is a fact that all the planets move in elliptical orbits around the sun and carve out equal areas in equal amounts of time depends, in part, upon our fashioning a concept of planet in such a way that it includes, for example, the Evening Star (Venus) but not the North Star. Public language may presuppose the existence of public objects. But it does not follow from this that these objects are what they are independent of any of our world versions.

The discussion so far may seem quite removed from the debate about multiculturalism and the canon, but the perception of distance here is illusory. For D'Souza, Kimball, and Searle, the notions of one system of truth and its corresponding, independently existing, ready-made reality undermine the case for multiculturalism while buttressing the canon along with its rather conservative approach to education. Further, the abandonment of a correspondence theory of truth and a ready-made reality supposedly leads to a denial of rationality, truth, and objectivity. And with these losses legitimate standards or goals for education crumble. Political manipulation replaces the search for truth in the classroom.

This conservative nightmare, however, doesn't relate to realities. Although support for a Eurocentric canon certainly is weakened by the criticism of metaphysical realism and the correspondence theory of truth, we shall find that the dreaded consequences of a loss of rationality, truth, and objectivity do not follow.

If we recognize multiple truths, some in conflict, pluralism gains support and with it the contention that there is good reason to expose students to multiple and varied approaches and voices. The notion that the world or worlds are malleable implies that worlds are made as much as discovered, that realities are, at least in part, human constructs and result from human symbolic activities. And this suggests that there may be true versions that are in conflict with our currently accepted (and, perhaps, even true) ones, whatever the field of inquiry. So, if D'Souza is correct and the primary goal, or at least one of the goals, of education is the pursuit of truth, then the curriculum needs to be opened up to multiple perspectives. The assumption that the

Eurocentric curriculum is and ought to be at the center of education and the core of all learning presupposes an untenable epistemology and metaphysics.

We've seen so far that replacing the search for truth with the search for truths, and the one ready-made independent reality with multiple human-made realities, provides firm support for multicultural education. But this is only the beginning. So far, we've introduced a somewhat radical idea into the traditional notion that there is a single objective reality and only one system of truths that captures that reality. But we need to push further; for even the appealing and popular idea that education primarily involves the search for truth must be abandoned. This is not because there are multiple and conflicting truths but rather because much of what learning and education is or ought to be about concerns issues and areas where questions of truth do not properly arise.

Truth applies to statements, and indicative statements at that. So to focus our curriculum solely on the pursuit of truth is to ignore such nonverbal symbol systems as painting and music. And even if we were to restrict ourselves (mistakenly) to a study of verbal systems, we would discover that much creative cognitive verbal activity does not concern truth, because it does not involve making statements; for example, when we devise systems or schemes of classification—of planets and stars, mammals and fish, or projectible and nonprojectible predicates. Schemes of classification are neither true nor false, but they may be appropriate or right, or inappropriate or wrong. Further, in our preoccupation with statements and questions about their literal truth value, we may often ignore other (and often more) important features even of statements; for example, what the statement expresses or exemplifies, or whether the statement, although literally false, may not be metaphorically true.

So, for example, we may learn and gain insight and understanding from a study of the thought of traditional people, not because what is being said is literally true, but rather because of the novel associations produced by the metaphors. And we can learn and gain understanding from a study of rituals of non-European societies, not because what is being said is literally true, but because of what is being expressed or exemplified. As Peter Winch has argued, "What we may learn by studying other cultures are not merely possibilities of different ways of doing things, other techniques. More importantly we may learn different possibilities of making sense of human life, different ideas about the possible importance that the carrying out of certain activities may take on for man, trying to contemplate the sense of his life as a whole."

Truth, therefore, is not only multiple and conflicting, but inapplicable to many of the educational studies and activities we need to engage in to understand our worlds. But this is not the end of the matter; for even where questions of truth are relevant, we often must settle for justified or rational belief and hope for truth. Surely, an important goal of education is to provide students with the tools to weigh evidence, critically evaluate alternatives, challenge cherished beliefs, distinguish between sophistry and sophistication, and thereby develop and understand the nature of rational beliefs. We need to consider, then, whether the elusive notion of justified or rational belief, unlike that of truth, is nonrelativistic.

Here we clearly are on less controversial ground, for even according to standard conceptions of knowledge, justified belief, unlike truth, is relative to the evidence. For example, although it is true that water is composed of hydrogen and oxygen and we are now justified in believing it, Thales, living in the very different evidential situation of the seventh century B.C.E., would not have been justified in holding this belief. A belief P, unjustified at time *t*, may be justified at time *t'*. But, so the standard story goes, there is only one truth about the composition of water.

My concern about rationality is different from the traditional one. My claim is not that, as a result of changes in the evidence, what is justified or rational to believe at one time may not be rational to believe at another time. That point is noncontroversial. Rather, my point is that, given the same evidence, what is justified or rational to believe in one community may not be rational or justified in another. Hence it becomes increasingly important to open up our educational system to the perspectives of other communities and cultures, to other voices, in order to expose us to other conceptions of rationality and to other possibilities of rational beliefs. . . .

Consider now some final curricular issues. Searle insists that the debate over multiculturalism and the canon focuses primarily on the study of literature. Quite rightly, he believes, the debate is not found in the sciences or even in philosophy. However accurate this analysis, the foregoing defense of relativism and pluralism suggests that the debate should in fact be widened. And, *pace* Searle, in philosophy at least there has been considerable discussion about the need to incorporate multicultural perspectives into the curriculum. Further, the examples cited here in support of pluralism came not from literature but from the worlds of common sense, science, and mathematics. If these worlds are malleable and multiple, it is not surprising that so are the worlds of literature.

Of course, any serious and realistic discussion of the curriculum must take into account the realities of the classroom. As Searle correctly notes, neither proponents nor opponents of multiculturalism have "much to say about what actually happens in most college classrooms." It is one thing to defend multiculturalism on metaphysical and epistemological grounds. It is another to show how the resulting curriculum will be an effective pedagogical tool, given the nature of the students and the training and strength of the faculty. This is so even if one grants further that a major concern in curricular design is to promote what Matthew Arnold termed "the best that is known and thought in the world."

Following Arnold, there may be many good reasons for choosing to include Kant rather than King (Martin Luther) in an introductory philosophy course, or Paz (Octavio) rather than Pope in a poetry class. Yet to focus on the former case, we might find out, as many of us have, that Kant (like Paz!) is inaccessible to many of our students, no matter how hard they and we try, but that King, although not an original thinker or a major philosopher, raises fundamental issues about natural rights and natural law, about the relationships between law and morality, and he does so with examples (unlike Kant's) that are alive and moving and engaging. As a result, King, not Kant, may prove most effective for introducing many students to philosophy, not only because he presents an eloquent and stirring voice for the voiceless, but perhaps even more important, because his writings successfully engage students in fundamental, persistent, and perplexing moral problems. As such, King rather than Kant may prove more effective initially in promoting yet another important goal of education, getting students to learn to learn.

Although multiculturalism conforms, I believe, to the most plausible and defensible metaphysical and epistemological positions, there is still the haunting fear expressed by Kimball that "far from being a means of securing ethnic and racial equality, [multiculturalism is] an instrument for promoting ideological separatism based on . . . age, class, ethnicity, institution, gender, nation, tribe, race, rank, religion, sexuality." Until multicultural curricula are implemented and tested it is difficult to evaluate these concerns. We do know, however, that Eurocentric curricula have been implemented and are well established in universities, and that they have in fact been "instrument[s] for promoting ideological separatism based on . . . age, class, ethnicity, institution, gender, nation, tribe, race, rank, religion, sexuality." Is it not worth trying to counter the elitism and chronic provincialism of many of our students by opening up the curriculum to those powerful voices of previously unrepresented groups that have not found a prominent place in the Eurocentric curriculum?

If Matthew Arnold's dictum is to be taken seriously, then the curriculum should reflect the best that is known and thought *in the world.* If, in addition, the curriculum should provide an understanding of *our* cultural heritage, then the curriculum should reflect the perspectives and cultures of *us.* But to study our heritage is to study diversity, and that increasingly includes, and means hearing about and from, women, African Americans, Native Americans, gays, lesbians, Latinos, Asian Americans, and so on. It is difficult to believe that a curriculum that provides students with the opportunity to understand the contributions and cultures of the peoples of our country and world would be more conducive to promoting separatism than a curriculum that kept students ignorant of others.

The promotion of multiculturalism along with an appreciation of its metaphysical and epistemological underpinnings would go a long way, I believe, toward the development of a sense of tolerance and respect for others. Epistemological relativism and metaphysical pluralism (or irrealism) lend credence to the idea that one's truths and one's rational beliefs and one's world may not exhaust the universe. Some alternative views, even if in conflict with ours, may be equally reasonable and correct and may participate in making other worlds. The worlds stand really malleable.

The idea that more than one world version may be rational or true should be sobering as well as liberating, for it should encourage us to try to understand, to come to grips with, and to get inside of, other perspectives and worlds. So relativism and irrealism lead to tolerance, not in the sense that anything goes, for it doesn't, in fact much doesn't go, but rather because they provide intellectual support for concern and curiosity about other peoples and other worlds. Given the multicultural makeup of this country and the strong case for epistemological relativism and metaphysical irrealism, the failure to provide students with rich multicultural curricula amounts to an insupportable provincialism that is intellectually without warrant.

AGAINST MULTICULTURALISM

Jan Narveson

INTRODUCTION: POLITICIZATION

Our subject is a contemporary syndrome—the not entirely homogeneous set of phenomena known as "political correctness." Intriguingly and perhaps significantly, this phrase, originally stemming from the bad old days of the Bolsheviks and meant, I suppose, to be cute and rather derogatory, has been embraced by its friends almost as readily as by its enemies. It's hardly to be taken literally: the tendency to refrain from assassinating adherents of rival political views, or of rival candidates for political office, is not to be so classified, even though it is political, certainly, and it is indeed "correct." There are good and strong reasons of principle for having and cultivating that tendency, but it is not the sort of thing designated by the expression "politically correct." That phrase was born to live between scare-quotes: it suggests that the operative considerations in the area so called are *merely* political, steamrollering the genuine reasons of principle for which we ought to be acting and to promote which, we hope, our political institutions are designed. Presumably the friends of political correctness could not accept that characterization. They surely suppose that the policies they advocate are defensible via broadly acceptable principles. In this, I think, they are wrong, and I shall try to make a detailed case for that in the following pages. The focus here, at any rate, is on principles and arguments—on the *conceptual status* of the policies we are considering.

There is one attitude toward subjects such as the present one to which, I think, objection should be made right away, and analysis of which will serve as a prelude to the rest of this essay. It is often enough said nowadays that "*everything* is political," or words to some such effect; and those who say that often invoke it in support of positions on currently controversial matters. I'm not at all sure how seriously the claim is made by those who make it, or what, if anything, they really suppose it means. But it might be worth opening this discussion by pointing out why the slogan can be no more than that—that insofar as one can attach any kind of serious meaning to it, the effect can hardly be what was intended by anyone purporting to provide *reasoned* support for any describable view on any discussable subject.

To see this, let us ask what would be the range covered by the word "everything" in our slogan? One supposes it applies at least to the realm of discourse generally, and of decision making in particular. Consider, then. Is the question *whether one proposition implies another* intended for inclusion? If it is, presumably the idea is that whether or not proposition q actually *follows* from proposition p is to be regarded as itself just as "political" as whether p is true in the first place. But if that is what is meant, then what is the point of invoking the slogan on behalf of any *particular* view, as opposed to other views? For if the question whether the view follows from the slogan, or from anything, is itself a political matter, rather than a matter of logic or fact, then there is evidently no way to know whether the slogan "supports" one view or another about anything, including politics itself. (Try it . . !) Like so many other similarly uninhibited generalizations, this one has a remarkable capacity for undermining itself: if it were right, then a political decision could suddenly make it the case that the very theory of political correctness is itself false. I presume that proponents of political correctness don't think that is so.

Everything's being literally political is unimaginable. In no useful sense of "political" can one hold that the question of, say, whether there is global warming, or Snell's Law holds up, is political. What it would properly apply to, for example, might be committee deliberations that are suspected of being influenced by political rather than scientific reasons to declare for a particular scientific judgment when some other judgment, or none, was actually better supported by the evidence. Perhaps, for example, more money would be available from the granting agency if one side in the issue was declared to be the right one ("If your research is intended to support hypothesis H, then we'll give you a research grant of twenty thousand dollars; if not, forget it!" A current example: the belief that HIV "causes" AIDS, despite much contrary evidence.) In this perfectly clear and usable sense of "political," however, it is plainly false to say that "everything" is so. And it is also clear that the term is essentially pejorative in such contexts. If you do science by consulting political interests, that *impugns* your work as science: those who did such things should have their Ph.D.'s revoked and their labs turned over to people who will take the job seriously.

Why would anyone be tempted to suppose that "everything" is political? The argument seems to appeal to some such argument as this: (1) All judgments are formulated in words; but (2) words are social artifacts; and yet (3) society is political (because it has political institutions, which exercise control over it).

Of course we must grant all of those premises. But what conclusion are we supposed to draw? That molecular chemistry is really a branch of politics, perhaps? After all, its conclusions and reports of evidence are indeed written and spoken in some language. Or should we instead argue that politics is actually a branch of molecular chemistry, seeing that everything, including politicians, is composed of molecules? Better yet, the claim should be dismissed for the absurdity it is.

Nevertheless, the topic of political correctness is genuine enough. The claim that "everything" is political is used in practice to support a move *to politicize,* that is, to increase the incidence of political control in some domain that was not previously so treated. The argument we have just considered is readily seen to be nonsense. If its premise were correct, then whatever domain was in question must *already be* political, in which case there is no sense in proposing to *politicize* it. Its not having been literally so (or, as much so) in the past is an obvious presupposition of proposing to make it so, or more so, in future. On the other hand, if that presupposition *is* true, then the general covering premise is false—*not* everything is political. You can't have it both ways. But the argument requires precisely that.

Thus, the proponent now needs new, and this time *meaningful,* premises for supporting the proposal. And everything would turn on the plausibility of those premises. We can supply some meaning to the suggestion that everything is political by interpreting it to mean that everything that anything can be done about is conceivably something that can be legislated about. But the fact that something *can* be done hardly means that it ought to be: everyone is capable of murder, for instance.

Politicizing means that instead of being free to do as they think best, people are now directed by some authority to do something else. It means, then, an increase in administrators and an increase in taxation or other impositions on somebody, or on everybody, to support the costs of the politicization. Above all, it means a decrease in individual voluntary deliberation and decision. These are all evils, in my view, to be avoided unless there is a much greater gain from the new measures, to justify the extra costs. My argument, in each case, is that there is in general no gain to speak of from these policies for anyone except, perhaps, the administrators themselves, and much loss for everyone else. All of them are made in the interest of "justice," according to their proponents. But justice, as I will argue, is precisely what gets lost in the shuffle.

The Issues

Among the various issues clustered under the general heading of political correctness, I will discuss the following five:

1.   Should there be "canonical" bodies of literature in various academic disciplines or domains? To suppose that there are, says political correctness, is to be racist, sexist, or in some other way discriminatory.

2.   Should the study of this or that subject, especially in the humanities, reflect the multiplicity of cultures from which various contributors have stemmed? The politically correct view has it that the whole field should be reconceived so that various cultural expressions that have not hitherto been regarded as contributions to it are to be regarded as being so after all—and what's more, they get equal standing with the canonical ones.

3.   What about concepts such as truth, objectivity, and impartiality? Is there anything left of them after postmodernism, in particular after applying

the theory known as "deconstruction"? The politically correct view is that those notions must go—or be given political interpretations.

4. What about persecuted and oppressed groups? Should they be given preference in academic (and other) hiring, or the distribution of related rewards or distinctions? Political correctness supports what is now known as "affirmative action," supposedly to remedy the situation.

5. Finally, there are speech codes. Various spoken or written utterances are regarded as deprecatory or otherwise harmful when they previously weren't so considered, or perhaps made positively illegal when formerly they were regarded as minor matters that should be left to the persons involved. The political correctness view is that we should greatly expand the range of the notion of harassment, thus opening the doors to committees empowered to enforce politically clean talk.

These are all real issues in practice. In response to these questions, curricula have been revised, assorted cultural groups given various special privileges, speech codes and "zero harassment" provisions adopted, and hiring practices altered by requiring affirmative action on behalf of various groups (most prominently, women). And this is done on the basis of theories, ideals of what society should be like. Our question is whether those ideals and the theories underlying them are really acceptable. In each case, I argue, they are not. The basis for affirmative answers to these questions is lacking. On the other hand, there is ample reason for *not* doing the various things in question. Each involves in one way or another important losses to innocent people trying to get on with their lives.

The Theory of Political Correctness

It would be helpful if we could spot any common basis for the "political correctness" types of action in these domains. Do they actually have something substantial in common? Is there a single direction of departure from familiar norms that they all involve? There is indeed. They take shape as various applications of a single general idea. That idea and its associated principles form the fundamental subject of this essay, though my discussion mainly focuses on specific claims in the five areas identified.

The common structure that seems to me to be at work in all of these proposals is the pursuit of what is claimed to be *equality.* Individuals, firms, and associations have objectives, attainable in varying degrees by the exercise of skill and intelligence—especially the latter, in the academic cases concentrated on here. In the pursuit of academic ends, some people will be found who perform better than others, and those people are selected, in preference to others less talented, for positions in the institutions and associations working toward those ends. And in various other ways, too, they are recognized and rewarded more highly for their achievements. Yet political correctness takes the view that the ones who do less well, and who are correspondingly less rewarded by academic institutions, are being somehow cheated or mistreated. They are regarded as "oppressed," by that very fact, or because their lesser performance is claimed to be a manifestation of some other oppression, in the form of "domination" by some group: by the rest of us, say, or by the "winners" in the current arrangements, or by those who support them. It is then proposed that to rectify the situation we must do one or more of the following:

1. Alter the standards by which better and worse performance is appraised.

2. Create special avenues to the desired rewards, or to the attainment of higher levels of performance, for those who have hitherto done less well, thus smoothing the way so that they too will do better, as judged by the existing criteria.

3. Impose handicaps on those at the upper end of the spectrum, thus to some degree equalizing their situations as compared with those lower down.

The fundamental aim, in short, is *equality of outcome,* and the politically correct principle is that everyone has the right to that status, a right overriding any considerations of merit deployed within the offending field.

This analysis does not apply so readily to the fifth of the proposed topics. Even speech codes, though, may be viewed as attempts to equalize the situations of speakers and hearers in certain respects. The kinds of speech objected to are viewed as manifesting a kind of domination of the hearers by the speakers. Speech codes are meant to restore equality between them.

The case for these efforts at equalization depends on either a reassessment of the objectives of the field, or a claim that the standards employed in appraising efforts on behalf of those objectives are in some way objectionable— say, that those standards or even the objectives themselves are really the creations of the allegedly oppressing class, whose members get to define them. That some such move is essential to the program is clear when we reflect that the possibility of achieving objective truths about the subject matter in question is an intrinsic presupposition of the academic endeavour at hand. Inquiry, as we used to understand it, proceeds by patient tracking down of evidence that tends to support some hypotheses in preference to others, sometimes to the complete epistemic exclusion of some of the latter, and to support them quite independently of what the inquirer might *like* to be the case. Human intelligence does the sleuthing, but nature itself confirms or disconfirms the answers. So long as that assumption is made, there are objective criteria of achievement, and it is hardly surprising that some do better and some worse, and thus that reasoned claims can be made about who should be preferred to whom for the purposes of that field of inquiry.

If you don't like this situation, one way to deal with it is to accuse those in the upper performance brackets, or their friends, of rigging the whole show, thus reconceiving the activity in question as mere power-tripping on the part of a self-appointed elite. Such an accusation must be taken seriously, for as we have seen, all non-political correctness theorists will agree that if that is what is actually going on, then our efforts at what we thought was objective science or scholarship are mere pretensions. The accusation, in fact, amounts to asserting that the subject in question is not really a *subject* at all, but just *politicking.* Aristotle is replaced by Machiavelli as the patron saint of the academic.

Political correctness advances these claims on the basis of more or less plausible-sounding premises. None of us approves of injustice or unfairness; all of us favor, in some sense, equal treatment of all. If those familiar principles can be brought to bear in these areas with the effects in question, then how can we object?

But in all this there is a mixture of ideology and misunderstanding. The latter is, I shall argue, extensive. Like all misunderstandings, especially those that drive ideologies, there are important truths on which the argument tries to build—but it builds in the wrong direction, leaving a theoretical jumble and leading to practical nightmares. The ideology involves a moral vision. But it is not what it claims to be. It is, instead, a flawed vision—actually *ressentiment,* in the guise of critical "theory." That is what I shall argue for in the ensuing pages.

THE CANON

We begin with the idea of there being a *canon* in some domain of the humanities: a smallish set of works that constitute the paradigms of achievement in that area, the works one must know if one is to qualify as an educated person. Or, since almost all of the attention in this area has been concentrated on works in the broad area known as the "humanities," acquaintance with the canon qualifies a person as educated in the humanities—though that is pretty near to being the area that many people would identify with being "an educated person," period.

This calls for specific comment. There are plenty of people with impressive knowledge in non-humanities areas. Yet in their areas, "canons" are largely out of the question. Scientists read Newton and Galileo only out of historical curiosity, not as useful sources of knowledge in their subjects. I shall say more about the ideal of a "liberal education," an ideal that still seems to me important. Insofar as there is an ideal of education for all, of the educated *person* as opposed to the paleontologist, economist, biochemist, etc., the ideal of a liberal education in the humanities is at its heart. But let us not delude ourselves into supposing that such persons are the intellectual aristocracy of our time, or that it is everyone's sacred obligation to acquire such an education.

We will suppose, then, that it is in the area of a liberal humanistic education that there arise questions about the legitimacy of any "canon" of masterworks or paradigm works, regarded as a "core," basic to the subject. That said, let us begin by agreeing that there is plenty of unclarity and imprecision in the idea. It would be silly for anyone to claim to know *precisely* how many items really are canonical in any given humanistic area. Moreover, the areas differ greatly. Are *all* the works of Jane Austen in the canon, or just one or two? If the latter, is it, then, *Pride and Prejudice,* or *Emma,* or some other?

Is George Eliot in the canon, or is she on the fringe? Faulkner? Virginia Woolf? Who would ever seriously advance *precise* claims about the canon? Among serious scholars, surely, the very idea of a precise list is laughable. Even if asked to name the ten most important works in the field, let alone the top hundred, most teachers and scholars of the subject, however eminent, would submit quite different lists.

Nevertheless, lists of that kind will also contain many common entries. Indeed, it is that very fact that gives the idea of a canon such credibility as it has. Very few will put Shakespeare far down the list. None will elevate the novels of Benjamin Disraeli (sometime Prime Minister though he be) to the top. Anyone who would seriously support an opposite classification would have to be written off as just out of it. But that is, in its place, an important fact. It is certainly this level of agreement that makes the idea of a "canon" a workable one. Without it, the idea couldn't get off the ground. There would then be genuine doubt on the validity of the field as a field: if the supposed knowledge and the supposed standards of this field are worth their salt, surely its practitioners would be able to agree enough to distinguish the best from the mediocre?

That said, some important qualifications are in order. First, it is not right to say that the canon consists, simply, of the *best* works in the field. We must instead speak, more guardedly, of important works: e.g., because they are seminal—as having inspired further work, and worthy of our interest for having done so, even if successors improved on them. Still others are recognized for certain special qualities, even though in other respects they would not be held up as models. There are flawed masterpieces, brilliant but eccentric works, minor masterpieces, small gems, and so on. The canon, in short, is bound to be a somewhat unruly collection. That should go some way toward dispelling any aura of sanctity about it.

What grounds might there be for attacking the very idea of a canon? To formulate these, we will have to be a bit more elaborate in our depiction of the idea. I have spoken, vaguely, of the objectives of a field, by reference to which we may identify better and worse practitioners within it. But how do we do that? We must be able to say more precisely what this or that person has accomplished—what it is about his or her work that makes it better. Thus we require a distinction between the general *objectives* of the field, on the one hand, and the *criteria* in terms of which meritorious performance is to be appraised, on the other. We shall then need to make a further distinction: between those criteria, which are the abstract categories within which appraisals are made, and the *standards* in terms of which we express and categorize particular appraisals. Standards indicate levels of achievement on the basis of the criteria in question. Thus in awarding grades to papers, we use such criteria as clarity, depth, and acquaintance with the relevant literature; and we then sort them into those meriting "A," "B," "C," and so on. In a body of literature, we look for imaginativeness, perceptiveness, delineation of character, and many other things; and we rate the various works as first-rate, second-rate, and so on.

But how do standards and even criteria come to be recognized in a field? People do not usually carry such things about in their heads when they look at works of art or read literature. Or at least, they do not have them in explicit form. It is safe to say that fields in which such appraisals are made tend to be based on reactions to particular works upon acquaintance, *not* formed *on the basis* of antecedently formulated criteria of appraisal. Having tried it and liked it, intelligent and interested people begin to figure out what it was that they liked about it, and perhaps reflection about that enables them to go on to further work, and sometimes to rethink the unreflective judgments themselves. Here is one main lead-in to a canon, then: the accumulation of items in the field that really catch and hold the interest and admiration of those interested in that sort of thing, and that do not undergo revision at the hands of further reflection and continued acquaintance with those and other works. Such works come to be looked up to, and to set standards: "A good philosopher, though no Aristotle," we say.

All the factors mentioned have to work together. If there are no objectives, then there are no criteria of appraisal; and in the absence of those, it makes no sense to call anything a "standard." A standard *for what,* we ask. In the case of many of the humanities fields in academia, it would not be very easy to say what the "objective" of its literature is. What is the purpose of a novel or a poem? We might say, taking a shot at it, that it's to be interesting, insightful, inspiring, to show us something about ourselves, and so on. Those descriptions of objectives, though, are obviously not informative enough to give anything like precise guidance. Seeing how some particular work measures up will itself require an exercise of insight, sensitivity, and taste: it won't be possible to say, "And there, you see, this is precisely what makes this poem fulfil that objective to such-and-such a degree."

For similar reasons, it is not easy to specify the goal of an academic teacher and/or student of literature. The very specification of goals is done in terms of value judgments. To those who have no feel for the field, this fuels the suspicion that it isn't really a "field" at all, and this in turn supports the political correctness analysis. Contrast this with, say, chess or many branches of engineering. The object of the chess-player in a game is very precisely specified: to checkmate one's opponent's king. Strategies are extensively studied, but they all have that single, clear, perfectly-defined objective. Whether x is a good move or not, though often debatable, is frequently decidable. And "canonical" practitioners are identified: Bobbie Fisher (in his prime) was a great player, whereas I, for example, am a very rank amateur. There is no real room for argument on the latter examples. Anyone who thinks that I, for example, am a "great" player has either mistaken me for someone else, or simply doesn't know what's going on in the game of chess.

But the case against the humanities fails for the same reasons. Take the case of this author (or, probably, yourself) as a pianist. With work, I just might be able to pass a first grade examination; with much more, I might someday get as high as grade four. But to mention me in the same breath with an Ashkenazy would be absurd. On the other hand, rating Ashkenazy as compared with Rubinstein or Perahia would be much more difficult. Luckily, it is also unnecessary for most purposes. If one were selecting recordings to play for a class, or for a group of music lovers, one would then have to make such choices; but one would be able to explain, usually, that other choices could also have been defended, that selection is to a degree arbitrary, and to a degree a matter of personal taste.

Why evolve a canon for purposes of teaching in college literature courses? For one thing, it is quite natural. People in the field read not only what they are assigned as students but very much else as well. Competent students of a body of literature read far beyond the confines of any canon: most of what is read, indeed, is by definition not in it. This puts them in a position to make informed judgments about relative merit, and those judgments tend, as a matter of fact, to converge on a modest body of works, which consequently are dubbed "classics." In undertaking to explore a field with a group of students, with limited time at both the teacher's and their disposal, a selection must be made. It makes sense to include some of the acknowledged best of the type under consideration. It also makes sense to include seminal works, the ones that have actually stirred up creative juices among authors. And it makes sense to include some work that is *not* the "best," for comparison.

QUESTIONS FOR DISCUSSION
MULTICULTURALISM AND POLITICAL CORRECTNESS

1. How do Lawrence Foster and Jan Narveson define cultural diversity (or "multiculturalism")? Discuss how their different understandings of this concept influences their evaluations.

2. What do you think Foster means by "relativism" and "subjectivism"? Why, according to him, does relativism not lead to subjectivism? Why, do you suppose, does he support relativism but not subjectivism?

3. Why does Foster think it likely that Martin Luther King's writings would be a better introduction to philosophy than those of Immanuel Kant? Why does Narveson think otherwise? Compare the two opposing views.

4. Comment on Foster's assertion that "to study our heritage includes, and means, hearing about and from women, African Americans, native Americans, gays, lesbians, Latinos, Asian Americans, and so on." Do you agree? Why or why not?

5. What does Narveson mean by "politically correct," and how does he relate it to multiculturalism?

6. What is the "canon," criticized by Foster and defended by Narveson as the core of a "liberal education"? What concessions does Narveson make to critics like Foster, and what reasons does he offer to maintain the ideal of a liberal education?

SELECTED READINGS

BAPTISTE, H. *Multicultural Education.* Washington, DC: University Press of America, 1979.

BERMAN, P. *Debating P.C.* New York: Dell, 1992.

BOULDING, E. *Building a Global Culture.* New York: Teachers College Press, 1998.

CHOI, J. *The Politics and Philosophy of Political Correctness.* Westport, CT: Praeger, 1992.

DEVINE, P. *Human Diversity and the Cultural Wars.* Westport, CT: Praeger, 1996.

D'SOUZA, D. *Illiberal Education.* New York: Free Press, 1991.

FELDSTEIN, R. *Political Correctness.* Minneapolis: University of Minnesota Press, 1997.

JOPKE, C., and S. LUKES, eds. *Multicultural Questions.* New York: Oxford University Press, 1999.

KATSIAFICAS, G., and T. KIROS, eds. *The Promise of Multiculturalism.* New York: Routledge, 1998.

LYNCH, J. *Multicultural Education.* London: Routledge and Kegan Paul, 1986.

WURZEL, J., ed. *Toward Multiculturalism.* Yarmouth: England Intercultural Press, 1988.

13

WAR AND TERRORISM

On September 11, 2001, most of the world was basking in the sunshine of peace when the sudden destruction of the World Trade Center and part of the Washington Pentagon took place. This was followed by the U.S. declaration of a war against terrorism. These events gave humankind reason to reflect on the causes of war and terrorism, and the possible ways to reduce, if not entirely eliminate, these two evils. The coupling of war and terrorism suggested by the preceding phrase, "these two evils," raises an important ethical question: Are they equally evil, or is war sometimes justifiable and terrorism never justifiable?

A question that must be answered before evaluating war and terrorism is this: What exactly is the difference between them? It is sometimes said that the difference between freedom fighters and terrorists is whose side they are on. Is this true? For example, in the 1980s the U.S. federal government subsidized and armed bands of rebels, known as "Contras," who laid waste to areas of Nicaragua in order to subvert its left-wing government. The U.S. Congress had passed a bill forbidding such intervention, but the Reagan administration acted covertly in alleged defiance of Congress. During the resulting "Iran-Contra" congressional investigation, defenders of the intervention called the Contras "freedom fighters," whereas opponents referred to them as "terrorists." Were they one, or the other, or both? If both, then cannot terrorism sometimes be justified? B. T. Wilkins says yes; A. R. Louch says no.

Wilkins argues that some acts of terrorism, understood by him as the infliction of harm against innocent persons for political or social goals, are justified if (1) the goals are morally acceptable, (2) there is no likely nonviolent alternative for achieving them, and (3) the victims, even if personally innocent, are in some reasonable sense collectively guilty. He gives as an example of justifiable terrorism any acts of sabotage or indiscriminate assault against the Nazis by their potential victims. He does not consider the U.S. use of atomic bombs against Hiroshima and Nagasaki in World War II to be examples of terrorism because, he claims, these were "acts of war" employing weapons of extraordinary power that were not unlike the bombs that were used by both sides.

A. R. Louch denounces all terrorism as abominable. Unlike Wilkins, he does not regard acts of violence against tyrannies like the Nazi regime as ter-

532

rorist, because their political goals are fairly clear and morally justifiable; this implies that for him, terrorism is the use of indiscriminate violence for vague, unjustifiable, and probably unrealizable goals. Terrorists, he claims, are arrogant fanatics, "unable to distinguish between the repressiveness of totalitarian regimes . . . and democracies," so that "the targets of these groups are neither evil enough nor powerful enough to warrant such extreme measures."

It is difficult to decide between the views of Wilkins and Louch without a clear, precise, and commonly accepted definition of terrorism, which, alas, is hard to come by. The reader is advised to formulate his or her own definition.

CAN TERRORISM BE JUSTIFIED?

B. T. Wilkins

Probably the most important division in moral philosophy is between consequentialists who believe that the rightness or wrongness of an action is determined by its contribution to an ideal end state such as the greatest happiness of the greatest number and deontologists who deny that this is so, at least in cases where the action in question would involve the violation of the rights of an individual or individuals. One of the few amusing aspects of the usually grim topic of terrorism is the way in which consequentialists such as R. M. Hare and Kai Nielsen seek to dissociate themselves from terrorism, treating it ever so gingerly as though fearful it might explode in their hands doing great harm to whatever variety of consequentialism they espouse. Yet it seems to me plain enough that if there were good reasons for believing that terrorism would contribute to bringing about some ideal end state, then the consequentialist would be hard pressed to reject it as a morally legitimate means to that ideal end state. What then is wrong with terrorism if it cannot be condemned on consequentialist grounds? The deontologist's case against terrorism can be stated fairly simply: terrorism involves the violation of the rights of persons who may be killed or harmed; even if no one is actually killed or harmed by the terrorist, there is the threat of harm, and threats are a species of coercion, making people behave in ways that they would not otherwise choose; moreover, the persons who are, or may be, the victims of terrorism are frequently not those whose conduct the terrorist wishes to affect. . . .

One thing that makes terrorism of interest philosophically is that it compels us to rethink from a somewhat different perspective the question of when, if ever, it is morally justifiable to do violence to another person. The traditional answers, while perhaps valid, will take us only so far. It is generally agreed that it is justifiable to do violence to another person in self-defense; some wars can be accommodated under the category of self-defense where this is construed in terms of a community of persons defending themselves against aggressors. It is also agreed, though less generally, that even violence against an innocent person can be justified in the name of self-defense, in cases where he or she is being used by an aggressor as a hostage or a shield. If in the Second World War the Japanese Army had dispersed crucial weapons and supplies throughout Hiroshima and Nagasaki, and if these weapons and supplies could only have been destroyed by attacks upon the entire cities, then we would, I think, be far less troubled about the moral legitimacy of our attacks upon them. (Here I assume that Japan was the aggressor.) But what about terrorism which seems to be no respector of innocence among persons, and which seems all too willing to sacrifice innocent lives as a means to social or political change? Can we fail to be shocked by the anarchist who justified tossing a bomb into a crowded café in Paris on the ground that there are no innocent bourgeois? (But would it be blasphemous to suggest that we might be somewhat less shocked had he deliberately chosen a café known to be frequented by captains of industry, whom he would have regarded as "class enemies"?)

Though the victims of terrorist acts may be oppressors or aggressors or tyrants, or their collaborators, often they are not. Often they are innocent, at least as innocent as civilian populations in wartime. If we condemn unjust wars, or unjust acts committed in wartime, are we not also committed to condemning any terrorism in which violence, or the threat of violence, is inflicted upon innocent persons, except in those instances where they are being used as hostages or shields? Terrorism poses this problem: can we ever justify inflicting violence upon innocent persons in circumstances other than self-defense? Will a "justification" of terrorism succeed only by shrinking the notion of what is to count as innocence and by extending the range of activities to be considered as self-defense? Is there such a thing as collective guilt, and if there is can it ever be used to justify acts of violence against persons on the ground that they are members of a certain community or group?

I believe that any adequate answer to the question of when, if ever, terrorism is justified must take into account the problem of collective guilt, which is surely one of the murkiest and least explored topics in moral philosophy and which, to my knowledge, has been entirely neglected by those who have written on terrorism. On the question of whether there is such a thing as collective guilt opinions differ: there are those who believe that we, all of us, are guilty of each and every wrong done by any human being, a view which Mohandas Gandhi seems to have held; there are those who believe that we can be guilty only of those wrongs which we have done in an individual capacity, a view which seems to be lurking just below the surface in the writings of some political libertarians, and there are those of us who are not satisfied with either of these extreme positions and who are attracted to, but disturbed by, the idea that guilt may be at least in some cases collective. If we are to make sense of the notion of collective guilt, I believe that solidarity in the sense of a shared common interest is our best guide, and that the absence of wrongdoing by individuals who are nevertheless said to share in some collective guilt remains perhaps the biggest stumbling-block. The reason why humanity at large fails to be a satisfactory basis for pronouncements about collective guilt, except for the Mohandas Gandhis of this world, may be that the interests we share with humanity at large tend to be too slight or fragile, though this shows signs of changing. There are, however, communities of a less extensive and more tangible sort where shared or common interests are already conspicuously present: in families, in neighborhoods, in business or cultural institutions, in political states, and perhaps, if Marxists are correct on this point, in social and economic classes. Pride or shame in what is done in, by, or on behalf of such communities is probably the best phenomenological clue we have to locating the interests and values we share with others. But where collective guilt is concerned we tend to balk at admitting to guilt for things done in, by, or on behalf of those communities whose interests and values we share, when as individuals we did not actively participate in the doing of the things in question. However, the tie between collective guilt and individual wrongdoing is not a conceptual one; and where collective guilt is concerned we can turn to the law for examples of liability without contributory fault. For example, even if personally entirely innocent of the offense, a bank officer may be held strictly liable for the wrongdoing of a bank employee; and a convincing rationale having to do with the vigilance which society can reasonably expect of bank officers in hiring and management procedures can be given for this practice. In addition, Joel Feinberg, the master taxonomist, has uncovered the following models of liability *with* fault: liability with a fault that is non-contributory; contributory group fault where the fault is collective and distributive; and contributory group fault where the fault is collective but not distributive. I shall return shortly to these three models and to some of Feinberg's examples, but first I wish to consider an example of collective guilt which is, I believe, especially relevant to the question of whether terrorism can ever be justified.

I would suppose that in the history of imperialism, of racial and religious persecutions, and in the economic exploitation of one group by another there are numerous instances of collective guilt, but to my mind the clearest and most indisputable example in recent history is to be found in the persecution of the Jews in Nazi Germany. After the Second World War there was in fact an admission of guilt by the newly established West German government, and Chancellor Adenauer acknowledged an obligation on the part of the German people to make moral and material amends for crimes perpetrated in the name of the German people; through treaty negotiations with Israel, West Germany agreed to pay out some 715 million dollars. As an example of penance this payment of reparations may be lacking somewhat in moral purity: Adenauer was under pressure from the American government and from world opinion, political considerations were obviously much involved, and the negotiations were between a new German government, perhaps even a new German state, and the newly created state of Israel. Nevertheless the example does fit, however awkwardly, the classic picture of guilt, confession, and repentance in the form of efforts to make amends through reparations. . . .

The persecution of the Jews by the Nazis was so heinous that, it seems to me, terrorism on the part of the Jews would have been a morally justifiable response, meeting terrorism with terrorism. What I have in mind is not terrorism thought of in terms of vengeance or even retribution but terrorism regarded as an instrument of self-defense on the part of the Jews. While Jews in Germany did to some extent resist their oppressors, they did not practice terrorism. Perhaps terrorism by the oppressed was an idea whose time had not come; perhaps the Jews did not want to "sink to the level" of their persecutors; or perhaps there was a fear of making bad matters worse. Where sinking to the level of their oppressors is concerned, the Jews might have reasoned as follows: they were being persecuted because they were Jews, and if they practiced terrorism in turn, would they not be initiating violence, or threats of violence, against Germans because of their Germanness? There is, however, a crucial disanalogy between the two cases, which is sufficient in my judgment to overcome this objection. The Jews had done no wrong, and the effort to discredit them consisted of a tissue of lies: they had betrayed Germany in the First World War causing its defeat, they were responsible for Germany's post-war economic collapse, and so on. On the other hand, Germans were collectively guilty of the persecution of the Jews—thus, if Germans were the victims of violence, or threats of violence, by the Jews it would not have been because of their "Germanness" but because of their collective guilt for the persecution of the Jews, for being Jews. As for making bad matters worse, perhaps one could find a point in the history of the persecution of the Jews and say that henceforth it would be difficult to see how anything could have worsened their plight. Perhaps terrorism aimed first against the Nazis and then against other Germans might at least have helped to focus German and especially world attention on what was happening in Germany. Even if terrorism by the Jews had done nothing to improve matters, striking out in self-defense is, I believe, a morally legitimate action on the part of anyone who has been condemned to death. State terrorism was being practiced against the Jews, terrorism not as a species of coercion but with the aim of the annihilation of the Jews. How much of what the Nazis were doing in this respect was actually sanctioned by German law remains a somewhat controversial topic, but surely whether legally or not the apparatus of the German state was being directed toward the extinction of the Jews. Under such circumstances Jews in Germany were in effect being driven into a Hobbesian state of nature, pursued by a Nazi Leviathan, and this is why I believe that terrorism was a morally acceptable option had the Jews elected to use it.

In summary, my thesis is that in the case of the persecution of the Jews, reparations by the German government for crimes done in the name of the German people was a morally appropriate response *after* the harm was done, but that terrorism as an instrument of self-defense by the Jews would have been a morally appropriate response *while* the harm was in process of being inflicted upon them. But what does this example of a case where terrorism would have been morally justifiable actually show? There is a tendency among some commentators on the topics of terrorism and assassination to maintain that while some instances of terrorism or assassination might be justified, in the name of moral necessity, this is a far cry from our being able to arrive at a moral rule which would justify terrorism or assassination: the thought seems to be that exceptions to a moral rule do not provide the basis for a new moral rule. There are some weighty metaphilosophical and methodological problems involved in all arguments of this kind which I shall, mercifully, not attempt to explore here. Instead, I shall conclude by proposing a rule for your consideration. There may be other rules which would justify terrorism, and the rule I shall propose is couched only in terms of sufficient conditions, although I believe that the first condition laid down by the rule I propose may well be a necessary condition which any justification of terrorism would have to satisfy. Here is the rule: terrorism is justified as a form of self-defense when: (1) all political and legal remedies have been exhausted or are inapplicable (as in emergencies where "time is of the essence"); and (2) the terrorism will be directed against members of a community or group which is collectively guilty of violence aimed at those individuals who are now considering the use of terrorism as an instrument of self-defense, or at the community or group of which they are members. Perhaps there may be other acceptable moral rules which would justify the use of terrorism, for example in cases where an entire people have been dispossessed of their homeland, or where one part of a country is occupied by a foreign power which prevents its being reunited with the country of which it is historically and culturally a part, or where one economic class or one race systematically exploits another economic class or race. Here the issue would be whether dispossession, separation, or exploitation as contrasted to violence against persons is sufficient to warrant terrorism as a response, and whether the struggle to remedy the wrongs in question could be regarded as falling somehow within the category of self-defense. Perhaps rationales for terrorism which do not depend upon whether self-defense is involved might be constructed, but I shall not explore this possibility here; nor shall I consider whether terrorism in the absence of any collective guilt in the group toward which the terrorism is directed might somehow be justified.

Where the application of the moral rule I have proposed is concerned, I believe that the employment of terrorism against members of a community which is collectively guilty of violence should be subject to certain constraints in which moral and prudential considerations are interwoven. There is no reason why terrorism should necessarily be indiscriminate, and there are good reasons why it should not be. The picture given by the popular press, . . . of the terrorist firing off an automatic weapon in a crowded airport misses the mark: most terrorists are in fact far more selective than this suggests, and even if they were not, there is nothing essential to terrorism which requires that its targets be randomly or indiscriminately selected. Here are the constraints I have in mind. First, the terrorism should be limited to the members of the community which is collectively guilty of violence. (It might be noted that the indiscriminate firing of a weapon in a crowded airport would be disqualified right off, on the ground that members of other communities, tourists and businessmen for example, commonly frequent such places.) Second, as far as possible terrorism should be confined to "primary targets," and where this is not possible the terrorist should pick a "secondary target" who is as guilty or nearly as guilty, in the sense of being responsible for initiating or participating in the violence which can be said to have "started it all" and which is continuing. An individual who simply shares the beliefs and attitudes of the "primary target" would not be an acceptable "secondary target." (Also, the choice of a morally inappropriate "secondary target" might backfire tactically in the sense of creating public sympathy for either or both of the targets involved—arguably, something like this may have happened in the Hearst case, which, of course, involved a terrorism different from the kind I am now considering.) Third, the terrorism in question should be directed initially at the perpetrators of violence and then at their accomplices in such a way as to reflect the part they played in the violence. If terrorism still fails to achieve its goal, the successful defense of the terrorists or the community or group to which they belong, then they should proceed to violence against those who, as individuals, are guilty of moral complicity in the violence in question. For example, the editors, the bankers, the university professors and the motion-picture makers who "knew what was going on"—and were handsomely rewarded for their silence and acquiescence—should be the next in line. But what about members of the "silent majority" who, it would seem, do no evil, see no evil and hear no evil, or if they do hear aren't really listening or dismiss what they hear as rumor? If the terrorists are seeking a change in the policies which have led to the violence directed against themselves or the community or group of which they are members, then perhaps the "silent majority" was their ultimate addressee all along, i.e. the addressee whose attention they had sought vainly to get by legal or political means and which they now seek by violent means. Certainly it seems reasonable to suppose, again using the German example, that no systematic persecution of significant numbers of innocent persons can continue over long periods of time if the "silent majority" is awakened from its lethargy or its preoccupation with the details of its daily existence. Terrorists can be pictured as saying, "We demand your attention." But what if they fail, in their campaign of violence against the perpetrators of violence and their criminal and moral accomplices, to awaken the conscience and the voice of the "silent majority"? Then it would seem that the "silent majority" itself would become tainted first with moral and perhaps eventually even with criminal complicity in the ongoing violence directed against the terrorists and the community or group they represent. Under these circumstances at least, some judicious, highly selective terrorism aimed at members of the "silent majority" might become morally appropriate and tactically necessary, as a reminder that no one is safe until the injustice in question is ended.

I shall conclude by giving a brief, explicit statement of how what I have done above relates to the questions I posed earlier. First, can we ever justify inflicting violence upon innocent persons in circumstances other than self-defense? Here my justification of terrorism applies where those who are considering it as an option either have themselves been the actual or intended victims of violence, or are members of a community or group which has been the actual or intended victim of violence. Thus, the terrorism I defend is a species of self-defense, but may it involve inflicting violence upon innocent individuals? Here, the answer is a yes and a no. Yes, it may involve inflicting violence upon those who in their individual capacity may have done or intended no harm to the would-be terrorists or to the community or group to which they belong; but no, the individuals in question by virtue of their membership in the community or group which has done or threatened to do violence to the would-be terrorists or the community or group to which they belong are collectively guilty of the violence in question. . . . Will my justification of terrorism succeed only by shrinking the notion of what is to count as innocence and/or by extending the range of activities to be considered as self-defense? The answer to the first part of this question is that no conceptual revision or change in the criteria for the use of the concepts we have is necessary: the concept of collective guilt is already in place in our moral vocabulary, and while my use of collective guilt as part of a justification of terrorism under certain circumstances may be original, I am not using the concept "collective guilt" in any novel way . . . The range of activities to be considered as legitimate self-defense may, however, be extended in the light of my justification of terrorism under certain circumstances. But if individuals and communities may justifiably kill or fight wars in self-defense, I believe that terrorism may also under certain circumstances be considered a legitimate instrument of self-defense. Of course, not all terrorism can be seen as involving self-defense, and I have said nothing to justify any terrorism in which self-defense, and self-defense against actual or intended violence, is not the central moral consideration. Is there such a thing as collective guilt, and if there is can it ever be used to justify acts of violence against persons on the ground that they are members of a certain community or group? Here, of course, my answer is that there is such a thing as collective guilt, but that to justify acts of violence against persons on the ground that they are members of a certain community or group is permissible only when "membership in a certain community or group" is clearly understood to be elliptical for "membership in a certain community or group which has done or intended to do violence against the would-be terrorists or the community or group to which they belong." In other words, it is not membership in a particular community *per se* but membership in a community or group which is collectively guilty of wrongdoing that is morally relevant; to regard community membership otherwise would involve a relapse into an unacceptable barbarism.

TERRORISM IS IMMORAL

Alfred Louch

Are there actions so abominable that no reasons could justify or contexts excuse them? Answers, I suppose, may differ. My list would include torture, killing for the fun of it, and blowing up the innocent in order to demoralize those one supposes guilty. Others will say, the first two surely, the Shah of Iran and Charles Manson, but the third, in spite of the apparent atrocity of it, is after all the response to atrocity. The innocent suffer and that is unfortunate, but their death and dismemberment are stages in a radical social surgery. At the end of that process is the millenium, when repression and exploitation will cease.

If we believe that only terror can bring about the millennium, we will be well on the way toward admitting its necessity. Even so, we may find it hard to shake off a rather different impression of the terrorist—the person who carries out the ghastly assignment. This may be so for two related reasons. First, terrorists, like kidnappers, put us in the unenviable position of acceding to their illegitimate demands or becoming accessories to their atrocities. If we comply we only make further demands more likely; if we refuse we feel a joint responsibility for the fate of their victims. Rage is the natural response to this dilemma, and rage does not exactly diminish feelings of moral, as well as personal, distaste.

Second, it is cowardly to attack the defenseless. It speaks of an indifference to violence that is not suitable psychological material for the millennium. Most of all, terrorists are arrogant, acting on beliefs about social causality that the available evidence does not license. Their moral perceptions are equally dulled, since they seem quite unable to distinguish between the repressiveness of totalitarian regimes—Hitler's, Amin's or Stalin's—and those, like the Western democracies, that, even if they limit human freedom, do so within recognizable constraints on political or economic power, and in an atmosphere that allows for some freedom of opinion. They are, in short, fanatics, and fanatics are not part of the good society. They are the effluvia of social unrest, ambition, frustration, and hatred. Even if we allowed that only through fanaticism are great social objectives ever attained, we would still be repelled by the fanatic.

Are we hypocrites if we tacitly approve the consequences while condemning the doer and the deed? It has been suggested to me by my friend

541

and former student, Professor Keith Quincy, that morality has to do with what is done, not with the agent who does it. So we might consistently approve a deed and condemn the doer—approve terror and condemn the terrorist. On the face of it, this distinction amounts to a utilitarian account of action. Of the act we ask: does it result in a balance of good over evil? Of the person: is he or she someone we could like, trust, or regard as a friend? But if we reject a utilitarian calculus—as unworkable or as false to our moral intuitions—we might believe that the judgments about persons are a better index of the morality of actions than the consequences that issue from them. If, along these lines, we saw that only a repulsive character could perform certain acts, we should find this a reason to condemn them.

And this applies to jailers, secret agents, soldiers, informers, and all sorts of people whose business and talent it is to do violent, sordid, and unpleasant things, as well as to terrorists. But most of us acknowledge the necessity of nasty functions, and try not to think about the agency of them, even while condemning noninstitutionalized terror. Are we in the position of Bolingbroke?—

> They love not poison that do poison need,
> Nor do I thee: though I did wish him dead,
> I hate the murderer, love him murdered.
> > Richard II; vi. 38–40.

So the first question is: do we have a leg to stand on in condemning terror?

Another question arises also from our equivocal attitude toward violence. We don't condemn all instances of random or sudden violence. We applaud the act, and from a distance admire the actor, where terror is directed against regimes so hideous and oppressive as Nazi Germany. Many, though obviously not all, will feel similarly equivocal about the methods of internal warfare employed to bring down Chiang Kai-shek, Batista, or Somoza, or to establish the state of Israel. We say that the evil against which we fight is both serious and powerful; only by fighting fire with fire can we hope for a remedy. If at the same time we condemn the PLO, the Red Brigade, the IRA, or the SLA, it must be because we think the targets of these groups are neither evil enough nor powerful enough to warrant such extreme measures. Or we may feel rather more fastidious than they about targets—it is one thing, we say, to blow up dictators, banks, or bridges, quite another to plant bombs in supermarkets where the victims are innocent. We must then ask, is our condemnation of terror selective? And if so, does our distinction between allowed and disallowed forms of terror rest on an assumption that Western societies are really not so bad? We shall doubtless feel at least somewhat tepid about this assumption—embarrassed, perhaps, at finding it in our ideological baggage. This is a second challenge to the moral condemnation of terrorism.

Finally, we shall need to face up to the moral strains under which terror places us. What are we to think of terrorists, and how are we to respond to them? Terrorists commit us to a response which is itself violent, for they are outside the reach of law because they do not acknowledge its authority. They are thus outlaws. But we have few, if any, instructive precedents for dealing with outlaws. This is perhaps the most important dimension of terrorism, but I have, alas, the least to say about it.

I.

Are we hypocrites in condemning terror? Or without sin in casting stones? Suppose we draw the following distinction: there is all the (moral) difference in the world between public institutional sanctions and random individual reprisals. The difference is that the first commands community consent and gives advance warning of the consequences of acting in certain ways. The second raises an idiosyncratic conception of the good, or the just, above the consensus, and applies sanctions without warning. In a community dominated by terror, there is no way that citizens could know their guilt or how to avoid it. In contrast, settled communities have at least institutionalized their barbarities (allowing for the sake of argument that all forms of force applied by the state on individuals are barbaric). An individual has grounds for predicting the state's use of force, and knows how to act in order to avoid it.

Now terrorists say the distinction is meaningless. Law and authority are illusions that tempt the imperceptive to cooperate in their own exploitation. It is odd that this argument has so often paralyzed moral judgment, for it is the most transparent instance of a *tu quoque*. We don't appeal to examples of admitted wickedness as models and justifications of our own conduct. Corporations, banks and the democratic process, in their various ways, may be instruments of exploitation and coercion; for that very reason they hardly serve as an excuse for greater violence. That would be like using the existence of capital punishment in one jurisdiction as a motive for another to resort to torture.

But to construe the argument this way is to miss its effect. Political societies are described in the language of exploitation not to license violence but to paralyze the will of those who give at least tepid allegience to such societies. We bourgeois feel, hearing the charges, the twinge of guilt at our own practices or those in which we have acquiesced. We are people in glass houses, and that is a frame of mind in which we lose our grip on the important distinction between practices admittedly needing improvement or rectification, and those that are incorrigibly evil.

Nonetheless, here is a sketch of an attempt to maintain that distinction. Unless we are fanatics, we don't believe that a perfect society is possible. Bourgeois regimes, which are so often vilified by revolutionaries as the paradigms of exploitation and repression, are marked by severe disparities of advantage and opportunity and by obstacles to legitimate pursuits and the airing of righteous grievances. Nonetheless, some mitigation of these evils is better than none. A state in which, for example, it is possible to appeal through the courts to win relief from police misconduct has to be preferred to one in which the police are wholly immune from citizen complaints, and brutality and torture are the rule. We shall not, having made that judgment, justify the brutality of our own police, or fail to take note of gross injustice, to which venality or race or class consciousness of public officials exposes us. But we will argue that a system like ours, with its partially working constraints on police power, is immensely to be preferred to one in which torture or imprisonment without trial are accepted practices. We don't want to be complacent about our faults, but neither do we want to obliterate the distinction between capricious and lawlike exercises of the police function, simply because both rest on coercion. The policeman's even reluctant reading of the *Miranda* warning to the quaking suspect is not to be compared to the interrogations of a secret police or the staged executions of terrorist justice. If we cannot find it in our hearts to condemn the terrorist because the police carry guns and sometimes use them too rashly, we evidently believe that violence is evil. Otherwise the example of police brutality would not embarrass us. If we do believe thus, we should be able to distinguish greater and lesser degrees of violence, or greater and lesser control over it. I therefore see no reason to suffer paralysis of judgment on account of *tu quoque* arguments. Let us agree: the act of terror is evil.

II.

If anything more is to be said, it must be by way of extenuation. The terrorist's reasons, or the context of his action, must make a difference. And here, I think, the friends of terror say one of two things. First, they say, you must sometimes fight fire with fire, a slogan designed to show that violence is the only means to a worthy or a necessary end. Second, they complain that systematic (and cunningly disguised) repression prevents legitimate points of view from being heard; violence is the only remaining way to express a certain range of beliefs about politics and society. Let us look at these apologies in turn.

1. If the fighting-fire-with-fire principle applies, terrorists must have good reason to believe either that worse things will happen unless he throws his bombs, or that a more than offsetting good will be brought about, and can only be brought about, in this way. Terrorists seldom trouble themselves about the eventual good; their future extends only to the destruction of present institutions. So we and they don't know what positive qualities of life the destruction of society aims at. To kill in the name of unspecified and unspecifiable benefits is to kill for no reason at all. This is gratuitous violence, for which no extenuation is produced or sought. It is an immorality of thought as well as act.

Terror as preventive action may seem more promising. Most of us allow that violence might be necessary in self-defense, or to subdue a madman, or to assassinate a tyrant. These cases sometimes—even in the critical light of hindsight—warrant violence. Hitler and Amin are not open to persuasion or vulnerable to other lawful pressures. We know, moreover, that they will certainly commit further atrocities if we fail to kill them. If we are lucky, a single bullet may put an end to the imminent evil. But usually the method is more like war. There will be regretted casualties, as war always brings in its wake; but still more will die, and still more rot in prisons, if the chance isn't taken.

The argument is not unpersuasive. But before it can be assessed to help the terrorist, distinctions must be made. The assassin and guerrilla soldier kill so that atrocities may cease. They may be mistaken, but it is at least plausible to believe that on occasion they are not. It is possible that the evidence supports their actions and excuses the suffering they cause.

But are guerrillas soldiers or terrorists? I have no zeal for definitional disputes, but a matter of importance hangs on the answer to this question. Terrorism, guerrilla warfare and assassination share a form of extenuation. Bloody work is done to prevent bloodier consequences. But in attempting wicked things for virtuous ends, stronger than usual evidence is required to show that the work will indeed bring about the desired future, that it will not have unforeseen effects that cancel out the accomplished good, and that other options for action are unavailable. The Vietnam War protester who sits on the White House lawn may or may not have adequate grounds for his views about the evil of the war or the consequences of withdrawing from it, but because his action is not itself morally momentous—causing at most minor inconvenience to public officials and passersby—we do not oblige him to prove his case beyond the shadow of a doubt. He is, we say, entitled to his opinion. But the assassin who supposes a president must die to end the conflict, or the terrorist who sees the war as a symptom of social malaise and attempts to destroy society by random violence, cannot claim immunity because these are privately held opinions. Can an assassin ever be sure that with the death of his or her target evil will cease, or that it will not bring other unforeseen evils in its wake? Rarely, we say. And those cases for which we may find the grounds sufficient are tyrannies in which present evils are so frightful that our inability to rule out untoward consequences of tyrannicide simply cannot matter. Can the terrorist's theories of social repression ever offer grounds for capricious violence? Here, I think, the answer is that the antibourgeois terrorist cannot profit by sharing a common label with the guerrilla or the assassin of lunatic despots. Those who rail against bourgeois society and attempt to bring it to its knees by leaving bombs in supermarkets cannot claim to be frustrating demonstrable and about to be committed evils. They do not know what specific evils they are preventing; the rhetorical flourishes of repression and exploitation do not serve to identify the alleged evils. They have no evidence to show that the social structure will crack under the pressure of their sporadic violence. And nothing, surely, is more horrifying than the use of tendentious slogans of social theories as bills of indictment against individuals. Yet this is the proposed extenuation offered on behalf of terrorists in the Western world, in Ireland, or in Palestine. No greater atrocity will be prevented by their exploding bombs. Such reasons do not mitigate violence, but simply make light of it.

2. Sometimes terrorists are described as seeking an audience for their views in the only way open to them. We cannot therefore accuse them of doing terrible deeds on the merest pretext of evidence as to their efficacy,

because efficacy is not part of the terrorists' immediate intention. Rather, their bombs dramatize their condemnation of the social order. I find this idea bewildering. The message of dismembered housewives is at the very least unclear. By what twisted reasoning can it be supposed that the exploitation of persons will succeed in stating a message about exploitation? Should I be awakened to my status as a wage slave or a manipulated consumer by contemplating this ultimate use of people as means? Why should I not learn instead the lesson that my current exploited state is much to be preferred to the exploitation I may expect at terrorist hands? Those who can say that terrorists are only expressing opinions they have a right to hold and express have failed to appreciate what the exploitation of persons means. They can demonstrate it in their social theories, and fail to notice it in dreadful fact. These are threadbare defenses indeed.

One last effort at extenuation. Sometimes it is argued that no man is innocent, therefore the terrorist is not guilty—or at least not of slaughtering the innocent. This argument shifts the grounds of mitigation from the reasons for acting to the context in which it takes place. But what can that mean? Not, surely, some Kafka-like eschatology, which when applied to practical affairs converts killers into agents of divine retribution, even though an element of just such madness can be detected in the minds of many terrorists. In a more mundane spirit, one might suppose that the loss of the status of being innocent means only that a state of total war exists. Many who could not be connected positively to the war effort died at Dresden and Hiroshima, but their presence there made them accidental victims of a strategy with a rightful cause, the defeat of the Axis powers. So terrorists are at war with society, fighting for its demise through tactics imposed on them by the logic of the situation. To argue in this way, whether about bombing Hiroshima or the Bank of America, sidesteps the issue as to whether the probabilities of good results can justify such atrocities. We might answer—as many friends of terrorism would—that we lacked such warrant in Dresden or Hiroshima. What, then, would lead us to suppose that the terrorist declaration of total war is any different? Indeed, it is ludicrous to suppose that a half-dozen self-appointed rescuers of humanity are in any position to declare war, total or otherwise, or to appoint themselves just executioners of the wicked against a nation of 50 or 250 million people. Such a defense is just another instance of banal reasons thought adequate for the commission of violent crimes.

It is, of course, part of the terrorist's eschatology to believe that citizens of modern states are hopelessly corrupted by their affiliation, and by their exploitation. To say no one is innocent may mean just this—some are exploiters and die for that, others are exploited and are thus past saving. So in pulling down prisons as centers of repression, guards should die as agents of repression, and the prisoners as victims of it. Such a bloody salvation can only be self-immolating; terrorists must be victims of the social order also. At least they do not, as far as I know, come down from the sky, though some of them, or their defenders on university campuses, may appear to have come up out of the earth.

III.

So much for extenuation. But what of us? Terror is a fact of life to which we must respond somehow or other. Terror tempts us to violent reprisal because it strikes us as irrationally violent. By the same token, we want to say that terrorists are mad. And so our minds are diverted to thoughts of therapy and commiseration. This response is self-deceiving, unless we remember Conrad's remark in *Lord Jim:* "how much certain forms of evil are akin to madness, derived from intense egotism, inflamed by resistance." On the other hand, a violent response to violence caters to the propaganda of terror. Our violence supports the terrorist's otherwise shabby case, or seems to do so for many. And so we seek accommodation, which appears as a sign of the success of terrorist methods. In the end, we must reluctantly admit that the terrorist's uncompromising position makes it impossible to treat him or her as other than the enemy—as an outlaw. Except in war we lack the conventions of violent reprisal. And even in war we maintain the minimum conventions of civility; we recognize that our enemies hold other, but still plausible, allegiances. Men and women who blow up supermarkets and glory in their deed have moved beyond the reach of that courtesy. But what it means to treat someone as an outlaw is a matter on which I fear I have no more to say, except to say that it is what we ought to think about.

QUESTIONS FOR DISCUSSION
WAR AND TERRORISM

1. Is there such a thing as collective guilt; that is, can all the citizens of a country be held responsible for the crimes of their government if they support it? What does B. T. Wilkins say? Do you agree? Defend your response.

2. When resistance fighters exploded bombs in French restaurants frequented by Nazi officers during the German occupation of France, were they committing acts of terrorism? Were they justified? Do you agree with Wilkins's discussion of this issue? Explain why or why not.

3. Wilkins raises the question of whether people should be coerced into doing what is right. Do you think they should? Should they ever be coerced into *not* doing what is morally wrong? Support your view with evidence or arguments from the readings.

4. Discuss Wilkins's claim that consequentialists (utilitarians—see Chapter 1) cannot condemn terrorists whose actions have good consequences in the long run; only deontologists like Kant and Adams can. Is that an argument for consequentialism or for deontology? Explain your response.

5. Is the attempt to change a social system or a way of life an essential feature of terrorism? If so, is it ever justifiable? Discuss this issue, using examples from anti-Nazi sabotage during World War II, or anti-communist terrorism practiced by "Contras" in Nicaragua during the 1970s.

6. Were the atomic bombings of Hiroshima and Nagasaki terrorist actions? What do Wilkins and Louch say? With whom do you agree? Explain why.

7. Louch writes: "Terrorists are at war with society, fighting for its demise through tactics imposed on them by the logic of the situation." Would you do the same in the same situation? Is Louch unfair to condemn them, if he believes that their tactics are imposed on them? Explain your response.

SELECTED READINGS

CAMERON, G. *Nuclear Terrorism.* Basingstoke, England: Macmillan, 1999.

FREY, R., and C. MORRIS, eds. *Violence, Terror and Justice.* New York: Cambridge University Press, 1991.

GROSSCUP, B. *The Explosion of Terrorism.* New York: Macmillan, 1987.

HEYMANN, P. *Terrorism and America.* Cambridge, MA: MIT Press, 1998.

KHATCHADOURIAN, H. *The Morality of Terrorism.* New York: Lang, 1998.

LAQUEUR, W. *The Age of Terrorism.* New York: Little Brown, 1987.

———. *The New Terrorism: Fanaticism and the Arms of Mass Destruction.* New York: Oxford University Press, 1999.

MORRIS, E., and A. HOPE. *Terrorism, Threat and Responsibility.* New York: St. Martin's Press, 1988.

OLIVIERO, A. *The State of Terror.* Albany: State University of New York Press, 1998.

RAPOPORT, D., and Y. ALEXANDER, eds. *The Morality of Terrorism*. New York: Pergamon, 1982.

VALLS, A. *Ethics in International Affairs*. Lanham, MD: Rowland and Littlefield, 2000.

WILKINS, B. *Terrorism and Collective Responsibility*. New York: Routledge, 1992.

ZULAIKA, J., and W. DOUGLAS. *Terror and Taboo*. New York: Routledge, 1996.

Name index

Subject index

abortion, 99, 169, 237-69
    dilemma of, 262-7
    on demand, 237
    right to, 247-61
absolutism
    ethical, 13
    rational, 23-41, 319
    religious, 20-8, 319
action
    affirmative, 412-47
    concept of, 142
    freely willed, 112-66
agent
    -centered ethics, 341-7
    moral, 128, 133
animals
    rights of, 449-78
    treatment of, 449-78
authority
    moral, 380-1
    of choice, 41, 216
    of the will, 41

benefit
    of research, 480-510
    social, 15, 42-52
    See also interest

cannibalism, 55
cause
    concept of, 139
    immanent and transeunt, 136-40, 167
    of action, 134
    of death, 196, 208
chance, 125, 167
charity, 319-20
children, 365
choice
    of action, 141
    of death, 193, 316-26

    of social policies, 273-301
    rational, 61, 273-4
collective guilt, 526-40, 548
commands
    divine, 14, 20-8, 109
    of duty, 32
    of reason, 32
    See also imperatives
compatibilism. *See* determinism, "soft"
compensation, 440
contractualism, 16, 60-90, 109
convention, 16, 53-9, 109
cost-benefit, 275, 276, 283
"could have done otherwise," 136,
    156-60, 167
counsels of prudence, 36-7
courage, 81-2
crime, 169, 270-303, 537
criteria
    of university admission, 412-47
    See also standards
cultural diversity, 512-31
    See also multiculturalism
culture
    Alexandrian, 84
    Buddhist, 84
    Socratic, 84-5
    tragic, 84

death
    misfortune of, 465-8
    See also suicide; choice of death;
        right, to die
deontology, 371
desire
    "categorical," 467-8
    sexual, 76
    See also motives
determinism, 112, 123
    "hard," 112, 115-22, 154-66